Practical P Windows 10
Security Essentials

- ☐ The Easiest
- ☑ Step-By-Step
- ☐ Most Comprehensive
- ☑ Guide To Securing Data and Communications
- ☑ On Your Home and Office Windows Computer

Marc L. Mintz, MBA-IT, ACTC, ACSP

Practical Paranoia: Windows 10 Security Essentials for Home and Business
Marc L. Mintz

Copyright © 2015, 2016 by Marc Mintz.

Notice of Rights: All rights reserved. No part of this document may be reproduced or transmitted in any form by any means without the prior written permission of the author. For information on getting permission for reprints and excerpts, contact marc@mintzit.com.

Notice of Liability: The information in this document is presented on an "As Is" basis, without warranty. While every precaution has been taken in the preparation of this document, the author shall have no liability to any person or entity with respect to any loss or damage caused by or alleged to be caused directly or indirectly by the instructions contained in this document, or by the software and hardware products described within it. It is sold with the understanding that neither the author nor the publisher is engaged in rendering professional security or Information Technology service to the reader. If security or Information Technology expert assistance is required, the services of a professional person should be sought.

Trademarks: Many of the designations used by manufacturers and sellers to distinguish their products are claimed as trademarks. Where those designations appear in this book, and the author was aware of a trademark claim, the designations appear as requested by the owner of the trademark. All other product names and services identified in this document are used in editorial fashion only and for the benefit of such companies with no intention of infringement of trademark. No such use, or the use of the trade name, is intended to convey endorsement or other affiliation within this document.

Edition Preview: 7/2015 • 1: 8/2015 • 1.1: 8/2015 • 1.2: 10/2015 • 1.3: 1/2016 • 1.4: 2/2016

Cover design by Ed Brandt

ISBN-10: 1514139545
ISBN-13: 978-1514139547

Dedication

*To Candace,
without whose support and encouragement
this work would not be possible*

*My great thanks to
Zachary Sandberg and Anthony Galczak,
our Windows and Network Consultants,
for their tireless research on this work*

Contents At A Glance

Dedication 3
Contents At A Glance 5
Contents In Detail 7
Introduction 17
1. Vulnerability: Passwords 29
2. Vulnerability: Updates 67
3. Vulnerability: User Account 77
4. Vulnerability: Storage Device 113
5. Vulnerability: Sleep and Screen Saver 141
6. Vulnerability: Malware 147
7. Vulnerability: Firewall 171
8. Vulnerability: Data Loss 175
9. Vulnerability: Recovery Drive 201
10. Vulnerability: Lost or Stolen Device 213
11. Vulnerability: When It Is Time To Say Goodbye 233
12. Vulnerability: Local Network 255
13. Vulnerability: Web Browsing 277
14. Vulnerability: Email 335
15. Vulnerability: Documents 459
16. Vulnerability: Storage Device Encryption 505
17. Vulnerability: Instant Messaging 535
18. Vulnerability: Voice and Video Communications 553
19. Vulnerability: Internet Activity 569
The Final Word 627
Mintz InfoTech, Inc. Windows 10 Security Checklist 629
Review Answers 633
Index 643
Mintz InfoTech, Inc. when, where, and how you want IT 647
Practical Paranoia Security Essentials Workshops & Books 648

Contents In Detail

Dedication 3
Contents At A Glance 5
Contents In Detail 7
Introduction 17
    Who Should Read This Book 18
    What is Unique About This Book 19
    Why Worry? 21
    Reality Check 23
    About the Author 25
    Practical Paranoia Updates 26
    Practical Paranoia Book Upgrades 27
1. Vulnerability: Passwords 29
    The Great Awakening 30
    Passwords 31
        Assignment: Create a Strong Password for Your User Account ... 33
        Assignment: Setting up a PIN in Windows 10 36
        Assignment: Removing a PIN in Windows 10 41
    Challenge Questions 47
    LastPass 48
        Assignment: Install LastPass 49
        Assignment: Configure LastPass 57
        Assignment: Use LastPass to Save Website Authentication Credentials ... 61
        Assignment: Use LastPass to Auto Fill Website Authentication 63
2. Vulnerability: Updates 67
    System Updates 68
        Assignment: Configure System Updates 69
    Application Updates with Ninite Updater 73
        Assignment: Install Ninite Updater 73
    Review Questions 76
3. Vulnerability: User Account 77
    User Accounts 78
    Never Log In as an Administrator 80

Contents In Detail

    Assignment: Create an Administrative User Account 81
    Assignment: Change an Administrator to a Standard User 86
    Application Whitelisting and More With Parental Controls 88
    Assignment: Create a Child Account 89
    Assignment: Configure your Child Account 98
    Assignment: Allowing Access to Websites Through Email 109
  Review Questions 112

4. Vulnerability: Storage Device 113
  Block Access to Storage Devices 114
    Assignment: Block Access to Storage Devices via Registry 114
    Assignment: Restore Access to Storage Devices via Registry 115
    Assignment: Block Access to Storage Devices via Device Manager 116
    Assignment: Restore Access to Storage Devices via Device Manager 119
    Assignment: Block Access to Storage Devices via USB Disabler 121
    Assignment: Restore Access to Storage Devices via USB Disabler 126
  Full Disk Encryption 127
    Assignment: Enable Encryption Using BitLocker 127
  Review Questions 140

5. Vulnerability: Sleep and Screen Saver 141
  General Security 142
    Assignment: Require Password After Sleep or Screen Saver 142
  Review Questions 145

6. Vulnerability: Malware 147
  Anti-Malware 148
    Assignment: Install and Configure Avira 151
    Assignment: Uninstall Avira Antivirus 159
    Assignment: Install and Configure Bitdefender Antivirus 160
  Review Questions 170

7. Vulnerability: Firewall 171
  Firewall 172
  Review Questions 174

8. Vulnerability: Data Loss 175
  The Need for Backups 176
    Assignment: Format the Backup Drive for Both Windows Backup &
    Restore and Parted Magic 179
    Assignment: Configure Windows Backup and Restore 184

Contents In Detail

        Assignment: Configure System Image Backup 192
        Assignment: Integrity Test the Backup 196
    Review Questions 200

9. Vulnerability: Recovery Drive 201
    Recovery Drive 202
        Assignment: Create a Recovery Drive 202
        Assignment: Test the Recovery Drive 205
    Review Questions 211

10. Vulnerability: Lost or Stolen Device 213
    Find My PC 214
        Assignment: Activate and Configure LoJack 214
    Prey 222
        Assignment: Activate and Configure Prey 222
    Review Questions 231

11. Vulnerability: When It Is Time To Say Goodbye 233
    Preparing a Computer for Sale or Disposal 234
    Primer: Solid State Drives vs. Rotating Magnetic Drives 235
    Secure Erase Magnetic Hard Drives 236
        Assignment: Secure Erase a Magnetic Drive Protected with BitLocker ... 236
        Assignment: Secure Erase a Magnetic Boot Drive Without BitLocker
        Encryption 236
    Secure Erase a Solid State Hard Drive (SSD) 238
        Assignment: Create a Bootable USB Drive of Parted Magic 238
        Assignment: Secure Erase a Solid State Drive Protected with BitLocker . 245
        Assignment: Secure Erase a Solid State Boot Drive without BitLocker
        Encryption 246
        Assignment: Secure Erase a Non-Boot Drive 249
    Review Questions 254

12. Vulnerability: Local Network 255
    Ethernet Broadcasting 256
    Ethernet Insertion 257
    Wi-Fi Encryption Protocols 258
    Routers: An Overview 259
        Assignment: Determine the Wi-Fi Encryption Protocol 260
        Assignment: Configure WPA2 On a Router 263
    Use MAC Address to Limit Wi-Fi Access 267

Contents In Detail

    Assignment: Restrict Access by MAC Address 267
  Router Penetration 272
    Assignment: Examine Router Security Configuration 272
  Review Questions 276

13. Vulnerability: Web Browsing 277
  HTTPS 278
    Assignment: Install HTTPS Everywhere 279
  Choose a Browser 285
  Firefox Private Browsing, Chrome Incognito, and Edge InPrivate Mode 287
    Assignment: Enable Firefox Private Browsing 287
    Assignment: Enable Chrome Incognito Mode 288
    Assignment: Enable Edge InPrivate Mode 290
  DuckDuckGo 292
    Assignment: Make DuckDuckGo the Default Search Engine 292
  Clear History 295
    Assignment: Clear Firefox Browsing History 295
    Assignment: Clear Edge Browsing History 298
    Assignment: Clear Chrome Browsing History 301
    Assignment: Secure the Firefox Browser 302
    Assignment: Secure the Chrome Browser 305
    Assignment: Secure the Edge Browser 307
  Web Scams 310
  Tor 311
    Assignment: Install Tor for Anonymous Internet Browsing 313
    Assignment: Configure Tor Preferences 324
  Onion Sites and the Deep Web 333
  Review Questions 334

14. Vulnerability: Email 335
  The Killer App 336
  Phishing 337
  Email Encryption Protocols 339
  TLS and SSL 340
    Assignment: Install Mozilla Thunderbird 341
    Assignment: Configure Mozilla Thunderbird to Use TLS 341
    Assignment: Configure Microsoft Outlook to Use TLS or SSL 345
  HTTPS 348

Contents In Detail

    Assignment: Configure Browser Email to Use HTTPS 348
  End-To-End Secure Email with Sendinc 349
    Assignment: Create a Sendinc Account 350
    Assignment: Send a Secure Email with Sendinc 352
    Assignment: Receive and Respond to a Sendinc Secure Email 353
  End-To-End Secure Email With GNU Privacy Guard 356
    Assignment: Install GPG and Generate Your Public Key 357
    Assignment: Add Your Other Email Addresses to Your Public Key 367
    Assignment: Install Your Friend's Public Key 372
    Assignment: Enable GPG in Thunderbird 374
    Assignment: Composing a GPG Encrypted Email in Outlook 382
    Assignment: Encrypt and Sign Files with Win4pgp 387
    Assignment: Decrypt files with Win4pgp 392
    Assignment: Send a GPG-Encrypted and Signed Email 395
    Assignment: Receive a GPG-Encrypted and Signed Email 397
  End-To-End Secure Email With S/MIME 399
    Assignment: Acquire a Free Class 1 S/MIME Certificate for Personal Use 400
    Assignment: Setup a Business Account to Purchase Class 3 S/MIME
    Certificates 415
    Assignment: Purchase a Class 3 S/MIME Certificate for Business Use ... 422
    Assignment: Download and Install a Business S/MIME Certificate 434
    Assignment: Importing a S/MIME Certificate in Microsoft Outlook 444
    Assignment: Exchange S/MIME Public Key with Others 449
    Assignment: Send S/MIME Encrypted Email in Microsoft Outlook 453
  Closing Comments on Encryption and the NSA 456
  Review Questions 457

15. Vulnerability: Documents 459
  Document Security 460
  Password Protect the Document within Its Application 461
    Assignment: Encrypt an MS Office Document 462
  Encrypt a PDF Document 465
    Assignment: Convert a Document to PDF for Password Protection 465
  Encrypt a Folder for Personal use in Windows 10 469
    Assignment: Create an Encrypted Windows Folder 469
    Assignment: Backup Encryption Keys for the Encrypted Folder 471
    Assignment: Import Previously Saved File Encryption Certificates 479

Contents In Detail

Encrypt a Folder for Any OS Use with VeraCrypt 486
    Assignment: Download VeraCrypt 487
    Assignment: Configure VeraCrypt 488
    Assignment: Create a VeraCrypt Container 490
    Assignment: Mount an Encrypted VeraCrypt Container 499
Review Questions 504

16. Vulnerability: Storage Device Encryption 505
BitLocker & UEFI/Legacy BIOS 506
    Assignment: Secure UEFI/BIOS Firmware 506
    Assignment: Verify TPM is Enabled 520
    Assignment: Test the UEFI/BIOS Password 522
    Assignment: Enabling additional UEFI/BIOS Security Features 523
Review Questions 534

17. Vulnerability: Instant Messaging 535
Instant Messaging 536
    Assignment: Install and Configure Wickr 537
    Assignment: Send a Secure Text Message with Wickr 548
Review Questions 552

18. Vulnerability: Voice and Video Communications 553
    Assignment: Sign up for an OStel account 555
    Assignment: Install the OStel App–Jitsi 557
    Assignment: Configure Jetsi 562
    Assignment: Make Your First Encrypted Call 563
Review Questions 567

19. Vulnerability: Internet Activity 569
VPN–Virtual Private Network 570
Gateway VPN 571
VPNArea 575
    Assignment: Install VPNArea on Windows 10 575
Mesh VPN 591
LogMeIn Hamachi 592
    Assignment: Create a LogMeIn Hamachi Account 592
    Assignment: Configure the Hamachi Network 600
    Assignment: Add Users to the Hamachi VPN Network 604
    Assignment: Deploy Hamachi 613
    Assignment: File Sharing Within a Hamachi VPN Network 620

Contents In Detail

Assignment: Exit the Hamachi VPN Network 622
Resolving Email Conflicts with VPN 624
Review Questions 625
The Final Word 627
Mintz InfoTech, Inc. Windows 10 Security Checklist 629
Review Answers.. 633
Index 643
Mintz InfoTech, Inc. when, where, and how you want IT 647
Practical Paranoia Security Essentials Workshops & Books 648

Practical Paranoia Windows 10 Security Essentials

Marc L. Mintz, MBA-IT

Introduction

Just because you're paranoid doesn't mean they aren't after you.
–Joseph Heller, *Catch-22*

Everything in life is easy–once you know the how.
–Marc L. Mintz

Introduction

Who Should Read This Book

Traditional business thinking holds that products should be tailored to a laser-cut market segment. Something like: *18-25-year-old males, still living at their parent's home, who like to play video games, working a minimum-wage job.* Yes, we all have a pretty clear image of that market segment.

In the case of this book, the market segment is *all users of Windows 10 computers.* Really! From my great-Aunt Rose who is wrestling with using her first computer, to the small business, to the IT staff for major corporations and government agencies.

Even though the military may use better security on their physical front doors– MP's with machine guns protecting the underground bunker–compared to a residential home with a Kwikset deadbolt and a neurotic Chihuahua, the steps to secure OS X for home and business use are almost identical for both. There is little difference between *home-level security* and *military-grade security* when it comes to this technology.

The importance of data held in a personal computer may be every bit as important as the data held by the CEO of a Fortune 500. The data is also every bit as vulnerable to penetration.

Introduction

What is Unique About This Book

Practical Paranoia: Windows 10 Security Essentials is the first comprehensive Windows 10 security book written with the new to average user in mind–as well as the IT professional. The steps outlined here are the same steps used by my consulting organization when securing systems for hospitals, government agencies, and the military.

By following the easy, illustrated, step-by-step instructions in this book, you will be able to secure your computer to better than National Security Agency (NSA) standards.

Hardening your computers will help your business protect the valuable information of you and your customers. Should your computer work include HIPAA or legal-related information, to be in full compliance with regulations it is likely that you will need to be using at least Windows 7, and I recommend Windows 10.

For those of you caught up in the ADHD epidemic, do not let the number of pages here threaten you. This book really is a quick read because it has lots of actual screenshots. Written for use in our *Practical Paranoia: Security Essentials Workshops* as well as for self-study, this book is the ultimate step-by-step guide for protecting the new Windows 10 user who has no technical background, as well as for the experienced IT consultant. The information and steps outlined are built on guidelines from Microsoft, the NSA, and my own 30 years as an IT consultant, developer, technician and trainer. I have reduced dull background theory to a minimum, including only what is necessary to grasp the need-for and how-to.

The organization of this book is simple. We provide chapters representing each of the major areas of vulnerability, and the tasks you will do to protect your data, device, and personal identity.

Although you may jump in at any section, I recommend you follow the sequence provided to make your system as secure as possible. Remember, the bad guys will not attack your strong points. They seek out your weak points. Leave no obvious weakness and they will most likely move on to an easier target.

Introduction

To review your work using this guide, use the *Mintz InfoTech Security Checklist* provided at the end of this book.

Theodore Sturgeon, an American science fiction author and critic, stated: *Ninety percent of everything is crap.* https://en.wikipedia.org/wiki/Sturgeon%27s_law. Mintz's extrapolation of Sturgeon's Revelation is: *Ninety percent of everything you have learned and think to be true is crap.*

I have spent most of my adult life in exploration of how to distill what is real and accurate from what is, well, Sturgeon's 90%. The organizations I have founded, the workshops I've produced, and the *Practical Paranoia* book series all spring from this pursuit. If you find any area of this workshop or book that you think should be added, expanded, improved, or changed, I invite you to contact me personally with your recommendations.

Introduction

Why Worry?

In terms of network, Internet, and data security, Windows users must be vigilant because of the presence of well over 1,000,000 malware such as viruses, Trojan horses, worms, phishing, and key loggers impacting our computers. Attacks on computer and smartphone users by tricksters, criminals, and governments are on a steep rise. In addition to Windows-specific attacks, we are vulnerable at points of entry common to all computer users, including Flash, Java, compromised websites, and phishing, as well as through simple hardware theft. How bad is the situation?

- According to a study by Symantec, an average enterprise-wide data breach has a recovery cost of $5 million.

- According to the FBI, 2 million laptops are stolen or lost in the U.S. each year.

- Of those 2 million stolen or lost, only 3% ever are recovered.

- Out of the box, a Windows computer can be broken into – bypassing password protection – in less than 1 minute.

- According to independent testing by AV-Comparatives *http://av-comparatives.org*, the built-in Windows anti-malware catches only 80% of known malware.

- The typical email is clearly readable at dozens of points along the Internet highway on its trip to the recipient. Most likely, that email is read by somebody you don't know.

- A popular game played by high school and college students is *war driving*: the act of driving around neighborhoods to find Wi-Fi networks, geographically marking the location for others to use and break into.

- The Cyber Intelligence Sharing and Protection Act (CISPA) *http://en.wikipedia.org/wiki/Cyber_Intelligence_Sharing_and_Protection_Act* allows the government easy access to all your electronic communications. PRISM *http://en.wikipedia.org/wiki/PRISM_ (surveillance_program)* allows government agencies to collect and track data on any American device.

Introduction

The list goes on, but we have lives to live and you get the point. It is not a matter of *if* your data will ever be threatened. It is only a matter of *when*, and how often the attempts will be made.

Introduction

Reality Check

Nothing can 100% guarantee 100% security 100% of the time. Even the White House and CIA websites and internal networks have been penetrated. We know that organized crime, as well as the governments of China, North Korea, Russia, Great Britain, United States, and Australia have billions of dollars and tens of thousands of highly skilled security personnel on staff looking for *zero-day exploits*. These are vulnerabilities that have not yet been discovered by the developer. As if this is not enough, the U.S. government influences the development and certification of most security protocols. This means that industry-standard tools used to secure our data often have been found to include vulnerabilities introduced by government agencies.

With these odds against us, should we just throw up our hands and accept that there is no way to ensure our privacy? Well, just because breaking into a locked home only requires a rock through a window, should we give up and not lock our doors?

Of course not. We do everything we can to protect our valuables. When leaving on vacation we lock doors, turn on the motion detectors, notify the police to prompt additional patrols, and stop mail and newspaper delivery.

The same is true with our digital lives. For the very few who are targeted by the NSA, there is little that can be done to completely block them from reading your email, following your chats, and recording your web browsing. But you can make it extremely time and labor intensive.

For the majority of us not subject to an NSA targeted attack, we are rightfully concerned about our digital privacy being penetrated by criminals, pranksters, competitors, and nosy people as well as about the collateral damage caused by malware infestations.

You *can* protect yourself, your data, and your devices from such attack. By following this book, you should be able to secure fully your data and your first device in two days, and any additional devices in a half day. This is a very small price to pay for peace of mind and security.

Introduction

Remember, penetration does not occur at your strong points. A home burglar will avoid hacking at a steel door when a simple rock through a window will gain entry. A strong password and encrypted drive by themselves do not mean malware can't slip in with your email, and pass all of your keystrokes – including usernames and passwords – to the hacker.

It is imperative that you secure all points of vulnerability.

- NOTE: Throughout this book we provide suggestions on how to use various free or low-cost applications to help enforce your protection. Neither Marc L. Mintz nor Mintz InfoTech, Inc. receives payment for suggesting them. We have used them with success, and thus feel confident in recommending them.

About the Author

Marc Louis Mintz is one of the most respected IT consultants and technical trainers in the United States. His technical support services and workshops have been embraced by hundreds of organizations and thousands of individuals over the past 3 decades.

Marc holds an MBA-IT (Masters of Business Administration with specialization in Information Technology), Chauncy Technical Trainer certification, and Post-Secondary Education credentials.

Marc's enthusiasm, humor, and training expertise have been honed on leading edge work in the fields of motivation, management development, and technology. He has been recruited to present software and hardware workshops nationally and internationally. His technical workshops are consistently rated by seminar providers, meeting planners, managers, and participants as *The Best* because he empowers participants to see with new eyes, think in a new light, and problem solve using new strategies.

When away from the podium, Marc is right there in the trenches, working to keep client Android, iOS, OS X, and Windows systems securely connected.

The author may be reached at:
Marc L. Mintz
Mintz InfoTech, Inc.
1000 Cordova Pl
#842
Santa Fe, NM 87505
+1 888.479.0690
Email: *marc@mintzIT.com*
Web: *http://mintzIT.com*

Practical Paranoia Updates

Information regarding IT security changes daily, so we offer you newsletter, blog and Facebook updates to keep you on top of everything.

Newsletter

Stay up to date with your Practical Paranoia information by subscribing to our free weekly newsletter.

1. Visit *http://mintzIT.com*
2. Select the *Contact Us* link, and then select the *Newsletter* submenu.
3. Enter your Name, Email, and then select the *Sign Up* button.

Blog

Updates and addendums to this book also will be included in our free *Mintz InfoTech Blog*. Go to: *http://mintzit.com*, and then select the *Blog* link.

Facebook

Updates and addendums to this book also will be found in our *Practical Paranoia Facebook Group*. Go to *https://www.facebook.com/groups/PracticalParanoia/*

Introduction

Practical Paranoia Book Upgrades

We are constantly updating *Practical Paranoia* so that you have the latest, most accurate resource available. If at any time you wish to upgrade to the latest version of *Practical Paranoia* at the lowest price we can offer:

1. Tear off the front cover of **Practical Paranoia**.

2. Make check payable to Mintz InfoTech for $30.

3. Send front cover, check, and mailing information to:
   Mintz InfoTech, Inc.
   1000 Cordova Pl
   #842
   Santa Fe, NM 87505

4. Your new copy of **Practical Paranoia** will be sent by USPS. Please allow up to 4 weeks for delivery.

1. Vulnerability: Passwords

For a people who are free, and who mean to remain so, a well-organized and armed militia is their best security.

–Thomas Jefferson

Knowledge, and the willingness to act upon it, is our greatest defense.

–Marc Louis Mintz

The Great Awakening

In June 2013, documents of NSA origin were leaked to The Guardian newspaper *http://en.wikipedia.org/wiki/NSA_warrantless_surveillance_controversy*. The documents provided evidence that the NSA was both legally and illegally spying on United States citizens' cell phone, email, and web usage. These documents, while causing gasps of outrage and shock by the general public, revealed little that those of us in the IT field already did not know/suspect for decades: every aspect of our digital lives is subject to eavesdropping.

The more cynical amongst us go even further, stating that *everything* we do on our computers *is* recorded and subject to government scrutiny.

But few of us have anything real to fear from our government. Where the real problems with digital data theft come from are local kids hijacking networks, professional cyber-criminals who have fully automated the process of scanning networks for valuable information, competitors/enemies and malware that finds its way into our systems from criminals, foreign governments, and our own government.

The first step to securing our data is to secure our computers. Remember, we are not in Kansas anymore.

1. Vulnerability: Passwords

Passwords

We all know we need passwords. Right? But do you know that *every* password can be broken? Start by trying *a*. If that does not work, try *b,* and then *c*. Eventually, the correct string of characters will get you into the system. It is only a matter of time.

Way back in your great-great-great grandfather's day, the only way to break into a personal computer was by manually attempting to guess the password. Given that manual attempts could proceed at approximately 1 attempt per second, an 8-character password became the standard. With a typical character set of 24 (a–z) this created a possibility of 24^8 or over 100 billion possible combinations. The thought that anyone could ever break such a password was ridiculous, so your ancestors became complacent.

This is funny when you consider that research has shown that the majority of passwords can be guessed. These passwords include: name of spouse, name of children, name of pets, home address, phone number, Social Security number, and main character names from Star Trek and Star Wars (would I kid you?) Most computer users are unaware that what they thought was an obscure and impossible-to-break password actually could be cracked in minutes.

A while back the first hacker wrote password-breaking software. Assuming it may have taken 8 CPU cycles to process a single attack event, on an old computer with a blazing 16 KHz CPU that would equate to 2,000 attempts per second. This meant that a password could be broken in less than 2 years. Yikes.

IT directors took notice.

So down came the edict from the IT Director that we *must* create "obscure" passwords: strings that include upper and lower case, numeric, and symbol characters. But in many cases this actually was a step backward. Since a computer user could not remember that his password was 8@dC%Z#2, the user often would manually record the password. That urban legend of leaving a password on a sticky note under the keyboard? I have seen it myself more than a hundred times.

Come forward to the present day. A current quad-core Intel i7 with freely available password-cracking software can make over 10 billion password attempts

1. Vulnerability: Passwords

per second. Create an army of infected computers called a botnet to do your dirty work (*http://en.wikipedia.org/wiki/Botnet*), and you can likely achieve over a hundred trillion attempts per second, unless your system locks out the user after x number of failed log on attempts.

What does this mean for you? The typical password using upper and lower case, number, and symbol now can be cracked with the right tools in under than 2 minutes. If using just a single computer to do the break in, make that a week. Don't believe it? Take a look at the *haystack* search space calculator at *https://www.grc.com/haystack.htm*.

If we use longer passwords, we can make it take too time consuming to break into our system, so the bad guys will move on to someone else.

But you say it is tough enough to remember 8 characters, impossible to remember more?

This is true, but only if we keep doing things as we have always done before. Since virtually all such attacks are now done by automated software, it is only an issue of length of password, not complexity. So, use a passphrase that is easy to remember, such as, "Rocky has brown eyes" (which at 100 trillion attempts per second could take over 1,000,000,000,000,000 centuries to break – provided Rocky is not the name of your beloved pet and thus more guessable).

How long should you make your password, or rather, passphrase? As of this writing, Microsoft's Security Chief recommends a minimum of 14 characters. Cisco recommends a minimum of 24. My recommendation to clients is a minimum of 14, in an easy-to-remember, easy-to-enter phrase.

In addition to password length, it is critical to use a variety of passwords. In this way, should a bad person gain access to your Facebook password, that password cannot be used to access your bank account.

Yes, pretty soon you will have a drawer full of passwords for all your different accounts, email, social networks, financial institutions, etc. How to keep all of them organized and easily accessed amongst all of your various computers and devices? More on that later in the *LastPass* section of this *Password* topic.

1. Vulnerability: Passwords

Assignment: Create a Strong Password for Your User Account

Computer security starts with strong passwords. No password is as important as the password for your user account. This is the password used to log in to your computer, and to authorize major changes such as installing software. It is the first guard at the entrance of your computer, and therefore your data.

In this assignment, we will create a strong password for your user account.

Create a Strong Password

1. Create an account password for yourself that consists of at least 14 easy-to-remember and easy-to-enter characters.

2. Test how difficult it is to break your password by opening a browser, visit haystack, and then enter your password: *https://www.grc.com/haystack.htm*.

3. If your password does not meet your or your organization's strength requirements, edit it until it does.

4. Record your new password in a way that you can find when you need it.

5. Exit the browser.

Change Your Old Password to the Strong Password:

1. Vulnerability: Passwords

6. Log into your computer using your user account.
7. Click on *Start* menu > *Settings* > *Accounts* > *Sign-in options*.
8. Select the *Password* > *Change* button.

1. Vulnerability: Passwords

9. Enter your original/old password, and then click the *Next* button.

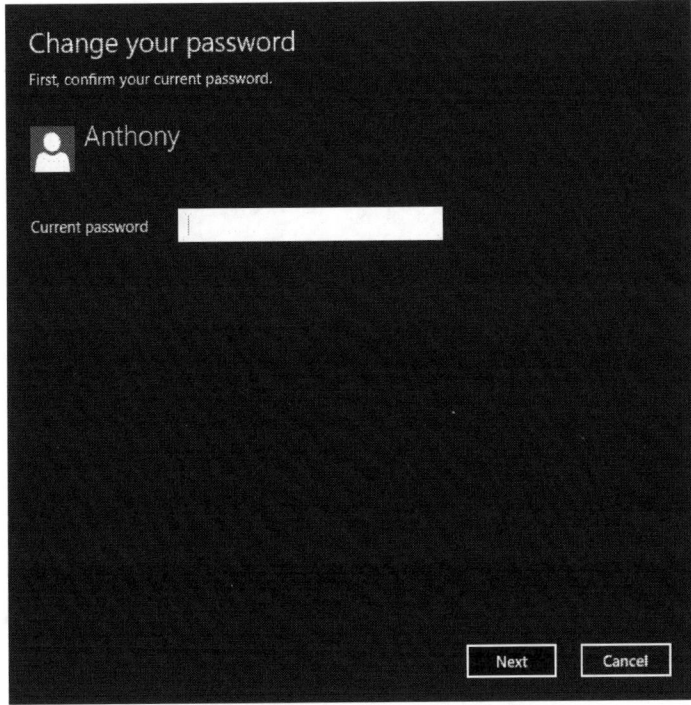

1. Vulnerability: Passwords

10. Enter your new strong password. Make sure you also enter the *Password hint*. This is required before proceeding to the next step in changing your password. Then click the *Next* button, and then the *Finish* button.

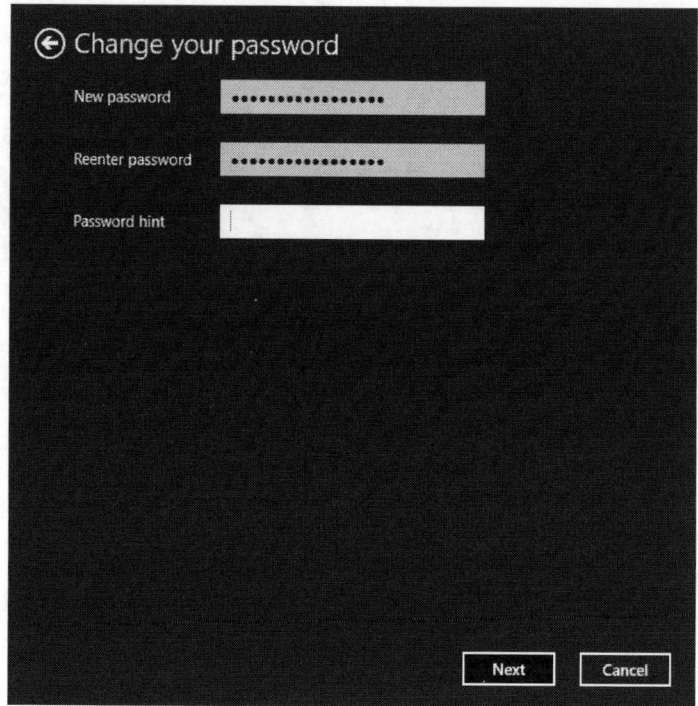

Your new, strong password now is in effect.

Assignment: Setting up a PIN in Windows 10

When setting up a Windows 10 installation for the first time it will ask you to setup a PIN. Microsoft has integrated FIDO 2.0 technology into their PINs. At this time, we do not recommend using a PIN and still standby using a standard password for security.

1. While in the installation process of Windows 10, a PIN setup screen will appear. Select *Set a PIN*.

1. Vulnerability: Passwords

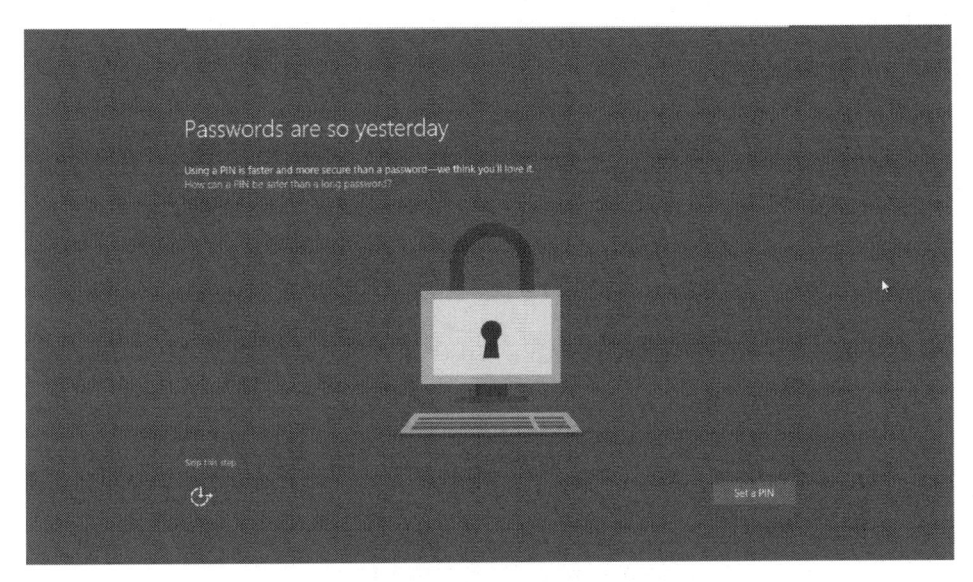

2. Enter a secure PIN, confirm it and press *OK*.

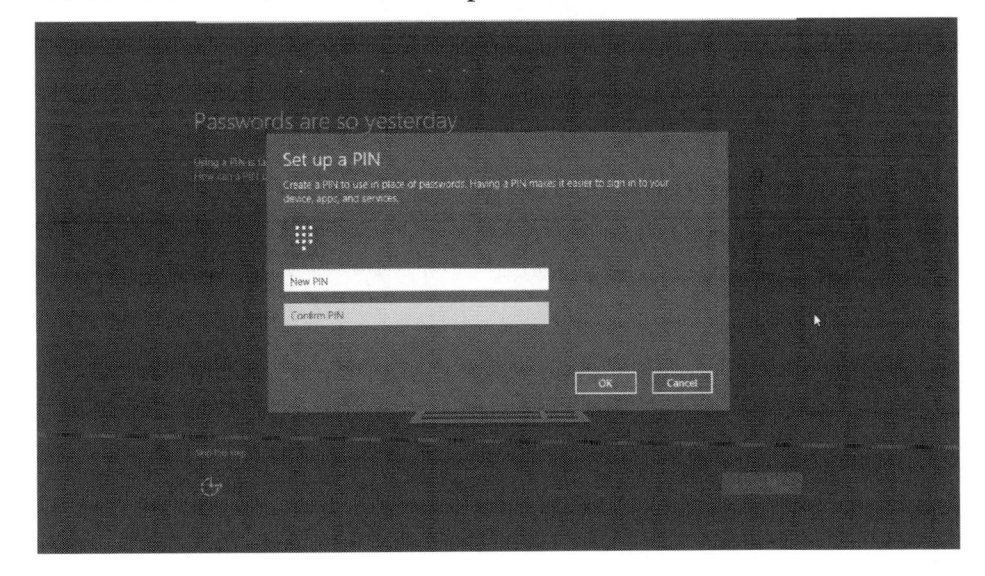

1. Vulnerability: Passwords

3. If you elected to not use a PIN on the initial Windows 10 installation then go to *Start > Settings*.

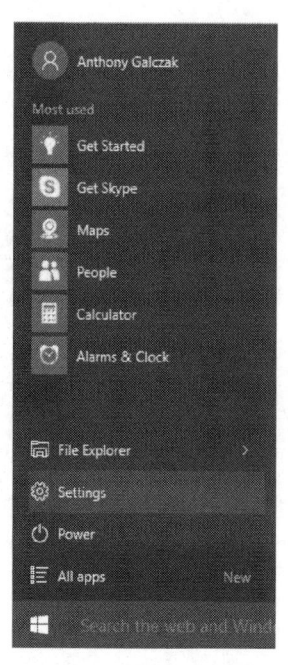

4. Select *Accounts*.

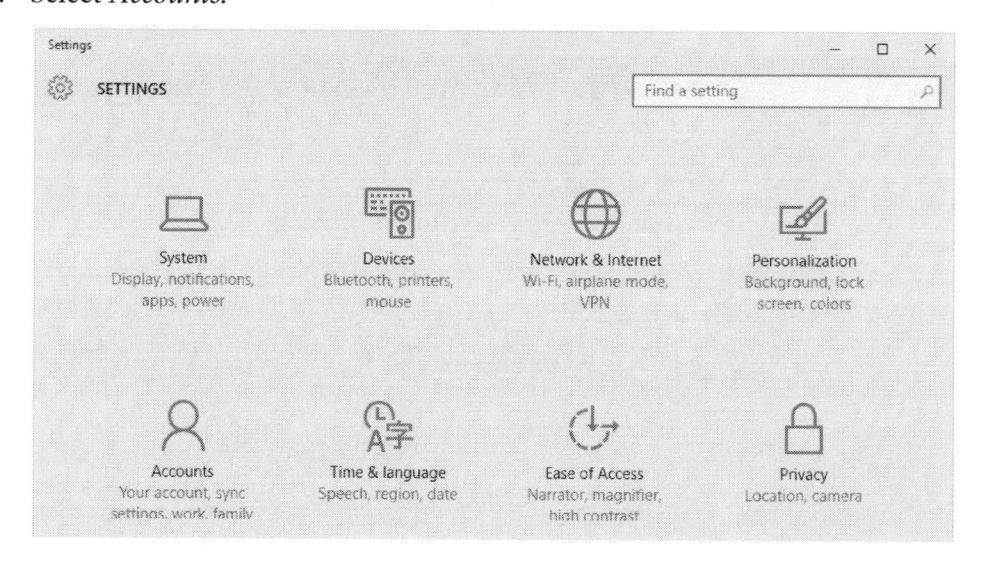

1. Vulnerability: Passwords

5. Select *Sign-in options* scroll to PIN and click *Add*.

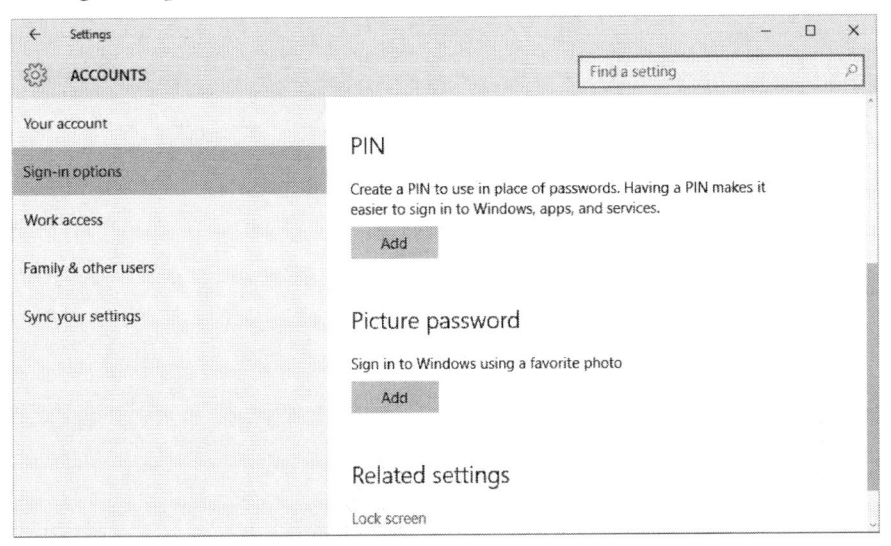

6. Enter your Microsoft credentials and select *Sign in*.

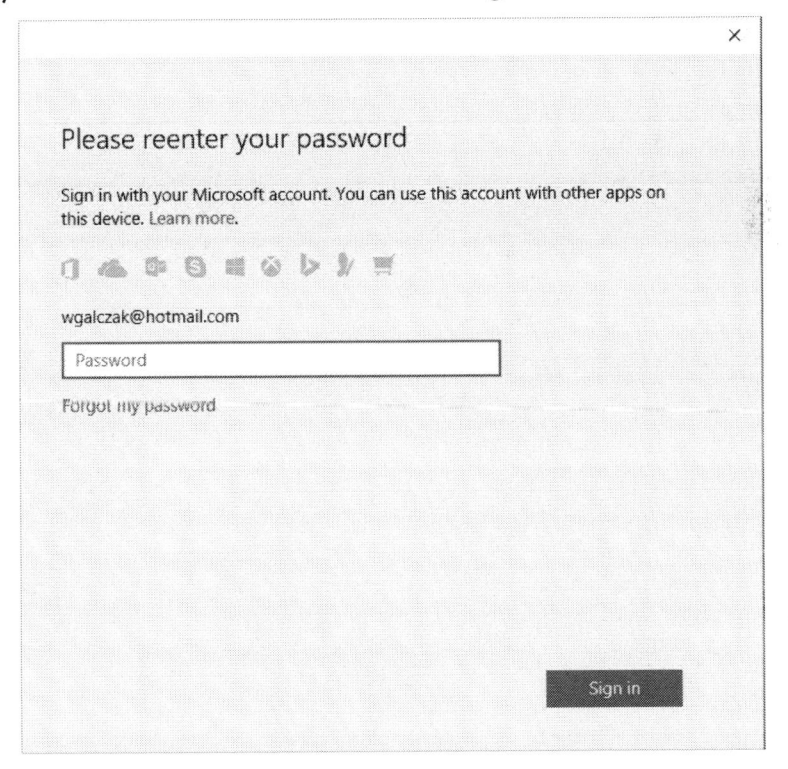

1. Vulnerability: Passwords

7. Setup a secure PIN, confirm it and press *OK*.

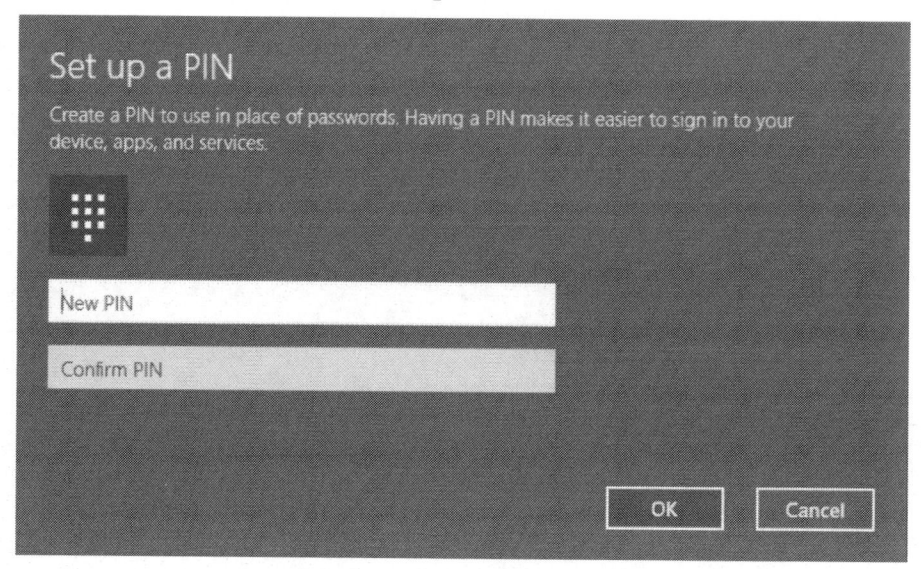

8. After your PIN is setup, it will show this message under PIN and give you the options for change.

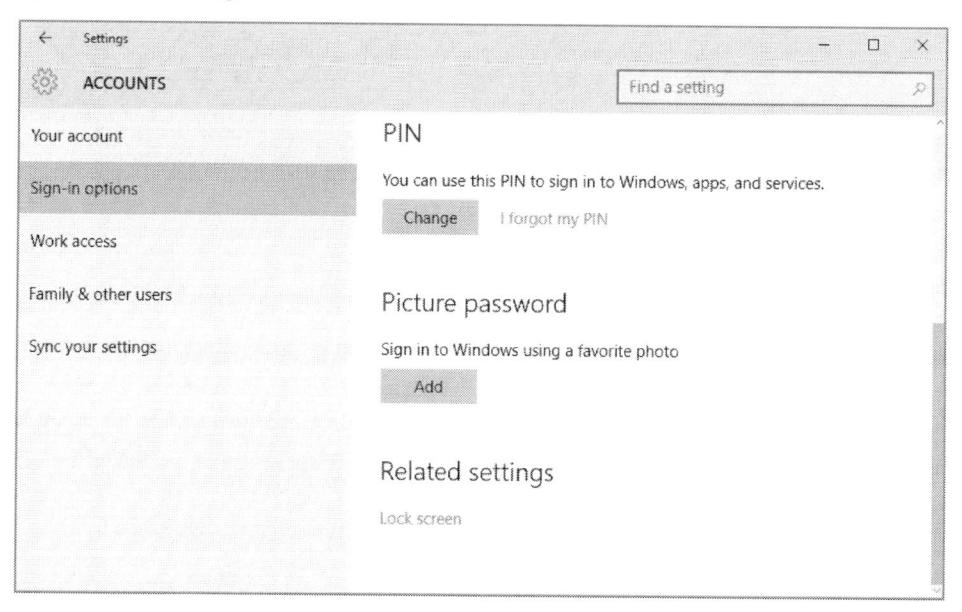

1. Vulnerability: Passwords

Assignment: Removing a PIN in Windows 10

Removing a PIN in Windows 10 is not as clear cut as it would seem. In previous versions of Windows, for removing a password or PIN there is a *Remove* button next to this type of authentication. In order to remove the PIN within Windows 10 you will need to act like you have forgotten your PIN number and after going through the authentication just not setting the PIN up again.

1. Go to *Start > Settings*.

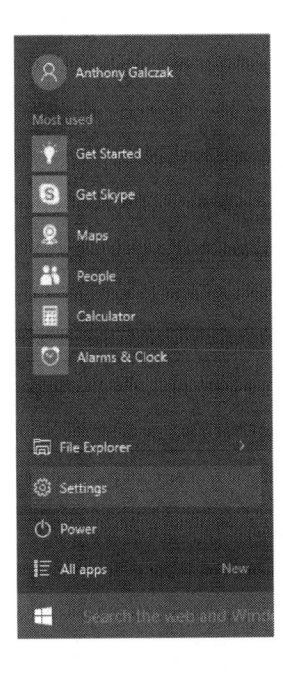

1. Vulnerability: Passwords

2. Select *Accounts*.

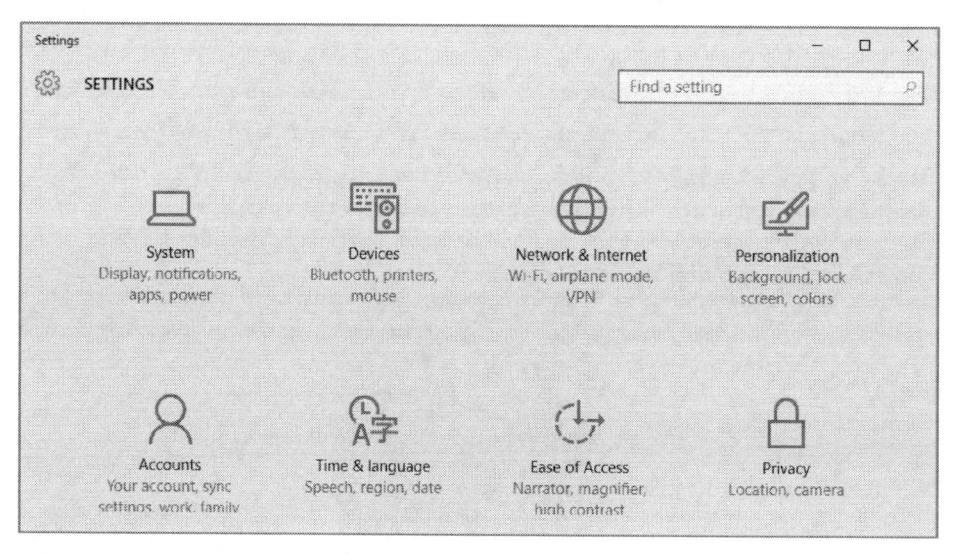

3. Select *Sign-in options*, scroll down to the *PIN* section, and then select *I forgot my PIN*.

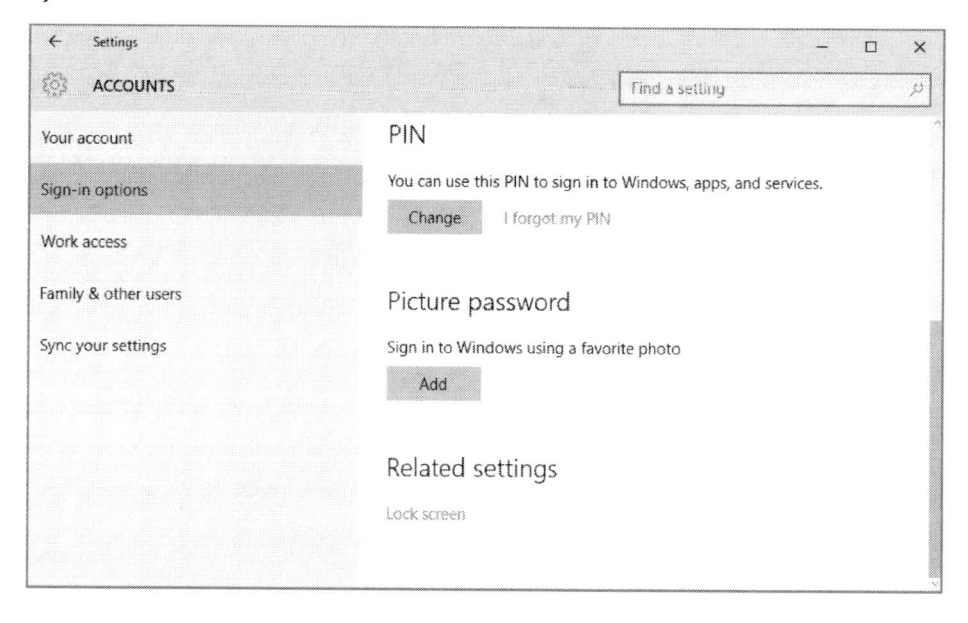

1. Vulnerability: Passwords

4. The dialog box will confirm that you are sure you want to go through with the PIN reset process. Click *Continue*.

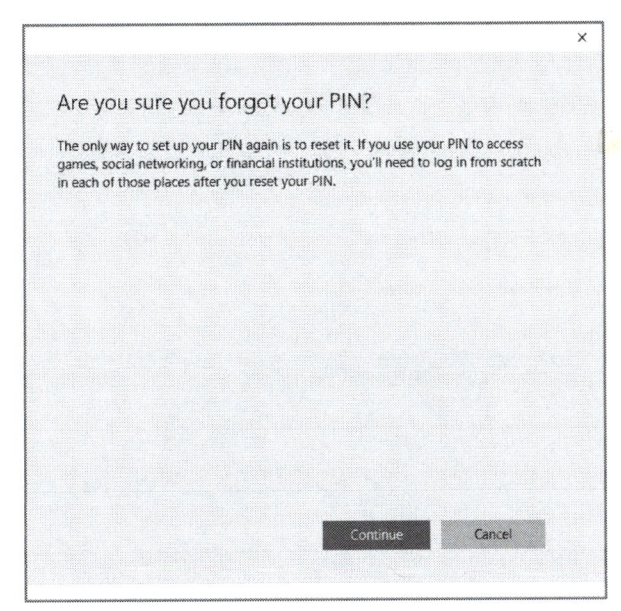

5. Log in with your Microsoft account. Enter your password, and then click *Sign in*.

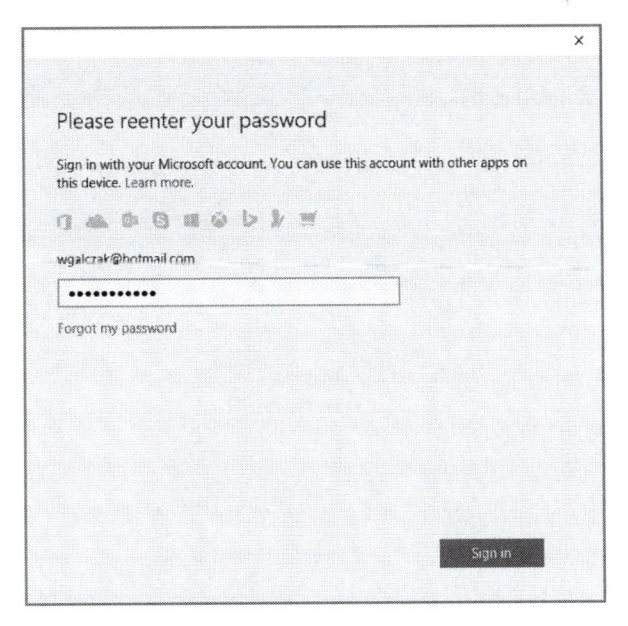

1. Vulnerability: Passwords

6. Select your authentication method for two-way authentication. This will generally be a phone or an alternative email. Enter the last 4 digits of your phone number or the full email address, and then click *Next*.

7. Once you have received the text or email with the code, enter the code here, and then click *Next*.

1. Vulnerability: Passwords

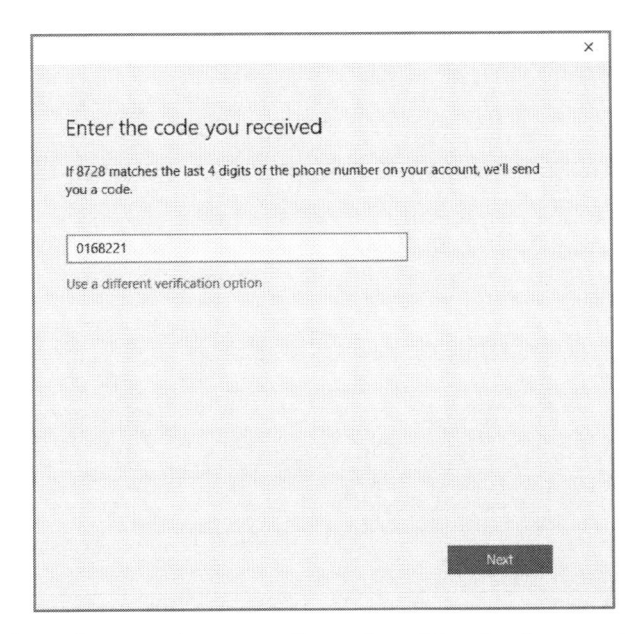

8. It is crucial that after you have confirmed and it asks for you to *Set up a PIN* that you just click *Cancel* to skip this process. You cannot leave it blank.

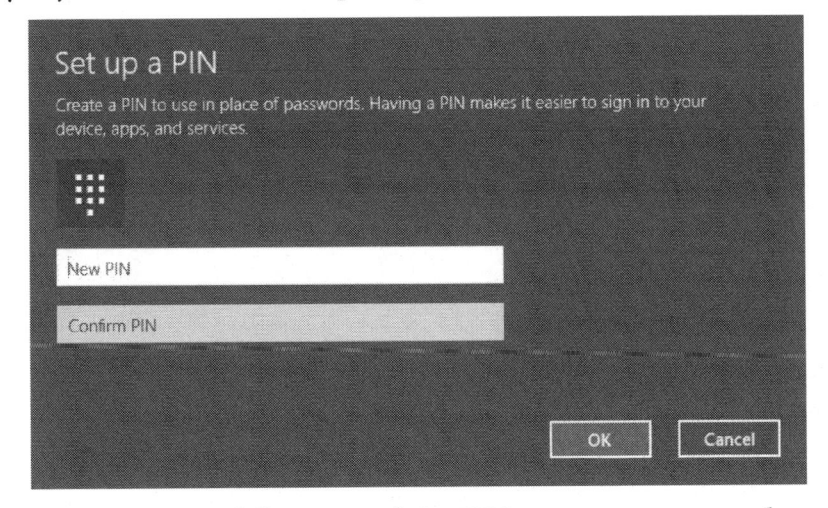

9. Now you have successfully removed the PIN on your account and can continue to use a traditional password or alternative authentication method.

1. Vulnerability: Passwords

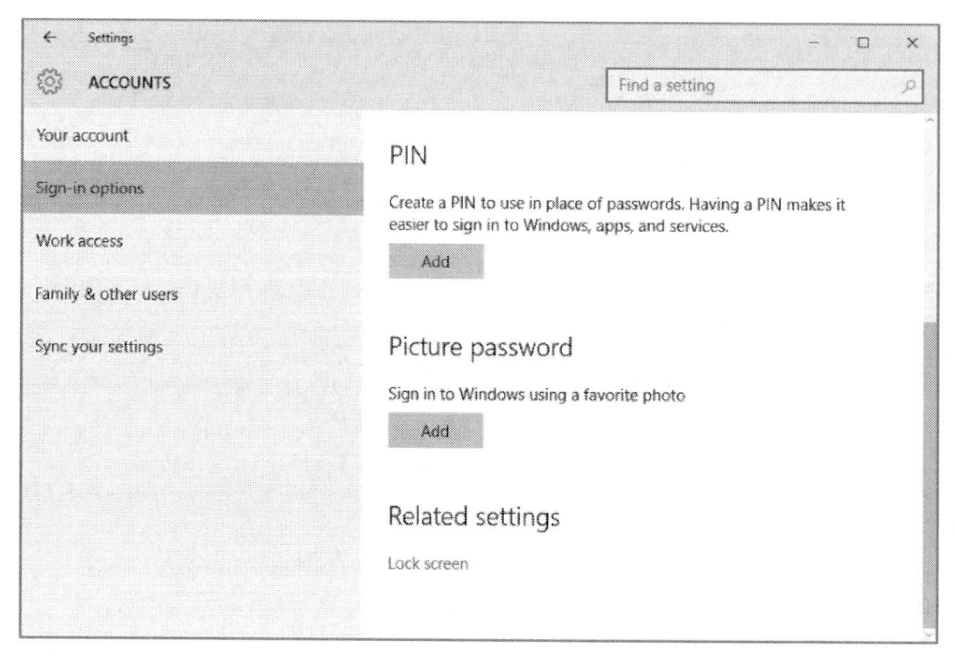

Your PIN has been removed and you can now use a secure password in lieu of an insecure 4 digit PIN. If you would like to return to using a PIN, follow the previous assignment for adding a PIN.

Challenge Questions

A Challenge Question is a way for websites to authenticate who you claim to be when you contact support because of a lost or compromised password.

For example, when registering at a website you may see: *Question: Where did your mother and father meet?* Or: *Question: Who is the most important person you have ever met?*

The problem with this strategy is that most answers easily are discovered with an Internet search either of your personal information or a bit of social engineering.

The solution is to give bogus answers. For example, my answer to the first question, *Where did your mother and father meet?* may be: *1954 Plymouth back seat*. It would not be possible for a hacker to discover this answer, as it is completely bogus. My mother tells me it was really a 1952 Dodge.

Unless you are some type of savant, there is no way you will remember the answers to your challenge questions. But there is no need to remember. We can use a utility that is highly secure and designed to hold secrets such as passwords and challenge questions. Consider *LastPass*.

1. Vulnerability: Passwords

LastPass

A great solution to the problem of password and challenge question management is *LastPass* at *http://www.LastPass.com*.

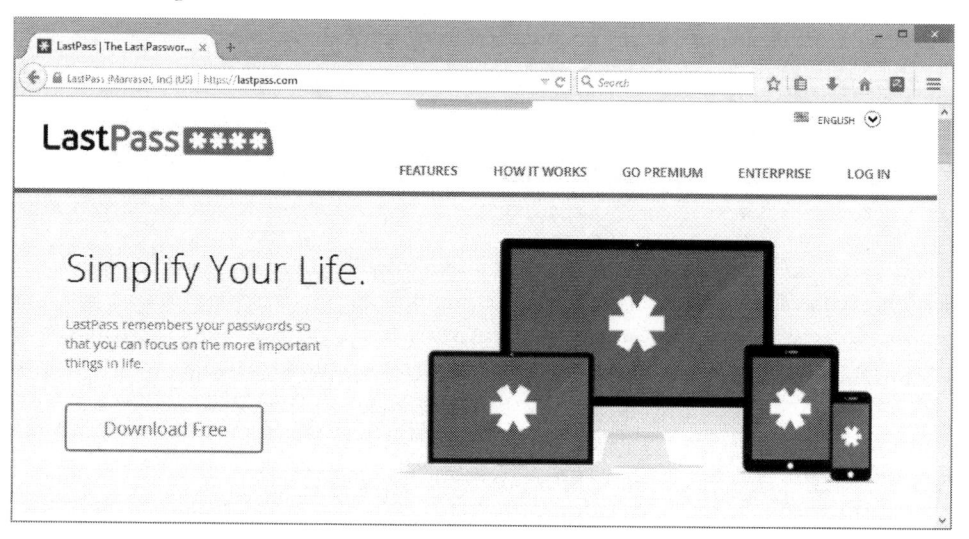

The most important advantage of LastPass is that you no longer have to concern yourself with Internet passwords – the correct response becomes automatic. LastPass will keep your Internet passwords available in each of your browsers and all of your devices – even across operating systems. It also securely stores manually entered data such as challenge questions. LastPass provides the following solutions:

- Provides free (ad supported) and premium (no ads) options
- Automatically remembers your Internet passwords, fully encrypted
- Auto fills web-based forms and authentication fields
- Stores notes and challenge questions and answers (Q&A), fully encrypted
- Synchronizes across multiple browsers
- Synchronizes across multiple computers
- Synchronizes across Windows, OS X, iOS, Blackberry, Windows Phone, Android

1. Vulnerability: Passwords

- Automatically generates very strong passwords, which since you do not need to remember them, provide even greater online security.

Assignment: Install LastPass

In this assignment, we will download and install LastPass on your Windows computer. As this is the free version, it will synchronize across all of your computers, but it will not synchronize with mobile devices. If you would like to be able to synchronize with mobile devices, after installing *LastPass Free*, upgrade to *LastPass Premium*.

1. Open a browser and surf to LastPass at *http://LastPass.com*. Select the Download Free button.

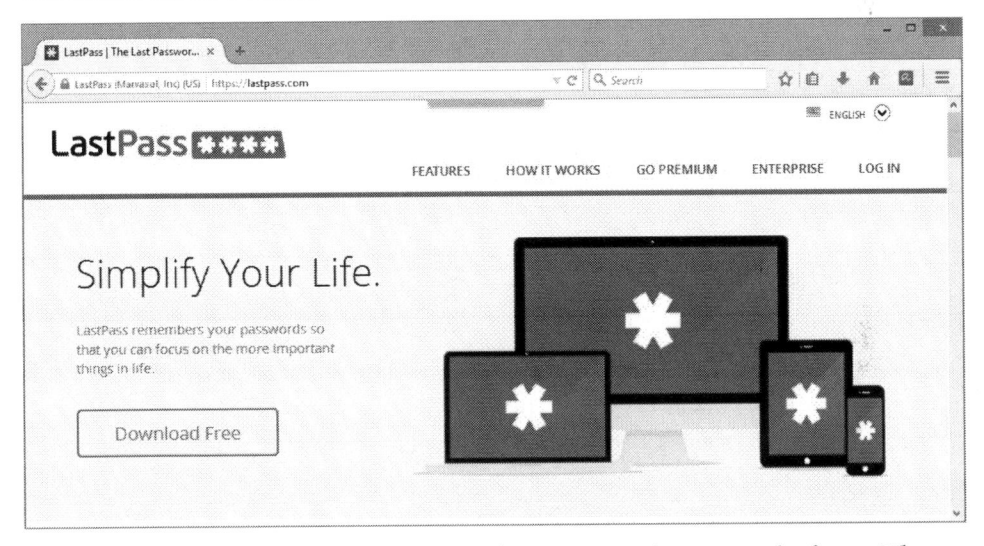

LastPass has a different download for each computer/browser platform. The website will automatically determine which platform combination you currently are on, and recommend the appropriate plug-in to download. As most PC users use more than one browser, I recommend downloading the universal installer.

1. Vulnerability: Passwords

2. In the *Recommended LastPass Download* page, click on *Windows*. This will take you to the LastPass for Windows

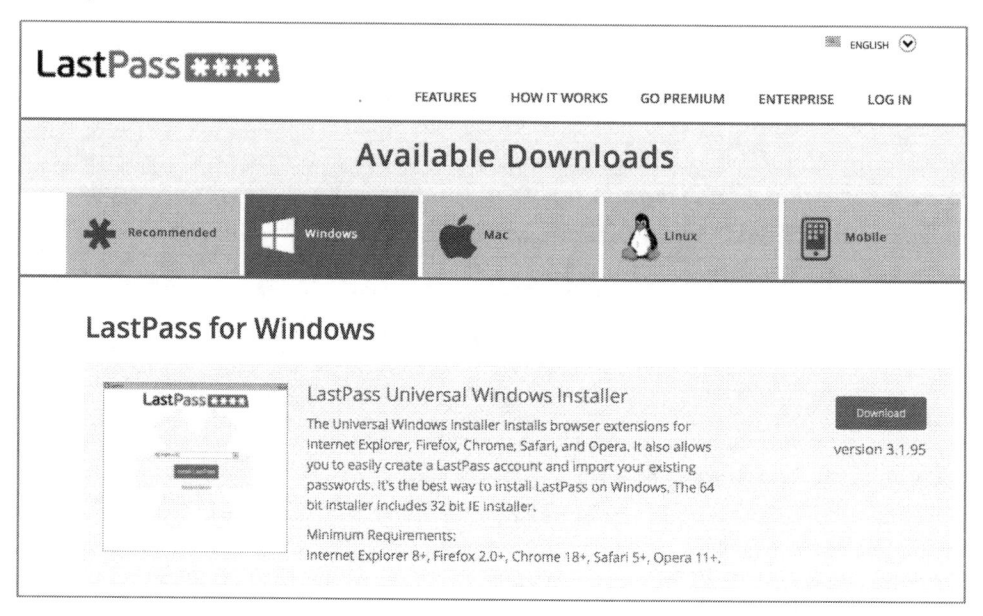

3. Select the *Download* button for *LastPass Universal Windows Installer*.

4. The *Opening lastpass_x64.exe (or x32)* window will appear. Select the *Save File* button.

5. When the window *User Account Control Do you want to allow the following program to make changes to this computer?* appears, select the *Yes* button. Once the installer has downloaded, click on Run and the installer will launch.

1. Vulnerability: Passwords

6. When the installer opens, click the *Advanced Options* button.

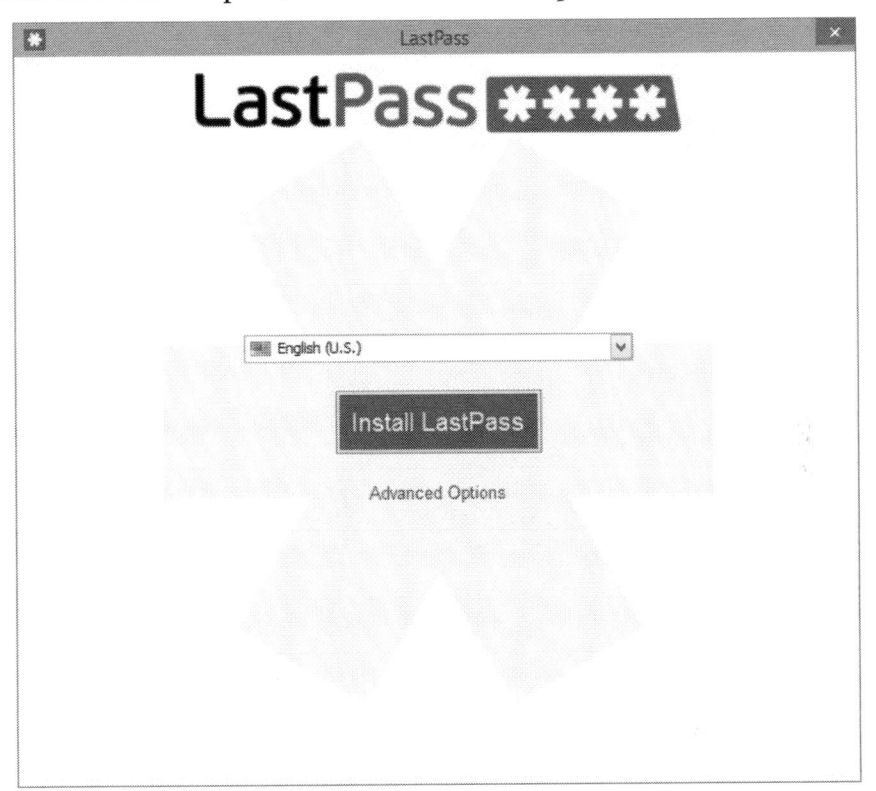

1. Vulnerability: Passwords

7. In the *Advanced Options* windows, configure to taste, and then select the *Install LastPass* button.

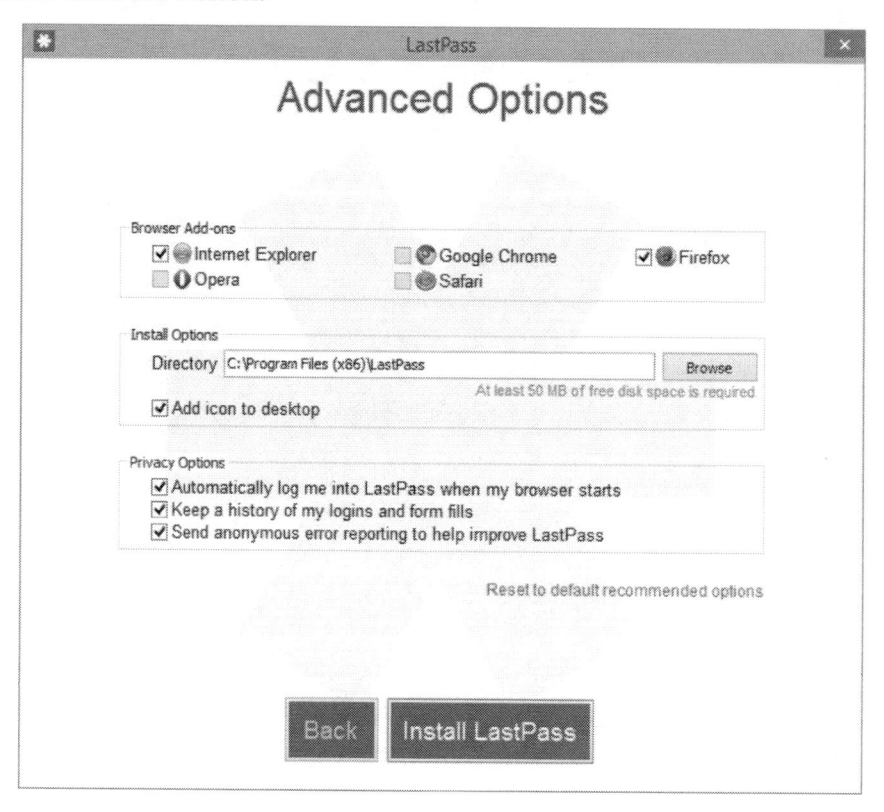

1. Vulnerability: Passwords

8. At the *Create or Log In* window, select the *Create a New Account* button.

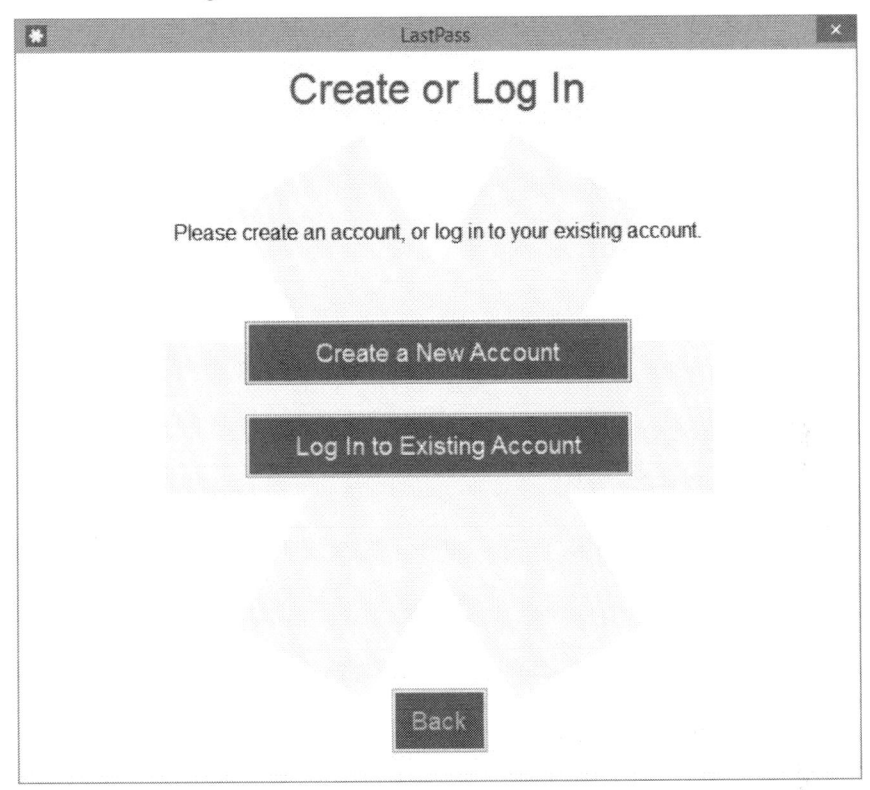

1. Vulnerability: Passwords

9. At the *Create a LastPass Account* window, enter the required information, including a strong password, and then select the *Create Account* button.

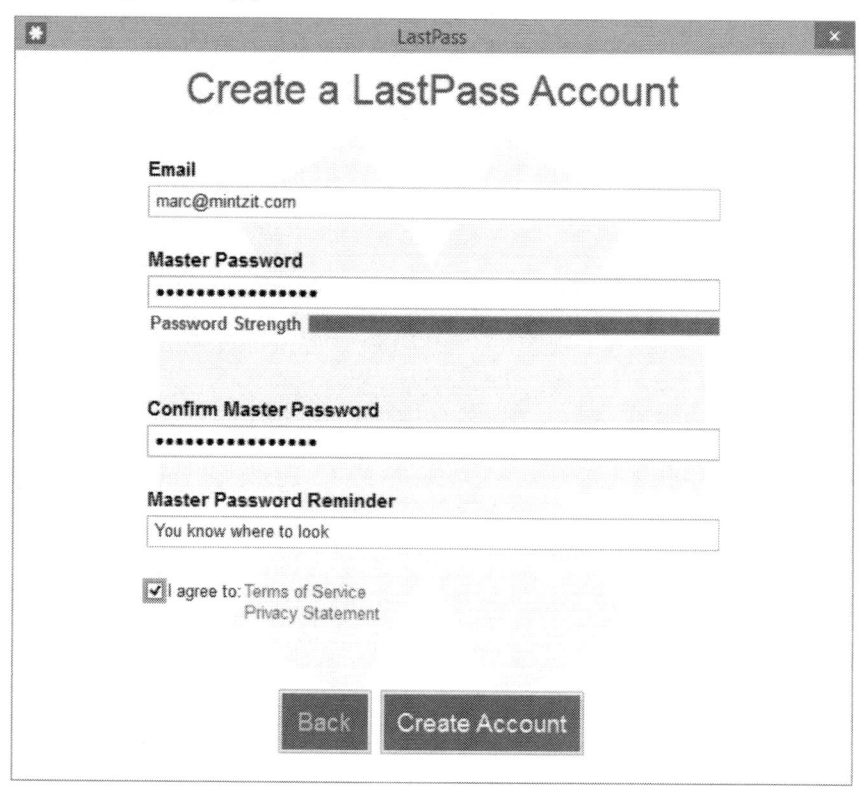

1. Vulnerability: Passwords

10. If prompted, follow the on-screen instructions to complete the LastPass installation.

> The LastPass browser add-on has been installed into Firefox. You're now just a few clicks away from signing in.
>
> *Please enable the LastPass browser add-on for Firefox by:*
>
> 1. *Switching to the 'Install Add-on' browser tab.*
> 2. *Checking the 'Allow this installation' checkbox.*
> 3. *Clicking on the 'Continue' button.*
> 4. *Clicking on the 'Restart Firefox' button to restart Firefox.*
>
> If your web browser does not display a browser tab labeled **'Install Add-on'**, please click here.

1. Vulnerability: Passwords

11. At the prompt, restart the browser, or exit and then open a browser to activate LastPass. You will see the LastPass icon in your browser tool bar.

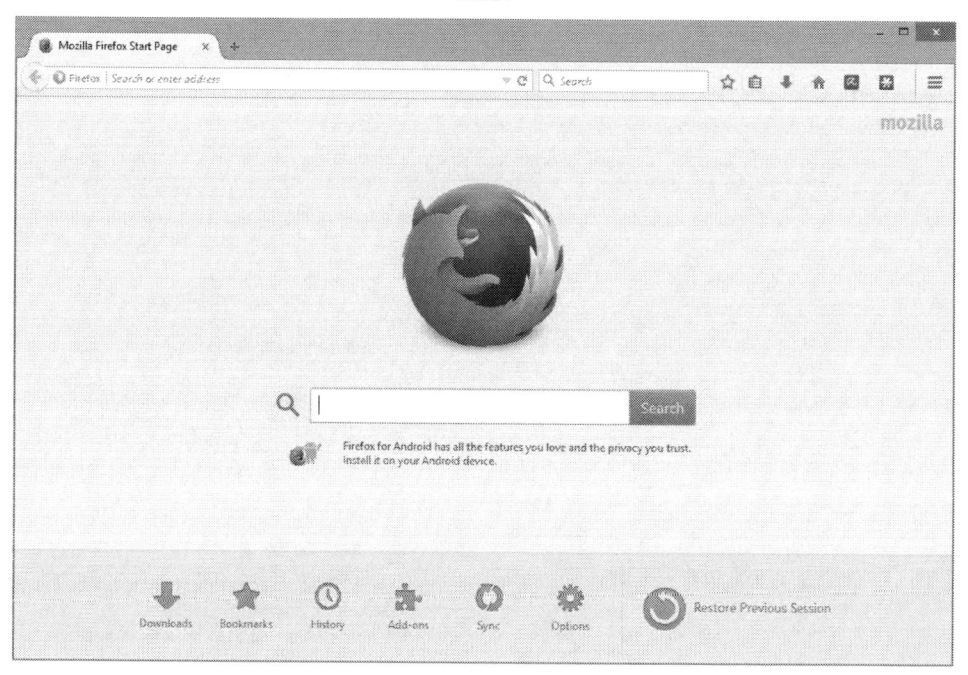

1. Vulnerability: Passwords

12. Select the LastPass icon in your browser's tool bar. The *LastPass Login* window appears. Enter the *Email* and *Master Password* used when registering, configure to taste, and then select the *Login* button.

13. In the LastPass window, select the *Settings* link.

You now are logged into LastPass in your browser.

Assignment: Configure LastPass

1. Once LastPass is installed, it must be configured. Open any of your browsers. You will find the *LastPass* button in the browser navigation bar.

Not logged into LastPass   *Logged into LastPass*

1. Vulnerability: Passwords

2. If you are not yet logged into LastPass, select the *LastPass* button, enter your credentials, and then select the *Log In* button.

3. Once logged into LastPass, select the *LastPass* icon in the tool bar, and then select *My LastPass Vault*. This will take you to your LastPass account page.

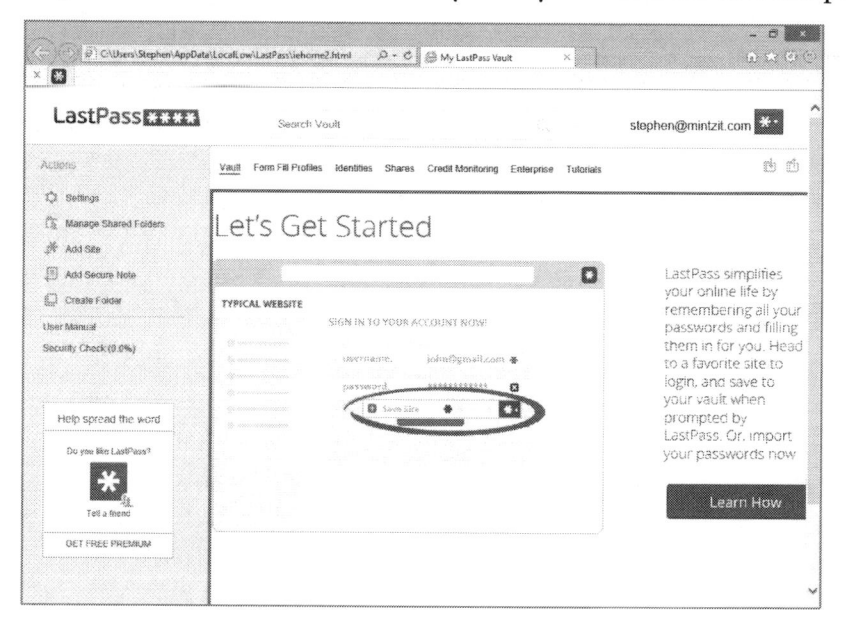

1. Vulnerability: Passwords

4. From the sidebar, select *Settings*. The *Edit Settings* window appears. Complete to your taste, and then select the *Update* button.

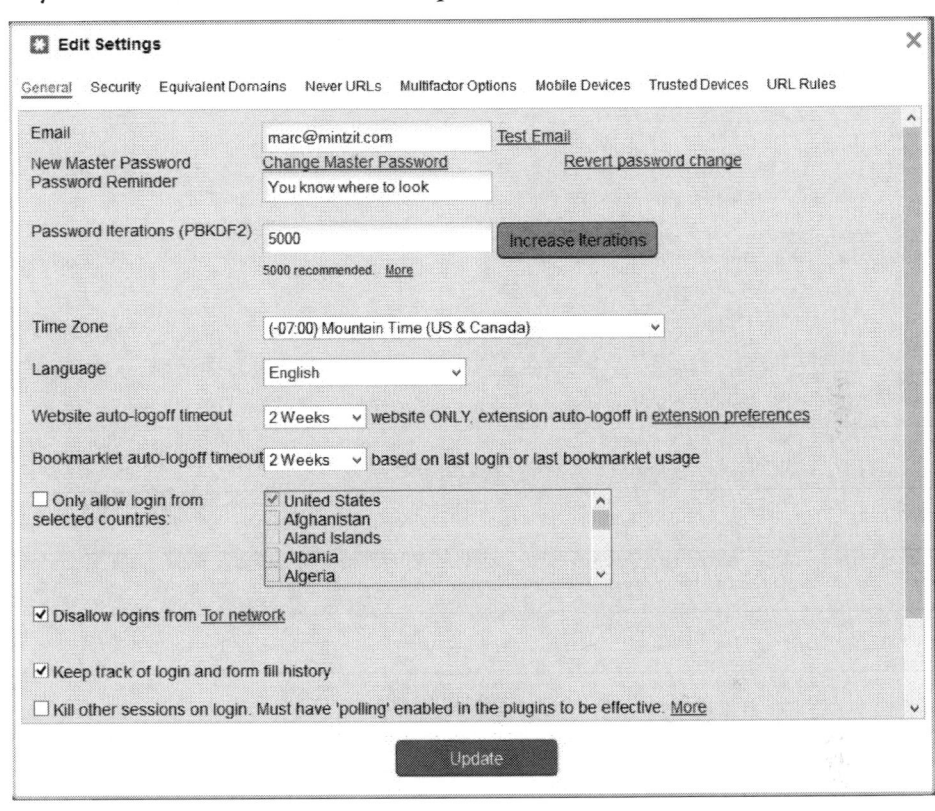

1. Vulnerability: Passwords

5. From the sidebar select *Settings*, then from the tabs select *Form Fill Profiles*, and then select the *Create A Profile* button.

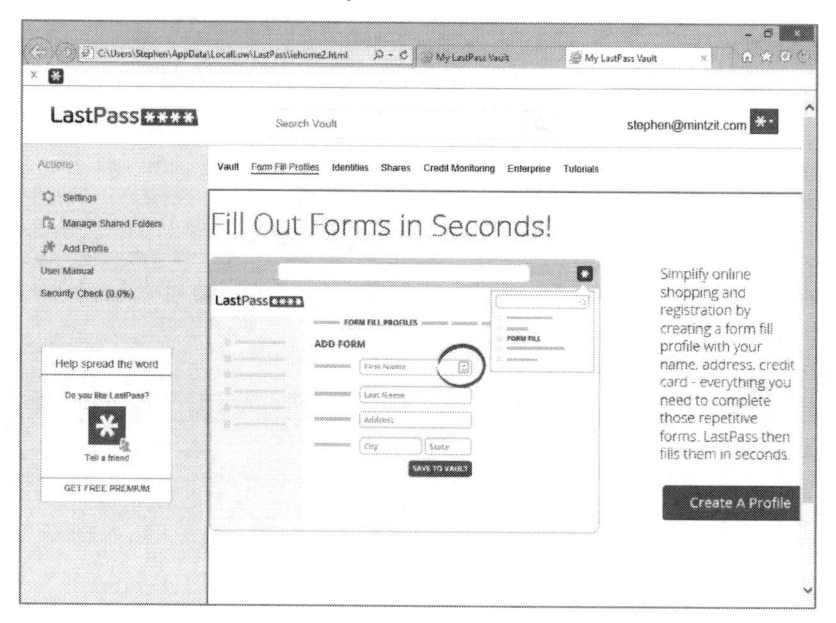

6. The *Add Form Fill Profile* window opens.

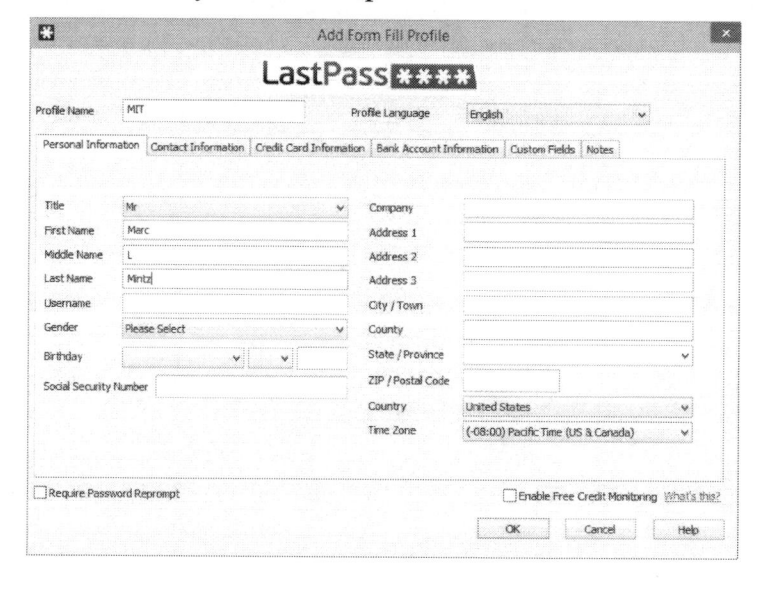

1. Vulnerability: Passwords

7. In the *Profile Name* field, enter a name for this profile.
8. Select the *Personal Information* tab, enter the requested information, and then select the *Ok* button. You will be returned to the main window.
9. Select the edit button ✏ to complete your profile.
10. Select the *Contact Information* tab, enter the requested information, repeat for all tabs, and then click on the *OK* button.

Assignment: Use LastPass to Save Website Authentication Credentials

Once LastPass is installed, put it to use. In this assignment we will use LastPass to store the user name and password for Facebook.

1. Open a browser, and go to Facebook: *https://facebook.com*.

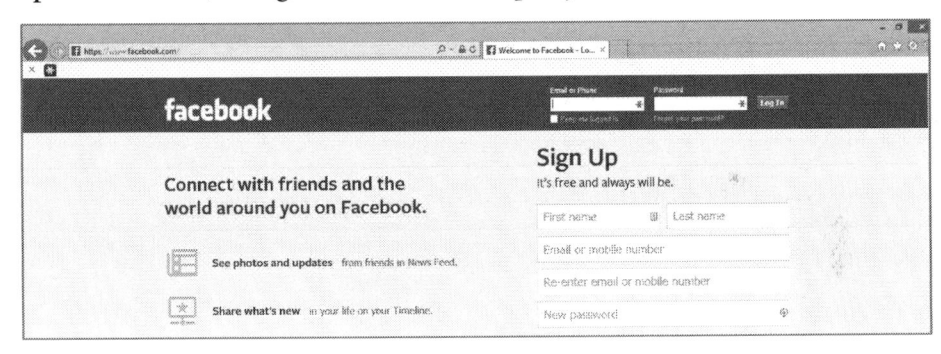

1. Vulnerability: Passwords

2. As this is the first time you have visited Facebook since installing LastPass, your log in credentials have not yet been stored in LastPass. Enter your Email or Phone and Password information, and then select the *Log in* button.

3. LastPass will detect that there is a form on this page, and present an option to remember your credentials. This will appear just under the navigation bar. Select the *Save Site* button.

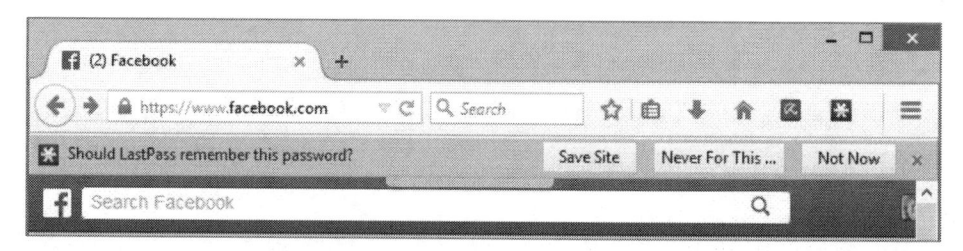

4. The LastPass *Add LastPass Site* window will open for the site. Configure to your taste and then select the *Save Site* button. This will return you to the Facebook page.

5. Click the *LastPass* icon and then click on *Sites*. You should see an item labeled *Social*, and if you click on this, you will find *facebook.com* under this section.

6. While in Facebook, take a moment to join our *Practical Paranoia* group. In the Facebook *Search* field, enter *Practical Paranoia*.

1. Vulnerability: Passwords

7. From the search results, select the *Practical Paranoia: Security Essentials Public Group*.

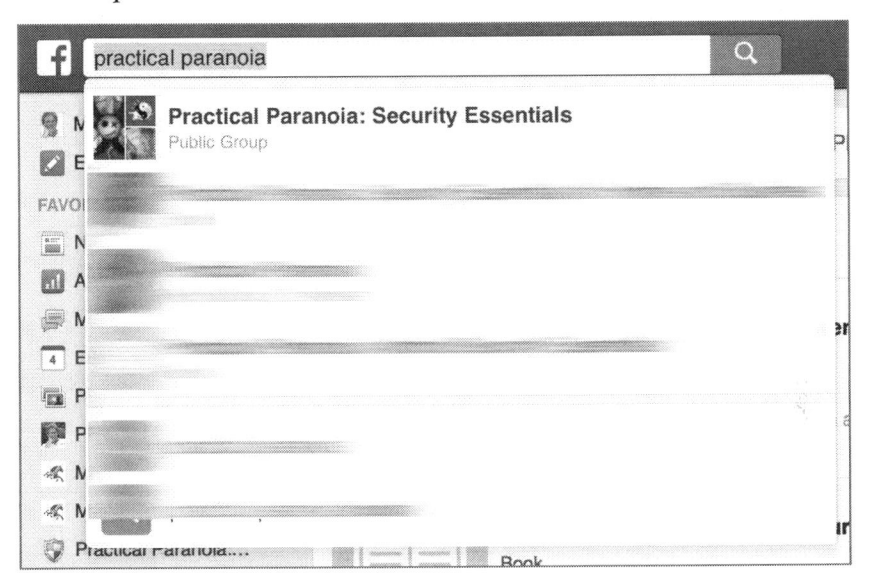

8. Select the *Join Group* button. Join requests are approved within 24 hours.

9. Quit your web browser.

Congratulations. Your Facebook account credentials are now stored in LastPass, so you do not need to remember them.

Assignment: Use LastPass to Auto Fill Website Authentication

When LastPass has saved user name and password information for a site, you will never need to manually enter that information again. For this assignment, we will revisit Facebook and allow LastPass to enter our credentials.

1. Launch a browser and surf to Facebook at *http://facebook.com*. Take note that the authentication credentials have been automatically entered by LastPass.

1. Vulnerability: Passwords

2. Quit the browser.

You have just successfully proved that LastPass is saving your credentials.

Review Questions

1. Microsoft Recommends at least 12 characters for passwords to meet minimum length requirements. (True or False)

2. Two-factor authentication ensures that an account is secured using one or more independent verification sources. (True or False)

3. It is helpful to pick obscure challenge questions, or provide bogus answers. (True or False)

4. What is one website that can be used to test the strength of a password?

2. Vulnerability: Updates

Every new beginning comes from some other beginning's end.
–Seneca, Roman philosopher, statesman, and dramatist

System Updates

The majority of Windows users simply fail to update their systems. In most cases they give the reason that updates slow down the computers, or they are concerned about introducing instability to their computers.

It occasionally is true that updates may introduce instability – but it is far more likely that not updating will create greater instability.

More important is that many updates actually are about patching vulnerabilities and security holes in the system. Fixing these security issues is so important that US-CERT (Homeland Security division responsible for cyber terrorism and IT security) strongly recommends that all users update all computers within 48 hours of an update release.

There are fundamentally three reasons for updates and upgrades:

- **Bug fixes**. All software and hardware have bugs. We simply never will be rid of them. Developers do want to squash as many as possible so that you are so happy with their product and will continue to pay for upgrades.

- **Monetization**. Updates to operating systems and applications almost always are free, or included in the price of the original purchase. Upgrades typically are for fee. But developers will include significant new features in an upgrade to encourage the market to purchase, so the developers can afford to stay in business.

- **Security patches**. Although rarely talked about, one of the most important reasons for an update is to patch newly discovered security holes. Without the update, your computer may be highly vulnerable to attack.

It is for this last reason alone that we implore clients to be consistent with the update process.

To protect your computer from security holes in the operating system, it is critical to check for updates daily. Fortunately, we can automate this process.

2. Vulnerability: Updates

Assignment: Configure System Updates

In this assignment, we will automate the process of updating the Windows operating system and Microsoft applications.

1. Click on the *Start* menu, and then click on *Settings*. On this screen, click on *Update & Security*.

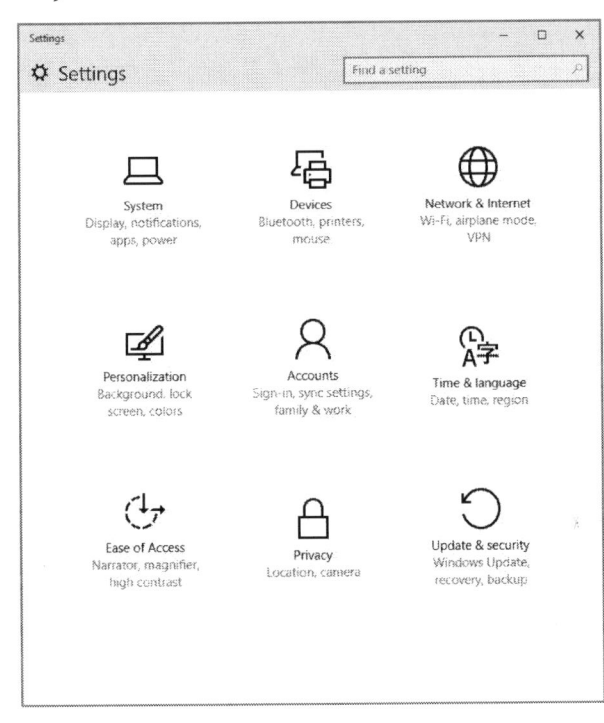

2. Vulnerability: Updates

2. From the *Update & Security* page, click on *Windows Update* and then *Advanced options.* Your window should look like this.

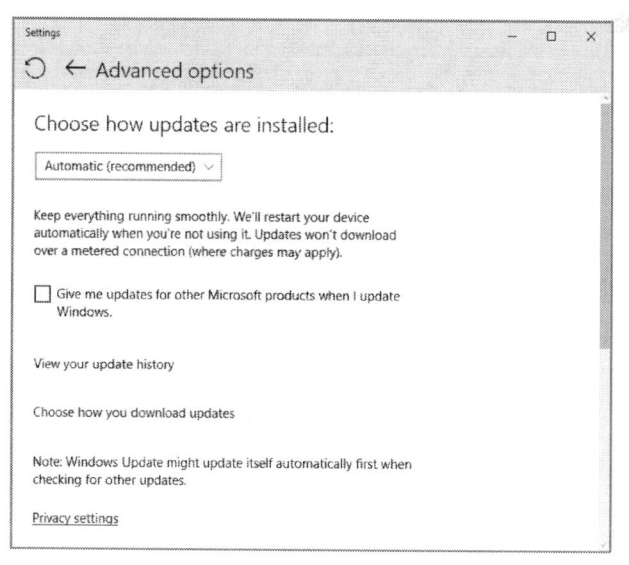

3. If you would like Windows to not automatically set a time to do updates, then click on *Automatic (recommended)* and change this option to *Notify to schedule restart.* This will prompt you to download updates and also prompt you to restart for those updates.

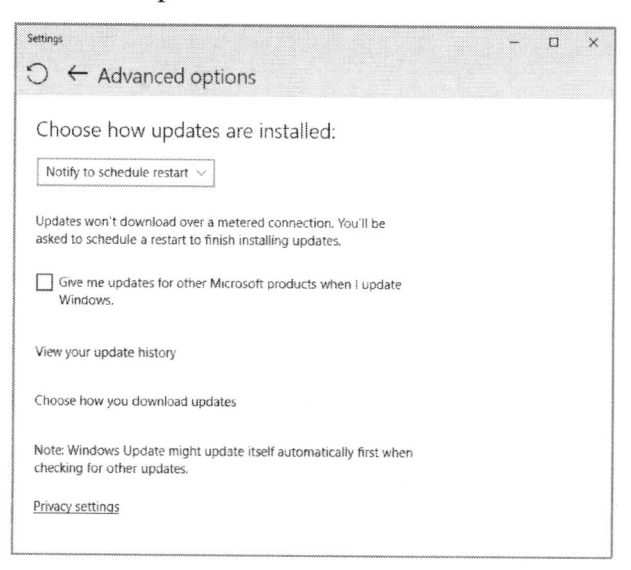

2. Vulnerability: Updates

4. If you would like to restrict how you download updates, then click *Choose how you download updates*. If you would like to only download your updates directly from Microsoft, then switch the toggle to *Off*.

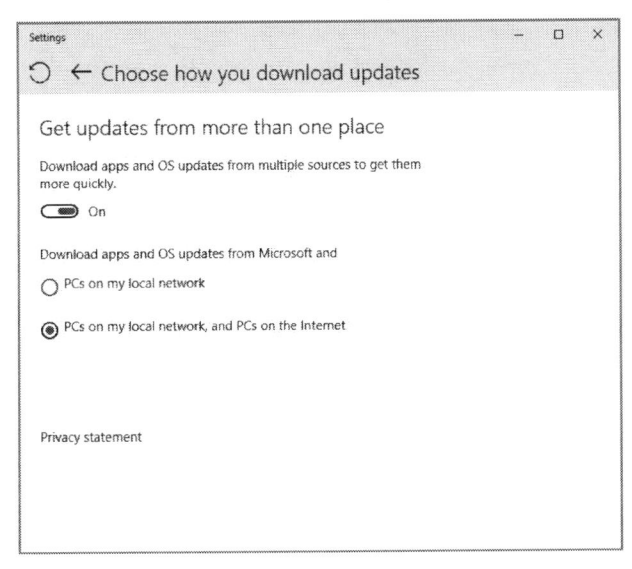

5. Press the back button in the upper left, and then click on *View your update history*. Review your updates here. If you would like to uninstall an update, select *Uninstall updates*.

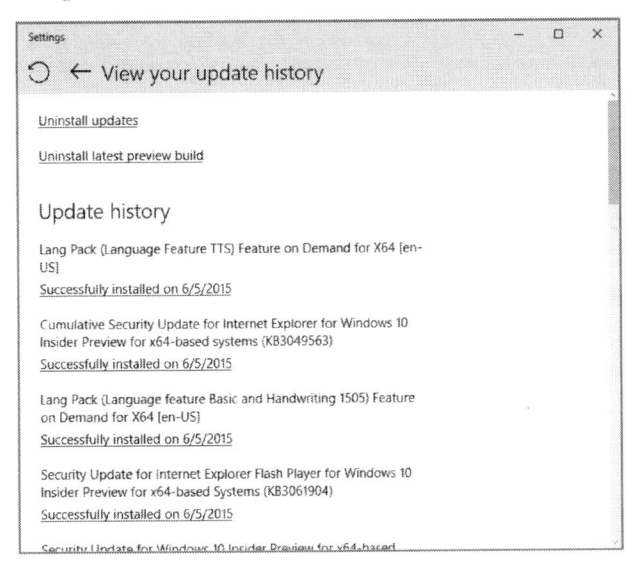

2. Vulnerability: Updates

6. A new dialog box will appear. In the *Installed Updates* window, select the update you would like to uninstall and click *Uninstall*. It will confirm your choice, and then click *Yes*.

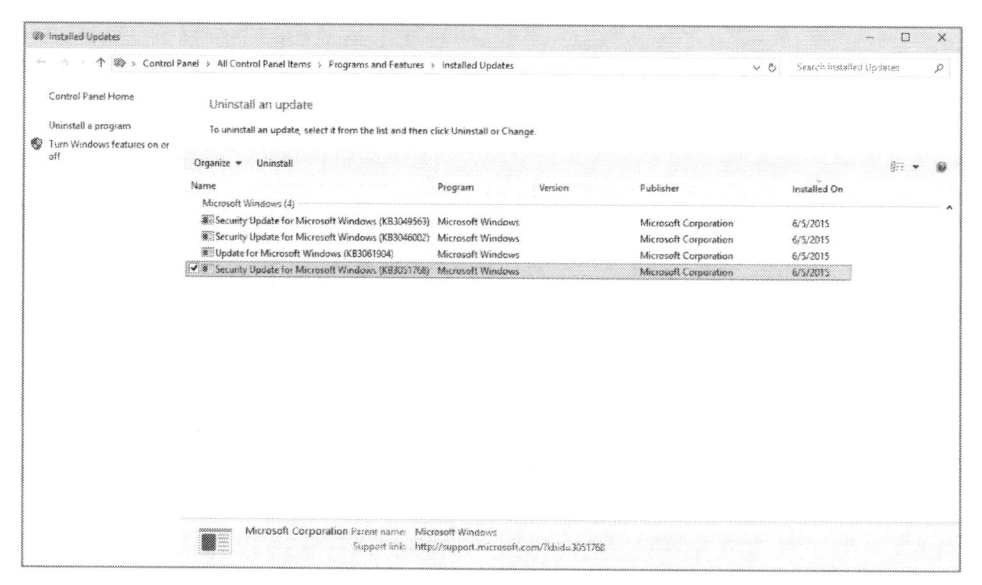

7. When done, press the *X* in the upper right to close both windows.

Congratulations, Windows will now do your updates for you.

Application Updates with Ninite Updater

Windows has built-in functions to update Microsoft applications only. It does not auto-update 3rd-party applications. Although some 3rd-party applications have built-in automatic updating, this is not the norm. Also, system preferences, plug-ins, and other software do not typically automatically update.

It is critical to keep all of your software up-to-date so that vulnerabilities can be secured. Recently, Adobe Flash and Oracle Java have been used by criminal elements to gain control over computers to access user data. Many other software points have been, can, and will be exploited.

As the typical user has over 100 applications, plug-ins, extensions, etc., by far the fastest, easiest, and most cost-effective way to do this is to automate the process. An inexpensive way to automate is to use *Ninite Updater* *https://ninite.com/updater* ($9.99/year license).

Assignment: Install Ninite Updater

In this assignment we will download, install, and configure Ninite to automate application updates.

2. Vulnerability: Updates

1. Open a browser and surf to *https://ninite.com/updater*. You will need to purchase this product. Click on the *Buy it* button.

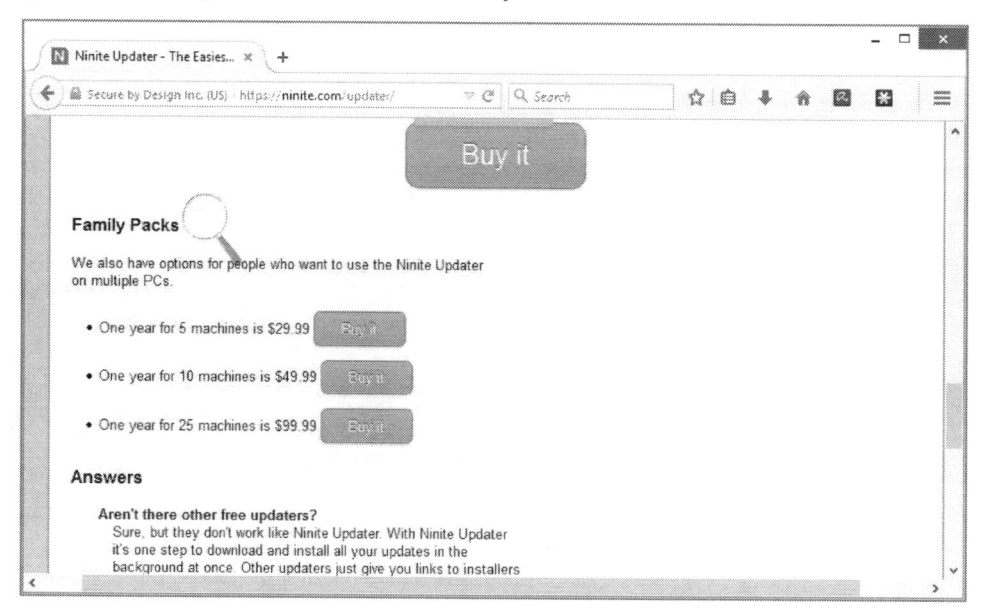

2. The application website appears. Purchase Ninite Updater and *Ninite Updater* will download.

3. Locate the download, which by default, is your *Downloads* folder.

4. Open the *Ninite Updater* and it will install and run a check of all apps currently installed.

5. The Ninite icon "N" will appear in the Taskbar. It will be green if it has found no updates.

2. Vulnerability: Updates

6. From now on, Ninite will run automatically and notify of any apps needing updates.

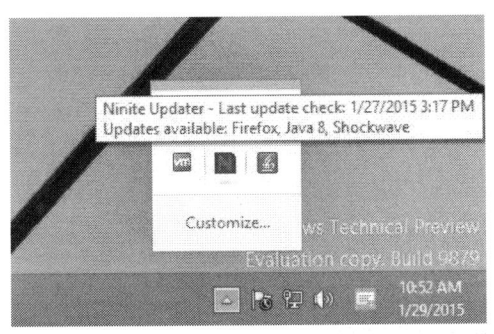

   - On the *Taskbar,* you will either see an icon that looks like a Red *N* or click on the arrow pointing up or then you will see the *Ninite* icon.
   - When hovering a cursor over the *Ninite* icon, you will see the available updates and when it last did a scan.

7. Click on the *Ninite* icon to display its pop-up menu.

8. Click on *Install updates* to display any updates *Ninite* has discovered.

9. Click the *Update* button and it will install the discovered updates.

2. Vulnerability: Updates

Review Questions

1. What are the three fundamental reasons for security updates and upgrades?
2. The department of Homeland Security recommends installing updates no later than 72 hours after their release. (True or False)
3. Name one way in which 3rd party applications can be monitored and patched as needed.

3. Vulnerability: User Account

If money is your hope for independence you will never have it. The only real security that a man will have in this world is a reserve of knowledge, experience, and ability.

–Henry Ford

User Accounts

Windows 10 allows 4 different types of user accounts, each with its own pros and cons, powers and limitations:

- **Administrator Account**. There should always be at least one, and may be an unlimited number of administrators, or administrative user accounts, each having identical power over the computer. Windows 10 automatically grants an Administrator account to the first person that signs in to a new PC. That person effectively owns the PC. What makes an Administrator unique above the Standard, Child, and Microsoft Account users are its abilities to:
    - Create new user accounts
    - Delete user accounts
    - Modify the contents of the root level of the hard drive
    - Authorize the installation or removal of applications and system updates
- **Standard Account**. There can be an unlimited number of Standard accounts. This is the recommended account level for most users working locally on the computer. Standard accounts can open and work without limitations with any application installed on your PC. The advantage of working as a Standard account is that it is not possible to damage the operating system or applications. Standard accounts come with limits that keep them from installing programs (and potential viruses).
- **Child Account**. This account is fundamentally a Standard account with the *Family Safety* controls turned on. Family Safety Controls further restrict the powers of the account by limiting:
    - Access to specific applications
    - Access to specific websites or any adult site
    - The hours for which the user may stay logged in
- **Microsoft Account**. Windows 8 introduced a new account called *Microsoft* account. It simply means that a person's account is tied to Microsoft's servers, making it easier to set up new devices (but making access more difficult when

3. Vulnerability: User Account

servers are down). When you log on using your Microsoft account it remembers all of your settings in Windows including:

- Choice of desktop wallpaper
- Wi-Fi network logon information
- Downloaded or purchased apps

Like Local accounts, Microsoft accounts can either be Administrator or Standard accounts.

In order to use the family safety features you must have a Microsoft or Outlook.com enabled account as the administrator of the children accounts.

3. Vulnerability: User Account

Never Log In as an Administrator

Maybe it is the human condition. We want power, authority, and more power. This carries over into how we log in to the computer. Everyone wants to be the administrator of his or her computer. Windows 10 enables this. When the owner of a new PC boots up for the first time, that person is prompted to create a user account, which is by default an administrator account.

But this is bad juju.

If you have the bad luck of opening a malware attack on your computer (most often unknowingly) while you are logged in as an administrator, the malware will take on your user account power. This means the malware has full control and power over the computer – including all other user accounts. Yikes.

On the other hand, if you have the lousy luck to launch a malware attack while logged in as a non-administrative user, the malware will typically take on your non-admin power. Under this scenario, the malware has full control over your home files (documents, pictures, and videos) but nothing else.

I can hear the wailing from here: *But I need to be an administrator. How else will I be able to install software and updates, and perform maintenance?*

Fear not. In Windows 10, you do not need to be logged in as an administrator to perform administrator tasks (adding/deleting user accounts, installing/updating the system and applications, and running system diagnostic and repair utilities.) You can be logged in with any type of user account except for the *Child* account. You only need to authenticate with an administrator name and password when prompted.

To do this, you need to have an administrative user account on the computer, but log in with a non-admin (standard) user account. When you are prompted for an admin name and password while performing admin duties, just enter them.

3. Vulnerability: User Account

Assignment: Create an Administrative User Account

In this Part 1 of the assignment, you will create an administrative user account on the computer. In Part 2, you will change your own account (which is probably administrative) back to a standard user account.

1. Log in to the computer with your normal administrator account.
2. Click on the *Start* menu > *Settings* > *Accounts* > *Family & Other users*. If you would like the account to be attached to your Microsoft account, click *Add a family member*. Otherwise, click on *Add someone else to this PC*.

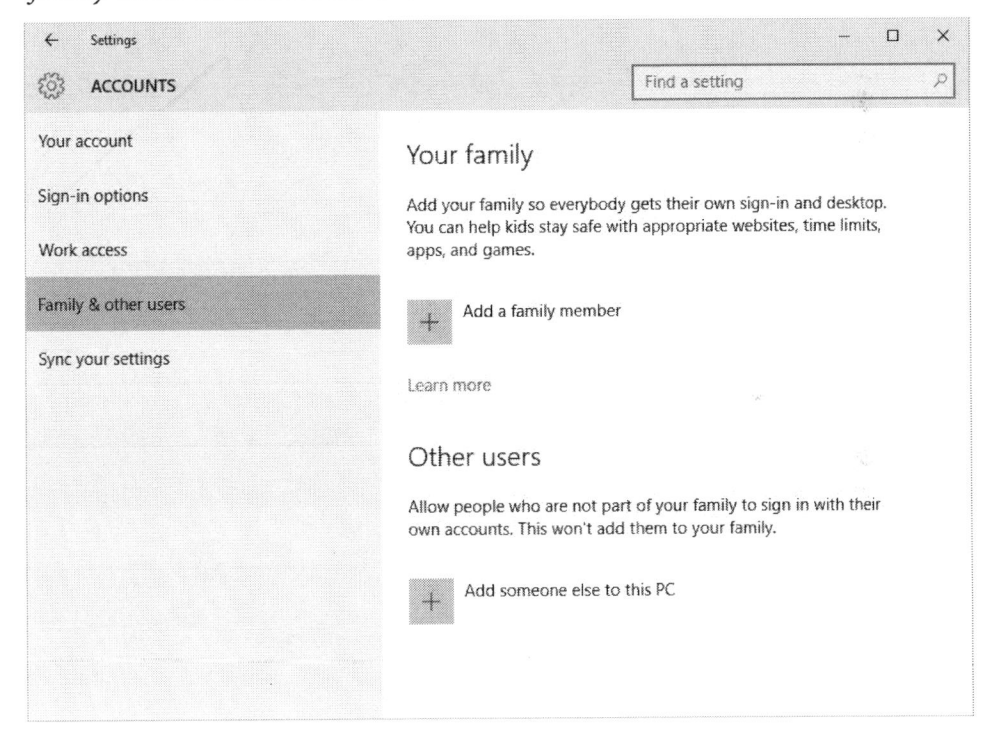

3. Vulnerability: User Account

3. You will be presented with a window to add a new user. By default, it will want you to create the new user with an email address. We will not be doing this. Click on the option *The person I want to add doesn't have an email address.*

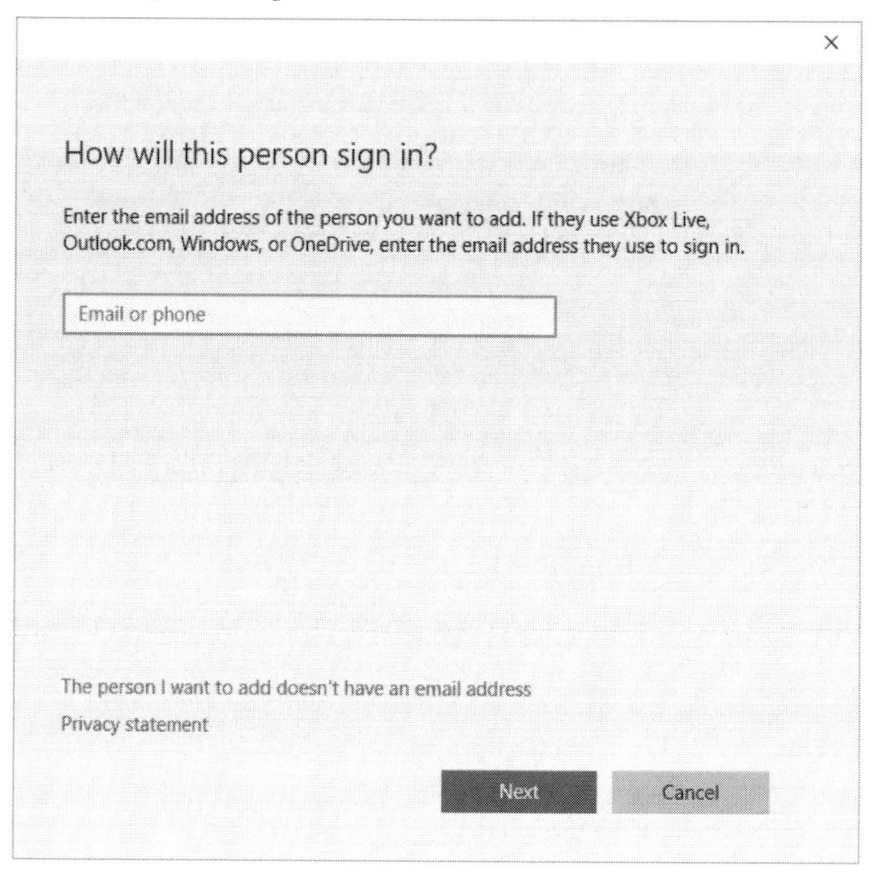

3. Vulnerability: User Account

4. Click on *Add a user without a Microsoft account*.

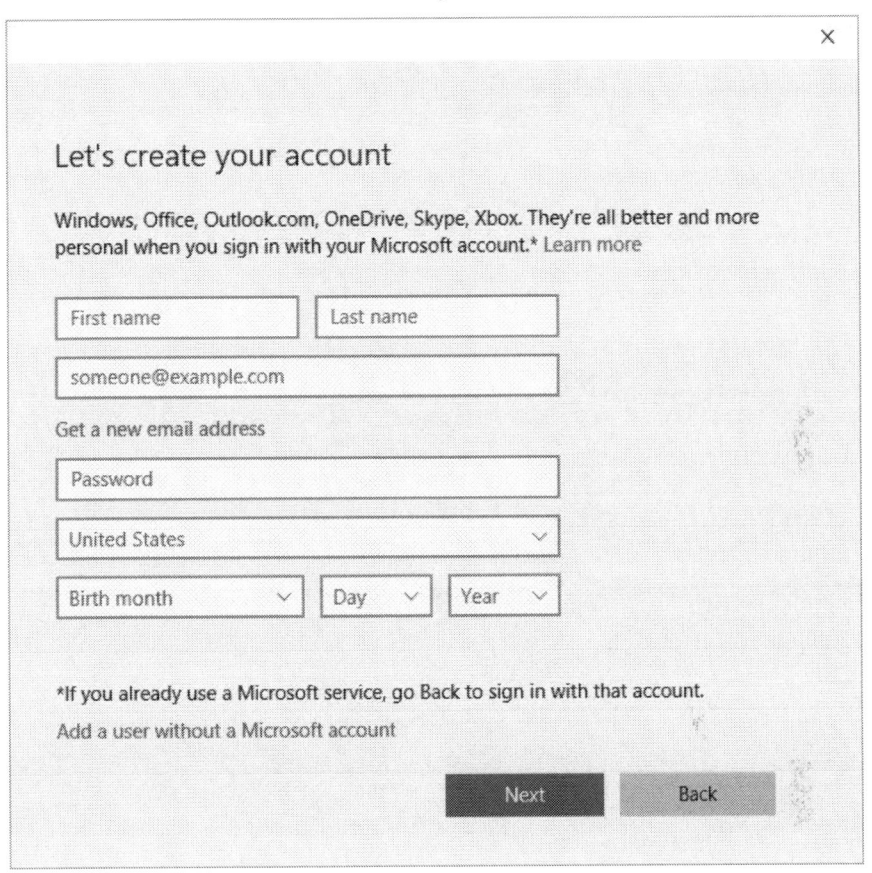

5. The *Create an account for this PC* opens. Enter the user name, password and password hint and click *Next*.

   - In the *username* field, enter *Admin*.

   - In the *password* field, enter a strong password. Reenter in the reenter password field.

   - In the *password hint* field, you must type a hint. Type a hint that will remind you of the password.

   - Click on the *Next* button to confirm your changes.

3. Vulnerability: User Account

Create an account for this PC

If you want to use a password, choose something that will be easy for you to remember but hard for others to guess.

Who's going to use this PC?

[Bob]

Make it secure.

[••••••••••••••••••]

[••••••••••••••••••]

[big dog]

[Back] [Next]

3. Vulnerability: User Account

6. On the Accounts window click on the account you created and click *Change account type.* This account is currently a standard user, we will now change it to an administrator account.

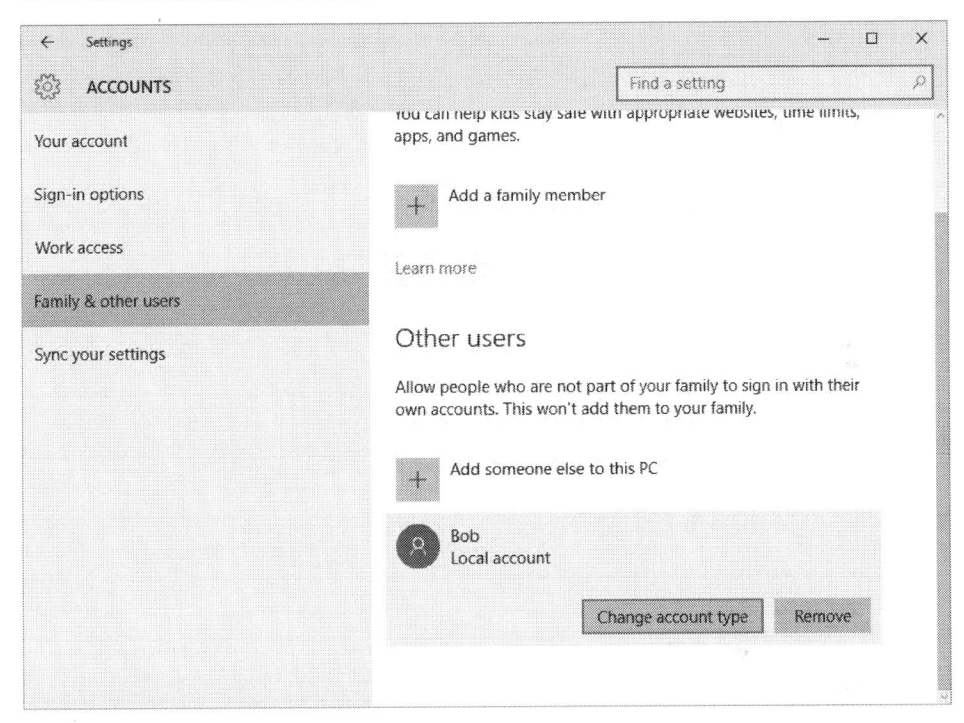

7. Select *Standard User* and change it to *Administrator.* Press *OK* to continue.

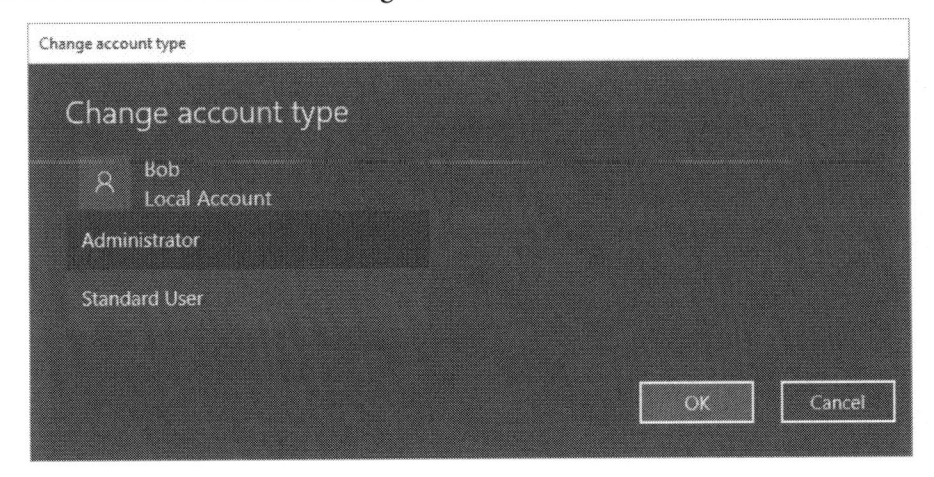

-85-

8. The *Accounts* window will now show your administrator account setup.

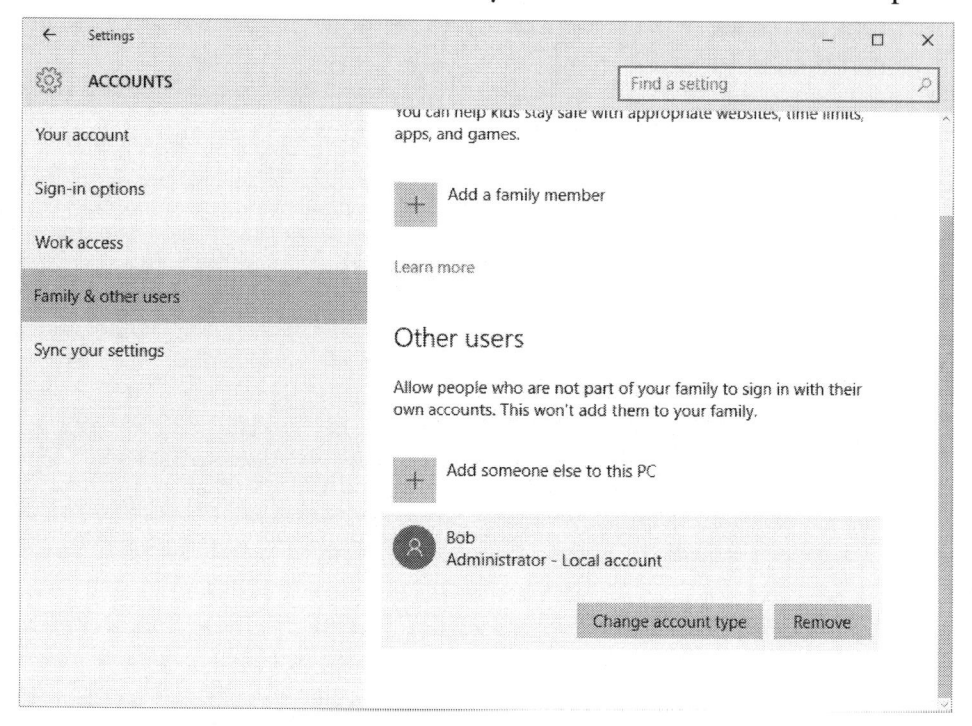

9. Click the *X* in the upper right corner to close the *User and accounts* window.

Congratulations. You have just created a new Administrator account.

Assignment: Change an Administrator to a Standard User

In Part 1 of this assignment (above), you created an administrative user account whose name and password can be used when needed. Now in Part 2, you change your own account to a standard user account, which will remain your regular log in account.

1. Click on the *Start* menu > *Settings* > *Accounts* > *Family & Other users*.

3. Vulnerability: User Account

2. Click on the account you want to change. Typically, this will be the account you currently use. Then click on the *Change account type* button to change account.

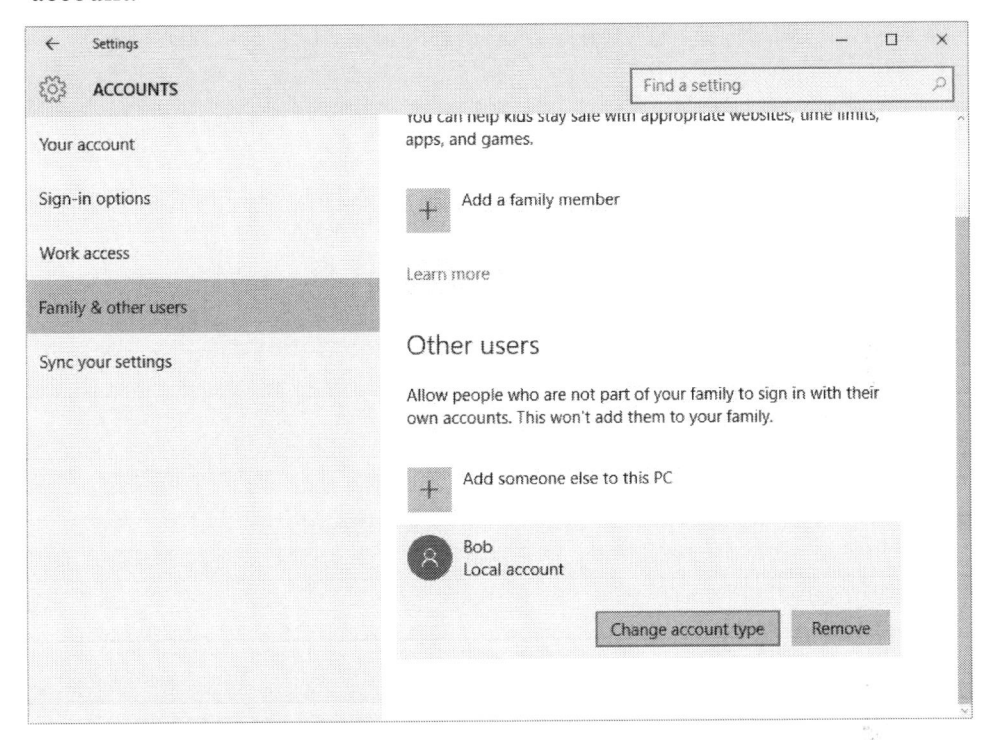

3. Click on the drop down menu, and then click *Standard user*.

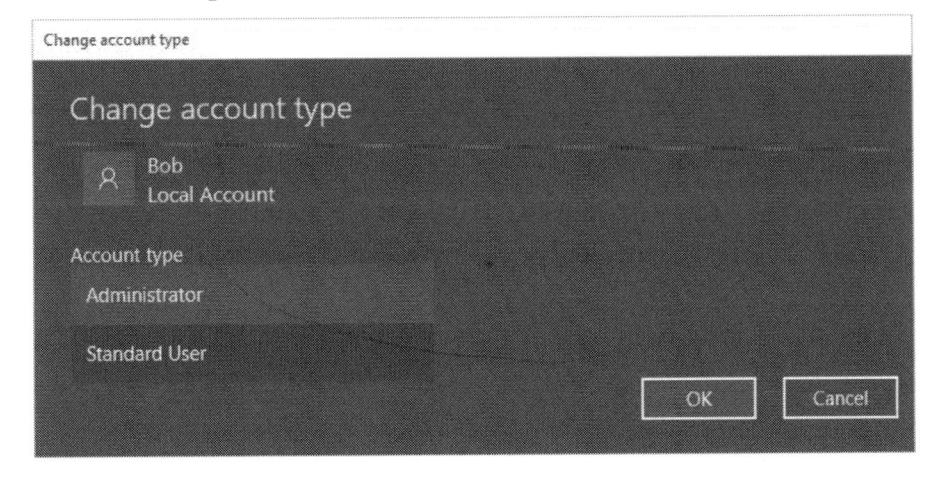

4. Click the *OK* button.

5. Click the *X* in the upper right corner to close the *User and accounts* window.

You have just changed an administrator account to a standard account.

Application Whitelisting and More With Parental Controls

In 2014, Target, Home Depot, and other major retailers were hacked for their customer databases. Although there were multiple breakdowns in the security protocols of these organizations, one step would likely have prevented all of the breaches–*Application whitelisting*. This same strategy should be used by both home and business systems to help secure computer systems.

Application whitelisting is a process that allows only authorized applications to run on a computer, blocking any executable that is not on the list. This is a vital ingredient to system security because even the very best anti-malware catches only 99.9% of the *known* bugs. What if your computer is penetrated by *unknown* malware? Anti-malware is of marginal use here. However, if your computer has application whitelisting in place, the unknown malware cretins are blocked from executing. In Windows 10, *Family Safety* can be used to perform application whitelisting.

Family Safety allows an Administrator to restrict access to only specific applications and services to any non-administrative user account. As the name implies, this feature was originally intended as a way for parents to better manage their children's account. It also is perfect for the business setting by restricting specific applications (disallowing Spotify, etc.), restricting access to specific websites (pornography, social media, etc.), or allowing access to the account only during work hours.

Once Family Safety has been used to implement application whitelisting, it will be necessary for the administrator to be available for a brief time while the unintended consequences shake out. It is common for some permitted applications to require the use of a restricted application or process. An administrator will need to be available to provide authorization.

Once Family Safety is established for a user account, the account is referred to as a *Child* account. Only non-administrative accounts may be managed. If creating a

3. Vulnerability: User Account

new user account, it can be initially setup as a *Child*. If the account already exists as a *Standard* account, it can be converted to a *Child*.

Assignment: Create a Child Account

For this assignment, we will be creating a child account. First, we will need to create the account within settings and then confirm the addition of a family member within Microsoft's *Family* service through your browser.

1. On the computer hosting the user account to be managed, click the *Start menu > Settings > Accounts > Family & Other Users*. In order to add a child account, they must be a part of your family. Click on *Add a family member*.

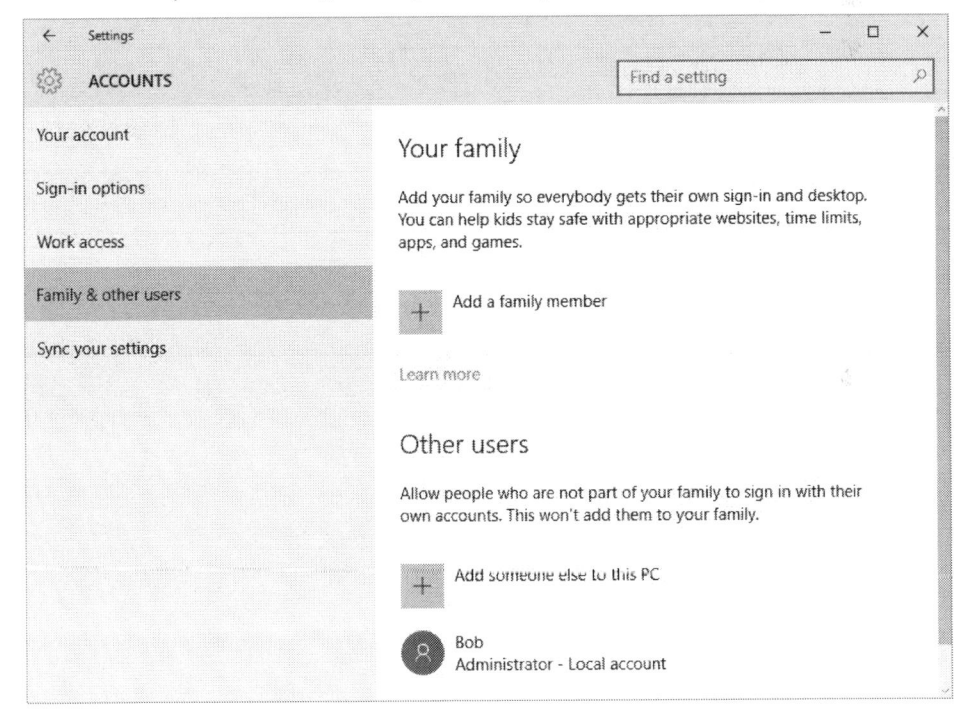

2. Click on *Add a child*.

3. Vulnerability: User Account

3. Enter the email address for the child account. If you do not have an email address for the account, you must set one up as family safety is an online-only feature. Click *Next*.

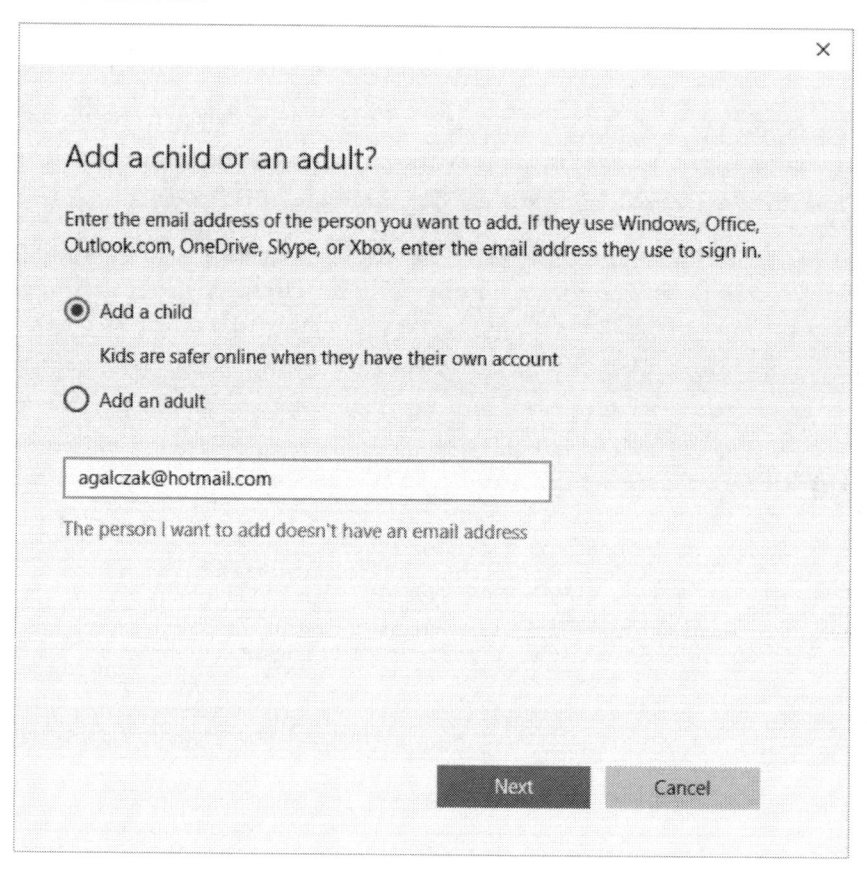

> ✕
>
> **Add a child or an adult?**
>
> Enter the email address of the person you want to add. If they use Windows, Office, Outlook.com, OneDrive, Skype, or Xbox, enter the email address they use to sign in.
>
> ● Add a child
>   Kids are safer online when they have their own account
>
> ○ Add an adult
>
> [agalczak@hotmail.com]
>
> The person I want to add doesn't have an email address
>
> [Next]   [Cancel]

3. Vulnerability: User Account

4. Click on *Confirm* to confirm the account that you would like to add as a child account.

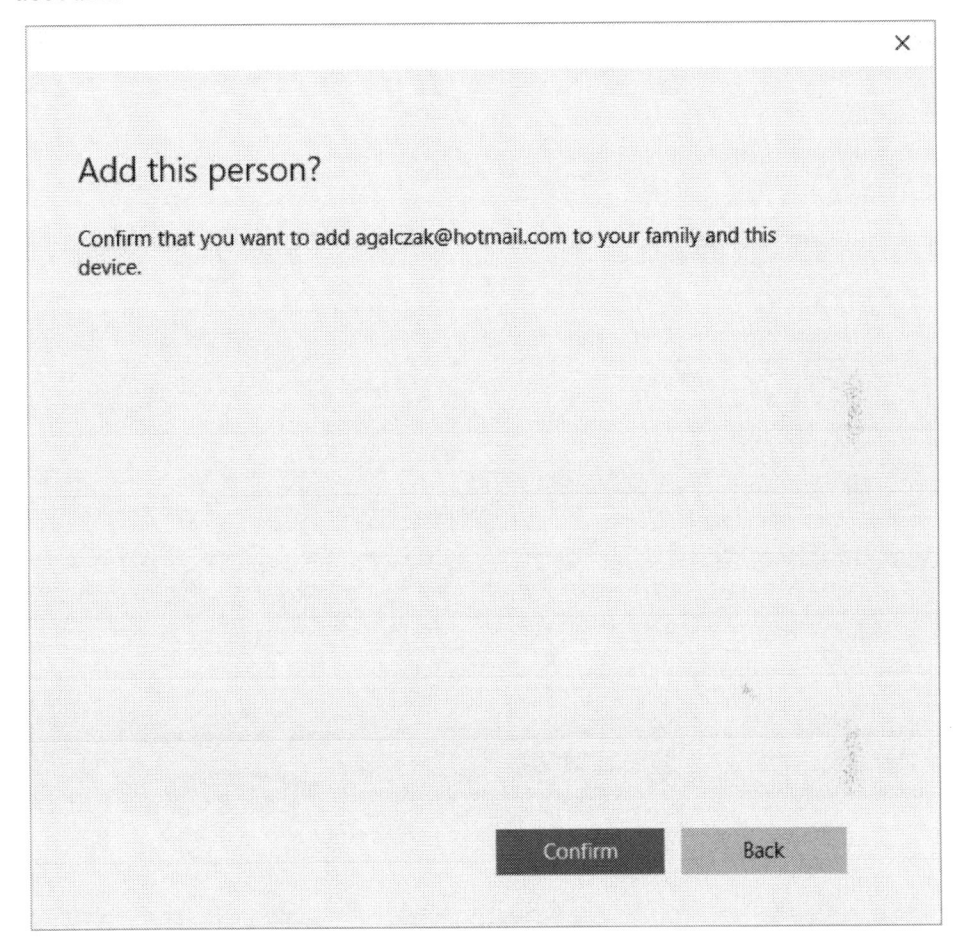

3. Vulnerability: User Account

5. The next screen will explain the email sent to the email for your child account. Click *Close* to close the window.

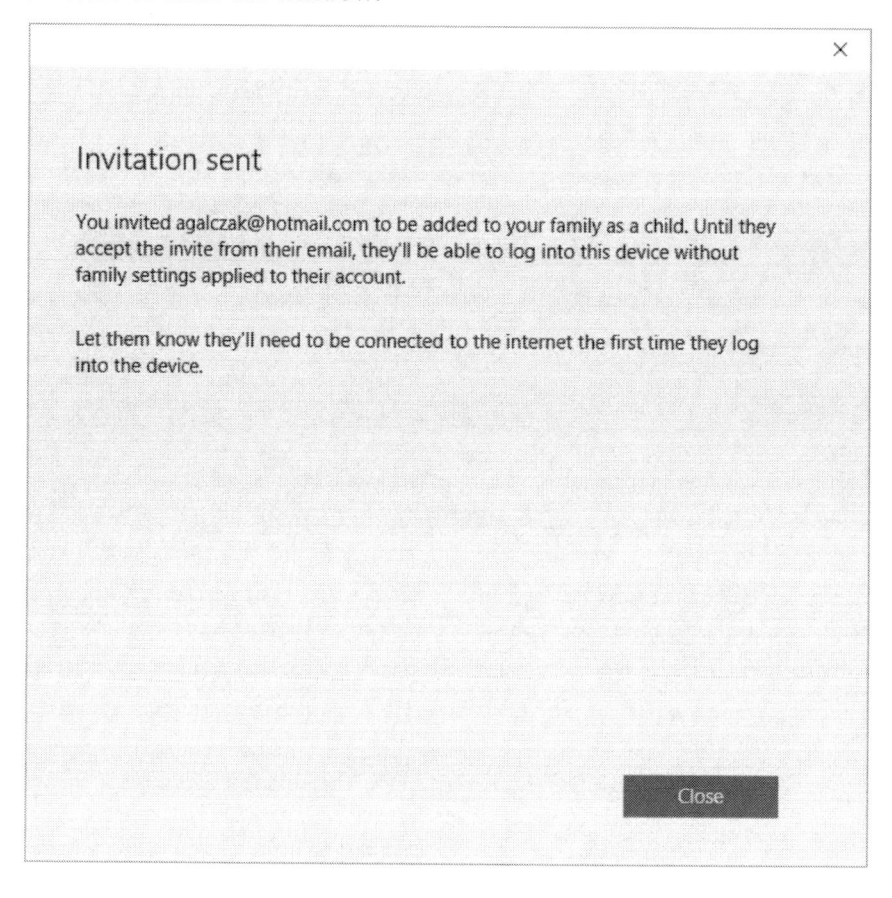

> **Invitation sent**
>
> You invited agalczak@hotmail.com to be added to your family as a child. Until they accept the invite from their email, they'll be able to log into this device without family settings applied to their account.
>
> Let them know they'll need to be connected to the internet the first time they log into the device.
>
> [Close]

3. Vulnerability: User Account

6. After you have hit *Close,* the regular *Accounts* window will appear and show your child account as pending. We now need to check the email for that account to accept the family invitation.

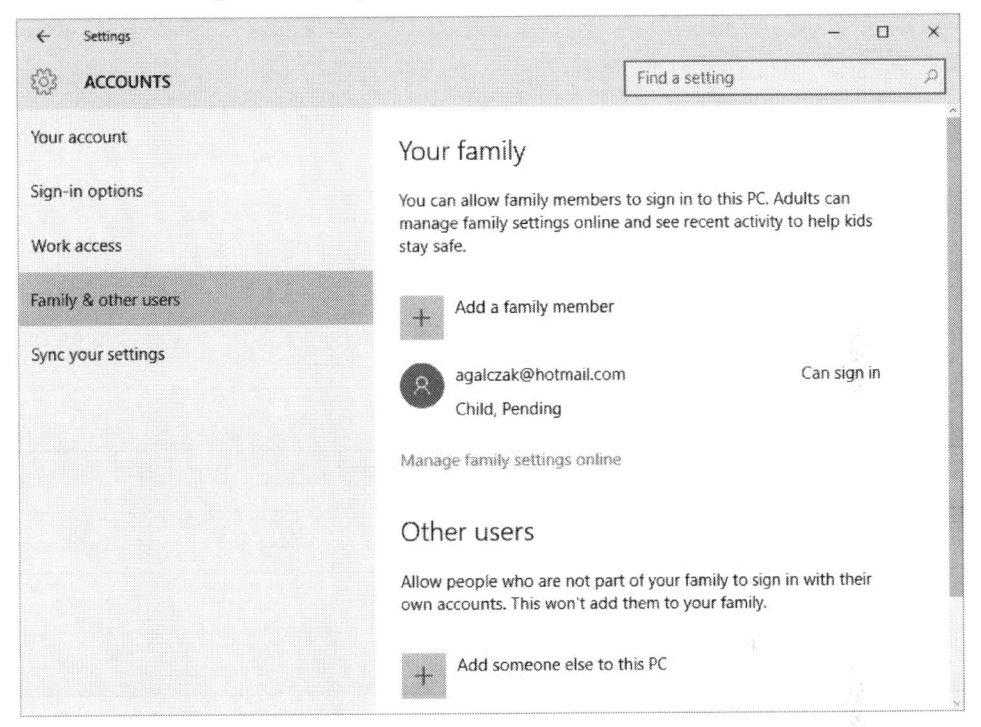

3. Vulnerability: User Account

7. Browse to *www.outlook.com,* and then login using your child account's email address and password. Click *Sign in.*

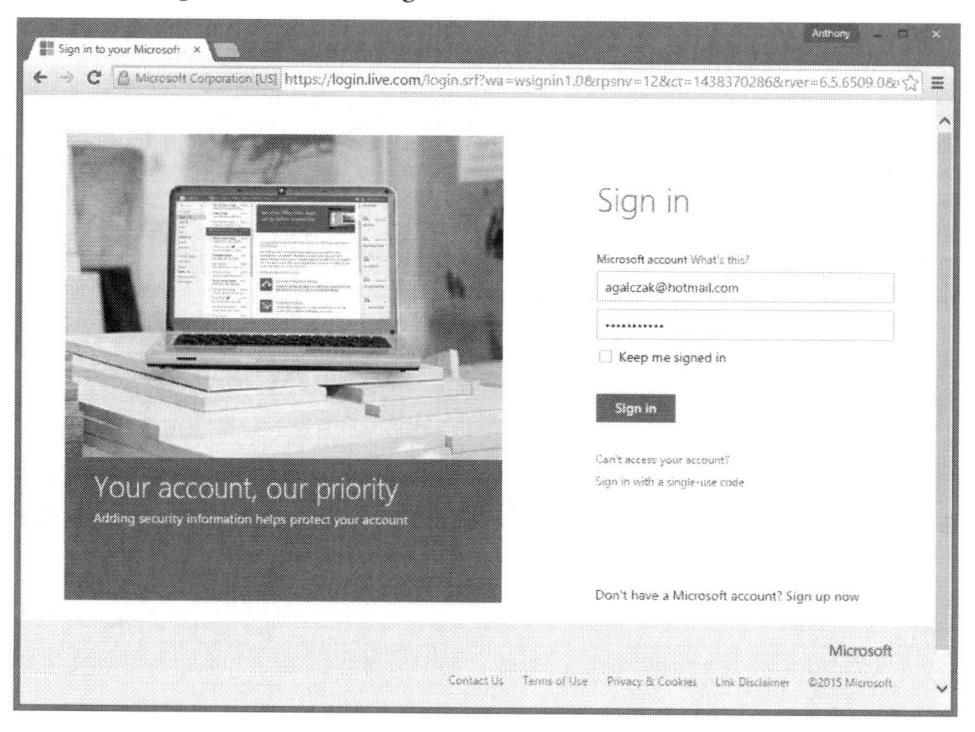

3. Vulnerability: User Account

8. Once you are into your mailbox, click on the email for joining the family.

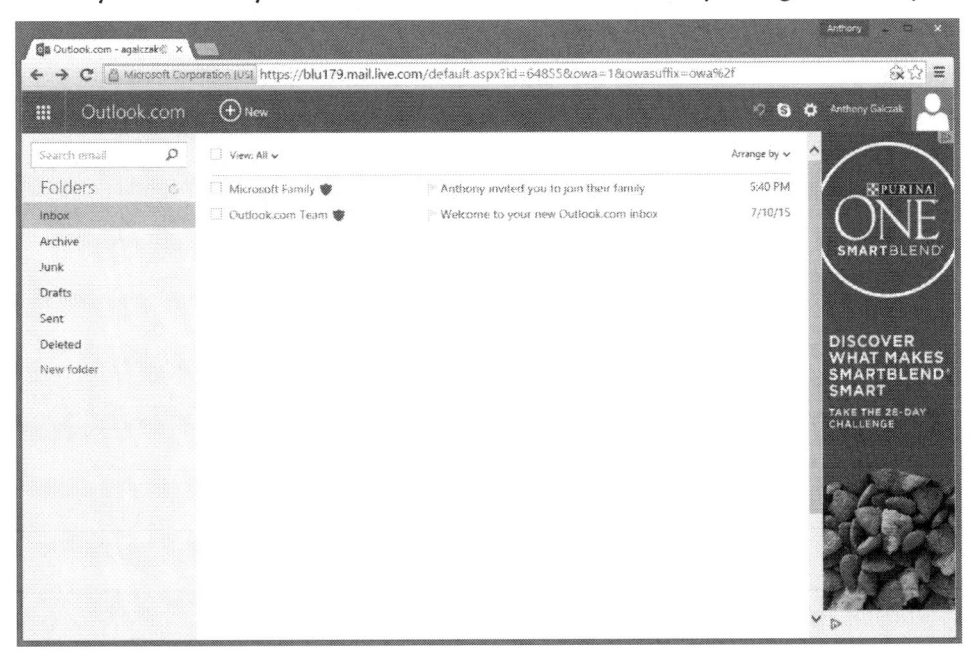

9. Click on *Accept Invitation*.

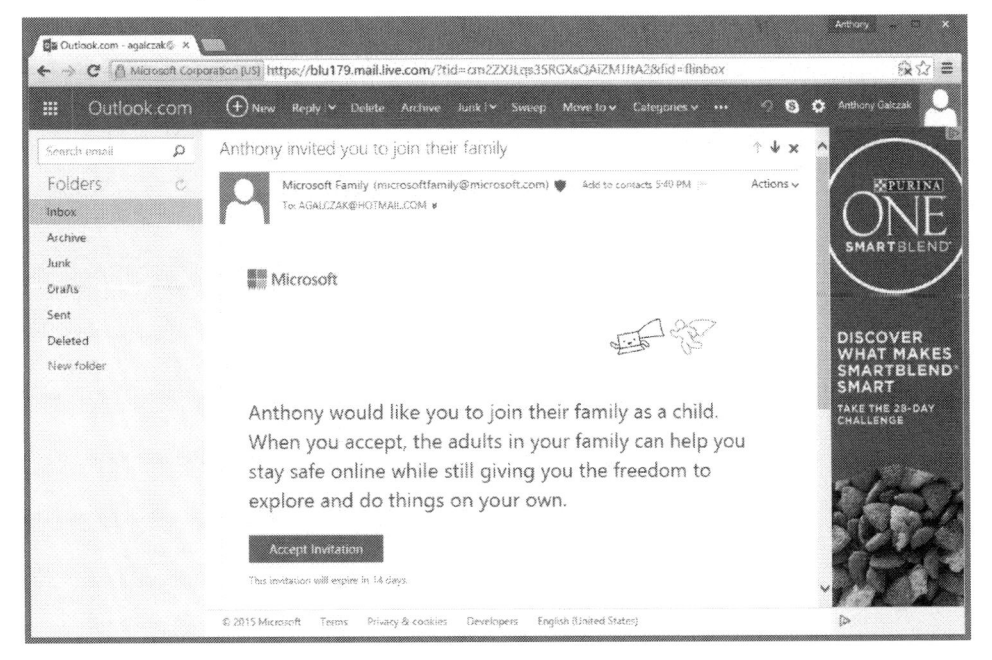

3. Vulnerability: User Account

10. Once you have accepted the invitation it will bring you into the Family settings and show you who is in your family. If necessary, you can remove yourself from the family on this screen as a child account.

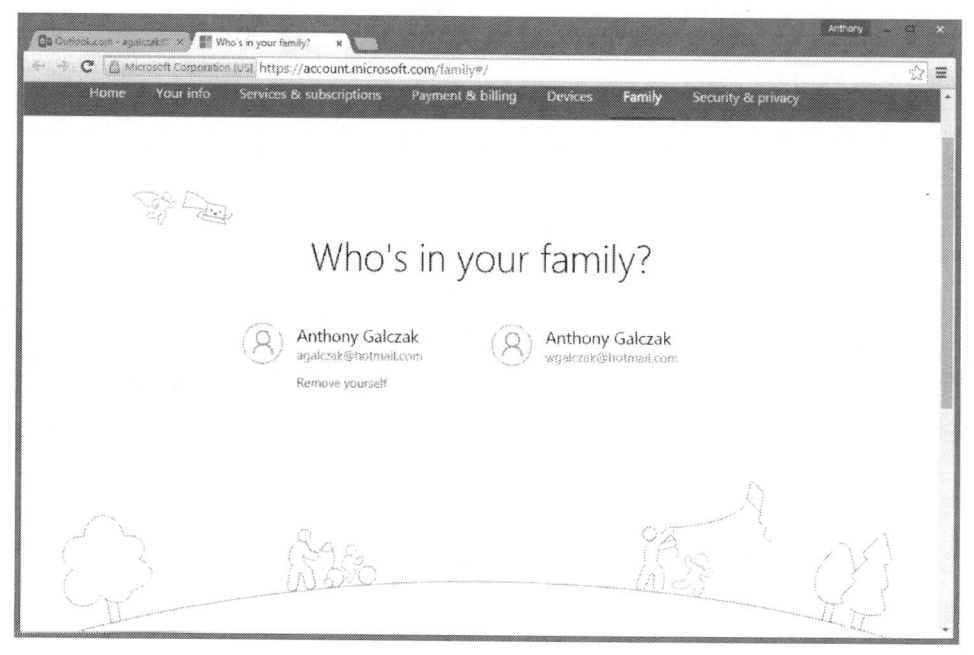

3. Vulnerability: User Account

11. We will need to log into the child account in order to finalize the process of adding the account as it will show as pending on the administrator account. Click the start menu, right click your user account and click *Sign out*.

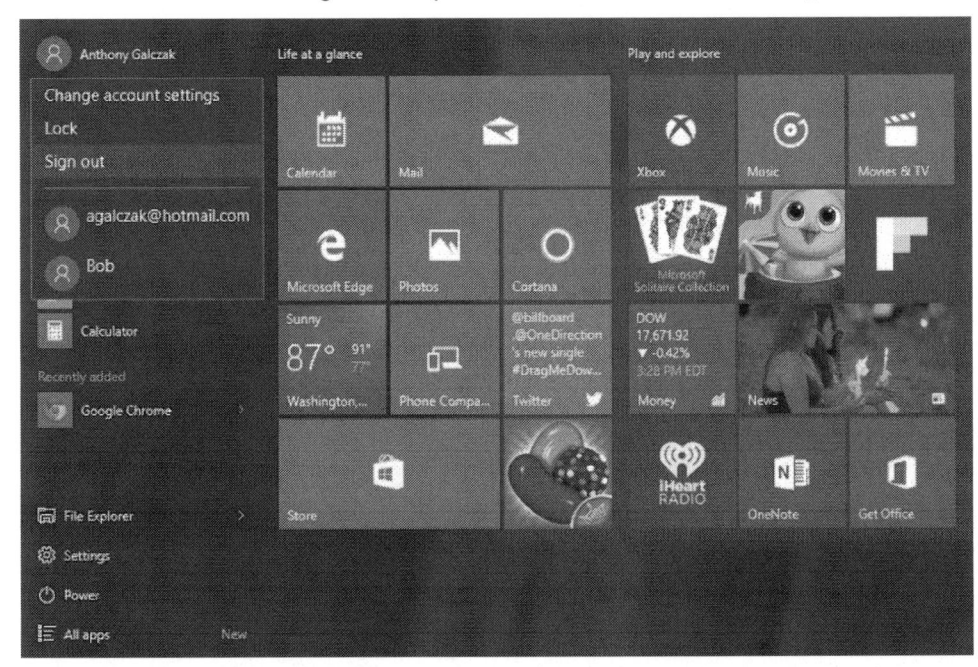

12. Log into your child account.

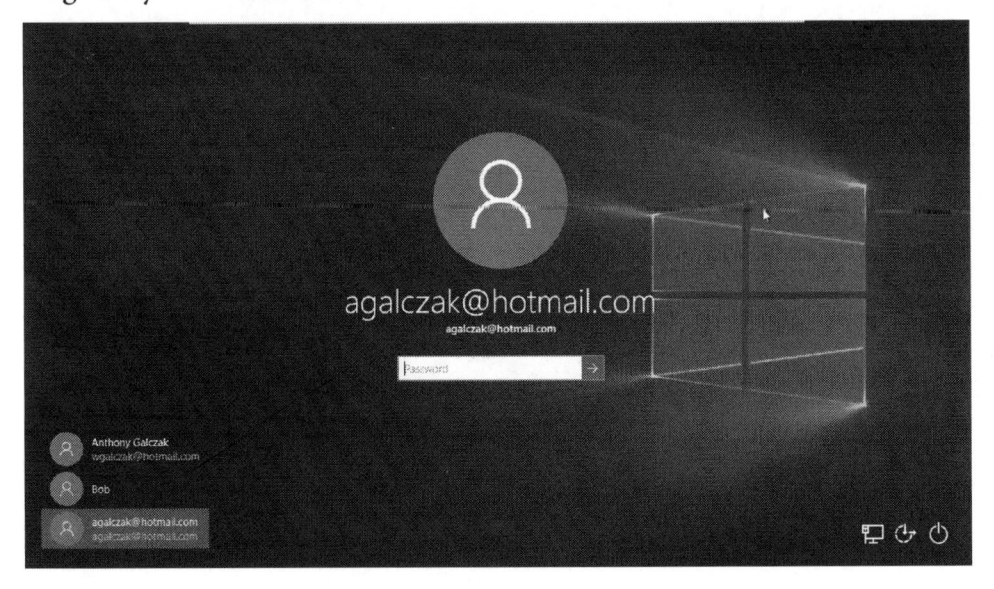

3. Vulnerability: User Account

After logging into the child account you have successfully created the account and can now configure restrictions on the administrator side of things with the family safety portal.

Assignment: Configure your Child Account

There are many ways to configure the new child accounts through the family safety portal. The fastest way to get to the portal is through *http://fss.live.com* and you will be able to manage anything from age restrictions on apps & games to specific websites to block and allow.

1. Log into your administrator account. If you followed the previous assignment then the child account should be setup and look like this.

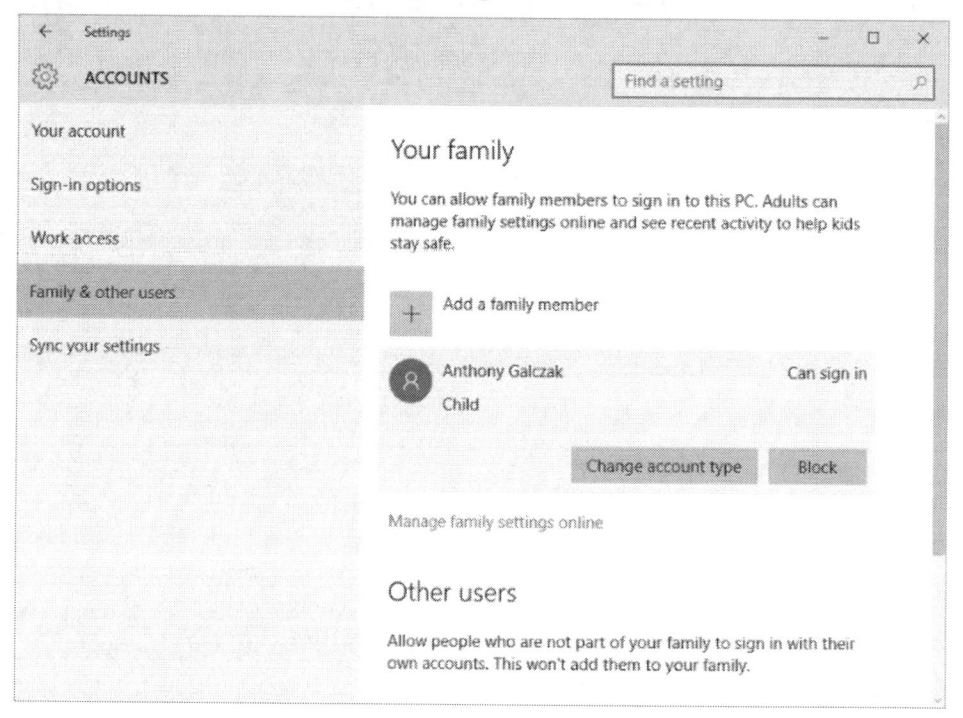

3. Vulnerability: User Account

2. In a web browser browse to *fss.live.com,* and then log into your administrator account's Microsoft account.

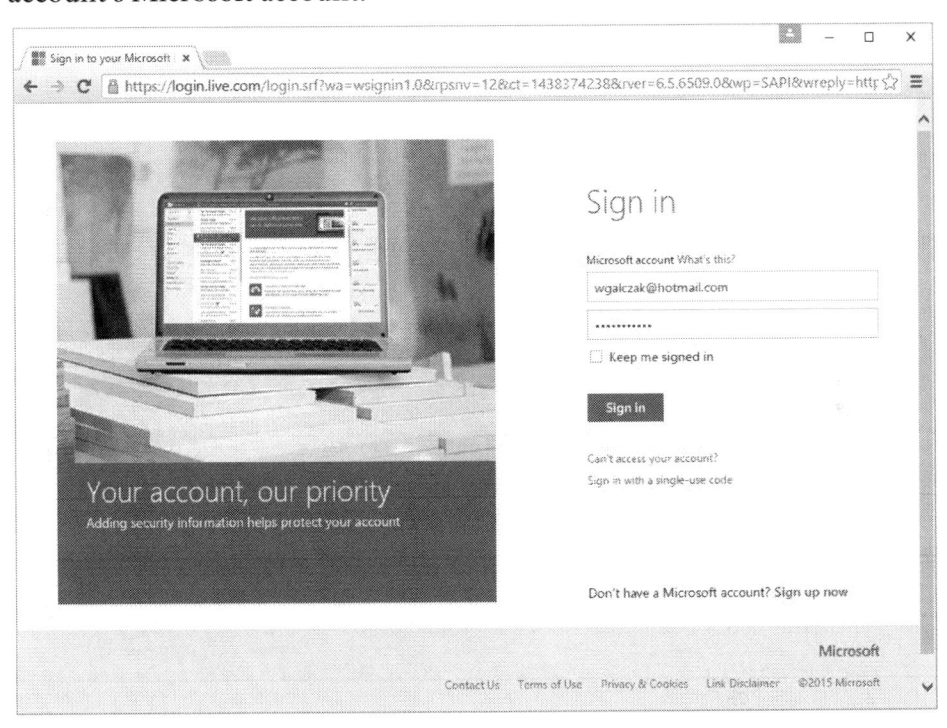

3. Vulnerability: User Account

3. On the *family safety portal,* you will see all the child accounts under you and the machines they are associated with. Click on the account that you would like to configure.

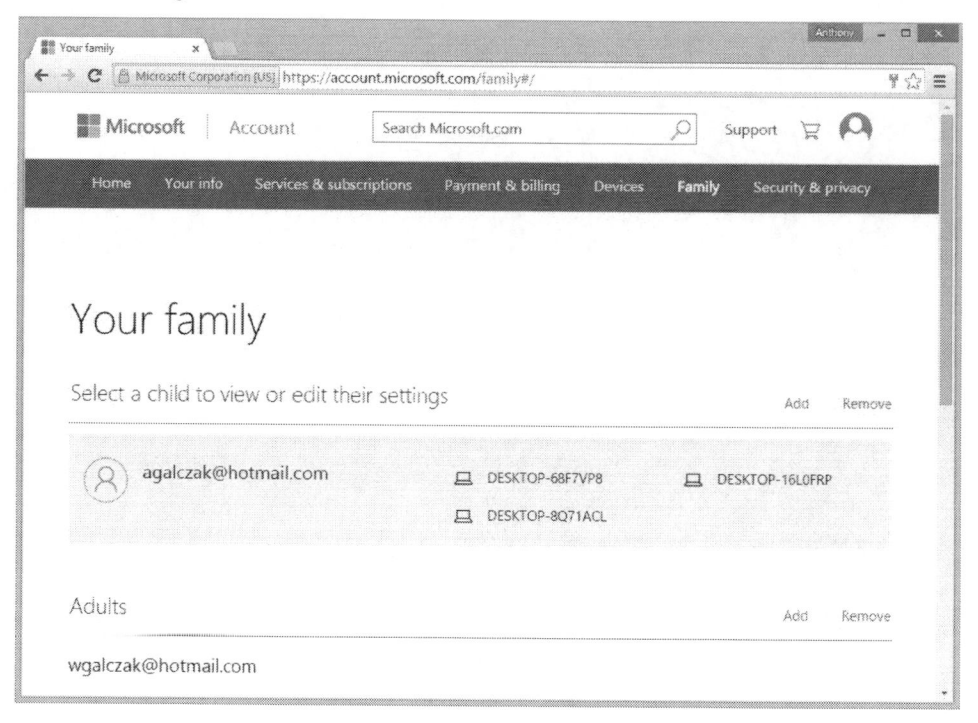

3. Vulnerability: User Account

4. The *Recent Activity* screen will give you the options to turn on/off activity reporting and have a weekly report sent to your Microsoft account. Also the usage for your child account will be shown down below as well. Click on Web Browsing on the left to go more in depth into browsing restrictions.

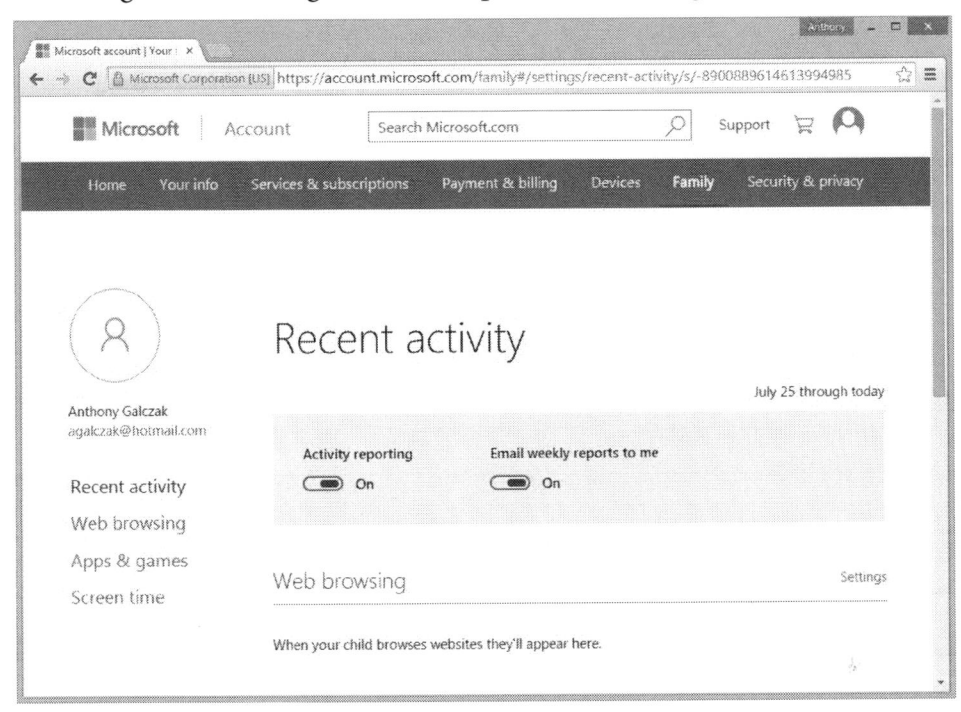

3. Vulnerability: User Account

5. On the web browsing screen, *Block inappropriate websites* is unchecked. I recommend you check this for a child account.

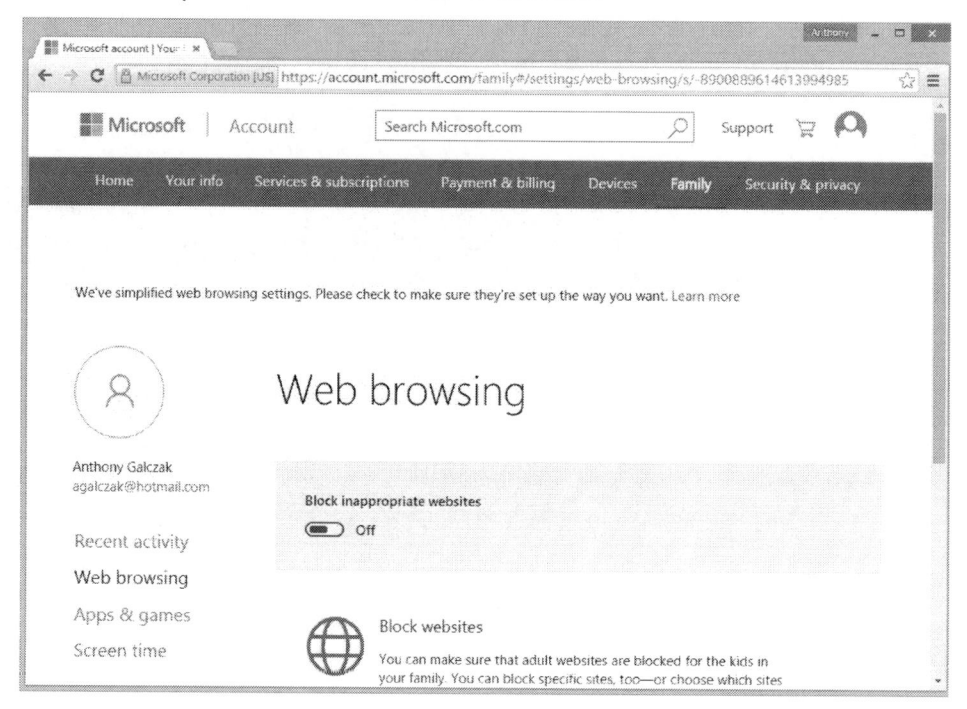

3. Vulnerability: User Account

6. Once you have checked the box for *Block inappropriate websites*, *Adult content* is blocked, *InPrivate browsing* is blocked and *Bing SafeSearch* is turned on. Also you will see *Allow website* and *Block website* at the bottom. In order to block or allow a website just enter a URL into the *example.com* field, and then click *Allow* or *Block*. When you are finished configuring websites to block or allow, scroll up and click *Apps & Games*.

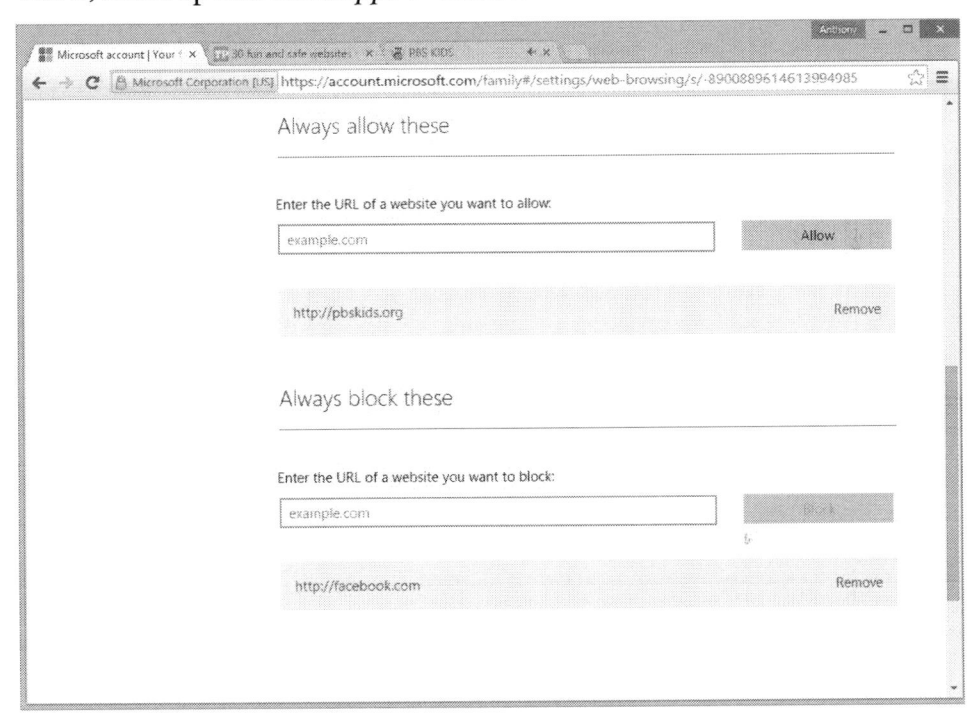

3. Vulnerability: User Account

7. By default, there is no ESRB limit on games within *Apps & Games.* Click on *Block inappropriate Apps & Games.*

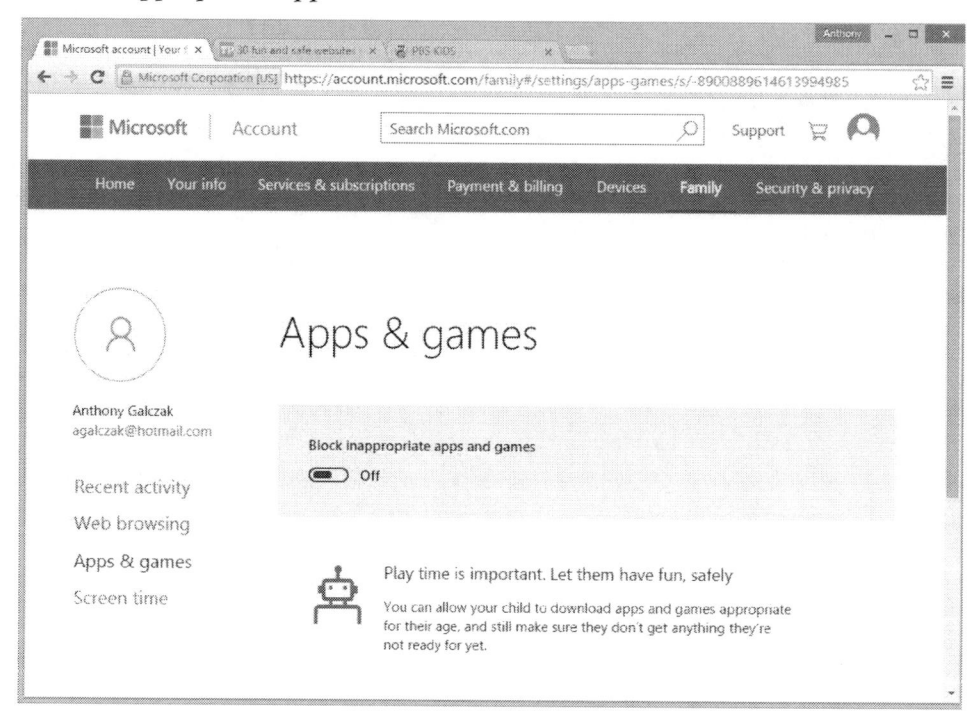

3. Vulnerability: User Account

8. Scroll down to see the drop down menu for age restrictions. Conveniently for us, the ESRB has already set stringent restrictions for each game. Configure to the appropriate age setting.

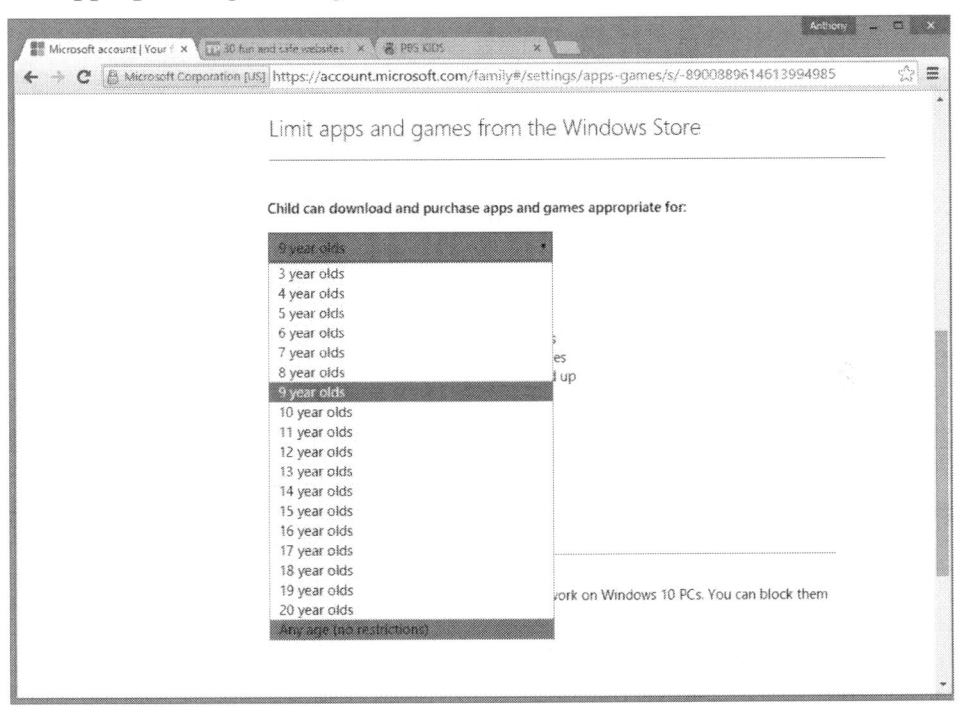

3. Vulnerability: User Account

9. Once you have set the age restriction, you will notice the ESRB symbol for the restriction is visible. Slightly below this is any games you may have specifically blocked in the past as well. Scroll up and click *Screen Time* to continue.

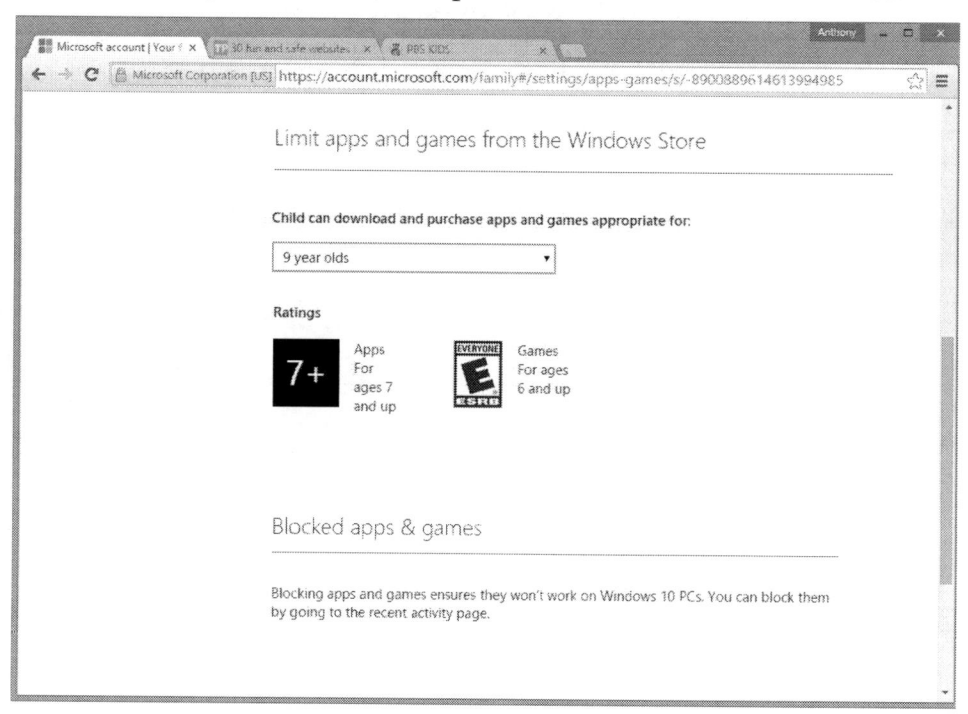

3. Vulnerability: User Account

10. *Screen time* may be the most important part of family safety. It will allow you to flat-out restrict that user from logging into the machine during pre-defined hours or days. By default, these limits are turned off, click *Set limits for when my child can use devices.*

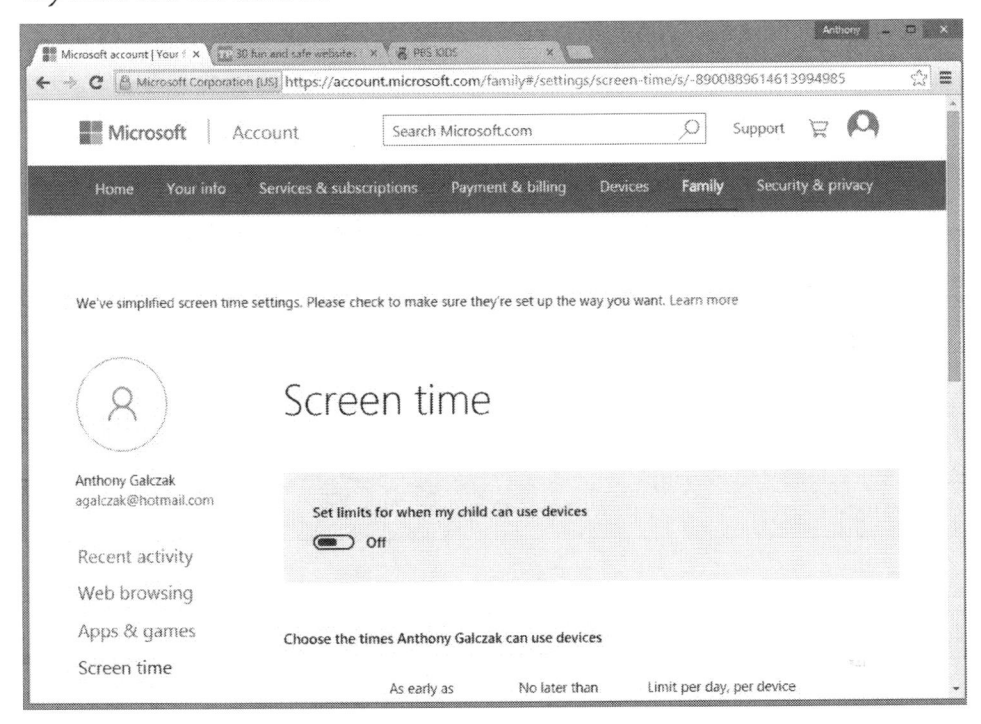

3. Vulnerability: User Account

11. Scroll down to see all the available options to restrict how early your child account can access the computer and when they should be off the machine. You can also limit the total time on the device per day. Keep in mind the Time settings in the Control Panel are restricted for child accounts so the old school method of changing the time will not bypass this.

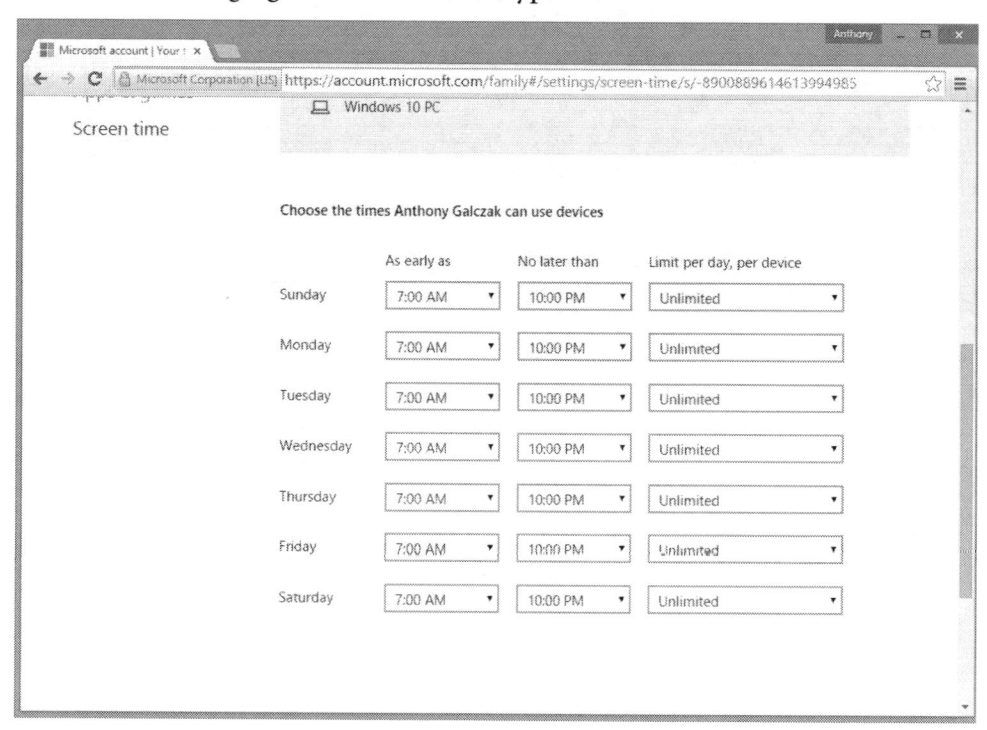

12. Here is what the screen time restriction looks like.

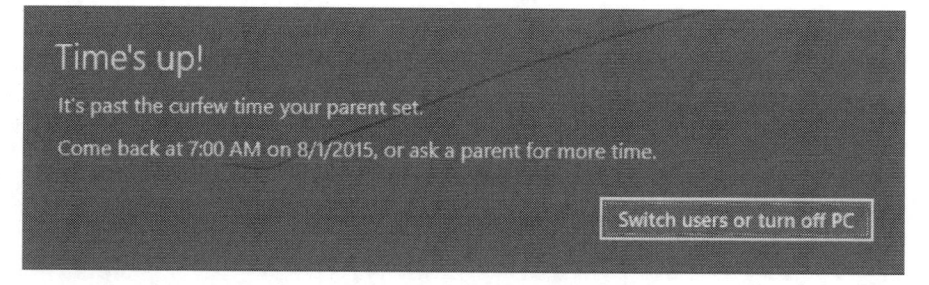

Congratulations! You have gone through and configured all of the screens in the family safety portal.

Assignment: Allowing Access to Websites Through Email

If you have set specific websites to be blocked for your child accounts, then you may end up receiving one of these requests for access emails. A prompt will appear when a website is blocked on the child account to *Ask by Email*. Of course you can ignore these emails and the website will continue to be blocked. But if you're feeling generous you can also allow access to the site through the email notification or the family safety portal.

1. If a child account is restricted from a website, it will show this screen. If the user wants access to this website, they can click *Ask by Email* and it will send an email request to all the adults in this family to give access.

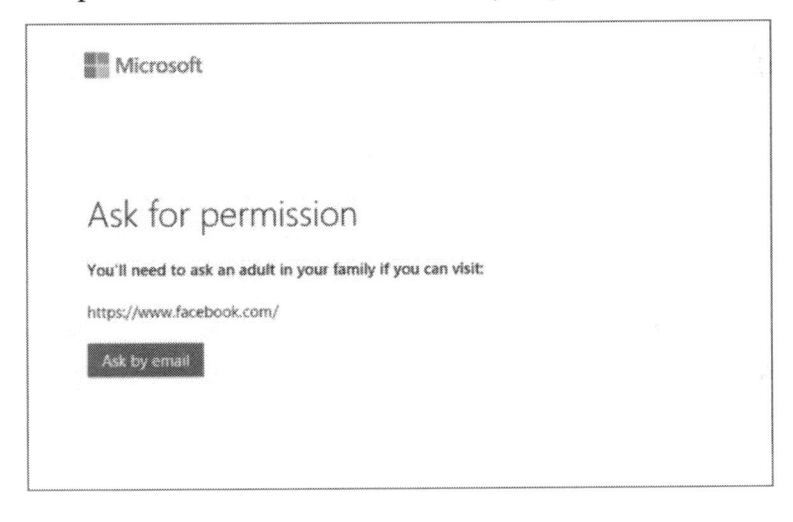

3. Vulnerability: User Account

2. Here is the screen for the email request.

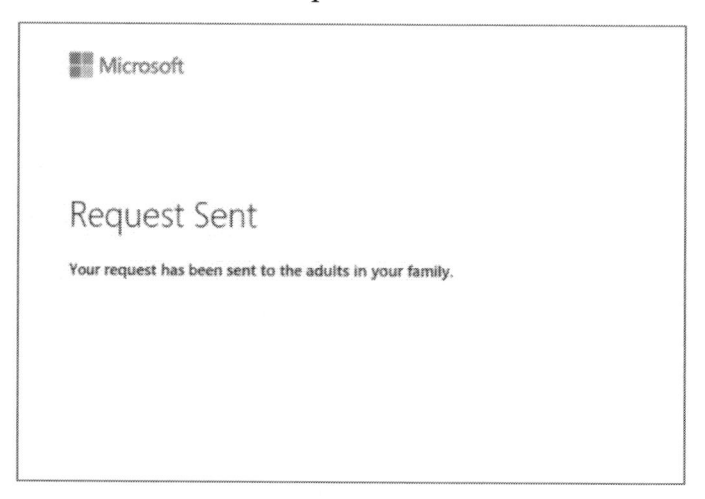

   Microsoft

   Request Sent

   Your request has been sent to the adults in your family.

3. If you do indeed want to give access once you've received the email. First log into your Microsoft Outlook account then click on the request for access email.

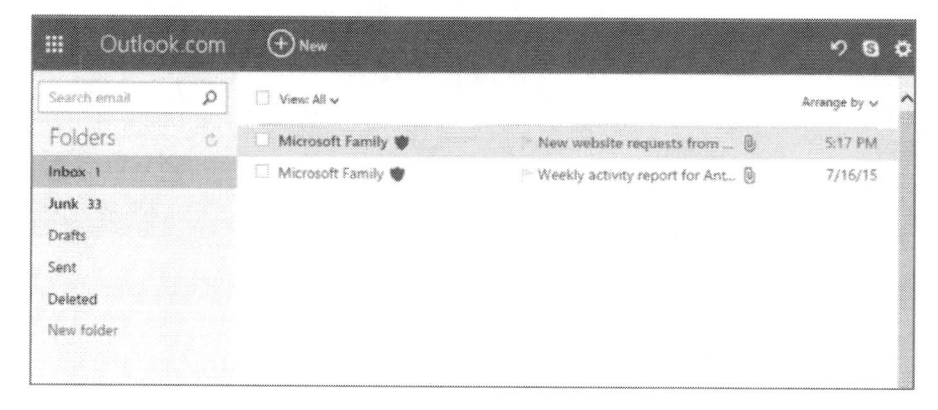

3. Vulnerability: User Account

4. From here you can choose to *Allow* the access or just simply delete the email and ignore it.

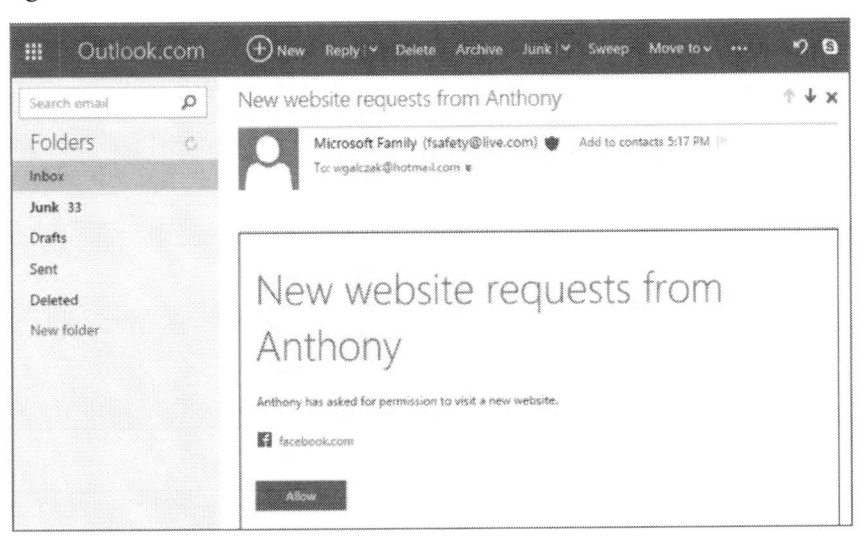

5. You can also view and allow the request through the family safety portal.

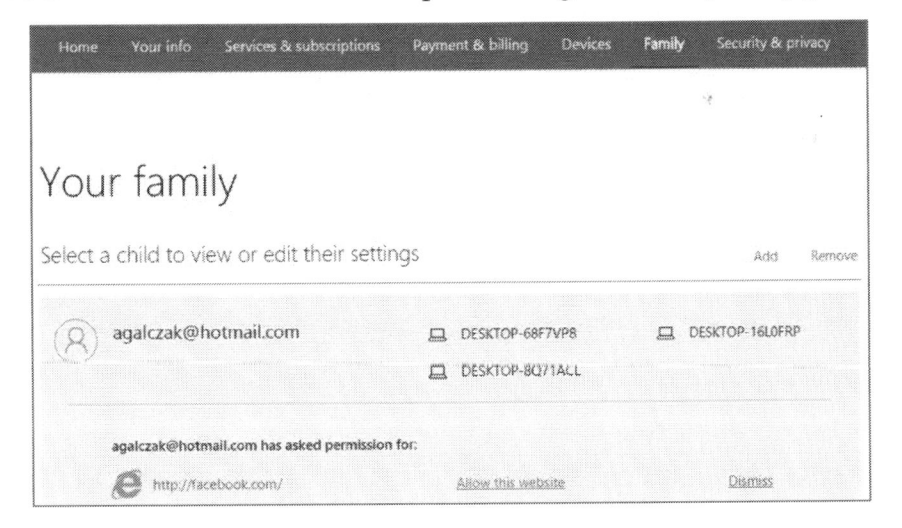

3. Vulnerability: User Account

Review Questions

1. What are the four different types of user accounts available in Windows 10?
2. What abilities does the Administrator have that other user accounts don't?
3. What are the minimum and maximum number of Administrator accounts?
4. What are the minimum and maximum number of Standard accounts?
5. What is the advantage of working in a Standard account?
6. A Child account is fundamentally a _____ account, with _____ turned on.
7. **Q:** Family Safety Controls restrict the powers of an account by limiting _____, _____, and _____.
8. A Microsoft account can only be an Administrator account. (True or False)
9. In order to use Family Safety on a Child account, the Administrator of the child account must have a Microsoft or Outlook.com enabled account. (True or False)

4. Vulnerability: Storage Device

I am disturbed by how states abuse laws on Internet access. I am concerned that surveillance programs are becoming too aggressive. I understand that national security and criminal activity may justify some exceptional and narrowly tailored use of surveillance. But that is all the more reason to safeguard human rights and fundamental freedoms.

–Ban Ki-moon, Secretary General of the United Nations

Block Access to Storage Devices

In some environments, it is appropriate to block access to external storage devices. This may be required so that users cannot copy sensitive data. There are three ways to accomplish this:

- Modifying the Registry
- Disabling USB Ports from the Device Manager.
- Using commercial software

Assignment: Block Access to Storage Devices via Registry

In this assignment, we will lock access to the USB ports through the *Registry*.

1. Login as an administrator.
2. Go to *Start* > type "*regedit*" and press enter to open the registry editor.

Back up the Registry:

3. Click on the *File* menu > *Export*.
4. A window will ask where to save backup. On the left side of the window, click on *Libraries* > *Documents* to save in this location.

5. In the *File name* field, type a name that will identify the registry backup, and then click on the *Save* button.

6. In the *Selected branch* field at the bottom of the window, navigate to the following key: HKEY_LOCAL_MACHINE\SYSTEM\CurrentControlSet\Services\USBSTOR

7. Click on *USBSTOR*, it will show items to the right. Locate *Start*. Double click on it to modify setting.

8. A window will pop up. Under the *Value data*, change the **3** to a **4**. This will disable the USB storage.

9. Close the *Registry* and reboot the PC for the changes to take effect.

10. Log back in and verify that the changes are in effect. What should happen is that a driver window may appear but when you go to *Computer,* you should not see any third party devices.

Assignment: Restore Access to Storage Devices via Registry

1. Login as an administrator.

2. Go to *Start* > type "*regedit*" and press enter to open the registry editor.

4. Vulnerability: Storage Device

3. Navigate to the following key:
   HKEY_LOCAL_MACHINE\SYSTEM\CurrentControlSet\Services\USBSTOR

4. Click on USBSTOR, it will show items to the right. Locate Start. Double click on it to modify setting.

5. A window will pop up. Under the *Value data,* change the *4* to a *3.* This will enable the USB storage.

6. Close the *Registry* and reboot the PC for the changes to take effect.

7. Log back in and verify that the changes are in effect. What should happen is that a driver window may appear but when you go to *Computer,* you should now see your third party devices.

Assignment: Block Access to Storage Devices via Device Manager

1. Login as an administrator.
2. Click *Taskbar > File Explorer* to open a file explorer window.
3. Right click on *This PC* and a menu should pop up. Left click on *Manage.*

4. Vulnerability: Storage Device

4. A *Computer Management* window will appear. On the left side, click on *Device Manager*.

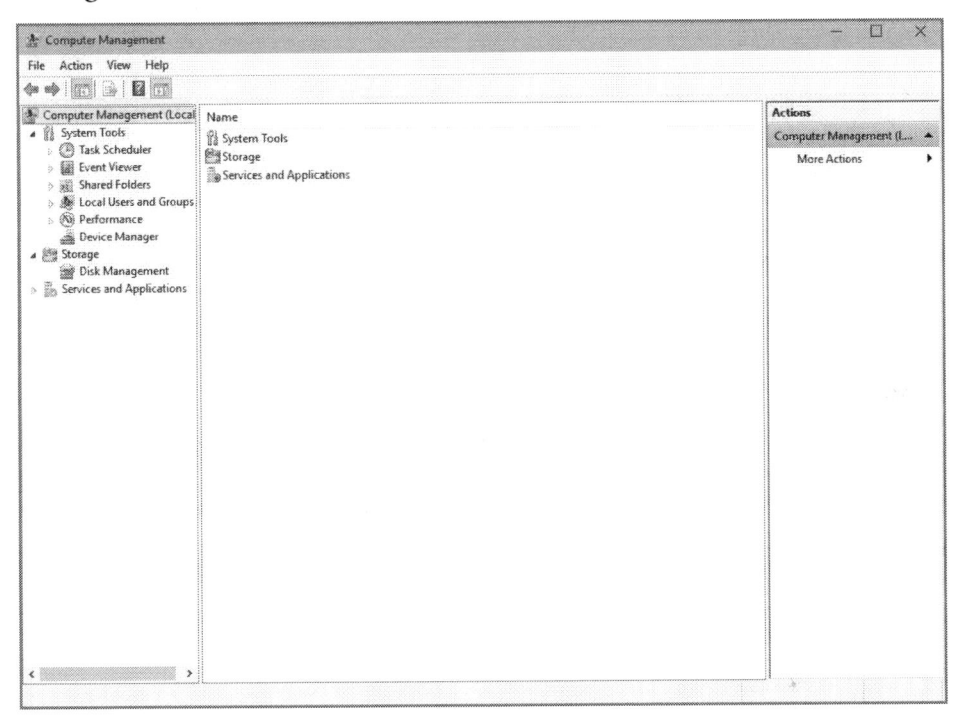

4. Vulnerability: Storage Device

5. To the right of the window will be a listing of devices. Click the *Universal Serial Bus controllers.* Click the small arrow to the left of this. It will drop down a listing of USB devices.

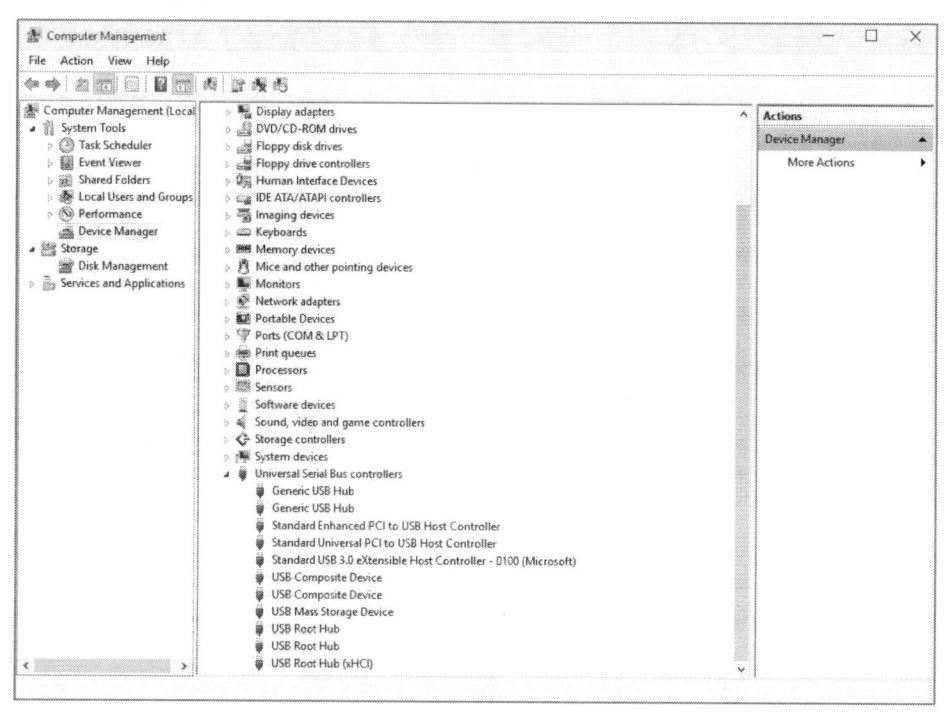

Disable each *Hub* and *Controller* one at a time:

6. Right click on of the device, and then click on *Disable*. This will disable this *Hub* or *Controller*.

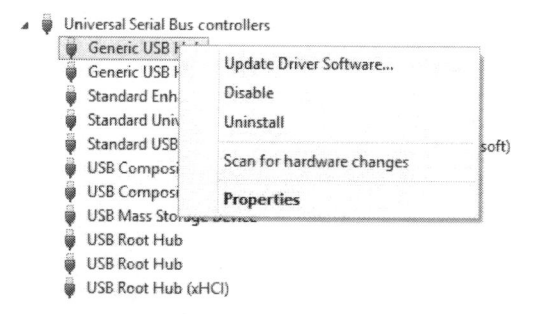

7. A window may appear confirming that you want to disable the device. Click the *Yes* button to disable device.

-118-

4. Vulnerability: Storage Device

8. Once you have disabled the *Hubs* and *Controller* you want, you can confirm this by looking at the devices and you should see an arrow on the device.

   - Universal Serial Bus controllers
     - Standard Enhanced PCI to USB Host Controller
     - Standard Universal PCI to USB Host Controller
     - Standard USB 3.0 eXtensible Host Controller - 0100 (Microsoft)

9. Close the *Computer Management* window, and then open a *File Explorer* to verify you have disabled the desired USB port. You should not see any USB devices loaded.

Verify that this change will affect all users on the PC:

10. Log out of the admin account.

11. Log in with another account.

12. Click on the *File Explorer* to see if you see any USB devices. You should not.

Assignment: Restore Access to Storage Devices via Device Manager

1. Login as an administrator.
2. On the *Taskbar*, click on the *File Explorer* to open a file explorer window.
3. Right click on *This PC* and a menu should pop up. Left click on *Manage*.

4. Vulnerability: Storage Device

4. A *Computer Management* window will appear. On the left side, click on *Device Manager*.

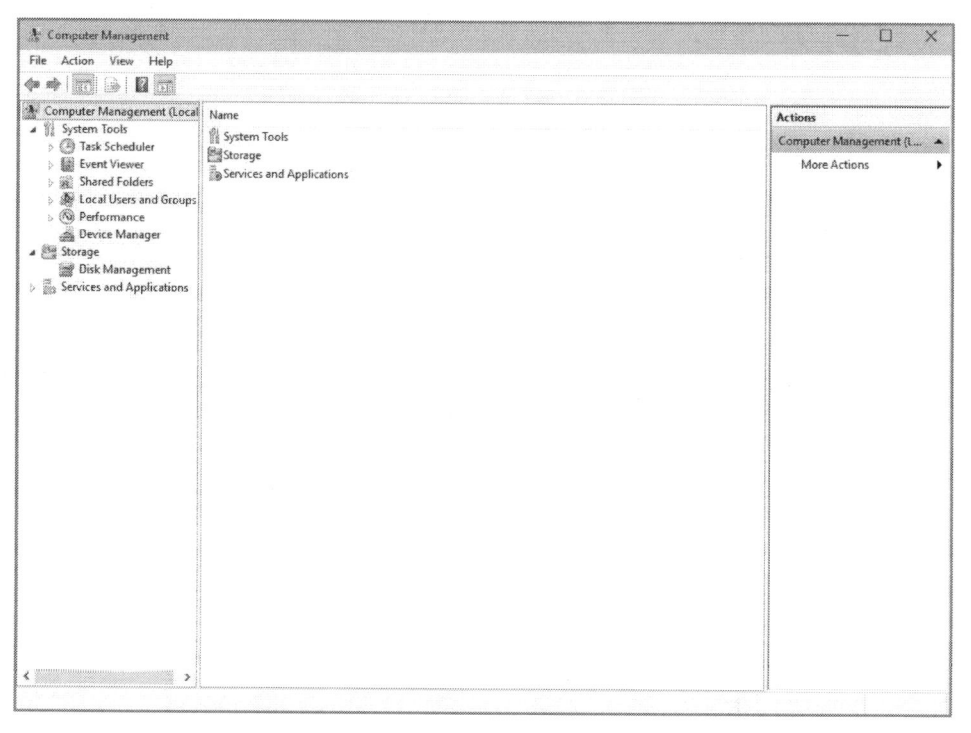

5. To the right of the window, you will see a listing of devices. Click on the *Universal Serial Bus controllers*. Click on the small arrow to the left of this. It will then drop down a listing of USB devices.

6. You will have to enable each *Hub* and *Controller* one at a time.

7. Right click on of the devices and a menu will pop. Click on *Enable* and this will enable this *Hub* or *Controller*.

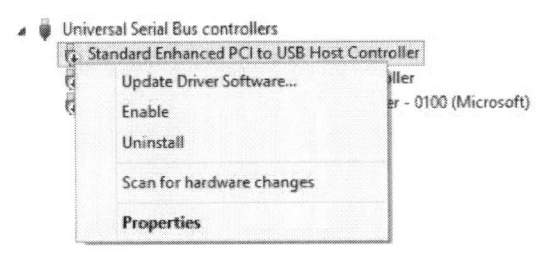

8. All the devices will start to load once you *enable* the *Hub* or *Controller*.

9. Once you have enabled all the *Hubs* and *Controller* you want, you can verify this by looking in the *File Explorer* window. If you now see your *USB devices*, you have successfully enabled your *Hub* and *Controller* devices.

Assignment: Block Access to Storage Devices via USB Disabler

1. Log in as an administrator
2. Open a web browser and enter the following link to download the *USB Disabler* app:
   http://www.intelliadmin.com/index.php/free-download/?filename=disableusb_free.exe

4. Vulnerability: Storage Device

3. At the *Free Download* page, enter your *Name* and *Email Address,* and then click *Get the Download Links* button. The developer will send you a web link to download the app.

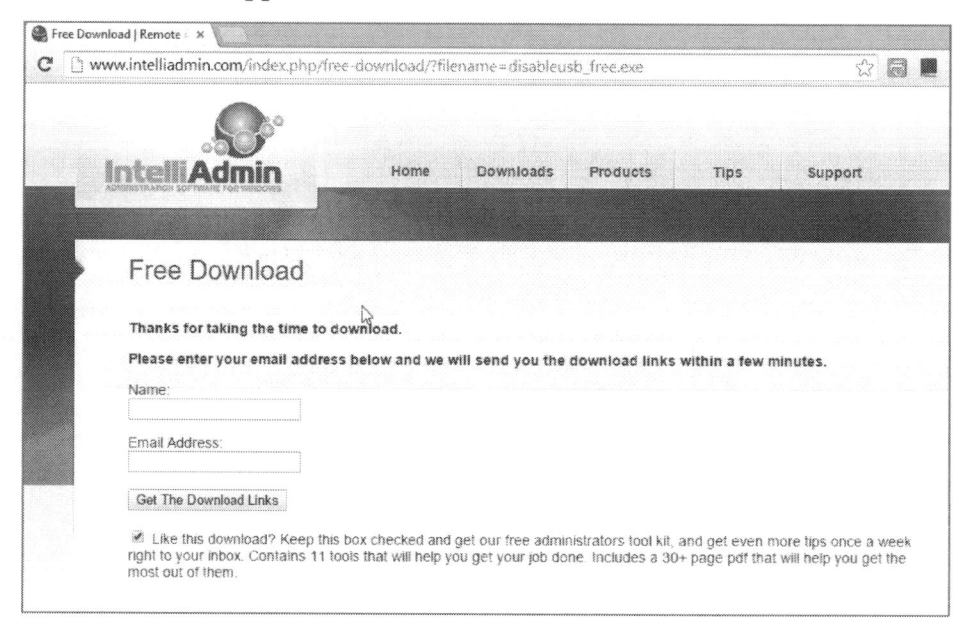

4. Open the email from the developer, and then click on the link for the download. It will download using your default web browser.

5. Most browsers will download files to the *Downloads* folder of your profile. Locate the file the file *disableusb_free.exe*.

6. Open this to install app. You may get a *User Account Control* window. Click the *Yes* button to continue.

4. Vulnerability: Storage Device

7. A *Setup* window appears. Click *Next*.

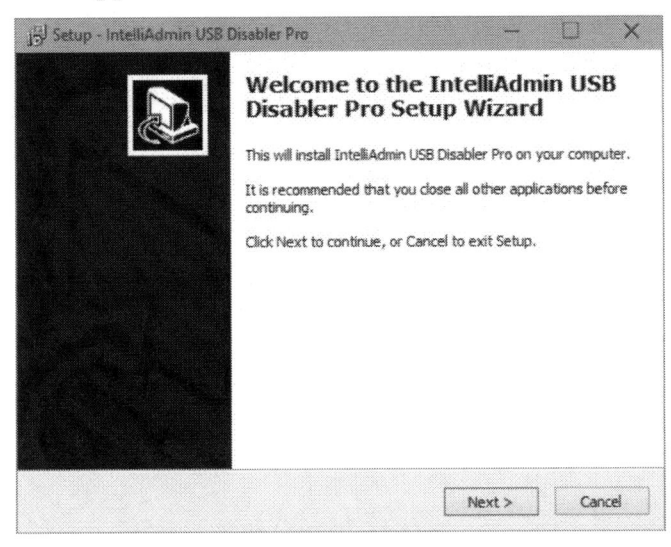

8. The *License Agreement* window opens. Click *I accept the agreement* radio button, and then click *Next*.

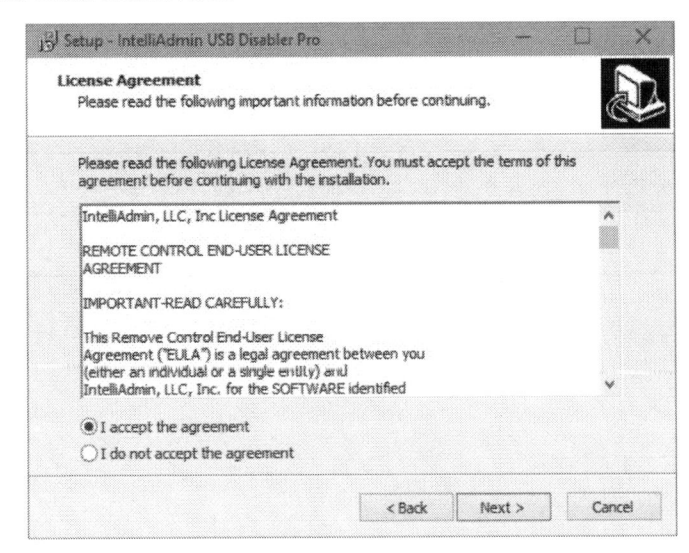

4. Vulnerability: Storage Device

9. The *destination location* window opens. Leave the location with the default settings, and then click *Next*.

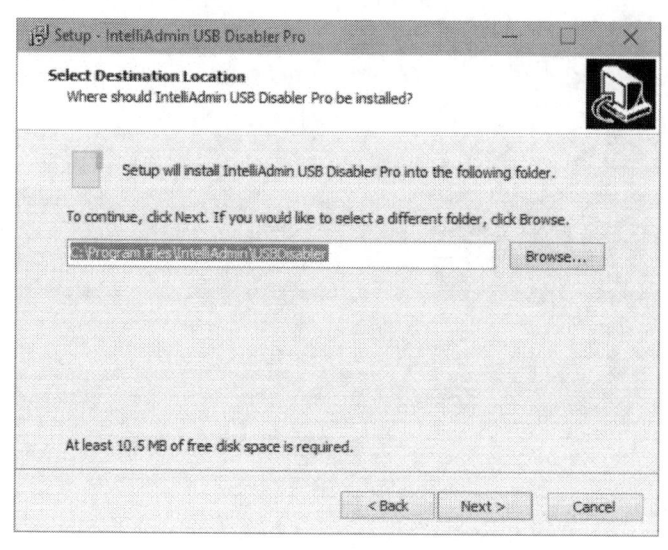

10. The *Ready to Install* window opens. Click the *Install* button.

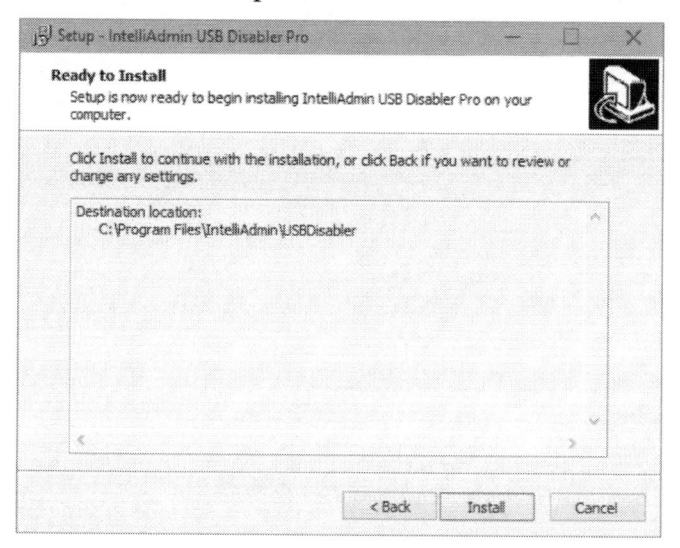

11. If you have a USB device connected to the PC, a window will appear. To clear this window, you may click *Add to allow list, System Settings,* or *Close.* Just click the *Close* button to clear window. Then click *Finish* to finish installation of software.

4. Vulnerability: Storage Device

- *Note:* This is a demo version. This app is recommended for a business since the Pro version is a *site license* version. For Home users, we recommend using the other methods mentioned in this section. The site license version is $599.

12. To access the app, you can either enter a *USB device* or you can go to the *Taskbar* and click on the arrow that is pointing up in the lower right corner. The icon is the one that is *dark gray* with a *USB* symbol. Click on this to open the app.

13. When a USB device is inserted, it will list under the *Blocked Devices*. You can decide if you want to block this particular *USB device* or not.

4. Vulnerability: Storage Device

14. Click on the *Options* tab. By default, *Block all users* is selected. You could leave this on but then administrators would not have to the *USB device.* We recommend selecting *Allow full access for administrators.*

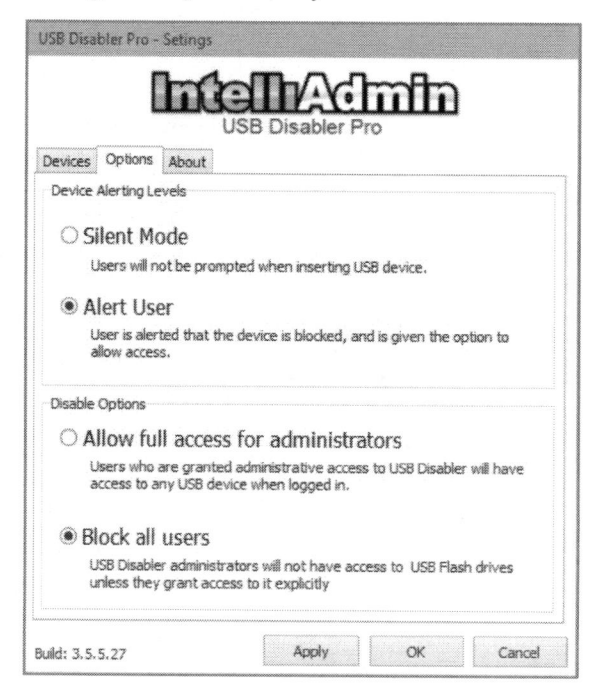

15. Once you have settings configured, click on the *Apply* button, and then *OK*.

Assignment: Restore Access to Storage Devices via USB Disabler

1. Log in as an administrator.
2. Click on *Search the web and Windows,* and then type *Control Panel.* When it displays the results, click on the first result, which will be *Control Panel.*
3. Under Programs, click *Uninstall a program.*
4. In the list of apps, click the *Intelliadmin* app, and then click on *Uninstall* above this window. The uninstall process will start.
5. Close the window.

Full Disk Encryption

Windows can encrypt hard disks using two methods–hardware encryption and software encryption. Hardware encryption is one of the most secure ways you can encrypt your hard disk. Encryption is accomplished using SEDs (self-encrypting drives). SEDs work by transferring the computational load of the encryption process to dedicated processors located within the drive unit, thus cutting the stress on the host system's CPU. In addition, because the encryption/decryption keys are stored in the hard drive controller and never sit in the system's memory, cold-boot attacks will not work.

Software encryption is done through *BitLocker* software that is included with Windows 10.

Assignment: Enable Encryption Using BitLocker

Using software encryption is simple and straightforward, but may take a few days to complete. In this assignment, you will enable full disk encryption using *BitLocker*.

1. Click the *Start* menu, type in the search field *Control Panel,* and then click on the *Control Panel* in the search results to open.

4. Vulnerability: Storage Device

2. Click on *System and Security > BitLocker Drive Encryption*.

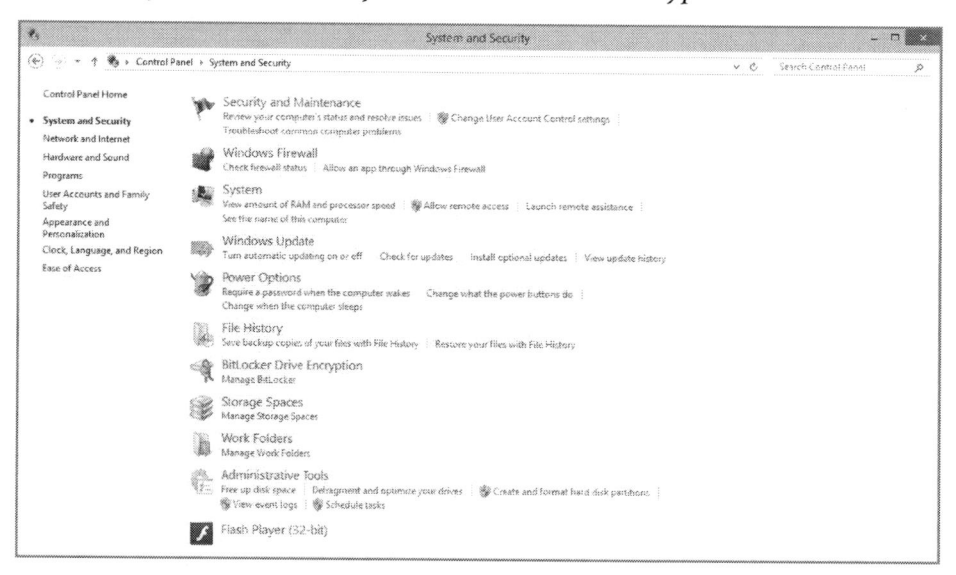

3. Under *Operating system drive*, you will see the *C* drive. To the right, you should see an option to *Turn on BitLocker*. Click on this to enable disk encryption.

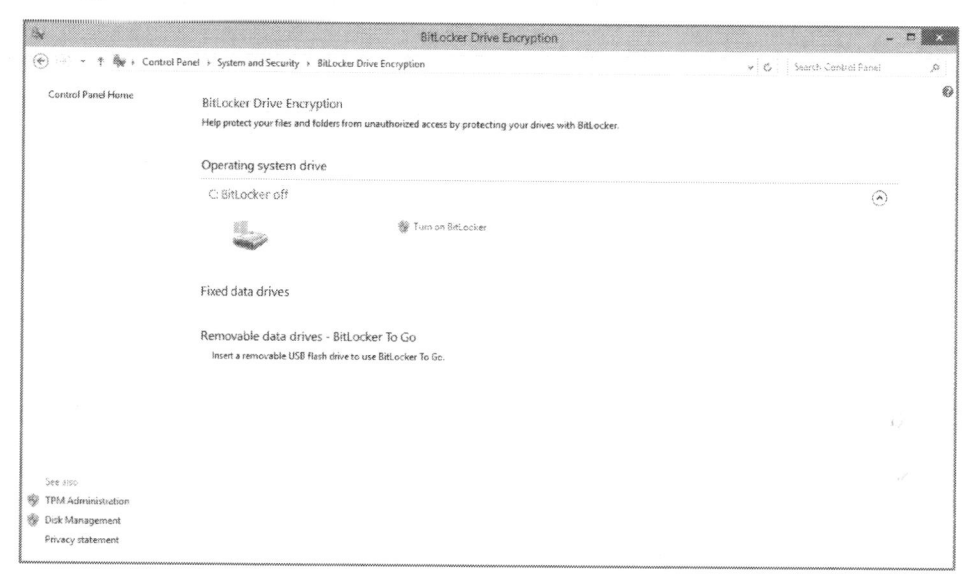

4. Vulnerability: Storage Device

4. If you do not get the following error message, skip to step 5.

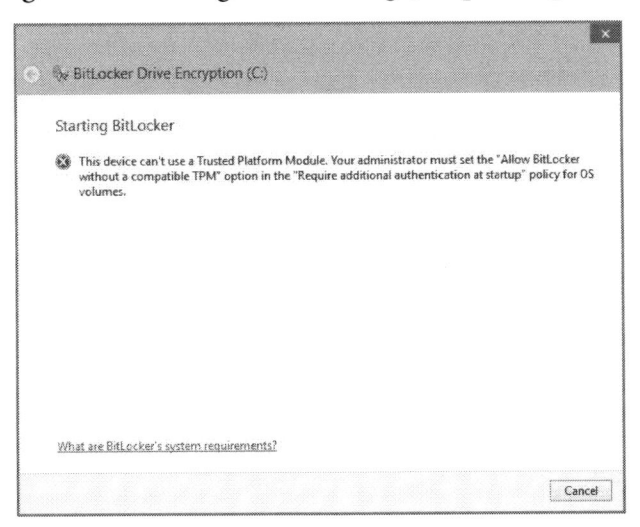

> **BitLocker Drive Encryption (C:)**
>
> Starting BitLocker
>
> ⊗ This device can't use a Trusted Platform Module. Your administrator must set the "Allow BitLocker without a compatible TPM" option in the "Require additional authentication at startup" policy for OS volumes.
>
> What are BitLocker's system requirements?
>
> [Cancel]

4. Vulnerability: Storage Device

If you do get this error message:

a. Click the *Start* menu, and then type *gpedit.msc* to access the *Group Policy* of the computer.

b. Click the arrow to the left of the *Administrative Templates* under Computer Configuration.

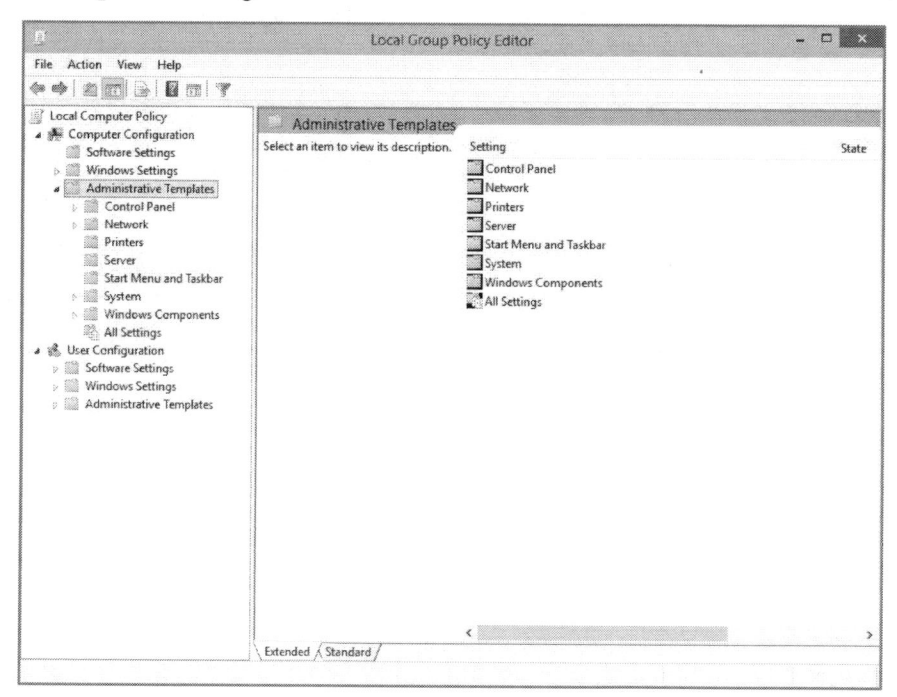

4. Vulnerability: Storage Device

c. Click on *All Settings*. Locate the following policy *Require additional authentication at startup*.

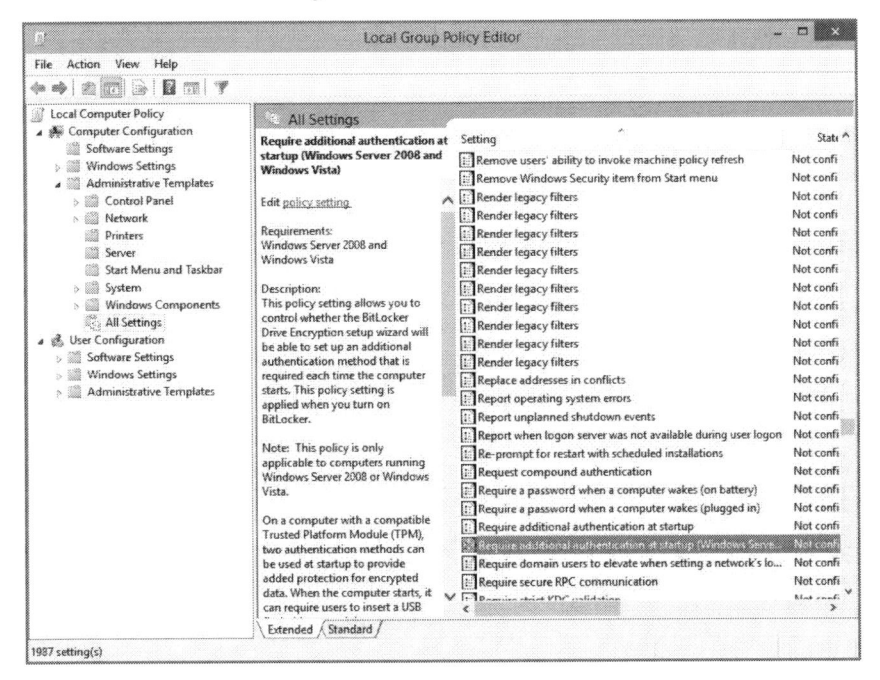

4. Vulnerability: Storage Device

d. Double click the policy to open it. It will be set to *Not Configured.* Click on *Enabled* to allow BitLocker without compatible TPM to be supported.

- TPM (Trusted Platform Module) *https://en.wikipedia.org/wiki/Trusted_Platform_Module* is a CPU dedicated to secure hardware. It is found only on higher-end business-class computers, but consumer-class devices may soon include TPM as chip costs come down.

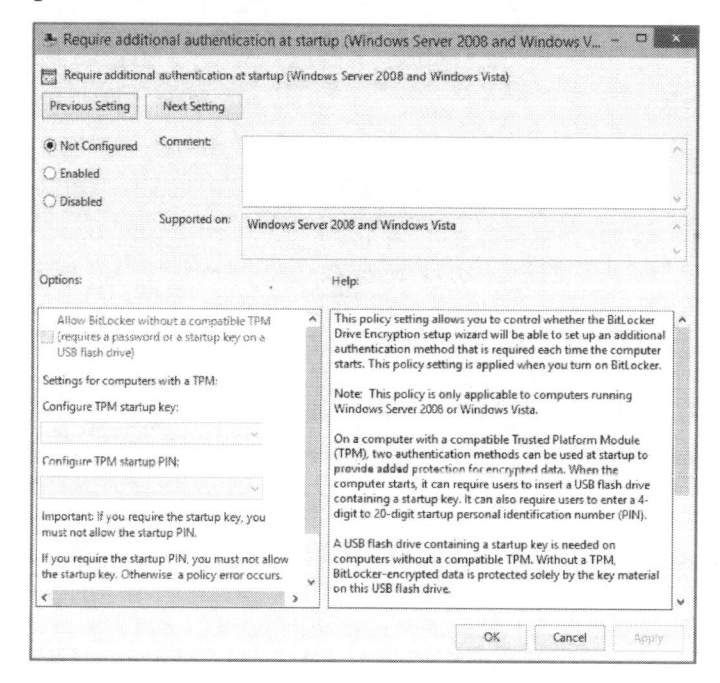

e. Click on the *OK* button to save changes, and then close the *gpedit.msc* window.

4. Vulnerability: Storage Device

5. Click on *Turn on BitLocker* to turn on encryption, and then click *Next*.

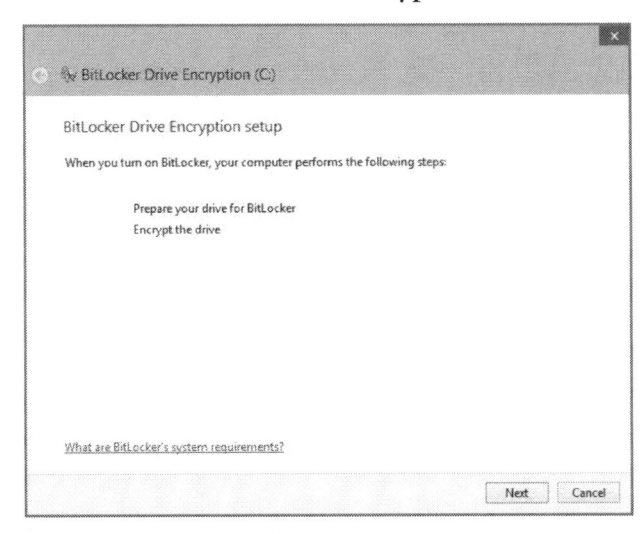

6. At the *Preparing your drive for BitLocker* window, click *Next*. The drive encryption process will begin.

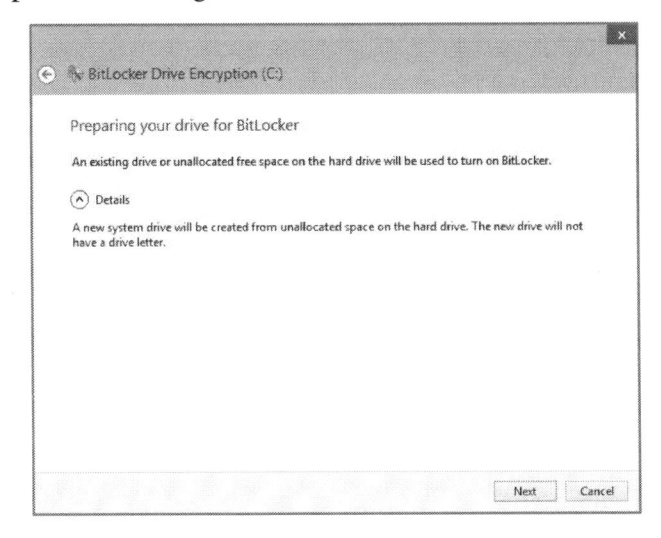

4. Vulnerability: Storage Device

7. Click on the *Restart now* button to reboot.

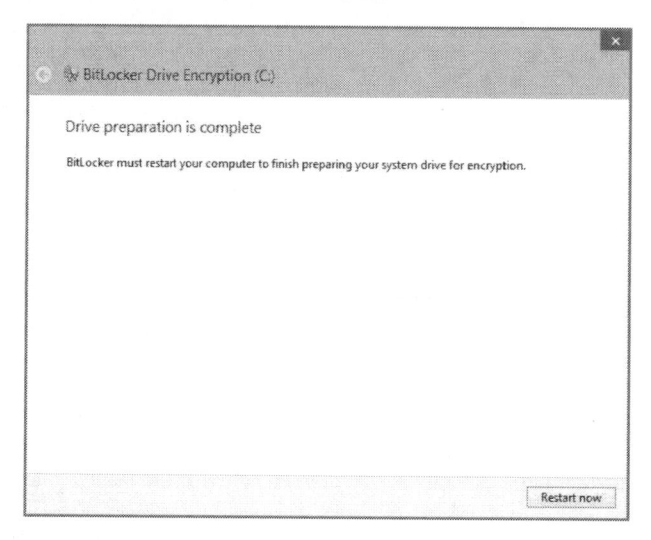

8. Once logged in, *BitLocker* will start the encryption process.

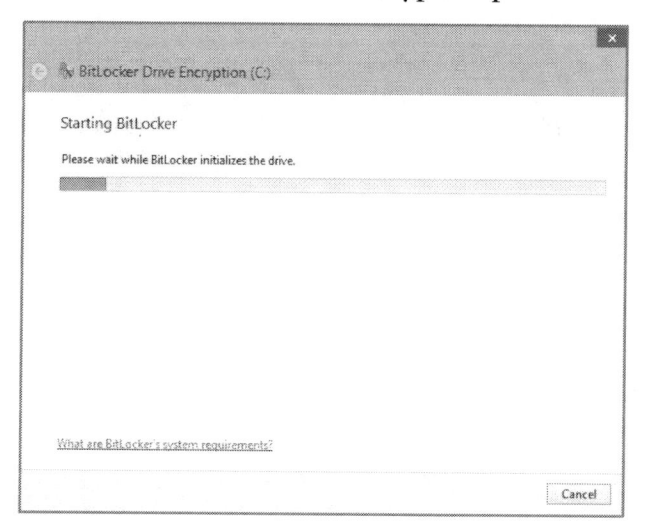

4. Vulnerability: Storage Device

9. When complete, click *Next*.

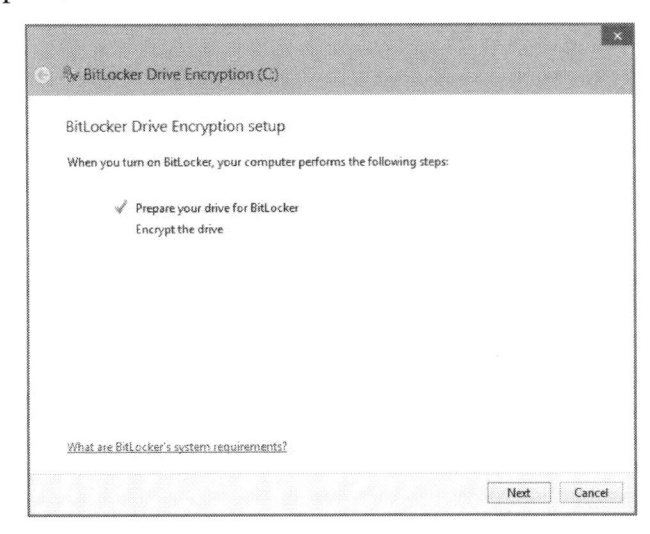

10. Select either a USB flash drive or a password as the method to unlock your drive at startup. We recommend a password. The following steps will show how to setup using a password.

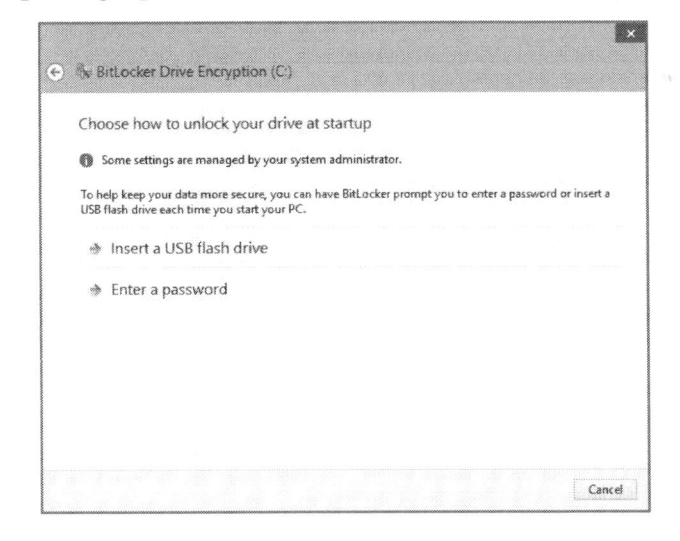

4. Vulnerability: Storage Device

11. Enter a desired strong password, and then click *Next*.

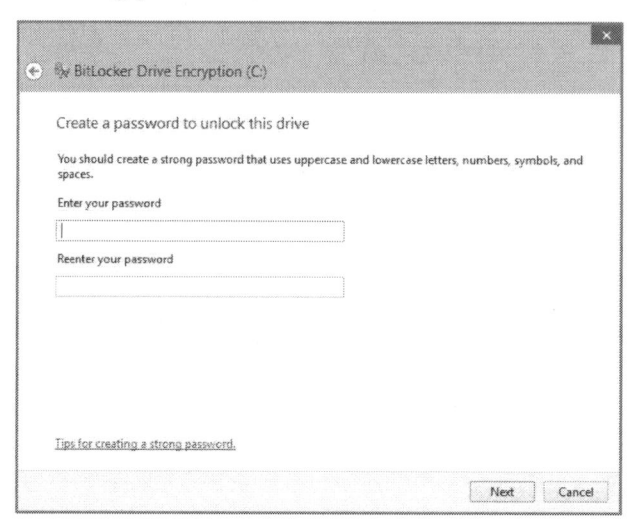

12. At the *How do you want to back up your recovery key*, select your desired option. We recommend *Print the recovery key*. Click on this option.

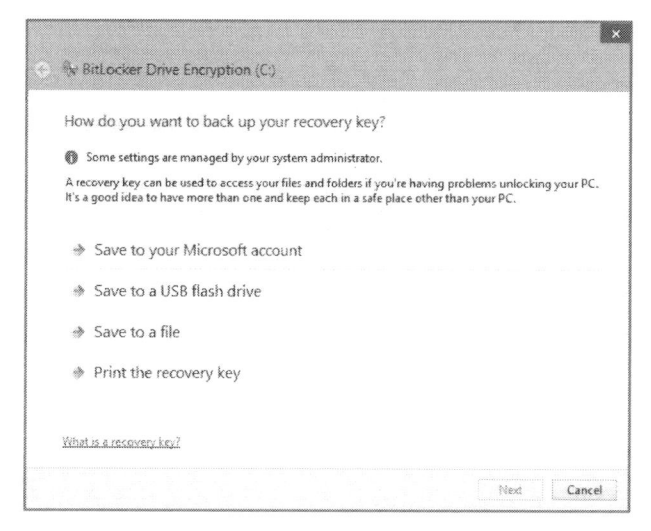

13. At the prompt, select the *Microsoft XPS Document Writer* and click the *Print* button.

4. Vulnerability: Storage Device

14. When asked where to save the file, we recommend saving it to your *Documents* folder.

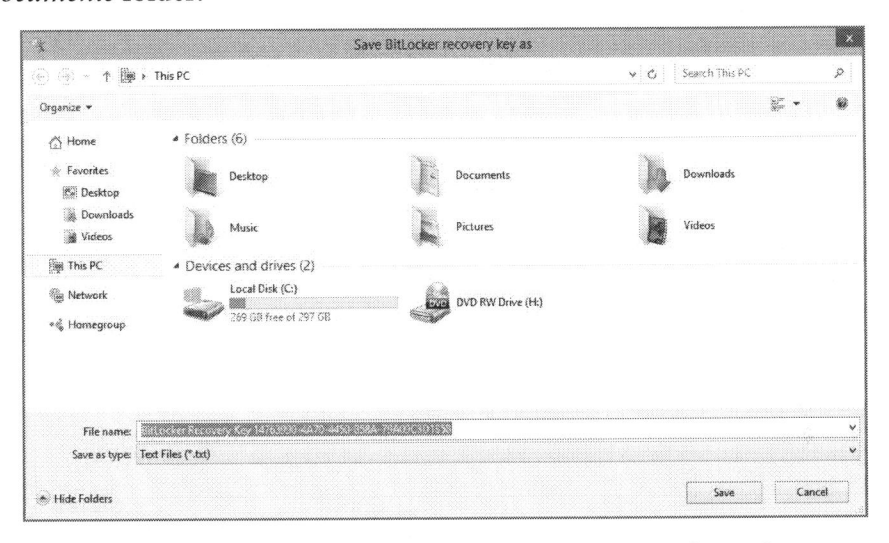

15. When opened, the file will look like the following. Keep this information in a safe place locked up for future reference.

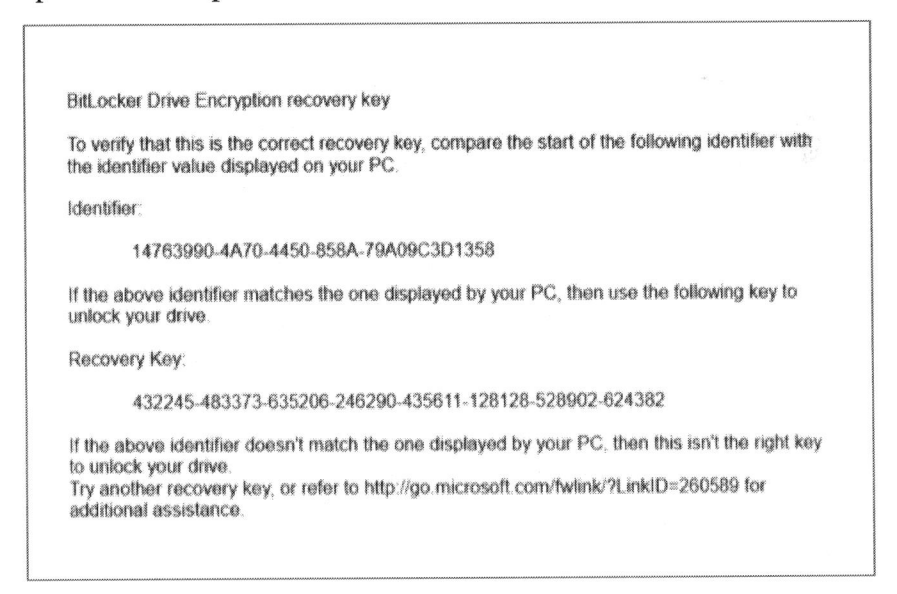

16. Click *Next*.

4. Vulnerability: Storage Device

17. At the window *Choose how much of your drive to encrypt*, select *Encrypt entire drive*, and then click *Next*.

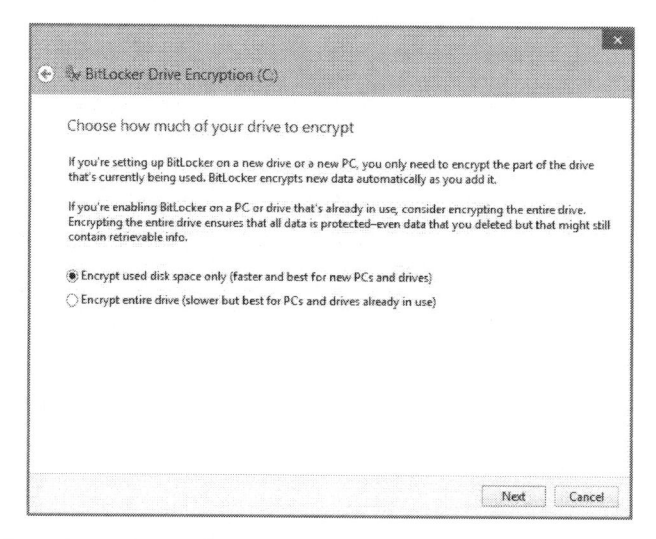

18. At the window *Are you ready to encrypt this drive?* click *Continue*.

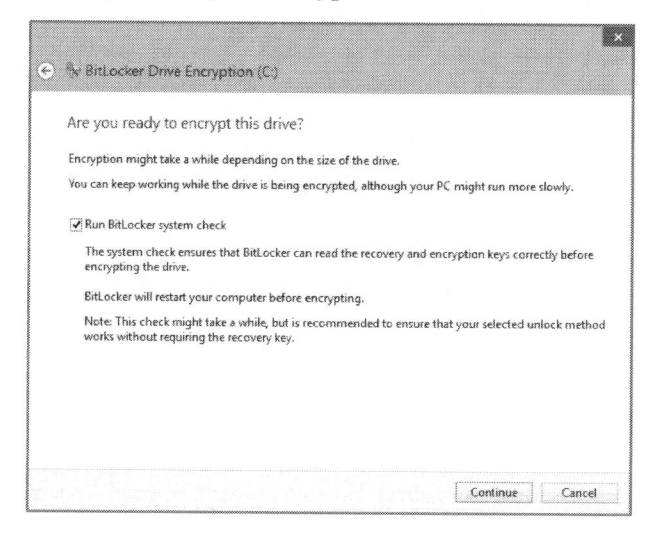

4. Vulnerability: Storage Device

19. At the window *The computer must be restarted*, click *Restart now* to start the encryption process.

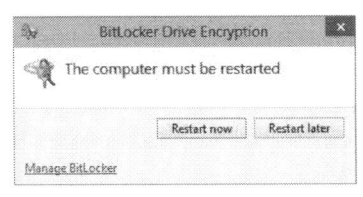

The encryption process may take as little as an hour or more than a day, depending on drive size, drive speed (5400 rpm, 7200 rpm, or SSD), CPU speed, and the availability of TPM.

4. Vulnerability: Storage Device

Review Questions

1. What are the three ways to block access to external storage devices?
2. What way(s) can Windows encrypt hard disks?
3. Hardware encryption is accomplished by using _____.
4. Software encryption is accomplished by using _____ software that is included with Windows 10.

5. Vulnerability: Sleep and Screen Saver

Do not take life too seriously. You will never get out of it alive.
–Elbert Hubbard, American writer, artist, and philosopher

5. Vulnerability: Sleep and Screen Saver

General Security

When you walk away from your computer, it is a trivial task for someone else to sit at the computer and access all of your data.

To help prevent this, configure your computer to lock down after a short period of inactivity, or upon command.

Assignment: Require Password After Sleep or Screen Saver

In this assignment, we will configure the computer to go into screen saver mode after 5 minutes of inactivity, and to require entering a password to remove the screen saver.

1. Click on *Search the web and Windows* and type *Control Panel*. Select *Control Panel* from the search results, and then select *Appearance and Personalization > Personalization > Change screen saver*.

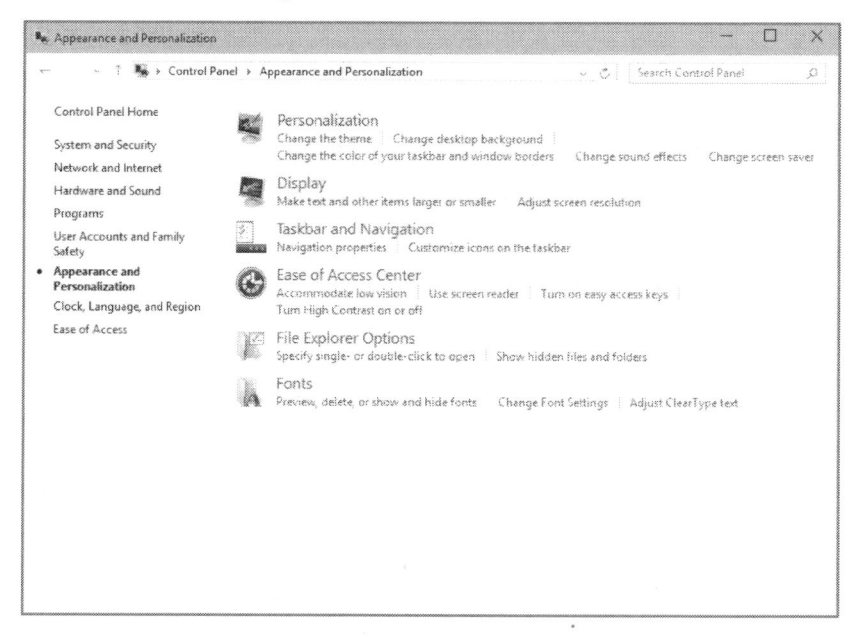

5. Vulnerability: Sleep and Screen Saver

2. The *Screen Saver Settings* opens. Set the *Wait* timer to *5 minutes*. Enable the *On resume, display logon screen* checkbox. Then click on the *Apply* button to save the settings.

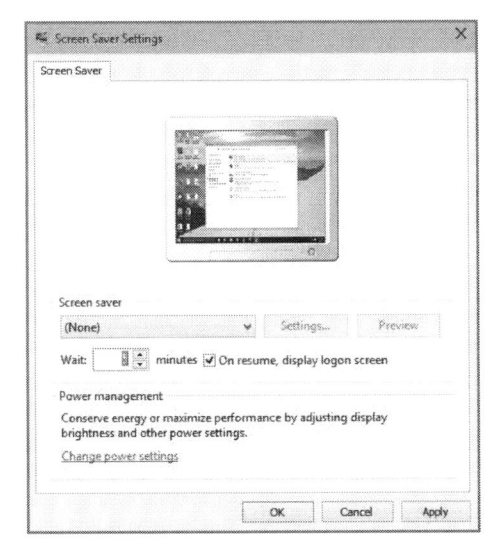

3. From the *Screen Saver Settings* window, click on the *Change power settings* to adjust the energy settings.

5. Vulnerability: Sleep and Screen Saver

4. Energy may be set to *Balanced*. To the right, you should see an option to change those settings for the plan you select. Click on *Change plan settings*.

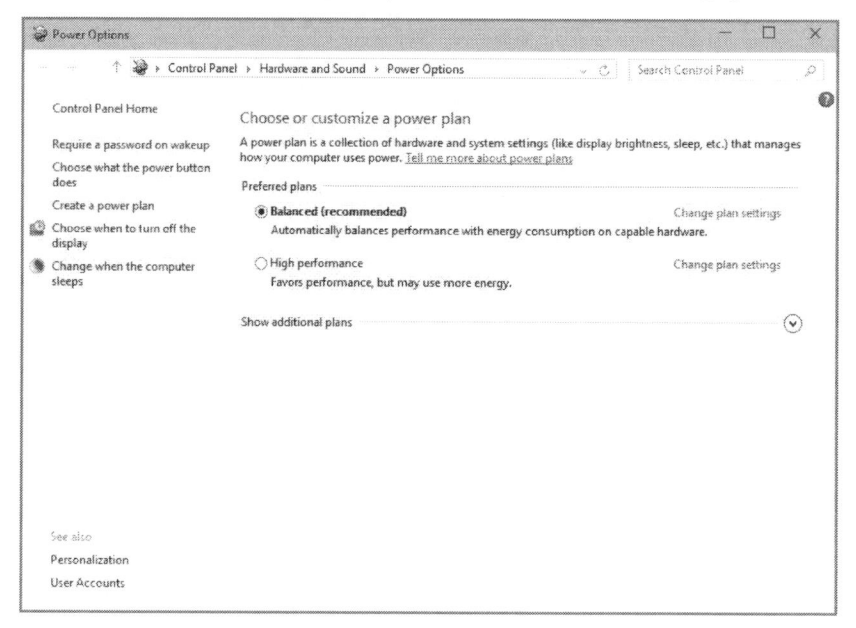

5. For *Turn off the display,* set this setting to 10 minutes. Remember, your screen saver will kick in after 5 minutes of inactivity.

6. For the *Put the computer to sleep,* set this to *Never*. Then click on *save changes* to set the settings.

At the time of this writing, Screen saver does not support *Hot Corners*. To activate an immediate lock of your PC, all you have to do is hit the *Windows* and the *L* keys.

5. Vulnerability: Sleep and Screen Saver

Review Questions

1. Where do you go to configure requiring a password after X minutes of inactivity?

6. Vulnerability: Malware

Behind every great fortune lies a great crime.
–Honore de Balzac, 19th-century novelist and playwright

6. Vulnerability: Malware

Anti-Malware

Most people know this category of software as *antivirus*, but there are so many other nasty critters out there (worms, Trojan horses, phishing attacks, malicious scripts, spyware, etc.) that the overarching term Anti-malware" is more accurate.

Depending on how one chooses to measure, there are from 500,000–40,000,000 malware *http://en.wikipedia.org/wiki/Malware* in the field that impact Windows. Symantec reports they receive as many as 40,000 new signatures in a single day.

As with previous version, Windows 10 bundles Windows Defender. Windows 10 will have hundreds of improvements–but no improvements to the built-in antivirus. Windows Defender only provides essential malware protection, which means it just a baseline protection for the PC. Windows Defender and Microsoft Security Essentials do not score very high in independent security tests. Microsoft has made it clear that these built-in solutions are only there to provide a *basic protection* for the PC and nothing more.

Should you and I care about malware? Yes. Not only can and will malware slow the computer and cause data and backup corruption (almost always an unintended malware consequence), but your every keystroke, passwords, email, and web browsing may be harvested. This information commonly is sold on hacker sites, allowing anyone with a few dollars to steal your identity, bank account, credit cards, etc.

It is for these reasons that I strongly recommend the installation of quality anti-malware on all computers. This raises the question of how to know that an anti-malware is quality software? We go by the results of independent testing organizations. One of the most highly regarded is AV Comparatives (AVC) *http://av-comparatives.org*. Although no testing organization tests all of the 100+ anti-malware products on the market, AVC tests the major players at least a few times each year against a wide range of the current bugs. The results of their Windows anti-malware product tests are made public at *http://chart.av-comparatives.org*. The report on Windows anti-malware product tests is available at *http://www.av-comparatives.org/wp-content/uploads/2014/12/avc_prot_2014b_en.pdf* .

6. Vulnerability: Malware

In their most recent testing of Windows anti-malware products, most of the tested software caught all of the Windows malware. So the deciding factors come down to ease of use, resource utilization (impact on computer performance), and ability to catch Windows malware.

For Windows home users without the need for the strictest security, we recommend either *Avira Free Antivirus* or *Bitdefender Antivirus Free Edition*. Avira catches all known Windows malware. It has advanced heuristic tools, which help catch unknown threats. Bitdefender is on par with any of the free antivirus programs. It can also scan the system right after booting into Windows to catch viruses before they load, and places a minimal toll on system resources.

The only product we currently recommend for both OS X and Windows business users is Bitdefender. This is due to its first-rate ability to recognize and remove both OS X and Windows malware, simple interface, low impact on computer performance, it has both an OS X and Windows applications, and can be centrally administered (although only from a Windows computer)–important factors for users running Windows on their Mac, as well as system administrators managing a mixed-platform environment.

6. Vulnerability: Malware

Turning to AVC for guidance, here is their chart on effectiveness of catching and removing malware from Windows:

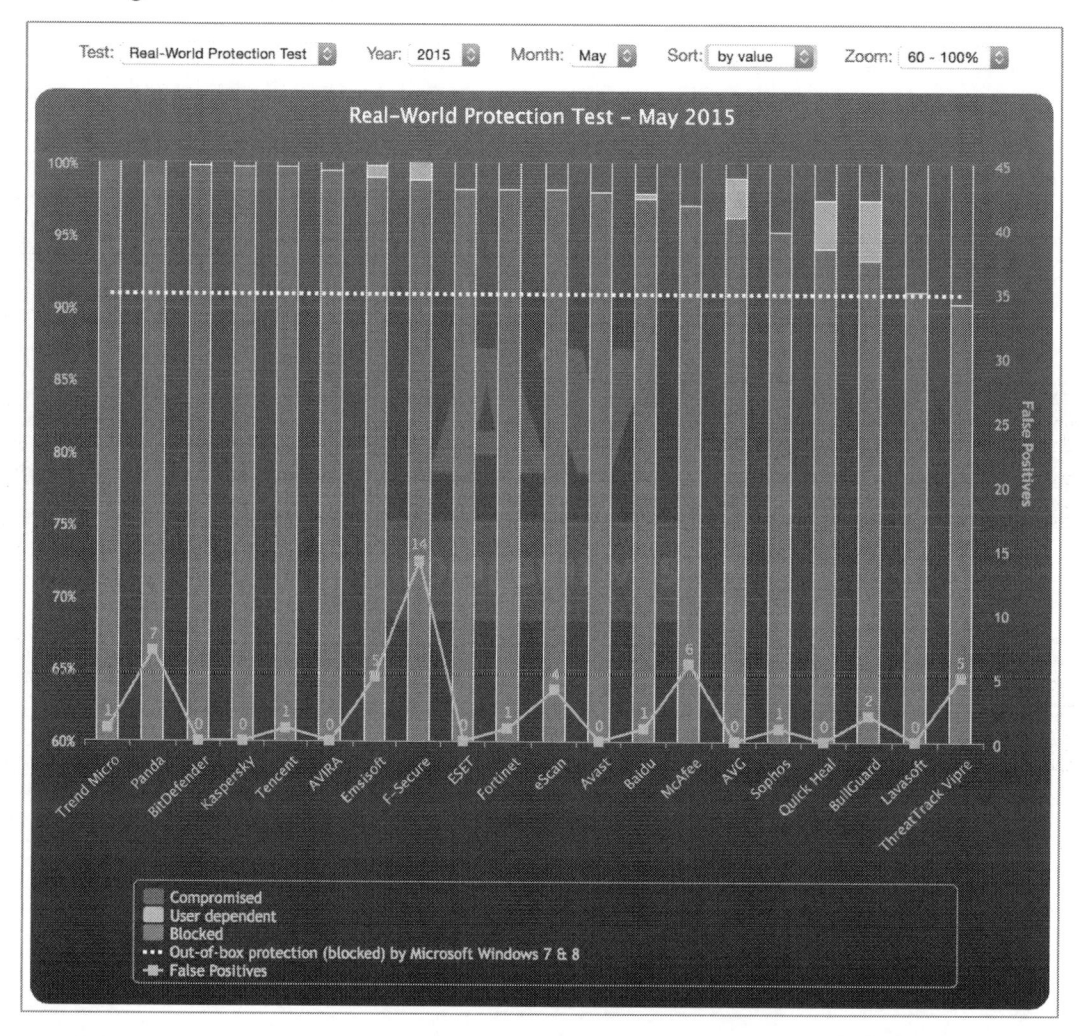

As of this writing, the top contender for effectiveness at 99.7% is Trend Micro. Panda, Bitdefender, Kaspersky, Tencent, and Avira complete the top effectiveness ratings. But effectiveness isn't the only important measurement. In this same chart we can see false-positives. It's a sad day when a clean file is flagged as infected and then automatically trashed. Of the leading brands, only Bitdefender, Kaspersky, and Avira have zero false positives.

6. Vulnerability: Malware

Another vital measurement is performance–the impact the anti-malware has on overall performance of your computer. Anti-malware should use as little system resources as possible.

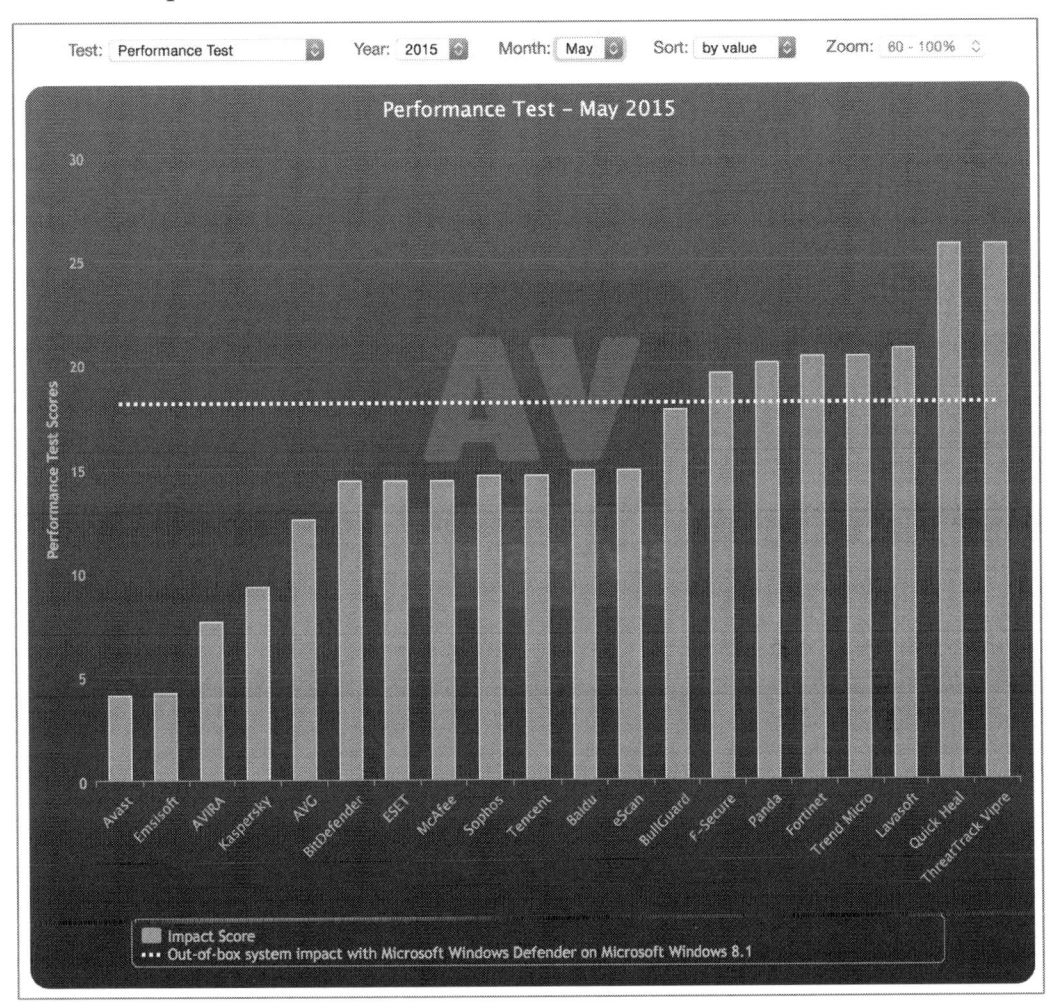

Assignment: Install and Configure Avira

In this assignment, you download, install, and configure *Avira Free Antivirus*.

1. Using a web browser, download *Avira Free Antivirus* at *http://www.avira.com*.

6. Vulnerability: Malware

2. Click the *Free tab > Antivirus > PC*.

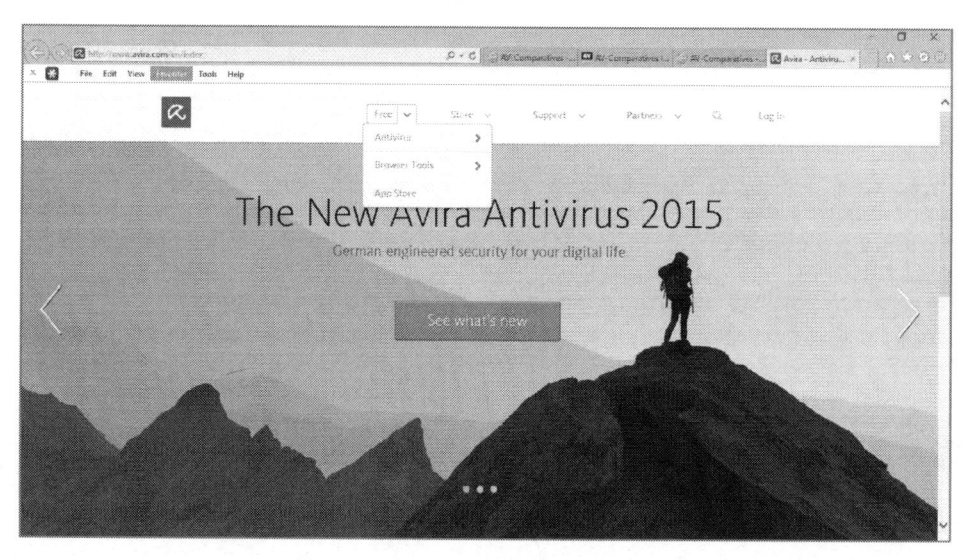

3. Click *Download Now*. The installer will download to your computer. You may be asked to either *Run* it or *Save* it. Click on *Save* to save the installer.

4. Locate the installer in your *Downloads* folder. It will be named something like *avira_en_av_5868561527_ws.exe*.

5. Right click on the installer, and then select *Run as administrator*. A *User Account Control* window will pop up. Click the *Yes* button to continue.

6. Click on the *Accept and Install* button to continue the installation. A window will appear stating that it is installing.

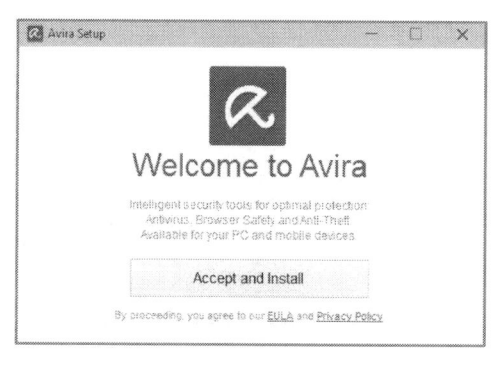

6. Vulnerability: Malware

7. When installation completes, another window opens stating the installation was successful, and the Avira menu icon will appear.

8. Click on the *Up Arrow*, and then click on the Avira *icon*. Click on *Open Avira*.

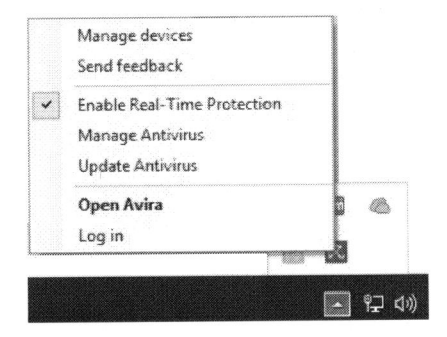

9. In the pop-up window, click on *Free Antivirus* to launch the app.

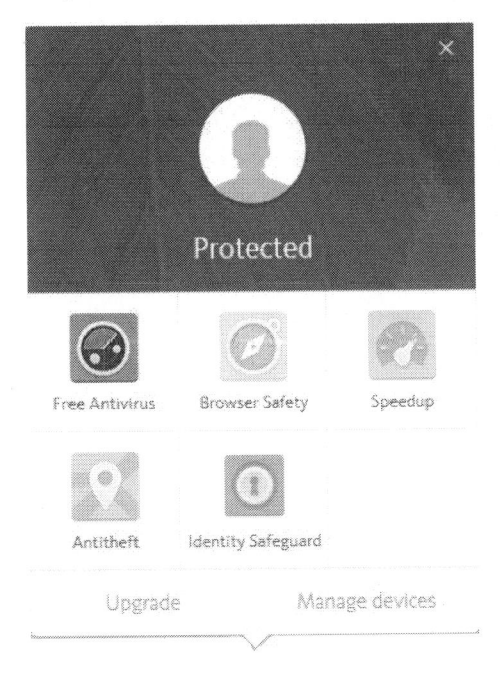

6. Vulnerability: Malware

10. Click the *Update* menu > *Start update* to start the update.

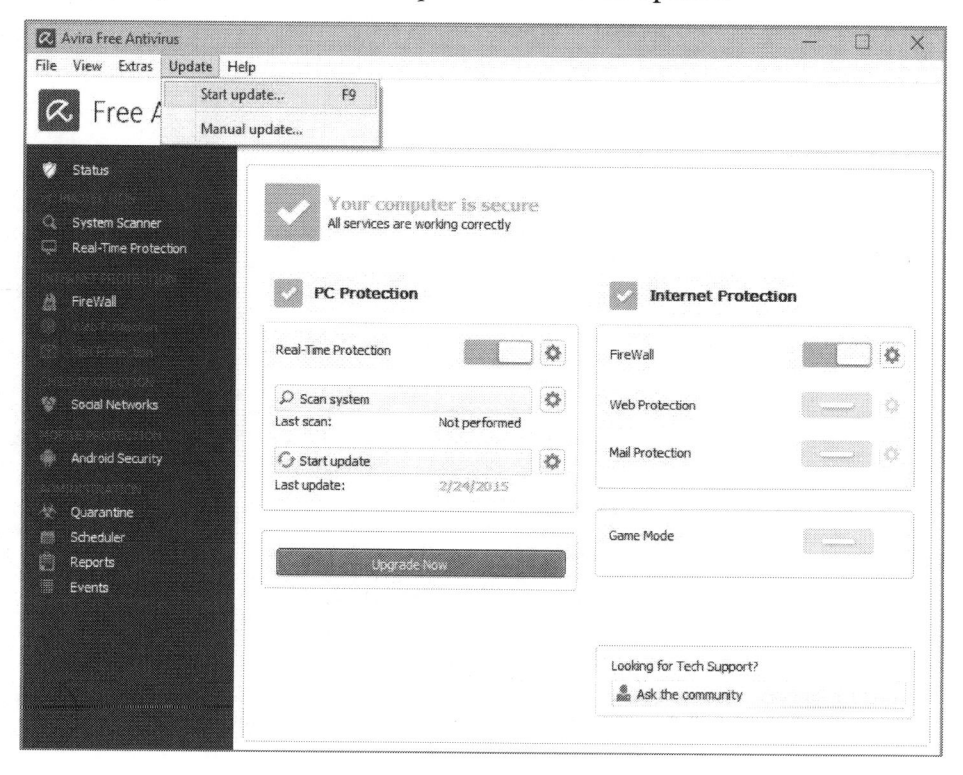

6. Vulnerability: Malware

11. In the side bar, click on *Scheduler* to start the process of scheduling a full scan.

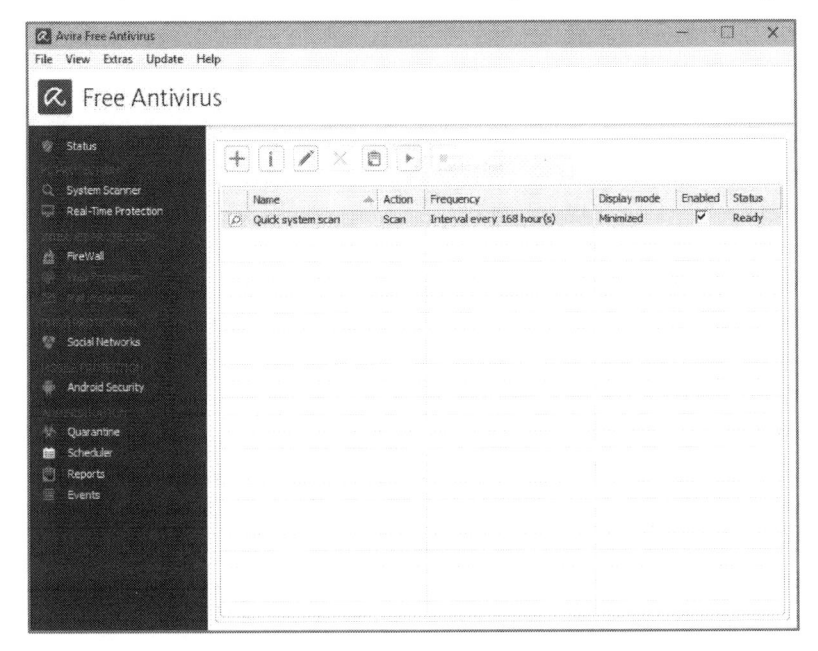

12. Click the + button to start a new scheduled scan.

13. In the *Name and description of the job* window, enter a *Name of the job* and a brief *Description of the job*, and then click *Next*.

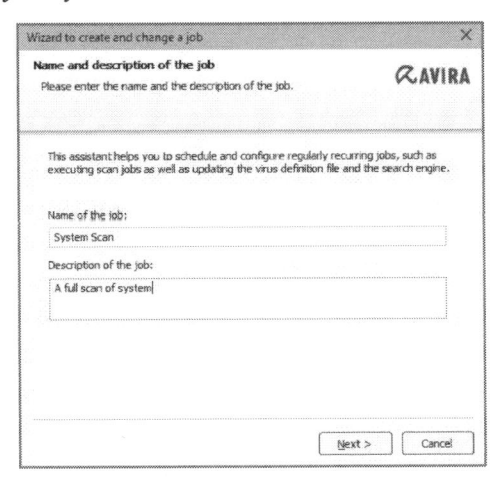

6. Vulnerability: Malware

14. In the *Type of job* window, select *Scan job,* and then click *Next.*

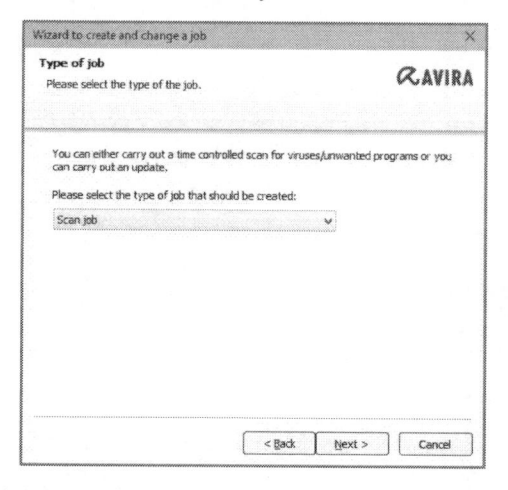

15. In the *Selection of the profile* window, select *Complete system scan,* and then click *Next.*

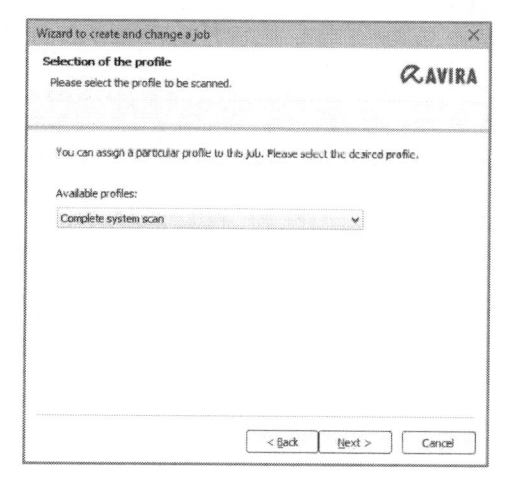

6. Vulnerability: Malware

16. In the *Time of the job* window, from the drop down menu select *Weekly,* set a time when your computer is usually awake, and then click the *Next* button.

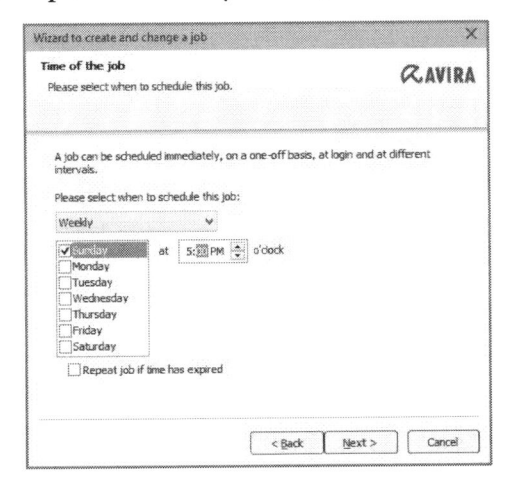

17. The last window will ask if you want to see a window. We recommend selecting *Invisible*. To select this, click on the *Display mode* drop down menu > *Invisible,* and then click *Finish* to save the new task.

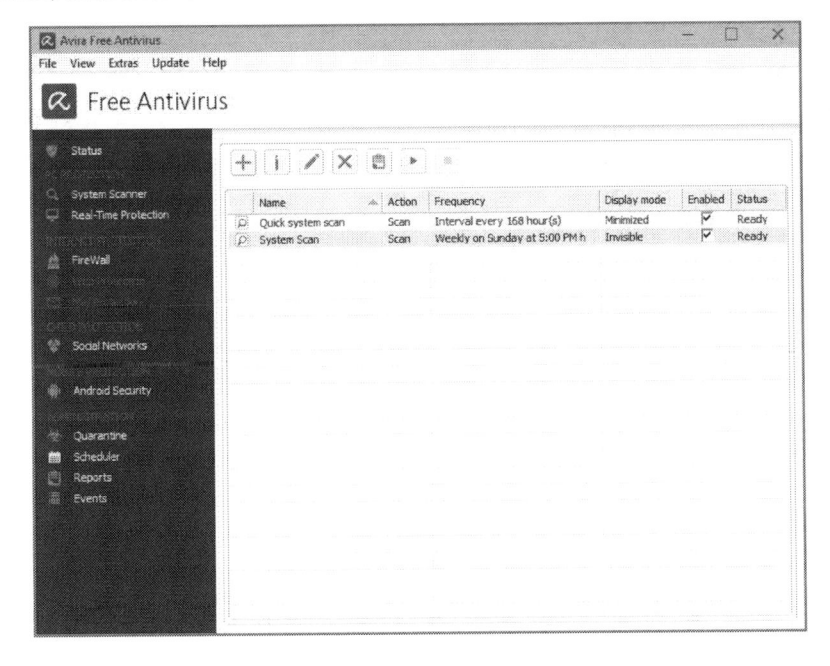

6. Vulnerability: Malware

18. Lastly, perform an initial scan on your entire system. Click *System Scanner* in the side bar, click on *Complete system scan,* and then click on the *Magnifier glass* to start the scan.

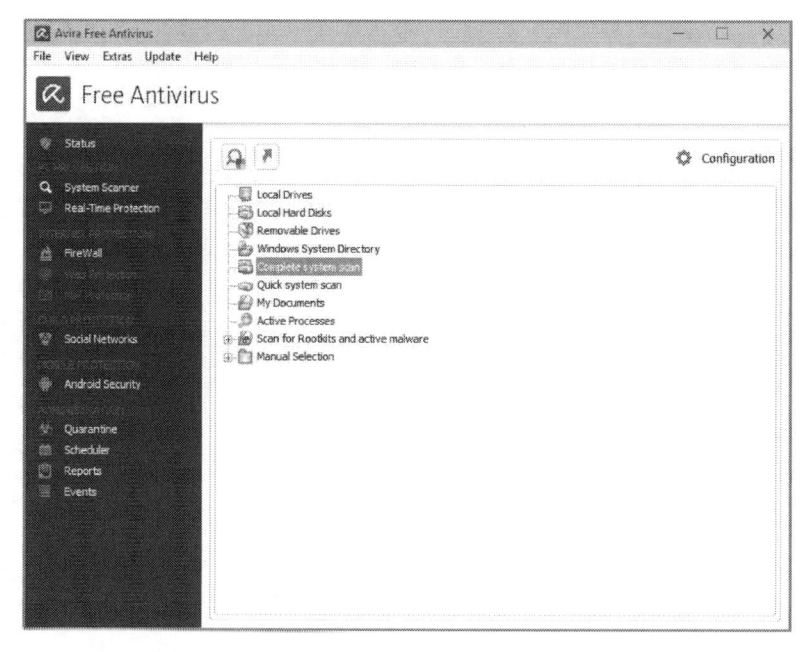

19. A window will display the system scan. Let it complete, then you can close the window, and then close the *Avira* window.

20. From the Avira menu icon in the *Taskbar*, click on the *Up Arrow,* left click on *Avira* and verify that *Enable Real-Time Protection* is enabled. If not, select *Enable Real-Time Protection* to enable it.

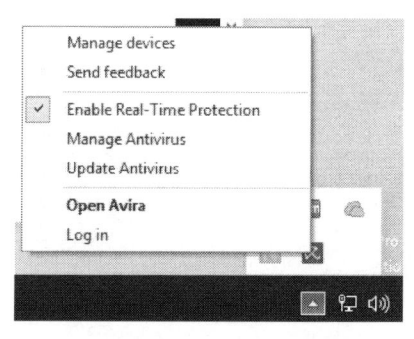

Your Avira is now installed, configured, and protecting your system.

6. Vulnerability: Malware

Assignment: Uninstall Avira Antivirus

Should you decide to remove Avira Antivirus from your computer, you will need to uninstall it from the *Control Panel*. In this assignment we will uninstall Avira.

- NOTE: If you wish to keep Avira installed, skip this assignment.

1. Click on the *Start* menu > *Control Panel*.
2. Under the Programs section, select *Uninstall a program*.
3. There will be 2 listings of *Avira*. Both need to be removed. Click on the first listing. Near the top of the window, click on *Uninstall*.

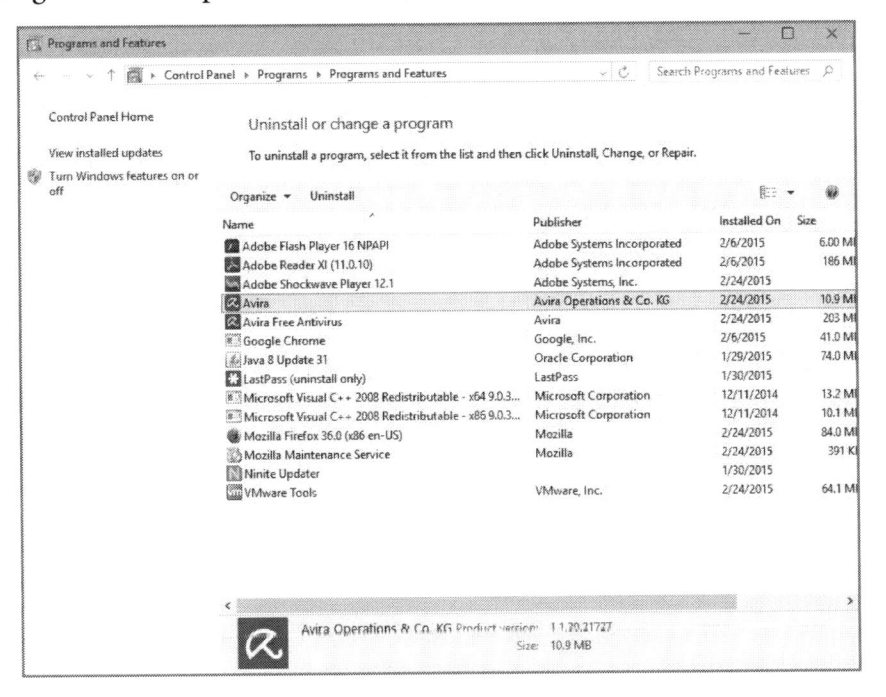

6. Vulnerability: Malware

4. In the next window, click on the *Uninstall* button.

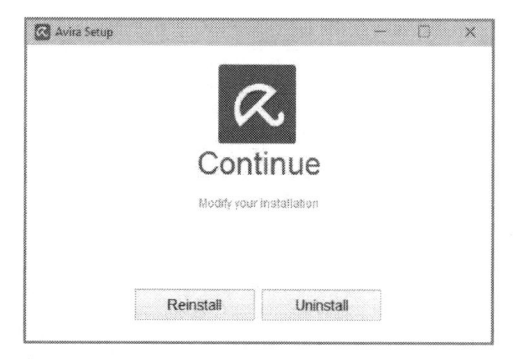

5. When the uninstall completes, click on the *OK* button.

6. Repeat this process for the second *Avira* item.

7. When prompted to reboot, click *Yes* to reboot and finish the uninstall process.

Assignment: Install and Configure Bitdefender Antivirus

In this assignment, you will download, install, and configure *Bitdefender Internet Security 2015*.

1. Using a web browser, visit and download *Bitdefender Internet Security 2015* at *http://www.bitdefender.com/Downloads/*. At the prompt, enter an email address you would like to register. Then click on the *Download Free Trial* button to start the download. At the prompt, click on the *Save* button to save the download.

6. Vulnerability: Malware

2. Locate the Bitdefender installer (*bitdefender_isecurity.exe*) in the Downloads folder. Right click on the installer, selecting *Run as administrator.* Click the *Yes* button to start the install.

3. Click the *Install* button to begin.

4. Once done, click *Get started*.

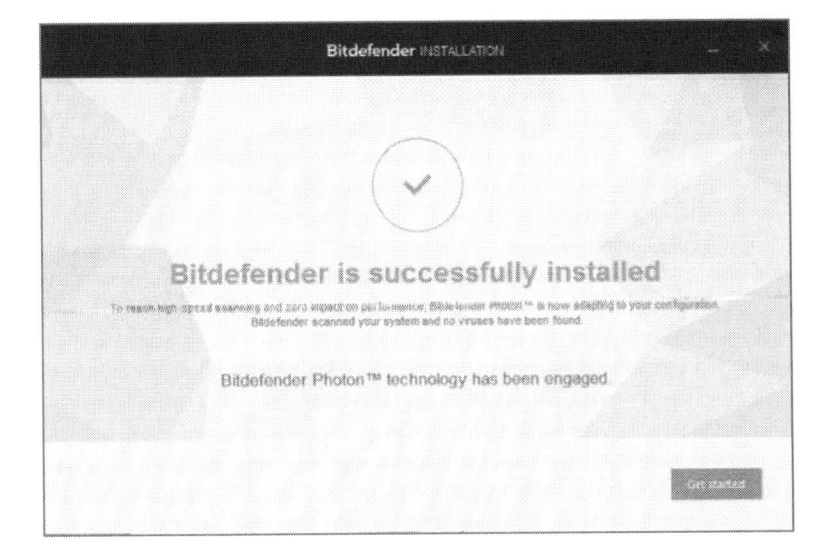

6. Vulnerability: Malware

5. Bitdefender opens a window to immediately perform a scan. If it finds issues with your PC, have it fix them for you.

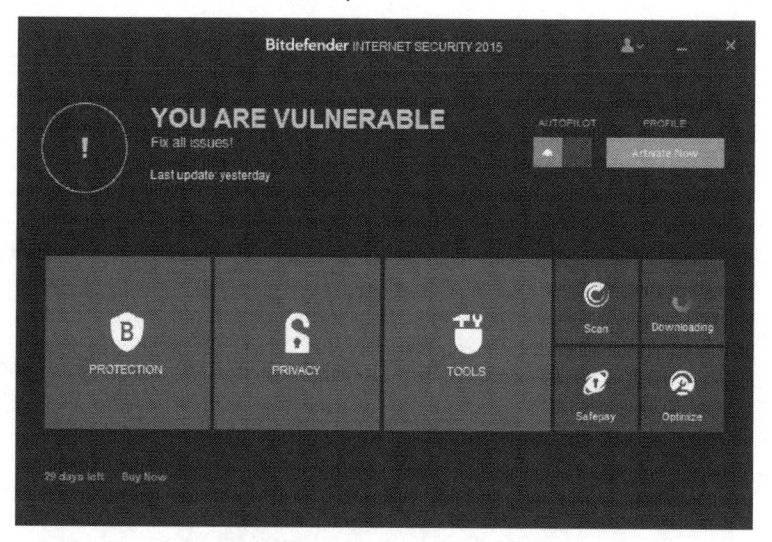

6. While in this window, click the *Activate Now* button to start the trial version. Bitdefender will be fully active in trial mode for 30 days.

7. Click the *Update* button to verify the virus definitions are fully updated. You may see an icon spinning to the lower right. This is Bitdefender updating the virus definitions.

6. Vulnerability: Malware

8. From the Bitdefender main window, click the *Protection* button. The *Protection* window opens. From the tool bar, select the *Protection* button.

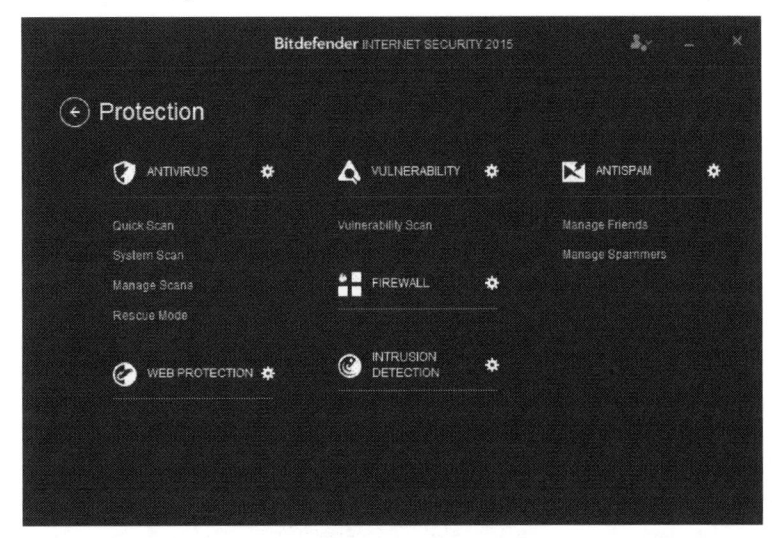

9. Select the *Antivirus* button. Configure as below.

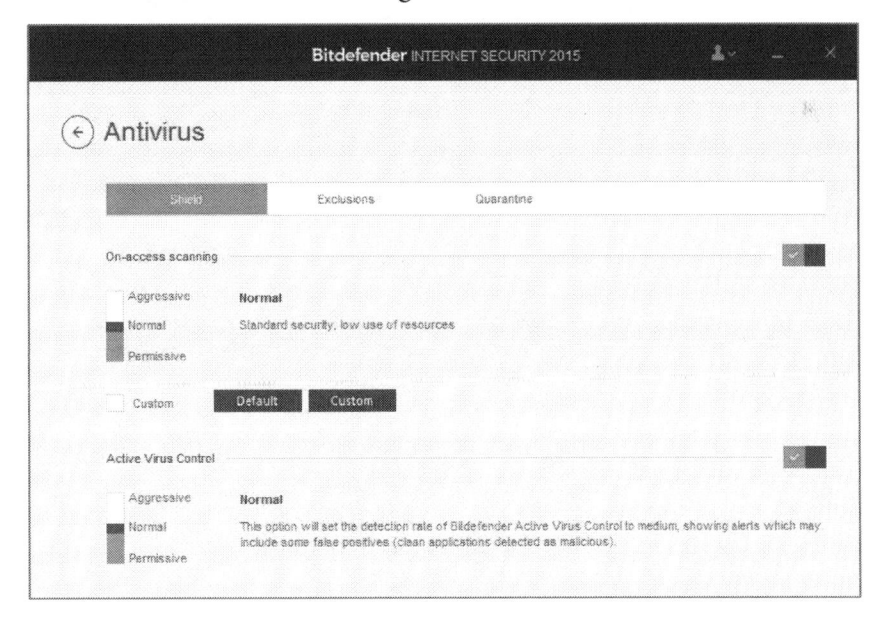

6. Vulnerability: Malware

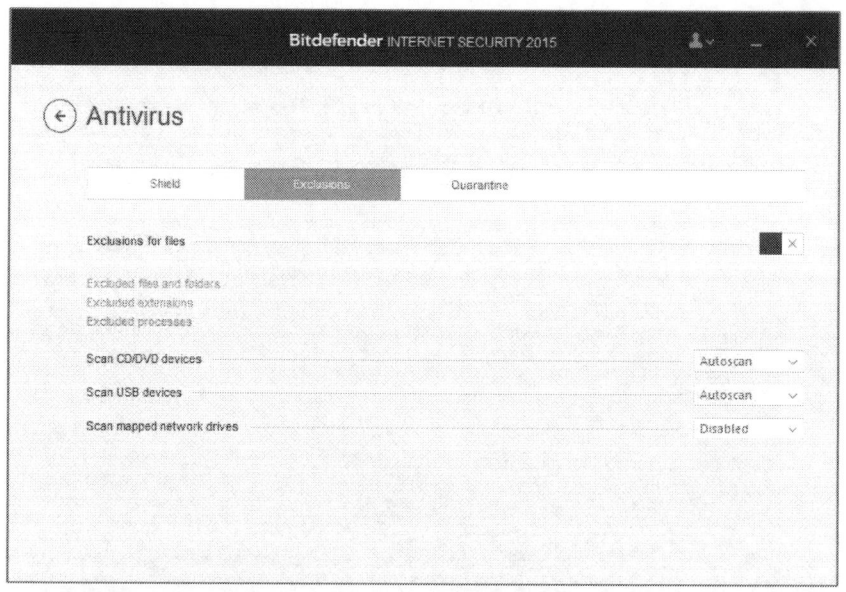

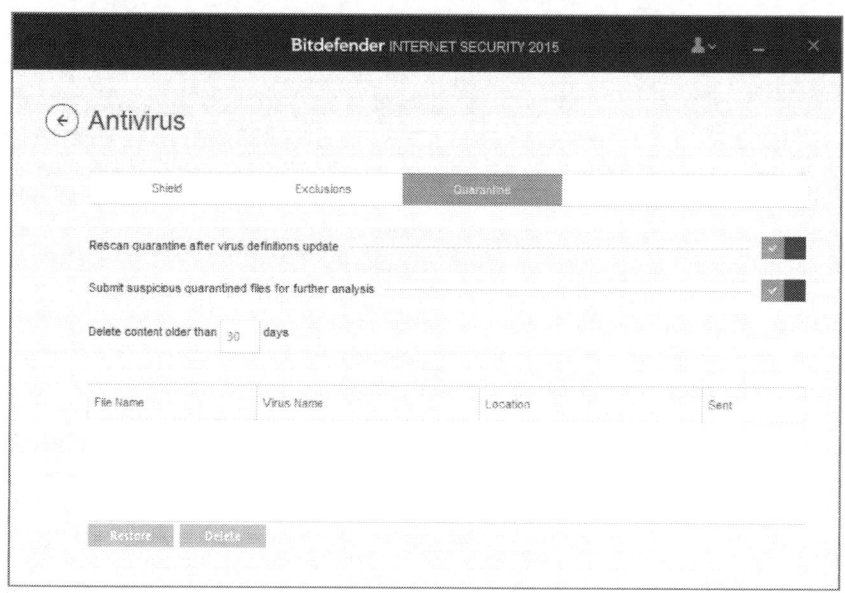

6. Vulnerability: Malware

10. Select the *Web Protection* button, and configure as below.

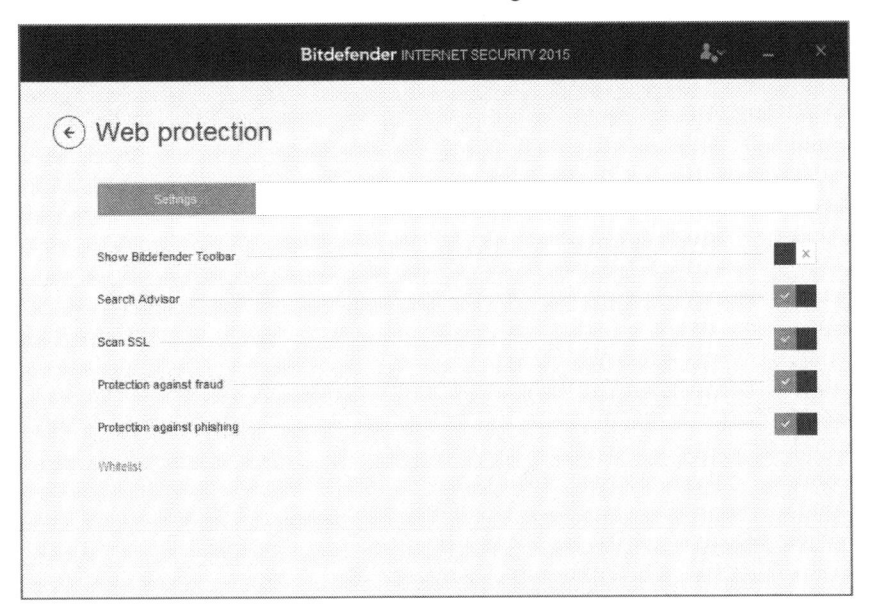

11. Select the *Vulnerability* button, and configure as below.

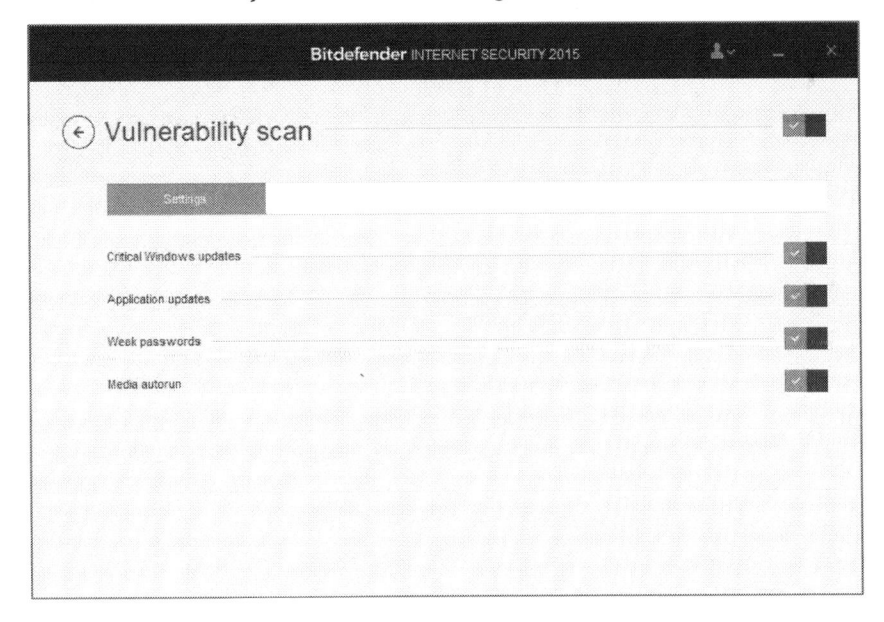

6. Vulnerability: Malware

12. Select the *Firewall* button, and configure as below. We will leave the *Rules* and *Adapters* sections alone, using the *default* settings.

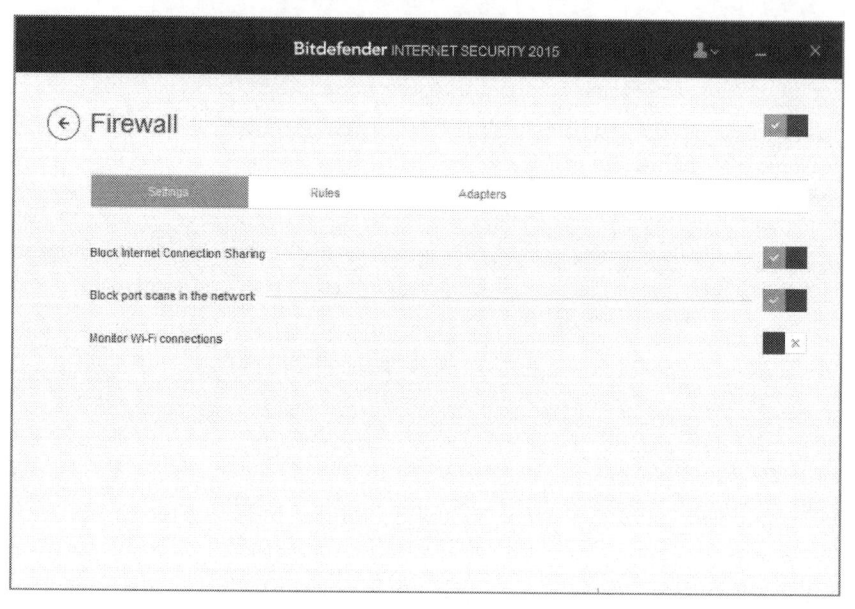

13. Select the *Intrusion Detection* button, and configure as below.

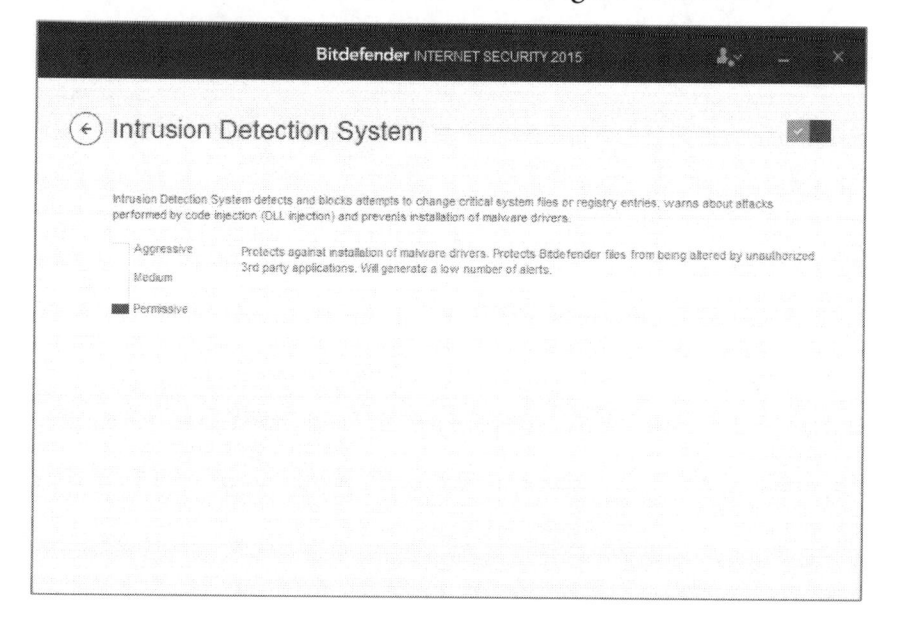

6. Vulnerability: Malware

14. Select the *Antispam* button, and configure as below.

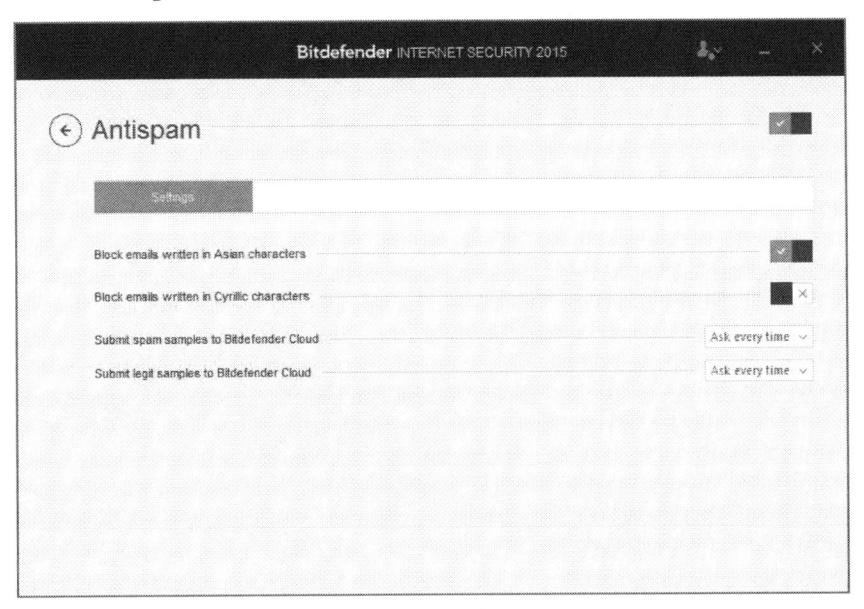

15. For *Manage Friends* and *Manage Spammers,* we will leave these alone. If you wanted to add a specific email address or domain to allow or deny, this is where to do so.

6. Vulnerability: Malware

16. Now we are ready to perform a full scan on your computer. Click the *System Scan* button under *Antivirus* section.

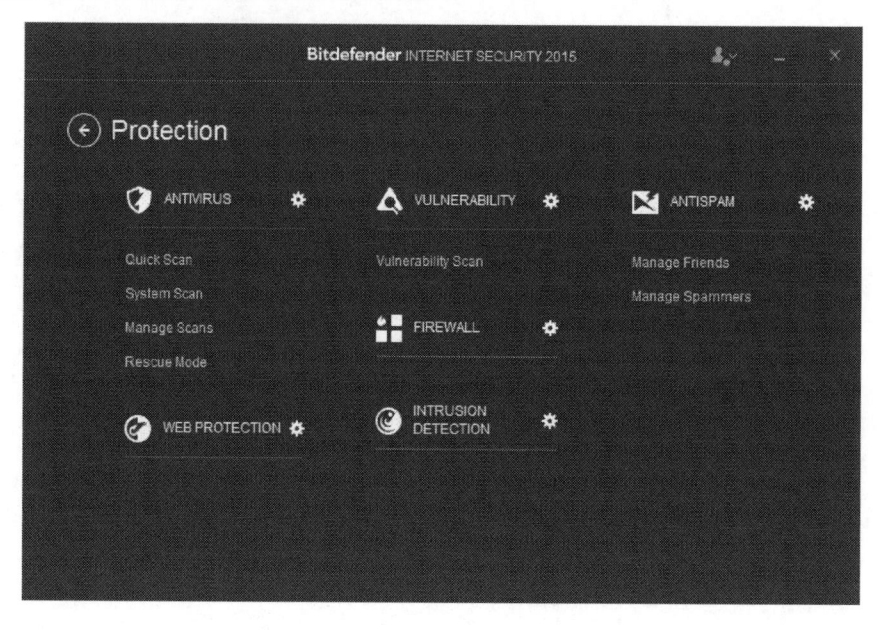

17. Depending on the speed of your computer and size of your drive(s), a full scan may take up to a full day to complete. Make sure that your *Power Options* preference for *Put the computer to sleep* is set to *Never*.

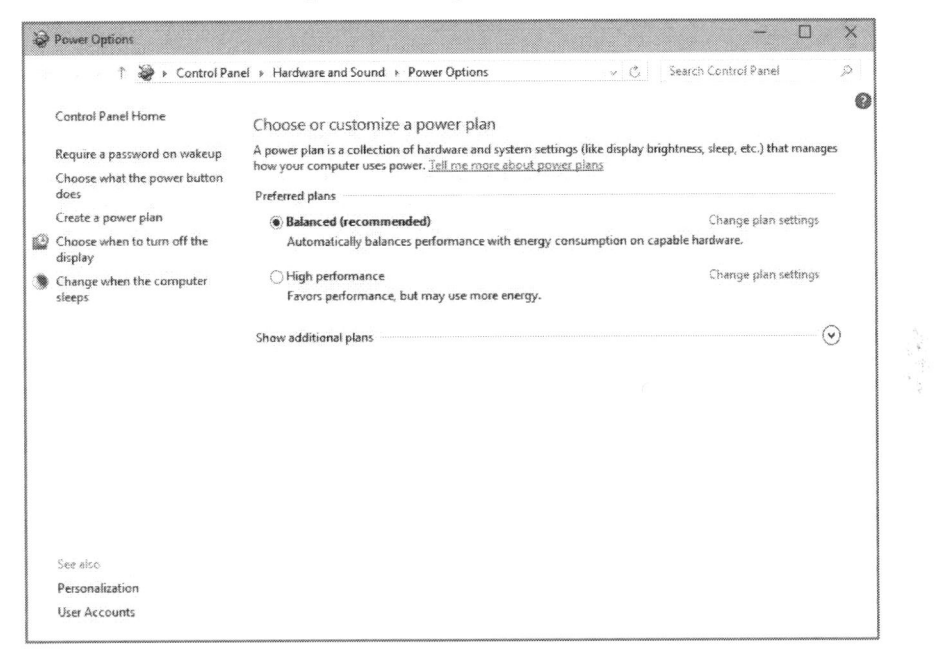

From now on Bitdefender will scan files in real-time, as they are opened. There should not be a need to perform another full scan. Bitdefender will automatically attempt to disinfect (remove malware) from an infected file. Failing that, it will delete the file.

6. Vulnerability: Malware

Review Questions

1. According to Wikipedia, there may be as many as _____ malware that impact Windows.

2. Name a URL of an independent anti-malware testing organization.

3. When selecting an anti-malware product, what are some of the selection criteria to consider?

7. Vulnerability: Firewall

If you could kick the person in the pants responsible for most of your trouble, you wouldn't sit for a month.

–Theodore Roosevelt

Firewall

Whenever a computer needs to communicate with the outside world–say, to print, receive or send email, or surf the web–it must "open a door" to that world. In the IT universe this is called "opening a port."

Ports are numbered from 1–65,535, with one port number assigned to any one communication task. For example, when using your browser to visit Google, you enter "http://www.google.com" in the address field. This can be translated into English as: "Using the language of the Internet (http) I would like to communicate with a server named www, within a domain named google.com."

The problem is that the www server at Google has 65,535 ports to which it may potentially need to listen. Invisible to the user, *:80* is been placed at the end of the address request. This translates into: "And please knock on port 80 (reserved for web server communications) so that www can respond to the web page requests that I send to it."

To best secure your computer, it is important to only have those ports open that are necessary to perform your work.

The purpose of a firewall *http://en.wikipedia.org/wiki/Firewall* is to block unwanted attempts to get into or communicate with your computer from the network or Internet through your 65,535 ports. It is about as simple as anything gets on a computer, and once activated you likely will never need to know about it again.

Since Windows 10 automatically activates the firewall, you can rest assured that the firewall puts guards at the gates to prevent unwanted visitors.

You never want to turn off your firewall. Leaving off the firewall is like an invitation for hackers to come and steal all your data and hijack your system. If you can, purchase a router with a firewall, to give you another layer of protection. Having a router on your network with firewall capabilities can your first line of defense for your network, whether hardwired or Wi-Fi. Keeping your firewall on gives you that second layer of protection from attacks or intrusions from the outside world.

7. Vulnerability: Firewall

- NOTE: If you have installed Bitdefender antivirus (previous chapter), it installed its own firewall, and deactivated the Windows 10 firewall. The Bitdefender firewall is more restrictive than the Windows firewall, meaning that you may receive alerts that some network processes need firewall attention to function properly with it enabled.

7. Vulnerability: Firewall

Review Questions

1. Network ports are number from _____ to _____.
2. The purpose of a firewall is _____.
3. By default, the Windows 10 firewall is off and must be configured to provide protection. (True or False)
4. Bitdefender installs its own firewall, and deactivates the Windows 10 firewall. (True or False)

8. Vulnerability: Data Loss

Weather forecast for tonight: Dark.

–George Carlin

8. Vulnerability: Data Loss

The Need for Backups

Data loss is a very real fact of life. It is not a matter of *if* you will experience data loss, just a matter of *when*, and how often. Only a small percentage of computer users back up on a regular basis. I suspect these are the folks who have experienced catastrophic data loss and never want a repeat.

There are many sources of data loss. The top contenders include:

- Computer theft
- Power surges
- Power sags
- Sabotage
- Fire
- Water damage. I personally have had 3 clients who have lost computers due to cats or dogs marking their territory, and my own cat took out a $4,000 monitor with nothing more than a hairball.
- Entropy / aging of the drive
- Malware
- Terrorist activities
- Criminal activities
- Static electricity
- Physical shock to the drive (banging the computer, dropping, etc.)

Best Practices call for three backups:

- **At least one full backup onsite**. This allows for almost immediate recovery of lost or corrupted documents, or full recovery of the OS, applications, and documents in the event of complete loss of the hard drive.

- **At least one full backup offsite**. This is your *Plan B* in the event of a catastrophic loss of both the computer and the onsite backup. This typically takes the form of fire or theft.
- **One Internet-based backup**. This is your *OMG, what do I do now?* fallback plan. Many people substitute the Internet backup for the offsite. A potential problem is that your Internet backup may take several days to weeks to download.

Onsite Full Backup with Windows Backup

Windows 10 comes with its own backup software–Windows Backup. Windows Backup has several advantages over other options, including:

- Free
- Highly reliable and stable
- Low resource requirements
- Allows new files to be added into backup
- Runs on your scheduled task
- Can back up to an external hard drive, USB or CD/DVD
- Can create a *System Image*, which is an exact image of your hard drive.

As a general rule, the backup drive should be at least double the size of your data, preferably quadruple. This allows for future growth and the maintenance of long-term document versioning.

When purchasing a USB hard drive or thumb drive, we highly recommend that it be USB 3.0. This has the fastest data transfer rate you can find today, and new PCs come standard with USB 3.0 ports. When recovering a Terabyte or more of data, speed will lessen the pain.

8. Vulnerability: Data Loss

Onsite Full Backup with Parted Magic

As great as Windows Backup and Restore is, there is one critical area in which it fails–it does not create a bootable clone. A bootable clone is an exact duplicate of the original drive. This is where Parted Magic comes in.

The need for a bootable clone backup becomes clear when you have a hard drive failure. Without a bootable clone, the recovery process looks like this:

1. Call a technician for assistance or rush to the store to buy a new drive.
2. Remove the old drive.
3. Install the new drive.
4. Install Windows.
5. Install all updates.
6. Get back to work–4 to 8 hours after the crash.

With a bootable clone, the recovery process looks like this:

1. Restart your PC with the Boot Manager. Then you can select the USB hard drive that is your clone.
2. Get back to work–5 minutes after the crash.
3. Call a technician for assistance. Let them know there is no rush.
4. At a time that is convenient (and not on overtime) the problem drive is replace and all data copied over.

So why use Windows Backup and Restore? It is the fastest and easiest way to recover lost or damaged documents.

Internet-Based Data Backup

There are several great and unique advantages to Internet-based backups:

- If a small black hole opens up devouring your computer, backup and offsite backup, your Internet backup will always be waiting for you.
- Should you find yourself far away from your computer, as long as you have any computer, your data can be accessed.

- A few of the Internet-based options are now including the ability to share access to any documents that have been backed up.

When looking for the right Internet-based backup service, in addition to cost, features, company and software stability, keep an eye out for document versioning. You want your service to keep at least one month of document versions. In the event that you accidentally delete a document, it will remain on the server for at least a month, or if a document corrupts, you want to be able to go back to a previous (presumably not corrupted) version.

My personal favorites include:

- **Backblaze** at *http://www.backblaze.com*. Easy to use, very fast uploads, rock solid stable, 30-day document versioning, backs up all user accounts.

- **Carbonite** at *http://www.carbonite.com*. Fast uploads, rock solid stable, limited document versioning, backs up all user accounts. 30-day document versioning, family and business accounts make it easier to administer multiple computers.

- **CrashPlan** at *http://www.crashplan.com* and *http://www.crashplanpro.com* -- my only choice for business. Fast upload, rock solid stable, document versioning, lifetime document versioning, individual and business accounts. Can meet your HIPAA or SEC compliance needs.

Assignment: Format the Backup Drive for Both Windows Backup & Restore and Parted Magic

My personal favorite strategy to back up a computer is to use one large external drive for both *Windows Backup & Restore* and clone backups. To do this, we must prepare the drive by formatting it for Windows, then partitioning it into two volumes, one for each of the two types of backup.

If you prefer to have only one type of backup, or to use two drives, each supporting one type of backup, these steps remain largely the same, just performed separately for each drive.

8. Vulnerability: Data Loss

Format the Backup Drive

1. Purchase an external hard drive that has at least four times the capacity of the data to be held on the host computer.

2. Connect the new drive to your computer.

3. Open an *Explorer* window and right click on *This PC*. Then select *Manage*, and the *Computer Management Console* will open.

4. From the list of drives, find the USB drive. The USB external is *Disk 1*. Right click on the name *Unallocated* to partition the hard drive into 2 partitions.

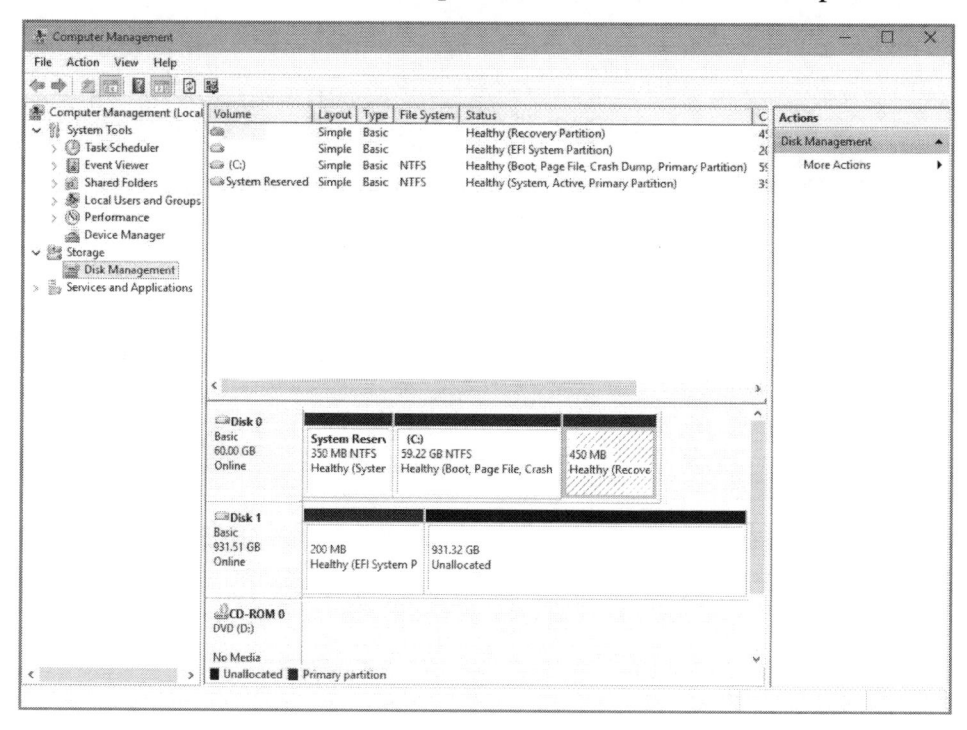

8. Vulnerability: Data Loss

5. A Wizard launches. Select *Next*.

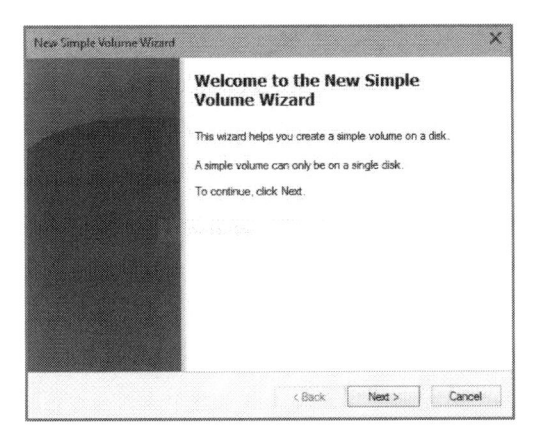

6. The *Specify Volume Size* window opens. We will divide the drive equally. You will have to manually enter equal amount of space, and then click *Next*.

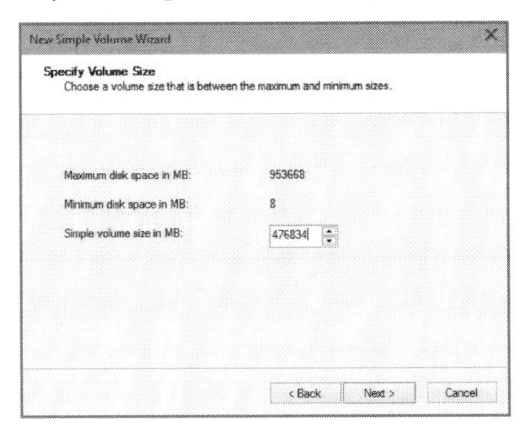

8. Vulnerability: Data Loss

7. At the *Assign Drive Letter or Path* window, you can assign any *Drive Letter* to the partition to distinguish this in your *Windows Explorer* window, and then click *Next*.

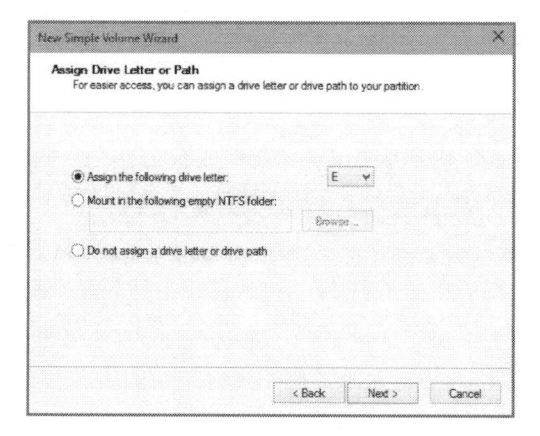

8. In the *Format Partition* window you can select which format the hard drive will be and to name the drive. Select *NTFS* as the *File System*, label the drive in *Volume Label* to distinguish the partition, enable the *Perform a quick format* checkbox, and then click *Next*.

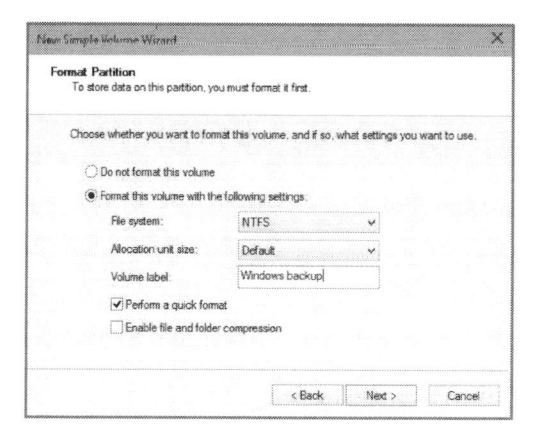

8. Vulnerability: Data Loss

9. In the *Completing the New Simple Volume Wizard,* click *Finish* to format and partition the hard drive.

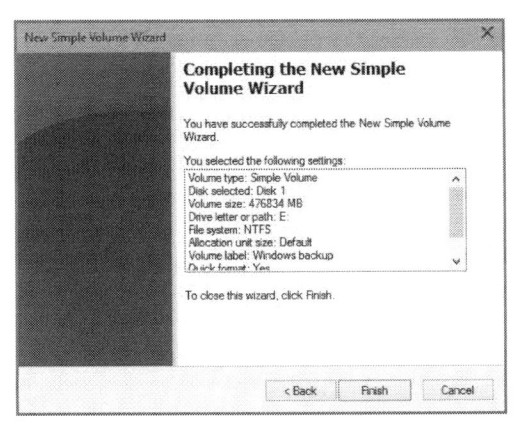

10. The new partition(s) will display.

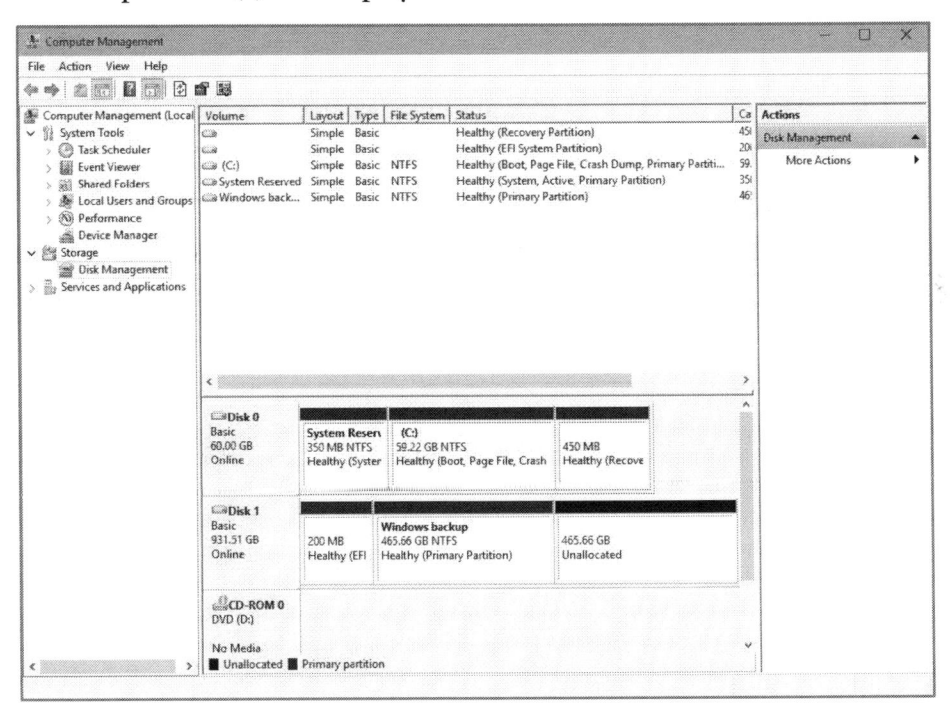

11. Repeat these steps to create the second partition for the clone.

8. Vulnerability: Data Loss

Assignment: Configure Windows Backup and Restore

In this assignment, we will configure the Windows Backup and Restore.

1. Attach the Windows Backup & Restore drive. If you have followed the steps above, it already is attached and mounted.
2. Click the *Start* menu > *Settings,* and then click *Update & recovery* to access the backup section.

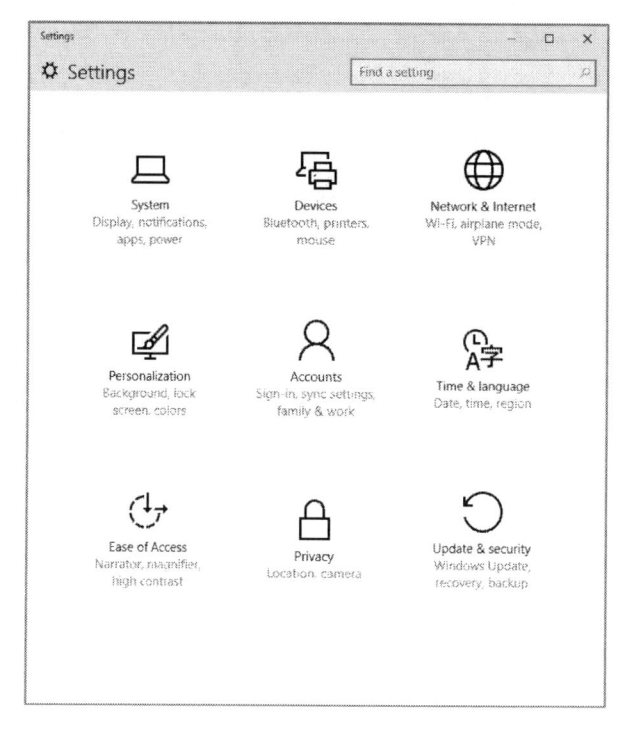

8. Vulnerability: Data Loss

3. Select Backup, and then click on Add a backup location on this PC.

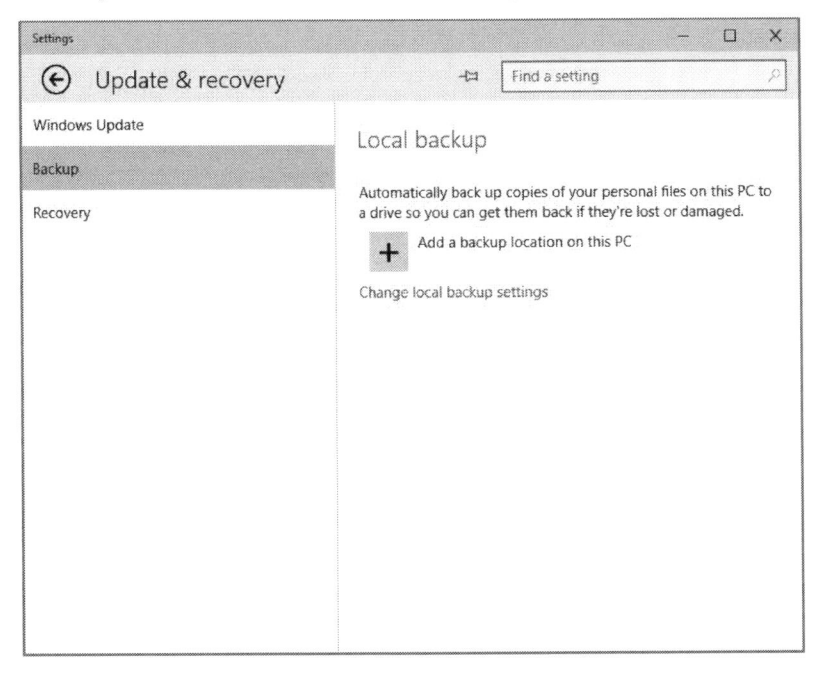

4. A scan for hard drives will start. It sees the partition you created, *Windows backup.* Click on the partition you want to use for the windows backup.

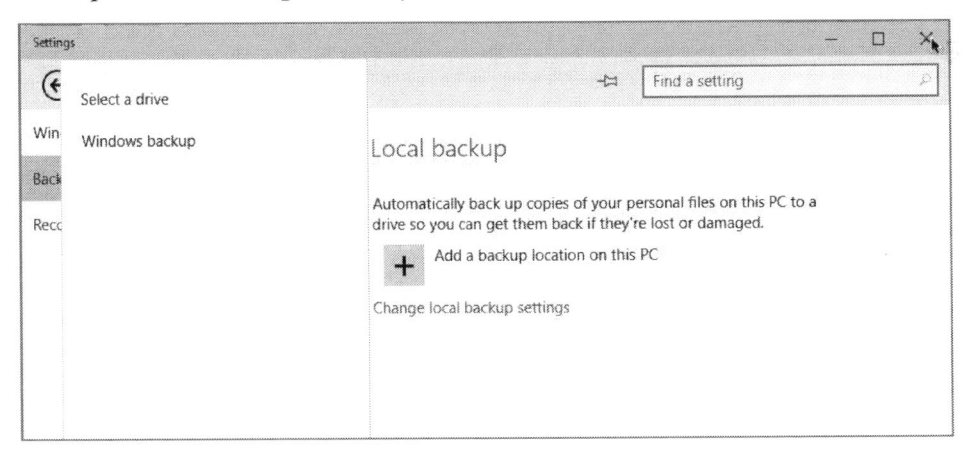

5. It may appear nothing is happening, but we must finish the setup. In the *Taskbar > Search* field, type *Control Panel* and hit the *Enter* key to open *Control Panel.*

8. Vulnerability: Data Loss

6. Click on *System and Security > File History*.

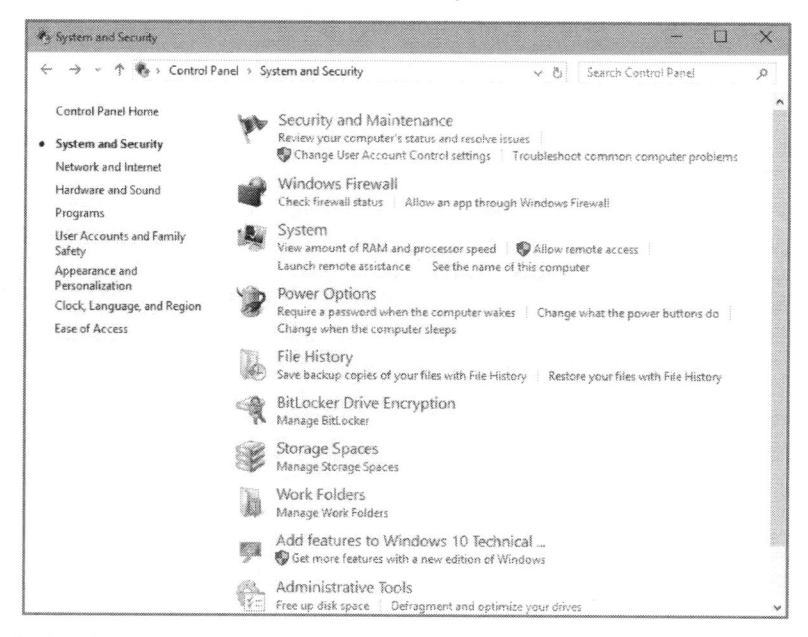

7. By default, this is *Turned Off.* Before we can turn this on, we need to encrypt the backup drive. Click on the link *Turn on BitLocker* in the yellow message.

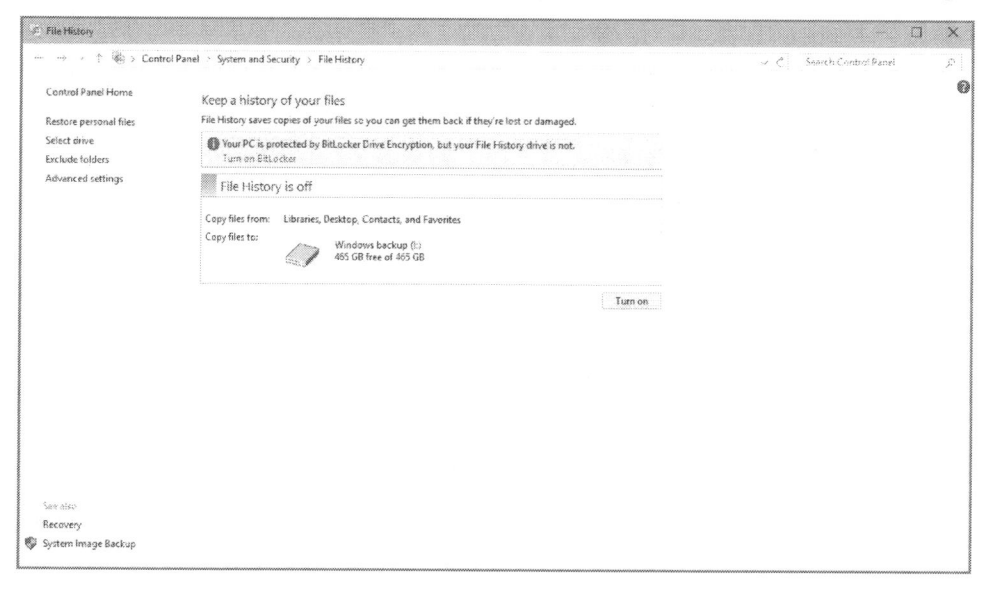

8. Vulnerability: Data Loss

8. See that the *C* drive is already Bitlocked. Below that is your backup hard drive. Click *Turn on BitLocker* for the backup drive.

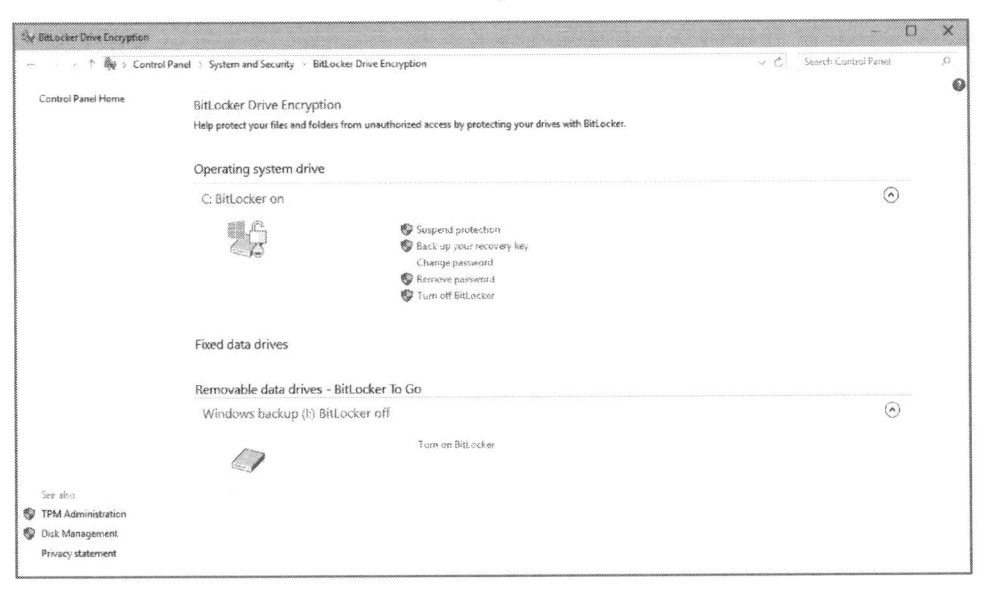

9. Enter a strong password for the hard drive *BitLocker*, and then click *Next*.

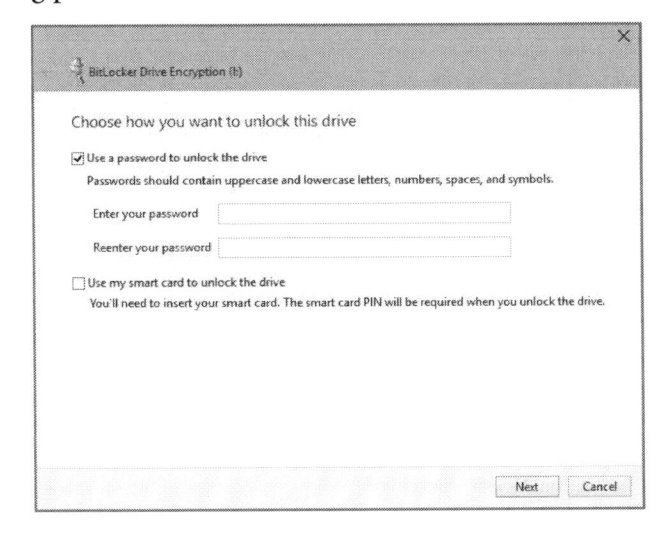

8. Vulnerability: Data Loss

10. Click *Save to a file*. When asked where to save the password file, select your *Documents* folder. If you get an error message, just click the *Yes* button to continue the save process, and then click *Next*.

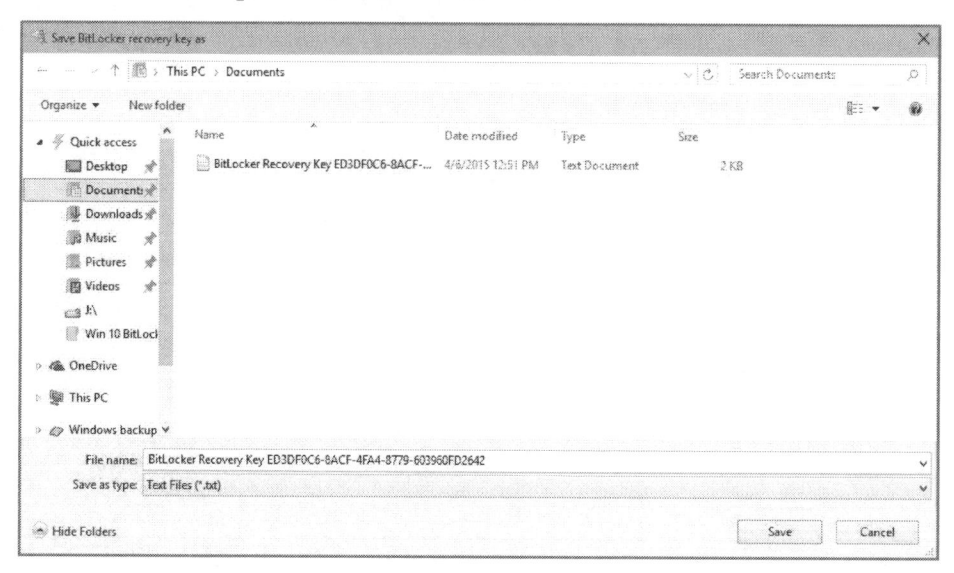

11. When asked how you want to encrypt the hard drive, select *Encrypt entire disk*, and then click *Next*.

We need to configure the encrypted backup hard drive to auto-unlock when you are logged into the PC.

12. Under System and Security, click on BitLocker Drive Encryption.

8. Vulnerability: Data Loss

13. Under the *Removable data drives* section, click the arrow to the right to show info of hard drive. Click the *Unlock drive* option, and then enter password for hard drive.

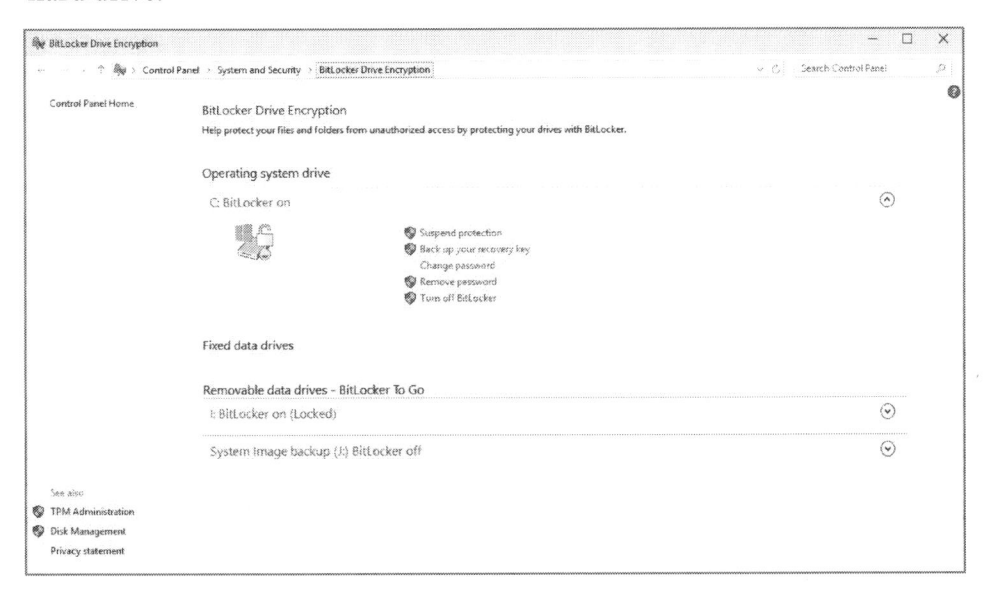

14. More options will appear. Click on *Turn on auto-unlock*. Doing this will set the hard drive to auto-unlock, allowing the windows backup to run on the scheduled time intervals.

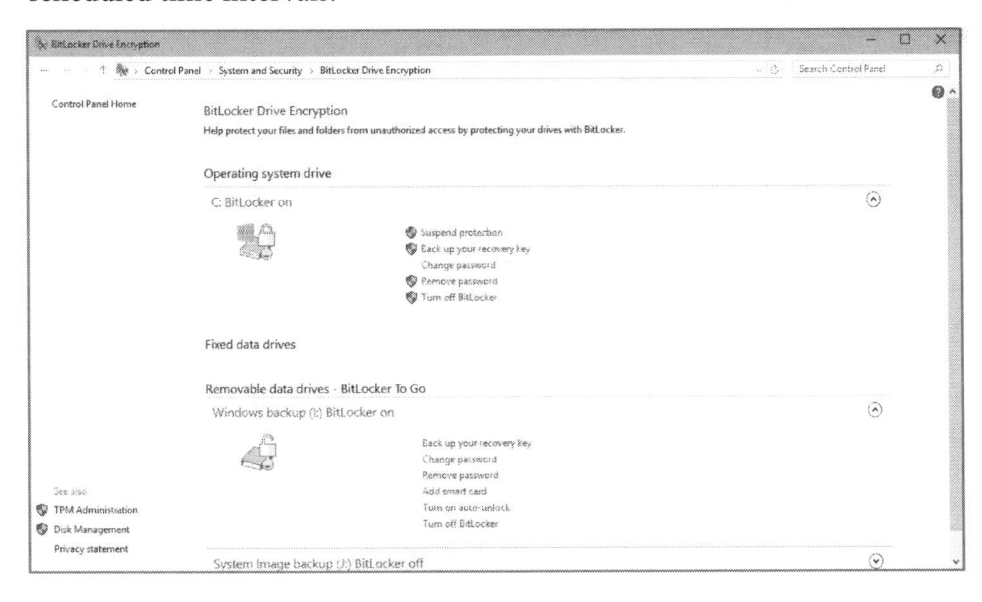

8. Vulnerability: Data Loss

15. The window will now show that you may turn this feature off, indicating it is currently on.

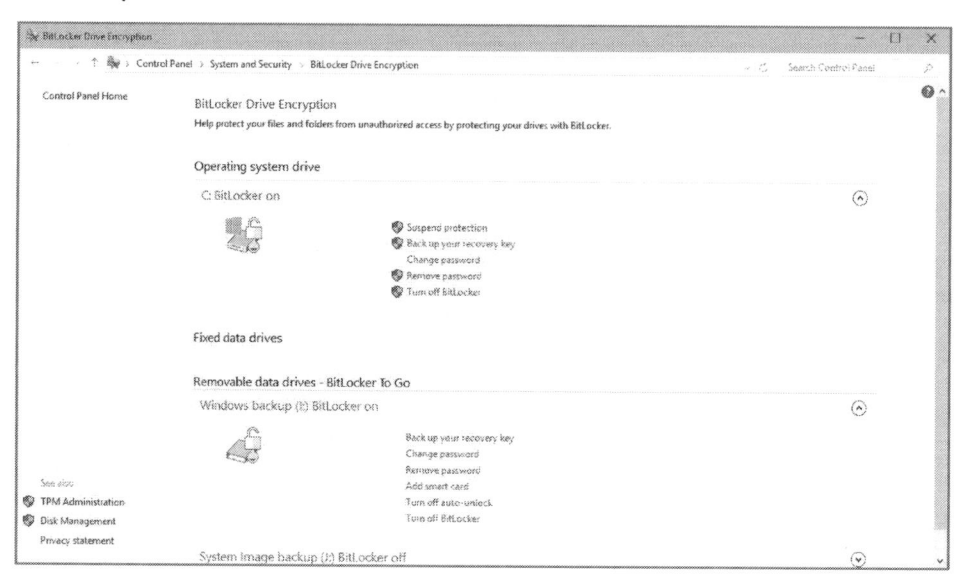

8. Vulnerability: Data Loss

16. By default, it will back up every hour. You can change this interval as well as how old to keep versions. We recommend that you leave *Save copies of files* at *Every hour,* and *Keep saved versions* at *Until space is needed.* You may change these settings by clicking on the *Advanced settings* to the left of the window. When complete, click *Save changes.*

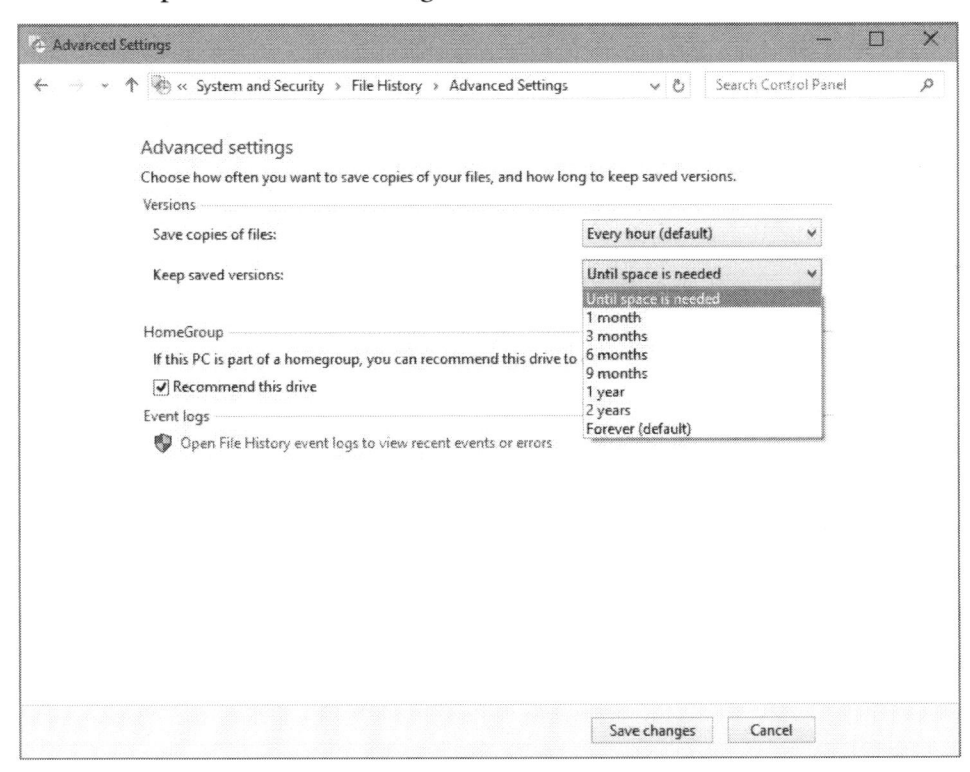

8. Vulnerability: Data Loss

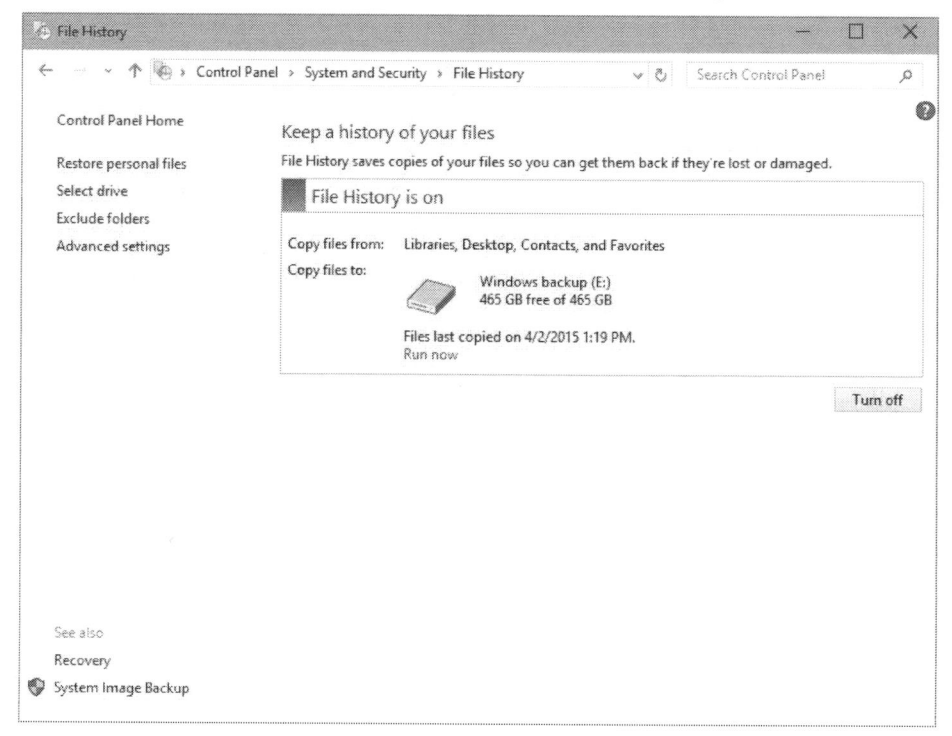

17. The *File History* window returns, confirming your settings.

Backups are now on autopilot. Just make sure that you leave your hard drive connected for the backups to run.

Assignment: Configure System Image Backup

Windows 10 can create a disk image of your system. This is would be used only if you wanted to restore your hard drive to its original state, or to have an image if you wanted to upgrade to a larger or faster hard drive. Because this will be a fairly large backup you will most likely want to use an external hard drive for this system image backup.

In this assignment you will configure the *System Image Backup*.

1. Connect an external hard drive on which the system image will be made.

8. Vulnerability: Data Loss

2. Click on the *Start* menu and type *Control Panel*. Then click on *Control Panel* to open it, click on *System and Security,* and then click on *File History*.

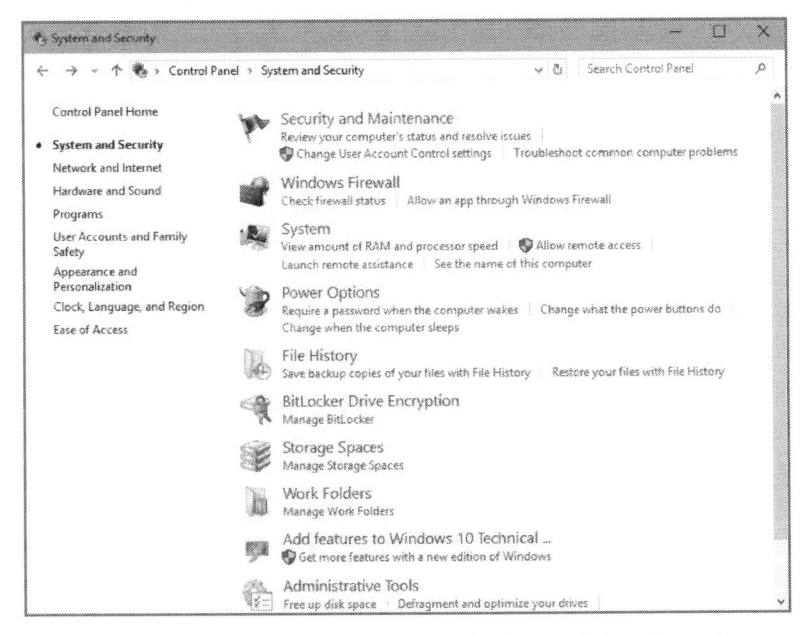

3. Click on *System Image Backup* located in the lower left of window.

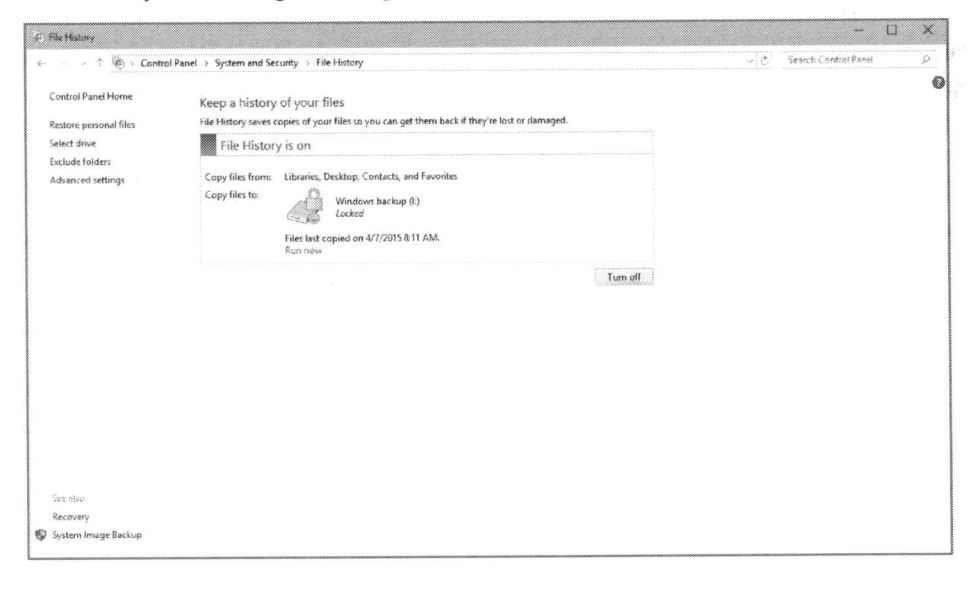

8. Vulnerability: Data Loss

4. A scan for available media will start. Make sure it sees the partition that you want to use for the system image. You can also create an image into CDs or DVDs. Once your media is selected, click *Next*.

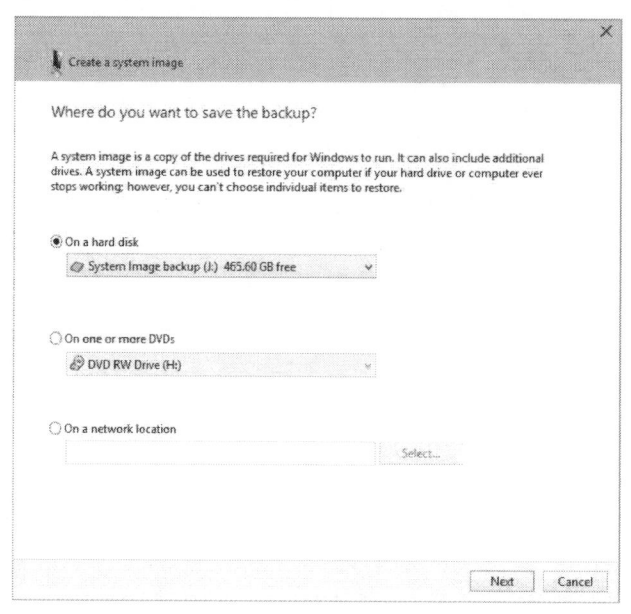

5. In the next window, select what is to be backed up. You may see 1 or more partitions. Make sure that you have the *C* drive selected, with the name *System* included. Once you do, click *Next*.

6. You may get an error message due to the fact that your *C* drive is encrypted. If you do, make sure you read the message and understand what it means, and then click the *OK* button.

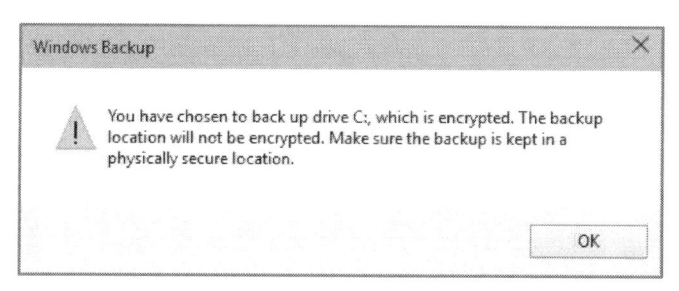

8. Vulnerability: Data Loss

7. The *Confirm your backup settings* window opens. Make sure the *Backup location* is good and the proper drives selected in *The following drives will be backed up*. Then click the *Start backup* button.

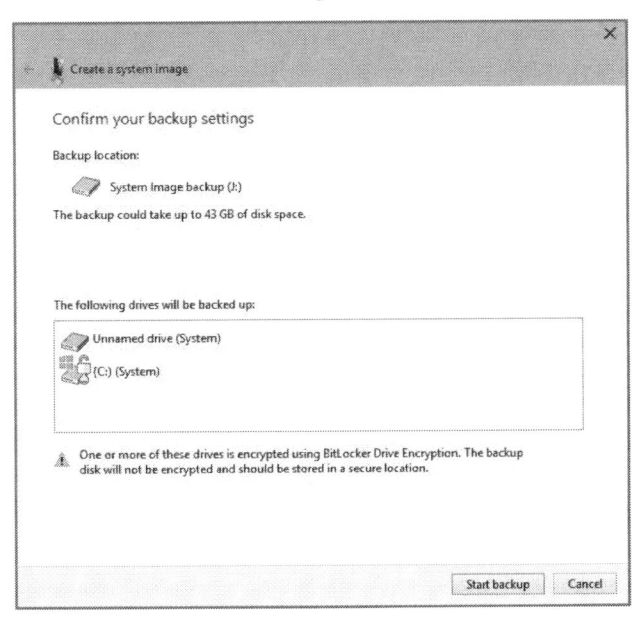

8. The *Windows is saving the backup* window appears, showing the status of the image creation. Let this finish before moving on.

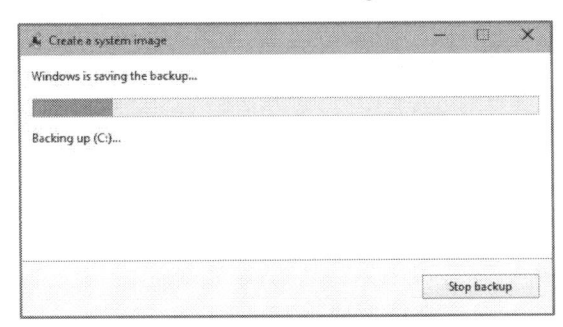

9. When complete, click *Close*.

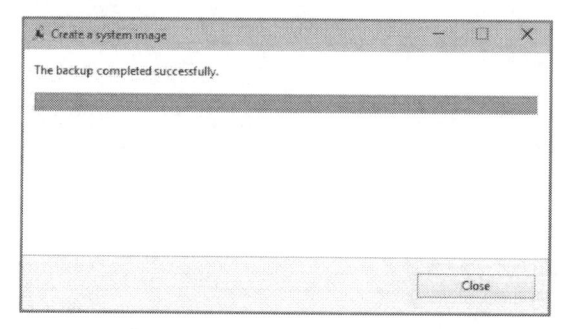

Congratulations. You have successfully created a system image of your hard drive.

Assignment: Integrity Test the Backup

The step missed by almost every user is testing the integrity of the backups. This testing process should be performed every month. Not a bad idea to put it on your calendar for the first workday of the month.

Integrity testing requires that your backup has completed at least one full cycle. If you have just completed the previous exercise, allow 24 hours of uptime before moving on.

To test your backup, you need to make sure your backup has the most current backup.

1. Select the *Start* menu > type *Control Panel* > click on it to open. Click on *System and Security* > *File History* and verify that your back up has a current date stamp.

2. Delete a test file, and then let backup run again.

3. The on the left side of window, click on *Restore personal files*. A window with a date stamp appears. At the bottom of the window click on the left arrow to the date and time you want to restore from.

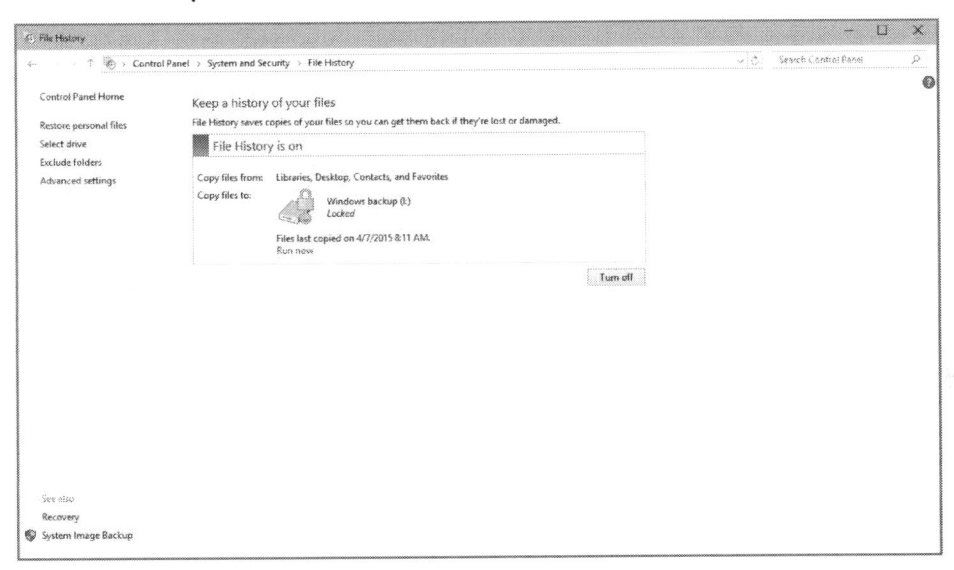

4. Open the *location* where the deleted file once was.

    - NOTE: in this exercise, we deleted some files from the Desktop, so that is where we are navigating.

8. Vulnerability: Data Loss

5. Double click the location to open it.

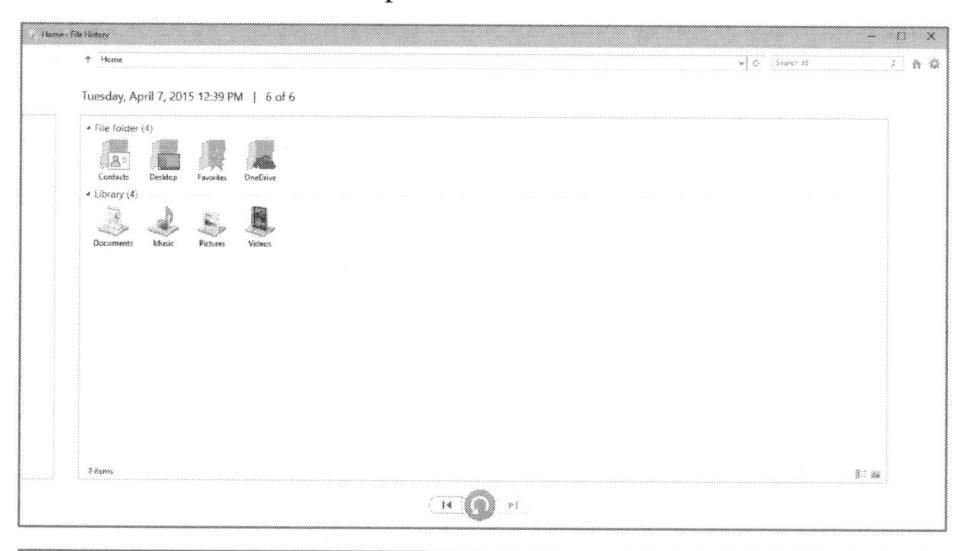

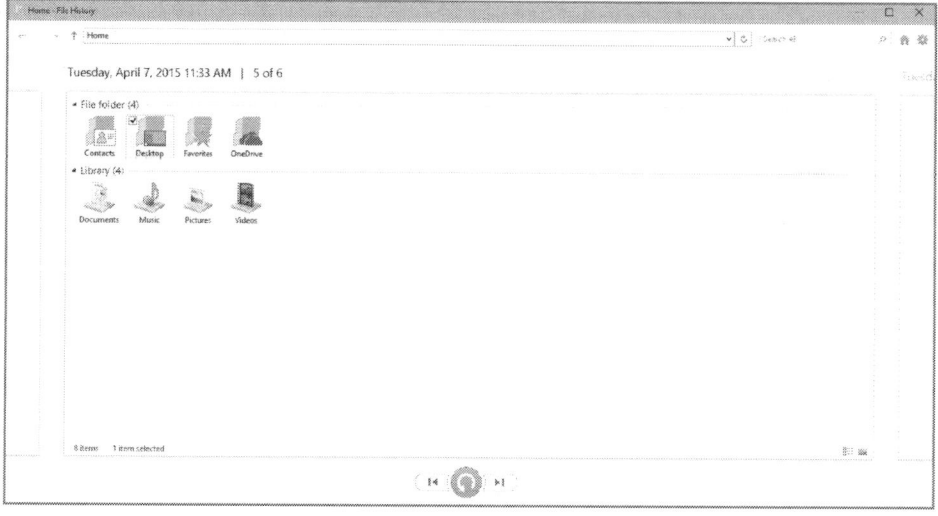

8. Vulnerability: Data Loss

6. Click the file(s) to be restored, and then click the *Green arrow* to restore the file(s) to its (their) original location.

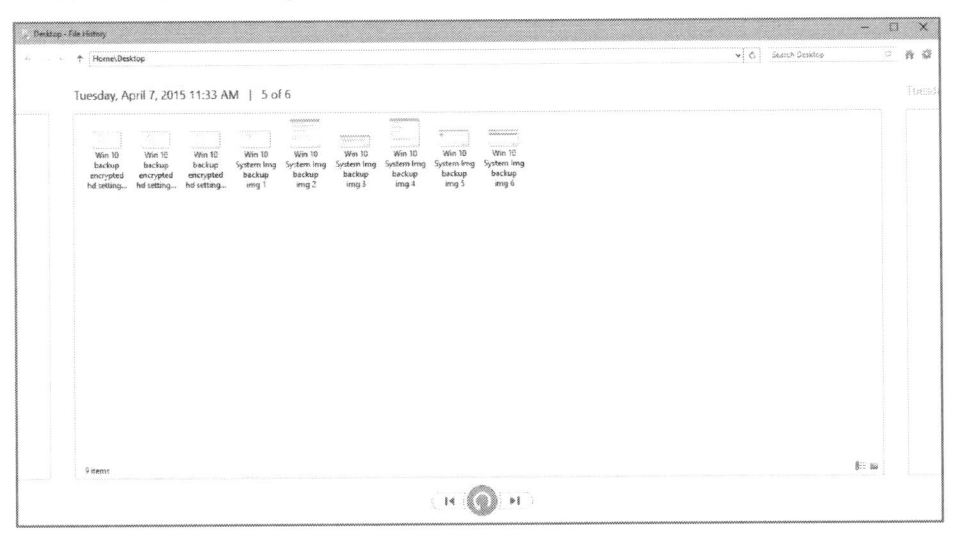

7. A new window opens, showing the restored file(s).

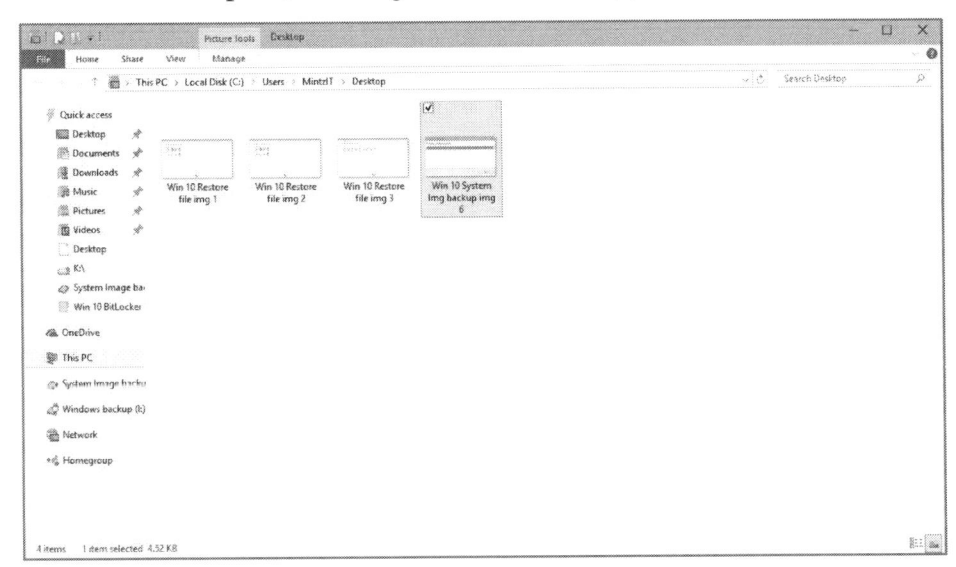

You have tested the integrity your *Windows Backup and Restore*. You can close the *Restore window*.

8. Vulnerability: Data Loss

Review Questions

1. Best Practices call for at least _____ backups.
2. The benefits of an on-site backup are _____.
3. The benefit of an off-site backup is _____.
4. Advantages of using Windows Backup for your backup include _____.
5. The advantage of using Parted Magic for your backup is _____.
6. The major advantage of using an Internet-based backup is _____.

9. Vulnerability: Recovery Drive

I have six locks on my door all in a row. When I go out, I lock every other one. I figure no matter how long somebody stands there picking the locks, they are always locking three.

–Elayne Boosler, American Comic

9. Vulnerability: Recovery Drive

Recovery Drive

If you are unable to boot into your Windows machine due to a virus, bad boot record or even just an overzealous nephew, a recovery drive can help. When we create a recovery drive it allows you to repair your operating system from an external drive (usually a flash drive) or if necessary re-install the entire OS. This is invaluable if you are stuck with a computer that is unable to boot or otherwise unworkable.

Assignment: Create a Recovery Drive

In this assignment, we will create a recovery drive on a blank USB flash drive.

1. Attach a blank USB flash drive to your computer. This will be used to store the recovery drive.
2. If a Create a recovery drive window opens, skip to step 3. If a Create a recovery drive windows does not appear, in the Search the Web and Windows field, enter Recovery, and then hit Enter. This will open the Recovery Control Panel.

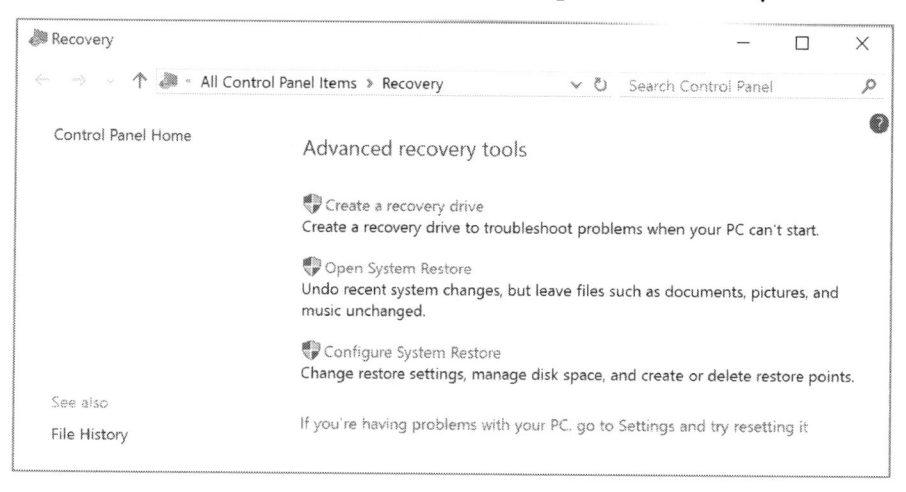

9. Vulnerability: Recovery Drive

6. Click *Create a recovery drive*.

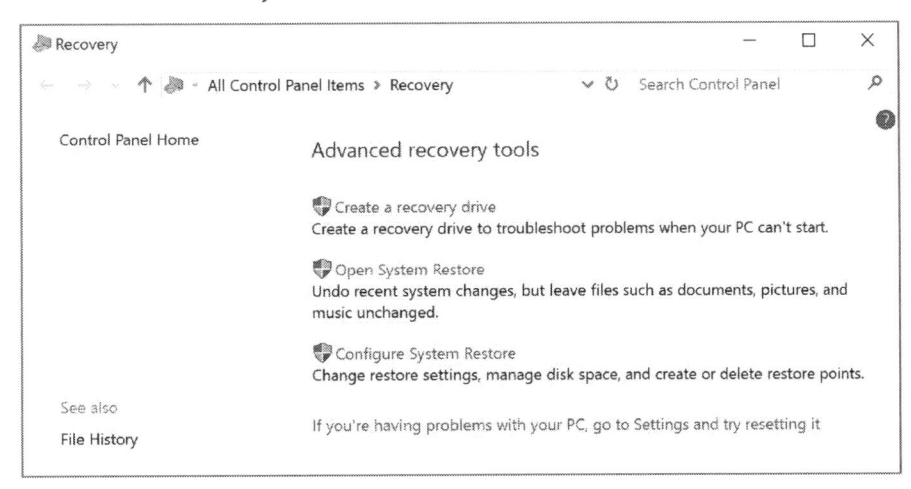

7. At the *Create a recovery drive* window, enable the *Copy the recovery partition from the PC to the recovery drive*, and then click *Next*.

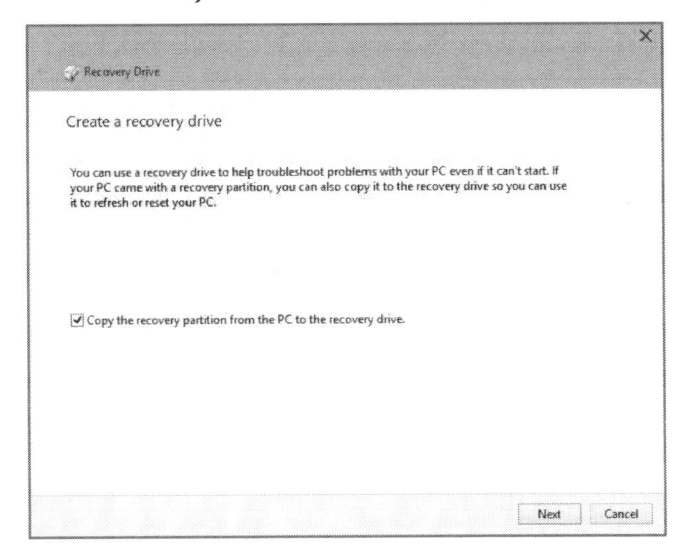

9. Vulnerability: Recovery Drive

8. In the *Select the USB flash drive* window, select the flash drive you attached for this exercise, and then click *Next*.

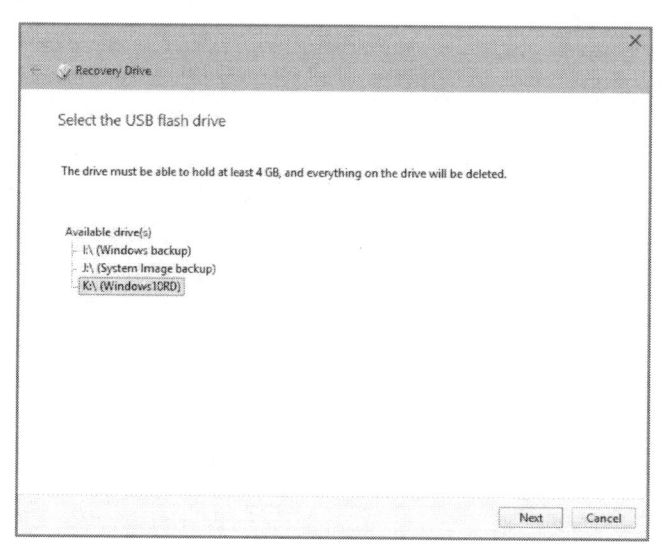

9. At the prompt asking *are you sure you want to do this*, click the *Create* button.

10. A window will announce *The recovery drive is ready*. Click *Finish* to complete the recovery drive creation.

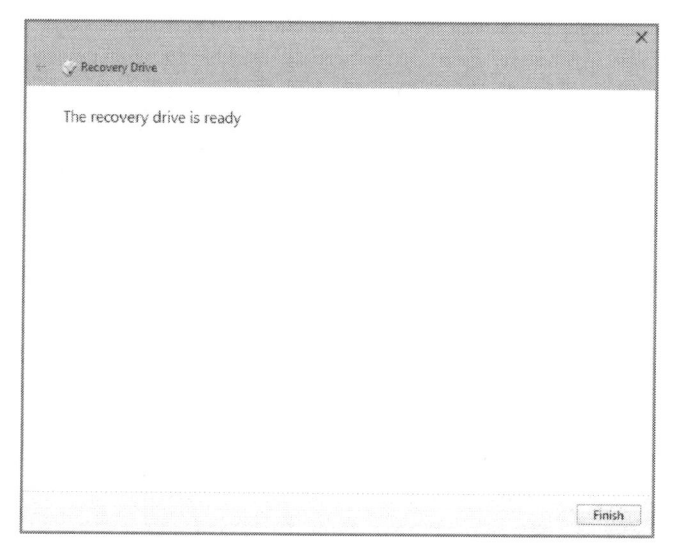

9. Vulnerability: Recovery Drive

We are done yet. It's vital to test the Recovery USB flash drive and the System Restore Image.

Assignment: Test the Recovery Drive

It is essential to make sure that the recovery drive just created is working. This will require booting into your BIOS settings in order to set the USB flash drive as the primary boot device. The keyboard shortcuts used may vary a bit depending on your hardware manufacturer as well.

1. Make sure the USB flash drive with the System Restore Image is inserted.
2. Turn on the computer while holding the F2 key (This is for Dell, it may vary for your manufacturer settings).
3. The BIOS screen will appear. You can only use your keyboard on this screen, no mouse control. Press the right arrow until you get to the startup options.

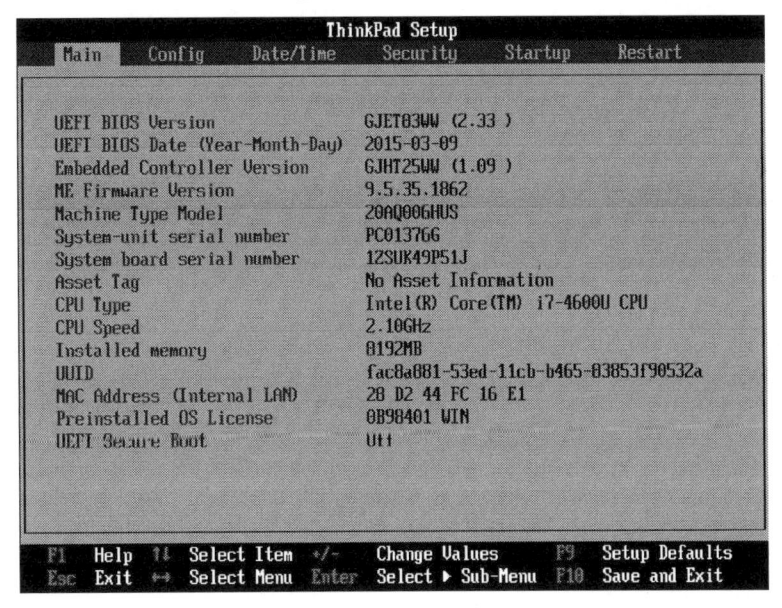

9. Vulnerability: Recovery Drive

4. Once you're under startup, select *Boot*.

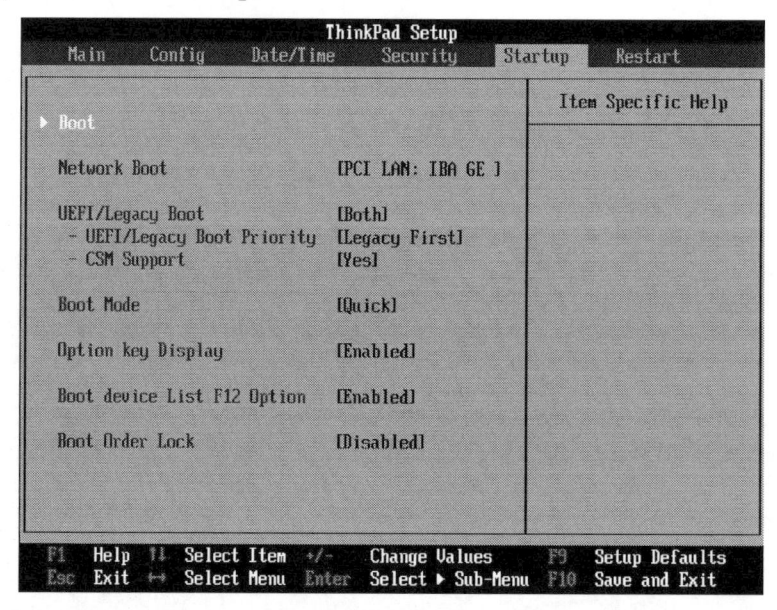

```
                         ThinkPad Setup
     Main    Config    Date/Time    Security   Startup    Restart

                                                   Item Specific Help
     ▶ Boot

       Network Boot              [PCI LAN: IBA GE ]

       UEFI/Legacy Boot          [Both]
        - UEFI/Legacy Boot Priority  [Legacy First]
        - CSM Support             [Yes]

       Boot Mode                 [Quick]

       Option key Display        [Enabled]

       Boot device List F12 Option  [Enabled]

       Boot Order Lock           [Disabled]


     F1  Help    ↑↓  Select Item   +/-    Change Values    F9   Setup Defaults
     Esc Exit    ↔   Select Menu   Enter  Select ▶ Sub-Menu F10  Save and Exit
```

5. Select the USB device you would like to boot from and send it all the way to the top of the boot order. If you do not have a boot priority in your BIOS we will instead use the manufacturer's boot menu.

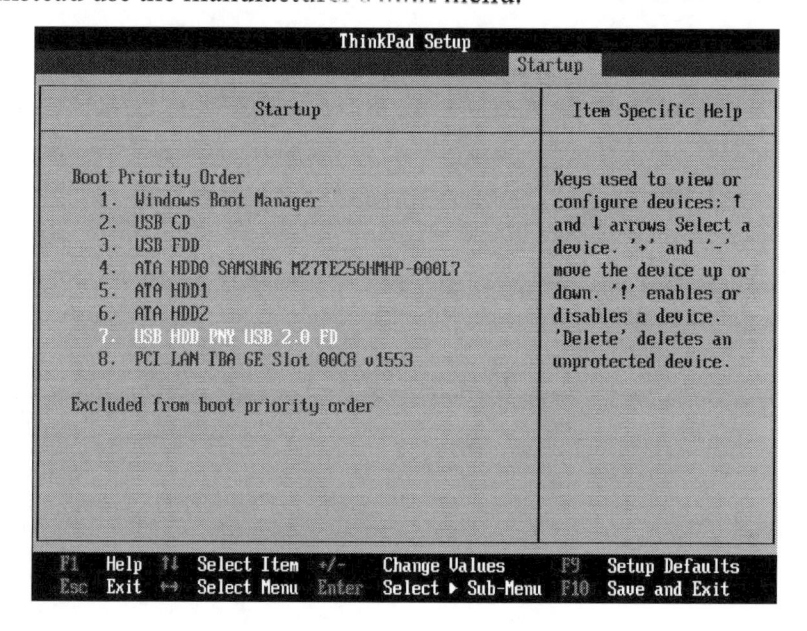

```
                         ThinkPad Setup
                                              Startup

                     Startup                        Item Specific Help

       Boot Priority Order                          Keys used to view or
         1. Windows Boot Manager                    configure devices: ↑
         2. USB CD                                  and ↓ arrows Select a
         3. USB FDD                                 device. '+' and '-'
         4. ATA HDD0 SAMSUNG MZ7TE256HMHP-000L7     move the device up or
         5. ATA HDD1                                down. '!' enables or
         6. ATA HDD2                                disables a device.
         7. USB HDD PNY USB 2.0 FD                  'Delete' deletes an
         8. PCI LAN IBA GE Slot 00C8 v1553          unprotected device.

       Excluded from boot priority order




     F1  Help    ↑↓  Select Item   +/-    Change Values    F9   Setup Defaults
     Esc Exit    ↔   Select Menu   Enter  Select ▶ Sub-Menu F10  Save and Exit
```

9. Vulnerability: Recovery Drive

6. Scroll to Restart and select *Exit Saving Changes*.

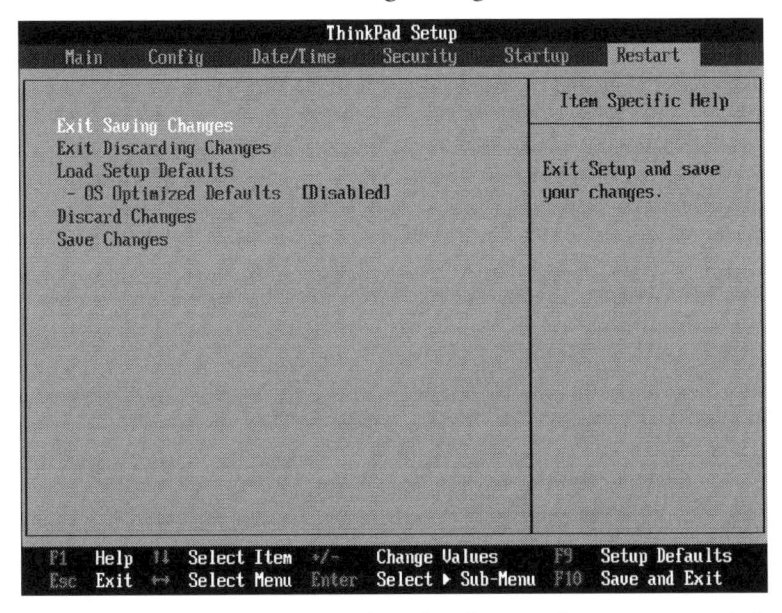

7. If you changed your boot priority already, skip to the next step. Otherwise, while the machine restarts press your boot options key (F12 for this computer). Select the USB device and press Enter.

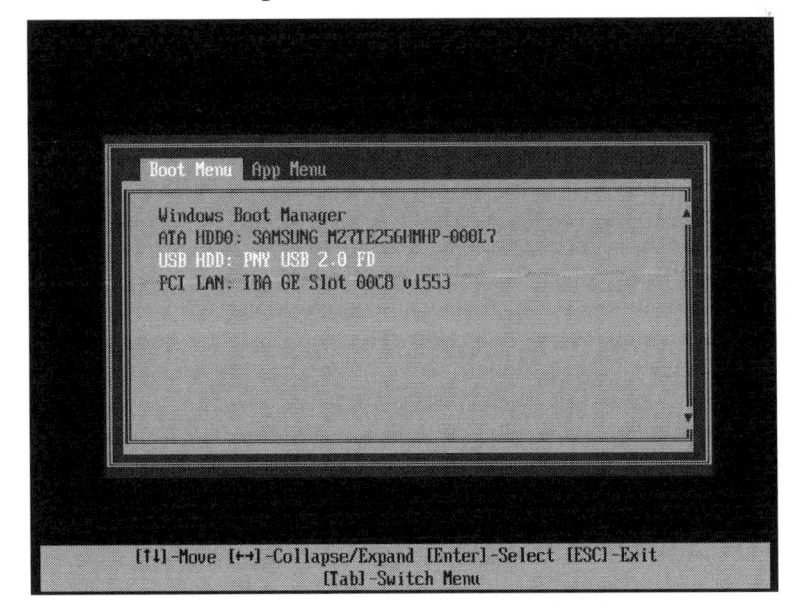

9. Vulnerability: Recovery Drive

8. When booted into your recovery drive it will ask you to select a keyboard layout. Use your arrow keys to scroll to *US* and hit *Enter*.

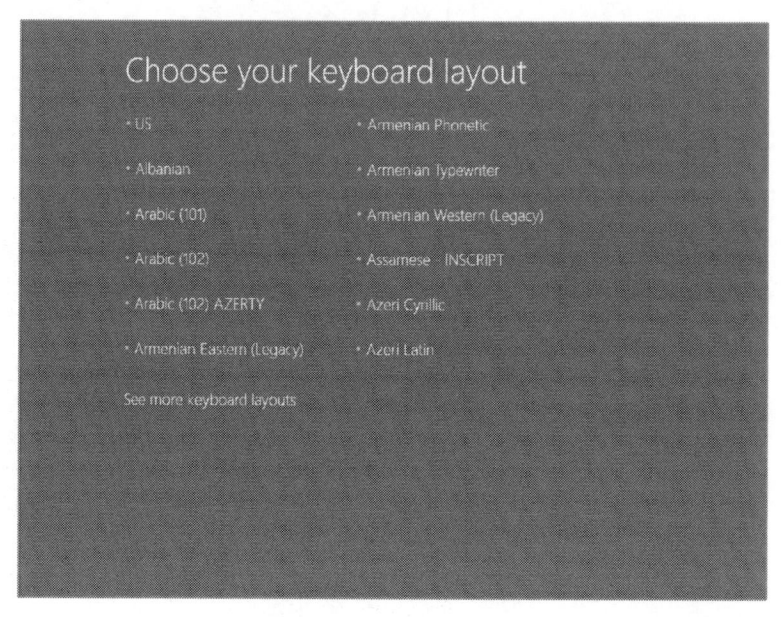

9. A menu appears with options to *Troubleshoot* or *Turn off your PC*. If you would like to troubleshoot, arrow key down to select *Troubleshoot*.

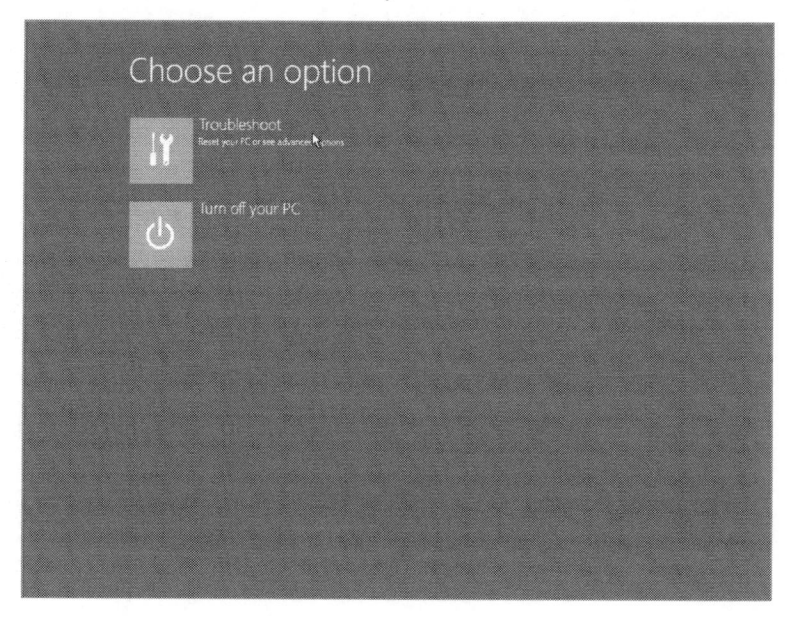

-208-

9. Vulnerability: Recovery Drive

10. From the troubleshoot menu you can reinstall Windows 10 or configure advanced options. Click on *Advanced Options.*

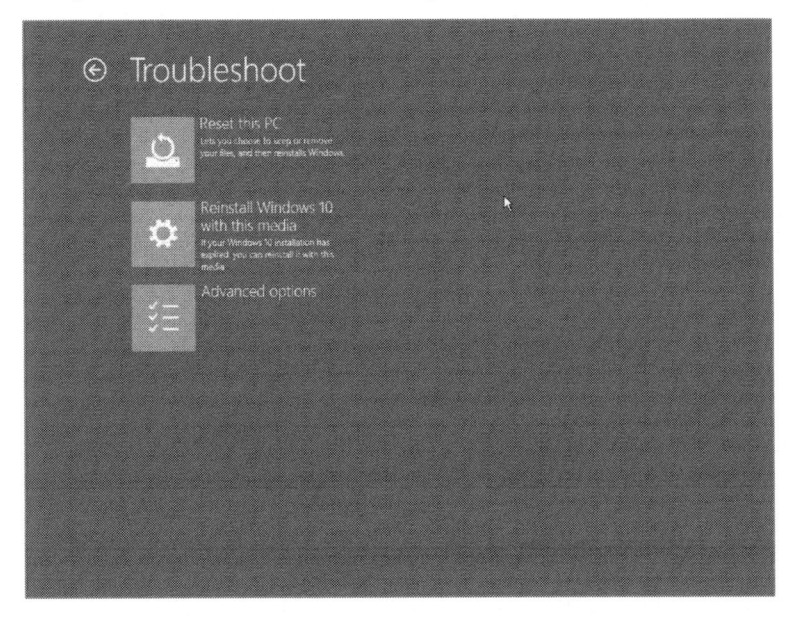

9. Vulnerability: Recovery Drive

11. *Advanced options* is where you can configure the repair of your operating system. You can restore Windows using a system restore, an image or just do a startup repair. Press the left arrow twice and *Turn off your PC*.

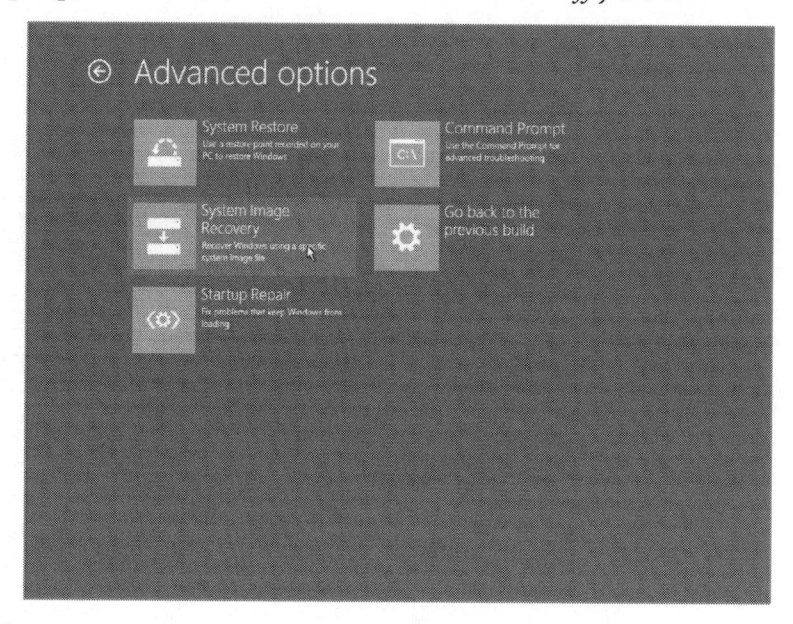

Congratulations. You have setup a recovery drive for your Windows 10 computer. You are now vastly more secure against operating system and software failures.

Review Questions

1. When would you use a Recovery Drive?
2. A Recovery Drive should be created on your boot drive. (True or False)
3. Where do you go to create a Recovery Drive?

10. Vulnerability: Lost or Stolen Device

It takes considerable knowledge just to realize the extent of your own ignorance.
–Thomas Sowell, American economist, social theorist, philosopher, and author

Find My PC

Millions of computers are stolen each year. If you have followed the steps above to enable *BitLocker* with strong passwords, as well as a BIOS password, nobody is going to break into your data.

But it would be nice to be able to get your computer back.

How are you to locate your stolen computer? One option is with is with *LoJack* at *http://lojack.absolute.com/en*. LoJack software comes with a yearly subscription and will locate your PC using GPS, Wi-Fi or IP geolocation. LoJack also works directly with law enforcement to recover your laptop once a police report for the theft has been filed via Phone or through the LoJack website.

Additionally, once LoJack is installed, you will be able to lock the laptop remotely, and erase either individual folders, or the entire system.

Since LoJack resides in a laptop's UEFI firmware, nothing a thief does will defeat it, short of replacing the system board–essentially the cost of the laptop itself.

Assignment: Activate and Configure LoJack

In this assignment we will download, install, and configure LoJack. Assuming that you have purchased a subscription from the LoJack website *http://lojack.absolute.com/en* and have downloaded the setup file, the LoJack installation is straightforward.

1. Open a browser and visit *http://lojack.absolute.com/en*.
2. Follow the on-screen instructions to download LoJack.

10. Vulnerability: Lost or Stolen Device

3. Double click the LoJack installer to launch the setup wizard. Click the *Next* button.

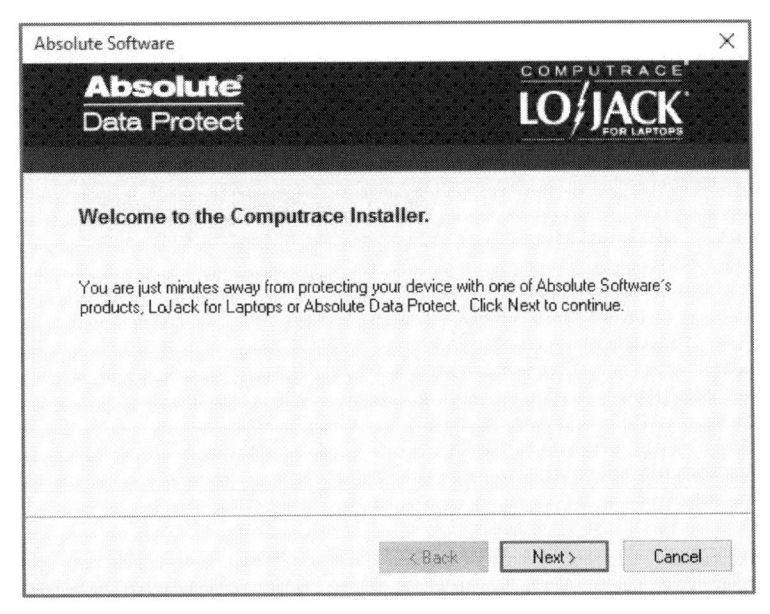

4. LoJack confirms an active Internet connection back to their servers and then proceeds with the installation.

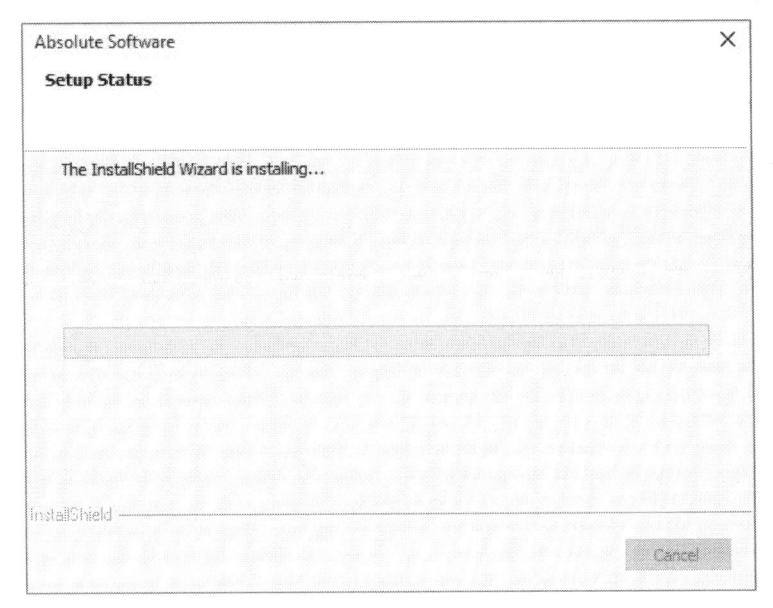

10. Vulnerability: Lost or Stolen Device

5. Click the checkbox after reading the EULA, and click *Continue*.

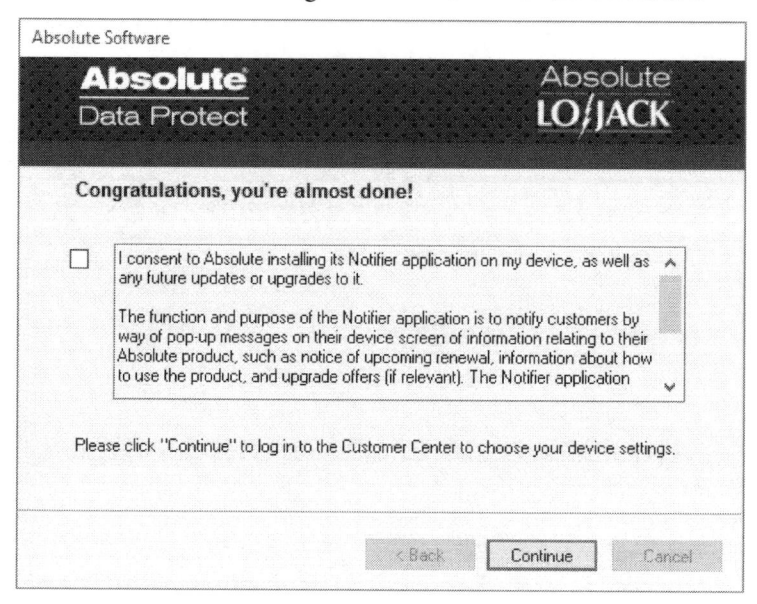

6. The installation wizard will quit, and a LoJack taskbar icon is created with a banner notification confirming that the device is protected.

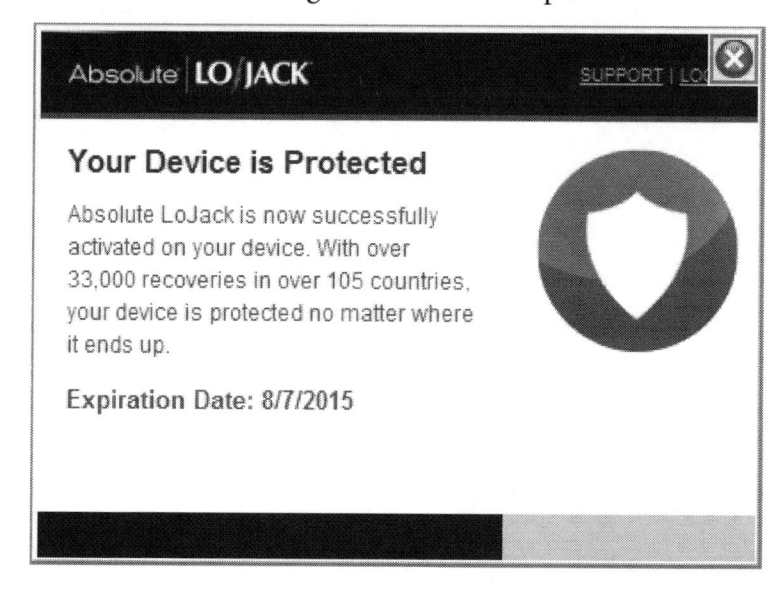

10. Vulnerability: Lost or Stolen Device

7. Logging into the LoJack website will reveal the location of your device on map, along with the status of your subscription at the top of the page.

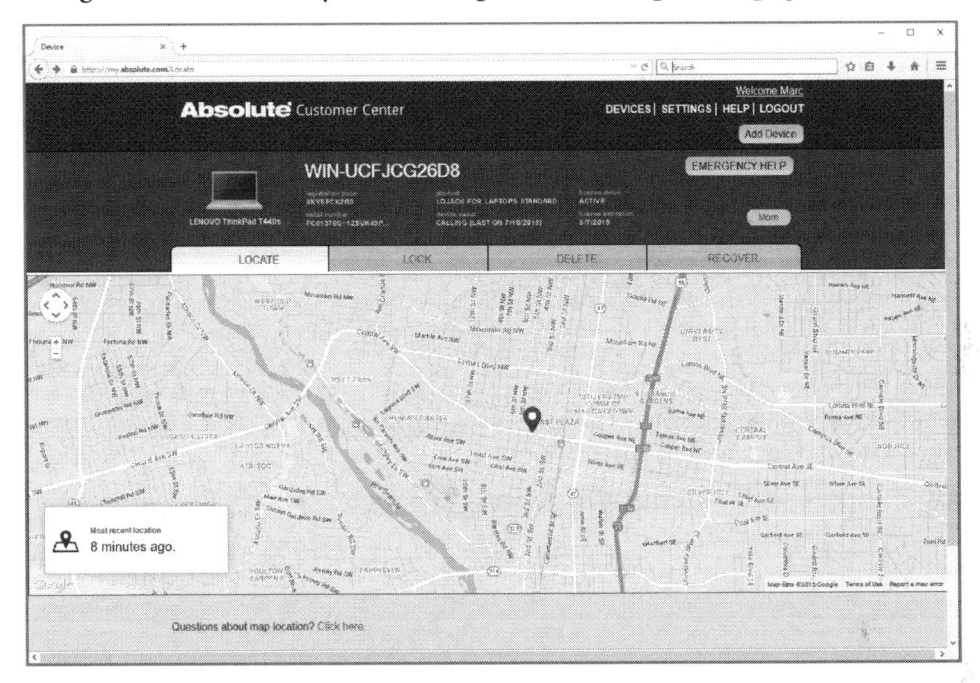

10. Vulnerability: Lost or Stolen Device

8. Clicking the *Lock* tab above the map displays a page that will allow you to Lock the laptop remotely, as well as display a message on the screen for the lawless new owner to see.

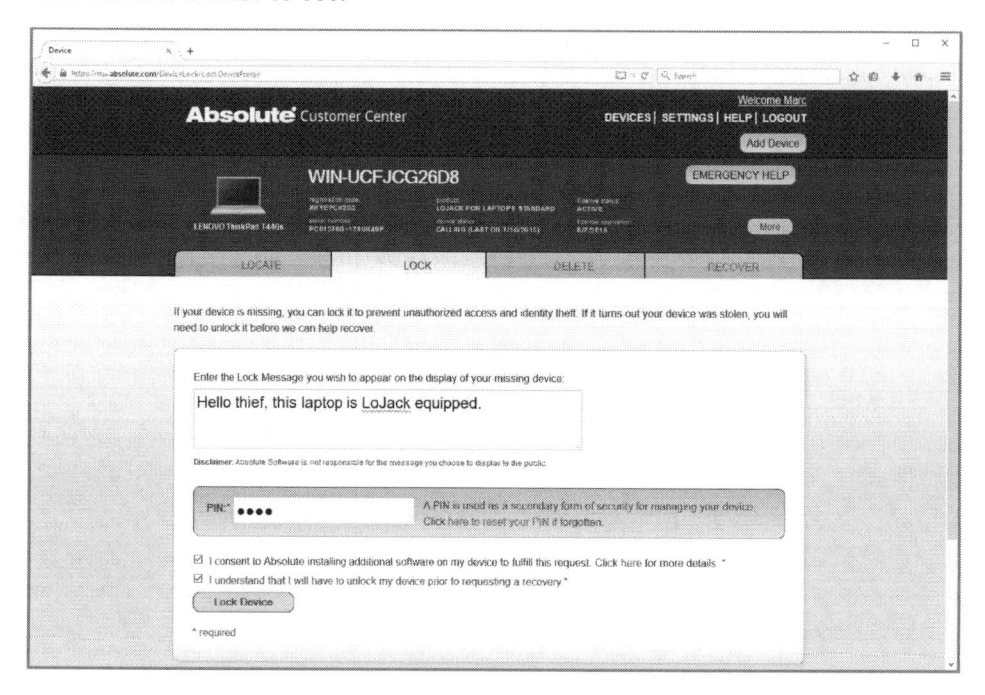

10. Vulnerability: Lost or Stolen Device

9. Clicking the *Lock* tab above the map displays a page that will allow you to Lock the laptop remotely, as well as display a message on the screen for the thief (or good Samaritan) to see.

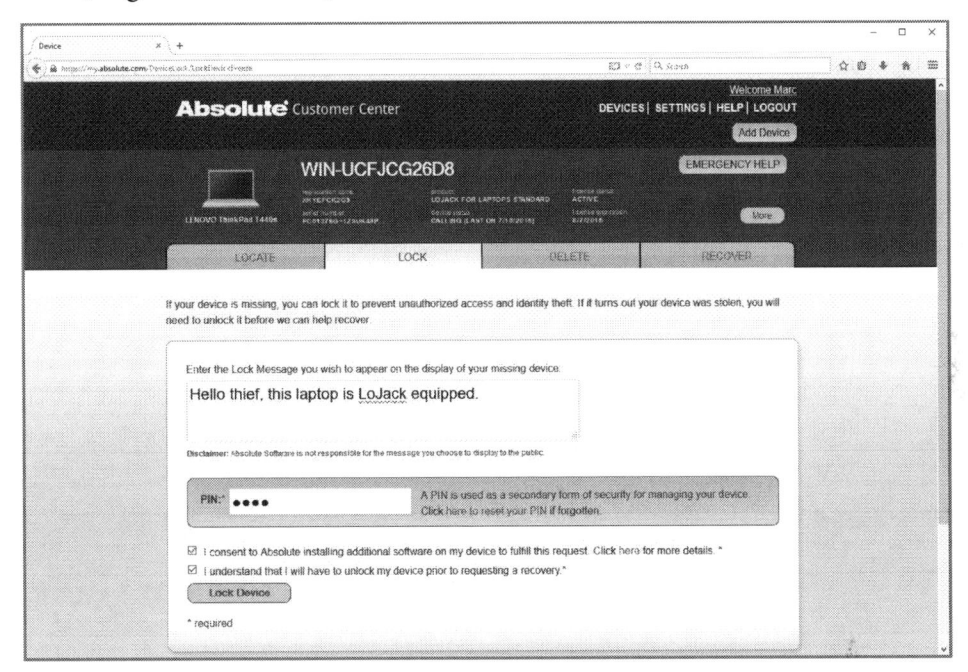

10. Vulnerability: Lost or Stolen Device

10. Clicking the *Delete* tab reveals one of the more interesting features of LoJack; the ability to remotely erase the entire hard drive, or just certain types of files or locations.

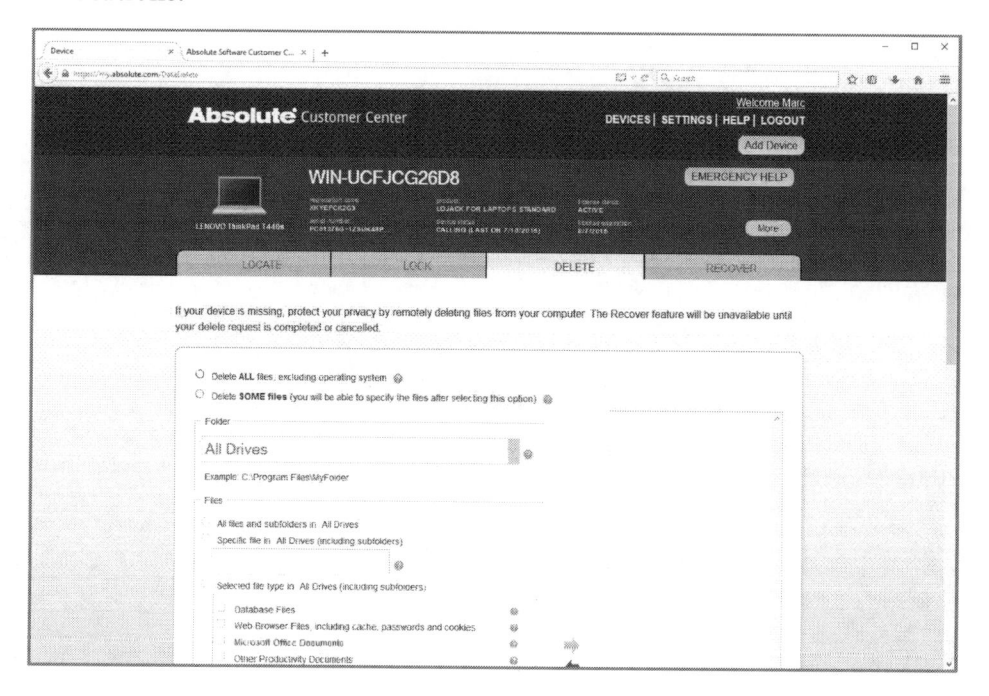

10. Vulnerability: Lost or Stolen Device

11. Clicking on the last tab, *Recover*, provides a web form to input the police report details for your theft. LoJack will then work directly with law enforcement if necessary to recover your stolen device.

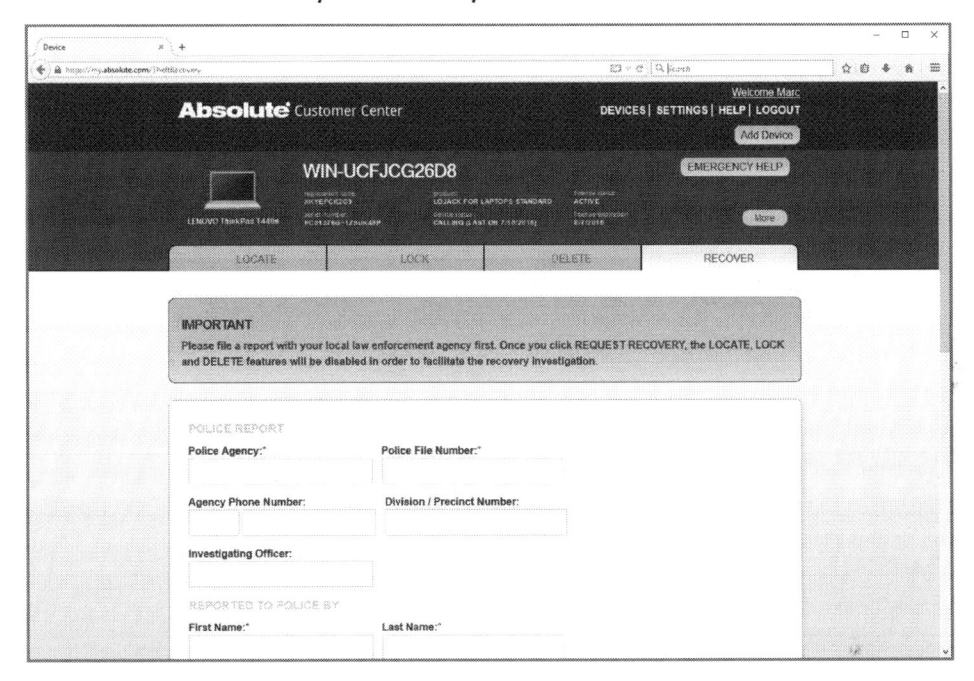

Prey

Another Laptop recovery option is *Prey*. Prey offers a free version, which has most of the features of their paid version. Although they have a subscription version, the free version will do all that you need.

With Prey you install an agent on your computer, tablet or phone, which silently waits for a remote signal to wake up and work its magic. This signal is sent from their hosted web service whenever you wish to gather information or trigger an action, like locking down the device. That's pretty much it. Let's go ahead and install and configure Prey.

Note: Unlike LoJack, Prey requires that a guest account be enabled to fully take advantage of its recovery features. Therefore, it is not recommended that Prey be used in conjunction with BitLocker, since using a guest account with BitLocker weakens its security.

Assignment: Activate and Configure Prey

1. Open a web browser and go to Prey's website to download their software: *https://preyproject.com/download*
2. Under the section *Prey 1.3.9 for Windows,* make sure you select the correct version of your OS.
    - NOTE: Since this is for Windows 10, select the *64-bit version.*
3. Let the file download.
4. Click *Save* to save the download.
5. Locate installer file *prey-windows-1.3.9-x64.exe* and open the installer.
6. Allow the installer to run by clicking the *Yes* button to continue.

10. Vulnerability: Lost or Stolen Device

The Prey installer wizard will open. Let's go through the process of installing Prey:

7. Click the *Next* button to start.

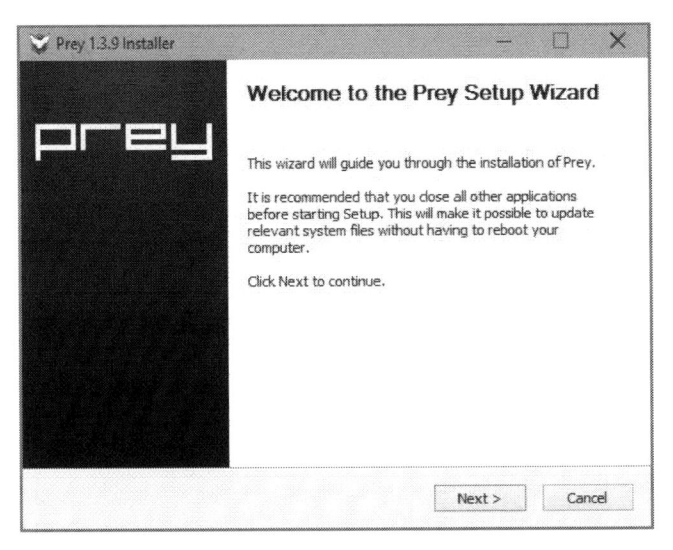

8. Click *I Agree* to continue.

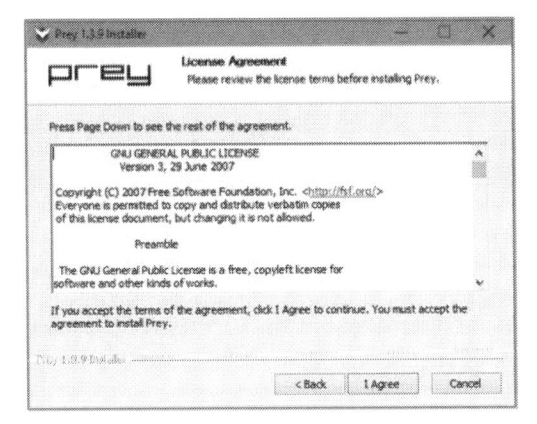

10. Vulnerability: Lost or Stolen Device

9. Click *Install* to continue.

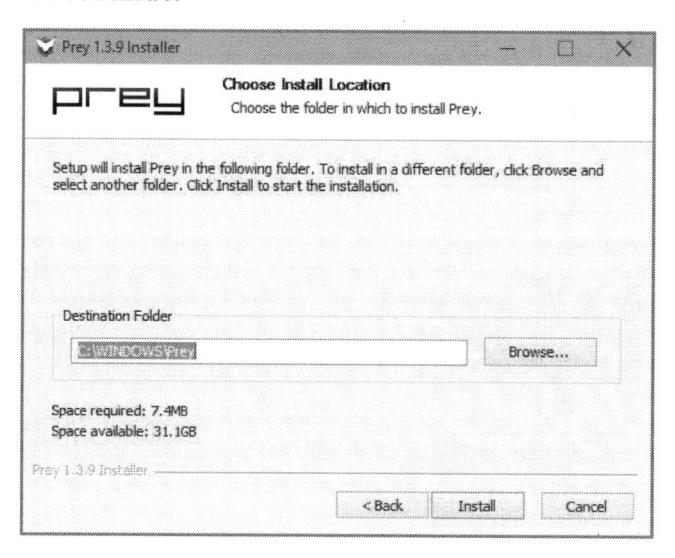

10. Vulnerability: Lost or Stolen Device

10. You may get an error message about software requiring *.Net Framework*. Click the *Yes* button to install software. Another window pop up. Click the *Download and install this feature* to install software.

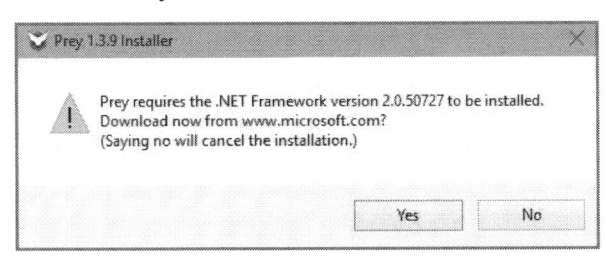

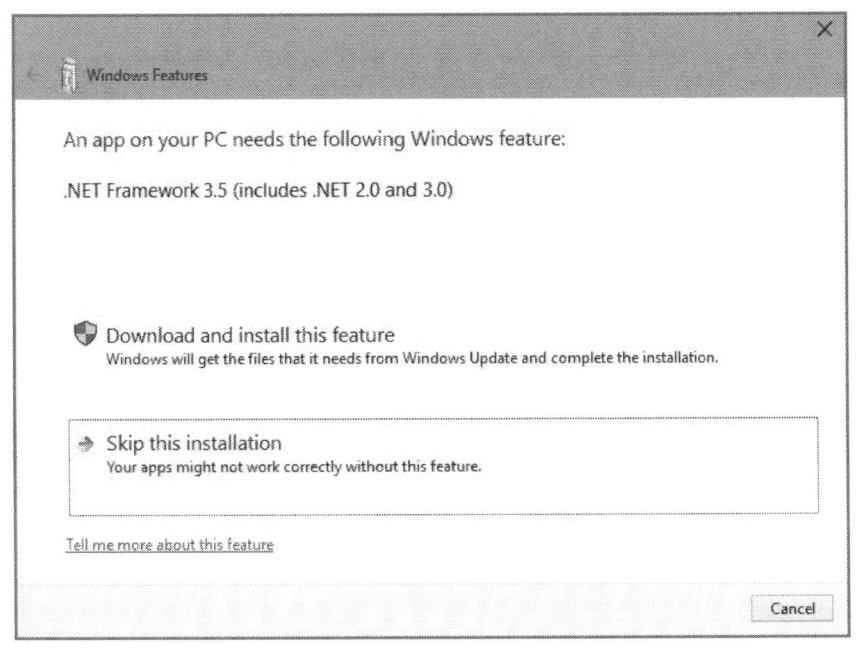

10. Vulnerability: Lost or Stolen Device

11. Software install should now be completed. Click *Close* to finish the install.

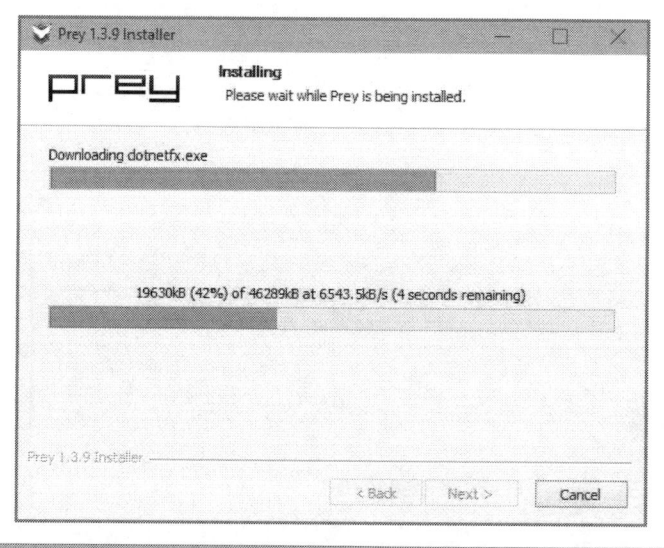

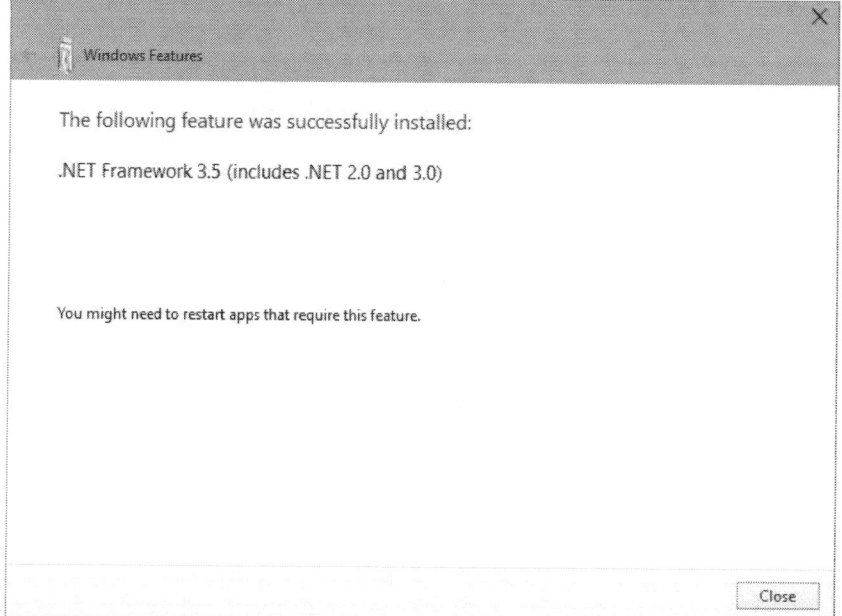

12. Click *Finished,* and then the setup process for the software will continue.

10. Vulnerability: Lost or Stolen Device

13. Click *OK* to continue.

14. If this is the first time using Prey, select *New user,* and then click *Next*. Once you create a user on Prey's website, you can select *Existing user* to add devices under your existing account.

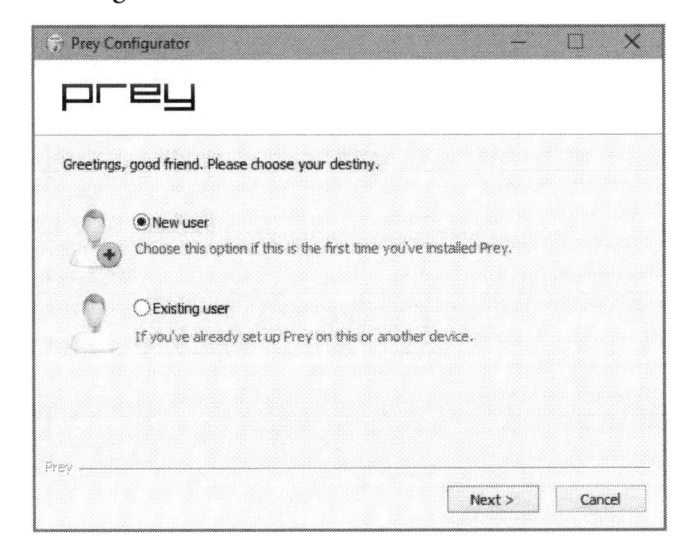

10. Vulnerability: Lost or Stolen Device

15. Enter your account information, and then click *Sign Up*.

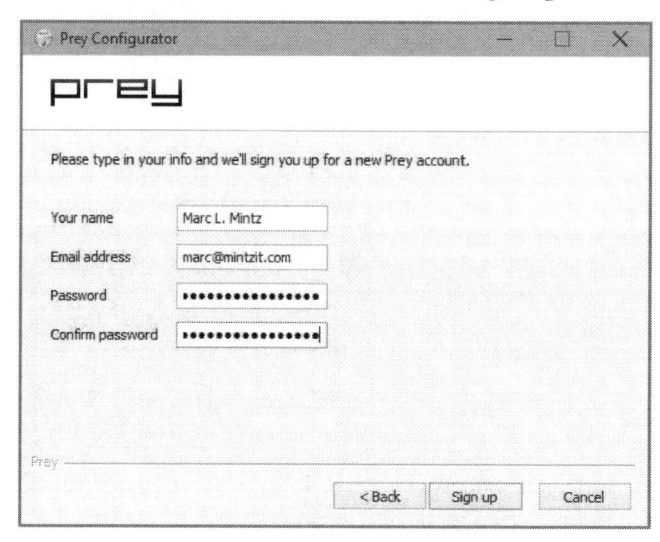

16. A confirmation window opens stating the computer is now protected. Click *OK* to continue.

17. To verify the account, open a web browser and log into your account.

10. Vulnerability: Lost or Stolen Device

18. Go to the Prey login page *https://panel.preyproject.com/login*, and then enter your account information.

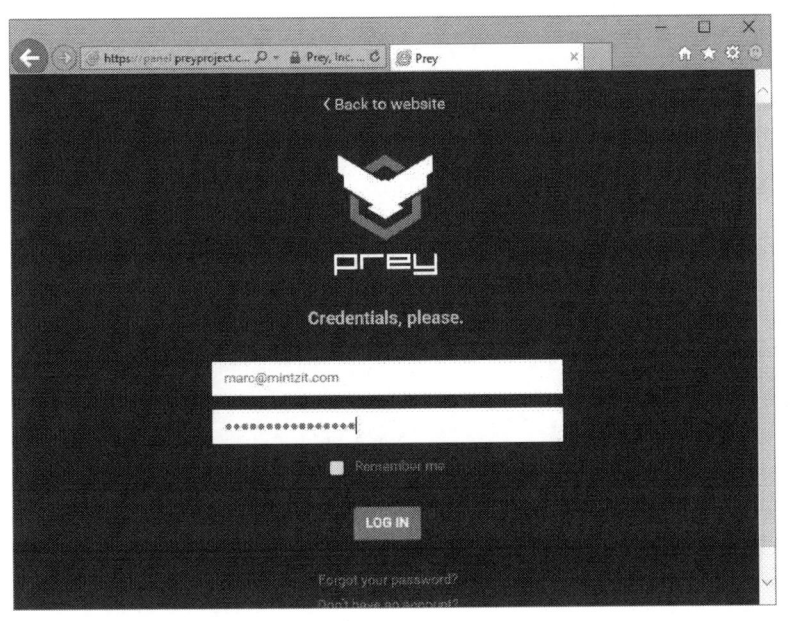

10. Vulnerability: Lost or Stolen Device

19. A *Tour* window will open. You may want to take it to quickly get familiar with the website. For now, we will continue with the verification of our install and configuration.

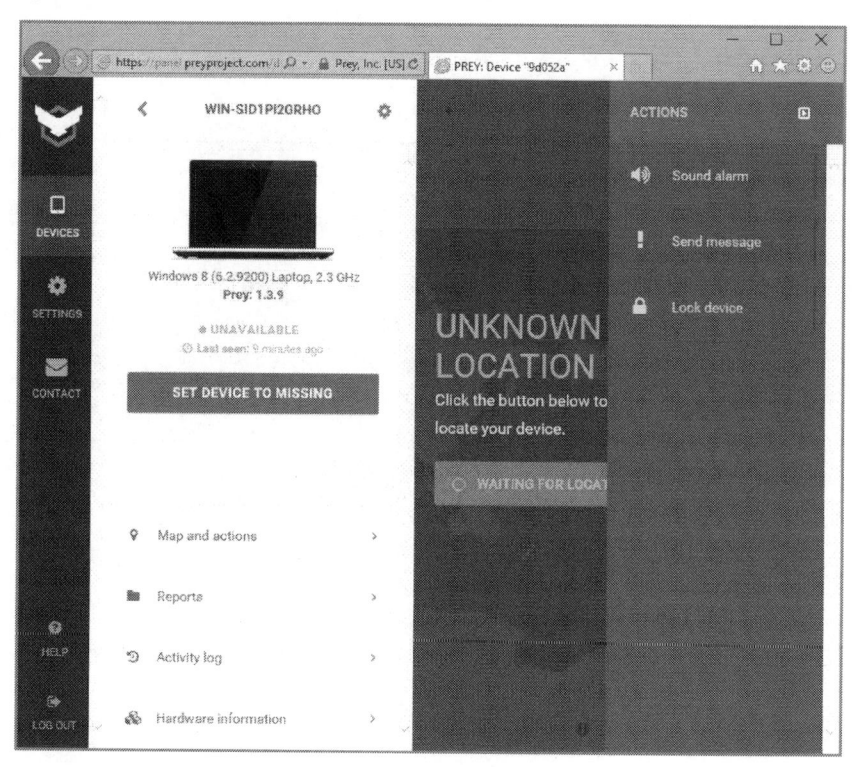

20. You should see your PC listed to the left. Click on it to start a search for the device. Once found, it will show your location.

-230-

Review Questions

1. LoJack can locate a PC using _____
2. Where is LoJack located on a PC?
3. Prey requires the guest account be enabled. (True or False)
4. What is the URL for Prey?
5. To use LoJack, a supported UEFI and a subscription are both needed for the service. (True or False)
6. Since LoJack is resident in the UEFI, it can remain on the device even if Windows has been erased, or the hard drive replaced. (True or False)
7. LoJack's primary purpose is theft deterrence. (True or False)
8. What feature does Prey rely on to allow for a stolen computer to be used and tracked by its owner?
9. Prey works in conjunction with full disk encryption software. (True or False)

11. Vulnerability: When It Is Time To Say Goodbye

Don't cry because it's over. Smile because it happened.

–Dr. Seuss

11. Vulnerability: When It Is Time To Say Goodbye

Preparing a Computer for Sale or Disposal

The time comes when all good things must end. This is just as true for your beloved PC. But, your PC holds all of your documents, passwords, pictures, web browsing history, etc. Not the items you would like someone else to see. Even if you are tossing your damaged computer into the trash, there is the very real probability that someone will find it, remove the drive, and harvest all your data.

So before selling, giving away, or trashing your PC, all data on the drive must be made inaccessible. There are two options:

- Securely erase the drive
- Physically destroy the drive

If you have to comply with DoD, DoE, NSA, or other top security regulations, you may have to physically destroy the drive. For the rest of us, we have a built-in application to securely erase a drive.

Primer: Solid State Drives vs. Rotating Magnetic Drives

Most desktops and older laptops will be equipped with the traditional rotating magnetic hard drives. These drives have spinning magnetic platters that store data in a way that both the hard drive's controller and operating system can understand. When it comes to securely erasing a standard magnetic drive, all the individual magnetic regions are written with random sequences of ones and zeros, effectively removing any "memory" they may have had prior to the procedure.

Solid State Drives (SSDs) operate a bit differently however. Like their magnetic counterparts, SSDs store information in ones and zeros, however unlike Magnetic disks, only the SSD's internal controller knows where in the memory cells the data is being stored. Because the SSD's controller uses wear leveling to maximize the life of the drive, the operating system has no idea where the controller ends up putting the ones and zeros.

When it comes time to securely erase your disk, a traditional wiping utility that writes the random sequences to the disk may end up not evenly erasing a solid state drive.

Because of this, it is important that the tool you choose for wiping is specifically compatible with SSDs. These utilities will use special SSD controller functions such as TRIM, and Secure-Erase to sanitize your data.

Secure Erase Magnetic Hard Drives

Assignment: Secure Erase a Magnetic Drive Protected with BitLocker

In this assignment, we will securely erase the boot drive. Unless you do wish to erase all of your data, skip this assignment.

Prerequisite: Completion of chapter 9, Recovery Drive, Assignment: Create a Recovery Drive.

1. Restart your computer and boot using the *Recovery drive*.
2. Click on the *US* (or your native language) for the keyboard.
3. Click on *Troubleshoot* to continue.
4. For this assignment, we will reset the computer to factory default. Click on *Reset your PC* to continue.
5. If the hard drive is using *BitLocker,* it will need to be unlocked by either entering the recovery key or loading the recovery key from a USB device. Make sure you have this key before wiping your hard drive using *BitLocker*.
    - **WARNING:** All data on this drive will be irrevocably erased.
6. At the warning window, click *Next*.
7. Click *Reset* to start the process. An alert will state it is resetting the system.
8. Select the *Erase* tab to begin the process.

Assignment: Secure Erase a Magnetic Boot Drive Without BitLocker Encryption

In this assignment, we will securely erase the boot drive. Unless you do wish to erase all of your data, skip this assignment.

Prerequisite: Completion of chapter 9, Recovery Drive, Assignment: Create a Recovery Drive.

11. Vulnerability: When It Is Time To Say Goodbye

1. Restart your computer and boot using the *Recovery drive* created in an earlier assignment. If you don't have one, refer to the section with the assignment *Create a Recovery drive.*
2. Click on the *US* (or your native language) for the keyboard.
3. Click on *Troubleshoot* to continue.
4. For this assignment, we will reset the computer to factory default. Click on *Reset your PC* to continue.
    - **WARNING:** All data on this drive will be irrevocably erased.
5. At the warning window, click *Next*.
6. Click *Reset* to start the process. An alert will state it is resetting the system.
7. Select the *Erase* tab to begin the process.

Secure Erase a Solid State Hard Drive (SSD)

Windows 10 includes a nice feature called *Recovery drive* that will allow you to fully clean the drive and reinstall a clean copy of Windows. Even though this same tool can be run on a solid state drive (SSD), it is not 100% effective, leaving some of your data accessible. For this reason, the DoD and many other governmental agencies do not permit simply the erasure of an SSD prior to sale, but require the SSD to be physically destroyed.

Assignment: Create a Bootable USB Drive of Parted Magic

Parted Magic is one of the best tools to partition, and securely erase all internal and external hard drives. It can be purchased in basic form for $9 from the Parted Magic website. In this assignment, you will create a bootable USB on which will reside Parted Magic.

11. Vulnerability: When It Is Time To Say Goodbye

1. Open a web browser and navigate to the Parted Magic home page at *http://partedmagic.com/*, and then click the *Download* button at the bottom of the page.

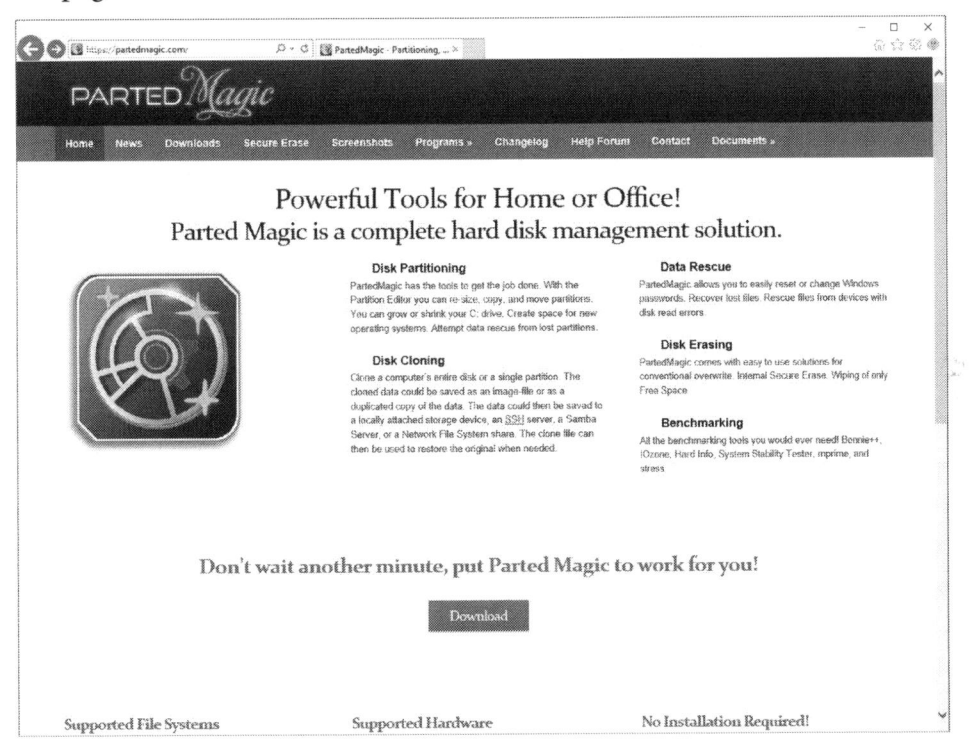

11. Vulnerability: When It Is Time To Say Goodbye

2. Choose the download that works for you (in this example, the $9 version)

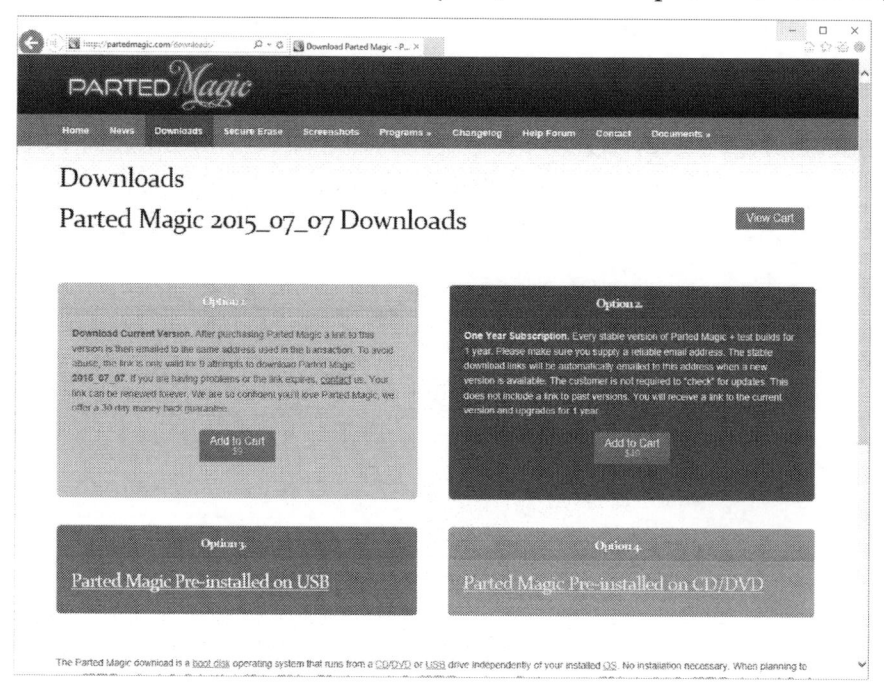

- **Note:** Once purchased, Parted magic needs to be written to a removable USB flash drive (or CD/DVD). This can be done using a free utility called *Rufus*, available at *https://rufus.akeo.ie/*. Once Downloaded, Rufus can be run from any location, since it is portable and requires no installation.

3. Open a web browser to Rufus at *http://rufus.akeo.ie/,* and then download Rufus.

4. Once downloaded, click the Rufus icon to launch the program

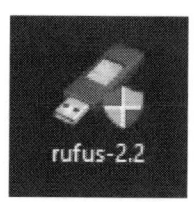

11. Vulnerability: When It Is Time To Say Goodbye

5. Rufus then opens, allowing you to select the *Device* at the top of the window. Select your removable USB drive from the drop down, and then continue to step 6.

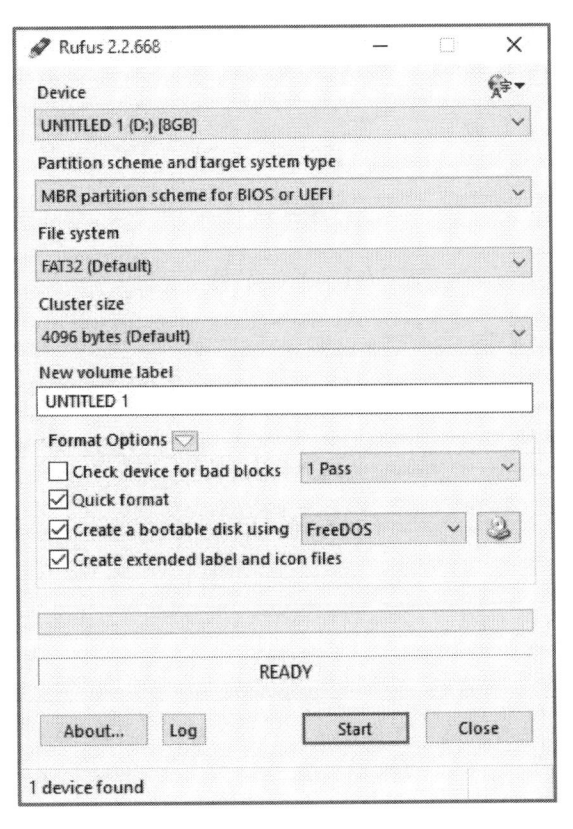

11. Vulnerability: When It Is Time To Say Goodbye

6. Click the icon circled below to open a file browser window.

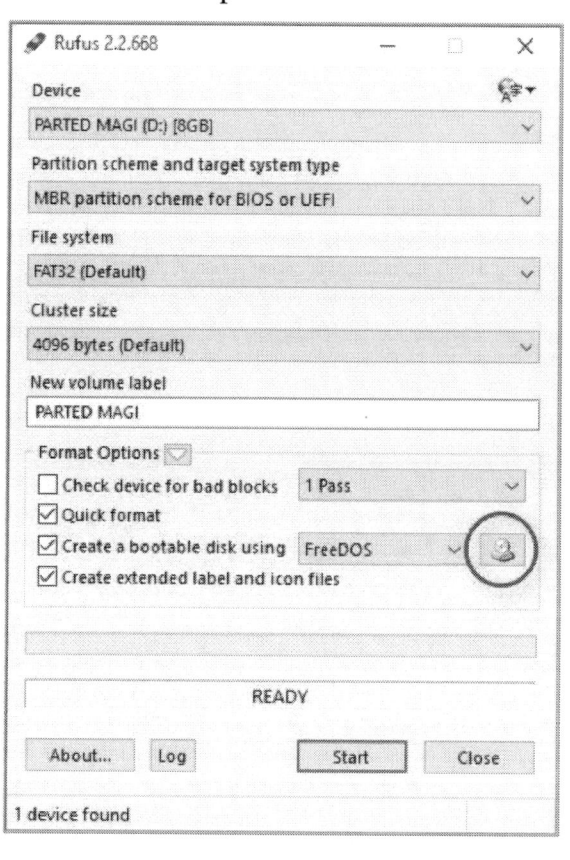

11. Vulnerability: When It Is Time To Say Goodbye

7. Navigate to where the Parted Magic ISO file was saved, select the file, and then click *Open*.

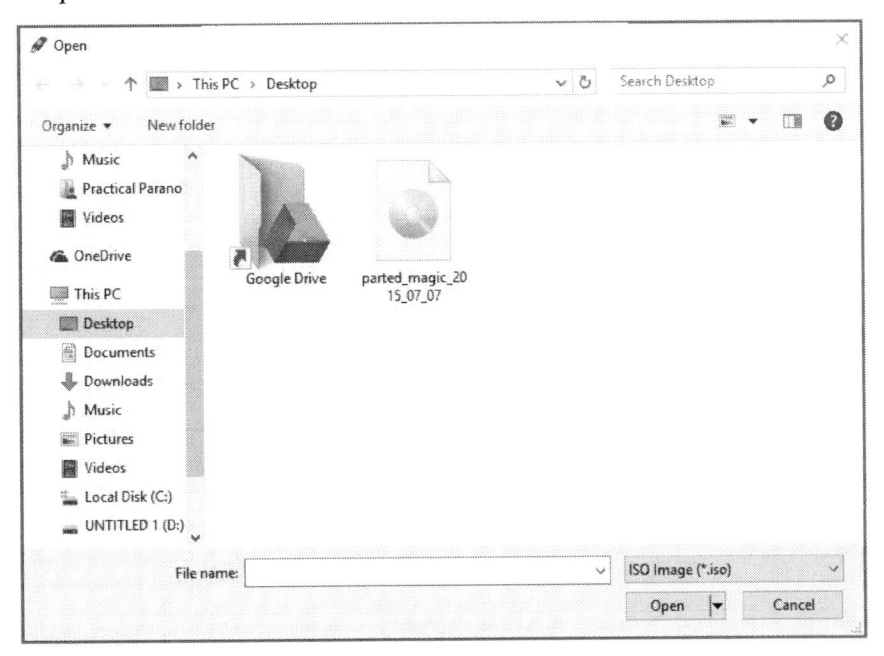

11. Vulnerability: When It Is Time To Say Goodbye

8. Click the *Start* button to kick off the creation process.

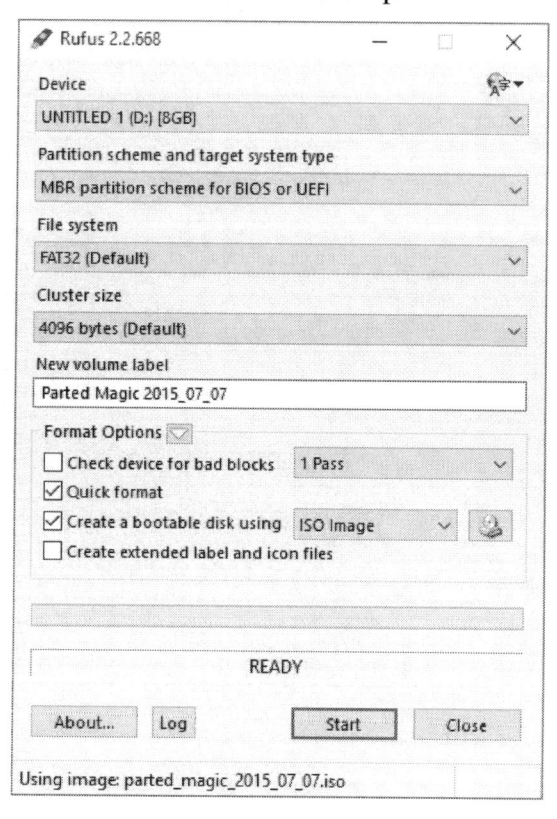

11. Vulnerability: When It Is Time To Say Goodbye

9. When complete, Rufus will display a green status bar and a *READY* dialog. Click the *Close* button.

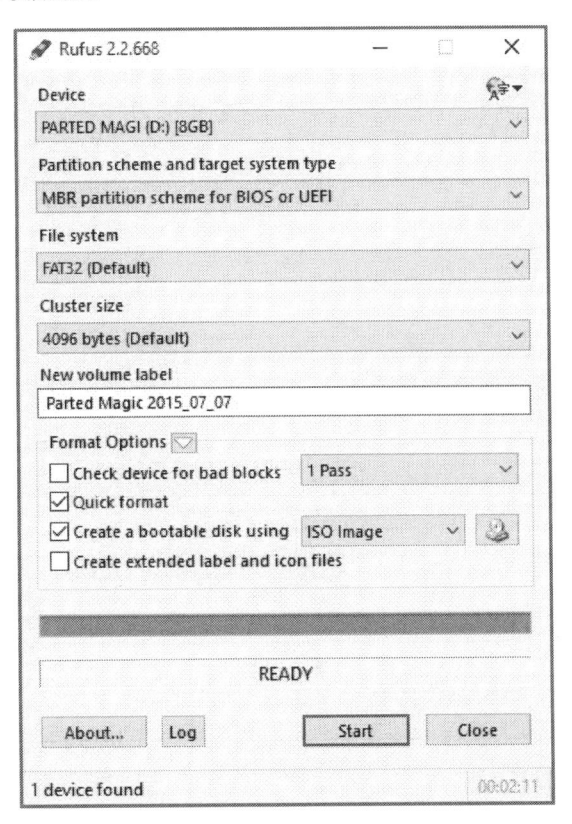

You now have a bootable USB drive with Parted Magic installed.

Assignment: Secure Erase a Solid State Drive Protected with BitLocker

In this assignment, we will securely erase the BitLocker encrypted boot drive. Unless you do wish to erase all of your data, skip this assignment.

Prerequisite: Completion of chapter 9, Recovery Drive, Assignment: Create a Recovery Drive.

1. Restart your computer and boot using the *Recovery drive*.
2. Click on the *US* (or your native language) for the keyboard.

11. Vulnerability: When It Is Time To Say Goodbye

3. Click on *Troubleshoot* to continue.

4. For this assignment, we will reset the computer to factory default. Click on *Reset your PC* to continue.

5. If the hard drive is using *BitLocker*, it will need to be unlocked by either entering the recovery key or loading the recovery key from a USB device. Make sure you have this key before wiping your hard drive using *BitLocker*.

    - **WARNING:** All data on this drive will be irrevocably erased.

6. At the warning window, click *Next*.

7. Click *Reset* to start the process. An alert will state it is resetting the system.

8. Select the *Erase* tab to begin the process.

Assignment: Secure Erase a Solid State Boot Drive without BitLocker Encryption

In this assignment, you will securely erase the boot drive. Unless you do wish to erase all of your data, skip this assignment.

Prerequisite: Completion of the previous Assignment: Create a Bootable USB Drive of Parted Magic.

1. Create a *Parted Magic* USB boot disk (See Assignment: Create a bootable USB drive of Parted Magic)

2. Power on the computer and boot from the USB drive with your computer manufacturer's *Boot List* key command

3. Choose the *Default settings 32* option from the boot screen

4. Once on the Parted Magic desktop, double-click the *Erase Disk* program on the Desktop

11. Vulnerability: When It Is Time To Say Goodbye

5. In the main Window, verify the *Internal* tab is selected, and then click the *ATA Secure Erase* button.

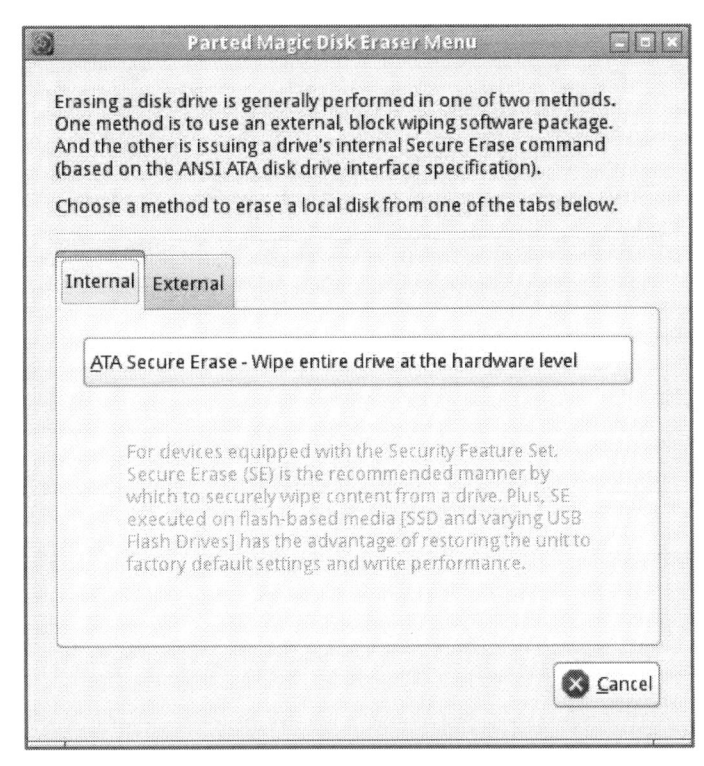

6. In the next window, the internal hard drive(s) are listed. Select the one you wish to securely erase and then click the *Continue* button. If a red notification is displayed that your drive is *Frozen* (as in the example below), you can try to unlock it using the sleep button. This will put the computer to sleep for a few seconds to trigger the hard drive controller to unlock.

11. Vulnerability: When It Is Time To Say Goodbye

7. When the drive is unfrozen, it should say *Not Frozen* in green letters. We are now ready to proceed.

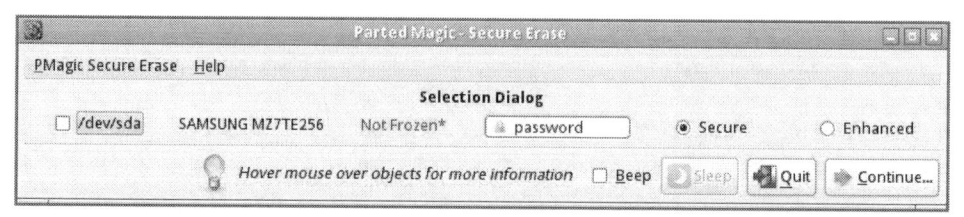

8. Click the drive(s) you wish to erase by selecting the left most checkbox next to the device name (in this example /dev/sda) and then click *Continue*. Optionally, you can check the *Enhanced* radio button for a multi-pass format. Leave the password field as it is, and then click the *Continue* button.

9. At the last screen, confirm that you wish to erase the entire SSD by clicking the checkbox *I allow this utility to erase the selected device(s)*. Then click the *Start Erase* button.

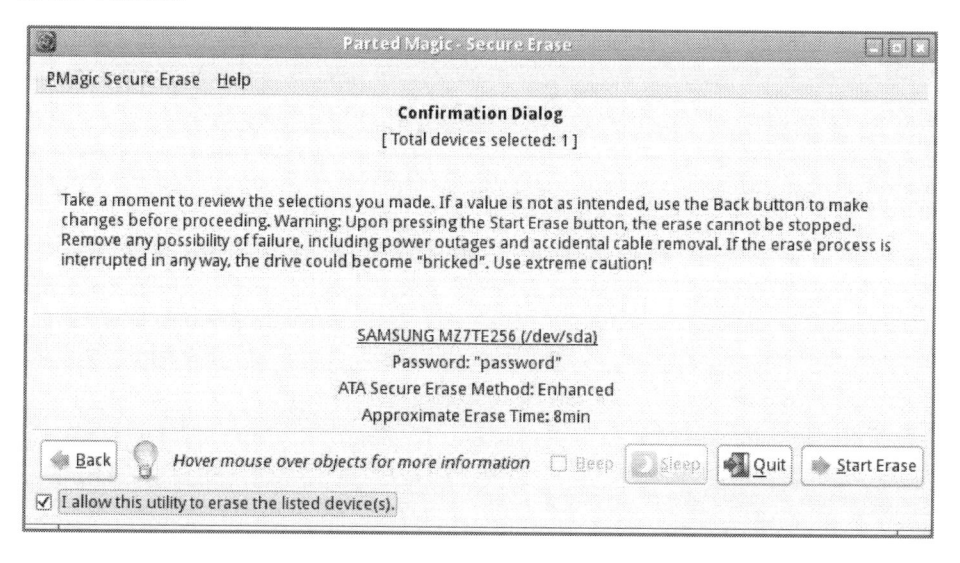

-248-

11. Vulnerability: When It Is Time To Say Goodbye

10. After the drive has been erased, close the confirmation dialog, and shut down your computer. You will need to insert bootable Windows 10 media to then reinstall Windows.

Assignment: Secure Erase a Non-Boot Drive

Many users have additional drives to store data that will not fit on the boot drive. There is a different strategy to securely erase these drives.

Prerequisite: Completion of the earlier Assignment: Create a Bootable USB Drive of Parted Magic, this chapter.

1. Power on the computer and boot from the Bootable Parted Magic USB drive with your computer manufacturer's *Boot List* key command.
2. Choose the *Default settings 32* option from the boot screen.
3. Once on the Parted Magic desktop, double-click the *Erase Disk* program on the Desktop.

11. Vulnerability: When It Is Time To Say Goodbye

4. In the main Window, click the *External* tab, and then click the *Nwipe* button.

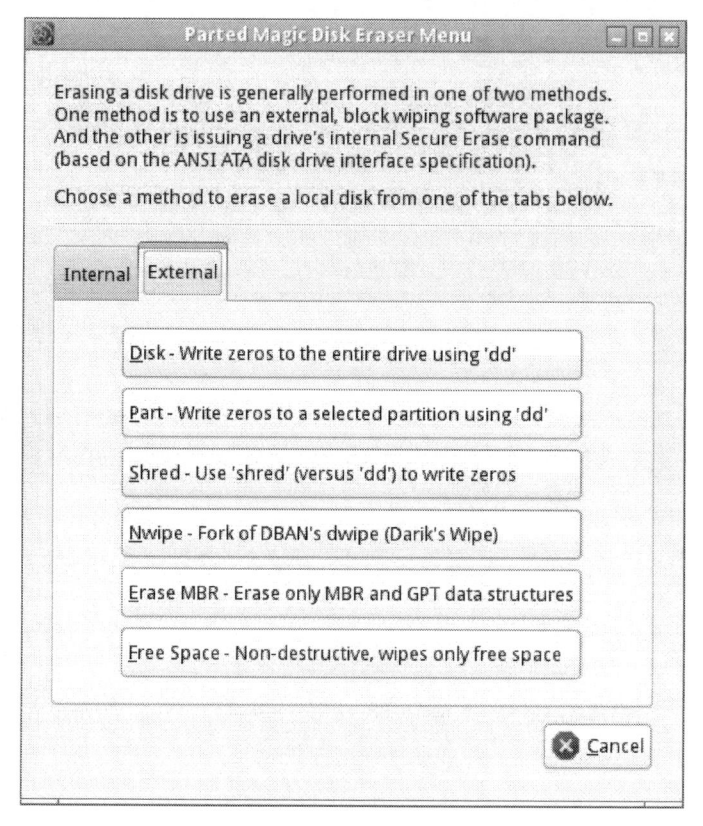

Parted Magic Disk Eraser Menu

Erasing a disk drive is generally performed in one of two methods. One method is to use an external, block wiping software package. And the other is issuing a drive's internal Secure Erase command (based on the ANSI ATA disk drive interface specification).

Choose a method to erase a local disk from one of the tabs below.

| Internal | **External** |

- Disk - Write zeros to the entire drive using 'dd'
- Part - Write zeros to a selected partition using 'dd'
- Shred - Use 'shred' (versus 'dd') to write zeros
- Nwipe - Fork of DBAN's dwipe (Darik's Wipe)
- Erase MBR - Erase only MBR and GPT data structures
- Free Space - Non-destructive, wipes only free space

[Cancel]

11. Vulnerability: When It Is Time To Say Goodbye

5. A new Window opens displaying Nwipe (Darik's Boot and Nuke). Select the external disk that you wish to wipe by moving the caret up and down with the arrow keys and selecting the disk by pressing the space bar.

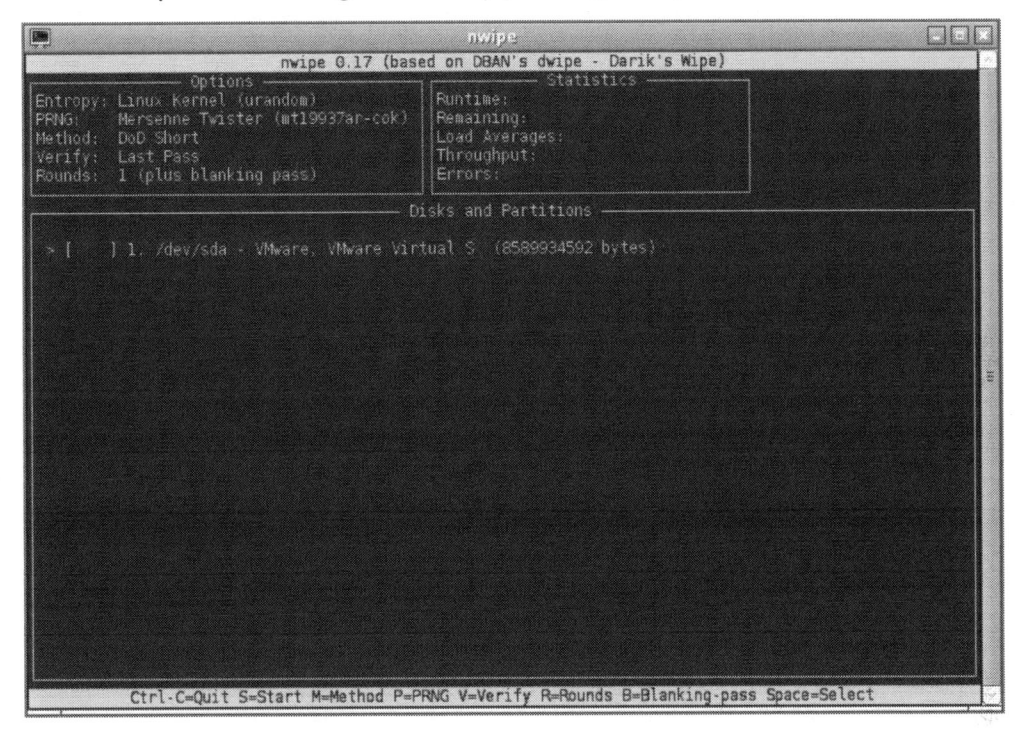

11. Vulnerability: When It Is Time To Say Goodbye

6. When a drive is selected it will display the words *wipe* between the brackets.

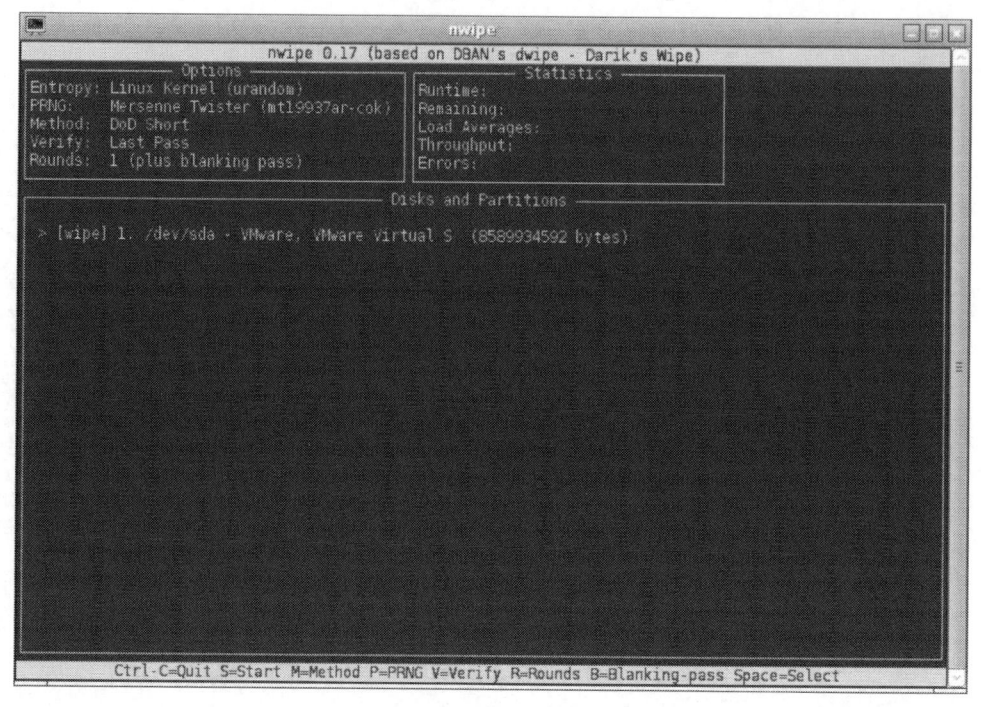

```
                                    nwipe
───────────────────── nwipe 0.17 (based on DBAN's dwipe - Darik's Wipe) ─────────────────────
─── Options ─────────────────────────────── Statistics ───────────
 Entropy: Linux Kernel (urandom)            Runtime:
 PRNG:    Mersenne Twister (mt19937ar-cok)  Remaining:
 Method:  DoD Short                         Load Averages:
 Verify:  Last Pass                         Throughput:
 Rounds:  1 (plus blanking pass)            Errors:
─────────────────────────── Disks and Partitions ───────────────────────────
> [wipe] 1. /dev/sda - VMware, VMware Virtual S  (8589934592 bytes)




 Ctrl-C=Quit S=Start M=Method P=PRNG V=Verify R=Rounds B=Blanking-pass Space=Select
```

11. Vulnerability: When It Is Time To Say Goodbye

7. Keep the default *DoD Short pass* option, and then press *Shift+S* to start the erasing process.

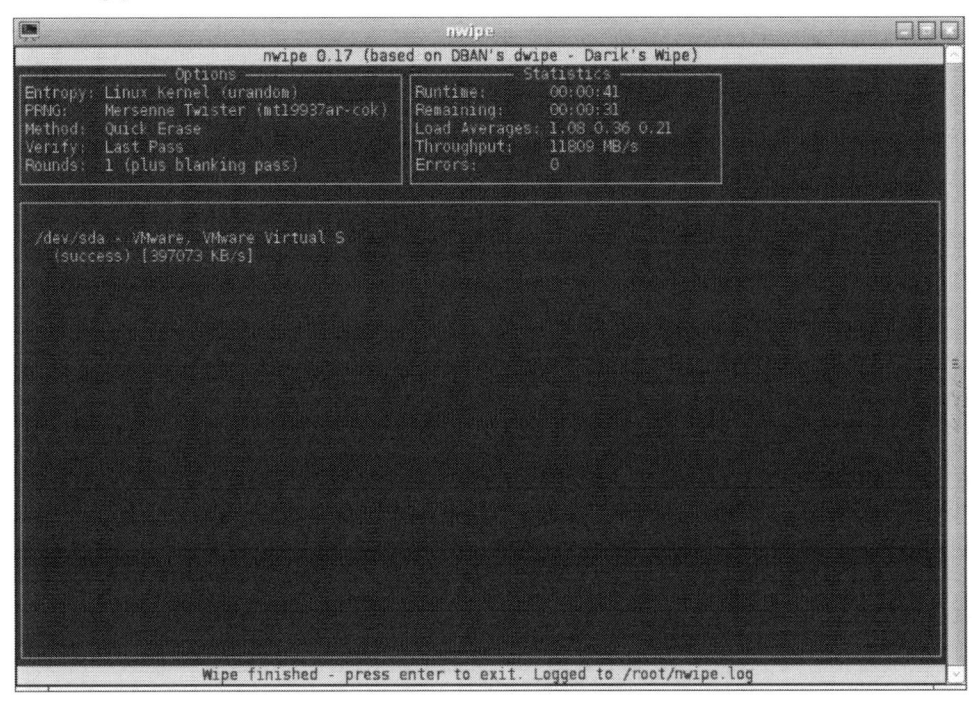

```
                              nwipe
              nwipe 0.17 (based on DBAN's dwipe - Darik's Wipe)
         Options                          Statistics
Entropy: Linux kernel (urandom)     Runtime:       00:00:41
PRNG:    Mersenne Twister (mt19937ar-cok)  Remaining:     00:00:31
Method:  Quick Erase                Load Averages: 1.08 0.36 0.21
Verify:  Last Pass                  Throughput:    11809 MB/s
Rounds:  1 (plus blanking pass)     Errors:        0

/dev/sda - VMware, VMware Virtual S
  (success) [397073 KB/s]




              Wipe finished - press enter to exit. Logged to /root/nwipe.log
```

8. When finished Nwipe will display a *Success* confirmation. Press the *Enter* key to close the window.

Congratulations. Your sensitive data is now scrubbed from your disks.

11. Vulnerability: When It Is Time To Say Goodbye

Review Questions

1. When selling, giving away, or trashing your PC, all data on the drive must be made inaccessible, which can be done by _____.

2. Using a traditional drive wiping utility will securely erase a SSD. (True or False)

3. To create a bootable USB drive with Parted Magic installed, use the _____ utility.

4. Secure-Erase and TRIM are controller functions that allow for secure erasure of Solid State Drives (True or False)

12. Vulnerability: Local Network

I am concerned for the security of our great Nation; not so much because of any threat from without, but because of the insidious forces working from within.

–General Douglas MacArthur

Ethernet Broadcasting

It is *common wisdom* that Ethernet is more secure than Wi-Fi. But as with most things we believe, this is not accurate.

There are two security issues with Ethernet: Broadcasting and Insertion. At the most fundamental level, what is happening when data travels through Ethernet is that electrons are traveling along a metal cable. There are two unintended consequences that occur whenever electrons go for a ride–heat generation, and the creation of an electromagnetic field. For our purposes, heat isn't an issue. But the electromagnetic field is.

Sending data through copper wire effectively turns that wire into a very large antenna that is broadcasting your data through radio waves. If you have the right receiver and translation software, you can easily capture every bit of data being sent and received along that cable.

This vulnerability is not something about which the average person or business would or should be concerned. On the other hand, if you or your business requires the utmost in security, it is mandatory to add encryption to your Ethernet network. This is accomplished using either a Linux, OS X, or Windows server running IEEE 802.1X protocol and software. More on this in a few paragraphs.

Speaking specifically about OS X, computer-to-computer communications are not encrypted, and so are strongly discouraged. When using computer-to-OS X Server communications, then all communications are encrypted. For business, this means that users should not do file sharing between any computer and an OS X computer, but instead copy files to a server for others to copy back to their own computers.

Ethernet Insertion

You would notice if someone came into your home, plugged a computer into your network, and sat there watching all the network data go by. But in the typical business, nobody would notice.

Ethernet networks can be protected from unwanted insertions by implementing the 802.1x protocol at *http://en.wikipedia.org/wiki/IEEE_802.1X* (often referred to as Radius). This protocol works with both Ethernet and Wi-Fi, mandating that anyone attempting to join the network authenticate with their own personal name and password. This is unlike the typical Wi-Fi authentication that uses the same password for everyone.

In order to have Radius security on your network, a Linux, OS X, or Windows server running Radius, or one of the many other 802.1x appliances that are available must be on the network. Details on how to configure 802.1x are beyond the scope of this book. Please consult the following for more information:

- Microsoft TechNet documentation
  http://technet.microsoft.com/en-us/library/hh831831.aspx

Wi-Fi Encryption Protocols

Right out of the box almost all Wi-Fi base stations are insecure. Anyone that can pick up the signal can connect. This allows them not only to use your bandwidth to access the Internet, but also to see all of the other data–such as usernames and passwords–that are travelling on that network. All that is needed to secure your Wi-Fi is to add strong password protection with encryption.

WEP (Wired Equivalency Protocol) *http://en.wikipedia.org/wiki/Wired_Equivalent_Privacy* was the first encryption protocol for Wi-Fi. Introduced in 1999, it was quickly broken, and by 2003 was replaced by WPA and WPA2 (Wi-Fi Protected Access). Any Wi-Fi base station manufactured in the past 5 years will offer WPA and WPA2, in addition to WEP.

There is only one reason to ever use WEP–you simply have no other option. Kids driving by your home can likely break into your WEP network before leaving the block.

WPA (Wi-Fi Protected Access) *http://en.wikipedia.org/wiki/Wi-Fi_Protected_Access* superseded WEP in 2003. Although it is a great advancement, it too has been broken. As with WEP, the only reason to use WPA is that you have no other option.

WPA2 *http://en.wikipedia.org/wiki/Wi-Fi_Protected_Access* is the only protocol considered secure. WPA2 superseded WPA in 2004. Although in the past year WPA2 has been broken, it is very difficult to do, and with strong passwords or with 802.1x still provides military-grade protection for your wireless networks.

There are two encryption algorithms that can be used–*TKIP* and *AES* (technically known as CCMP, but virtually all vendors refer to it as AES.) TKIP has been compromised and is no longer recommended. If your Wi-Fi device allows the option of AES, use only that. If it only allows for TKIP, trash the unit and purchase a more modern device.

12. Vulnerability: Local Network

Routers: An Overview

The connection point between your Internet Service Provider (ISP) and your Local Area Network (LAN) is most likely a router. A router is a device designed to connect two different types of networks, and provide resources for them to interact.

Common brands of routers include: Cisco, Linksys, Netgear, D-Link, Apple, and the many unbranded devices that Internet Service Providers lease to their customers.

Some newer routers, especially those provided by ISPs are all-in-one units containing several, if not all of the components below:

- **Modem**. The hardware that decodes and modulates the signal from your Internet provider to your cable or telephone jack. This is most likely to be a separate component if more than one device exists for your Internet connection.

- **Router**. A component that runs a specialized program, which allows hundreds of different devices to interact on a network, usually sharing a single IP address to the Internet. Routers use *Network Address Translation* (NAT) to convert and direct Internet traffic from websites to your computer and from your computer to other computers and peripherals on the *Local Area Network* (LAN).

- **Firewall**. Software which inspects data traffic between the internet and internally connected devices

- **Network Switch**. A hardware component that allows multiple devices to be connected simultaneously and interact with the router

- **Access Point**. A hardware component that allows tens or hundreds of wireless (Wi-Fi) devices to connect to it.

Every router has at least some basic security controls built in, including the ability to filter out what it thinks are attempts to hack into your network, and the ability to forward specific types of data packets to a specific computer within your LAN, or to point specific types of data packets to a specific computer on the Internet.

12. Vulnerability: Local Network

Malware sometimes attempts to alter these configurations so that either the malware or the criminals behind the malware have an easier time harvesting your data. Because of this, it is wise to routinely inspect the condition of your router. How often is "routine?" Within larger organizations such as Apple, and other security-conscious organizations with high-value data, it is common to have a network administrator dedicated to maintaining watch over the status of network equipment. For a small business or household, once every few months wouldn't be too often.

Assignment: Determine the Wi-Fi Encryption Protocol

You find yourself at a hotel with Wi-Fi and the need to access the Internet. You have the need to ensure that your data is not intercepted. How do you determine if the Wi-Fi network is using WPA or WPA2 instead of WEP? That is what this assignment is all about.

For this assignment, take yourself to a location that has an available Wi-Fi network. Your own home may do.

1. From the Taskbar, click the *Wi-Fi* icon. The *Network & Internet* window appears.

12. Vulnerability: Local Network

2. Select the wireless network to connect with.

12. Vulnerability: Local Network

3. The authentication window will appear, requesting the network's username and password.

    - If it does not appear, and this is the first time you have tried to access this network, this network does not have any security. It has allowed you to have access without a password, and should be not be used for any email, web surfing, or file sharing.

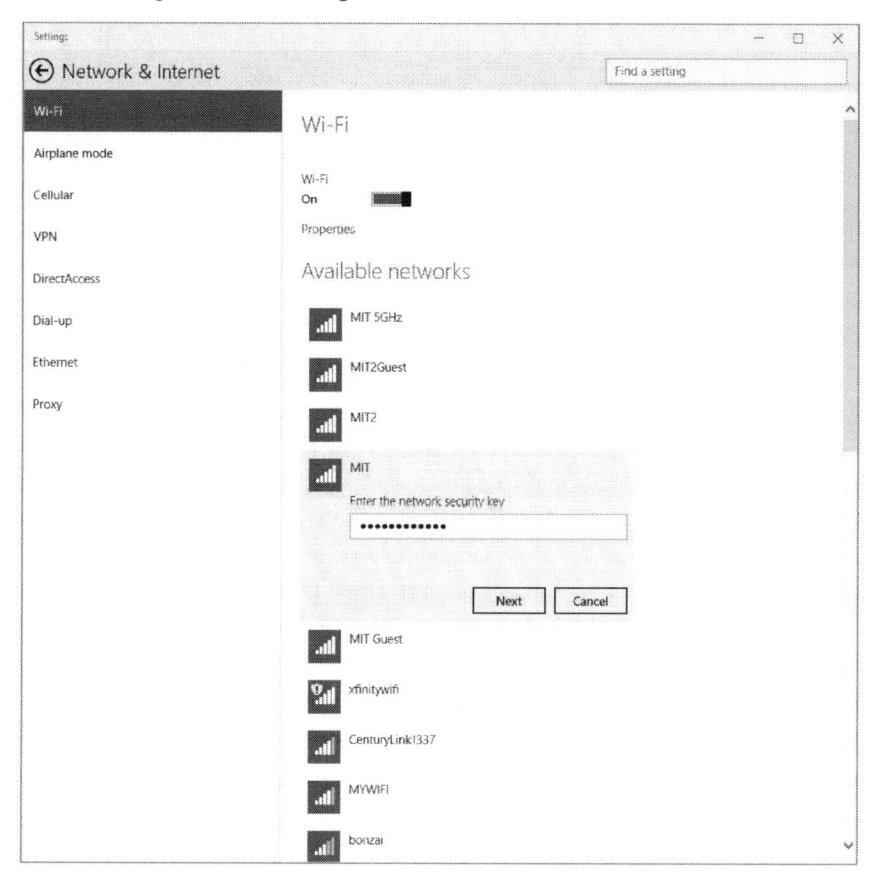

If you have already connected to the Wi-Fi network and don't recall which security protocol it uses, you can find it from your *Network Connection Preferences*.

4. Open the *Wi-Fi* menu from the Windows Taskbar.
5. At the top of the menu select *View Connection Settings*.

12. Vulnerability: Local Network

6. Under the *Wi-Fi* heading, select the current connected network.

7. In the *Properties* section > *Security Type*, you can see the current encryption protocol. In this example, the network is connected using WPA2-Personal encryption. This is sufficient for home needs if you are using it with it a long 15-character password.

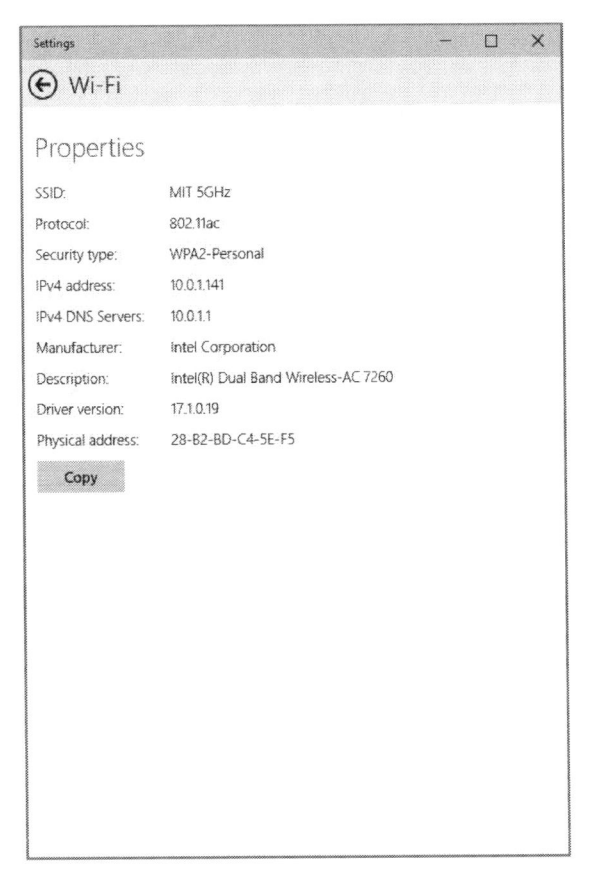

8. Close the window.

Assignment: Configure WPA2 On a Router

Although all Wi-Fi routers are configured differently, most follow a basic template. In this assignment we will be using a Netgear R7000. We assume you are on a network with this, or a similarly managed router.

12. Vulnerability: Local Network

Find the IP address of your Wi-Fi router:

1. Click the *Windows Start* button in the *Taskbar*.

2. In the *Search* field, enter *cmd*.

3. Select *ipconfig* from the top of the listings. The *ipconfig* window will open.

4. The *Default Gateway* will list the IP address of the router you are connected with.

Access the router:

5. Open a browser, and then in the *URL* or *Address* field, enter the IP address of the router.

6. At the *Authentication Required* window, enter the *administrator* user name and password. This will be the administrator of the router, not of the computer.

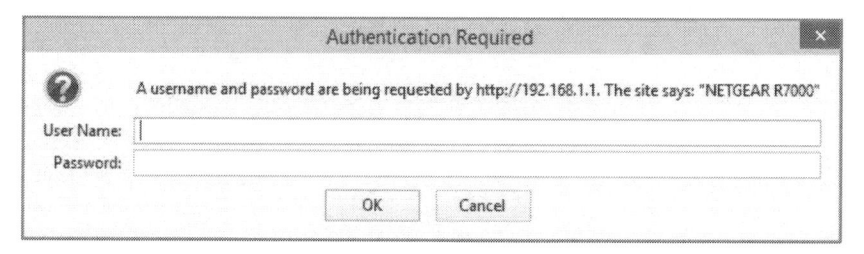

7. The router control panel will appear.

12. Vulnerability: Local Network

8. From the sidebar, select the *Wireless* button. In the main body area scroll to *Security Options*. Verify the Wi-Fi is configured to use the *WPA2* protocol. If it isn't, select it now, and then enter a desired strong password to access the network.

    - Note: Although the *WPA2 Enterprise* is the strongest security (even higher than WPA2), it requires network administrator skills and hardware that are outside the scope of this book.

12. Vulnerability: Local Network

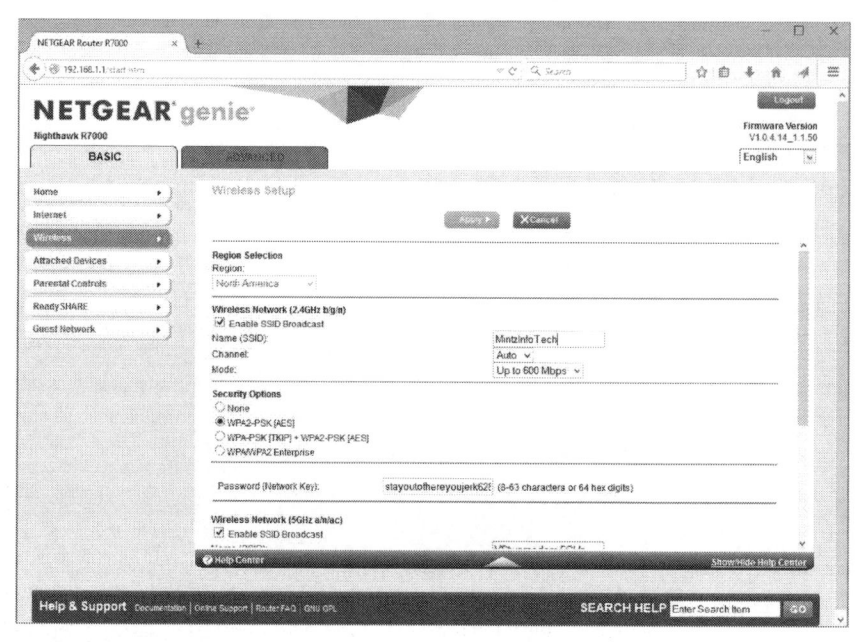

9. If any changes were made, click the *Apply* button to save the changes.
10. Close the browser window to exit out of your router.

Use MAC Address to Limit Wi-Fi Access

Every device that is capable of connecting to a TCP network has a unique *MAC Address* (Media Access Control) *http://en.wikipedia.org/wiki/MAC_address*. This address specifies the manufacturer of the device, and a device-specific number. Don't go to sleep on me yet. This MAC address can be used with most Wi-Fi routers to limit what devices can connect to the network.

Although every router has a unique interface to filter by MAC address, they all operate on the same principle–either allow anyone with the proper password to gain access to the wireless network, or allow anyone with the proper password *and* proper MAC address access to the wireless network. In this way, you can easily lock down your Wi-Fi to only approved devices. So even if an employee knows the password, they are unable to connect their personal computer to the network unless the MAC address for the device is on the list.

Assignment: Restrict Access by MAC Address

In this assignment we will configure our router to allow only desired devices to connect based on MAC address.

- NOTE: We will be using the Netgear R7000 router as our demonstration unit. Most routers follow a very similar process, although the specific menu names and paths may vary slightly.

12. Vulnerability: Local Network

1. Make a list of the devices to be permitted access to your Wi-Fi network. Include a few-word description, and the MAC address of the device.

   - The MAC address of a Windows device may be found with the *ipconfig* command in the command prompt.

   - The MAC address of an OS X device may be found from the *Apple* menu > *System Preferences* > *Network* > *Advanced* button > *Hardware* tab.

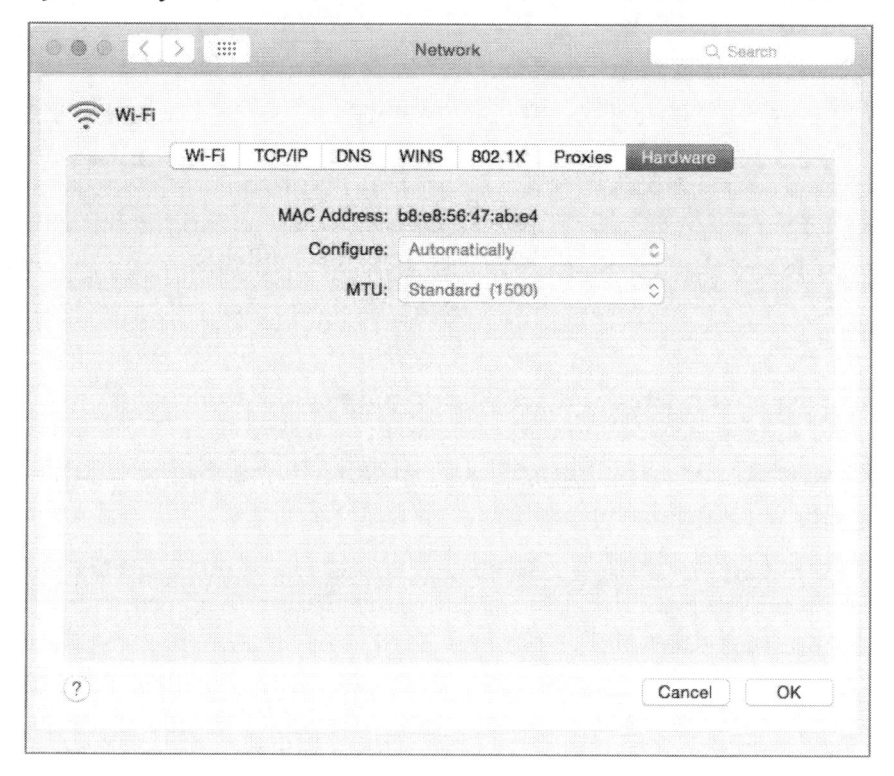

   - The MAC address of an android device may be found by tapping the *Menu* key > *Settings* > *Wireless & Network* > *Wi-Fi Settings* > *Advanced* heading > *MAC address* field.

12. Vulnerability: Local Network

- The MAC address of an iPhone may be found in the *Settings > General > About > Wi-Fi Address* field.

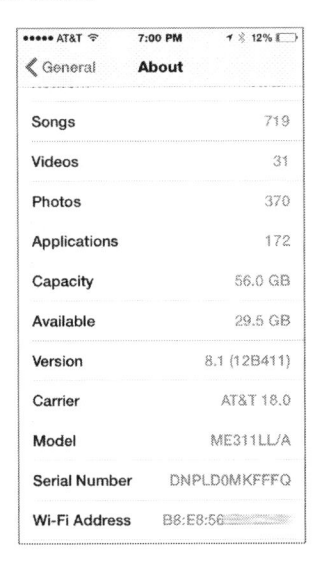

2. With your MAC address list in hand, launch a browser and enter the IP address of your Wi-Fi router.

3. At the authentication window, enter the user name and password of the administrator for the router.

4. The router control panel will appear.

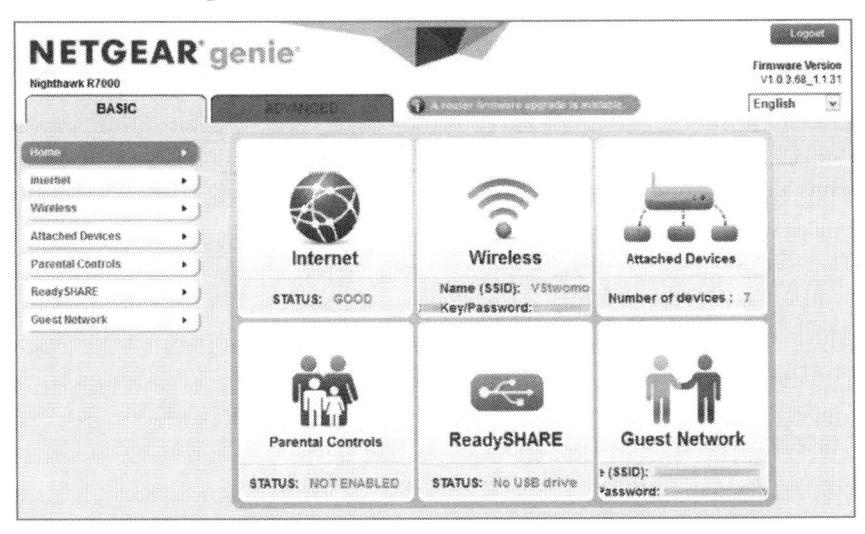

12. Vulnerability: Local Network

5. Select the *Advanced* tab.

   - NOTE: The router you are currently working on may have a different path to accomplish this same task.

6. From the sidebar, select *Security > Access Control*.

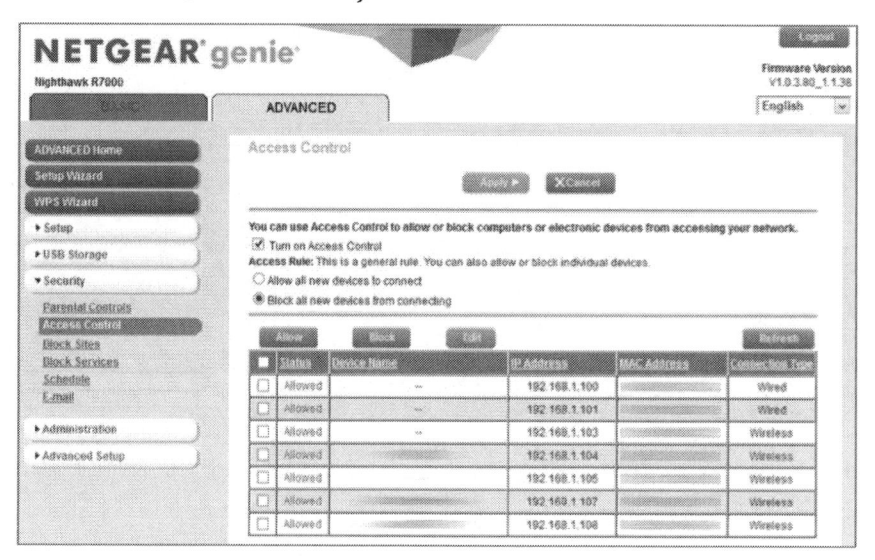

7. Enable the *Turn on Access Control* check box.

8. Enable the *Block all new devices from connecting* radio button.

9. Go through your list of devices to be allowed and compare to the devices currently connected.

   - If there are currently connected devices that are not on your list, verify if they should be on your list. If they should, add them to your list. If they should not, disconnect or block them from the currently connected list.

   - If there are devices on your list that are not connected, add them to the currently connected list. In this example, by selecting the *Allow* button, and then entering the device information.

10. Click the *Apply* button to save your changes.

11. Close the browser window to exit out of your router.

12. Vulnerability: Local Network

Congratulations! You have secured your wireless network so that only authorized devices are granted access.

Router Penetration

More recent phenomena are malware and hackers modifying router settings. This router modification enables easy data harvesting from network traffic. Common areas of router penetration include:

- **Port forwarding:** Port forwarding is useful if you have a service such as a web server running that you wish to be accessible from the internet. However, if ports are being forwarded without purpose, the firewall is being bypassed and your internal computers may be visible from the internet.

- **DMZ:** Related to Port Forwarding is the DMZ, or De-Militarized Zone. DMZ is typically used to route *all* external traffic for a specific IP address, regardless of service request, to a specific computer. Unless there is a unique need, it should remain disabled.

- **RAM-Resident Malware:** Many router malware make their home in the RAM of the router. In this way they can take control of your data traffic without showing in the interface.

- **Firmware:** It is vital to keep the router firmware up to date. Just as with any software, router firmware will always have vulnerabilities. Over time, criminals (including some government organizations) discover how to use these vulnerabilities to their benefit. Keeping the firmware updated helps to stay a step ahead of this.

Assignment: Examine Router Security Configuration

In the example below I'm using a Comcast Business-Class device. Comcast calls it a modem, but it is a router. Each router will have a slightly different interface.

1. Connect a computer via Ethernet to one of the Ethernet ports on the back of the Comcast unit.
2. Turn off Wi-Fi on your computer so that it can communicate only via Ethernet with the device.
3. In a browser, enter the IP address of the device; in this case it is *192.168.2.1*.

12. Vulnerability: Local Network

4. At the prompt, enter the administrator user name and password. You may need to ask your Internet provider for this information.

5. To verify there is no unwanted Port Forwarding, from the sidebar I select *Firewall*, and then the *Port Configuration* tab. Although Comcast refers to this as *Port Configuration*, in most devices this will be referred to as *Port Forwarding*.

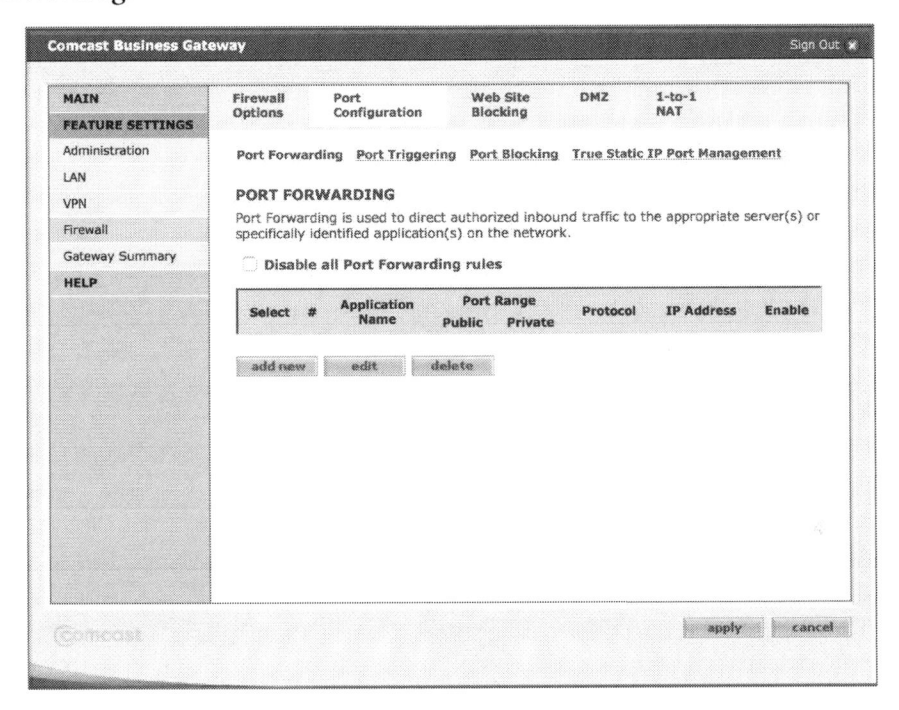

12. Vulnerability: Local Network

6. Related to Port Forwarding is *DMZ*. To check this I select *Firewall* from the sidebar, and then select the *DMZ* tab.

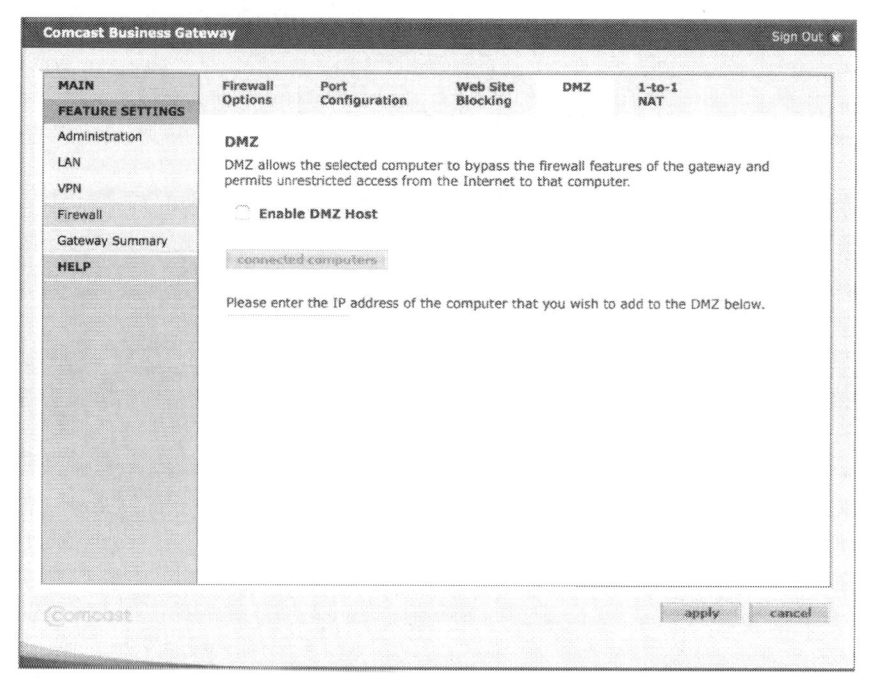

7. It is vital to keep your router firmware up to date. Just as with any software, router firmware will always have vulnerabilities. Over time, criminals (including some government organizations) discover how to use these vulnerabilities to their benefit. Keeping your firmware updated is mandatory to stay a step ahead in this cat and mouse game. Check with your Internet provider's technical support how to determine the firmware version currently installed, where to find updates, and how to install the updates.

12. Vulnerability: Local Network

8. A common form of router-targeted malware makes its home in the device's RAM. After performing your routine maintenance, power-cycle your router. This is nothing more than:

    a. Power off the router.

    b. Remove any internal battery (if present).

    c. Wait two minutes.

    d. Reinstall the internal battery (if present).

    e. Power on the router.

Any bug resting in your router RAM has just been eradicated.

Congratulations! You have updated the firmware and removed potential malware from your router.

12. Vulnerability: Local Network

Review Questions

1. The WEP Wi-Fi Encryption protocol should be used whenever possible. (True or False)
2. The WPA Wi-Fi encryption protocol should be used whenever possible. (True or False)
3. The WPA2 Wi-Fi encryption protocol should be used whenever possible. (True or False)
4. Of the two encryption algorithms–TKIP and AES–which should be used?
5. The network hardware that decodes and modulates the signal from your Internet provider to your cable or telephone jack is called a _____.
6. The network hardware that allows hundreds or thousands of devices to interact between the local network and Internet is called a _____.
7. The network hardware or software that inspects data traffic between the Internet and local network devices is called a _____.
8. The network hardware that allows multiple devices to connect and interact with each other and the router is called a _____.
9. The network hardware that allows tens or hundreds of wireless devices to connect to a network is called a _____.
10. A _____ address includes a unique manufacturer code, and a unique device code.

13. Vulnerability: Web Browsing

Distrust and caution are the parents of security.
–Benjamin Franklin

13. Vulnerability: Web Browsing

HTTPS

Due to an extraordinary marketing campaign, everyone knows the catchphrase: *What happens in Vegas, stays in Vegas*. With few exceptions, web surfers think the same thing about their visits.

Most websites use HTTP (Hypertext Transport Protocol) to relay information and requests between user and website and back again. HTTP sends all data in clear text–anyone snooping on your network connection anywhere between your computer and the web server can easily see everything that you are doing.

Typically, the only exceptions you will come across are financial and medical sites, as they are mandated by law to use HTTPS (Hypertext Transport Protocol Secure). HTTPS uses the SSL (Secure Socket Layer) encryption protocol to ensure that all traffic between the user and server is military-grade encrypted.

- **NOTE**: With the recent changes in Google SEO guidelines that give a higher priority to HTTPS sites, it will soon become common for sites to use encryption.

Although it is unlikely that you would ever be in the position to enter your password or bank account into an unsecure web page, you are almost guaranteed to enter your identity information, such as full name, address, phone number, and social security number. It is effortless for an identity thief to copy this information.

Anytime that you visit a web page that is secured using https, it will be reflected in the URL or address field of your web browser.

In the following example, I visit Wikipedia.org, which uses HTTPS by default:

Note how the address field reflects that I am now connected securely by displaying *https* and the *Lock* icon. Each browser will indicate security slightly differently–some displaying just the https, some just the lock.

Now that I am connected securely to Wikipedia, snoops will not be able to see my actions. However, they still can see that I am connected to Wikipedia. If you would like to shield yourself completely, continue reading to our chapter on using a Virtual Private Network (VPN.)

Having to remember to connect via HTTPS for each web page is an impossible task. First, you have other, more important items to store in your synapses. Second, many websites do not have an HTTPS option, resulting in many error pages and wasted time during the day.

There are two options to resolve this:

- Automate the attempt to connect to sites via HTTPS
- Encrypt your entire online session using VPN

Using VPN is covered in a later chapter. Automating the attempt to connect via HTTPS is both easy and free. All it requires is a freeware plug-in, *HTTPS Everywhere*.

HTTPS Everywhere is available for Firefox, Opera, and Chrome. If you are happy to use these browsers instead of Edge, there is no reason not to install HTTPS Everywhere!

Assignment: Install HTTPS Everywhere

HTTPS Everywhere is available for Firefox, Chrome, Opera, and Firefox for Android. For this example we will be using Firefox.

1. If the Firefox browser is not currently installed, open Edge, and the go to *http://firefox.com* to download Firefox.
2. Open Firefox.
3. Select the *Tools* menu > *Add-ons*.

13. Vulnerability: Web Browsing

4. Select *Get Add-ons* from the sidebar.

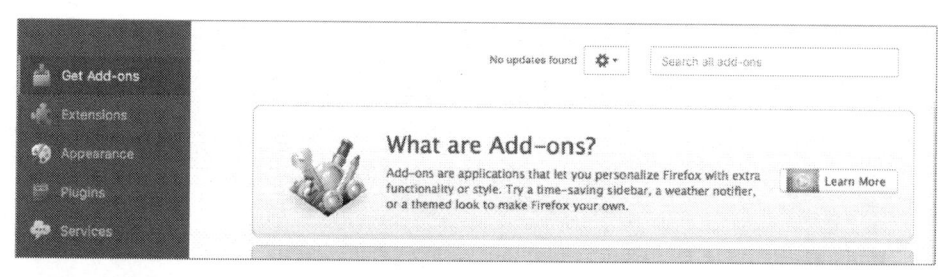

5. In the *Search* field, enter *https everywhere,* and then press the *Return* key. Matching items will appear below.

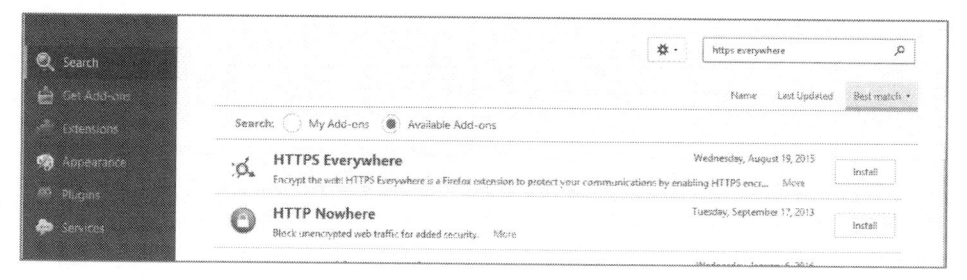

6. Select the *Install* button to the right of *HTTPS Everywhere*. HTTPS Everywhere will download.

7. When the download completes, select the *Restart Now* link.

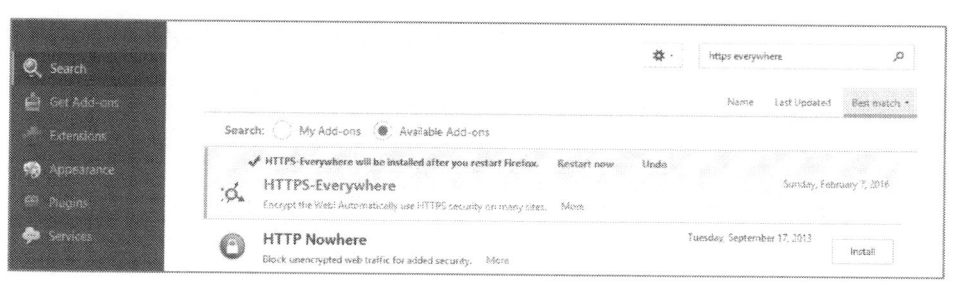

8. Firefox will restart.

13. Vulnerability: Web Browsing

9. The *HTTPS Everywhere* page opens. Take a few minutes to read up on this important addition to your security toolkit.

13. Vulnerability: Web Browsing

10. The *HTTPS Everywhere* icon can be found in the Firefox menu.

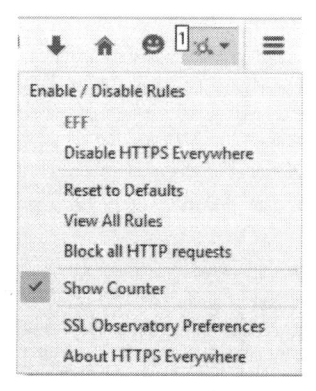

11. From the *HTTPS Everywhere* menu, select *SSL Observatory Preferences*. The *SSL Observatory* preferences window opens.

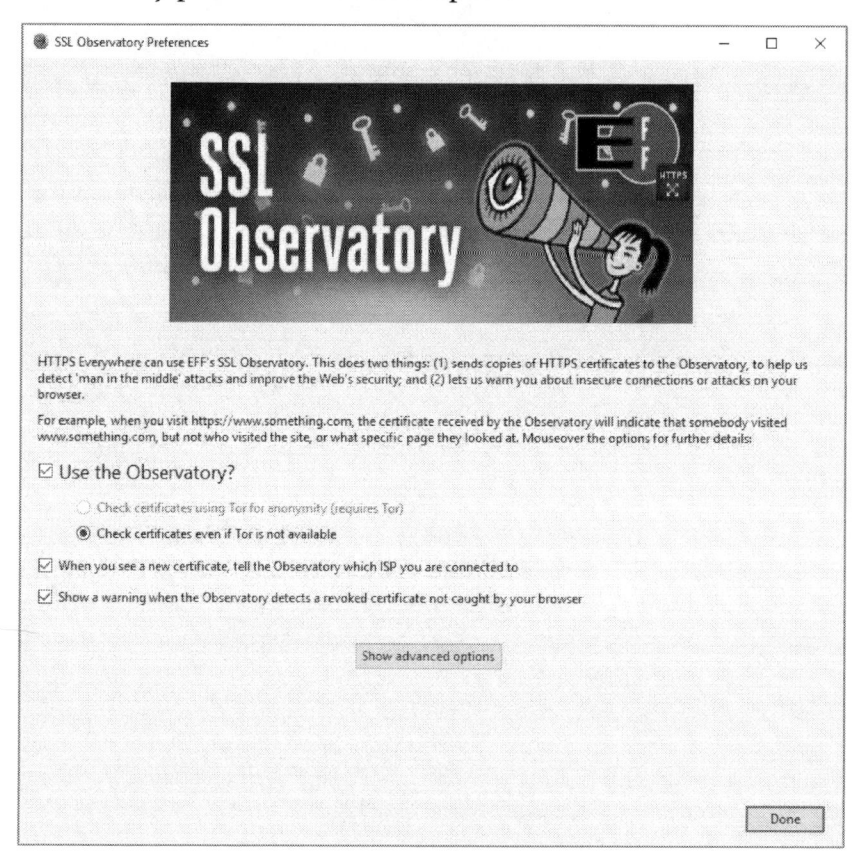

13. Vulnerability: Web Browsing

- Enable the *Use the Observatory?* Checkbox.

- If you have *Tor* installed (if not, you will install it later in this chapter), select *Check certificates using Tor for anonymity.* If not, select *Check certificates even if Tor is not available.*

- Enable the *When you see a new certificate, tell the Observatory which ISP you are connected to* check box.

- Enable the *Show a warning when the Observatory detects a revoked certificate not caught by your browser* check box.

12. Select the *Show Advanced Options* button.

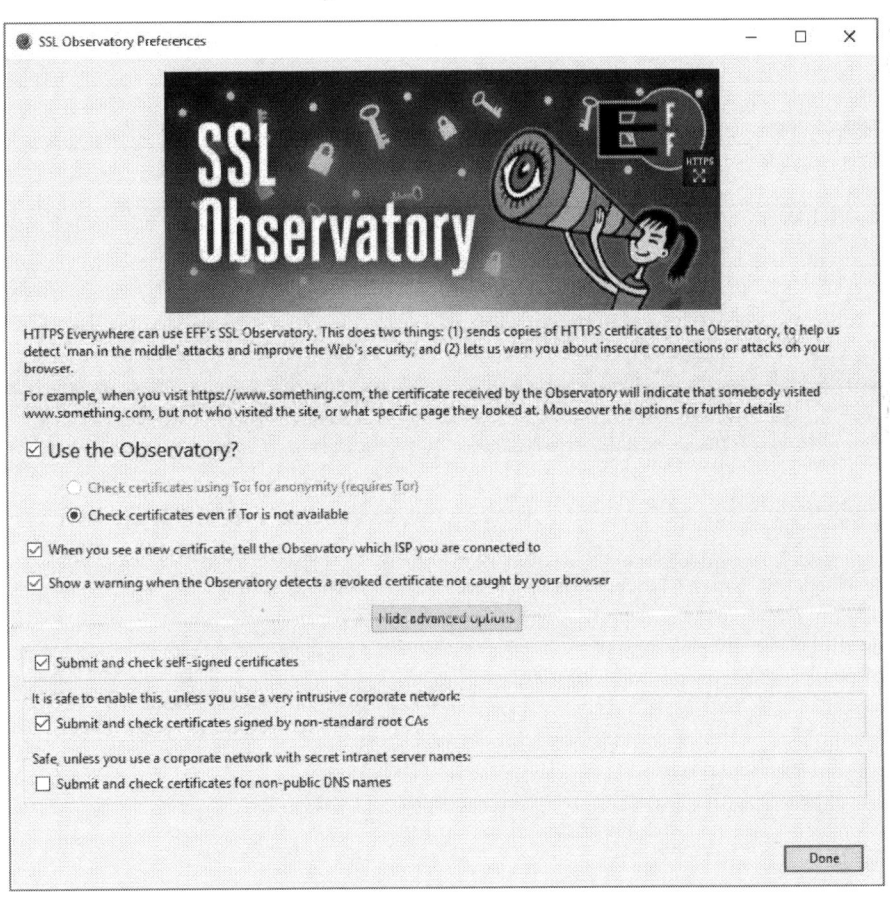

13. Vulnerability: Web Browsing

- Enable *Submit and check self-signed certificates* check box.
- Enable *Submit and check certificates signed by non-standard root CA's* check box.
- Select *Done*.

From now on, if a website has an HTTPS option (not all do), then you will be routed automatically to that page instead of the default unsecure page. If the site does not have an HTTPS option, the default unsecure page will load.

13. Vulnerability: Web Browsing

Choose a Browser

There many web browsers available on the market, with each placing a different emphasis on certain features, however the three most popular browsers for Windows include Microsoft Internet Explorer (its successor called *Edge*), Mozilla Firefox, and Google Chrome. Internet Explorer is included with Windows, while Chrome and Firefox are available for download. Why might you want to replace Internet Explorer (or Edge) with another browser? Chrome integrates tightly with Google's own services, offering features such as direct voice translation and an ultra-minimalistic interface. Firefox touts itself as the most privacy-respecting browsers, and while that is a subjective claim, Firefox does not transmit your data to Google or any other 3rd party company every time you search using the address bar box. While Google considers this "non-identifying information", IP addresses are identifying at the Internet Service Provider level. This functionality can be changed however, and with some tweaking, it is possible to make Chrome more privacy focused. Internet Explorer operates similar to Chrome, transmitting search queries to Bing, Microsoft's search engine. Like Chrome, it is possible to prevent Internet Explorer from sending searches automatically to Microsoft. However, Internet Explorer makes it difficult to change from using Bing as a default search engine and doesn't include a single click option to use Google or DuckDuckGo instead.

Browser	Platform	Price	Notable Features	Privacy
Chrome	Android, iOS, Linux, OS X, Windows	Free	Speed Google Services Integration	Fair
Edge	Windows 10	Free (included with Windows 10)	Active X Windows Integration	Fair
Firefox	Android, iOS, Linux, OS X, Windows	Free (Open Source)	Add-ons Privacy	Good
Internet Explorer	Windows	Free (Included with Windows	Active X	Fair

13. Vulnerability: Web Browsing

		prior to Windows 10)	Windows Integration	
Safari	OS X, iOS, Windows	Free (included with OS X and iOS)	History can be shared between all of your OS X and iOS devices	Fair

13. Vulnerability: Web Browsing

Firefox Private Browsing, Chrome Incognito, and Edge InPrivate Mode

Private Browsing (Firefox), *Incognito Mode* (Chrome), and *InPrivate Mode* (Edge) is a feature that prevents any normally cached data from being written to the hard drive while using a browser. This data includes browsing history, passwords, user names, list of downloads, cookies, and cached files. This is an essential tool if you work on a computer where your account is shared (what's with that?.), or if there is the possibility that someone else will examine your browsing habits.

Assignment: Enable Firefox Private Browsing

In this assignment we will enable Private Browsing within the Firefox browser.

1. Open Firefox.
2. Click the menu icon (3 lines), and then select *New Private Window*.

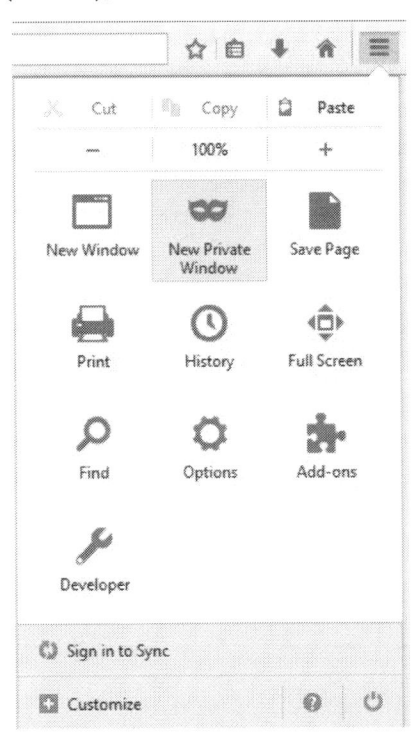

3. When selected, Firefox opens a new Window or tab with a mask icon, signifying that the window (or tab) is a private.

Keep in mind this does not mean your visit to websites has been anonymized; it only means that your browser is not remembering anything about the sites that you visited. For example, even in private browsing mode, if your troubled cousin visits Google.com and searches for something illegal, Google will still have a record of that search based on IP address, even if Firefox doesn't show a history of it. Aside from Google, your Internet Service Provider may also have records of your cousin's searches as well.

Assignment: Enable Chrome Incognito Mode

Incognito mode for Google Chrome works in just the same way as Firefox Private Browsing. The main difference between Chrome and Firefox is that Chrome does not sync your Incognito mode browsing with your Google account as it does with normal web browsing. Your information and browsing history will not be stored anywhere on your hard drive.

In this assignment we will enable Incognito Mode from within Google Chrome.

1. Open Chrome.

13. Vulnerability: Web Browsing

2. Click the menu icon (3 lines), and select *New incognito window*.

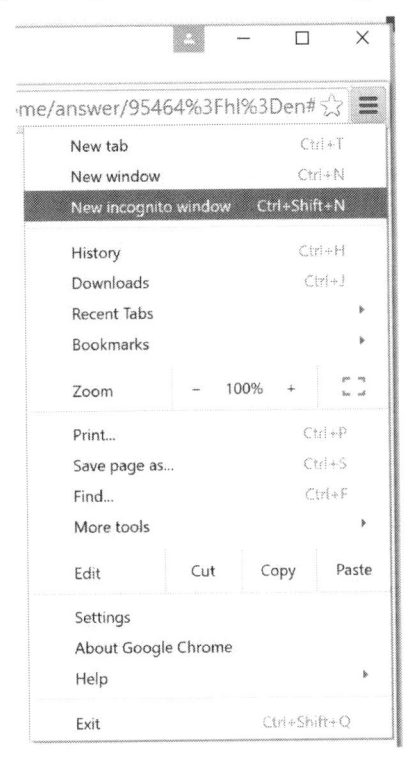

13. Vulnerability: Web Browsing

3. A new tab appears with a detective icon. There is also a small write-up explaining exactly what Incognito mode is.

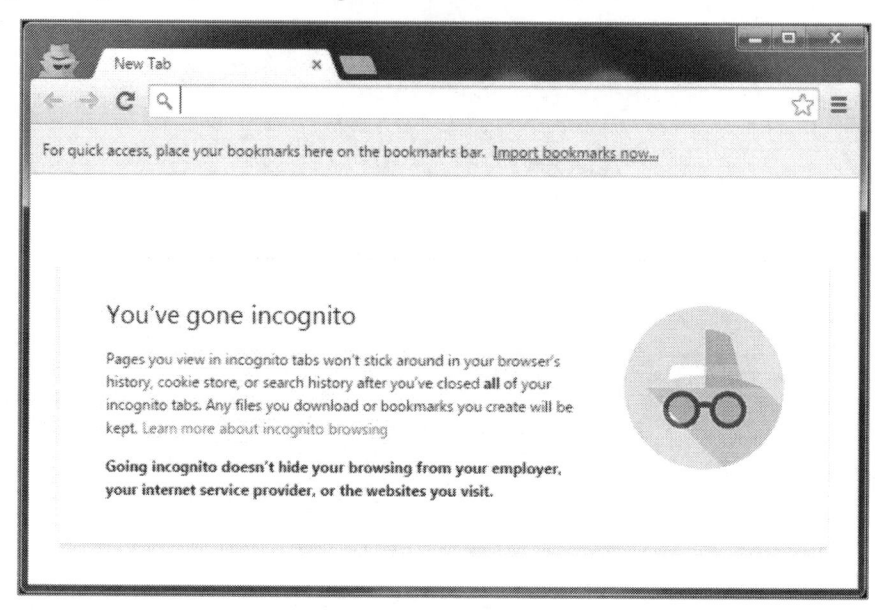

As with Firefox Private Browsing, you are only protecting your local machine and account from accessing your browsing history. If anything illegal or nefarious is done while in this mode, your ISP and the servers you make contact will still have logs all activity.

Assignment: Enable Edge InPrivate Mode

Windows 10 includes a new browser, Edge. Microsoft Edge is the successor to Internet Explorer and definitely improves on the many mistakes of IE. Flash and PDF-reading support will be built-in and its performance has been benchmarked as high as Chrome. Edge also comes with its own version of private browsing called *InPrivate*. While browsing in InPrivate mode, browsing data such as cookies and history are not stored on your PC, and when the tabs/windows are closed any temporary data is deleted.

In this assignment we will activate InPrivate mode.

1. Open Edge.

13. Vulnerability: Web Browsing

2. Click on the menu item (3 dots), and select *New InPrivate Window.*

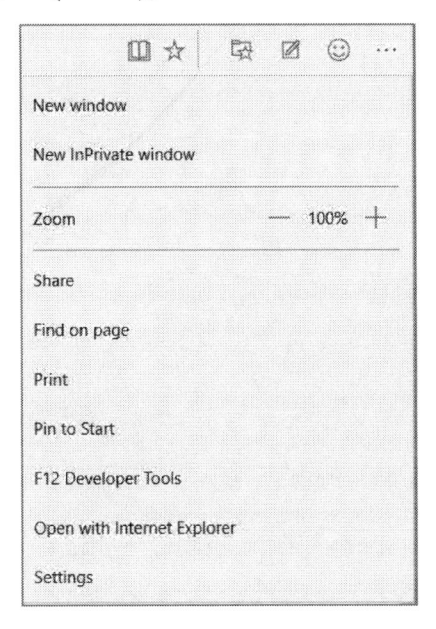

3. A new window appears with an *InPrivate* icon in the upper left. This verifies you are in InPrivate mode.

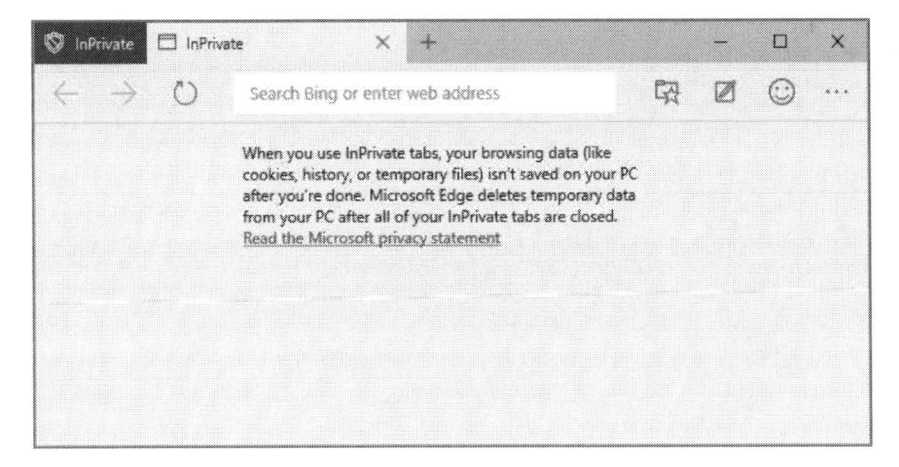

13. Vulnerability: Web Browsing

DuckDuckGo

With most web browsers, when performing a search, the search criteria and sites visited are collected and stored by the search engine. The Cookies assigned from one website can communicate with other sites and webpages you open. Also, most search engines record your searches and build a profile of your search history so that your search results will be unique and tailored to your interests.

Not so with the *DuckDuckGo* search engine. DuckDuckGo's policy is that it keeps no information on user searches, nor does it track search queries via IP addresses. Subsequently, all search results are identical for everyone.

Assignment: Make DuckDuckGo the Default Search Engine

In this assignment, you will change the default engine to DuckDuckGo.

1. Open a browser.

    - NOTE: As of this writing, neither Internet Explorer nor Edge allows setting DuckDuckGo as the default search engine. Firefox will be used in this example.

2. Point the browser to *http://duckduckgo.com*.

3. Click the button found at the bottom of the page *Set DuckDuckGo as your default search engine*.

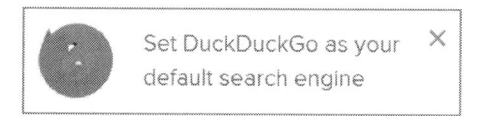

13. Vulnerability: Web Browsing

4. In the *Set as Default Search Engine* window, follow the instructions.

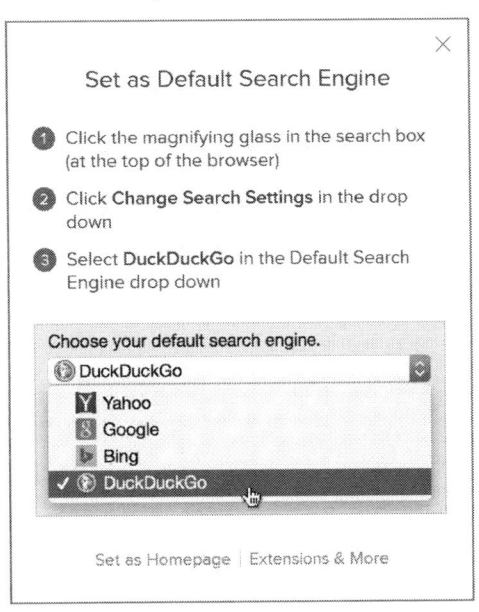

   Set as Default Search Engine

   1. Click the magnifying glass in the search box (at the top of the browser)
   2. Click **Change Search Settings** in the drop down
   3. Select **DuckDuckGo** in the Default Search Engine drop down

   Choose your default search engine.
   - DuckDuckGo
     - Yahoo
     - Google
     - Bing
     - ✓ DuckDuckGo

   Set as Homepage | Extensions & More

5. Click the magnifying glass in the search box, and then click the *Change Search Settings* in the drop down window.

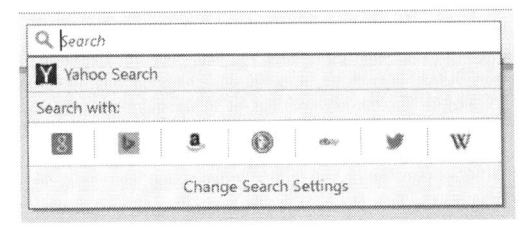

13. Vulnerability: Web Browsing

6. In the *Search* window drop down menu, select *DuckDuckGo*, and then close the window.

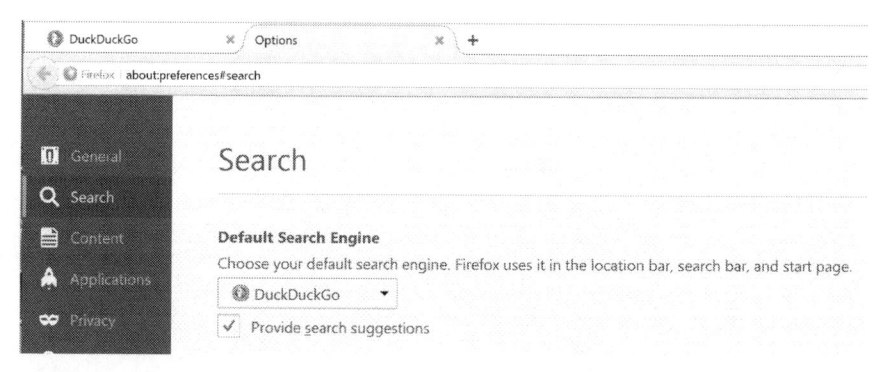

Congratulations. From now on your web searches will be private to you.

Clear History

You just realized that: 1) Your mother just called letting you know she is on her way over, 2) You have been naughty on the web all day, 3) You did not turn on private browsing, and 4) Your mom will feel insulted if you insist that an account for her must to be created instead of accepting her protest: *Oh, baby, I only need to check my AOL email. Just let me get on your account for a minute.*

Is it time to panic?

Not yet. You can erase your entire (steamy) browsing history in one click.

Assignment: Clear Firefox Browsing History

In this assignment you will clear your Firefox browsing history. Firefox provides you with fine-grained options for which aspects of your browsing history you can delete, and for how far back you wish the deletion to extend.

13. Vulnerability: Web Browsing

1. Open Firefox, and then select the menu (3 lines) > *History*.

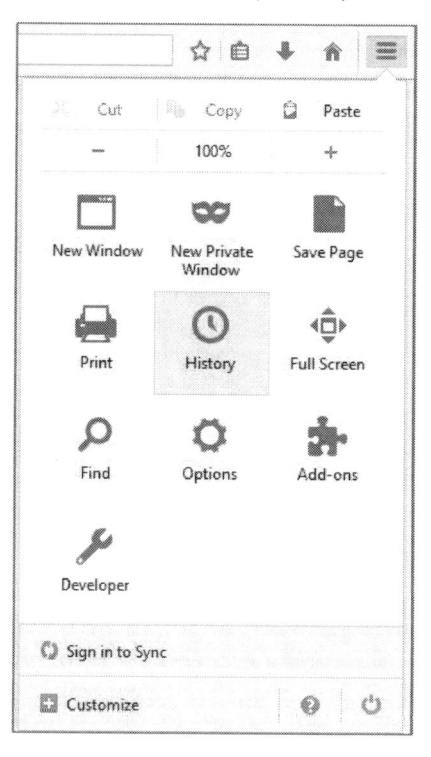

13. Vulnerability: Web Browsing

2. In the History window, select *Clear Recent History*.

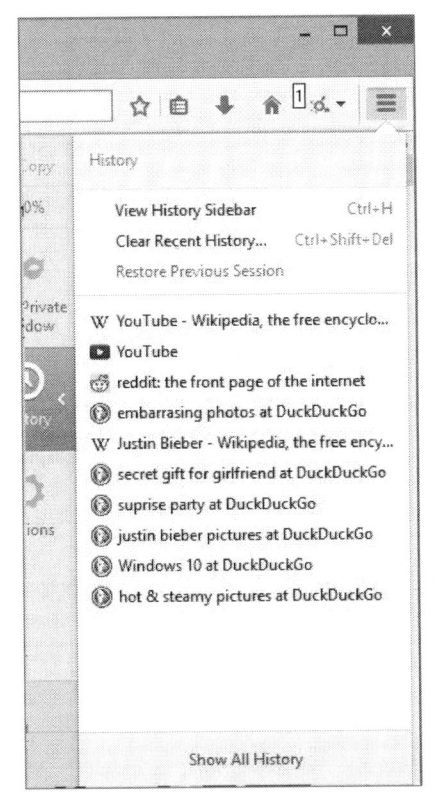

3. In the *Clear Recent History* window, click the *Time range to clear* drop down menu.

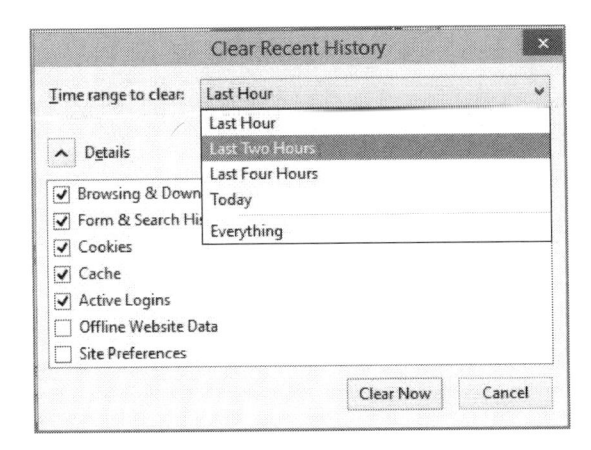

13. Vulnerability: Web Browsing

4. Click the *Clear Now* button to complete the history deletion.

Crisis averted.

Assignment: Clear Edge Browsing History

Edge provides browser history clearing similar to Firefox, but with a bit less granular control. In this assignment, we will clear the browser history in Edge.

1. Open Edge.
2. Click the menu (3 dots) > *Settings*.

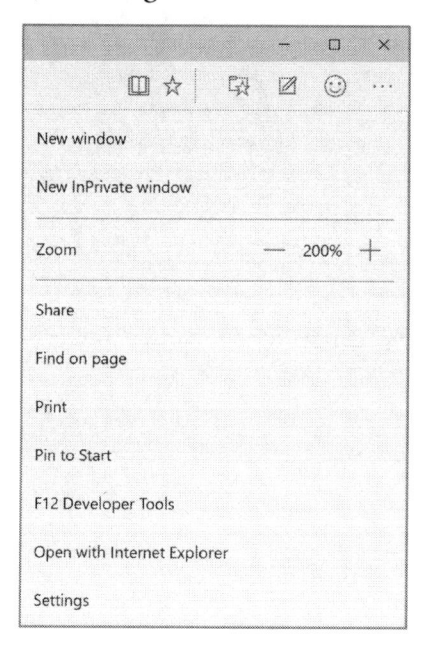

13. Vulnerability: Web Browsing

3. In the *Settings* window, click the *Choose what to clear* button.

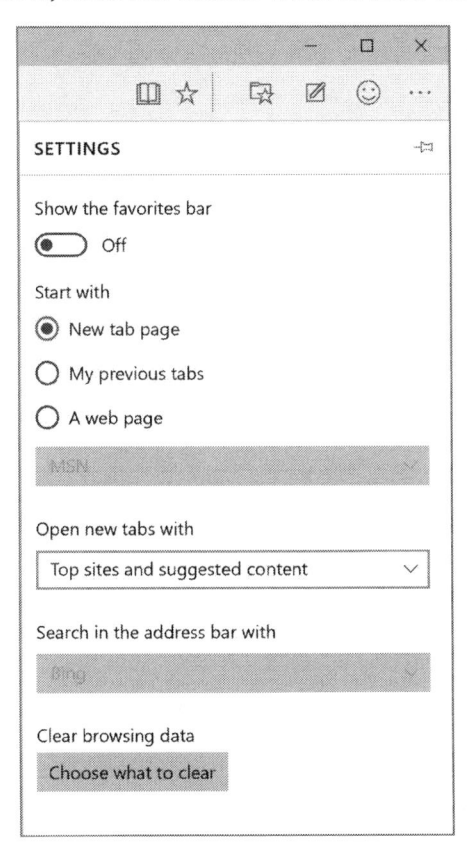

13. Vulnerability: Web Browsing

4. In the *Clear browsing data* window, enable the *Browsing history* checkbox and any other items to be deleted, and then click the *Clear* button.

Once again you have made a clear escape from those close to you knowing you are spending far too much time searching for aunts Noodle Koogle recipe.

13. Vulnerability: Web Browsing

Assignment: Clear Chrome Browsing History

1. Open *Chrome*, select the menu item (3 lines) > *History*.

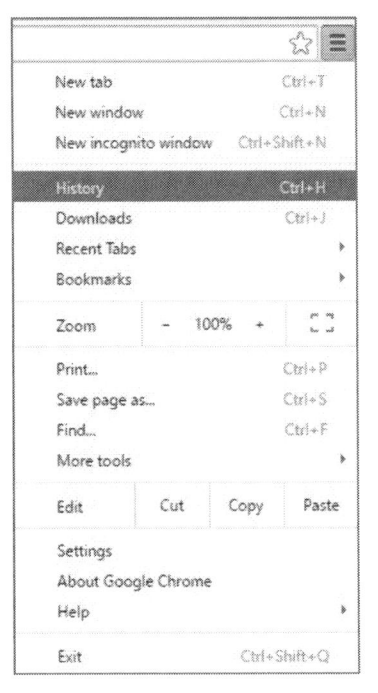

2. Click *Clear browsing data*.

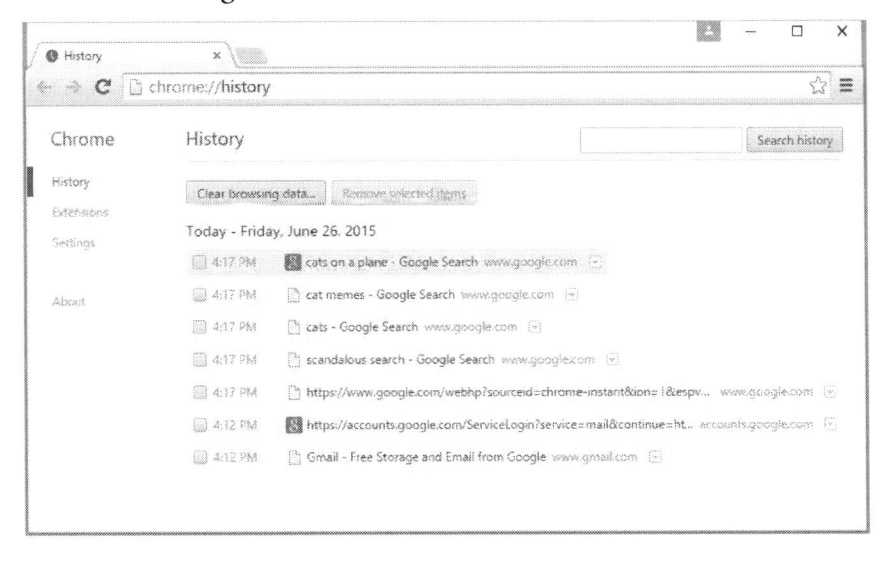

-301-

13. Vulnerability: Web Browsing

3. Select the amount of time that you'd like to delete as well as the specific browsing information such as Cookies or Download History and click *Clear browsing data*.

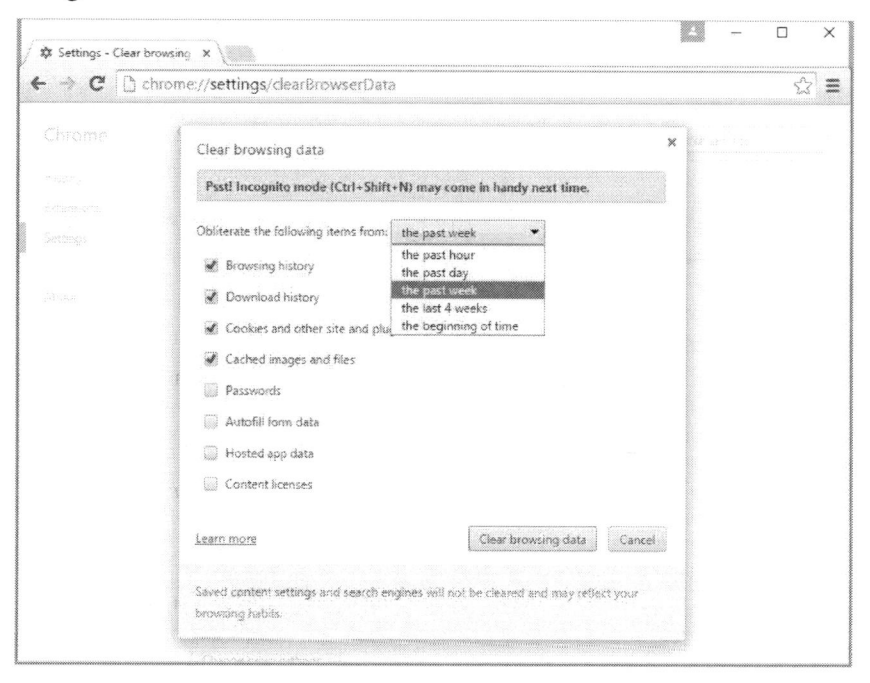

Assignment: Secure the Firefox Browser

Even if you are doing your due diligence and using best practices when browsing the web, it is still very important to make sure that your browser itself is secure. There are a few settings in Firefox that can be very useful for making sure that it is protecting you against simple attacks and also not tracking your every move on the web.

13. Vulnerability: Web Browsing

1. Open Firefox, and then select the *Options* button in the *Firefox Menu* toolbar.

13. Vulnerability: Web Browsing

2. In the Options window, click on *Privacy* in the left-hand pane. I recommend enabling the *Tracking* checkbox to automatically ask sites not to track your activity (sure, they have the option to ignore your request, but it's better than a stick in the eye).

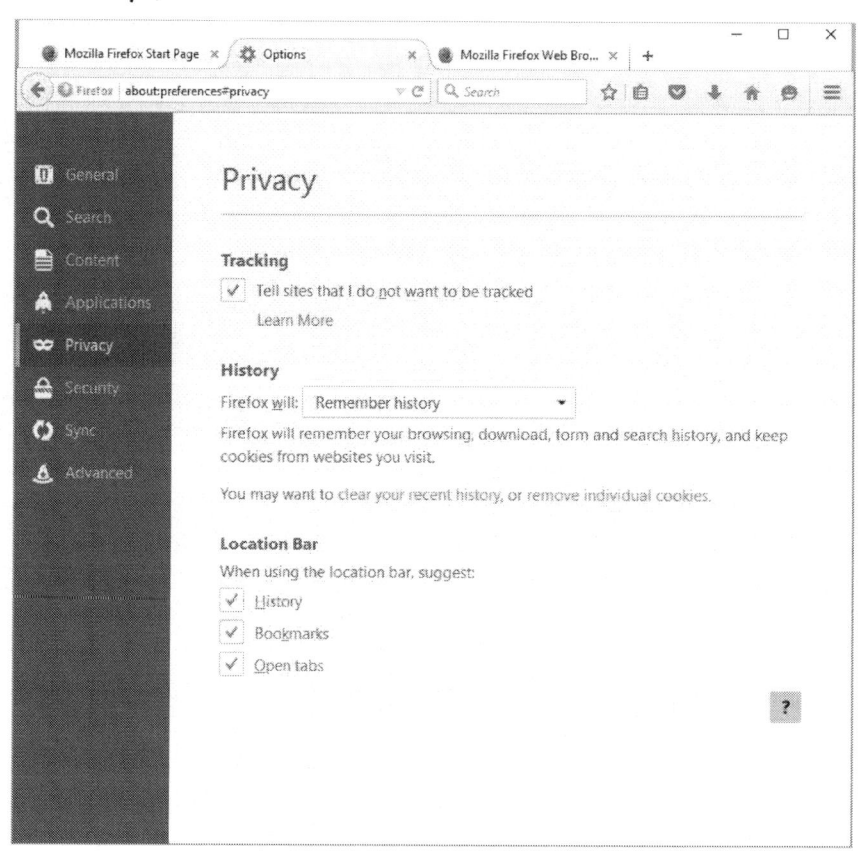

13. Vulnerability: Web Browsing

3. Click on *Security*. Check to enable *Warn me when sites try to install add-ons*, *Block reported attack sites*, and *Block reported web forgeries*.

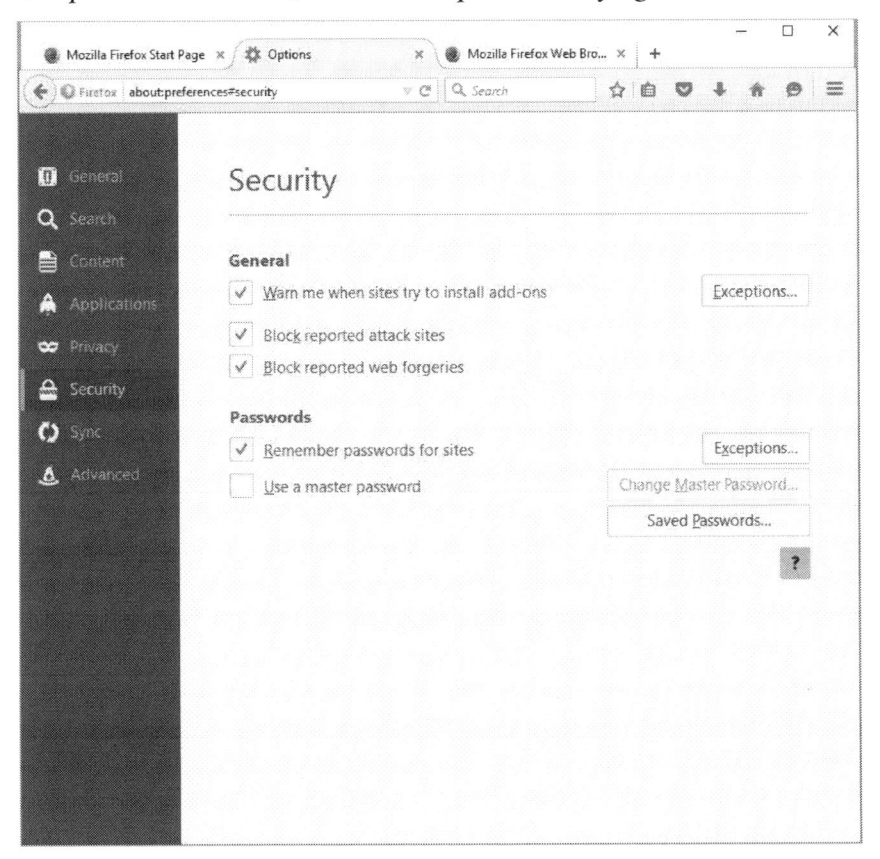

Congratulations. Your Firefox Browser is now secure from phishing attacks, third-party advertisers and known malware sites.

Assignment: Secure the Chrome Browser

Just the same as with Firefox, there are settings within Chrome that will keep you properly secured against the bad guys.

13. Vulnerability: Web Browsing

1. Open *Chrome*, select the menu item (3 lines), and click *Settings*.

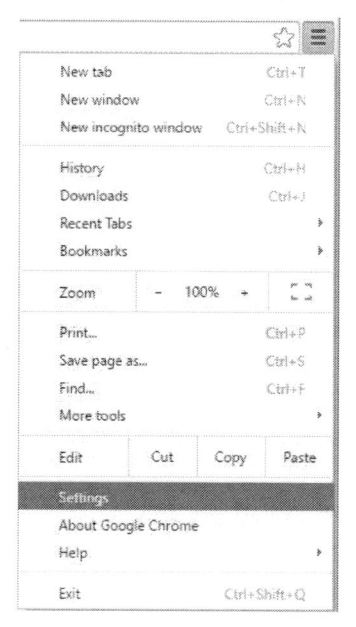

2. Scroll down to *Privacy*. Enable *Enable phishing and malware protection* and *Do Not Track*.

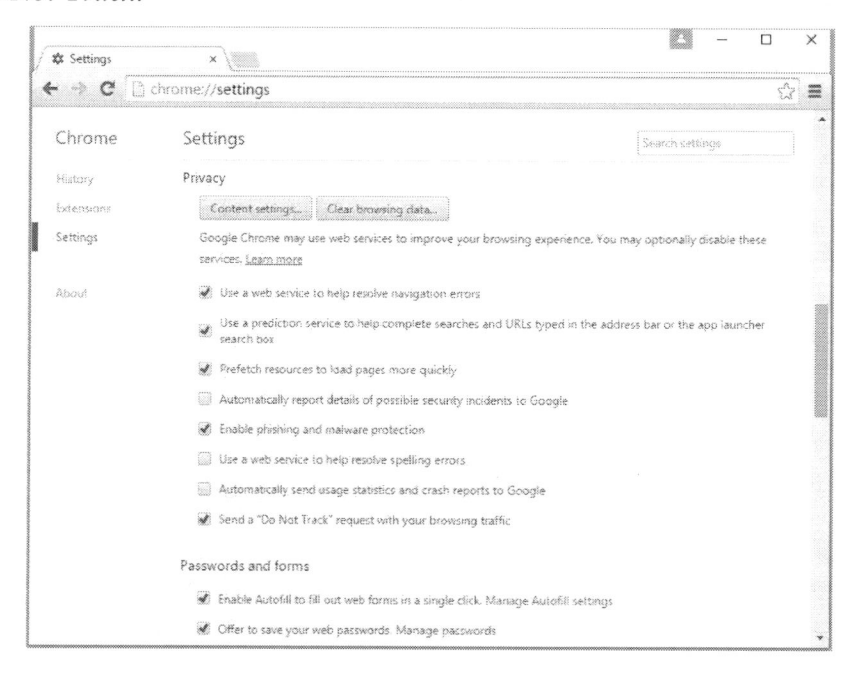

13. Vulnerability: Web Browsing

Assignment: Secure the Edge Browser

The Edge browser settings for proper security are very similar to the ones for Firefox and Chrome.

1. Open *Edge* and click on the menu item (3 dots), and click *Settings*.

13. Vulnerability: Web Browsing

2. Scroll down and click *Advanced Settings*.

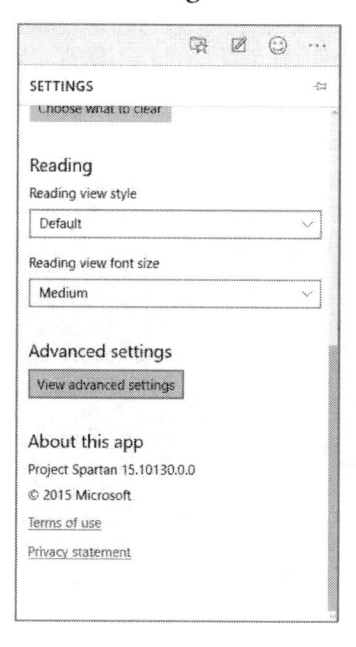

13. Vulnerability: Web Browsing

3. Scroll down again and set *Cookies* to *Block only third party cookies*, *Do Not Track* to *on*, and *Help protect me from malicious sites and downloads with SmartScreen Filter* to *on*.

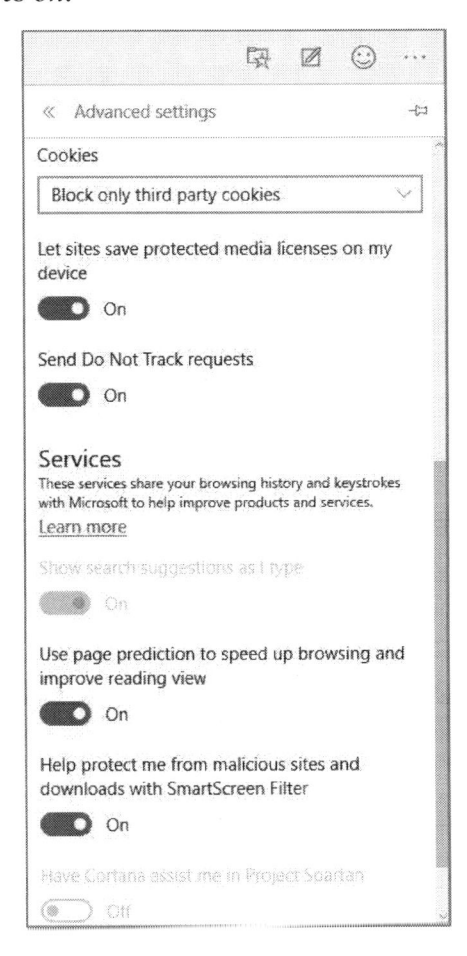

13. Vulnerability: Web Browsing

Web Scams

Over the past couple of years, a new type of scam has become popular. Instead of directly compromising the user computer, web sites are either compromised, or are deliberately designed to be malicious.

When a user visits such a site, they may receive a pop-up window stating something to the effect of: *Your computer has been found to be infected with XX viruses. Please call Apple at XXX-XXX-XXXX to have this infection removed.*

Upon calling the provided toll-free phone number (which, of course, is not really Apple, but that of the scammer), with your permission, they will install remote control software. After looking around your computer, they will assure they can remove the malware for only $$$.

There are two problems here. First, they have installed remote control software that allows the criminal access any time they wish. This gives them access to your usernames, passwords, banking, and other information. The second is that they now have your credit card information.

What to do if this happens to you?

1. Don't call!

In most cases, the malicious website has modified your web browser preferences to make the malicious page your home page.

13. Vulnerability: Web Browsing

Tor

Tor *http://en.wikipedia.org/wiki/Tor_(anonymity_network)* is a technology developed by the US Department of the Navy that enables anonymous web browsing. It has long since been released to the open source community for the public to use in the form of the *Tor Browser*. Many people within the security community are strong supporters of Tor, including Edward Snowden. Entire books have been written on just Tor. I'm not so sadistic as to subject you to that. What we are going to do is cut to the core of Tor, and learn the basics of how to surf the web anonymously.

The advantages of Tor include:

- Strong anonymity for all activity on the Internet.

- Can be used with Tails at *https://tails.boum.org*, which is a bootable, self-contained, flash drive that can run on most Windows, Linux, and Apple computers that leaves no trace behind

- The bootable Tails flash drive can be immediately disconnected from the host computer, causing the computer to erase memory of all trace of your session, and reboot.

These features make Tor ideal for those in oppressed countries, journalists working undercover, and anyone who may need to use someone else's computer and leave no trace behind.

Tor works by encrypting your packets as they leave your computer, routing the packets to a Tor relay computer hosted by thousands of volunteers on their own systems, many of which are co-located at ISPs. The relay knows where the packet came from, and the next relay the packet is handed to, but that is all. The user computer automatically configures encrypted connections through the relays. Packets will pass through several relays before being delivered to the intended destination. Tor will use the same relays for around 10 minutes, and then different relays will be randomly selected to create the next path for 10 minutes.

Alas, there is no free lunch. The encryption process and the relay process combine to create *latency*, which mean a delay in processing. Most users will experience around a four-fold performance degradation. So, if accessing a web page without Tor normally takes 3 seconds, it may take 12 seconds with Tor.

Something that Tor proponents tend to minimize is that Tor was developed by the U.S. Department of the Navy for military use, and then made available to the open source community. It is no secret that the U.S. government (and very likely other governments) host relays with the purpose of being able to monitor traffic over Tor. Several high-profile arrests have been made because of this tactic.

Even though Tor does as good a job as anything to keep you anonymous on the Internet, you must take precautions to protect your identity. These steps include:

- Don't enable JavaScript when using Tor. This has been used to track users within the Tor network.

- Don't reveal your name or other personal information in web forms.

- Don't customize the Tails boot flash drive. This will create a unique digital fingerprint that can be used to identify you.

- Connect to sites that use HTTPS so your communication is encrypted point to point.

For many security-conscious users, Tor becomes their only tool for defense. However, Tor by itself is a partial solution at best. It can protect your anonymity while surfing the web. At the very least, this still leaves email and messaging to be secured. A bigger issue is what to do when you need to use a computer and leave no trace behind on that system. This is where *Tails* comes into play.

Tails is a Linux Debian fork designed with two primary purposes in mind:

- Provide a highly secure operating system in a format that can be booted from either DVD or thumb drive on almost any PC or Apple computer, and

- Include the tools and applications necessary to provide a secure, anonymous Internet experience

What this means is that you can create a thumb drive that has an operating system capable of booting almost any computer, whereby you can then run Tor for secure anonymous Internet activity, send and receive email that is securely encrypted with GPG/PGP, and message with others in complete privacy. Then, when you

13. Vulnerability: Web Browsing

remove the Tails thumb drive, there is absolutely no record of your activity on either the computer *or* the thumb drive!

For those of you chomping at the bit to just use Tor, we will start there. When your curiosity has been satisfied, please take the next step to learn Tails at *https://tails.boum.org*.

Assignment: Install Tor for Anonymous Internet Browsing

Tor is a stripped down, simplified Firefox browser, designed to provide an encrypted, anonymous browsing experience. In this assignment, we will download and install Tor.

1. As a first step, we need to know our public IP address. This information will be used a few steps away to verify Tor has hidden our address. Open a web browser to *http://whatismyip.com*. Write down *Your IP Address*.

13. Vulnerability: Web Browsing

2. Open a web browser and go to *https://www.torproject.org*. Select the *Download* button.

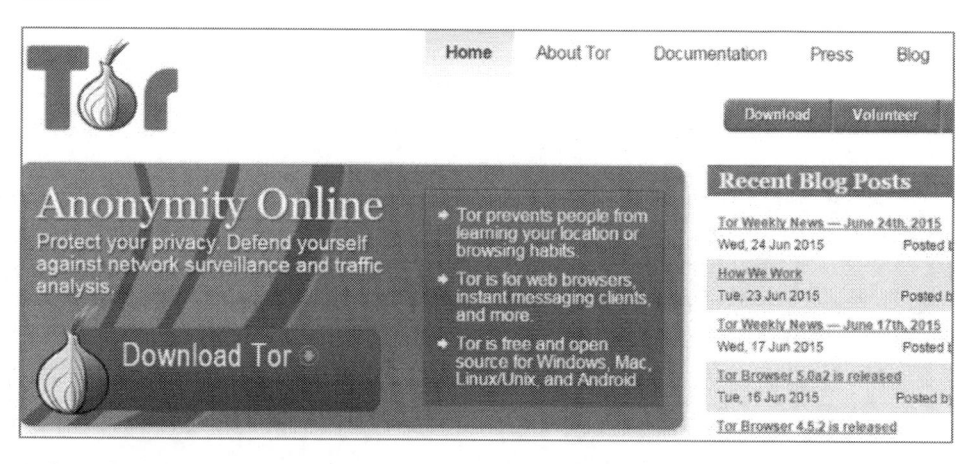

3. Select the *Download Tor Browser* button. The Tor installer will begin to download.

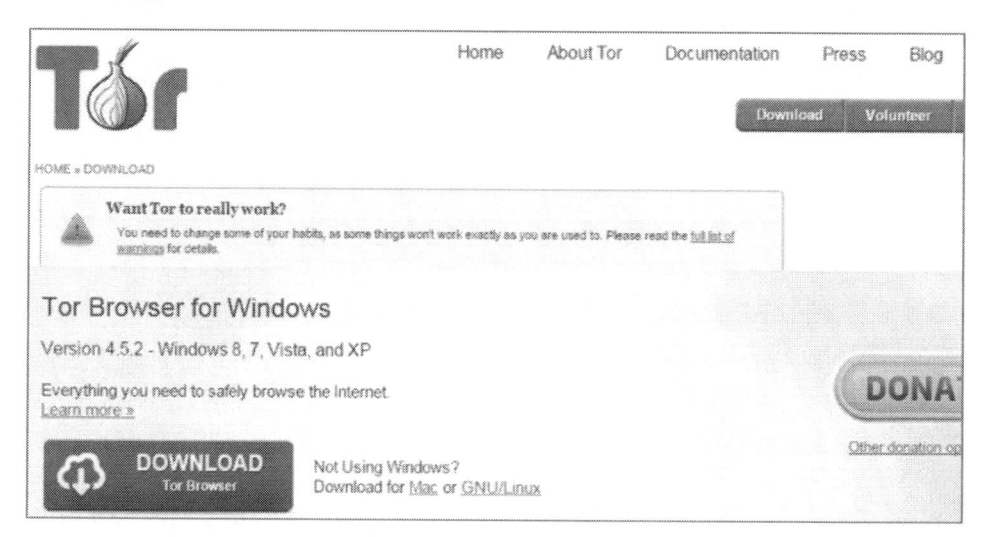

4. While the download is in progress, scroll down the page to read all the other steps that one must take to ensure your privacy is maintained. These include:

   - **Use the Tor Browser.** If you are concerned about protecting your privacy and security, do not use other browsers.

- **Don't torrent over Tor.** If you wish to file-share via torrent, don't use Tor. It is painfully slow; it slows down others using the Tor network, and in many cases, torrent software bypasses all of the security and anonymity precautions built into Tor.

- **Don't enable or install browser plugins in Tor.** Tor is designed to protect your security and anonymity. Many innocuous-looking plugins break that security.

- **Use HTTPS versions of websites.** Tor has *HTTPS Everywhere* built in (more on HTTPS Everywhere later in this book.) It will force a secure connection if a website has an option for https. This will enable a point-to-point encryption between your computer and the web server.

- **Don't open documents downloaded through Tor while online.** Many documents – particularly .doc, .xls, .ppt, and .pdf – contain links or resources that will force a download when the document is opened. If they are opened while Tor is open, they will reveal your true IP address and you will lose your anonymity and security. If you are concerned about these issues, we strongly recommend that you instead:

    - **Open the documents on a computer fully disconnected from the Internet.** This prevents any malicious files from "phoning home" or infecting your computer.

    - **Install a Virtual Machine (VM) such as Parallels, Fusion, or VirtualBox, configured with no network connection, and open documents within the VM.** This is an alternate way to prevent malicious files from phoning home or infecting your computer.

    - **Or use Tor while within Tails.** This is an alternative way to prevent malicious files from phoning home or infecting your computer.

- **Use bridges and/or find company.** Tor cannot prevent someone from looking at your Internet traffic to discover you are using Tor. If this is a concern for you, reduce the risk by configuring Tor to use a *Tor Bridge relay* instead of a direct connection to the Tor network. Another option is to have many other users running Tor on the same network. In this way, your use of Tor is hidden.

5. Click on the Tor installer. When the security screen appears, press *Run*.
6. Run through the install wizard. When installation is finished, press *Finish*.
7. The *Tor Network Settings* window appears. Select how you would like to connect to the Tor Network

    - *I would like to connect directly to the Tor network.* This will work in most situations. This option provides a faster Internet experience with no additional configuration. The possible downside is that a network administrator or your ISP is able to see that you are using the Tor Network.

    - *This computer's Internet connection is censored or proxied. I need to configure bridge or proxy settings.* This option provides a more secure and anonymous Internet experience because a network administrator or ISP is unable to see you using the Tor Network. The downside is a slower Internet experience, and some additional configuration.

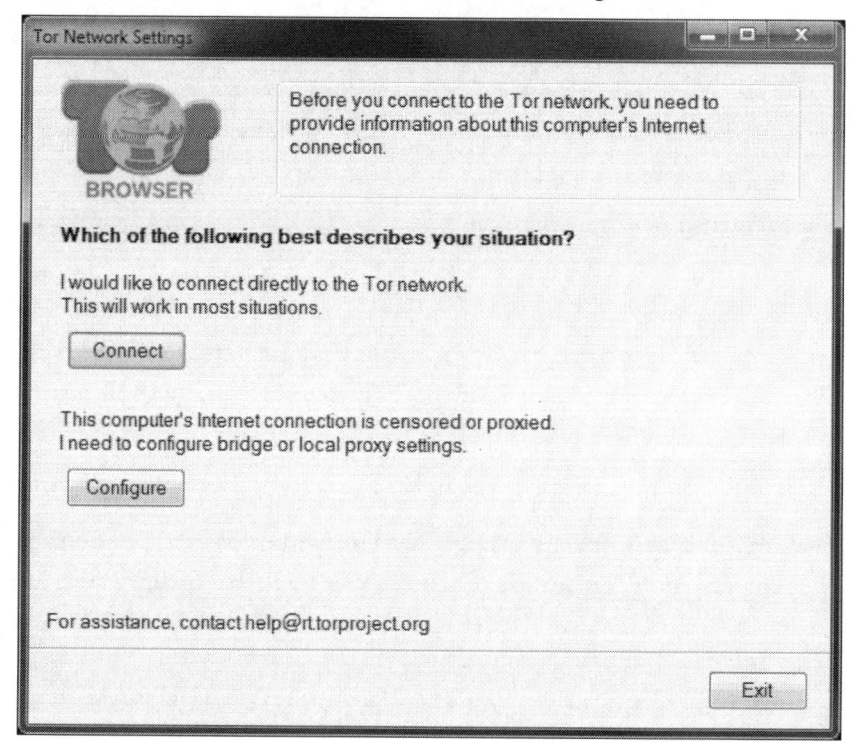

13. Vulnerability: Web Browsing

8. If you selected *This computer's Internet connection is censored or proxied. I need to configure bridge or proxy settings*, then continue. If you selected *I would like to connect directly to the Tor network*, skip to step 12. Select *Next*.

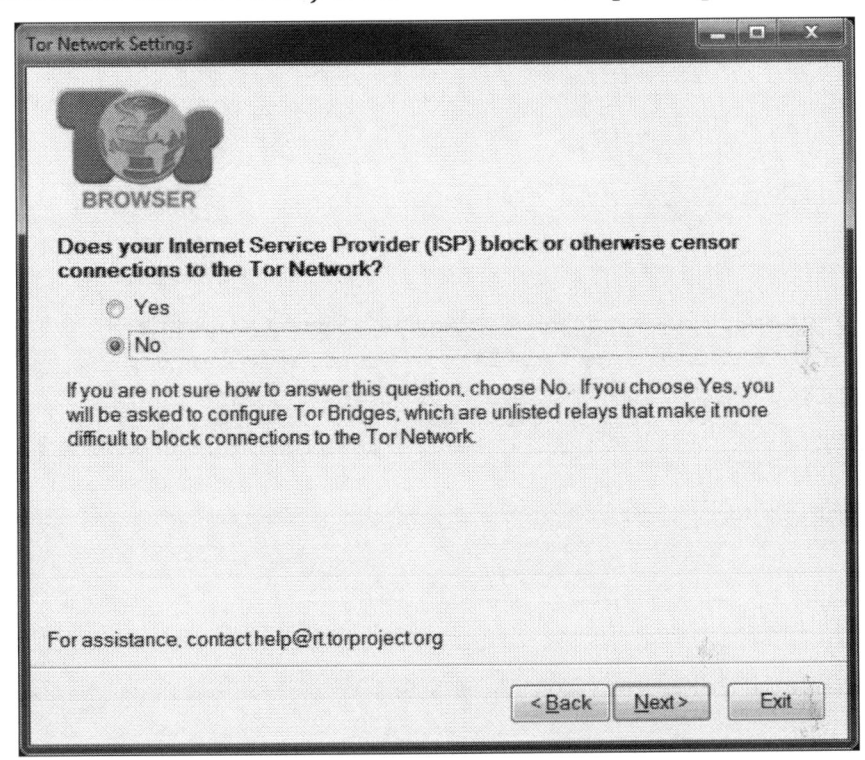

13. Vulnerability: Web Browsing

9. If you selected *Yes* to the *Does your ISP block or otherwise censor connections to the Tor Network* window, you now see the *You may use the provided set of bridges or you may obtain and enter a customer set of bridges* window. Select *Connect with provided bridges, Transport type obsf3 (recommended)*, and then select the *Connect* button.

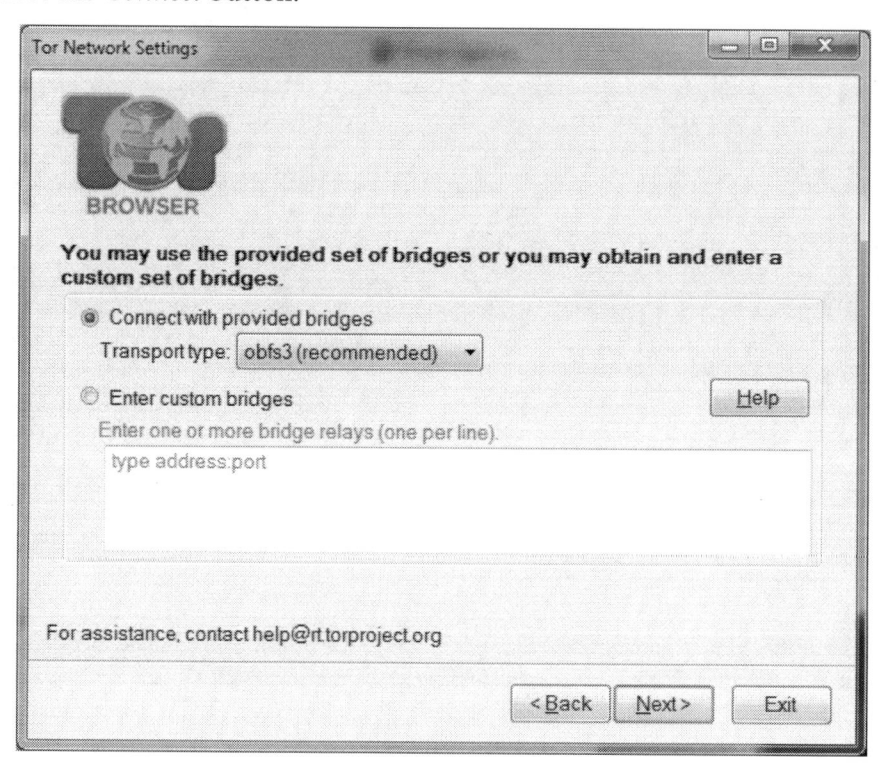

-318-

13. Vulnerability: Web Browsing

10. If you elected to use a Tor bridge relay, the following window appears. If your network requires a proxy to access the Internet, go to the next step and select *Continue*. Otherwise, select *No, then* select the *Connect* button and skip to step 12.

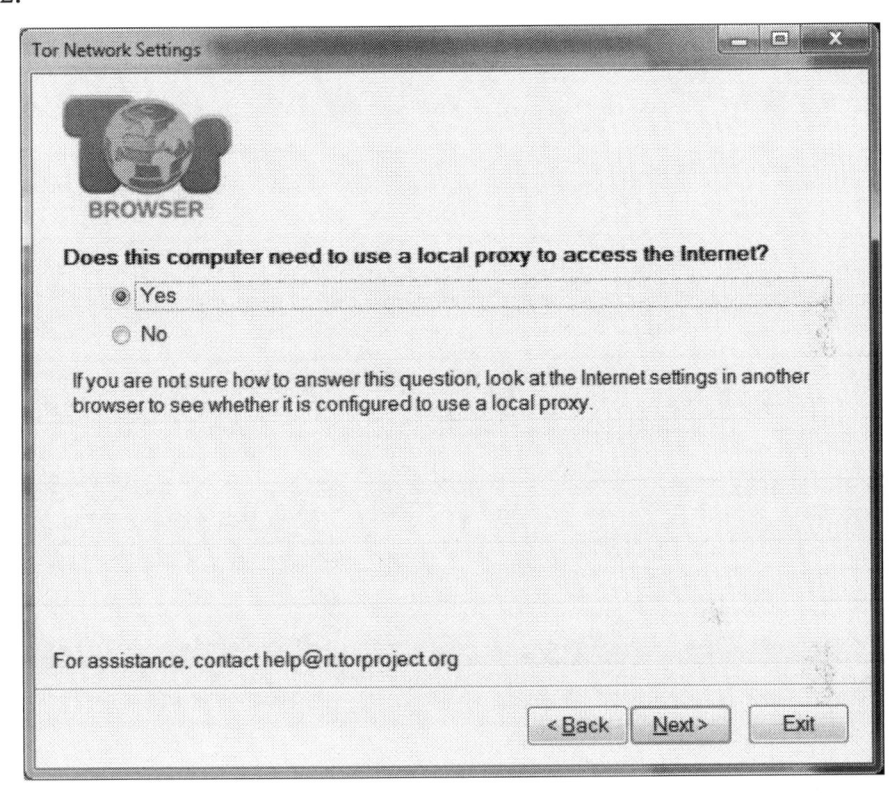

13. Vulnerability: Web Browsing

11. If you selected *Yes* to *Does this computer need to use a proxy to access the Internet,* you will now see the *Enter the Proxy settings* window.

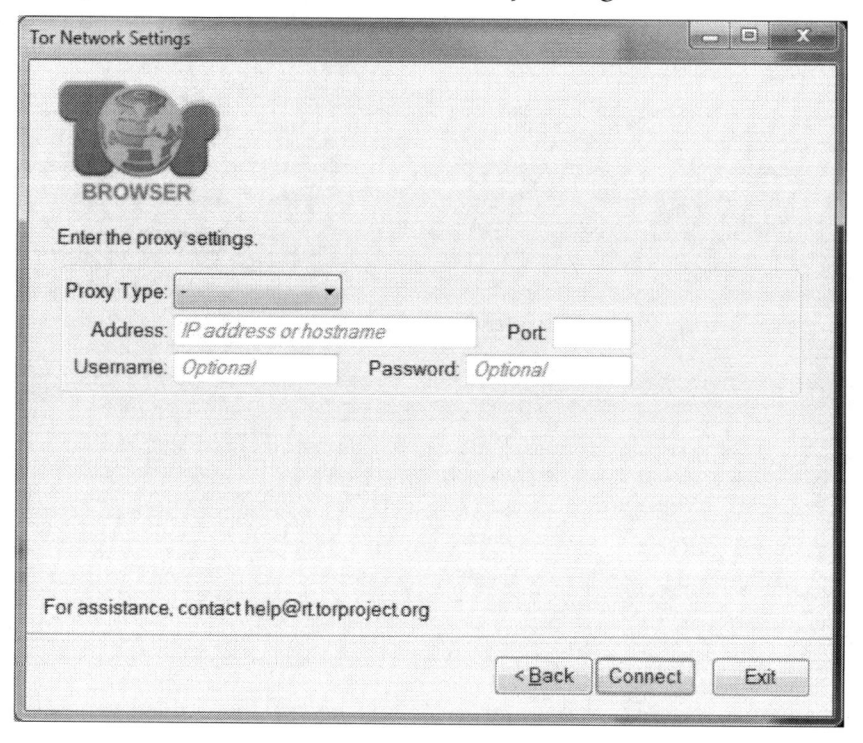

13. Vulnerability: Web Browsing

12. These will be the same settings your computer requires normally, and if used, will be found in *Control Panel > Internet Options > Connections* tab. Copy your settings from this pane into the Tor window, and then select the *Connect* button. Copy the proxy settings from *Internet Options* and then select *Connect*.

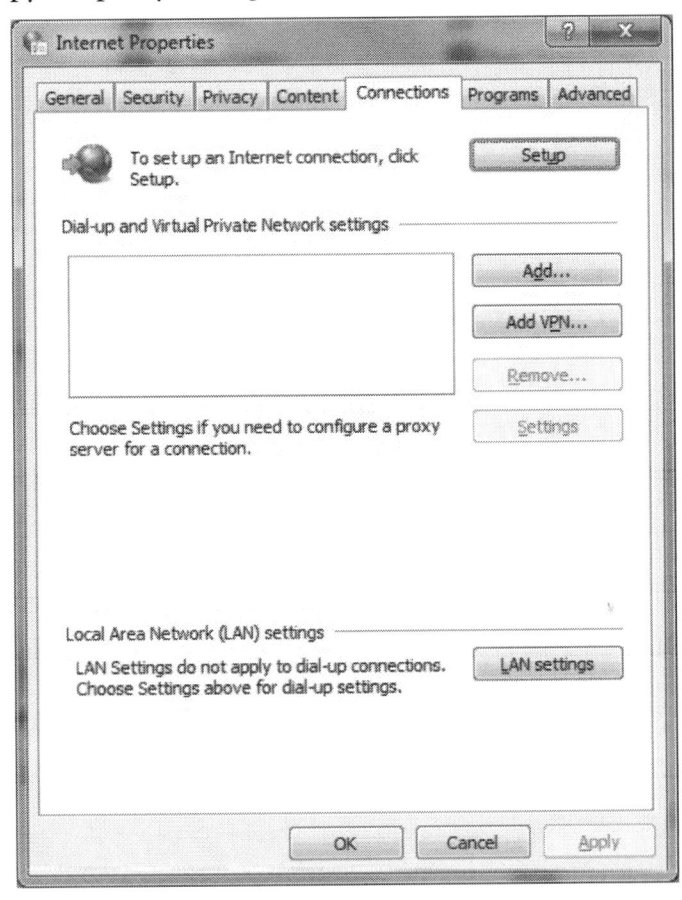

13. Vulnerability: Web Browsing

13. The TorBrowser updates often. If your copy is out of date, you will be welcomed by a message asking you to update. Follow the instructions, clicking on the *onion* icon > *Download Tor Browser Bundle Update*...to update. Once the download is complete, quit Tor Browser, and then replace it with the new version. Otherwise, if you are up to date, skip to the next step.

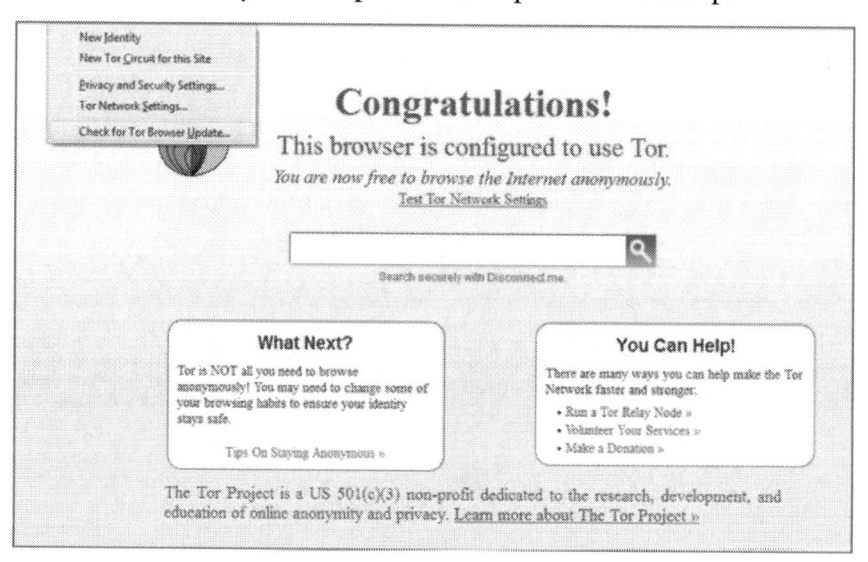

13. Vulnerability: Web Browsing

14. It is vital to test your connection to verify your IP address is hidden. On the Tor home page, select the *Test Tor Network Settings* link. You can also return to *https://whatismyip.com* as well.

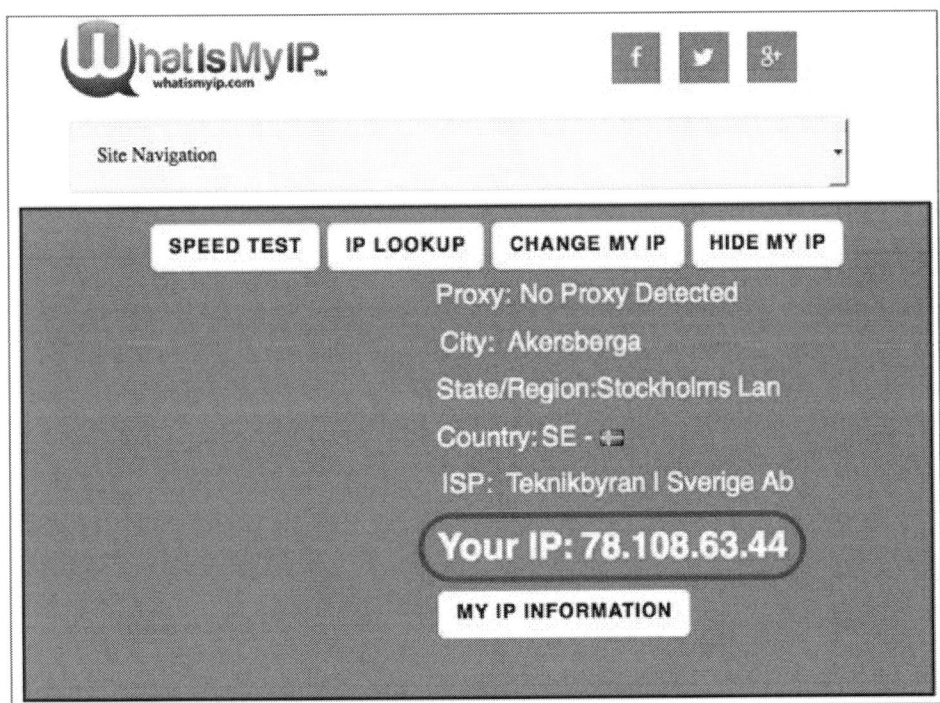

Congratulations. This browser is configured to use Tor.

Your IP address appears to be: **78.108.63.44**

WhatIsMyIP
whatismyip.com

Site Navigation

SPEED TEST | IP LOOKUP | CHANGE MY IP | HIDE MY IP

Proxy: No Proxy Detected
City: Akersberga
State/Region: Stockholms Lan
Country: SE -
ISP: Teknikbyran I Sverige Ab

Your IP: **78.108.63.44**

MY IP INFORMATION

Wahoo–you are now on Tor, completely anonymous and encrypted on the Internet.

The next step is to configure Tor.

Assignment: Configure Tor Preferences

One of the first things one should do when launching an application for the first time is to configure its preferences. No different for Tor. In this assignment, we will configure Tor preferences.

1. Open TorBrowser, and then select the *TorBrowser menu* (3 lines) > *Options* > *General* tab. This pane may be configured to taste.

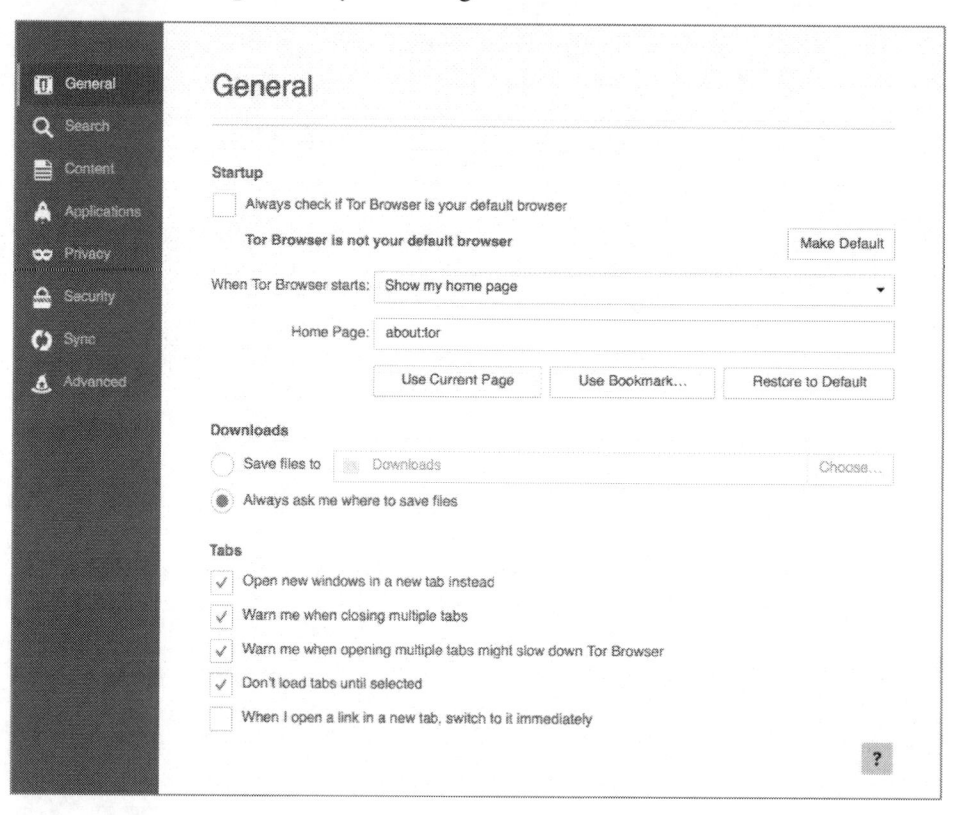

13. Vulnerability: Web Browsing

2. Select the *Search* tab.

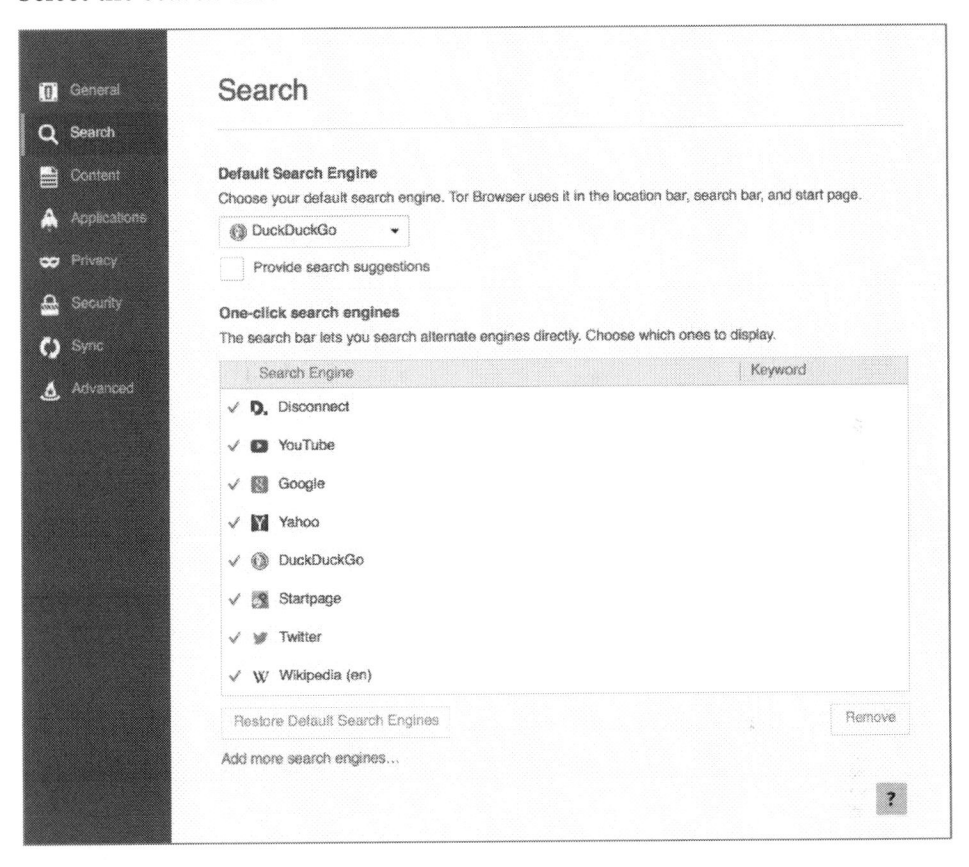

- For *Default Search Engine*, select *DuckDuckGo*.
- Other settings may be configured to your taste.

13. Vulnerability: Web Browsing

3. Select the *Content* tab. Configure to your taste.

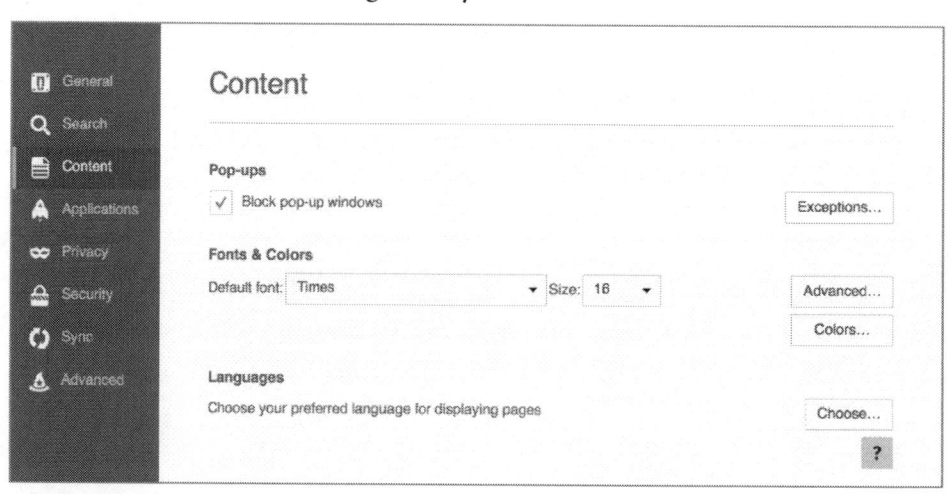

4. Select the *Applications* tab. Configure to your taste.

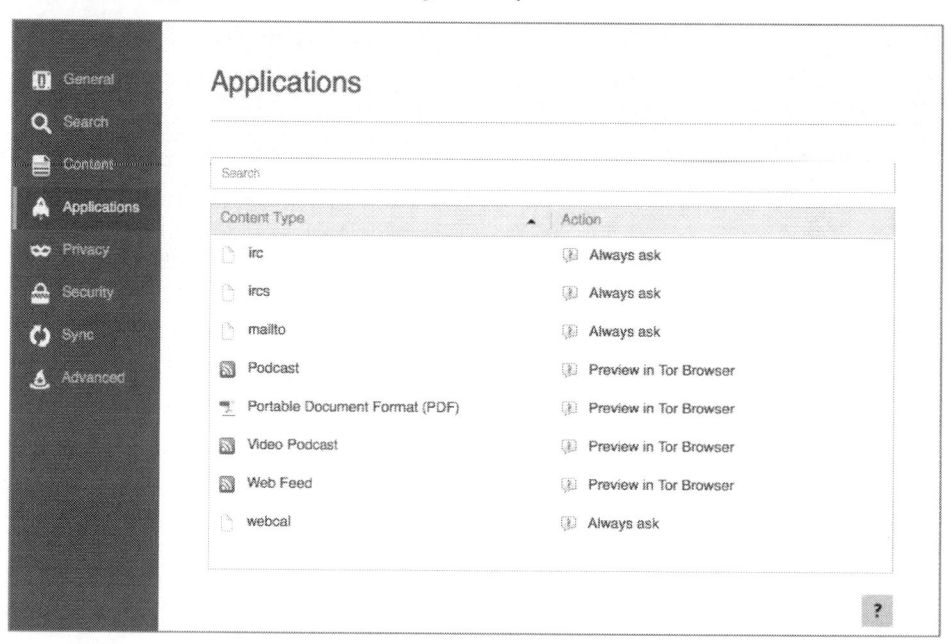

5. Select the *Privacy* tab.

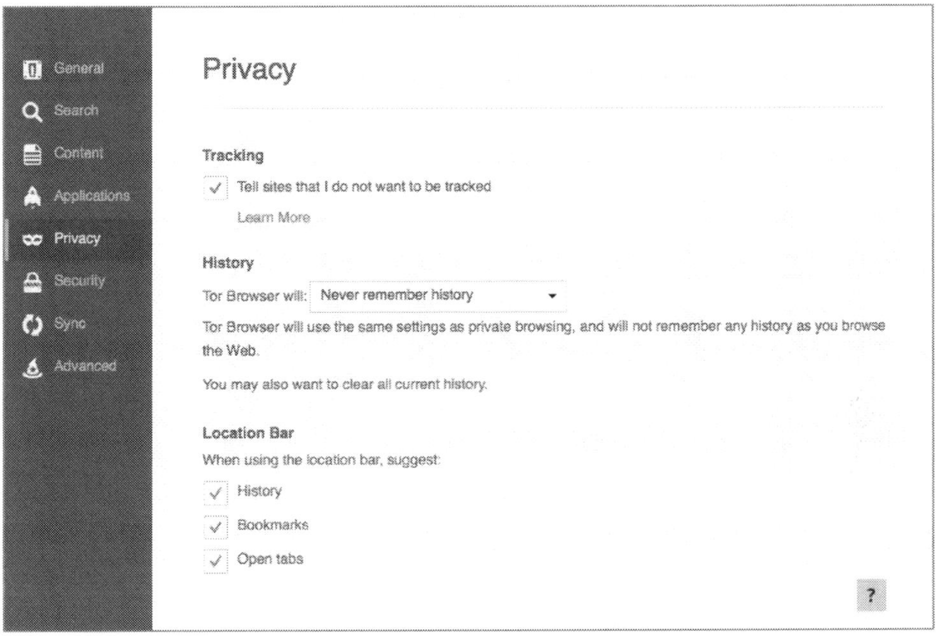
General
Search
Content
Applications
Privacy
Security
Sync
Advanced
Privacy
Tracking
Tell sites that I do not want to be tracked
Learn More
History
Tor Browser will:
Never remember history
Tor Browser will use the same settings as private browsing, and will not remember any history as you browse the Web.
You may also want to clear all current history.
Location Bar
When using the location bar, suggest:
History
Bookmarks
Open tabs
?

- Enable *Tell sites that I do not want to be tracked.*
- Configure other settings to your taste.

13. Vulnerability: Web Browsing

6. Select the *Security* tab.

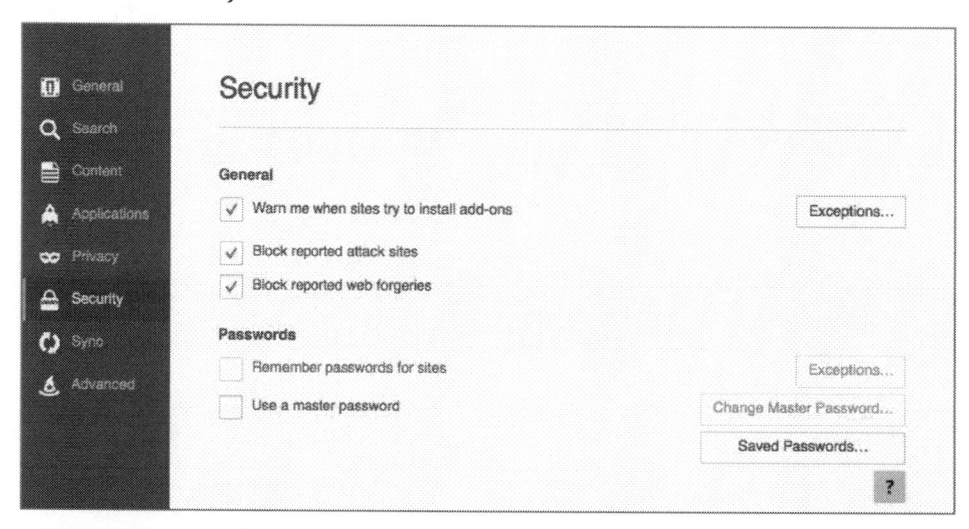

   - Enable *Warn me when sites try to install add-ons.*
   - Enable *Block reported attack sites.*
   - Enable *Block reported web forgeries.*
   - Configure other settings to your taste.

7. Select the *Sync* tab.

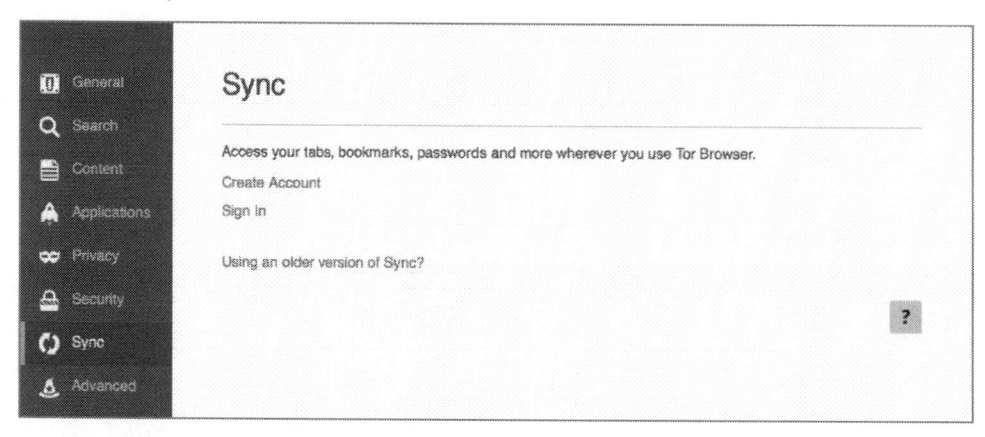

   - Configure to your taste.

13. Vulnerability: Web Browsing

8. Select the *Advanced* tab, and then select the *General* tab.

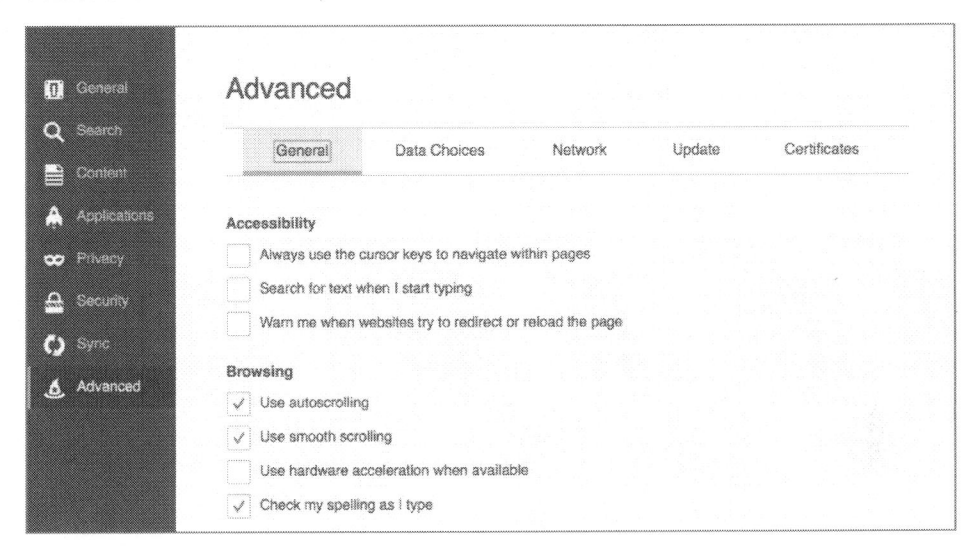

- Configure to your taste.

9. Select the *Data Choices* tab, and configure to your taste.

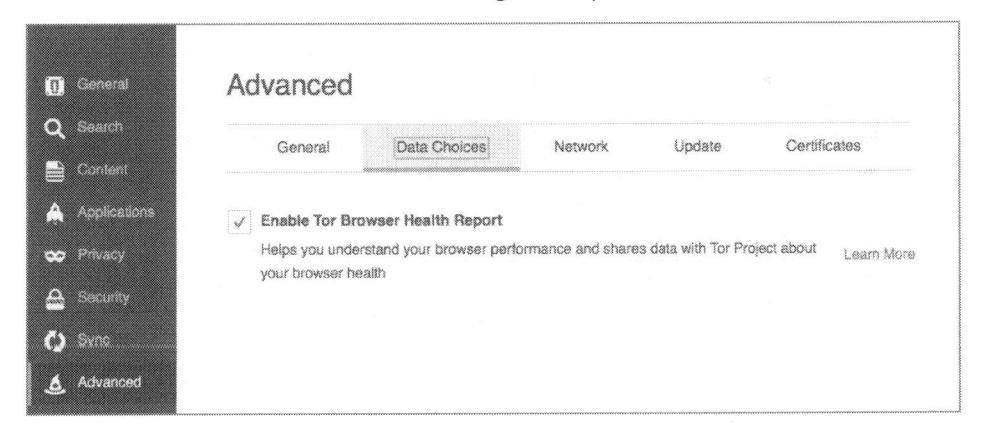

13. Vulnerability: Web Browsing

10. Select the *Network* tab.

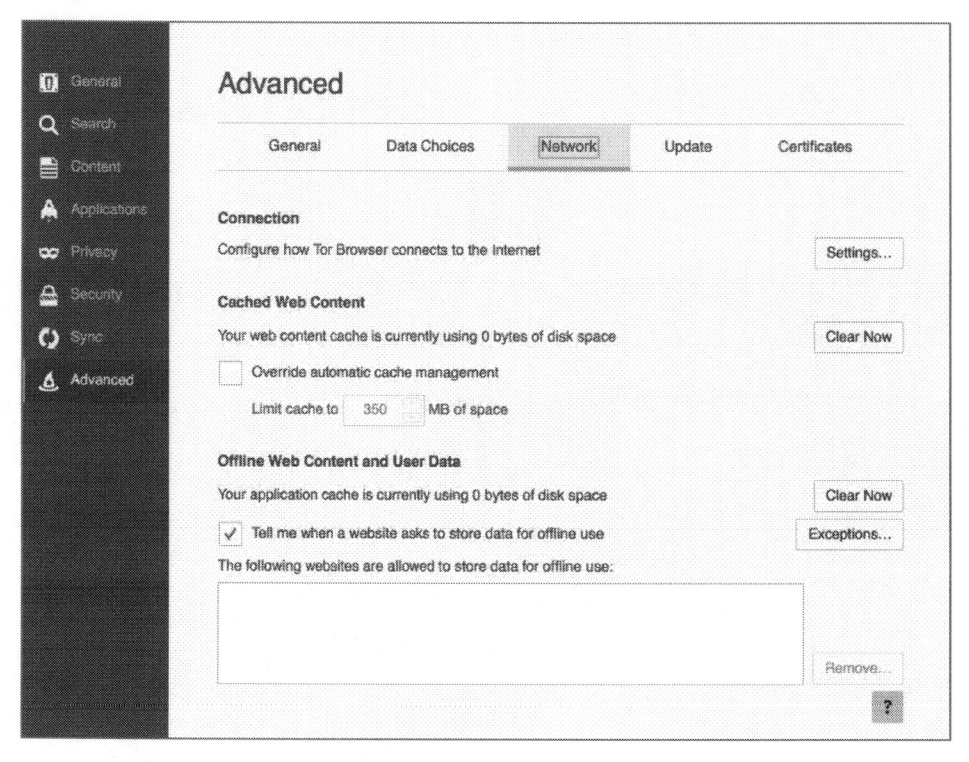

- Enable *Tell me when a website asks to store data for offline use.*
- Configure other settings to taste.

13. Vulnerability: Web Browsing

11. Select the *Update* tab.

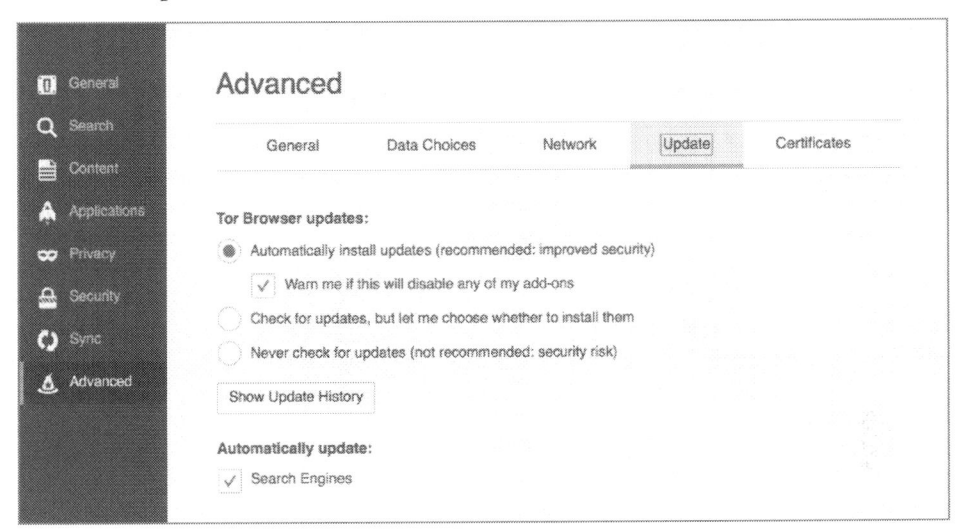

- Enable *Automatically install updates (recommended: improved security)*.
- Enable *Warn me if this will disable any of my add-ons*.
- Enable *Automatically update: Search Engines*.
- Configure other settings to taste.

13. Vulnerability: Web Browsing

12. Select the *Certificates* tab.

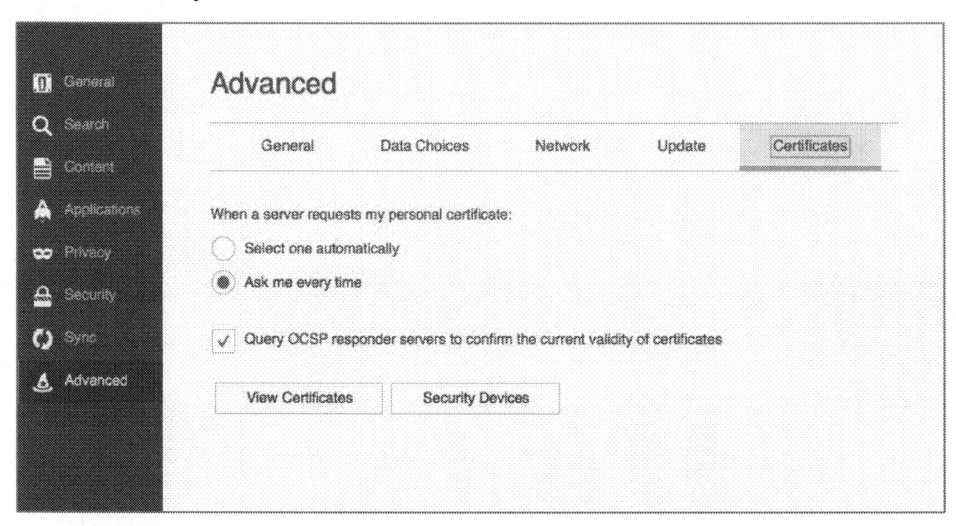

- Enable *Ask me every time.*
- Enable *Query OCSP responder servers to confirm the current validity of certificates.*

13. Close the preferences tab in Tor.

Great work! You are now ready to use Tor to securely and anonymously browse the Internet.

But remember, Tor is just one small part of *real* anonymity and security on the Internet. Many in the Internet Security field (including Edward Snowden) believe that to do this right, you will want a bootable Tails thumb drive. Learn all about it in our upcoming *Practical Paranoia: Tails Security Essentials* book. In the meantime, visit the Tails home page at *https://tails.boum.org.*

Onion Sites and the Deep Web

Tor not only allows you to have anonymous access to your regular web sites, it is also the only gateway to the *Deep web https://en.wikipedia.org/wiki/Deep_web_(search)*. The deep web is also known as the *Invisible Web*. It consists of web content deliberately not indexed with standard search engines, and only accessible by Tor. These sites are also called *Onion sites,* as they end with *.onion.*

Although the deep web is primarily thought of as a collection of sites to sell illegal products and services, it is also good and responsible uses for it. For example, in repressive countries such sites provide an avenue for freedom workers to work, for reporters to securely exchange information with sources (Ed Snowden did this), and there are sites to provide resources for whistleblowers.

As the deep web is not indexed by Google, Bing, or any other standard search engine, how do you go about discovering its resources? The list is in constant flux, but as of this writing, here are some good starting points:

- TorLinks *http://torlinkbgs6aabns.onion*
- Torch *http://xmh57jrzrnw6insl.onion/*

13. Vulnerability: Web Browsing

Review Questions

1. HTTPS uses the _____ encryption protocol.
2. To ensure your browser goes to https even if entering https, install the _____ plug-in.
3. To ensure your browser doesn't store browsing history, passwords, user names, list of downloads, cookies, or cached files, enable _____ mode.
4. By default, any two people will have the same results for a given Google search. (True or False)
5. By default, any two people will have the same results for a given DuckDuckGo search (True or False)
6. TOR is based on the _____ browser.
7. It is OK to install browser plug-ins to TOR. (True or False)

14. Vulnerability: Email

Human beings the world over need freedom and security that they may be able to realize their full potential.

–Aung San Suu Kyi, Burmese opposition politician and chairperson of the National League for Democracy

14. Vulnerability: Email

The Killer App

It can be rightfully argued that email is the killer app that brought the Internet out of the geek world of university and military usage and into our homes (that is, if you can ignore the overwhelming impact of Internet pornography.) Most email users live in some foggy surreal world with the belief they have a God or constitutionally given right to privacy in their email communications.

No such right exists. Google, Yahoo., Microsoft, Comcast, or whoever hosts your email service all are very likely to turn over all records of your email whenever a government agency asks for that data. In most cases, your email is sent and received in clear text so that anyone along the dozens of routers and servers between you and the other person can clearly read your messages. Add to this knowledge the recent revelations about PRISM *https://en.wikipedia.org/wiki/PRISM_(surveillance_program)*, where we now know that the government does not have to ask your provider for records. The government simply *has* your records.

If you find this distasteful, then here is how to put an end to it.

14. Vulnerability: Email

Phishing

The act of phishing is epidemic on the Internet. Phishing *https://en.wikipedia.org/wiki/Phishing* is the attempt to acquire your sensitive information by appearing as a trustworthy source. This is most often attempted via email.

The way the process often works is that you receive an email from what appears to be a trustworthy source, such as your bank. The email provides some motivator to contact the source, along with what appears to be a legitimate link to the source website.

When you click the link, you are taken to what appears to be the trustworthy source (perhaps the website of your bank), where you are prompted to enter your username and password.

At that point they have you. The site is a fraud, and you have just given the criminals your credentials to access your bank account. In a few moments your account may be emptied.

The key to preventing a successful phishing attack to be aware of the *real* URL behind the link provided in the email.

14. Vulnerability: Email

The link that appears in an email may have nothing at all to do with where the link takes you. To see the *real* link, hover (don't click) your cursor over the link. After 3 seconds, the *real* link will pop-up.

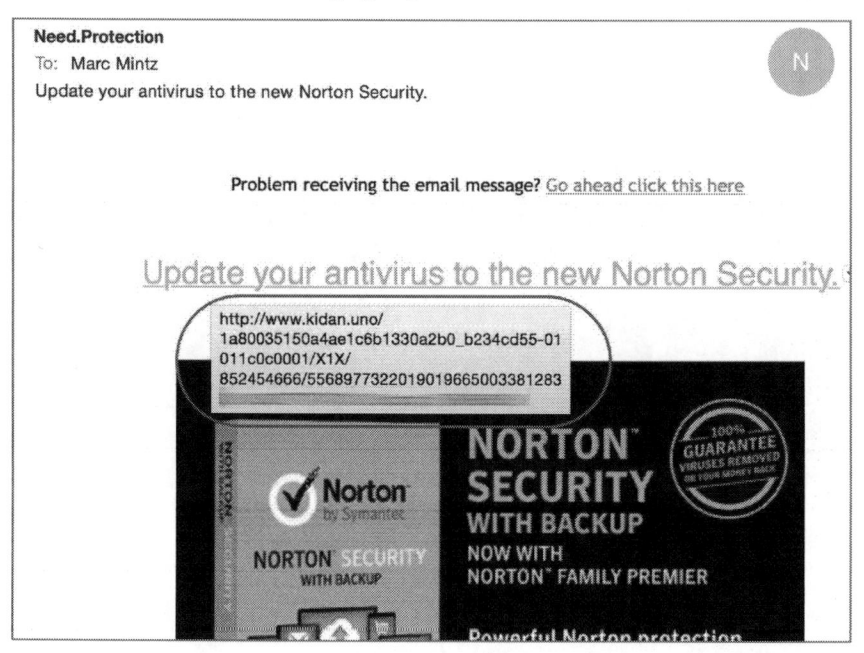

Some of these scams are getting a bit more sophisticated in their choice of URL links, and attempt to make them appear more legitimate. For example, the email may say it is from *Bank of America*, and the link say *bankofamerica.com*, but the actual URL will be *bankofamerica.tv*, or *bankofamerica.xyz.com*.

If you have any doubts at all, it is best to contact your bank, stockbroker, insurance agent, etc. directly by their known email or phone number.

14. Vulnerability: Email

Email Encryption Protocols

There are three common protocols that provide encryption of email between the user's computer and the user's email server:

- **TLS**, (Transport Layer Security)
  http://en.wikipedia.org/wiki/Secure_Sockets_Layer

- **SSL**, (Secure Socket Layer) the TLS predecessor:
  http://en.wikipedia.org/wiki/Secure_Sockets_Layer

- **HTTPS**, (Hypertext Transport Layer Secure)
  http://en.wikipedia.org/wiki/Https

Understand that these protocols only encrypt the message as it travels between your computer and your email server and back. Once your encrypted mail passes from your computer to your email server, it becomes clear text from your email server, through dozens of Internet routers, to the recipient email server.

TLS and SSL

In order to use TLS or SSL, the following criteria must be met:

- Your email provider offers a TLS or SSL option. Unfortunately, many providers do not offer TLS or SSL. If your provider does not, RUN DON'T WALK TO ANOTHER PROVIDER. If you are not sure which email provider to select, I'm a fan of Google mail.

- You are using an email application as opposed to using a web browser to access your email.

- Your email application supports TLS or SSL.

- Your email provider has configured your email service to use TLS or SSL.

- You have configured your email application to use TLS or SSL

- Lastly, although not a requirement for TLS or SSL, a requirement to stall off breaking your password is that your email provider allows for strong passwords, and you have assigned a strong password to your email (many providers still are limited to a maximum of 8 character passwords.)

If you only use a web browser for email, you may skip this assignment and move on to the next where we configure your browser-based email to use https. If you use a local email application for managing your email or aggregating multiple accounts, then this assignment is for you.

There are dozens of stand-alone email clients on the market, some are included with the Operating System, such as Windows's Mail app, others, like Microsoft Outlook, need to be purchased. Along with these bundled and purchased applications, there are others that are completely free.

Since Windows 8, Microsoft has included a basic email app called *Mail* that requires a *Microsoft Account* to use, even if (like me) you only have a Google email address. A *Microsoft Account* is the unified name of previously separate and individual accounts such as Microsoft Passport, .NET Passport, and Windows LiveID. Microsoft heavily pushes a *Microsoft Account* to store your personal data, email, Windows preferences and settings on their cloud servers, thereby

14. Vulnerability: Email

increasing your dependency on them, and allowing them to collect usage data about you.

As a Windows 10 user, a Microsoft Account is completely optional, even if Microsoft persistently nags you to sign up for one. If you don't already have a Microsoft Account in Windows (as opposed to a *Local Account* in Windows), and prefer to use Gmail as your email provider, then I would recommend downloading and installing the open source Mozilla Thunderbird email client to maintain as much privacy and control over your data as possible.

Thunderbird can be downloaded for Windows as well as Mac and Linux at *https://www.mozilla.org/en-US/thunderbird/*

In the following section, we will be walking through configuration of Mozilla Thunderbird (Free), Microsoft Outlook (Paid) and the Windows 10 Mail app (Included with OS).

Assignment: Install Mozilla Thunderbird

Downloading and Installing Mozilla Thunderbird is easy. Simply point your browser to *https://www.mozilla.org/en-US/thunderbird/* and click the download button. Launch the Thunderbird installer from the location the file was saved to, and then choose the default installation options.

Adding an email account in Thunderbird requires knowledge of your email provider's server settings–such as IMAP and SMTP servers and ports–and of course the username and password. Once you have these items, Thunderbird usually auto-configures the technical settings behind the scenes. In the next section, we're going to confirm the technical settings that your email provider uses are secure.

Assignment: Configure Mozilla Thunderbird to Use TLS or SSL

First we need to verify if your email currently uses TLS or SSL:

1. Open Mozilla Thunderbird.

14. Vulnerability: Email

2. Select the *Thunderbird* Menu (3 lines) > *Options* > *Account Settings*.

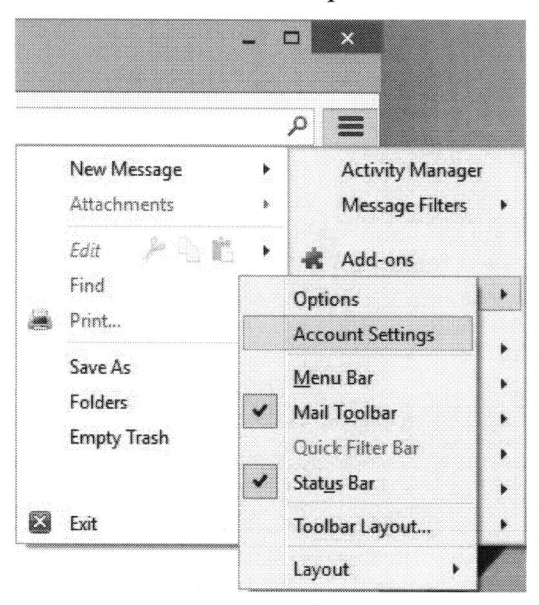

14. Vulnerability: Email

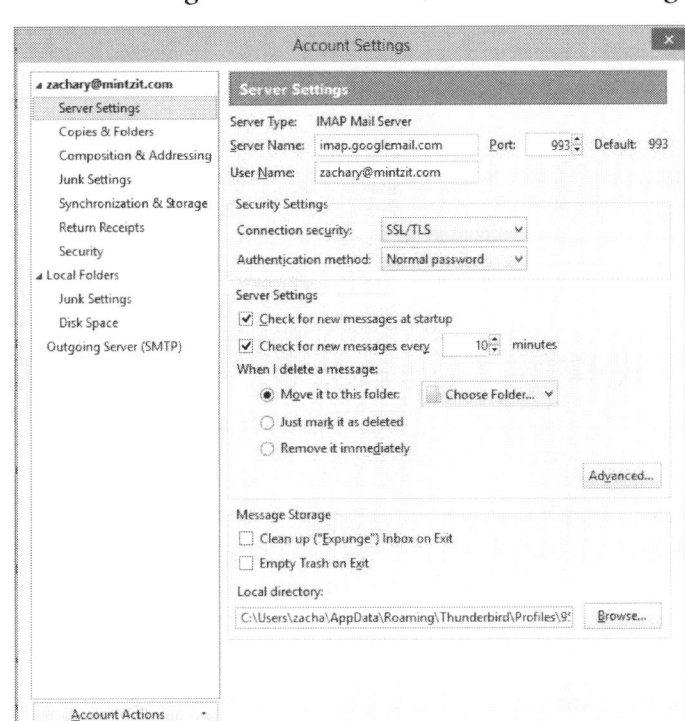

3. From the *Account Settings* window side bar, select *Server Settings*.

   ![Account Settings window showing Server Settings with IMAP Mail Server, imap.googlemail.com, Port 993, SSL/TLS connection security, Normal password authentication]

4. Look at the Security Settings section, and make sure that *SSL/TLS* or *STARTTLS* is selected in the dropdown settings. Most email providers use one of these two connectivity settings. If your connection security is set to *None*, you should contact your email provider for help in securing your mail. If for some reason your email provider does not support SSL/TLS or STARTTLS, change providers immediately.

Next, make sure that all outgoing email from your computer is sent over an encrypted connection.

14. Vulnerability: Email

5. In the left-hand pane, select *Outgoing Server (SMTP)* under your email account.

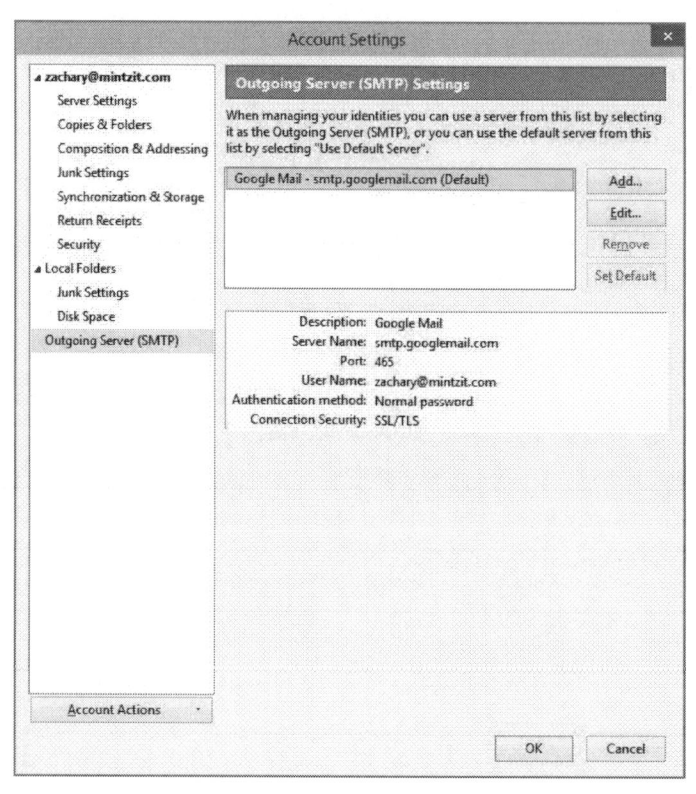

6. In the *Connection Security* section, verify that *SSL/TLS* or *TLS* exists. If no connection security is enabled, or *Password, Transmitted in Plaintext* is listed as the *Authentication Method*, contact your email provider and ask if they do work with TLS or SSL. If they don't, change providers immediately.

7. If they do support TLS or SSL, find out if there are any special settings that need to be changed in this window, and then make the changes.

8. If your password isn't strong (a minimum of 14 characters), now is the time to contact your email vendor's technical support to have it changed. Once changed at that end, enter the new longer password in the *Mail Preferences > Account Information* tab.

You now are sending and receiving encrypted email between your computer and your email server.

14. Vulnerability: Email

Assignment: Configure Microsoft Outlook to Use TLS or SSL

In this assignment we will configure Microsoft Outlook to encrypt email to and from your mail server. First we need to verify if your email currently uses TLS or SSL:

1. Open Microsoft Outlook. In this example, I am using version 2013.
2. Select the *Account Settings > Account Settings* drop down.

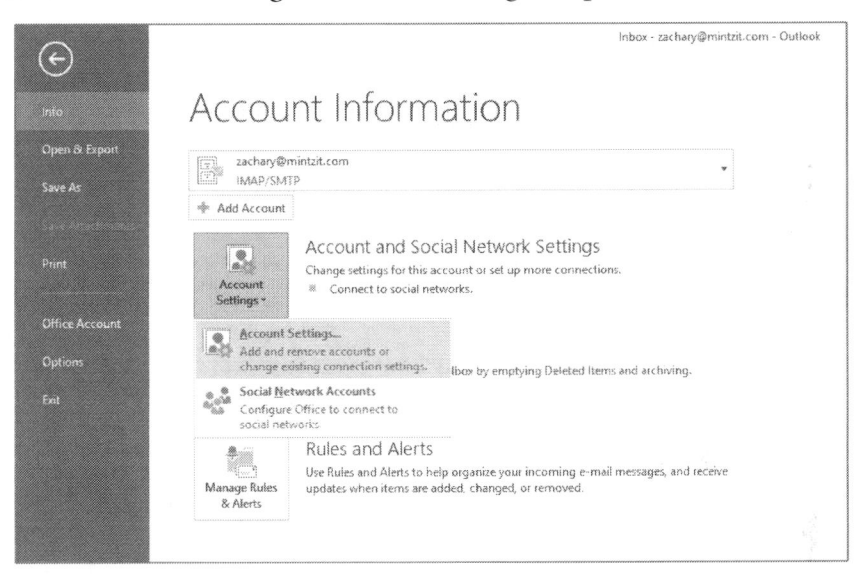

14. Vulnerability: Email

3. In the *Account Settings window,* double-click the name of the account that you would like to inspect.

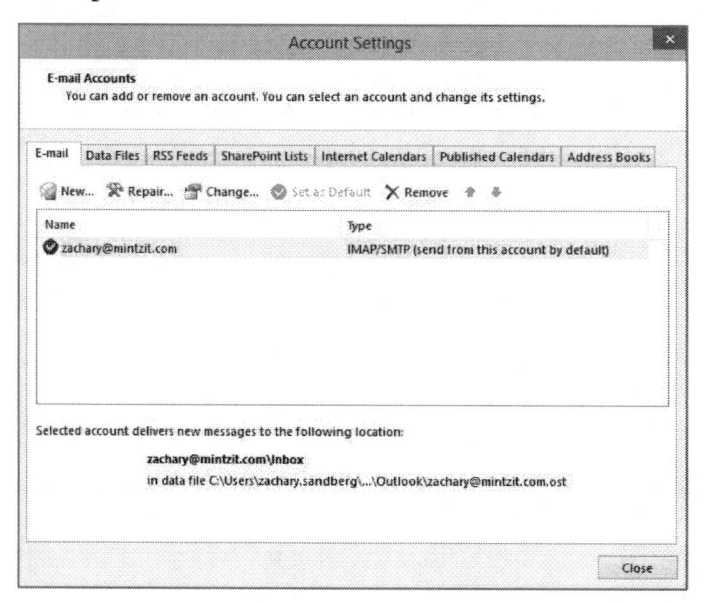

4. Click the *More Settings* button at the bottom right of the window.

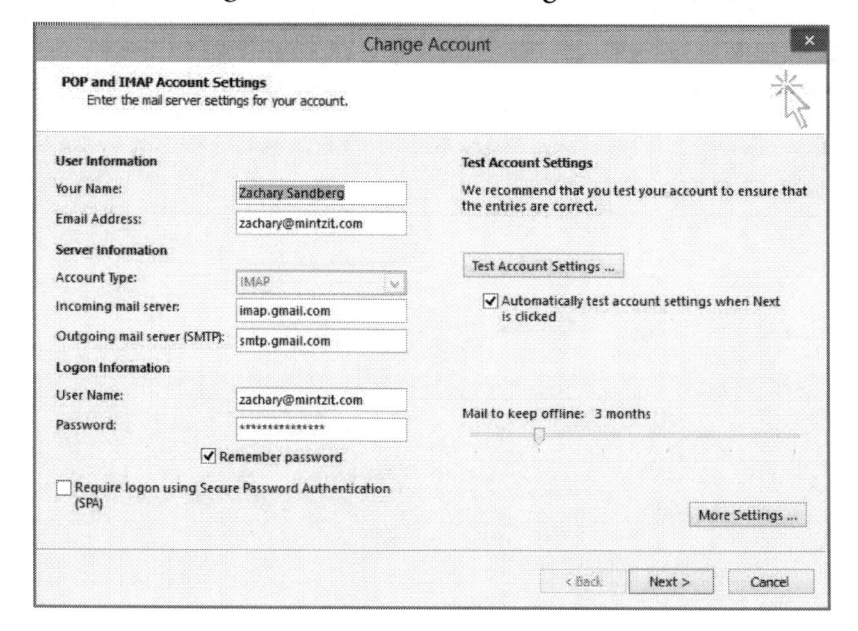

14. Vulnerability: Email

5. Click the *Advanced tab* at the top of the window, and make sure that *SSL* or *TLS* is selected in the drop down settings for both the *Incoming* and *Outgoing* server.

   - Most email providers use one of these two connectivity settings, but if your connection security is set to *None*, you should contact your email provider for help in securing your mail. If for some reason your email provider does not support SSL or TLS, change email providers immediately.

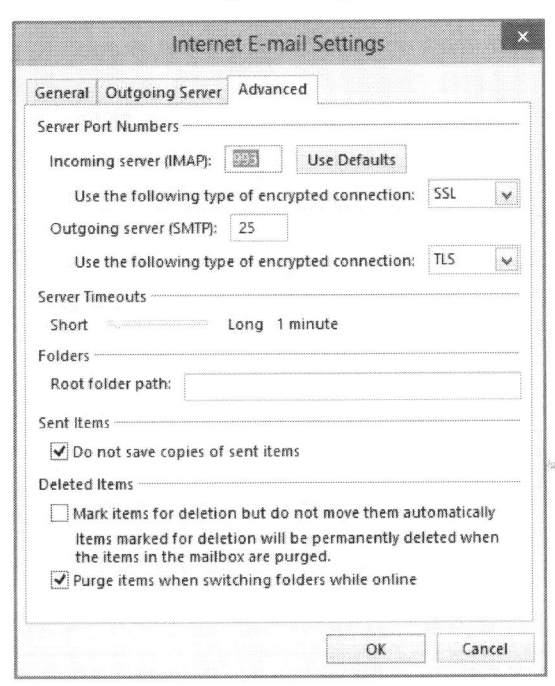

6. If your password is not strong (you want a minimum of 14 characters), now is the time to contact your email vendor's technical support to have it changed. Once changed at that end, enter the new longer password in the *Mail Preferences > Account Information* tab.

Congratulations. You now are sending and receiving encrypted email between your computer and your email server.

14. Vulnerability: Email

HTTPS

HTTPS is an encryption protocol used with web pages. It also can be used to secure email that is accessed via a web browser. When using HTTPS your user name and password are fully encrypted, as are the contents of all email that you create or open.

When using a web browser to access email, it is vital that your email site use the HTTPS encryption protocol to help ensure data and personal security.

Assignment: Configure Browser Email to Use HTTPS

If using a web browser to access your email, it is critical that your web connection use HTTPS. In this assignment we will verify that your browser-based email uses HTTPS:

1. Launch a web browser.

2. Go to your log in page for your email. In the example here we will be using Google Mail (Gmail).

3. As in the screen shot below, make sure that the URL field shows either the lock to the left of the URL, or *https://* and not *http://*. The *s* indicates you are communicating over a secure, encrypted pathway.

4. If instead your browser shows the URL to be *http://*, try revisiting your email log in page, but this time manually enter *https://*.

5. If you get to the log in page, all is good. Just bookmark the https:// URL and use it instead of the previous non-secure URL.

6. If you cannot get to your log in page, your email provider isn't giving you a chance to work securely, and you should change your email provider NOW.

14. Vulnerability: Email

End-To-End Secure Email with Sendinc

Using TLS/SSL or HTTPS for email is a good start. Unfortunately, as these only encrypt the path between computer and email server, this is much like locking your front door when leaving for vacation, while leaving the back door open.

If you are serious about email security, then you need to use an end-to-end secure email solution.

There are two ways to approach this:

- Use an email encryption utility. This works well as long as both sender and recipient are using the same encryption utility. Our next section will cover this strategy using *GNU Privacy Guard* and *S/MIME*.

- Use a cloud-based option. This method requires no special software for either sender or recipient, just access to a web browser. The downside is that instead of using an email client, a website is used to send and receive mail.

Our recommendation for cloud-based secure email is to use *SendInc* at*https://Sendinc.com*. Sendinc has several advantages for the typical user. These include:

- Free and pro service is offered.

- The pro service is only $5/month.

- Military-grade end-to-end encryption of username and password, email, and attachments are included.

- The free version automatically self-destructs email after 7 days. The pro version allows the user to determine the destruction date and includes unlimited retention.

- The free version allows up to 20 recipients/day. The pro version allows 200.

- The pro version allows retraction of a sent email (if it has not yet been opened), and offers mail that will delete after opening (straight out of *Mission: Impossible*).

- The pro version allows for rich text email. The free version is text-only.

14. Vulnerability: Email

When sending from Sendinc, you log into an HTTPS home page that also serves as your email composition page. Once the message is sent (fully encrypted), your recipient receives an email stating that a secure message is waiting. The recipient clicks the link, taking the recipient to an authentication page. Upon entering the password (which is automated if this is other than a first visit), the recipient then sees the message. The recipient can directly reply securely to the message, and you then receive an email informing you a secure message is waiting.

Although not quite as convenient as using your own email software, when security, convenience, and cost are taken into consideration against the impacts of violating HIPAA requirements, or the potential drama of confidential communications being intercepted, we find Sendinc to be an easy choice.

Assignment: Create a Sendinc Account

In this assignment we will begin our exploration of end-to-end secure email by creating a Sendinc account.

1. Using your web browser, visit *Sendinc* at *http://Sendinc.com*. Select the *Send Securely Now* button.

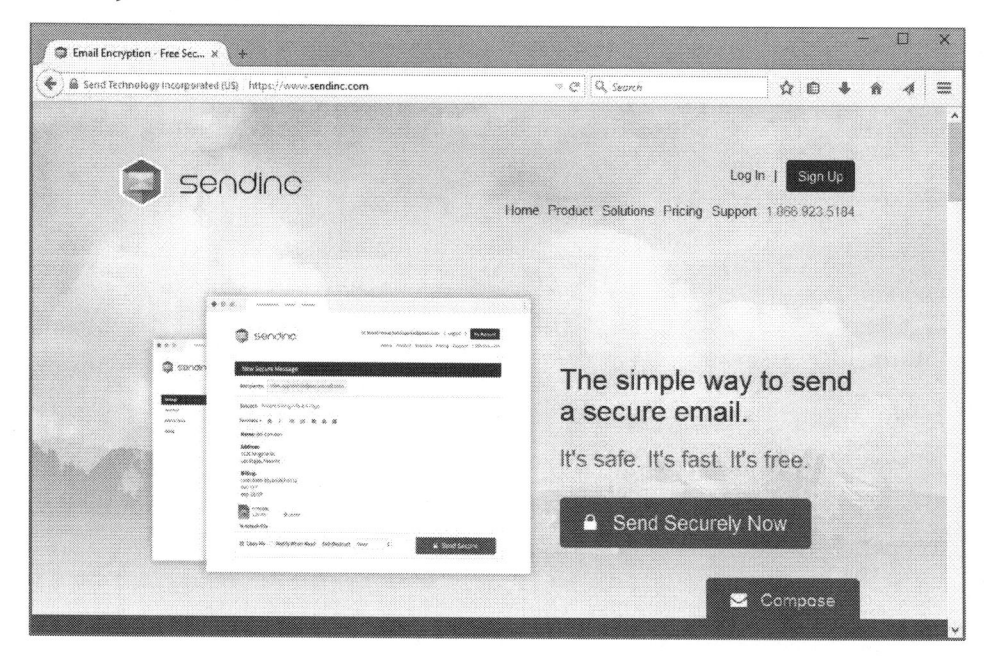

14. Vulnerability: Email

2. The *Send a secure email now* page opens. You can compare upgrade options in the two columns, but for this exercise, select the small text underneath the two bottom buttons that reads *Or get Sendinc Basic for free...*

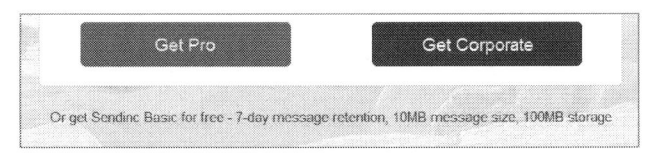

3. As this is the first time you have used Sendinc, you will be prompted to create a free account. Enter your email address and select the *Continue* button.

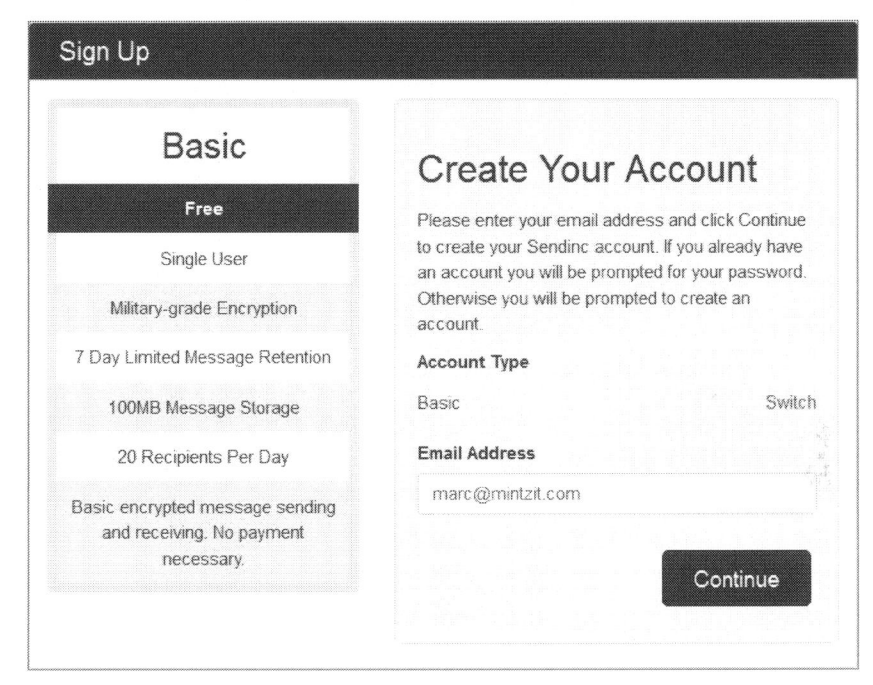

14. Vulnerability: Email

4. The *Create Account* window appears, and an email has been sent to your address behind the scenes with an activation code. Enter the requested information in the window, along with the activation code, and then select the *Create Account* button.

5. If all went well you will see a message box prompting creation of a new secure message. Your free Sendinc account is now active.

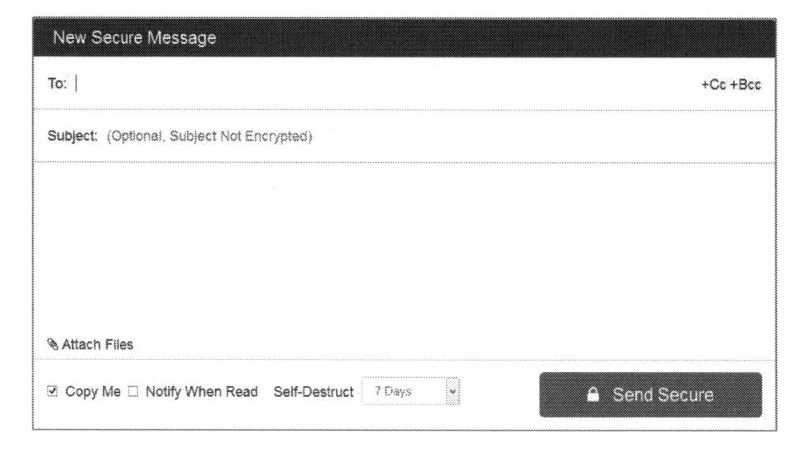

Assignment: Send a Secure Email with Sendinc

This next assignment requires that you currently have a Sendinc account. If you do not, please complete the previous assignment.

1. If you have just completed the previous assignment, the *New Secure Message* window is open. If not, use your web browser to visit *Sendinc* at *http://Sendinc.com* and select the *Login* link, and then log in.

2. In the *Recipients* field, enter the email address of the recipient.

3. In the *Subject* field, enter a subject message.

4. In the *Message* field, enter the text of your message.

5. If you want to include an attachment, select the *Attach Files* button, and then select the file to attach.

6. From the *Self-Destruct* pop-up menu, the default time period for the free account is 7 days. This can only be changed with the *Pro* or *Corporate* accounts.

7. Select the *Send Secure* Message button.

Your email has been sent to the recipient.

Assignment: Receive and Respond to a Sendinc Secure Email

In this assignment we reply to our first Sendinc secure email. The previous two assignments must first be completed.

14. Vulnerability: Email

1. The recipient gets the following email. Select the *View Secure Message* button within the email.

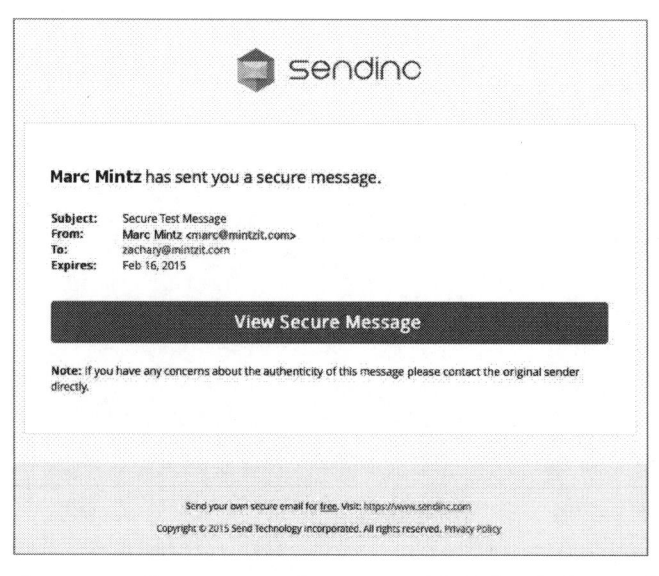

2. If this is the first time the recipient has visited SendInc, they will be prompted to create an account (as you did two exercises back.) If the recipient already has a Sendinc account, go to step 3.

3. At the *Log In* window, the recipient will enter their account password.

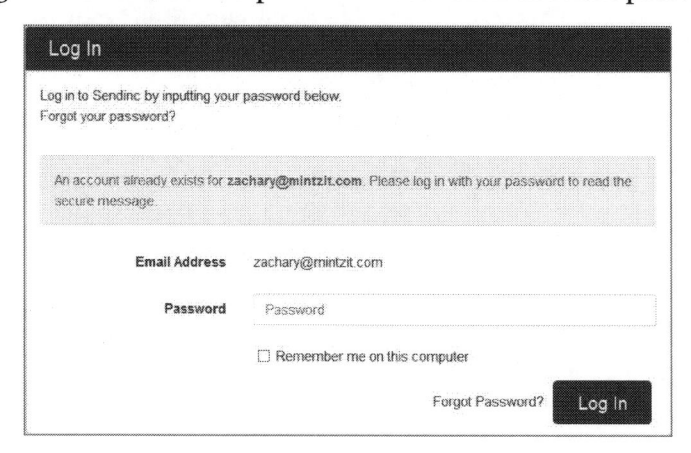

14. Vulnerability: Email

4. The Sendinc message from Marc to Zachary is now decrypted and is fully viewable.

Secure Message

↩ Reply ↩ Reply All ➔ Forward   ⚠ Report 🖨 Print 📄 Save as PDF

Secure Test Message

From: "Marc Mintz" <marc@mintzit.com>   Created: Today at 3:32 PM
To: zachary@mintzit.com   Expires: 02/16/2015

Hi Zachary,

Here is a secured test message.

Congratulations. You now have mastery over the easiest tool to create hardened secure email communications.

End-To-End Secure Email With GNU Privacy Guard

The gold standard for email security is to use an application to fully encrypt the message at the sender's computer in a format that only the intended recipient can decrypt. This tool also must be capable of alerting the recipient if the message has been tampered with in any way (i.e., a man-in-the-middle attack.) The leader in this arena is PGP (Pretty Good Privacy), now owned and maintained by Symantec. Fortunately, there is an open source utility that provides all of the core functionality and security of PGP, for free.

Setting up *GPG* (GNU Privacy Guard)–available for Linux, OS X, and Windows–takes a few more steps than our previous strategies in this section, and those with whom you wish to exchange secure email will need to also install GPG. But once both sender and recipient have their GPG in place, it is effortless to share fully encrypted messages.

Both PGP and GPG use the same strategy to securely encrypt email communications. Each user creates a *public key* and a *private key.* The Public Key typically is stored at a GPG server in the cloud, which can be found with a search for your name. The Private Key remains only on the user's computer. When sending an email to another person, your email application will automatically use the recipient's Public Key to encrypt the message. When the recipient receives the email, only the recipient' Private Key is able to decrypt and open the message.

If there are shortcomings to PGP and GPG, one is that there are only a few iOS apps that can use it–oPenGP and SecuMail. Also, GPG is designed to work within an email client application, not a web browser. Although there are plug-ins for FireFox to allow for GPG, you are best to stick with a mail application. Another issue is that before one can exchange encrypted email with someone else, both need to manually retrieve each other's public key. This typically is just a two-click process, but still…

Cryptography can quickly become Ph.D.-level material. I will cover everything you are likely to need to fully enable encryption and digital signing using GPG. Should you wish to delve deeper, visit the GPG4win Support site at *http://www.gpg4win.org*.

14. Vulnerability: Email

Assignment: Install GPG and Generate Your Public Key

To encrypt your email, you must have GPG installed, and have your recipient's Public Key installed in your GPG keychain. In order for your intended recipient to decrypt and read your email, the recipient must have:

- GPGtools, found at *http://gpgtools.org,* if using OS X,
- Gpg4win, found at *http://www.gpg4win.org,* if using Windows, or
- GPA, *http://www.gnupg.org/related_software/gpa/index.en.html,* if using Linux.

The recipient will also need to have your Public Key stored in their computer.

In this first assignment, you will install GPG on your computer, and upload your Public Key to the *GPG Public Key Server*, making it available to anyone wishing to send encrypted email to you.

1. Use your browser to visit the GPG4win home page at *http://www.gpg4win.org/.*
2. Select the *Go to Download* button.

3. Select the top (latest) *Gpg4win* button to start the download. The software will begin to download to your computer.
4. Go to your Downloads folder, locate and then double-click on the *gpg4win-x.x.x.exe* file. (with the x's being the version number for your particular download). This will mount the GPG disk image to your desktop, and then open the disk image to reveal the GPG Suite window.

14. Vulnerability: Email

5. Double-click the *Install.pkg* icon inside of the GPG Suite window to launch the *Install GPG Suite installer*. Click *Next*.

6. Read the *License Agreement*, and if in agreement, click *Next*.

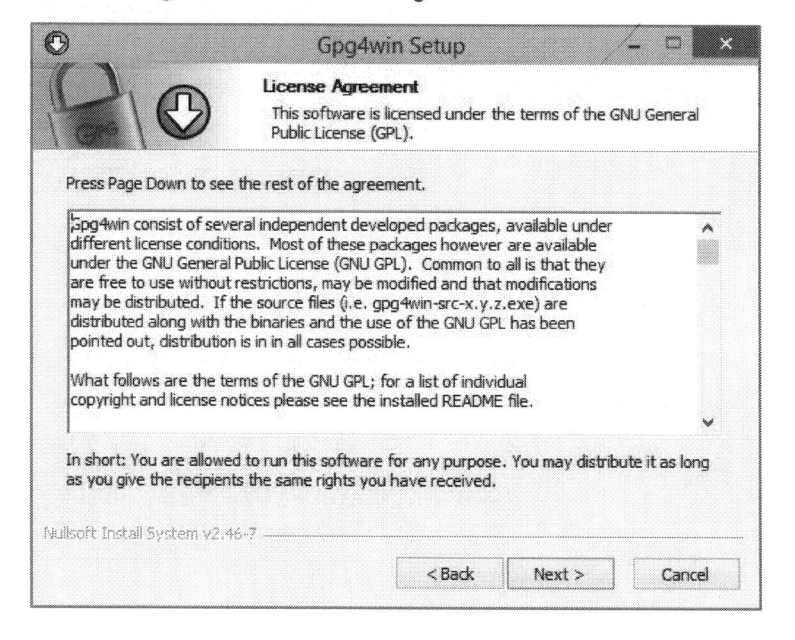

14. Vulnerability: Email

7. At the *Choose Components* screen, click *Next*.

8. At the *Install Location* screen, click *Next*.

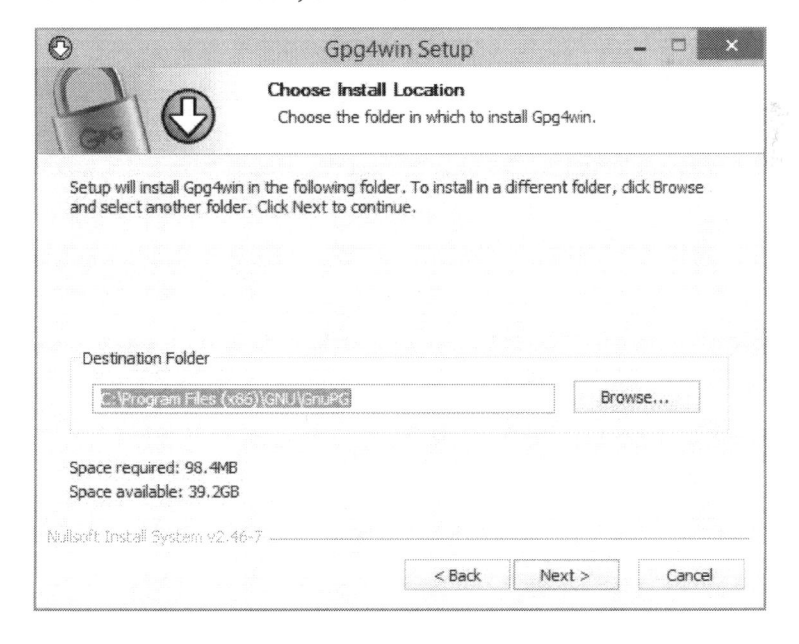

14. Vulnerability: Email

9. At the *Install Options* screen, select where Gpg4win will install links, and then click *Next*. Then click on the *Start Menu*.

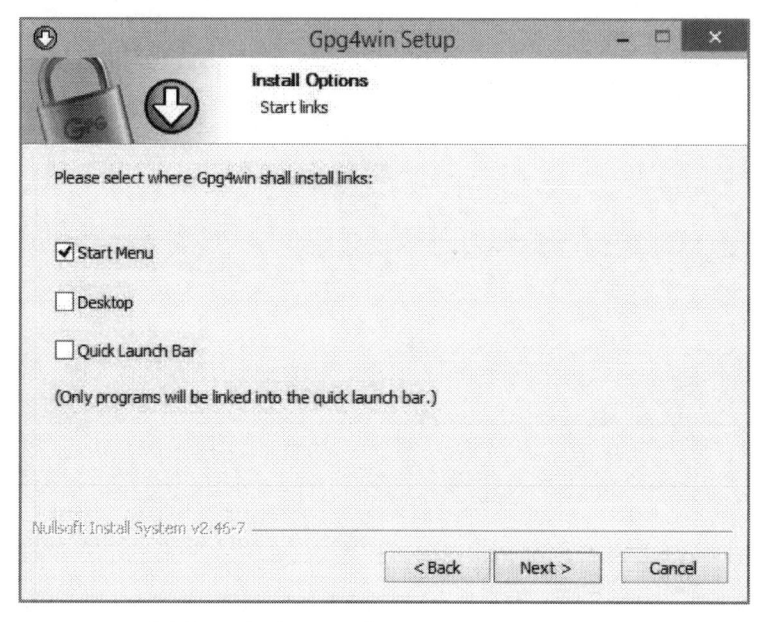

10. In *the Start Menu* folder, click *Install*.

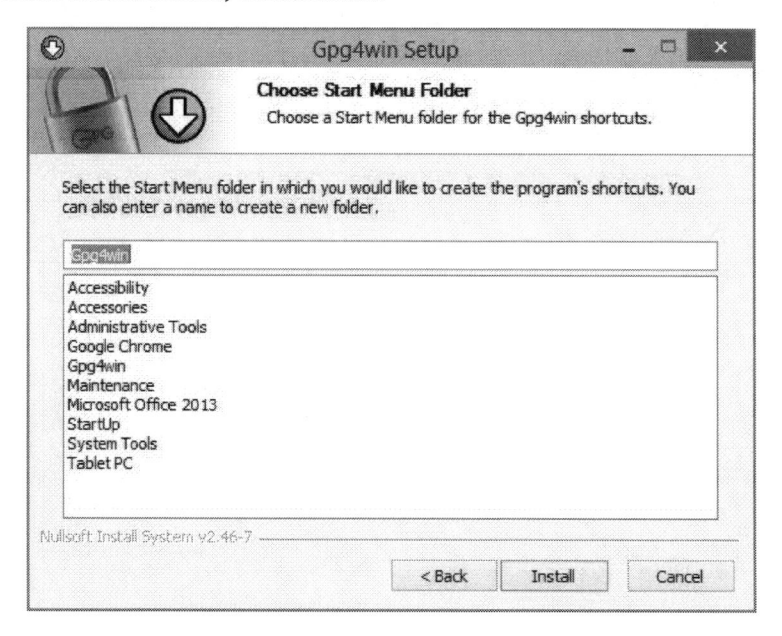

-360-

14. Vulnerability: Email

11. After the installation has completed, click *Finish* to close the setup window.

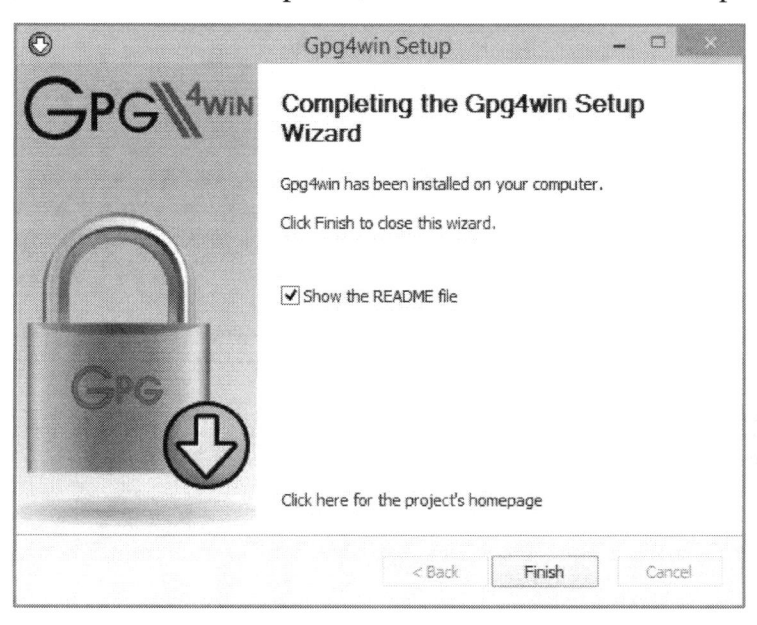

14. Vulnerability: Email

12. In the *Start* Menu, in the *Gpg4win* folder, select the *Kleopatra* Application. *Kleopatra* is Gpg4win's main configuration application.

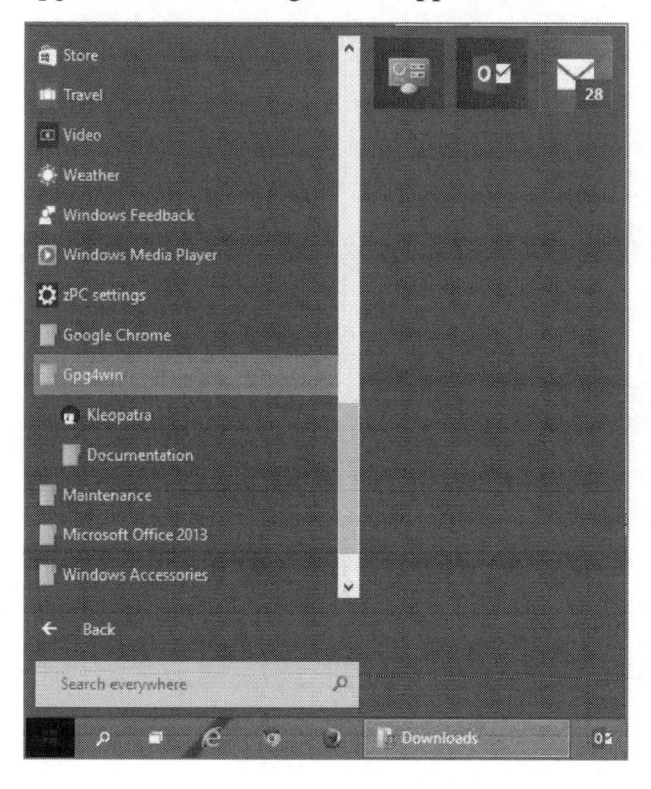

14. Vulnerability: Email

13. Once Kleopatra opens, click the *File* Menu and select *New Certificate*. From here we will create a new Certificate.

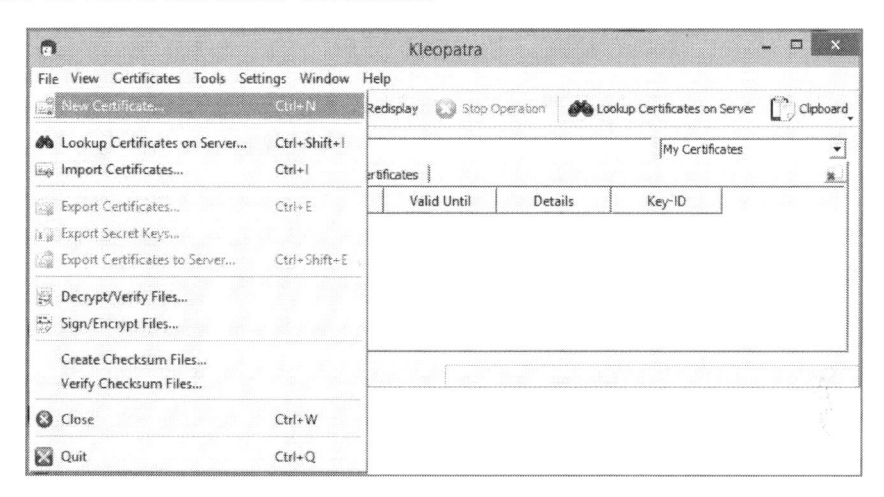

14. The *Create Certificate Wizard* will open, prompting you for the type of Certificate Format that you wish to create. For this exercise we will be choosing the top selection, *Create a personal OpenPGP key pair*.

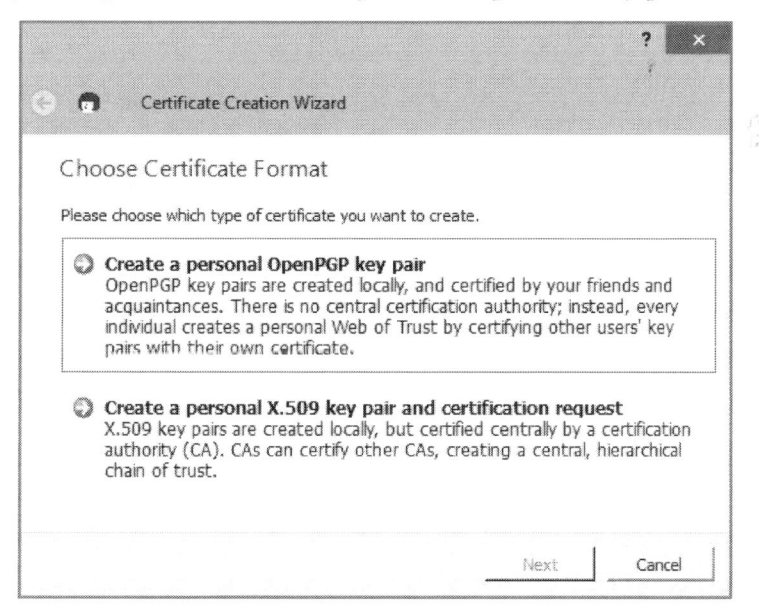

15. At the next screen, type your name, the email address you would like associated with your GPG certificate, and additionally a comment to identify this certificate (assuming that you may create others in the future).

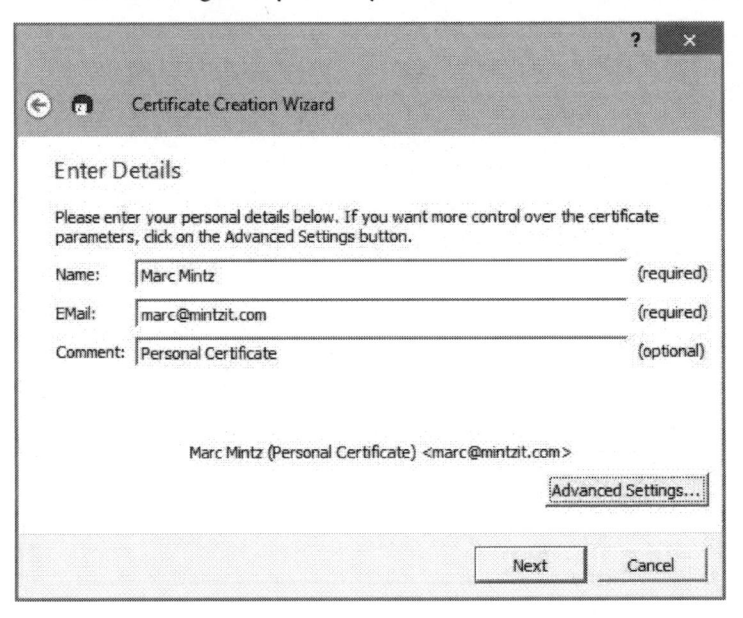

14. Vulnerability: Email

16. Click the *Advanced Settings* button to open a child window with additional configuration options.

- *Key Material*: Select *RSA* (default).

- *Length*: Select *4096*. The default is 2048. However, the larger the encryption bit depth, the more secure.

- *Valid Until*: I typically leave this disabled, allowing any of my encrypted email to be accessed (given the proper credentials) forever. However, if you prefer to set your key to self-expire, making any sent emails created with it unreadable after a certain date, then by all means enable this option.

17. Select the *OK* button.
18. Back at the *Create Certificates Wizard* window, click the *Next* button.

14. Vulnerability: Email

19. Review the *Certificate Parameters* previously input, and click the *Create Key* button.

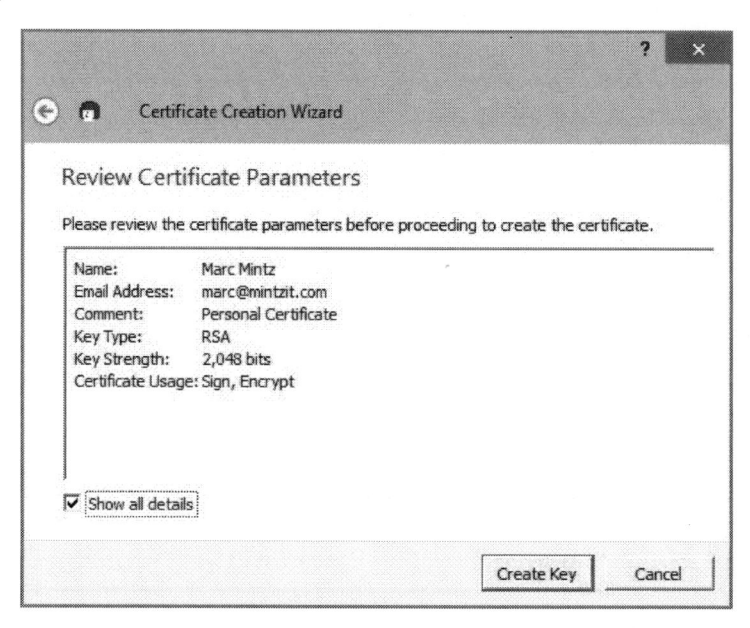

20. An authentication window appears asking for you to create a password for the new GPG key. Enter a strong password. Record this in a secure location.

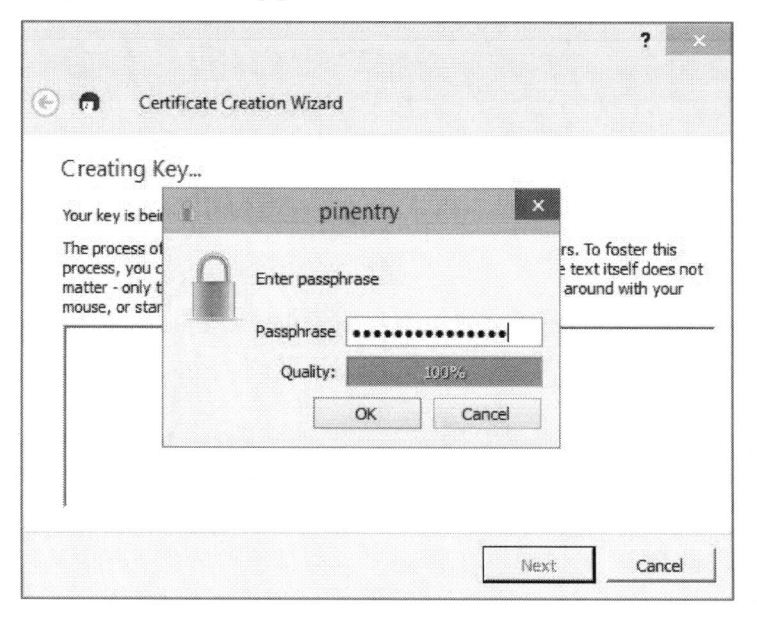

14. Vulnerability: Email

21. When your Public Key generation completes, the *Key Pair Successfully Created* window will display your new key.

22. Several options are presented in the completion window providing various options on how to transport or store your newly created certificates. Creating a backup of your newly created encryption keys.

    - Note that if you choose the option to *Upload Certificate to Directory Service*, that key cannot be removed from the key server. Be certain that the name you are using is the one you want others to be able to find you by via a server search.

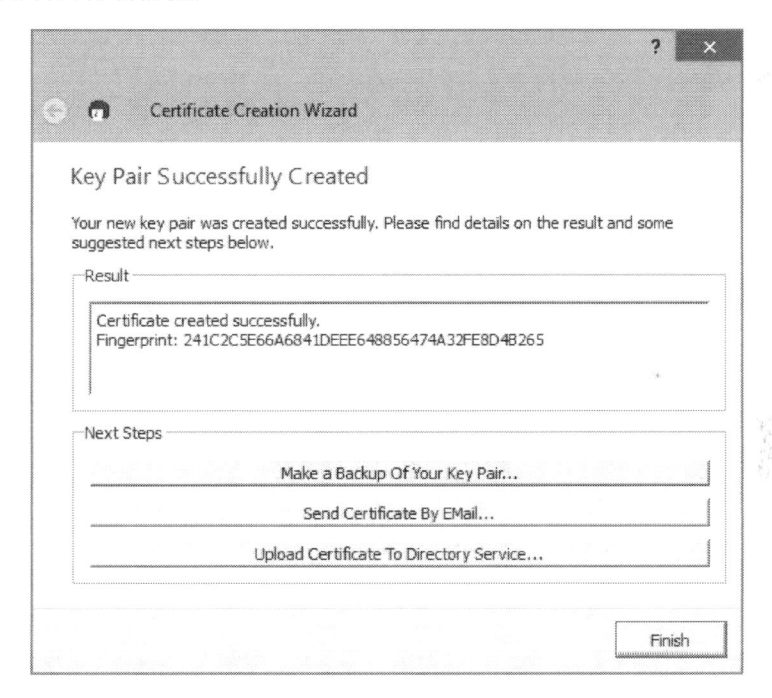

Assignment: Add Your Other Email Addresses to Your Public Key

Prerequisite: Gpg4win must be installed.

It's common to have multiple email addresses. It's wise to give each the ability to communicate securely. If you wish, you may create keys for each of your other

14. Vulnerability: Email

addresses simply by repeating each of the steps in the previous assignment. However, you may find that both tedious and somewhat redundant.

An alternative is to bind all of your email addresses together under one key. In this assignment we will do just that.

1. Open *Kleopatra*, located in *Start > Gpg4win*, and then double-click on your entry from the previous assignment.

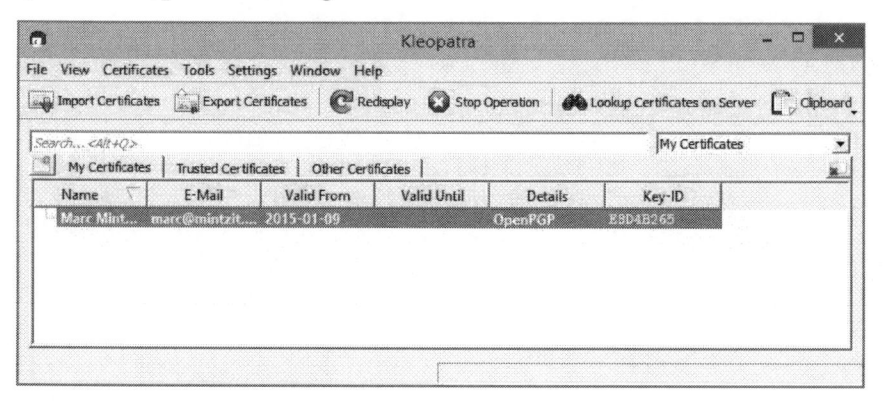

14. Vulnerability: Email

2. A new window will open. Select the *User IDs & Certificates* tab, and then click the *add* button.

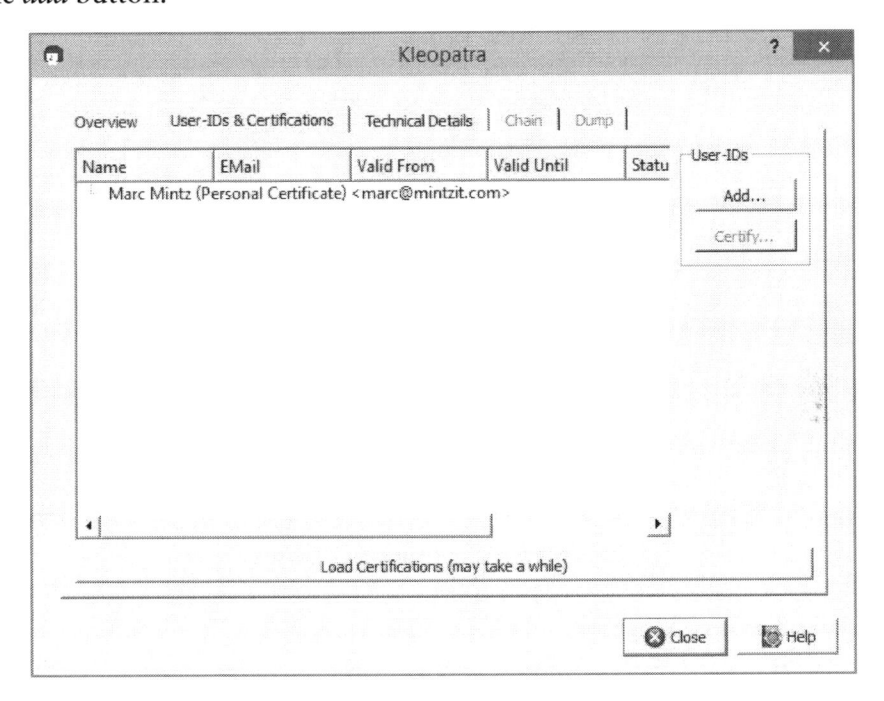

3. In the window that opens, enter your *Full name,* along with the new *Email address* you want to be bound to your original email/key combination, and then select the *OK* button. Confirm the password of the Key, and the new email address will be added to the list.

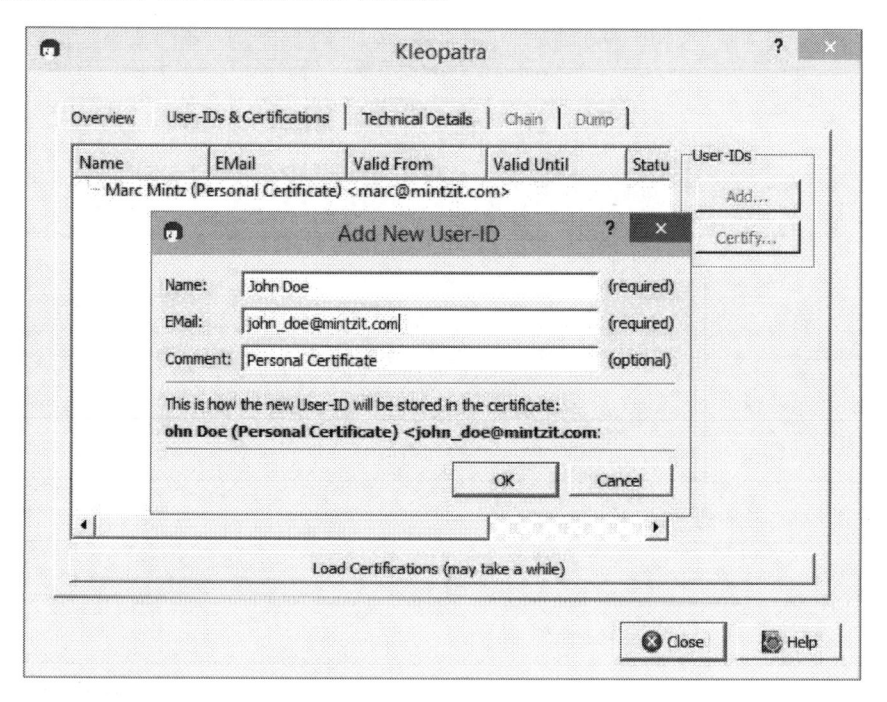

14. Vulnerability: Email

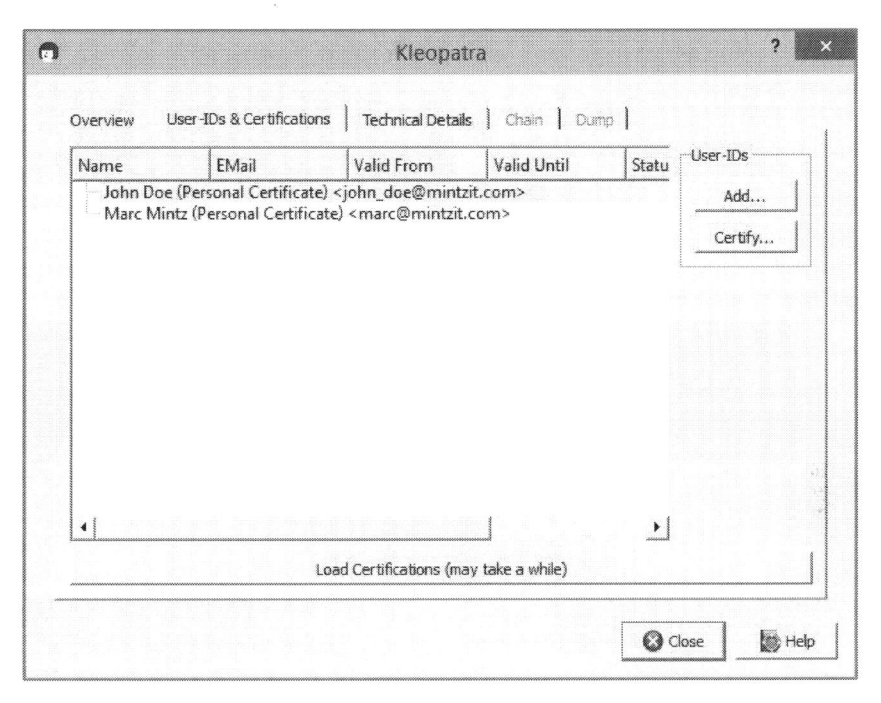

4. Repeat steps 2 and 3 for each of your email addresses.

5. Lastly, upload your changes to the Public Key Server. Select the *File* menu > *Export Certificates to Server*.

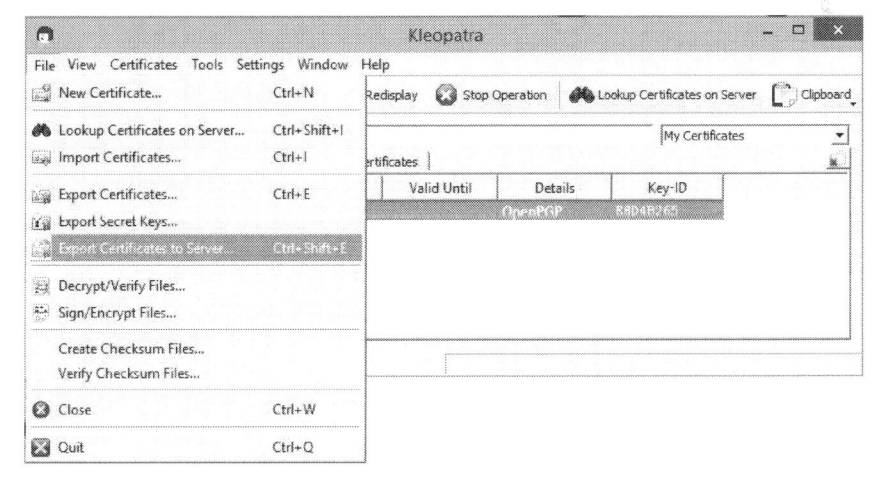

Whew. All of your email accounts can now send and receive encrypted mail.

14. Vulnerability: Email

Assignment: Install Your Friend's Public Key

Prerequisite: Gpg4win must be installed.

In order for you to send encrypted mail to someone else, it is necessary to have his or her *GPG Public Key*. In this exercise, you will find a friend's Public Key and add it to your GPG Keychain Access.

1. Open the *Kleopatra* application from the *Start > Gpg4win* folder
2. Select the *File* menu > *Lookup Certificates on Server*.

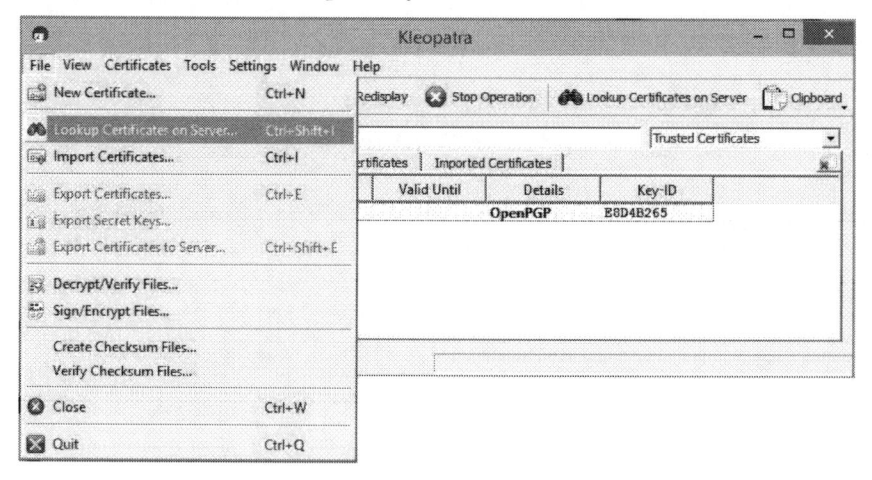

14. Vulnerability: Email

3. The Certificate server window will open, allowing you to enter the full name of the person you wish to either send encrypted mail to, or receive from, and then select the *Search key* button. A list of possible matches appears. If you don't yet know anyone with a GPG key, feel free to use *Marc Louis Mintz*. Shown below are the search results for the mythical person *Max Mustermann*.

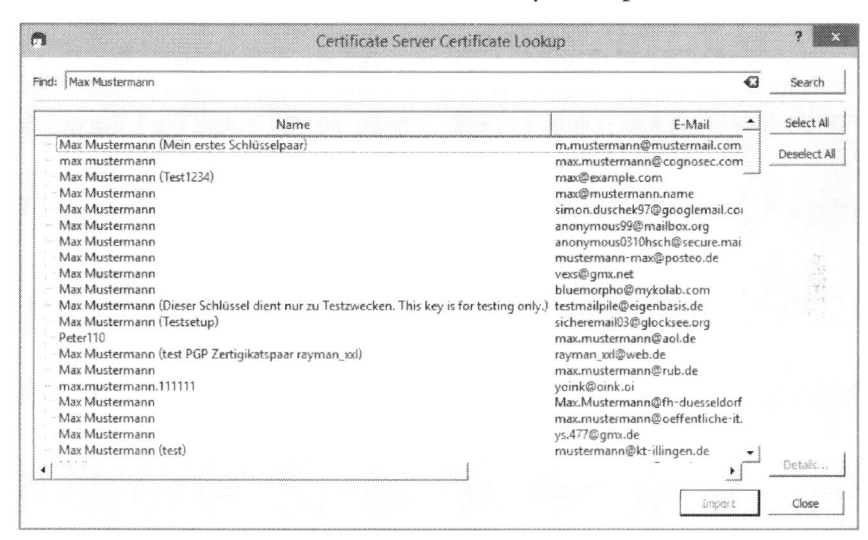

4. Select the target public key and then select the *Import* button. A notification window will appear showing that (for this example) Max Mustermann's encryption certificate was successfully imported into Kleopatra.

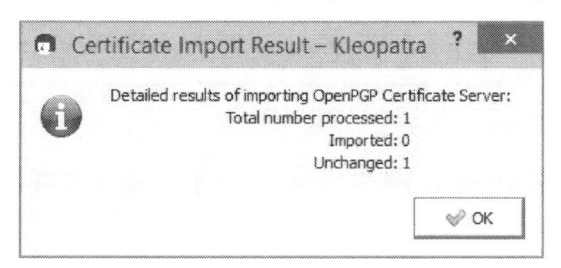

5. The Public Key is now added to your Kleopatra Keychain.

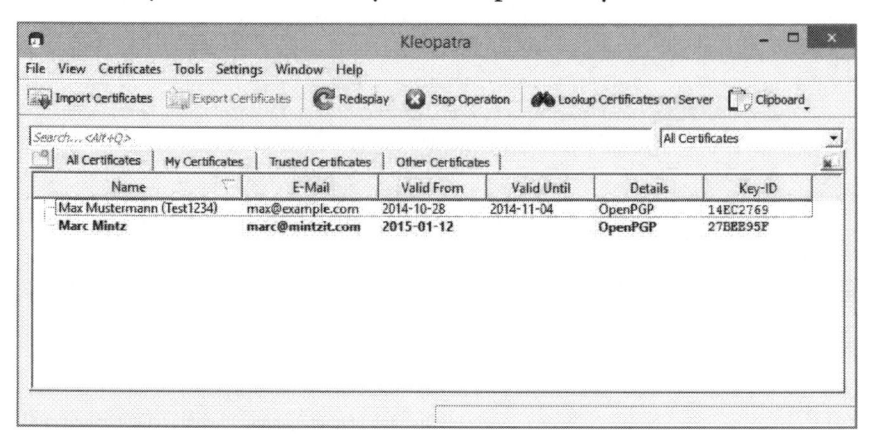

You are now ready to send encrypted email to your friends.

Assignment: Enable GPG in Thunderbird

With Gpg4win installed, the next step is to configure the *Preferences* within your email application. Since the basic Windows 10 Mail app does not support OpenPGP encryption, we will work with Mozilla Thunderbird.

14. Vulnerability: Email

1. Open the Mozilla Thunderbird application, and from the Thunderbird Menu and select *Add-ons*.

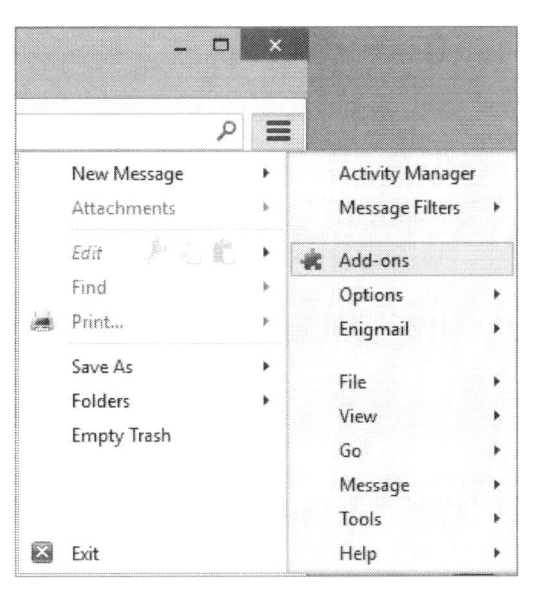

2. In the search box, type *Enigmail*. Click the *Install* button for the Enigmail plugin, and then restart Thunderbird at the prompt to do so.

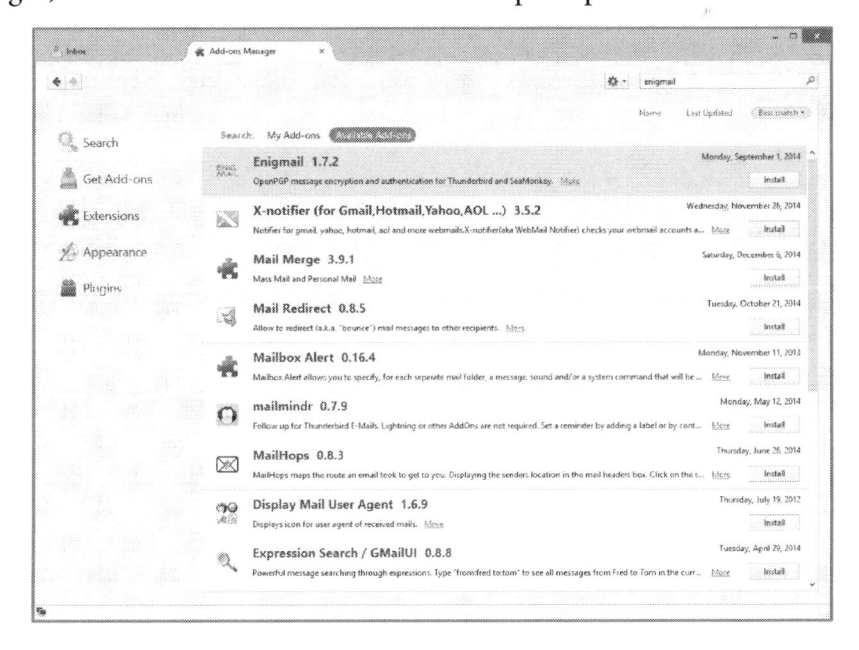

14. Vulnerability: Email

3. When Thunderbird restarts, the Enigmail setup wizard will automatically run. Click *Yes, I would like the wizard to get me started*, and then click *Next*.

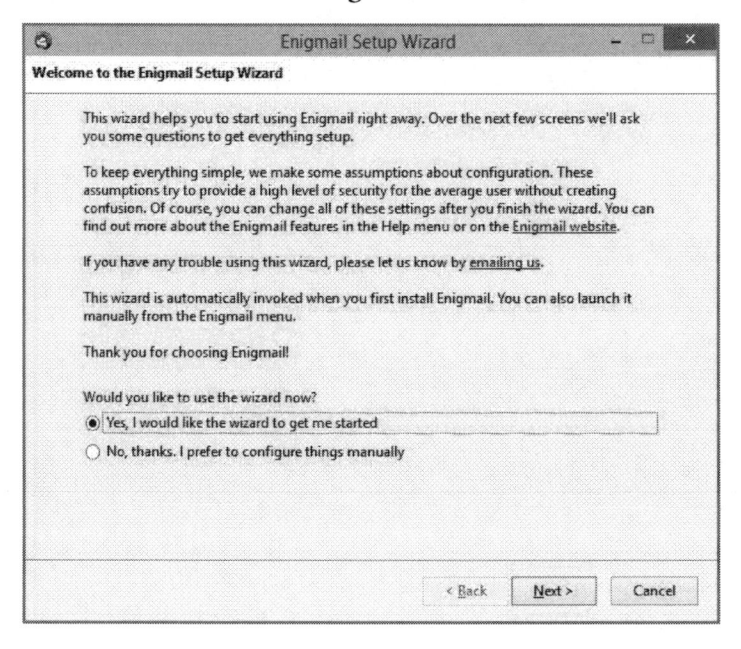

14. Vulnerability: Email

4. When prompted for the encryption mode to use for outgoing emails, select *Convenient auto encryption*, and then click *Next*.

14. Vulnerability: Email

5. The next option in the Wizard provides signing options. With the *Sign all my messages by default* option, your personal certificate will sign all emails, making it easy to identify that the email you send is really from you.

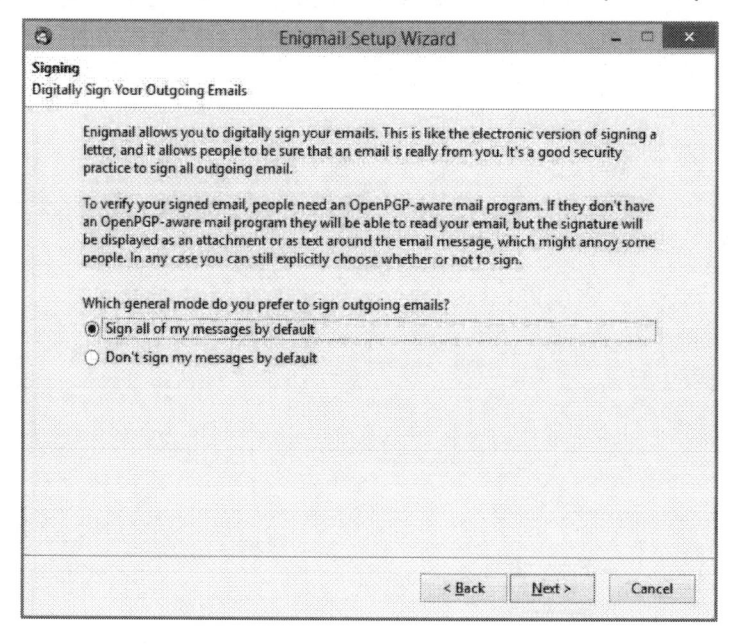

14. Vulnerability: Email

6. Allow Enigmail to optimize connectivity by allowing for optimized default settings to be applied. Select *Yes*, and then click *Next*.

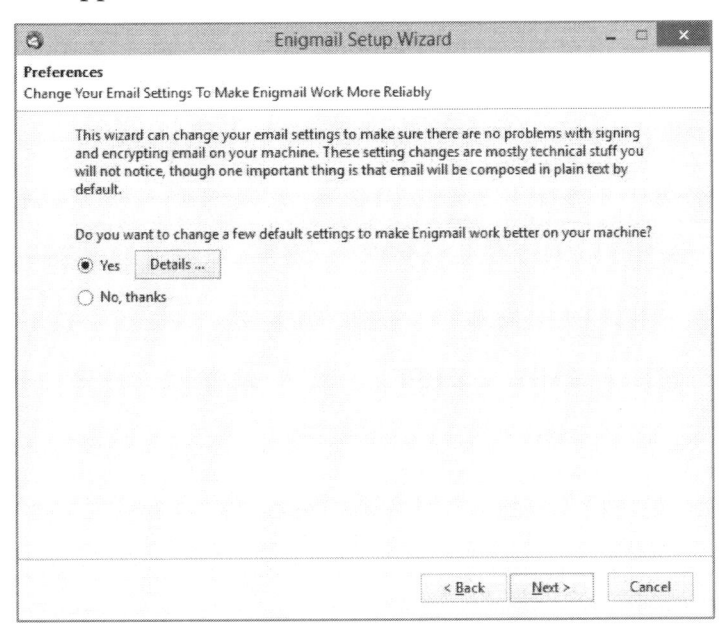

14. Vulnerability: Email

7. The Enigmail wizard is smart enough to see that we have previously created keys in Gpg4win's Kleopatra application. Select your name from the existing key list, and then click *Next*.

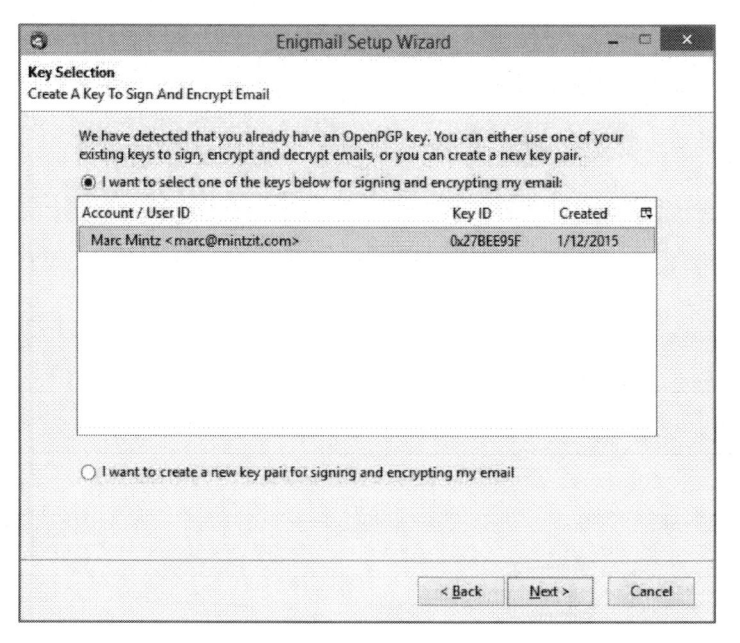

14. Vulnerability: Email

8. At the *Summary* window click *Next* to apply the options selected during the course of the wizard.

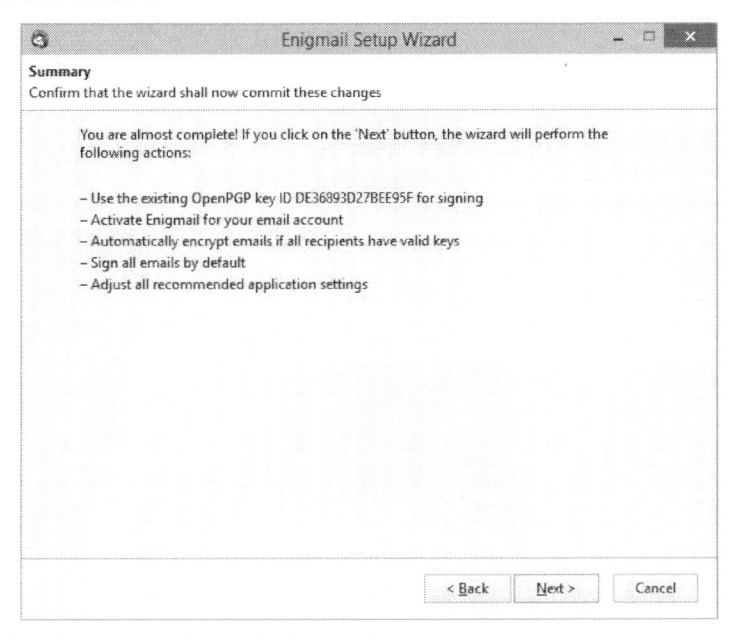

9. At the *Thank you* window, click *Finish*.

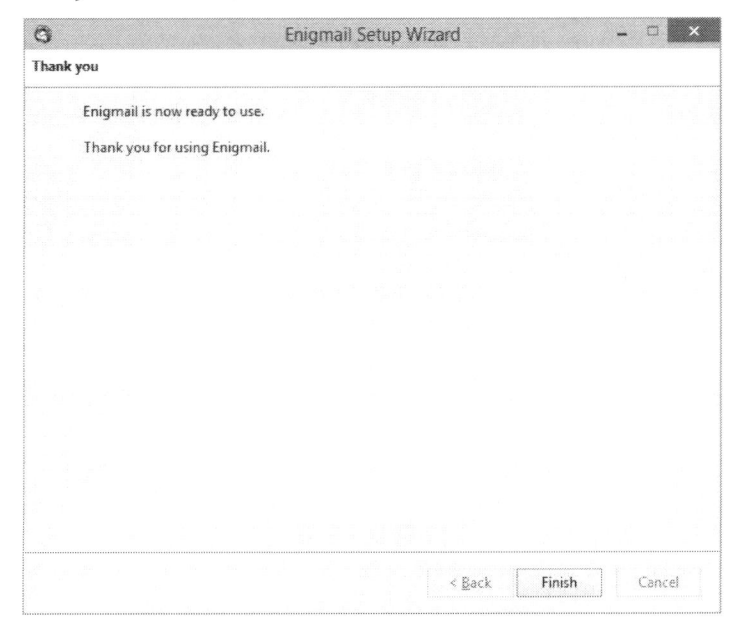

10. With Enigmail configured, Thunderbird will display an Enigmail button and toolbar in the message composition window. You can modify the per-message encryption and signing default options in these menus (*Advanced Users*).

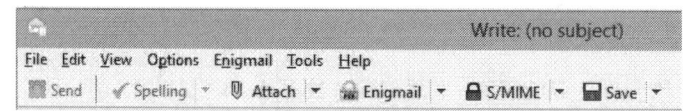

At this point you have email certificates installed and ready to use. Lastly, make sure you export and backup your certificate keys in a secure location, such as a CD-ROM that can be tucked away in a safe location.

Assignment: Composing a GPG Encrypted Email in Outlook

With Gpg4win installed, the next step is to configure the *Preferences* within your email application. If you are using Microsoft Outlook there is a way to configure S/MIME and PGP encryption. Within the Gpg4win installation there is a utility called GpgOL that we installed already. This will activate by default in your Outlook after your first restart of Outlook. The way that you use your PGP key within Outlook is a bit different than how Thunderbird/Enigmail configures it. You will have to encrypt and sign each message individually through the GpgOL tab. Don't fret, it is rather easy to set which certificate you'd like to encrypt or sign with through the GpgOL plug-in.

14. Vulnerability: Email

1. Open Microsoft Outlook. If you do not have the GpgOL tab then you may have to restart Microsoft Outlook. Click *New E-mail*.

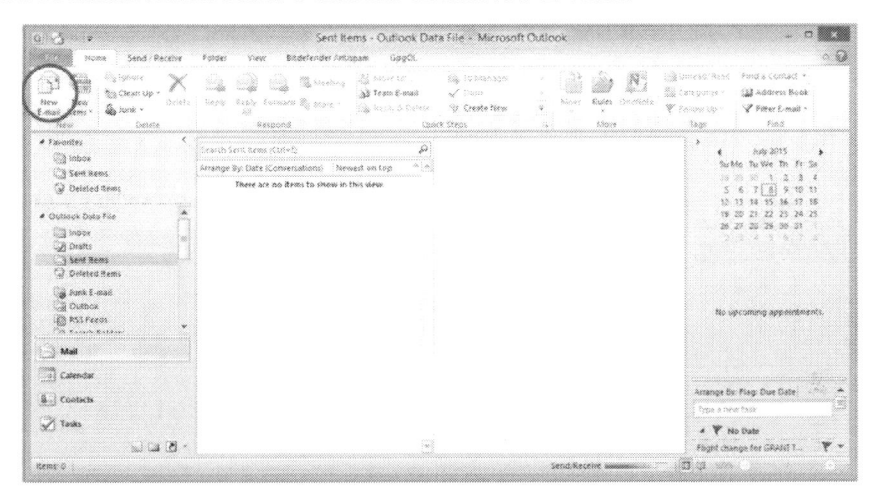

2. Enter all your information into your email including recipient, subject and body. Then click on *GpgOL*.

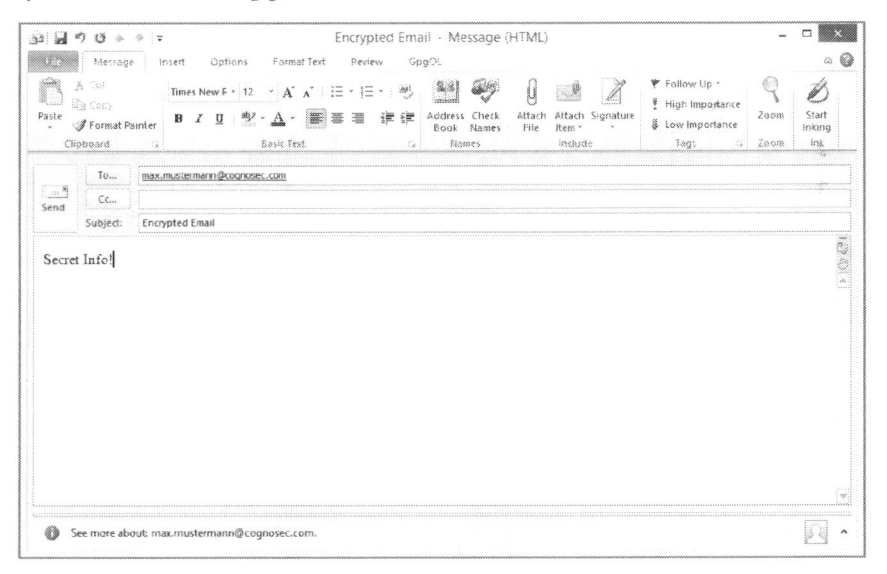

14. Vulnerability: Email

3. In order to encrypt your message with your OpenPGP key, click on *Encrypt*.

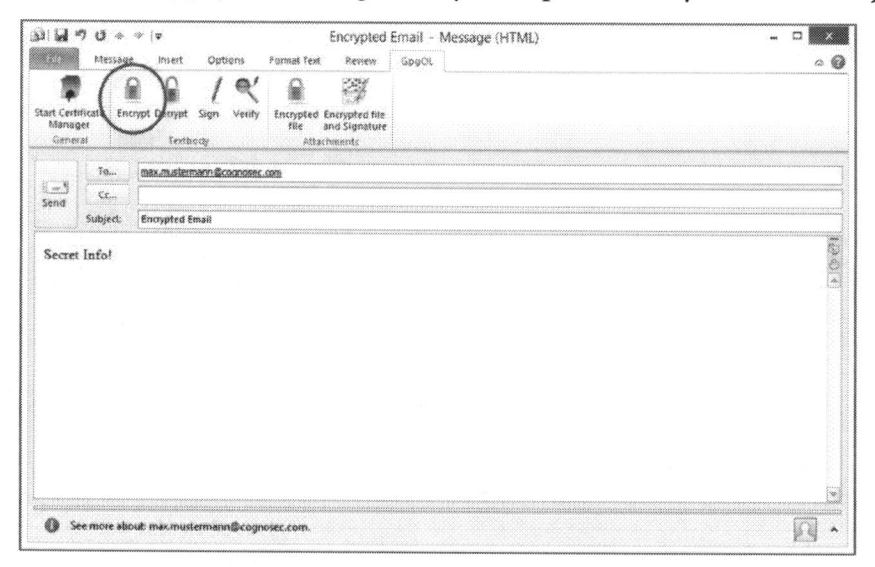

4. A new dialog box will appear. It should auto-populate the certificates for the email addresses. If it does skip to step 7, otherwise continue on.

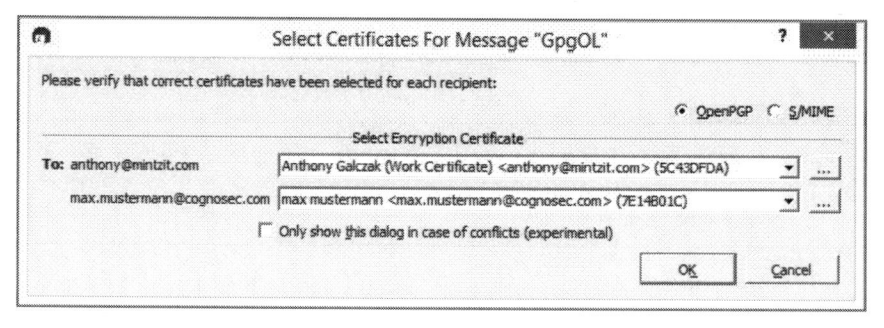

14. Vulnerability: Email

5. Select *OpenPGP*. Click on the 3 dots box to the right of the recipient. You want the certificates to match the email address.

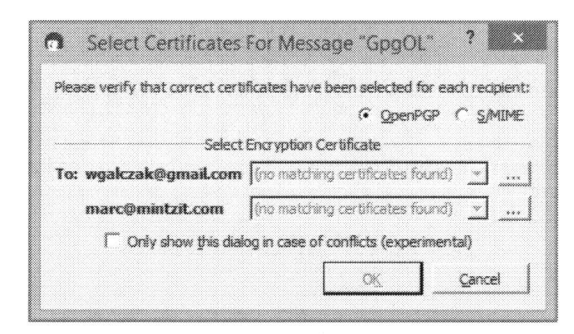

6. This will open Kleopatra. Double click on the appropriate certificate. Do this for all recipients listed. If they do not have a certificate in Kleopatra, then do not use a key. Click *OK*.

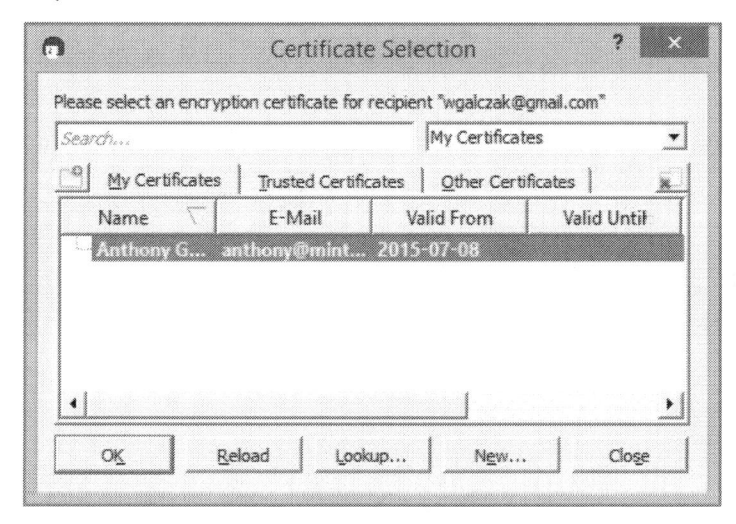

14. Vulnerability: Email

7. This will encrypt your message with your PGP key and should look something like this.

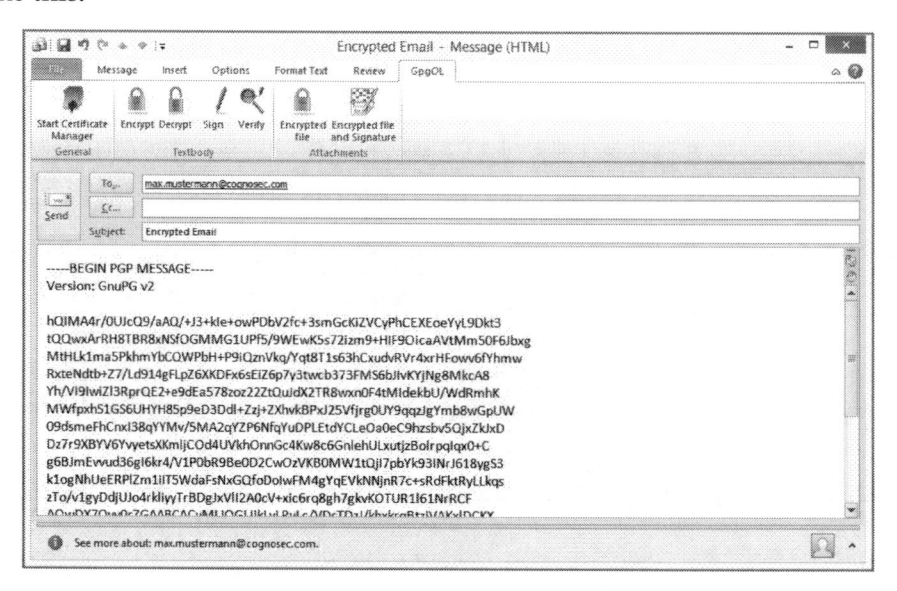

8. If you would also like to sign your message with your public key (and why wouldn't you?), click on *Sign*.

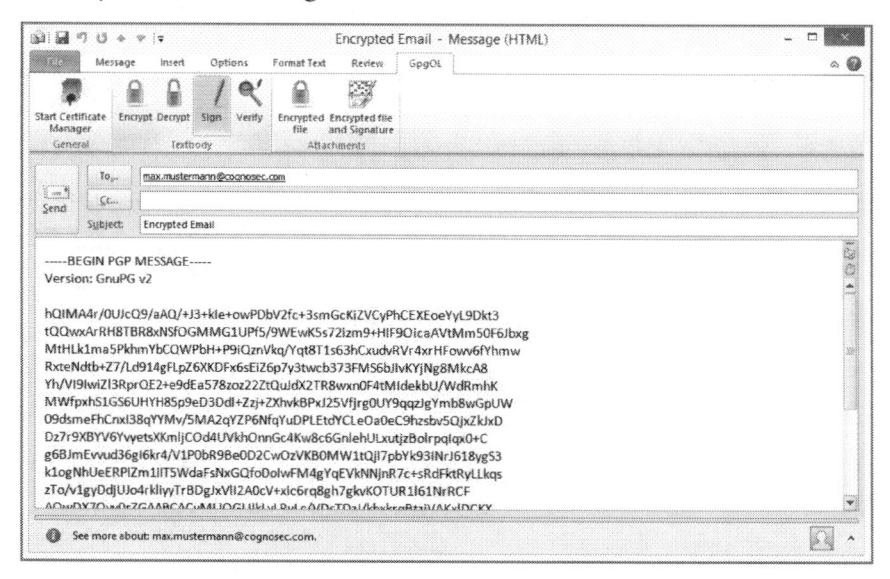

9. The certificate should auto-populate your signature from Kleopatra. If it does not, then click on the 3 dots and double click the certificate that you want to sign with.

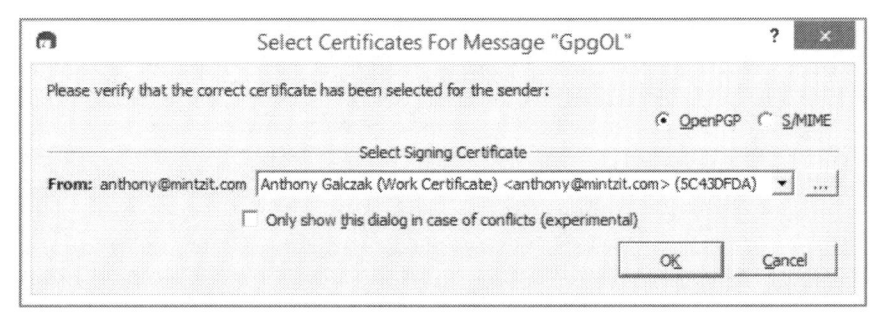

10. Enter your passphrase and click *OK*.

11. This will create a 2nd PGP message that will sign with your public key in your email. From here you are ready to send your encrypted email. Go ahead and hit Send.

Assignment: Encrypt and Sign Files with Win4pgp

Gpg4win allows encryption, decryption, and signing of files. This means that even if you can't directly encrypt and sign an email to a recipient, you can still use email transport to send an encrypted and/or signed document.

Prerequisite: You will need to have Gpg4win installed for this functionality. (See previous exercises.)

14. Vulnerability: Email

1. To sign or encrypt a file or folder, right-click on it. From the pop-up menu, select *Sign and encrypt*. In this example, I am using a Microsoft Word file called *Private Document*.

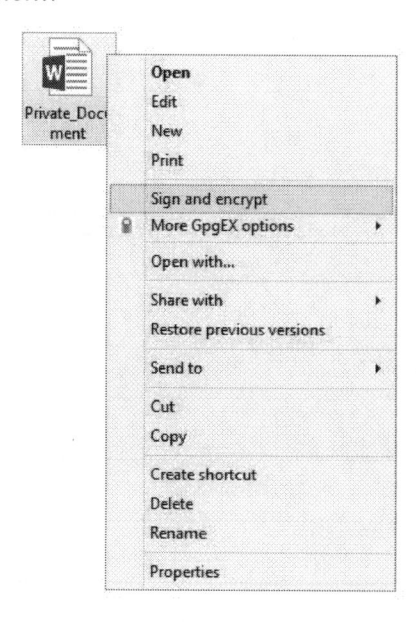

14. Vulnerability: Email

2. Select the *Sign & Encrypt* option, then click *Next*.

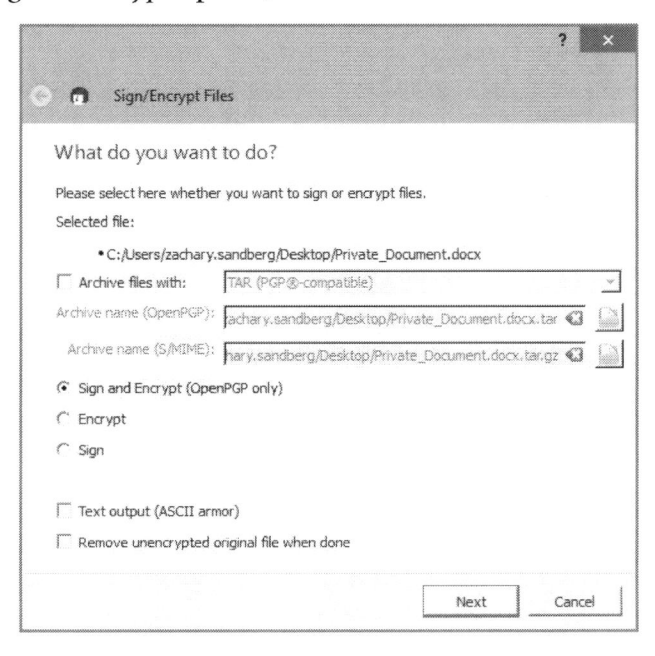

14. Vulnerability: Email

3. Using the *Add* and *Remove* buttons, select the keys you would like to be used for encrypting and decrypting the file. For this example, Zachary will share with Marc. Both of our keys to the bottom box.

   - NOTE: Zachary's key (the sender) is bolded, indicating it is a private key, while Marc's public key is not bold.

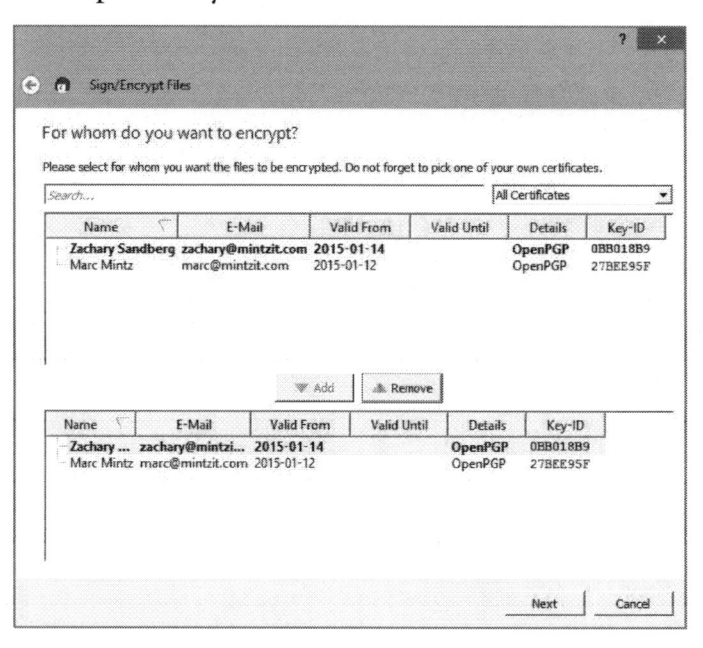

14. Vulnerability: Email

4. In the drop down box, select your own name as the signer of the file.

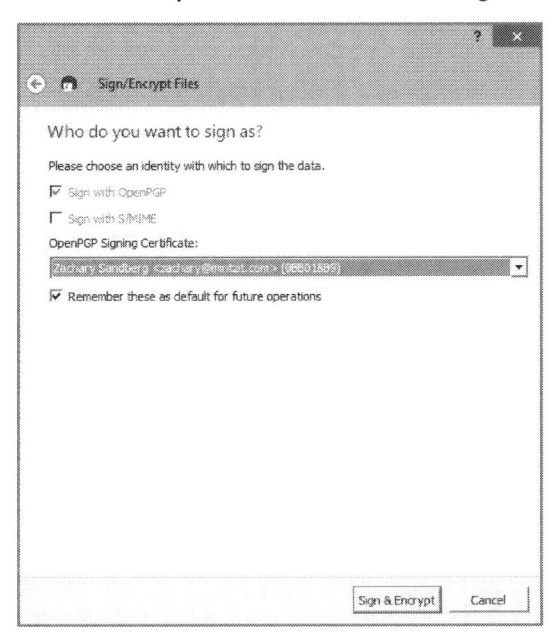

5. At the prompt, enter your private key passphrase, and then click *OK*.

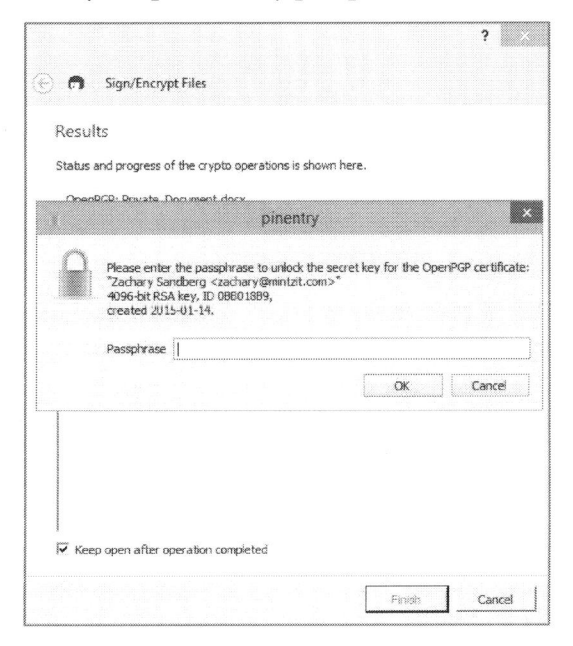

6. When the *Encryption Results* window appears, select the *Finish* button.

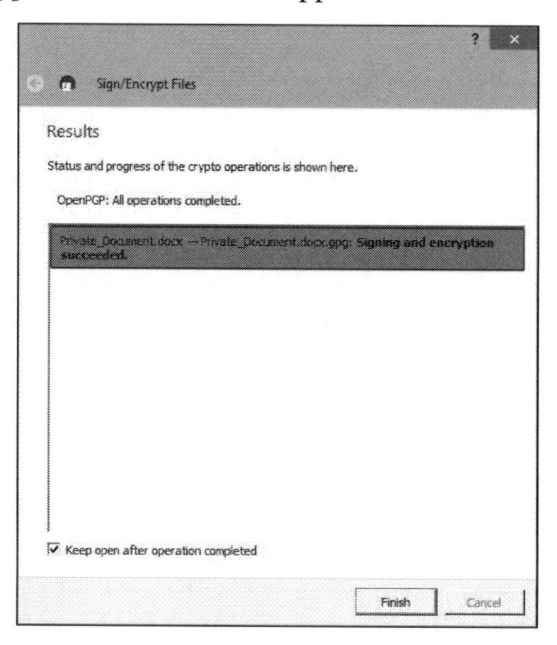

7. The newly encrypted file will be found next to the original, with a *.gpg* file extension. If desired, it can now be attached to an email and securely sent to the recipient(s) for whom the file was encrypted. The recipient(s) would then use their private key to decrypt the file.

Assignment: Decrypt files with Win4pgp

In the previous exercise we encrypted a Microsoft Word file called *Private_Document.docx*. Assuming that we have sent this file to someone, they will need to decrypt the file using their private key.

14. Vulnerability: Email

1. As the recipient, right-click on the encrypted *Private Document.docx.gpg* file, displaying a pop-up menu, and then select the menu option *Decrypt and verify* to start the Gpg4win decryption wizard.

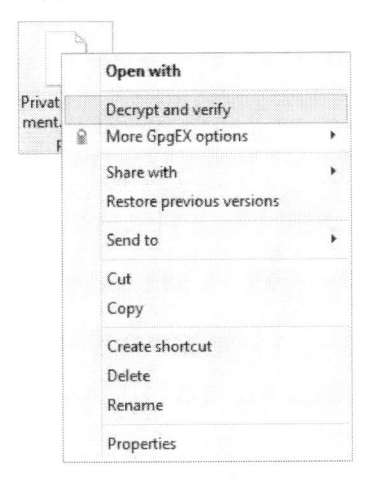

2. At the *Decrypt/Verify Files* screen, the recipient clicks the *Decrypt/Verify* button to start the decryption of the document into the output folder. By default, the output folder is the same location as the encrypted file.

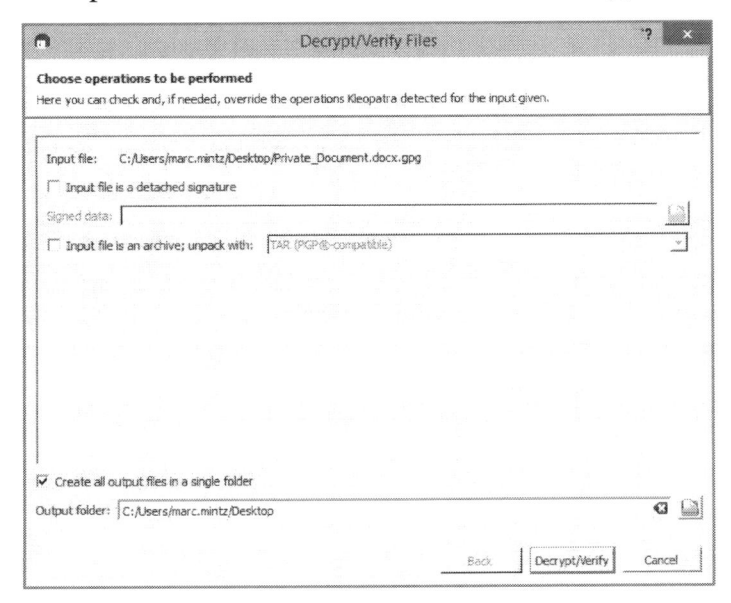

14. Vulnerability: Email

3. Enter the private key passphrase, and then click the *OK* button to start the decryption process.

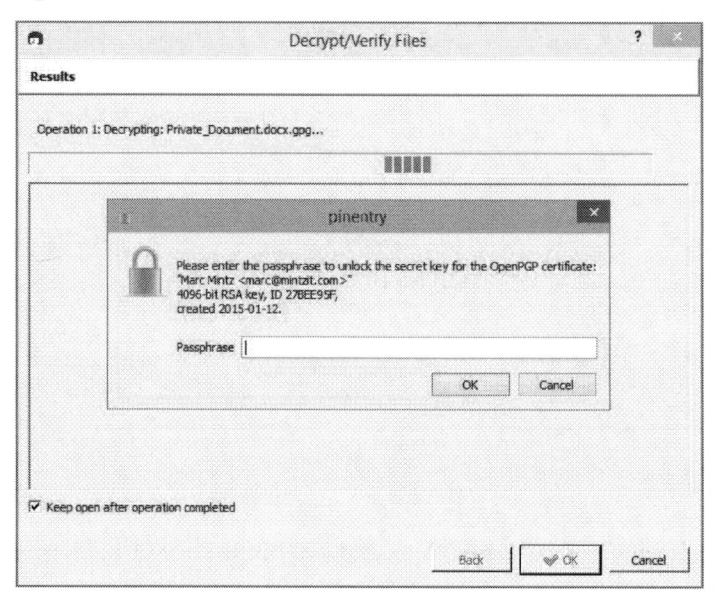

4. Once the file decrypts, the green field will display the signing verification, confirming that the authentic sender was indeed the one who initially signed and encrypted the file.

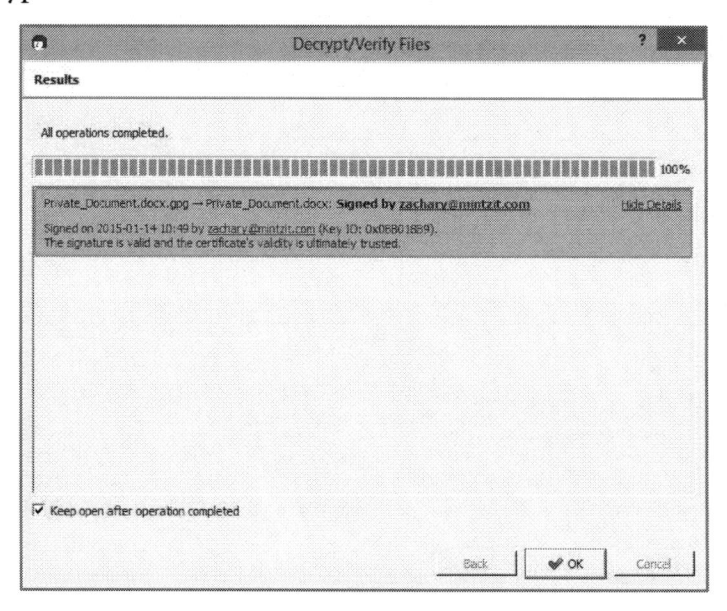

5. If for some reason the recipient does not have the senders public key installed, (or set to trusted), the signing box will be yellow, indicating that the signer's signature could not be verified. However, the file will still decrypt properly. Click the *OK* button to close the wizard.

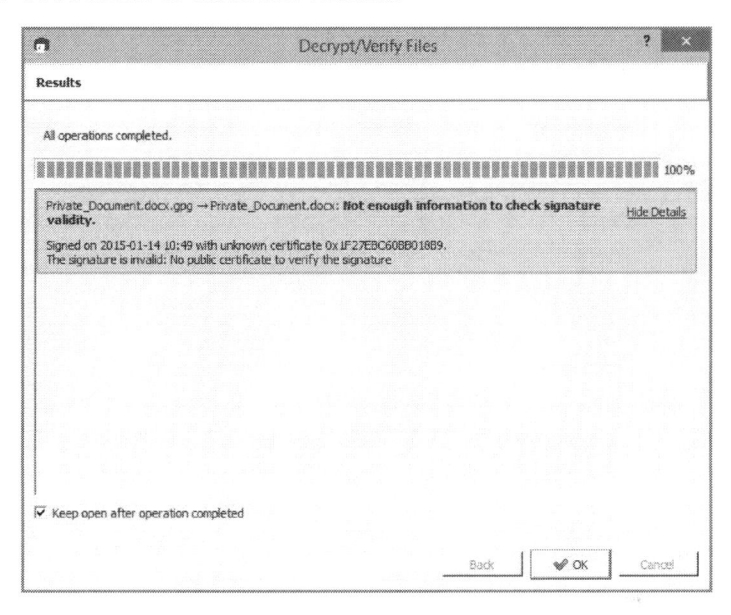

6. When decryption completes, the recipient will have both files on their Desktop.

Assignment: Send a GPG-Encrypted and Signed Email

Once you have created your key and have the Public Key of the intended recipient from the previous assignments, you are ready to send your first encrypted and signed email.

14. Vulnerability: Email

1. Open Mozilla Thunderbird and create a new outgoing email.

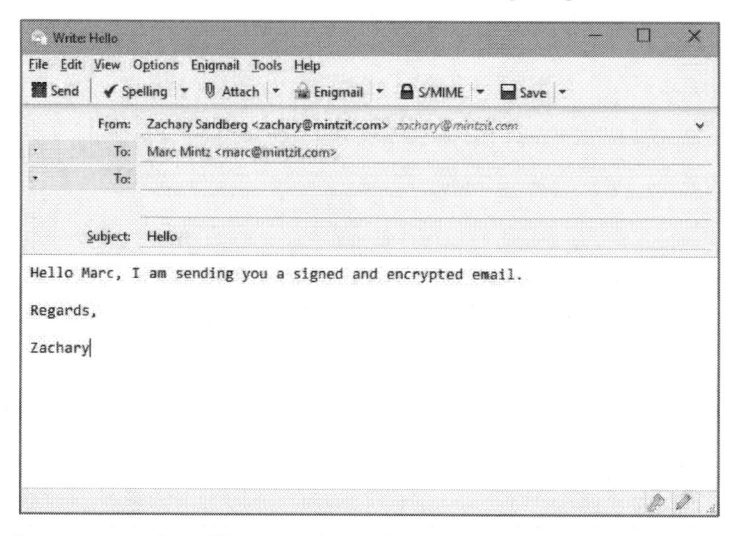

2. Expand the *Enigmail* toolbar entry, and notice the settings for signing and encrypting email. Make sure that encryption is set to *Force Encryption*.

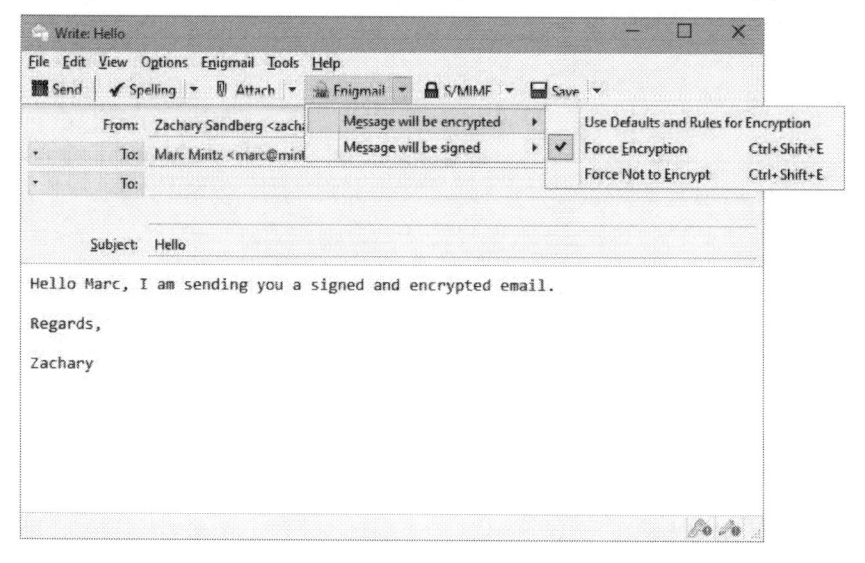

14. Vulnerability: Email

3. In the *To:* field, enter the email address of someone with GPG enabled on his or her computer (feel free to use my address of marc@mintzinfotech.com for your test).

4. Select the *Send* button, and your email is on its way to the recipient, fully secure because only the designated recipient will be able to read the email.

Assignment: Receive a GPG-Encrypted and Signed Email

1. When the email arrives at the recipient, it automatically is decrypted (assuming the recipient also has followed the steps detailed in the *Get Your Friend's Public Key* assignment). The message will have an indicator lock or envelope icon if it is encrypted or signed.

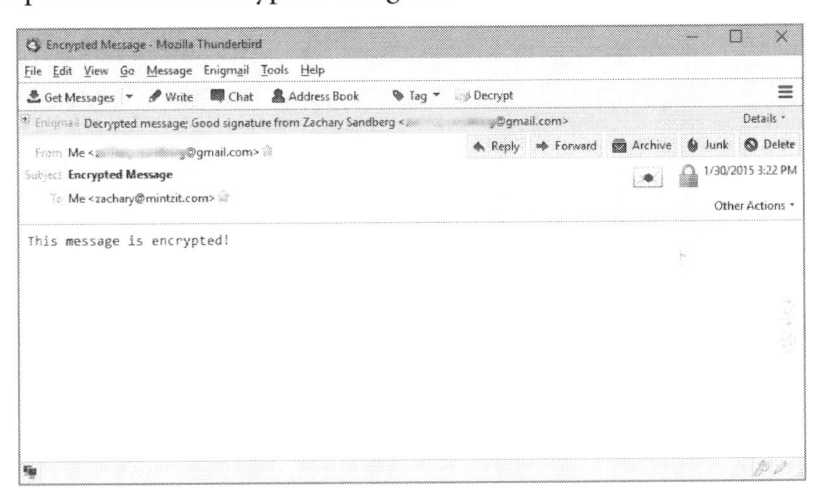

14. Vulnerability: Email

2. Should the recipient have any doubts as to the authenticity of the email, click on the lock icon. The certificate will display. Note the Key ID *1DB02505* on the 4th line.

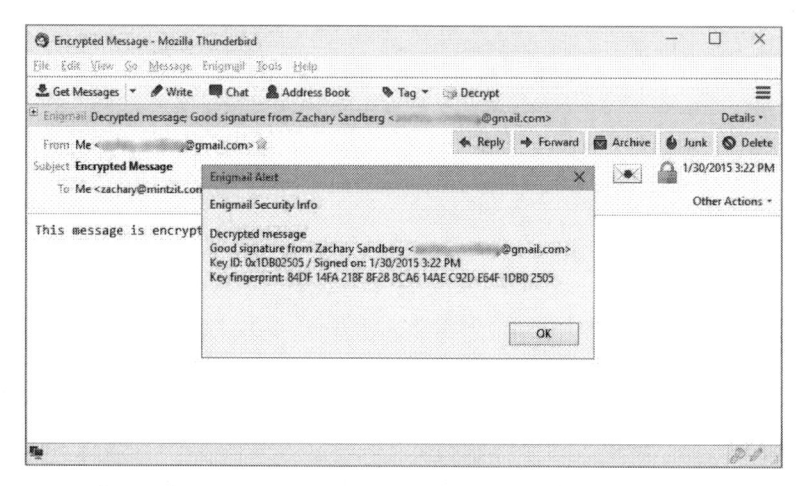

3. This *Key ID* from the email matches the Key name and ID stored in Kleopatra.

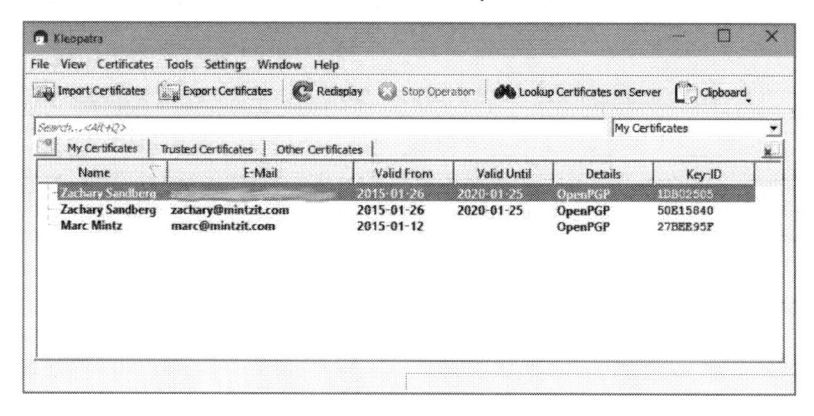

14. Vulnerability: Email

End-To-End Secure Email With S/MIME

S/MIME (Secure/Multipurpose Internet Mail Extensions) *http://en.wikipedia.org/wiki/S/MIME*, uses the same fundamental strategy of employing both Public and Private Keys to secure email as do PGP and GPG. Each person has a Private Key to decrypt a received email, and a Public Key that others may use to encrypt email to send out. An advantage of S/MIME over GPG is that there is no need to manually retrieve the other person's Public Key. Simply by signing an email and sending it to the other person, that person now has your Public Key. When the other person has done the same for you, the two of you may exchange encrypted email.

Unlike GPG, you will need to acquire an *email certificate* from a *Certificate Authority (CA)*. There are many Certificate Authorities available. Your Internet Provider or Web Host may be able to do this for you. Free certificates for personal use, which are valid for one year, are available, but using these can become tedious, as you will need to repeat all the steps below every year. Purchasing a commercial certificate will set you back $10 to $100 per year, but you will only have to go through the process once.

S/MIME offers three certificate classes:

- **Class 1**: This level of certificate is acquired without any background check or verification that the person requesting it has anything to do with the email address it will be assigned to. In fact, it is even possible to roll your own certificate. That said, it will verify that the email address in the *From* field is actually the address that sent the email, and do the job of encrypting email so that only the intended recipient can decrypt and read it.

- **Class 2**: This level takes it a step further, validating that not only is the email address in the *From* field the one that actually sent the email, but that the name in the *From* field is tied to that email address.

- **Class 3**: This is the highest-level validation, with a background check performed to verify not only the name of the individual or company, but physical address as well. **This is the only class suitable for healthcare (HIPAA), legal, and corporate use.**

14. Vulnerability: Email

Assignment: Acquire a Free Class 1 S/MIME Certificate for Personal Use

In this assignment you will sign-up for a free 1-year free S/MIME certificate for personal use from a leading Certificate Authority, Comodo, in Windows 10. This can be converted into a long-term commercial certificate.

1. Open your web browser and surf to *Comodo* at *https://comodo.com*.
2. From the navigation bar, select *Home & Home Office > Free Email Certificate*.

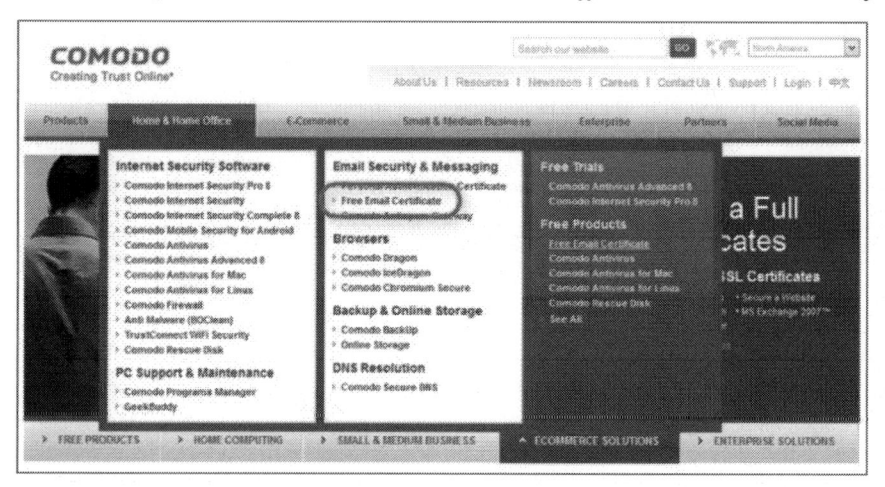

3. This takes you to the *Free Secure Email Certificate* page. Select the *Free Email Certificate* button:

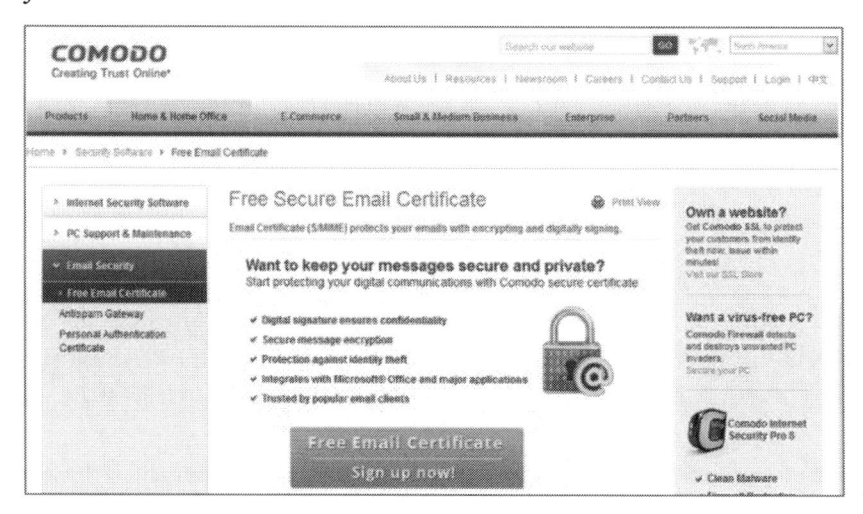

14. Vulnerability: Email

4. The *Application for Secure Email Certificate* page opens. Complete the form, specifying *High Grade* for your *Key Size*, and then select the *Next* button.

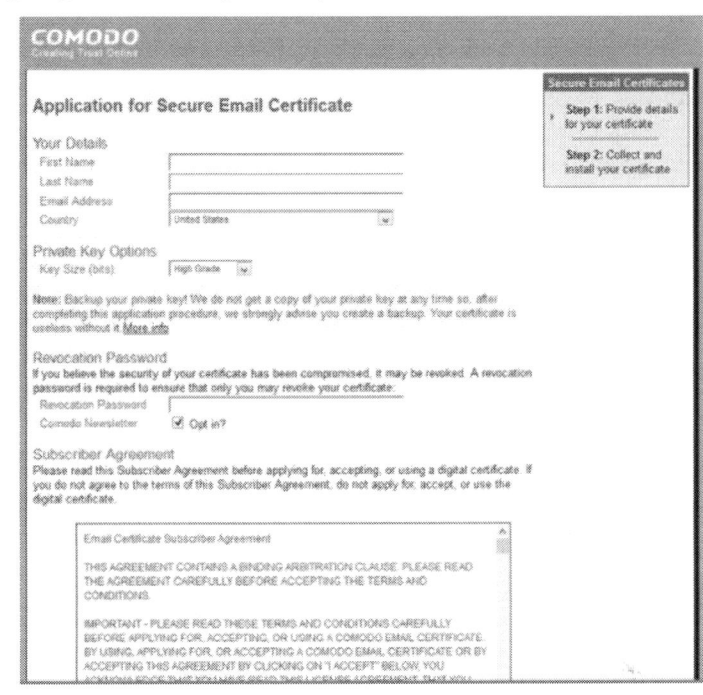

5. If all was completed correctly, you will see the *Application is Successful* page.

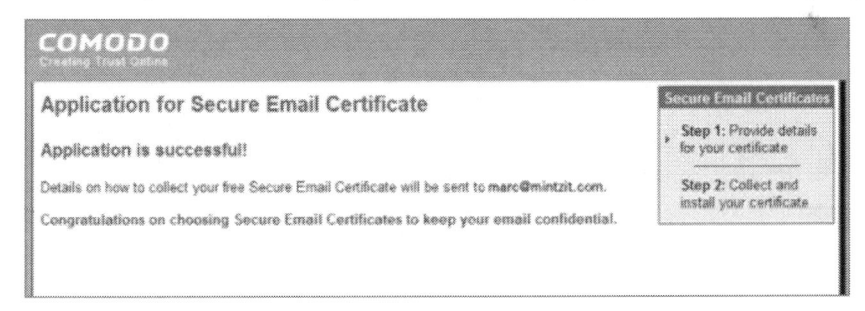

14. Vulnerability: Email

6. The certificate will be sent to the email address you specified.

7. Open your email to find the mail from Comodo, and then select the *Click & Install Comodo Email Certificate* button. You will be taken to the Comodo website to install the certificate on your computer

8. Assuming you are using Firefox, upon visiting the Comodo page, the Comodo certificate will automatically install in your browser. If using a different browser, you may be prompted to *install* or *download the certificate* manually.

9. Once installed in your browser, it's time to export the certificate and the associated private key to your email application. For this example we will be using Mozilla Thunderbird.

10. Go to the Firefox Menu and select the *Options* button

14. Vulnerability: Email

11. In the Options pane, select the *Advanced* tab, and then the *View Certificates* button.

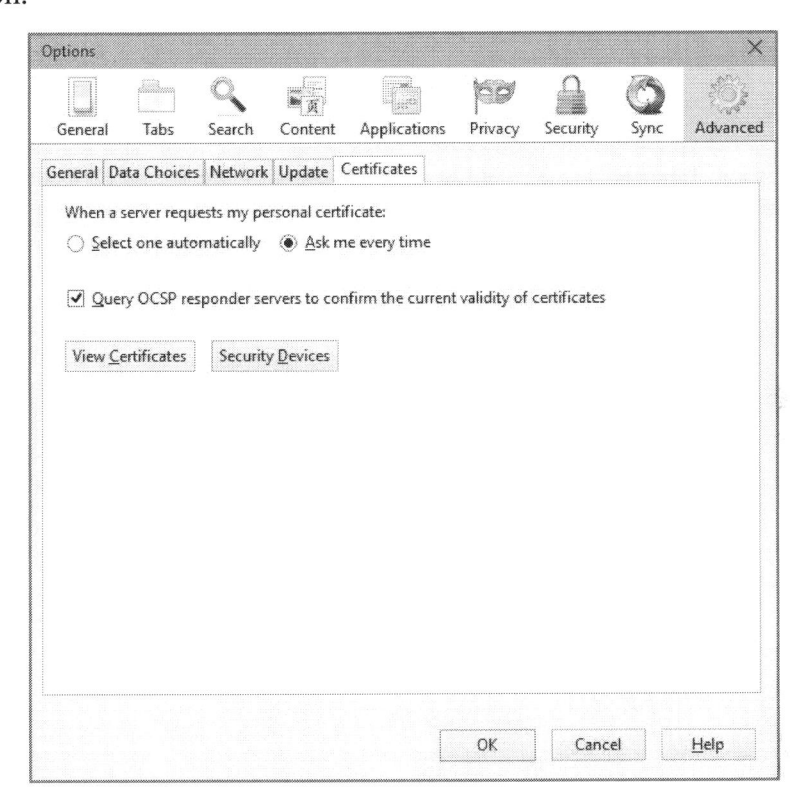

14. Vulnerability: Email

12. Once *View Certificates* opens, click the *Your Certificates* tab at the top. Select the certificate that was just installed, and then select the *Backup* button.

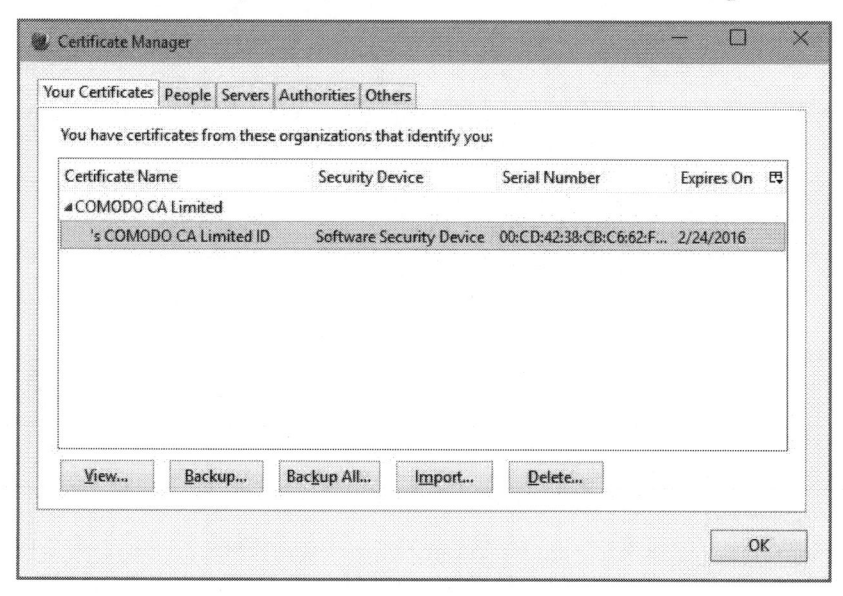

13. Select the *Save* button.

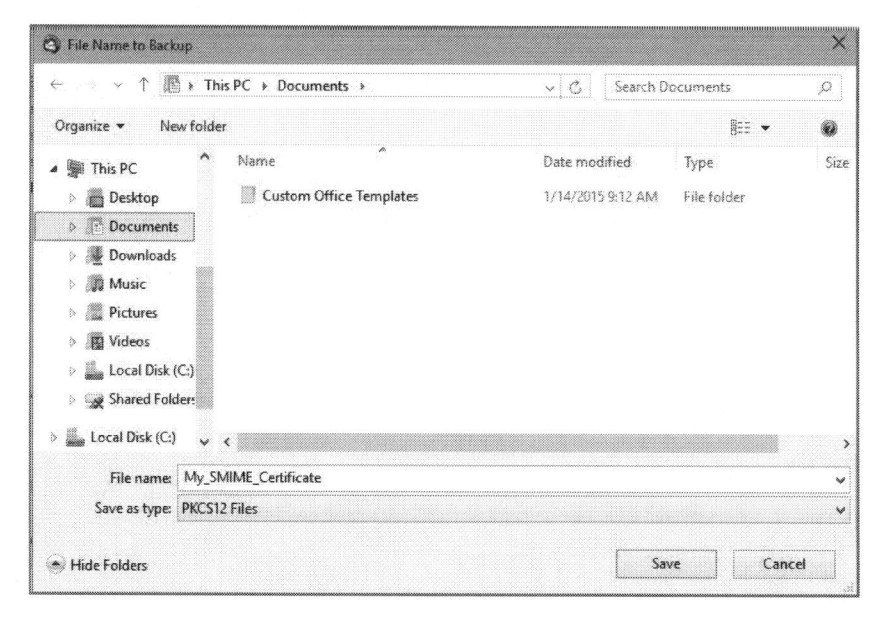

14. Vulnerability: Email

14. Name your personal certificate and click the *Save* button.

15. In the *Choose a Certificate Backup Password* window, enter a secure password, so that your exported Certificates will be secured with strong encryption, and then select the *OK* button.

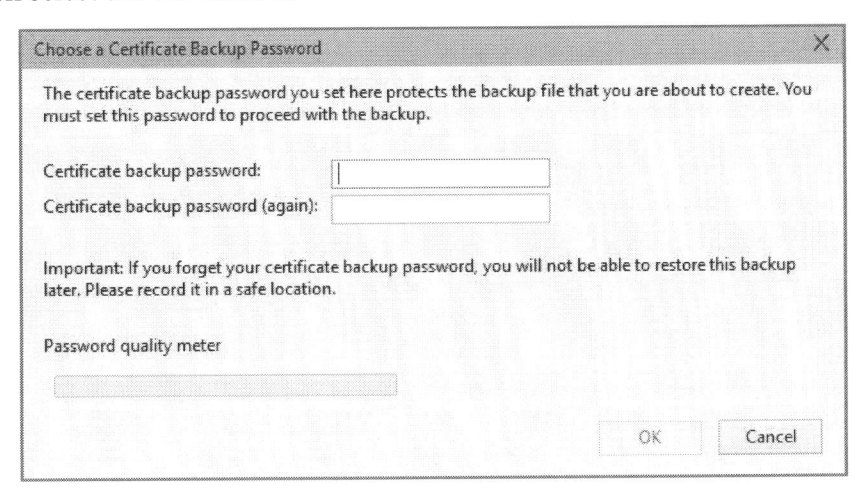

16. A dialog box will appear confirming that your new E-mail certificate has been successfully exported. Select the *OK* button.

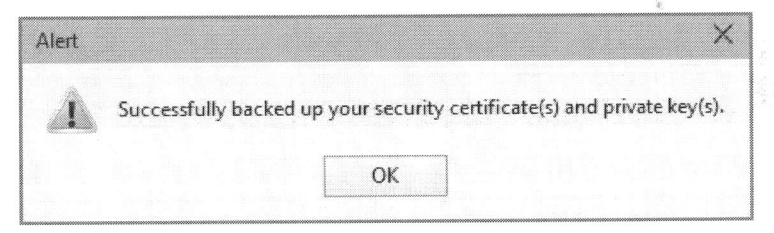

14. Vulnerability: Email

17. Assuming you are using Mozilla Thunderbird, open Thunderbird, click the *Menu Button*, and then select *Options* from the list.

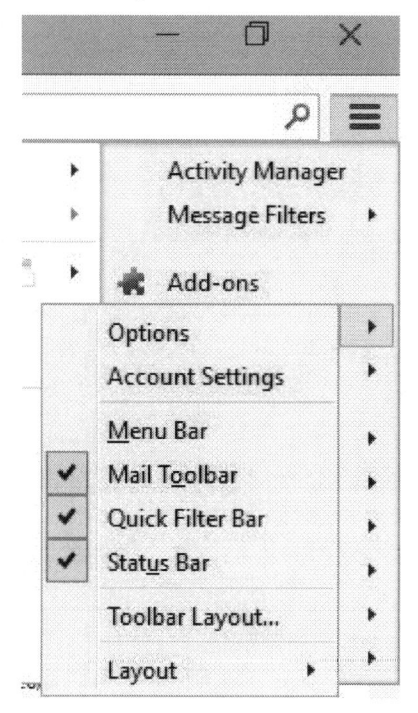

18. Click the *Certificates* tab, and then the *View Certificates* button (similar to what we previously did in Firefox.)

14. Vulnerability: Email

19. In the *Certificate Manager* window, click the *Import* button, and then select the saved Certificate file we created in the previous exercise.

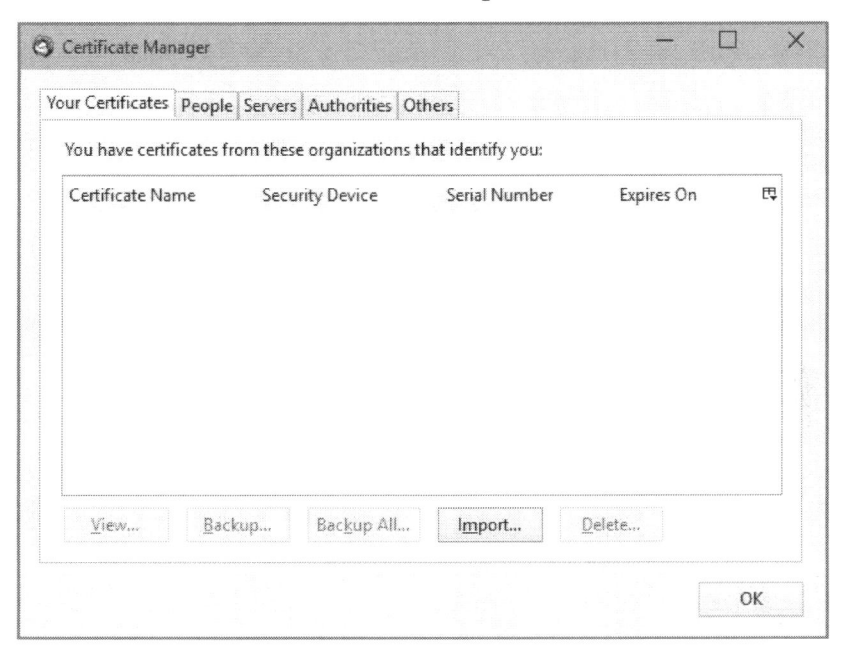

14. Vulnerability: Email

20. Select the path to the location where the previously exported certificate was saved (In the above example, we used the user *Documents* folder. Select the certificate and click the *Open* button.

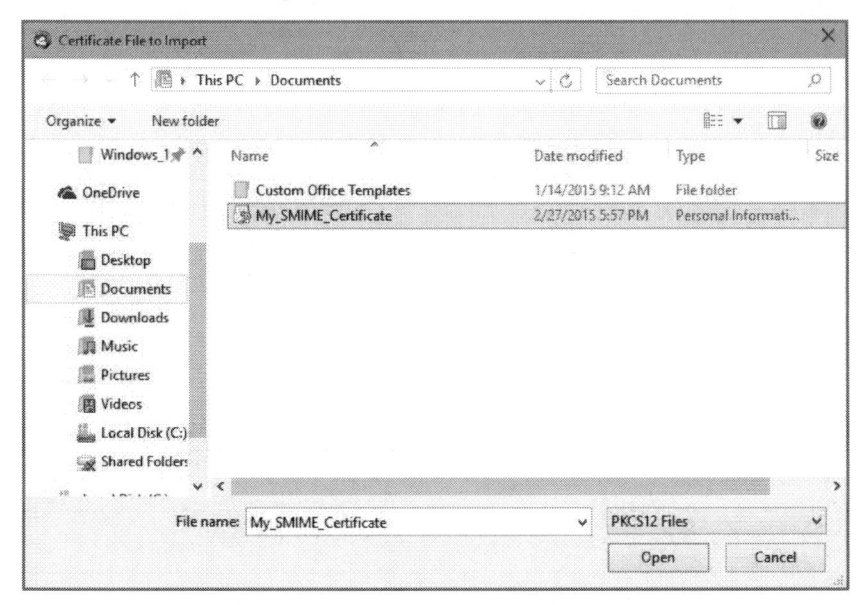

14. Vulnerability: Email

21. Enter the password previously created for the exported certificates.

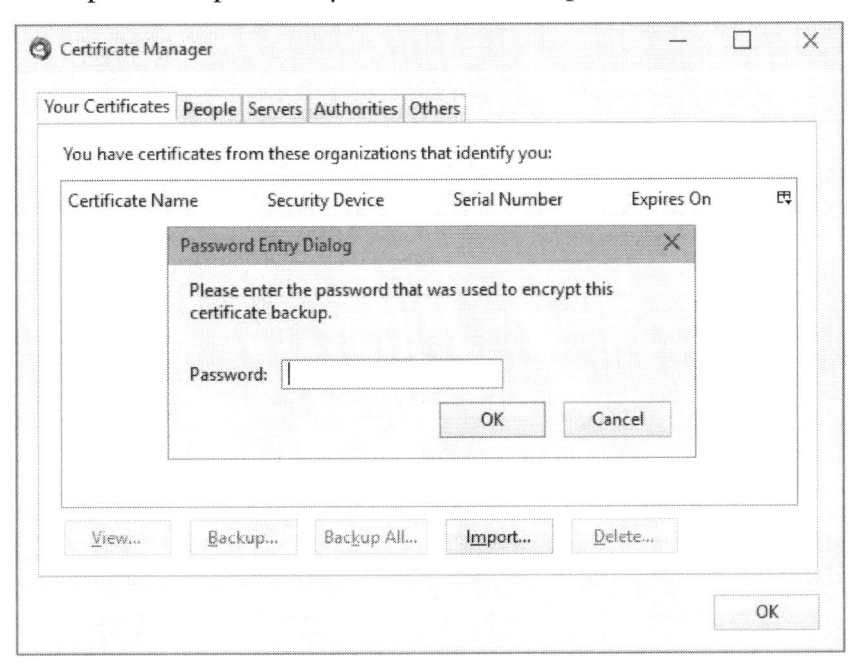

14. Vulnerability: Email

22. The certificate is now installed in Thunderbird. Click the *OK* button to close the dialog box.

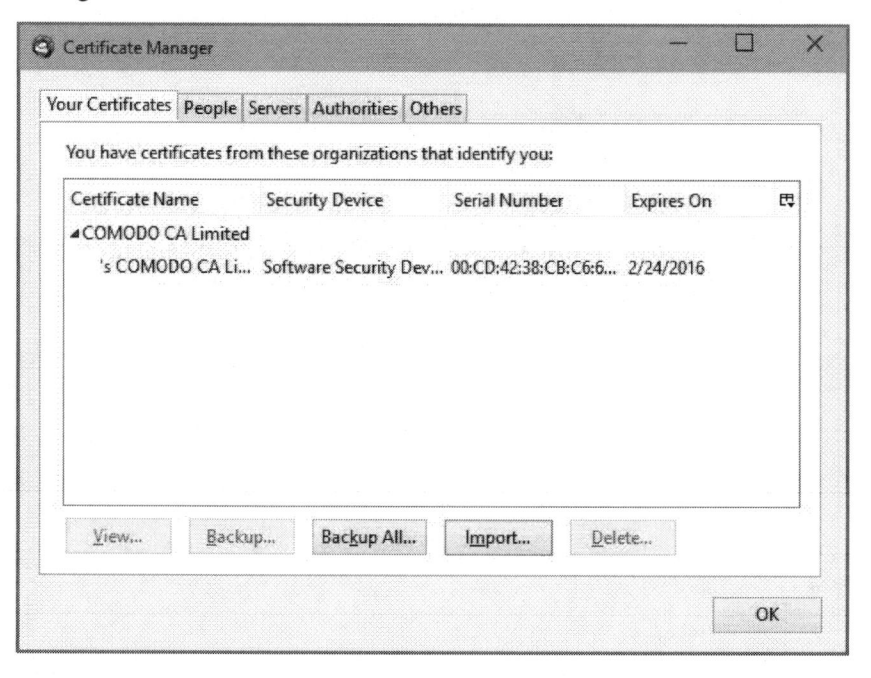

14. Vulnerability: Email

23. The last step of installing an S/MIME certificate in Thunderbird is to configure your email account to use the newly imported certificate. Click on the Thunderbird *Menu Button*, select *Options*, and then *Account Settings*.

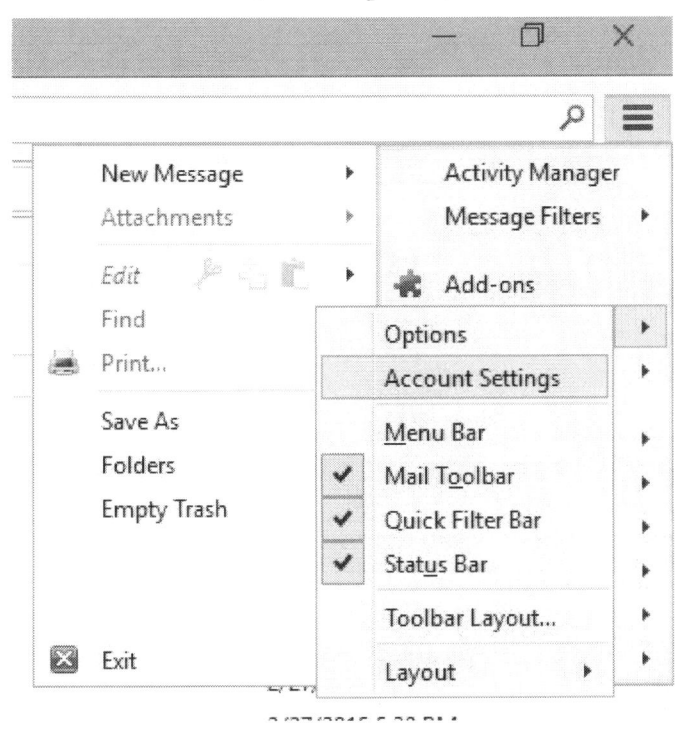

14. Vulnerability: Email

24. In the *Account Settings* sidebar, locate the appropriate account and select *Security*. Then, in the *Digital Signing* section, click the *Select* button.

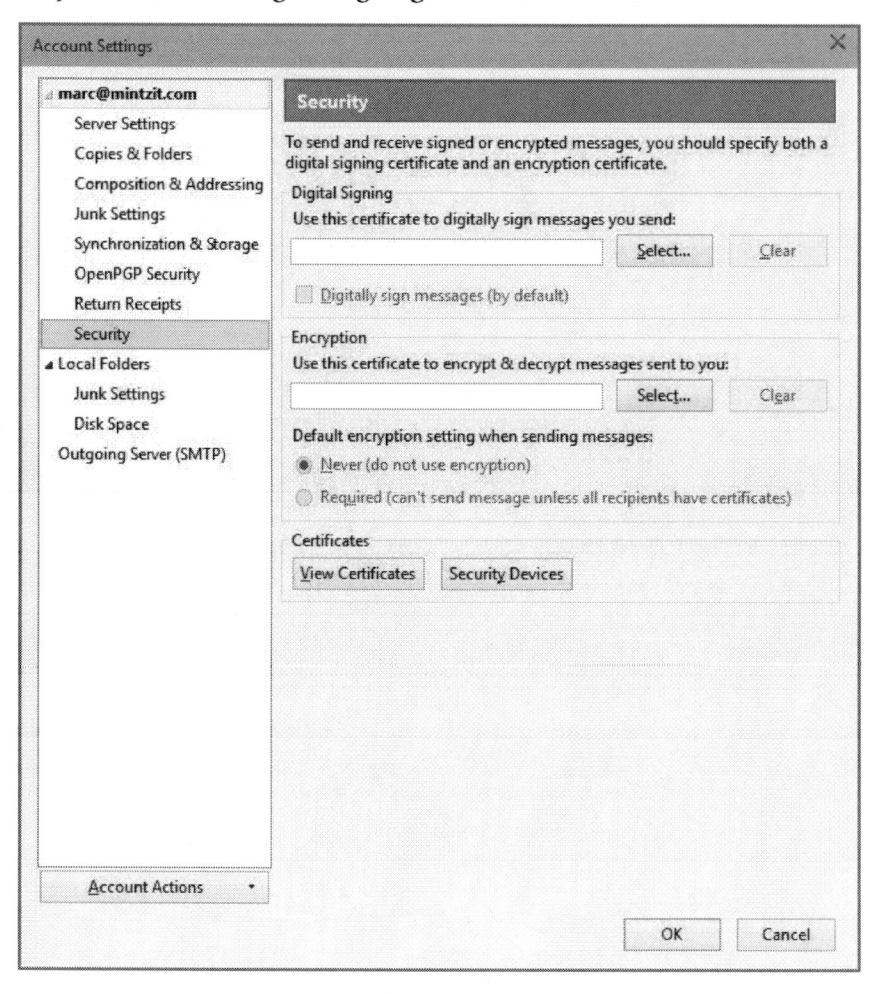

14. Vulnerability: Email

25. Select the Comodo S/MIME certificate that was installed earlier from the drop-down menu. Click the *OK* button.

26. Thunderbird then prompts you to choose whether or not this certificate should also be used for encrypting email. Click *Yes* to close the dialog.

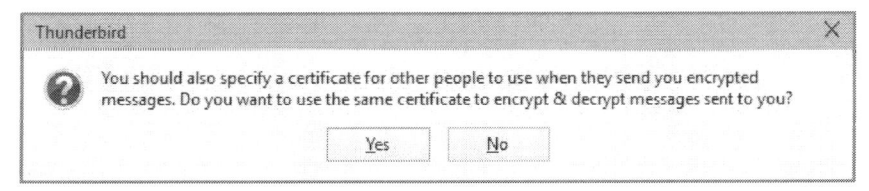

14. Vulnerability: Email

27. Within the *Encryption* section, select *Never (do not use encryption)*.
    Encryption can instead be enabled *à la carte* for individual messages. Click the *OK* button.

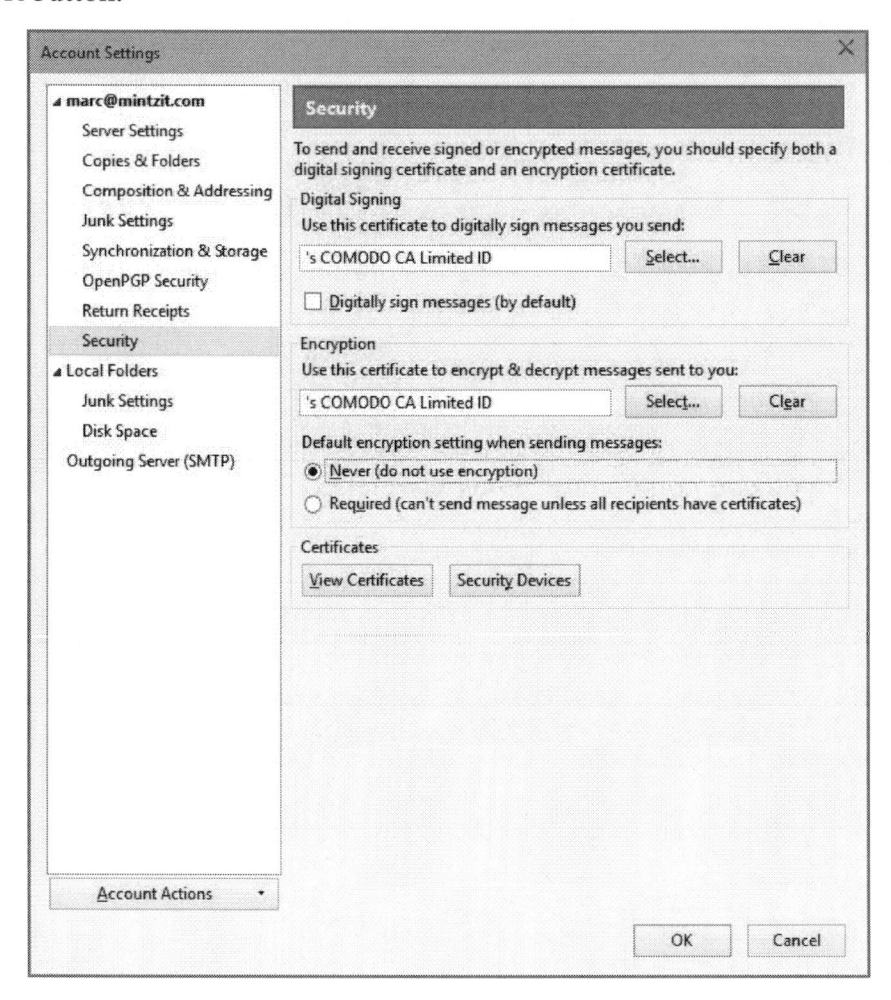

Wahoo. The hard part is over. You now are the proud owner (at least for a year) of email certificates for each of your email accounts. Next step is to start using your new powers.

14. Vulnerability: Email

Assignment: Setup a Business Account to Purchase Class 3 S/MIME Certificates

Getting a Class 3 certificate is significantly more involved than that of a Class 1. This is in part due to the need for identity verification, but also to the need for an infrastructure to help with managing potentially thousands of email addresses within an organization.

In this assignment we will start the process of acquiring a class 3 certificate from Comodo.

1. Using your web browser, visit *Comodo.com*
2. From the Navigation bar, select *Business & Enterprise > Email and Identity > Secure Email Certificate*.

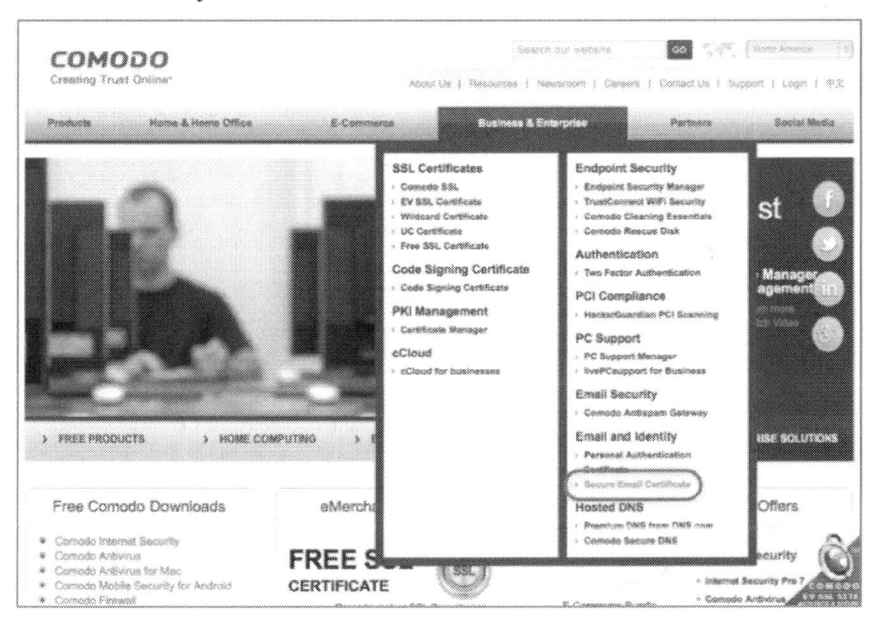

14. Vulnerability: Email

3. In the Secure Email Certificates page, select the *Email Certificate Buy Now* button.

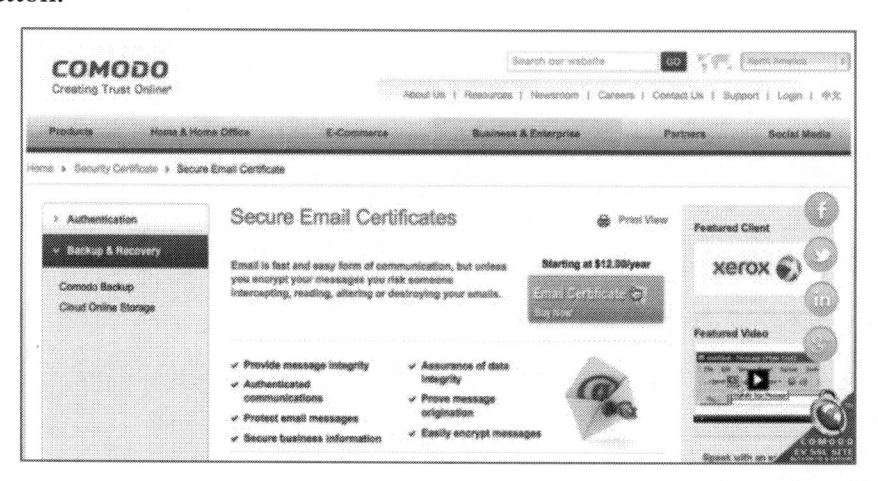

14. Vulnerability: Email

4. In the *Purchase Corporate Secure Email Digital Certificate* page, enter your desired *Term* and *Quantity*. And then select the *Next* button.

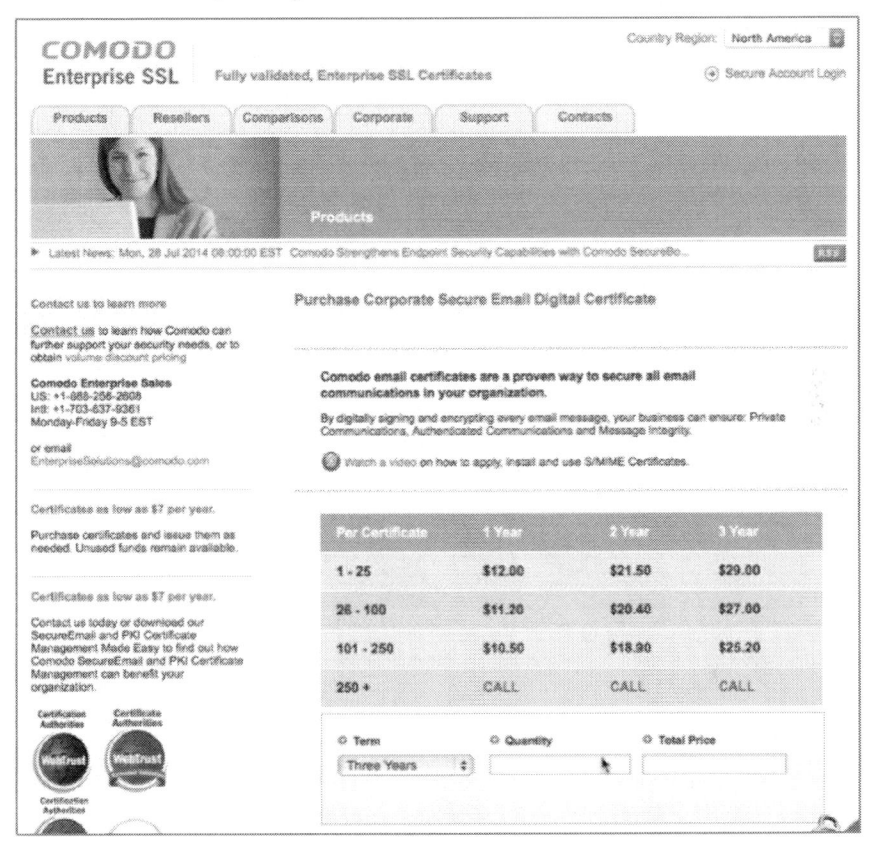

14. Vulnerability: Email

5. In the *Open an Enterprise S/MIME Enterprise PKI Manager (E-PKI) Account* window. Enter a domain name for your certificates, and then select the *Next* button.

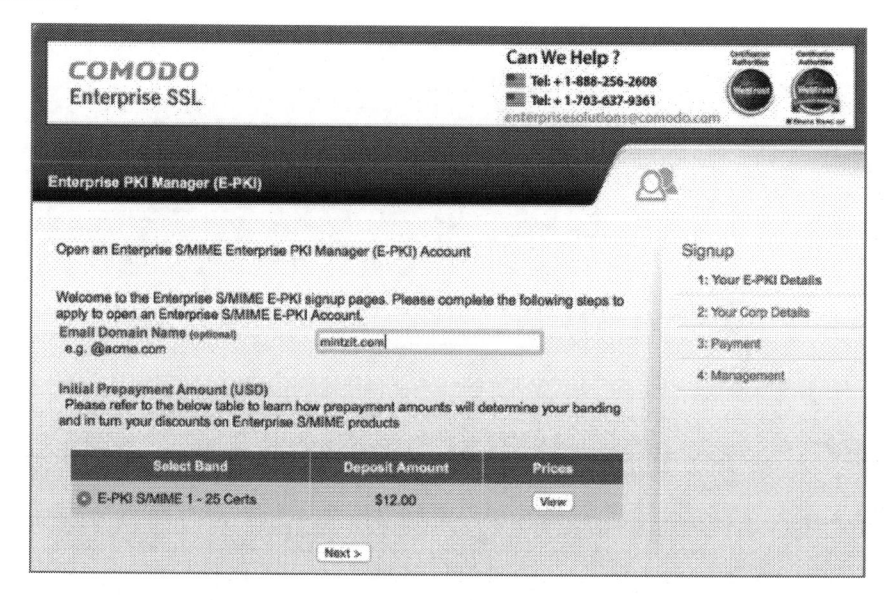

14. Vulnerability: Email

6. In the *Step 2: Your Corporate Details* page, enter all requested information, and then select the *Next* button.

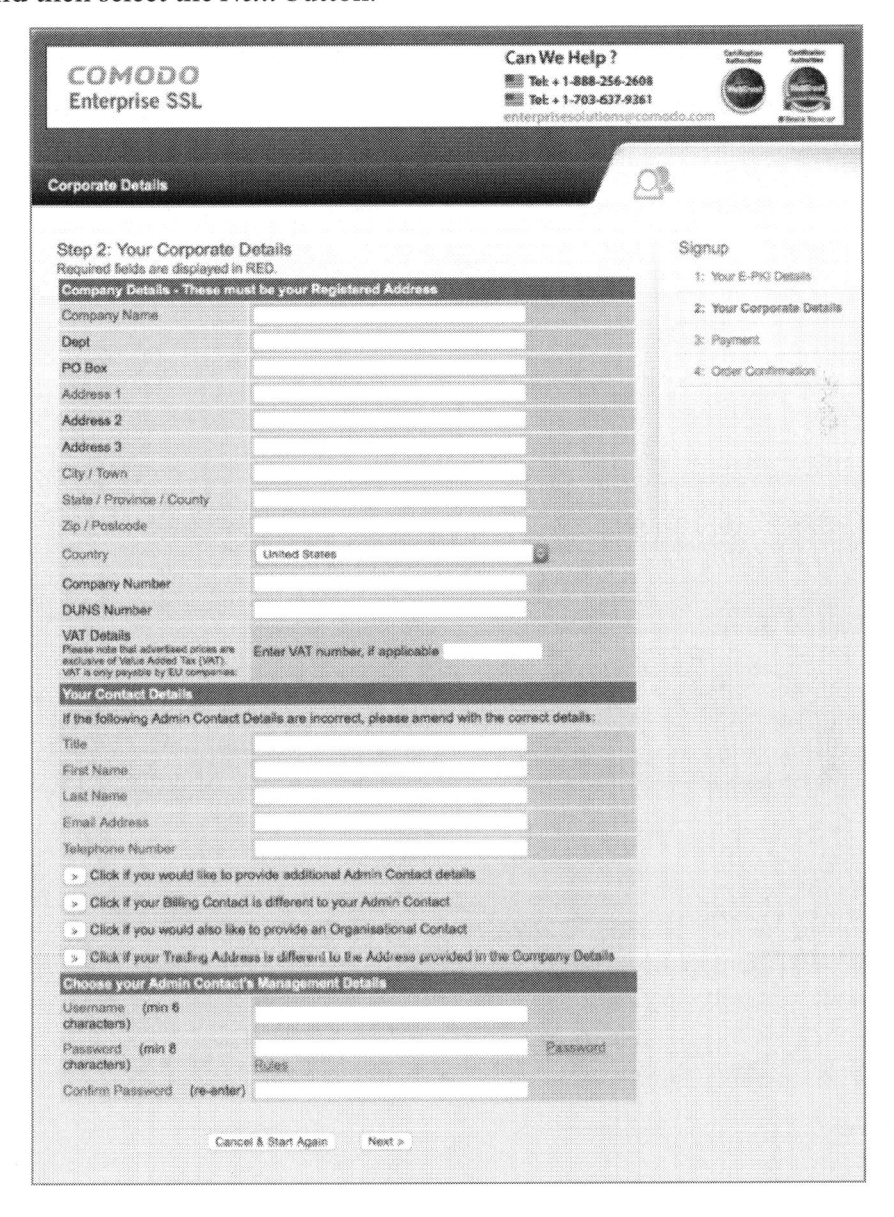

14. Vulnerability: Email

8. At the *Agreement* page, select the *I ACCEPT* button.

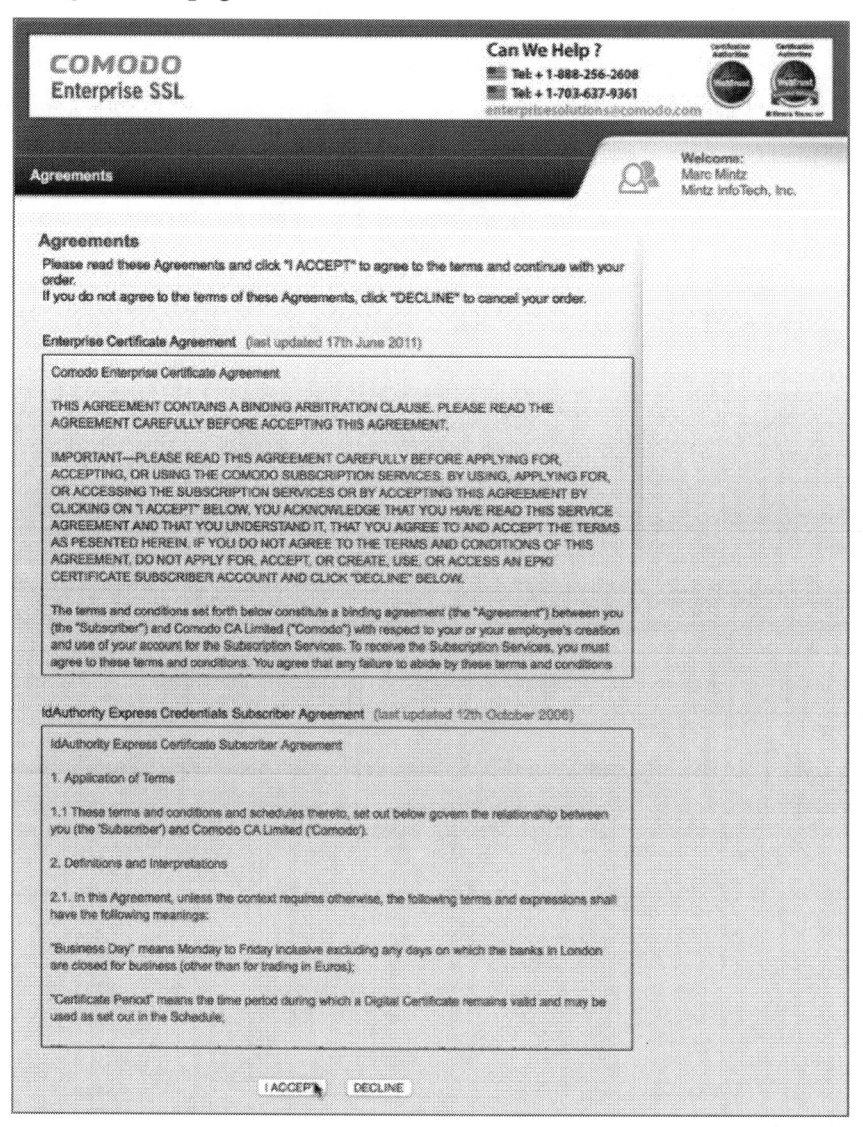

14. Vulnerability: Email

9. In the *Secure Payment Page,* enter your credit card information, and then select the *Make Payment* button.

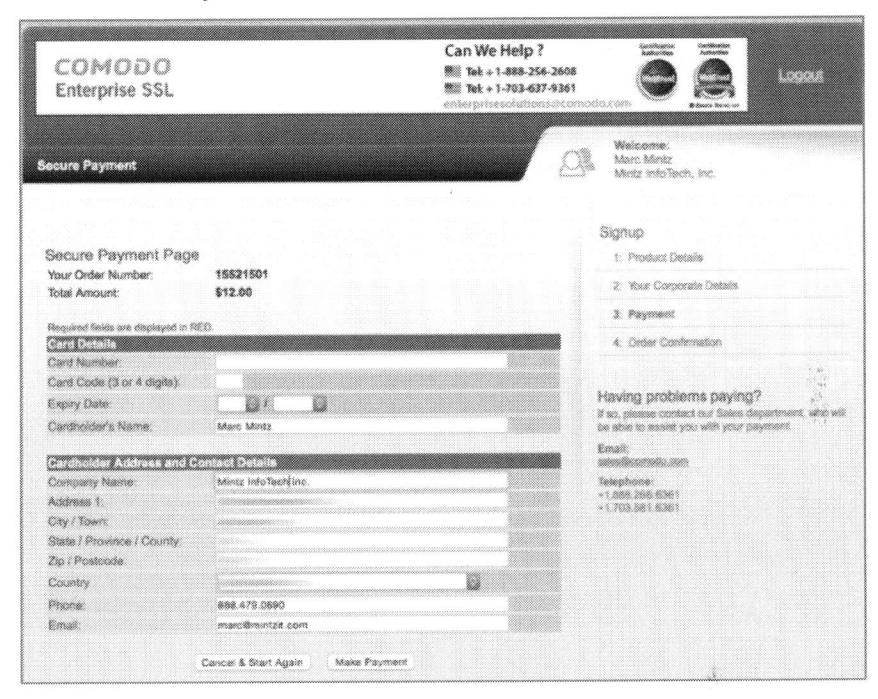

10. You will receive an email from Comodo informing you of receipt of your order, and stating that you will soon be receiving another email requesting documents to validate your identity.

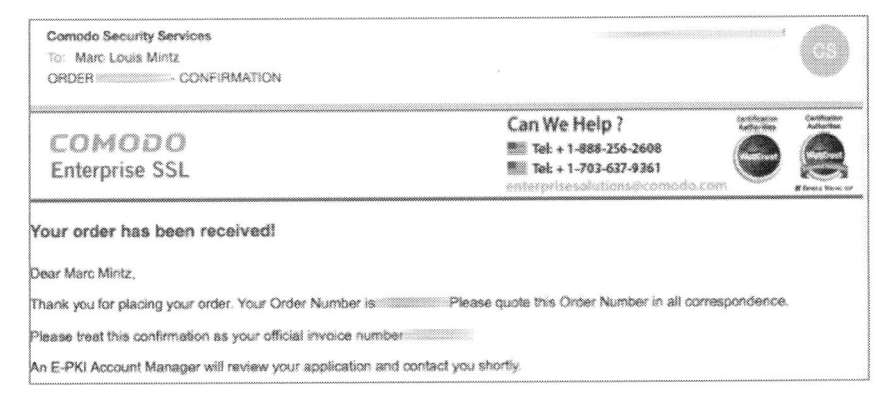

11. Soon you will receive an email requesting the validation documents. Submit the requested documents and information.

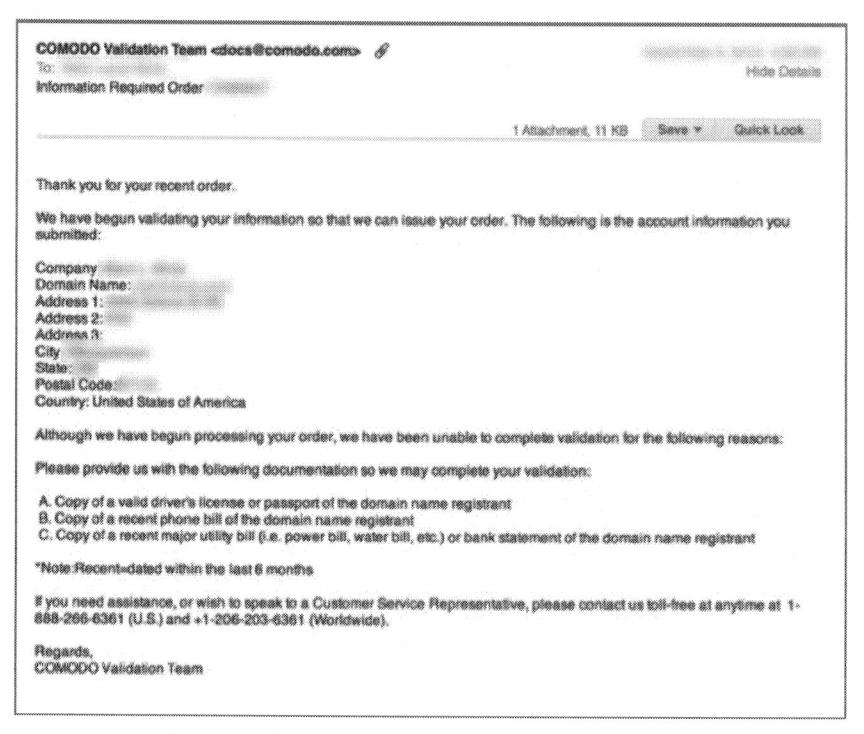

> **COMODO Validation Team** <docs@comodo.com>
> To:
> Information Required Order
>
> 1 Attachment, 11 KB
>
> Thank you for your recent order.
>
> We have begun validating your information so that we can issue your order. The following is the account information you submitted:
>
> Company
> Domain Name:
> Address 1:
> Address 2:
> Address 3:
> City
> State:
> Postal Code:
> Country: United States of America
>
> Although we have begun processing your order, we have been unable to complete validation for the following reasons:
>
> Please provide us with the following documentation so we may complete your validation:
>
> A. Copy of a valid driver's license or passport of the domain name registrant
> B. Copy of a recent phone bill of the domain name registrant
> C. Copy of a recent major utility bill (i.e. power bill, water bill, etc.) or bank statement of the domain name registrant
>
> *Note:Recent=dated within the last 6 months
>
> If you need assistance, or wish to speak to a Customer Service Representative, please contact us toll-free at anytime at 1-888-266-6361 (U.S.) and +1-206-203-6361 (Worldwide).
>
> Regards,
> COMODO Validation Team

12. You will receive an email informing you that your account has been created, with a link to their *Getting Started Guide*. Although the steps outlined in this book will take you through the process, it is not a bad idea to download and read the Guide as well. Download the *Getting Started Guide*.

13. Register for Comodo technical support by clicking the link provided in the email, and then follow the on-screen instructions. This will save you significant time and headaches if you ever need technical support from Comodo.

Assignment: Purchase a Class 3 S/MIME Certificate for Business Use

Once you have set up your Class 3 business account with Comodo, you are able to order S/MIME certificates for you and your staff at any time. In this exercise, you will purchase your first certificate.

14. Vulnerability: Email

1. From the Comodo email (see above), select the link to *Access your account here*. This will open the *Enterprise PKI Manager (E-PKI) Area* page. Enter the email address and password used to start your account with Comodo.

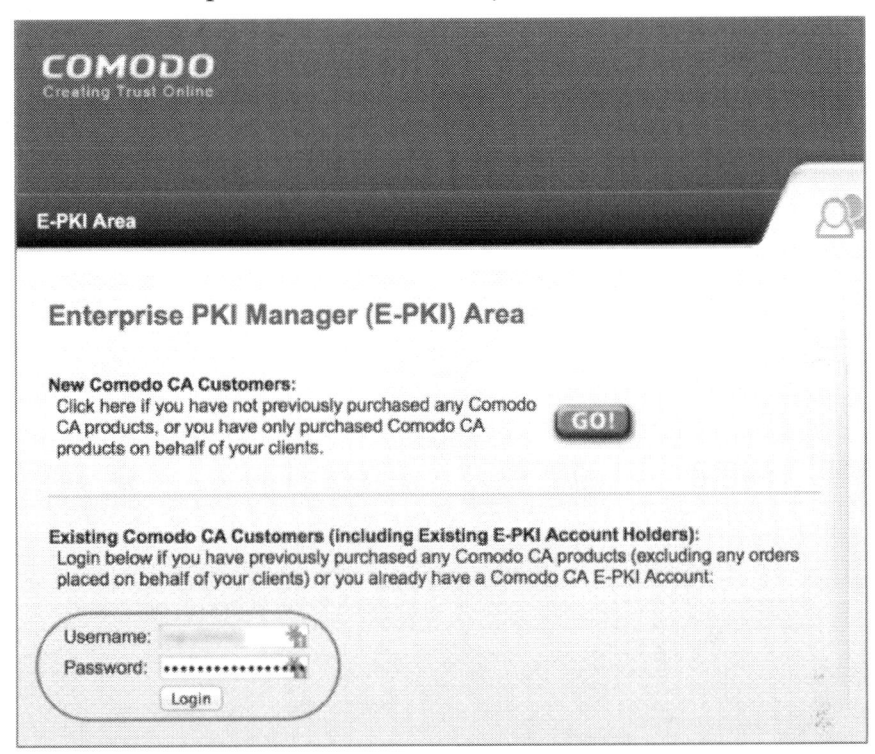

2. This will take you to the *Account Options: Management* page. Select the *E-PKI Manager* link.

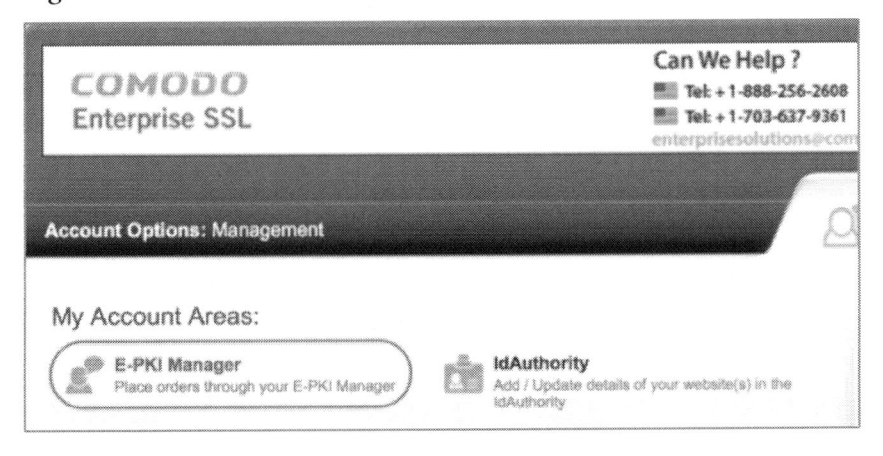

3. The *E-PKI Manager: Account Options: Management* page opens. With Comodo, you pay for certificates not directly, but by pulling from monies on deposit with Comodo. If there are inadequate funds on deposit, you will need to deposit money now. To do so, select the *Deposit additional funds* link.

14. Vulnerability: Email

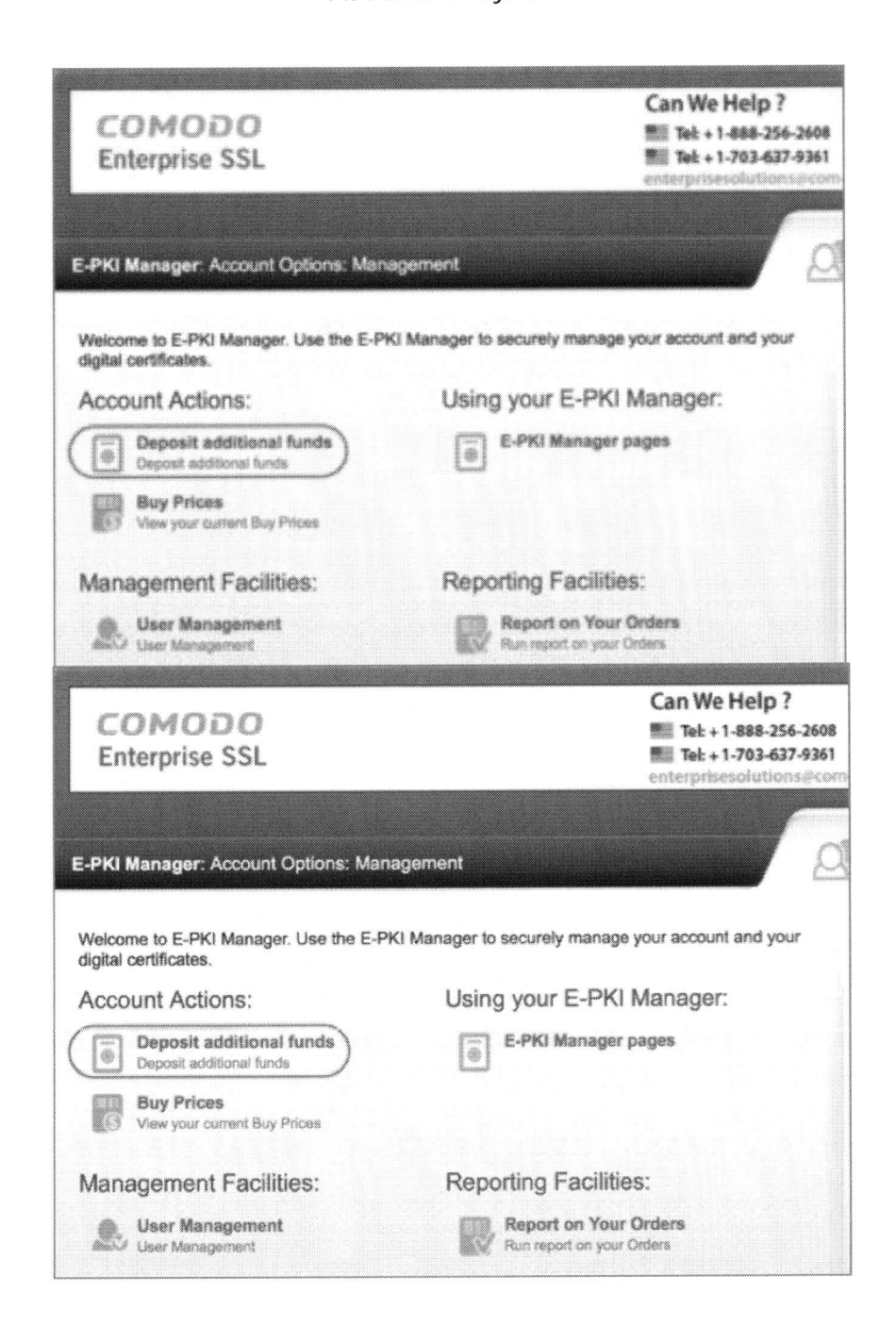

14. Vulnerability: Email

4. In the *Deposit Funds: Account Options: Management* page, enter at least the amount needed to purchase your S/MIME certificates. Rates per certificate as of this writing are.

Per Certificate	1 Year	2 Year	3 Year
1 - 25	$12.00	$21.50	$29.00
26 - 100	$11.20	$20.40	$27.00
101 - 250	$10.50	$18.90	$25.20
250 +	CALL	CALL	CALL

5. In the *Secure Payment* page enter your credit card information, and then select the *Make Payment* button.

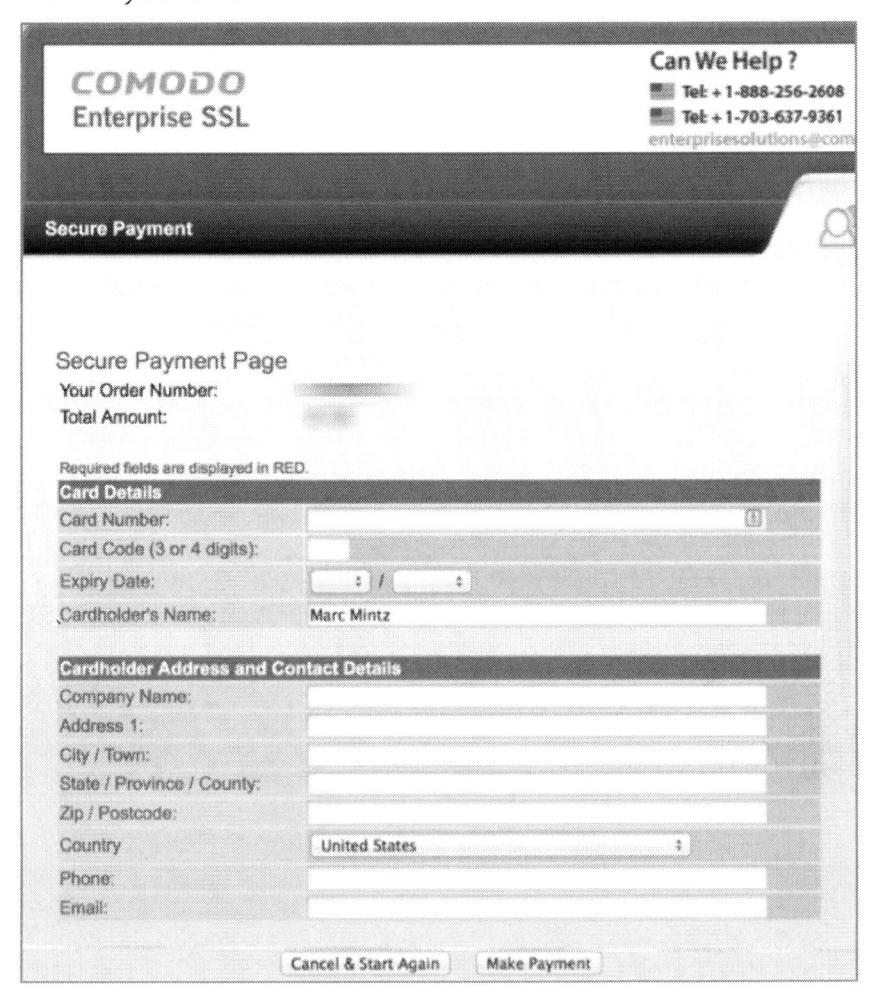

14. Vulnerability: Email

6. Return to the *Account Options: Management* page, and then select the *E-PKI Manager* link.

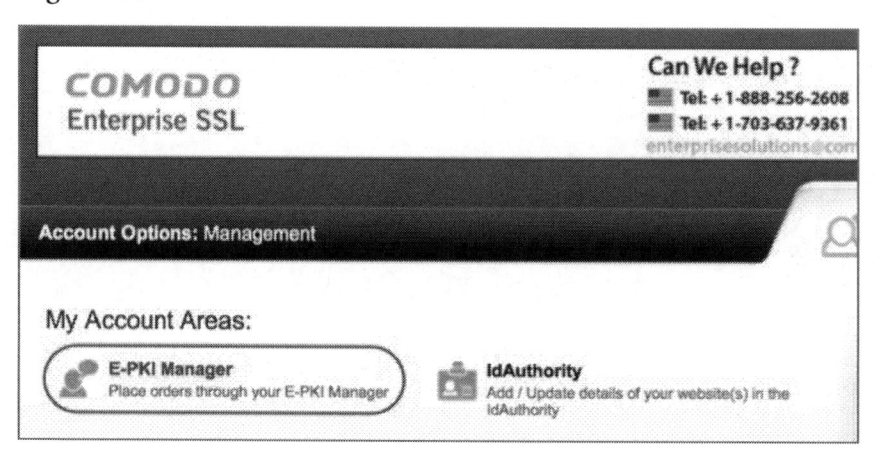

7. In the *E-PKI Manager: Account Options: Management* page, select the *User Management* link.

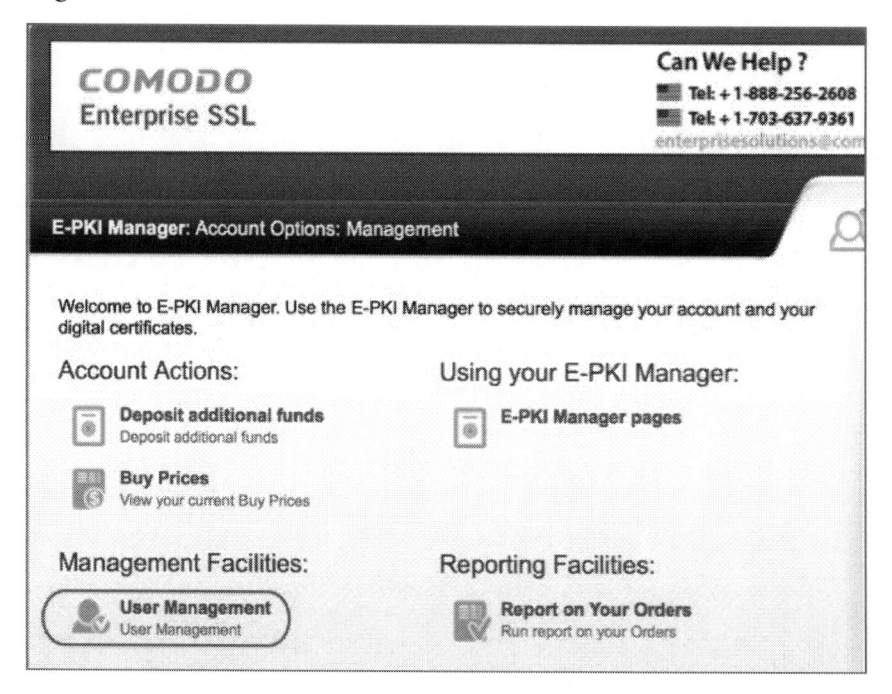

14. Vulnerability: Email

8. In the *User Management: Account Options: Management* page, select the *New User* button.

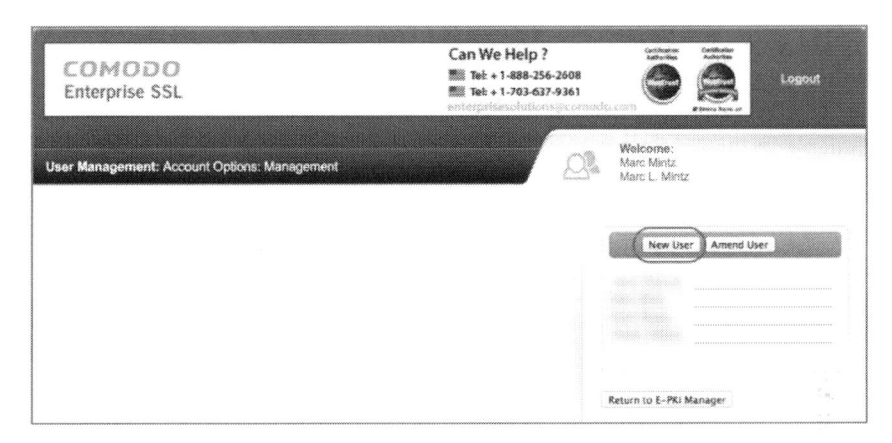

9. In the *New User* window, enter all information for your new user, select the *Save Changes* button, and then *Close* the window.

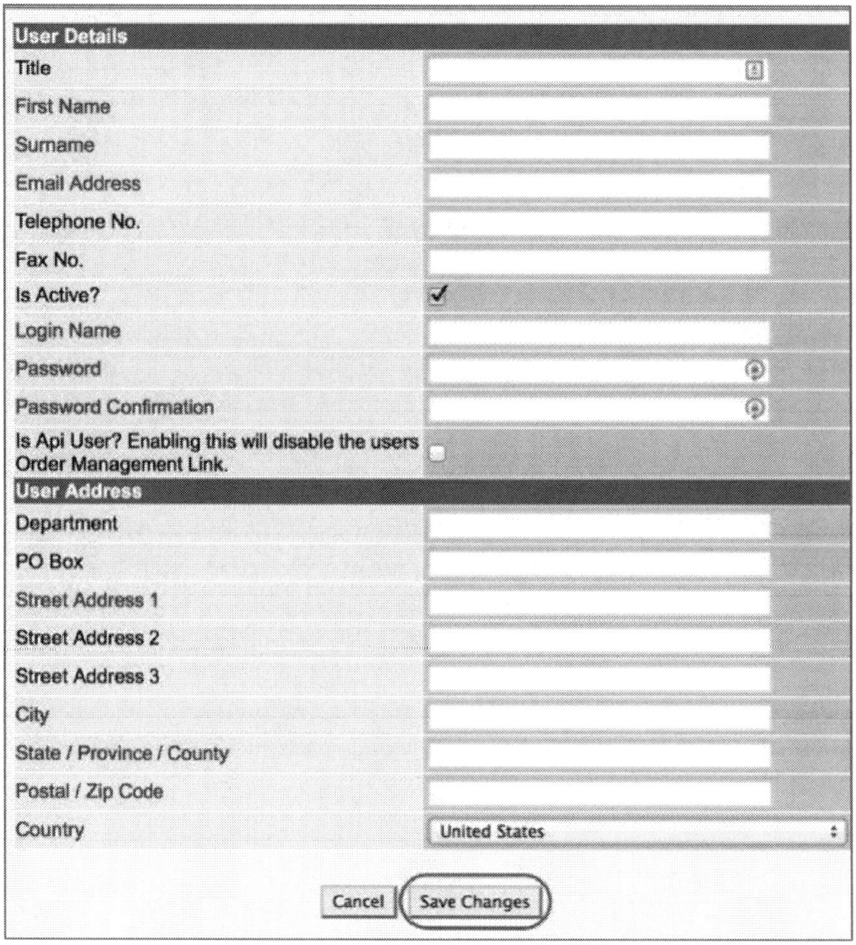
User Details
Title
First Name
Surname
Email Address
Telephone No.
Fax No.
Is Active?
Login Name
Password
Password Confirmation
Is Api User? Enabling this will disable the users Order Management Link.
User Address
Department
PO Box
Street Address 1
Street Address 2
Street Address 3
City
State / Province / County
Postal / Zip Code
Country
United States
Cancel
Save Changes

10. Repeat steps 7-9 to enable each user/email account to have an S/MIME certificate.

14. Vulnerability: Email

11. When all certificates have been requested, return to the *User Management: Account Options: Management* window, and then select the *Return to E-PKI Manager* button.

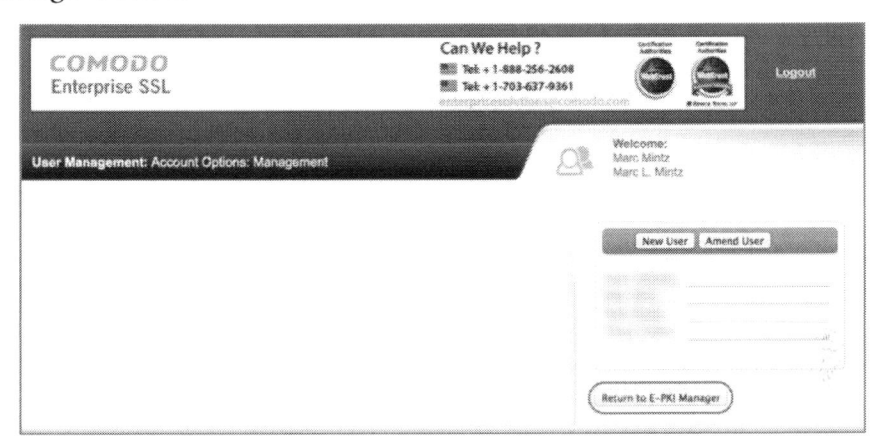

14. Vulnerability: Email

12. In the *E-PKI Manager: Account Options: Management* page, scroll to the bottom, and then select the *Corporate Secure Email Certificate Buy* button.

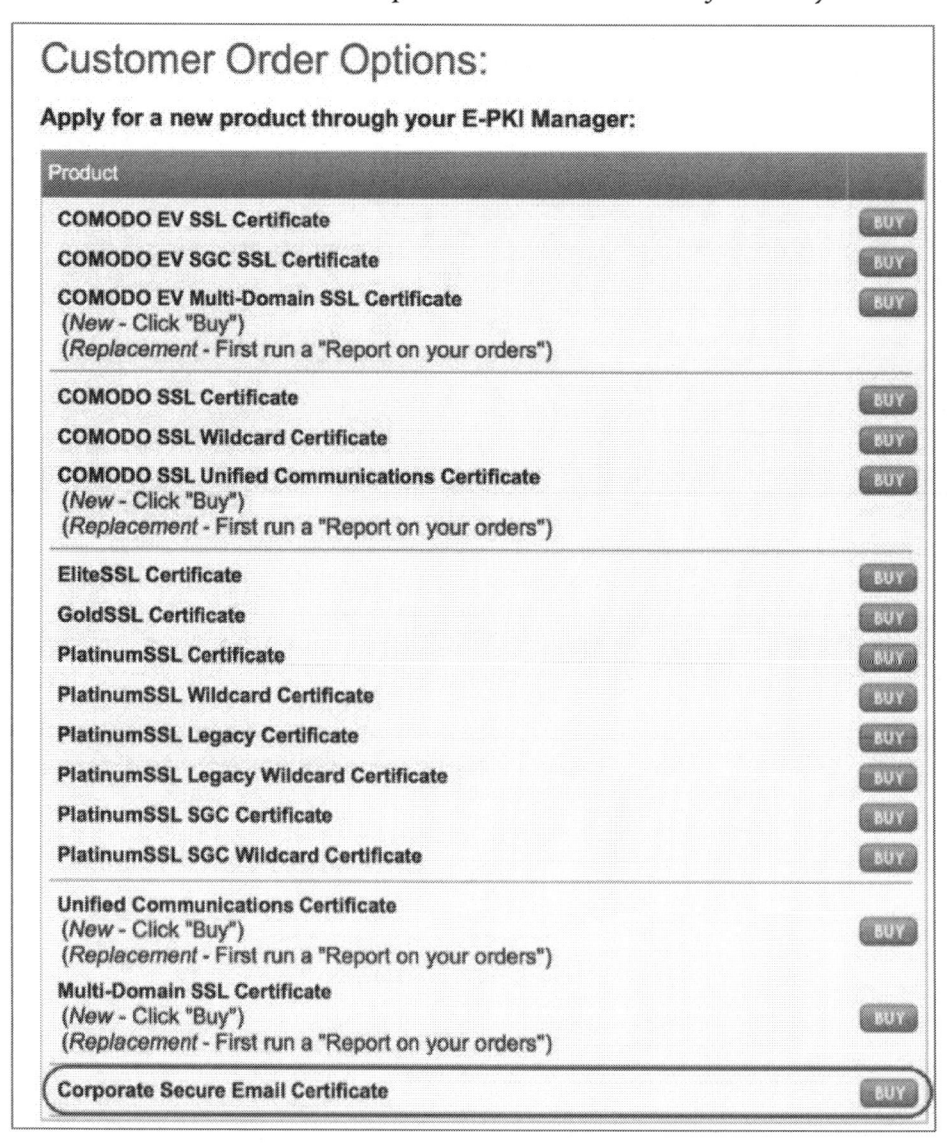

Customer Order Options:

Apply for a new product through your E-PKI Manager:

Product	
COMODO EV SSL Certificate	BUY
COMODO EV SGC SSL Certificate	BUY
COMODO EV Multi-Domain SSL Certificate (*New* - Click "Buy") (*Replacement* - First run a "Report on your orders")	BUY
COMODO SSL Certificate	BUY
COMODO SSL Wildcard Certificate	BUY
COMODO SSL Unified Communications Certificate (*New* - Click "Buy") (*Replacement* - First run a "Report on your orders")	BUY
EliteSSL Certificate	BUY
GoldSSL Certificate	BUY
PlatinumSSL Certificate	BUY
PlatinumSSL Wildcard Certificate	BUY
PlatinumSSL Legacy Certificate	BUY
PlatinumSSL Legacy Wildcard Certificate	BUY
PlatinumSSL SGC Certificate	BUY
PlatinumSSL SGC Wildcard Certificate	BUY
Unified Communications Certificate (*New* - Click "Buy") (*Replacement* - First run a "Report on your orders")	BUY
Multi-Domain SSL Certificate (*New* - Click "Buy") (*Replacement* - First run a "Report on your orders")	BUY
Corporate Secure Email Certificate	**BUY**

14. Vulnerability: Email

13. In the *Corporate Secure Email Certificate: E-PKI Manager: Management* page, complete the information for the user/email address you wish to assign an S/MIME certificate, and then select the *Submit* button.

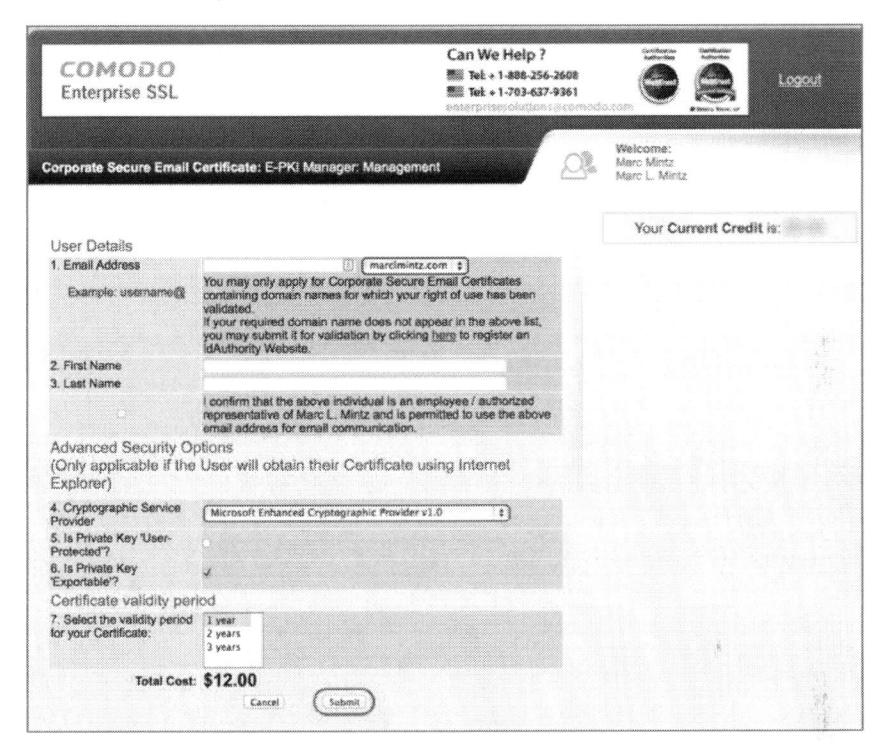

14. Vulnerability: Email

14. At the *Order Confirmation: E-PKI Manager: Management* page, print your receipt, and then select the *Return to* button.

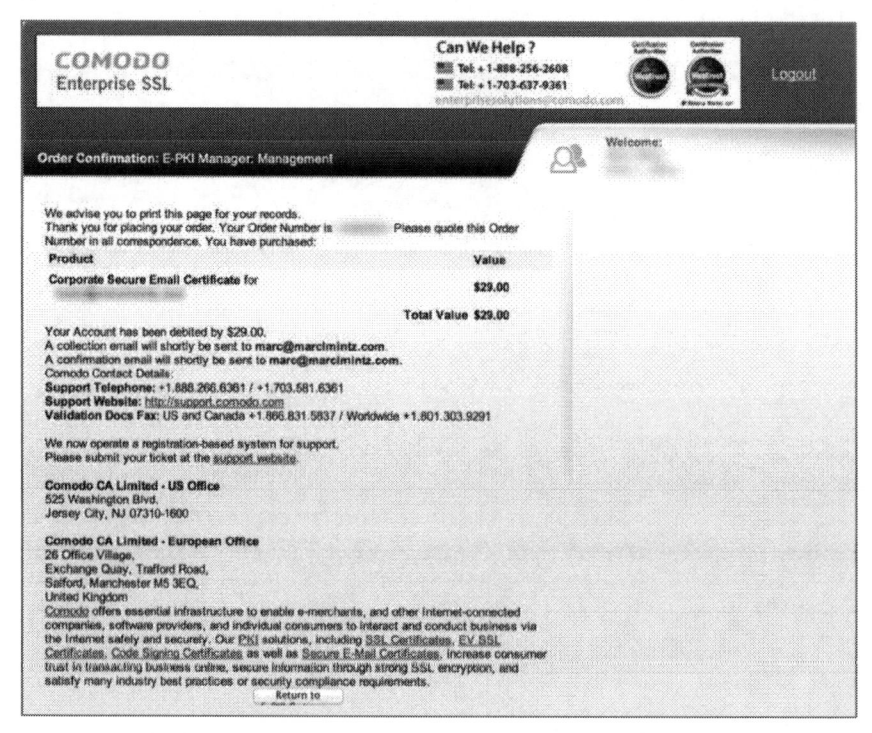

15. Repeat steps 12-14 for each user/email account to be assigned an S/MIME certificate.

Assignment: Download and Install a Business S/MIME Certificate

Once you have completed the steps above to provide a user/email account, that email address will receive notification of S/MIME certificate availability.

14. Vulnerability: Email

1. At the user's computer, check email for a message from *Comodo*, select and copy the *Your Certificate Password,* and then select the *Begin Corporate Secure Email Certificate Application* button.

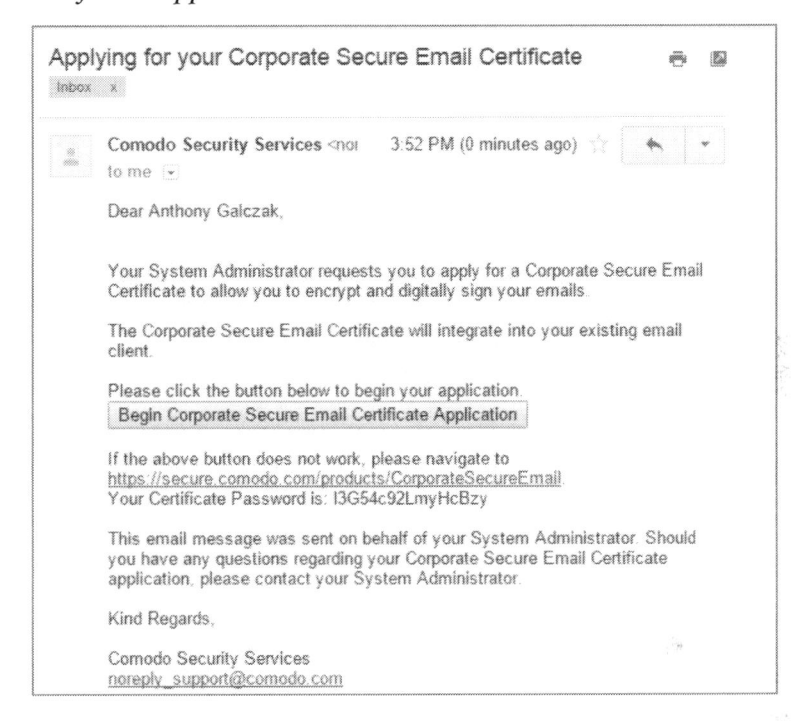

> **Applying for your Corporate Secure Email Certificate**
> Inbox x
>
> **Comodo Security Services** <nor   3:52 PM (0 minutes ago)
> to me
>
> Dear Anthony Galczak,
>
> Your System Administrator requests you to apply for a Corporate Secure Email Certificate to allow you to encrypt and digitally sign your emails.
>
> The Corporate Secure Email Certificate will integrate into your existing email client.
>
> Please click the button below to begin your application.
> [Begin Corporate Secure Email Certificate Application]
>
> If the above button does not work, please navigate to
> https://secure.comodo.com/products/CorporateSecureEmail
> Your Certificate Password is: I3G54c92LmyHcBzy
>
> This email message was sent on behalf of your System Administrator. Should you have any questions regarding your Corporate Secure Email Certificate application, please contact your System Administrator.
>
> Kind Regards,
>
> Comodo Security Services
> noreply_support@comodo.com

14. Vulnerability: Email

2. Click *Request My Certificate Now*.

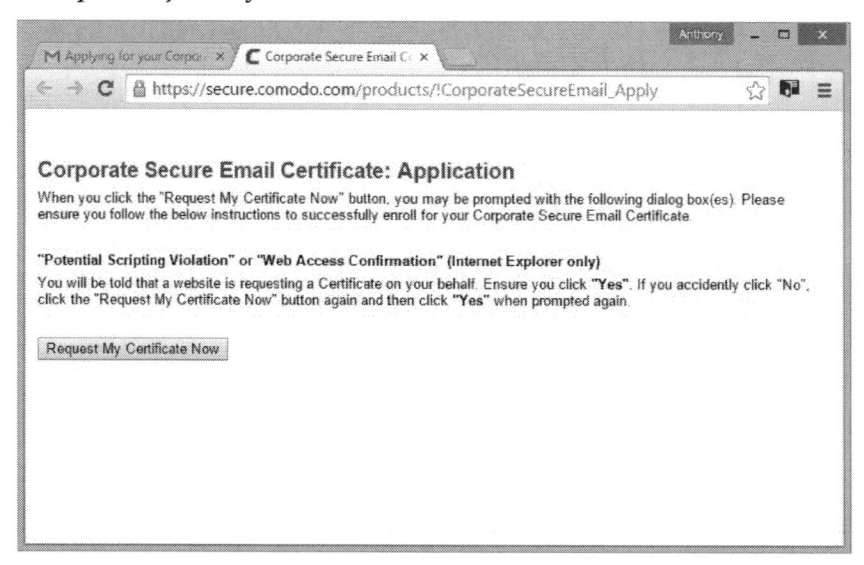

3. You will then receive an email for collecting your corporate email certificate. Click on *Begin Corporate Secure Email Certificate Collection*.

14. Vulnerability: Email

4. It will open an external web page that will save your certificate to your browser. Once you have collected your certificate, click on *View*. This may vary by browser, but we want to be able to access the certificate wizard for Windows.

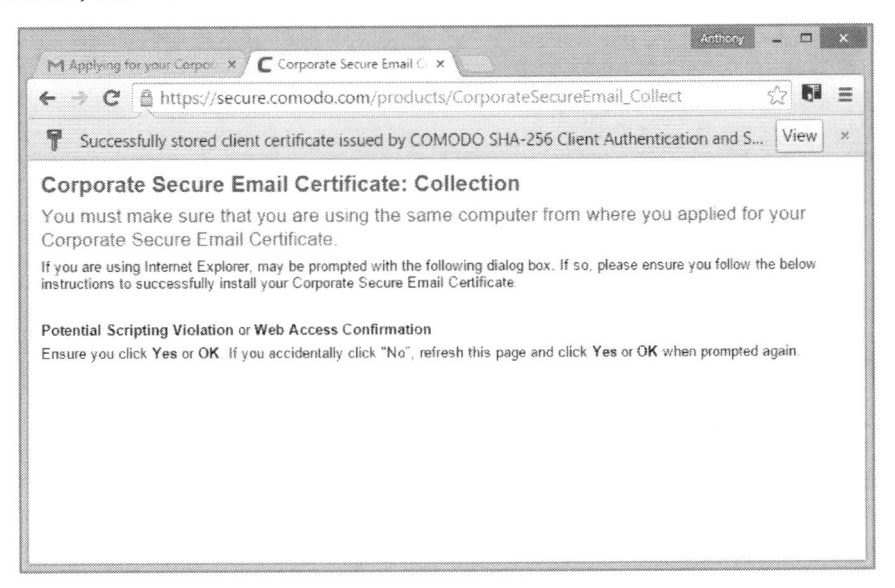

14. Vulnerability: Email

5. Under the certificate dialog box that opens, click on the *Details* tab.

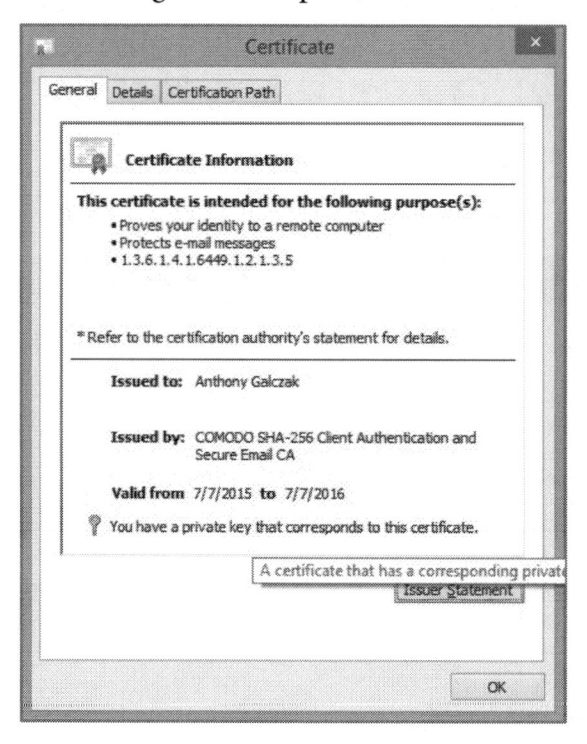

14. Vulnerability: Email

6. Click on *Copy to File.*

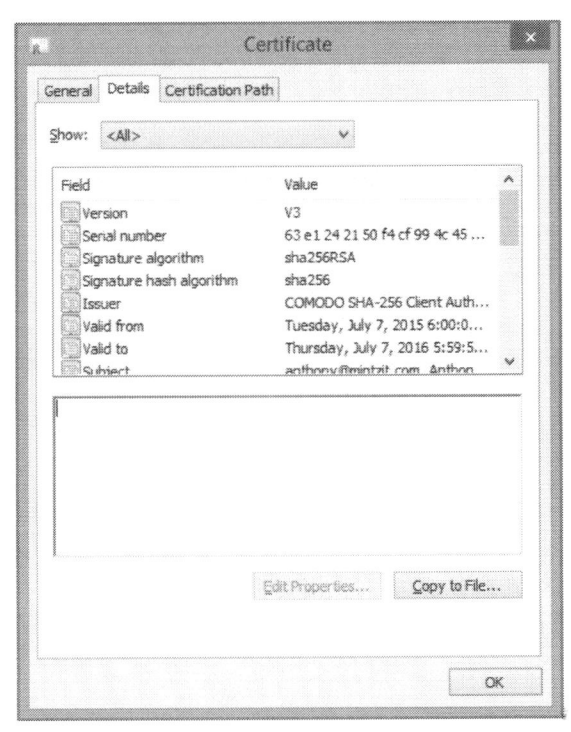

14. Vulnerability: Email

7. This will bring you to the certificate wizard. Press *Next* until the *Export Private Key* screen. From here select *No, do not export the private key* and hit *Next* again.

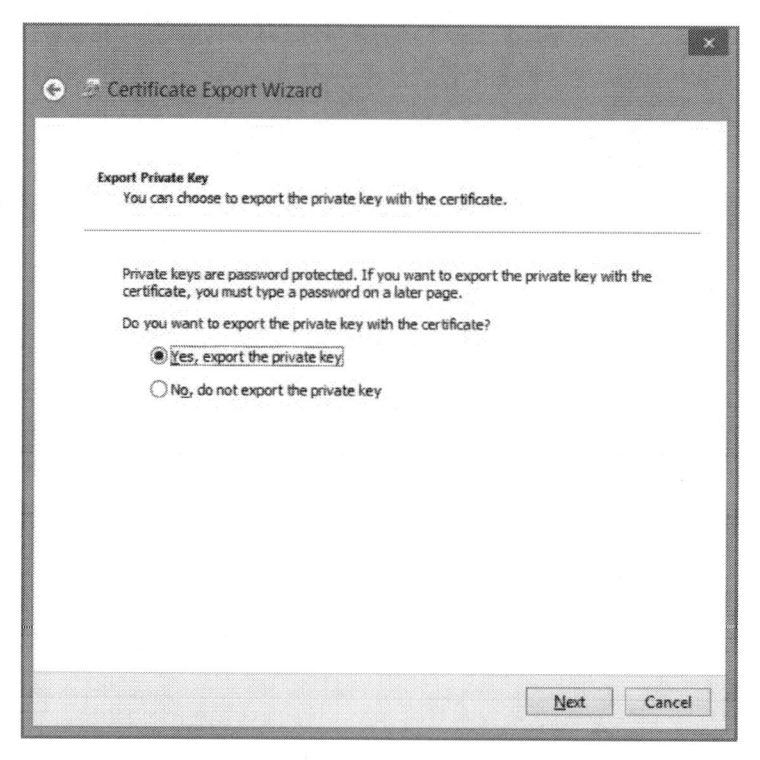

14. Vulnerability: Email

8. Click *Next* with these settings.

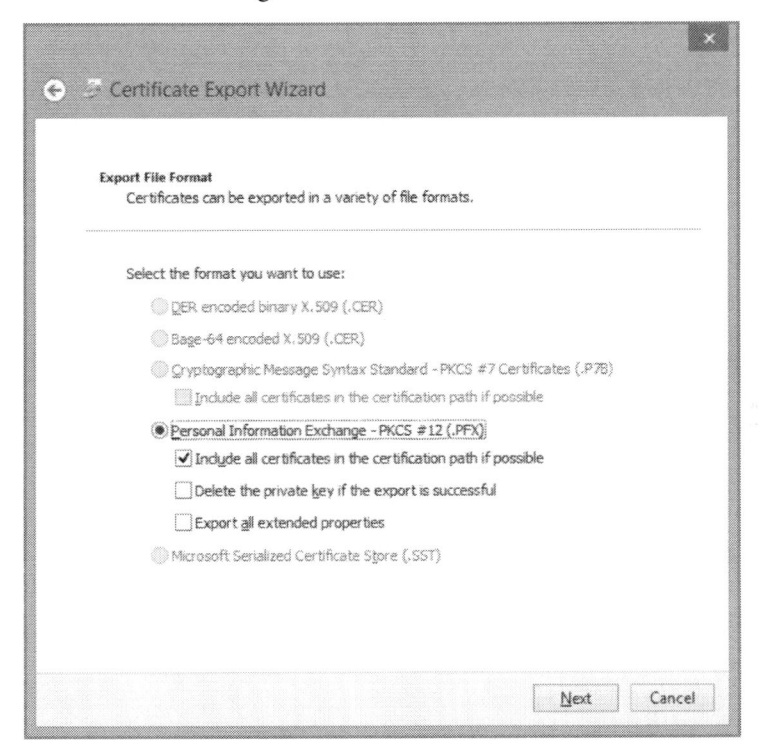

14. Vulnerability: Email

9. Click on the *Password* box and enter a strong password to secure the file you are about to create.

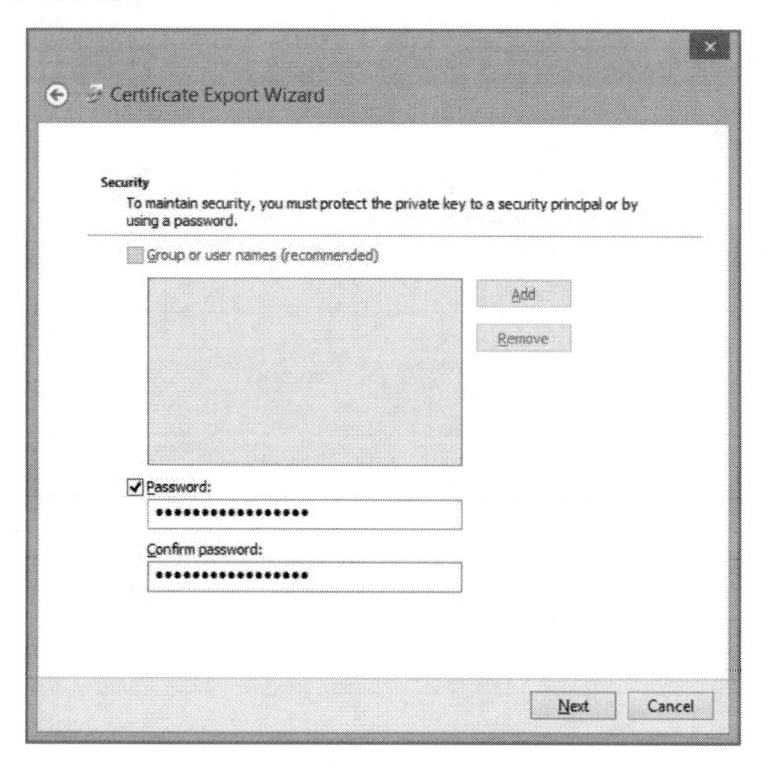

14. Vulnerability: Email

10. Browse to a memorable location to save your .pfx file. Click *Save* and then *Next*.

14. Vulnerability: Email

11. Click *Finish* to exit the wizard and save your .pfx file. You will get a message saying *The export was successful.*

Done.

Assignment: Importing a S/MIME Certificate in Microsoft Outlook

In order to use your S/MIME certificate within Microsoft Outlook you will need to import it as a Digital ID. Make sure that you exported a .pfx as Outlook will not accept a .cer.

14. Vulnerability: Email

1. Open Outlook. Click *File > Options*.

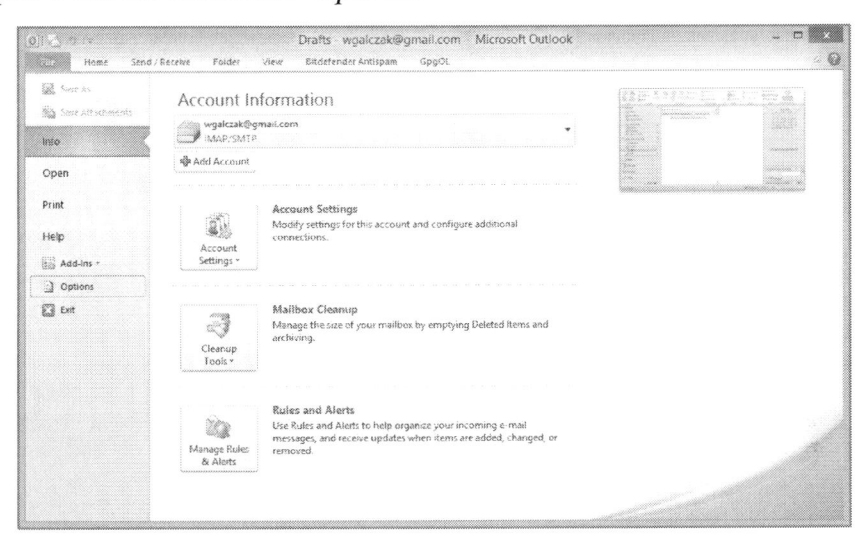

2. This will open *Outlook Options*. Click on *Trust Center > Trust Center Settings*.

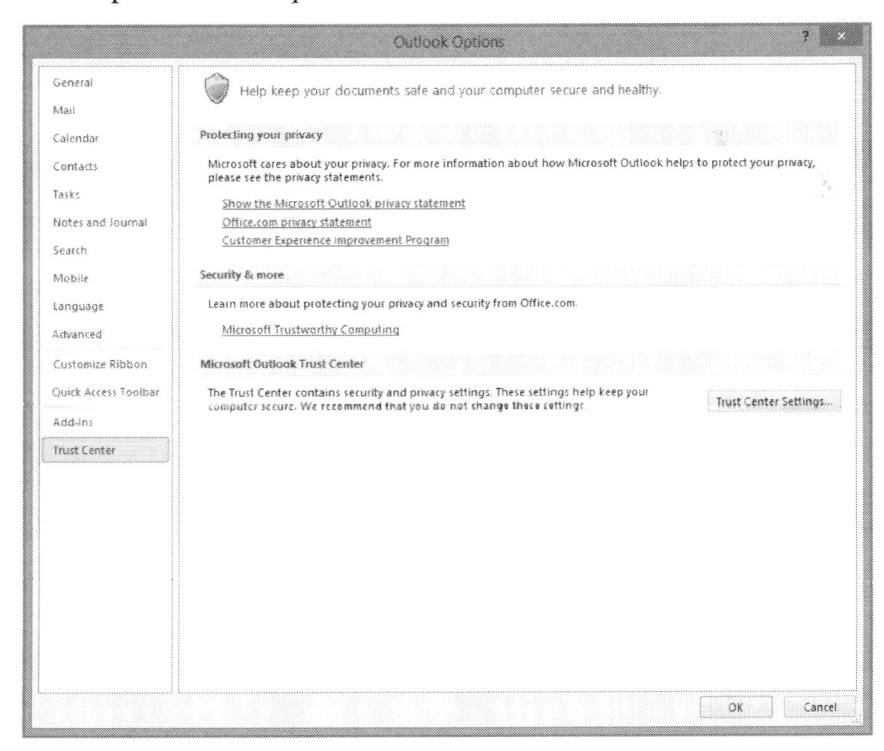

14. Vulnerability: Email

3. Click on *E-mail Security > Import/Export.*

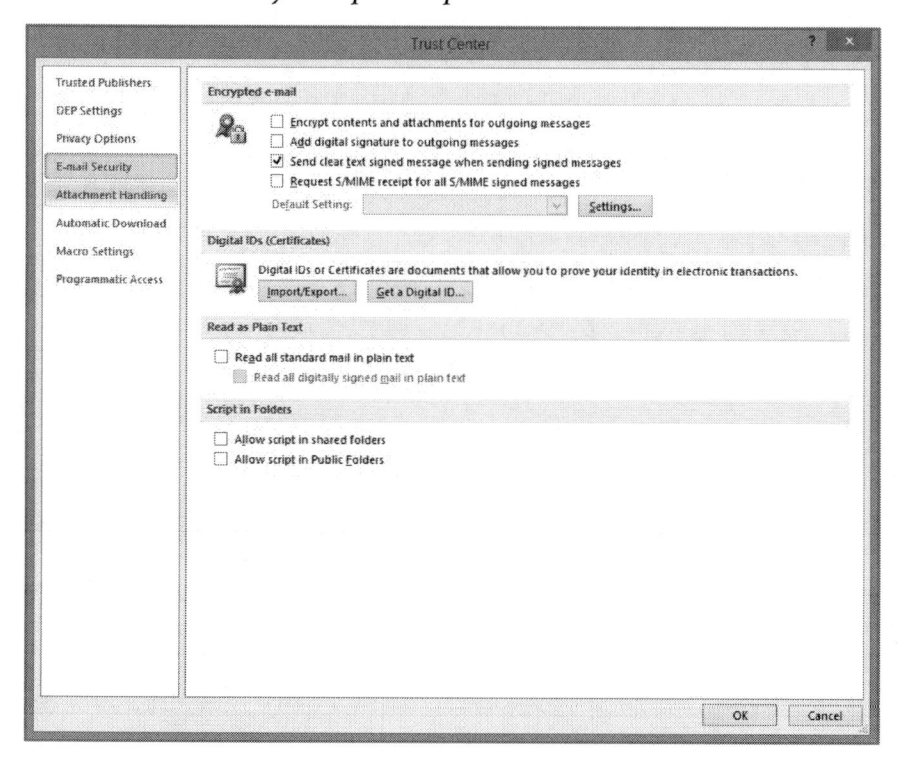

14. Vulnerability: Email

4. This will open the *Import/Export Digital ID* dialog box. Browse to the .pfx file you have saved.

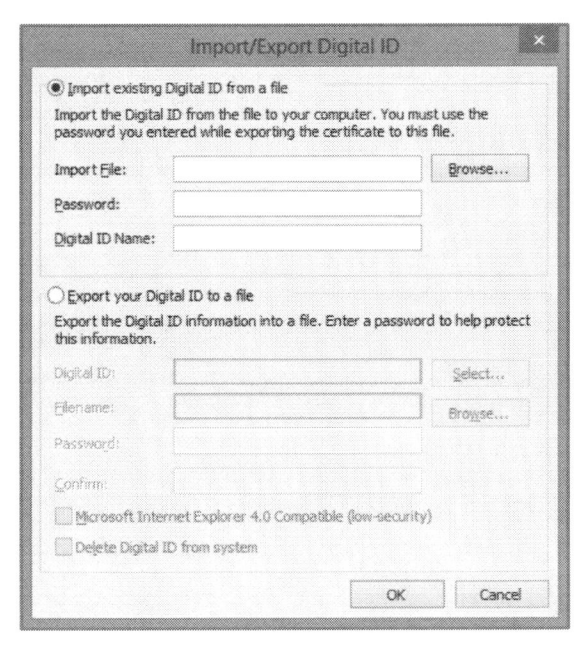

14. Vulnerability: Email

5. Enter your password for your .pfx and give your certificate a name under Digital ID Name. Click *OK* twice.

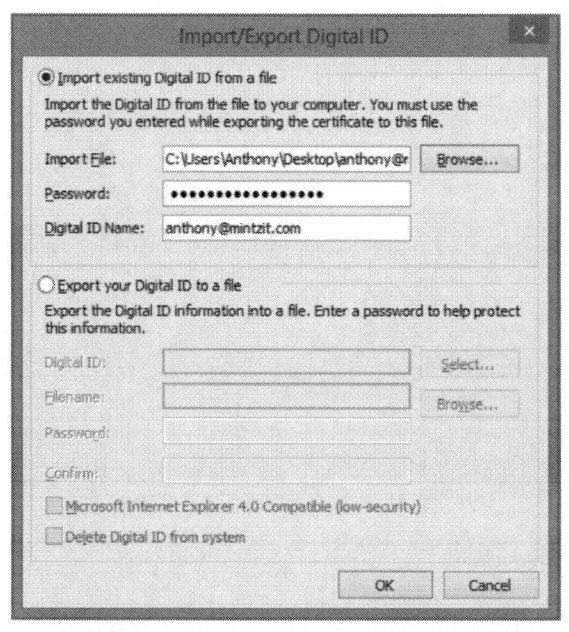

6. Check the box for *Add digital signature to outgoing messages.* Click *OK* twice.

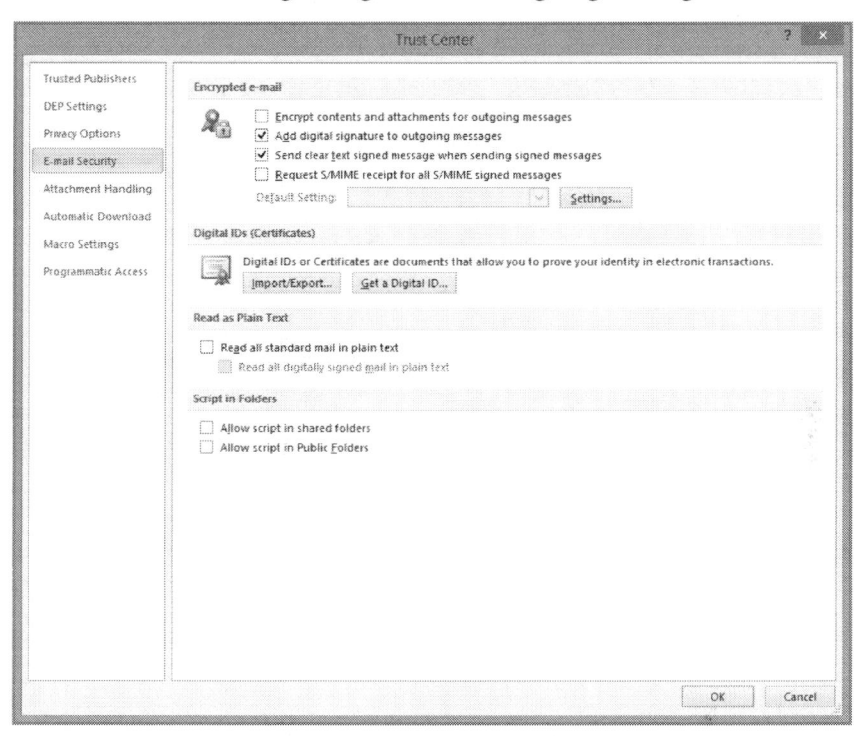

7. Checking this box will now add your S/MIME signature to each email you send out. This allows whoever you send email to send back an encrypted message using your public key. If you would like all outgoing emails to be encrypted, then check *Encrypt contents and attachments for outgoing messages.*

Assignment: Exchange S/MIME Public Key with Others

Before you are able to send or receive encrypted email with others, you need to exchange Public Keys with each other. This is as simple as sending a signed email to each other. This is assuming that you have set your e-mails to be digitally signed by default. To start, you will send a signed email to a friend. This will give this recipient your Public Key, as well as instructions for the recipient to set up S/MIME on their own system.

1. From a computer that now has your newly acquired email certificates, *Open* Microsoft Outlook.

14. Vulnerability: Email

2. Click *New Mail*.

3. Enter the recipient you would like to share your public key with. In the Subject line, be clear about the intent of the email by noting something like: *My S/MIME Public Key.*

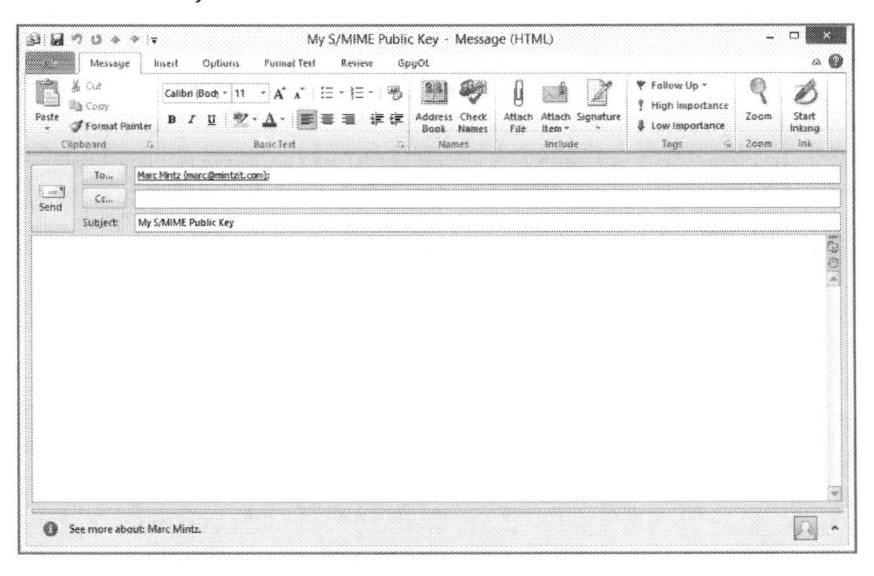

14. Vulnerability: Email

4. Click on the *Options* tab. Make sure the *Sign* button is clicked.

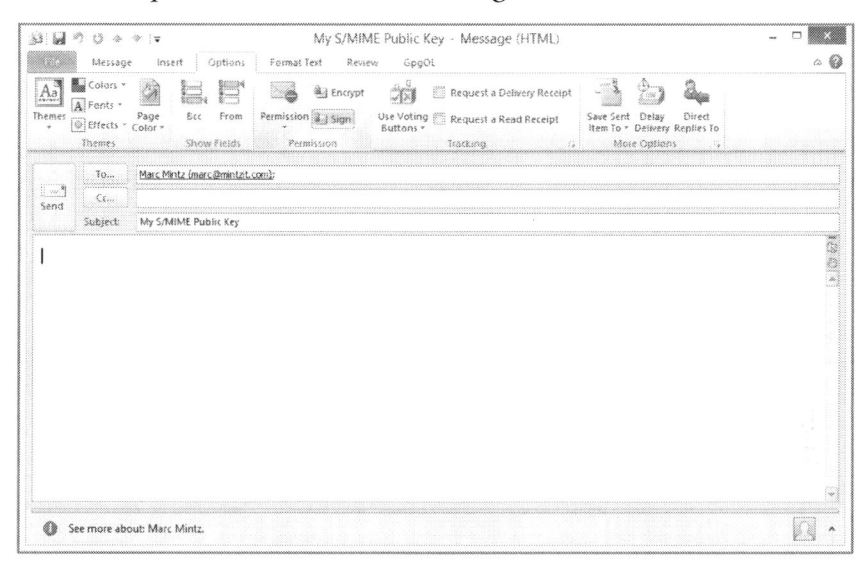

5. In the body area you may want to include instructions for how to acquire an email certificate–or better yet–point to this book at its website *http://thepracticalparanoid.com*:

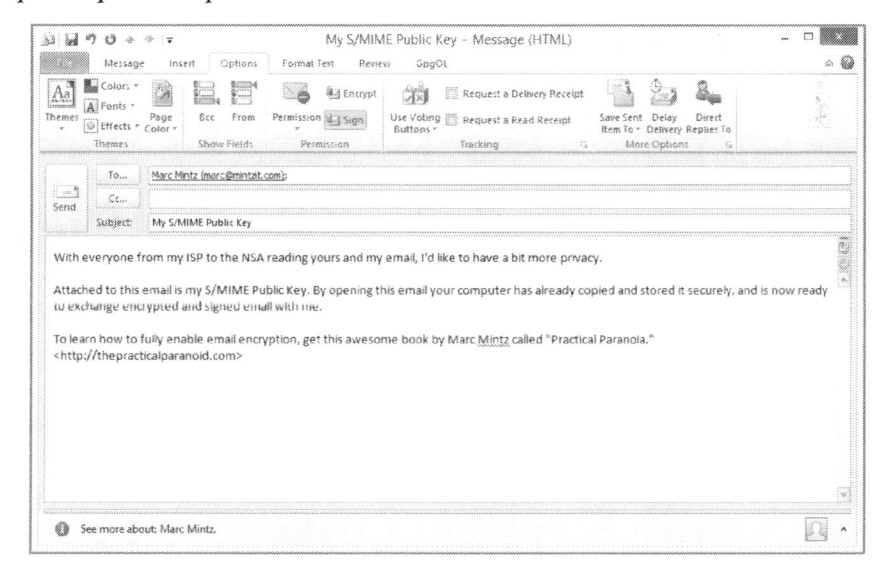

14. Vulnerability: Email

6. Click *Send* and then *Allow*.

7. When the recipient receives and opens the email, that recipient now has your Public Key and can determine that the email truly did come from you due to your signing the email with your certificate.

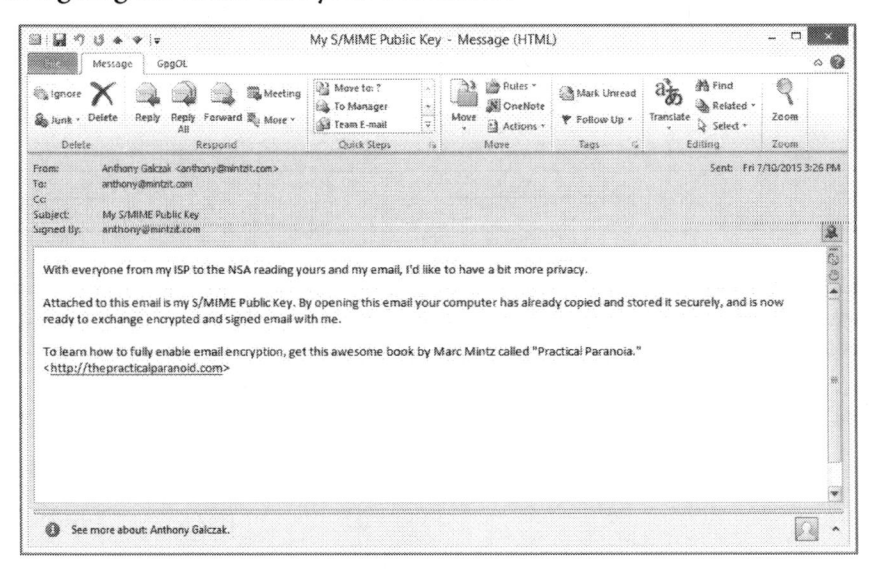

8. The recipient then needs to repeat the steps in this and the previous assignments to acquire an email certificate, and then send a signed email to you.

Once this is done, the two of you may exchange encrypted email.

14. Vulnerability: Email

Assignment: Send S/MIME Encrypted Email in Microsoft Outlook

To exchange S/MIME encrypted email, you and the other party must have exchanged S/MIME signed emails. Microsoft Outlook automatically imports any signatures that it receives from your emails and stores them in the contact. If you send encrypted email to a recipient that has already sent you their signature Outlook will automatically use their public key to encrypt the email when you send an encrypted email to that same contact.

1. Open Microsoft Outlook.
2. Click on *New E-mail*.

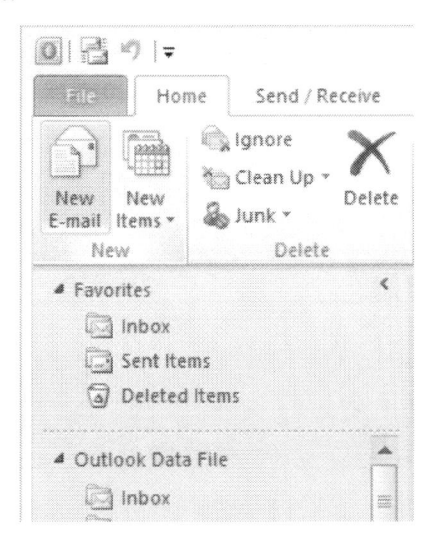

14. Vulnerability: Email

3. Compose your message and then click on *Options*.

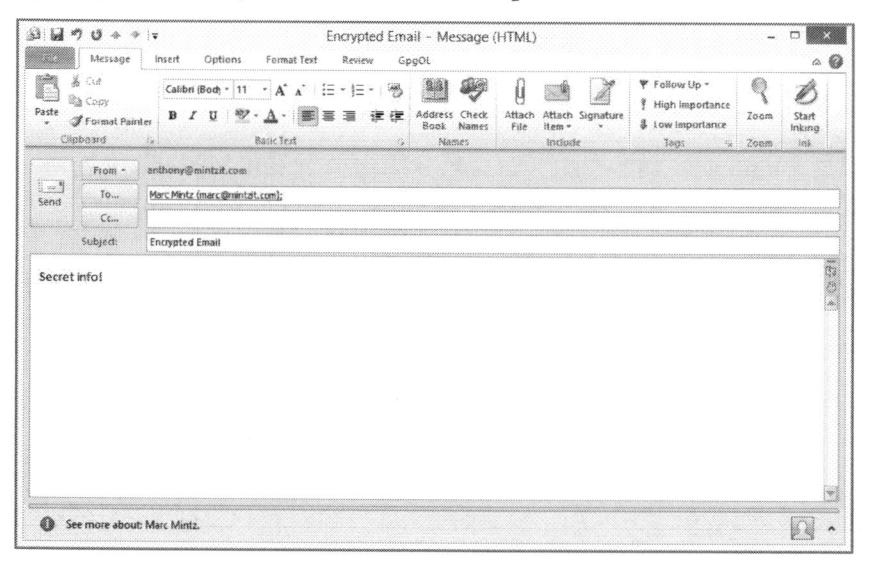

4. Notice the *Sign* button is already selected. To encrypt the message, click *Encrypt* also. Click *Send* to send your message.

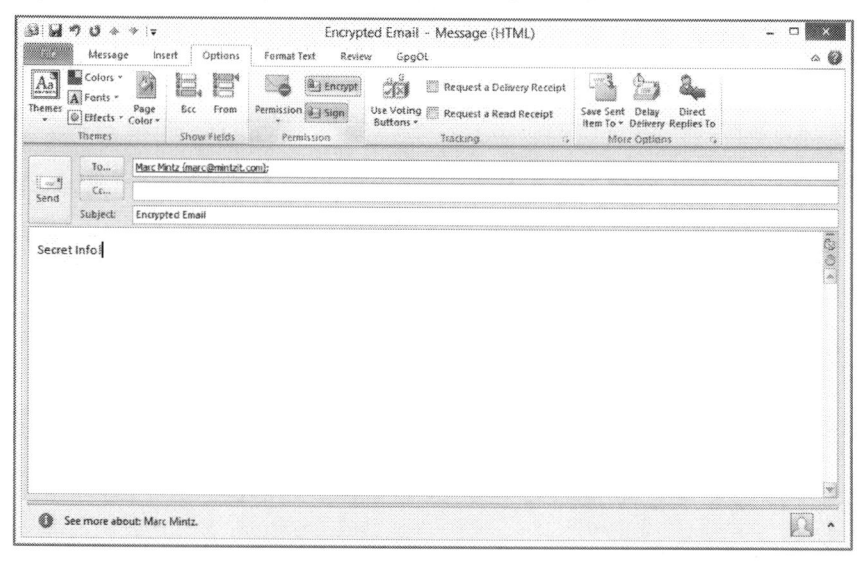

5. A Windows Security dialog box will appear asking if you'd like to let Outlook access your private key. Click *Allow*.

14. Vulnerability: Email

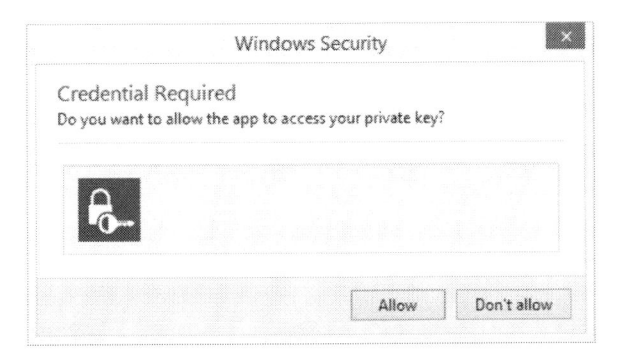

Congratulations. You have sent an encrypted email from Outlook.

14. Vulnerability: Email

Closing Comments on Encryption and the NSA

Using PGP, GPG, S/MIME, or secure email hosts will give 100% protection against your communications being intercepted or eavesdropped by pranksters, criminals, master criminals, and virtually all government personnel (my apology for being redundant.) The bad news is that the NSA may have the ability to bypass virtually any security system should the NSA take a strong enough interest. The question then becomes: *Am I someone of such strong interest to the NSA that they will focus their full legal (and illegal) powers upon me?* If so, you may want to consider a change of career or lifestyle.

14. Vulnerability: Email

Review Questions

1. The attempt to acquire your personal or sensitive information by appearing as a trustworthy source is called _____.
2. Three common protocols to encrypt email between email server and user are _____, _____, and _____.
3. The encryption protocol used for web-based email is _____.
4. Email encrypted with either PGP or GPG can be decrypted with either.
5. S/MIME Class 1 certificate is designed for business use. (True or False)

15. Vulnerability: Documents

Tradition becomes our security, and when the mind is secure it is in decay.

–Jiddu Krishnamurti, speaker and writer of philosophical and spiritual matters

15. Vulnerability: Documents

Document Security

If your documents never leave your computer, and you have encrypted your storage devices using BitLocker, there is no need to go the extra step to encrypt your documents. But should you ever need to email your sensitive data to someone else, or pass a sensitive document along via any storage device, encrypting the document goes a long way to a good night of sleep.

There are several options to document encryption, each with its own benefits and drawbacks. We will discuss each here.

Password Protect the Document within Its Application

A few applications are designed with document security in mind, and offer their own encryption scheme. Microsoft Office and Adobe Acrobat Pro are common examples.

Although Microsoft Office products make it an easy process to password protect your documents, prior to Office 2007, it was an equally easy process to break the encryption. There are many freeware and commercial utilities that can bypass the password and open the document for reading in older versions.

Starting with Microsoft Office 2007, Microsoft has changed the encryption standard to use the secure AES-128 algorithm. Assuming an adequate password length has been selected, it is estimated by some researchers that it would take millions of years to brute-force crack an AES-128 password with current computing power. For the purpose of security during this lifetime, the AES-128 encryption standard should be enough to protect your documents as long as an adequate password has been chosen.

In the next assignment, we will walk through how to encrypt your Microsoft Office documents. The example below is Microsoft Word, however, Excel, and PowerPoint methods are similar.

15. Vulnerability: Documents

Assignment: Encrypt an MS Office Document

1. Open the target document in Microsoft Word 2011.

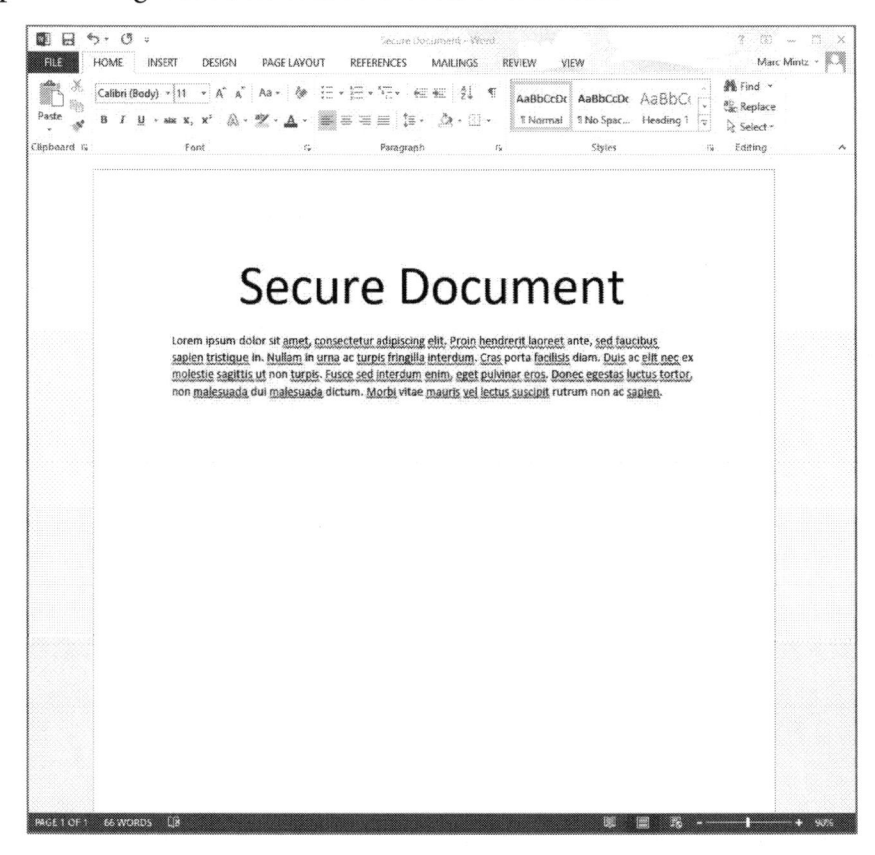

15. Vulnerability: Documents

2. Select the *File* menu > *Info* > *Protect Document,* and then select the *Secure with Password* option in the dropdown menu.

15. Vulnerability: Documents

3. The *Encrypt Document* window opens. Enter a strong password in the *Password* field. Then, select the *OK* button.

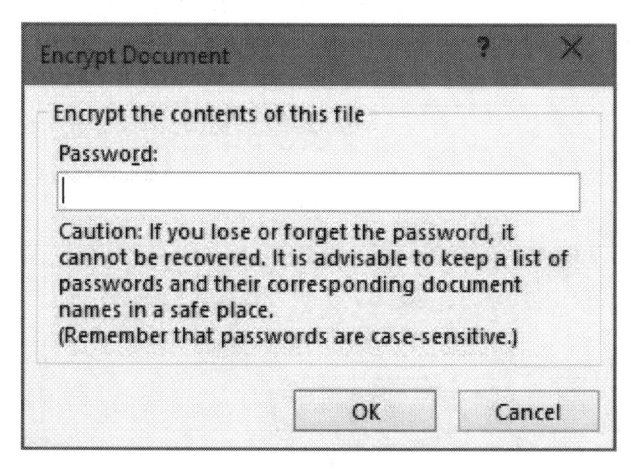

4. The *Confirm Password* window will open. Re-enter your password, and then select the *OK* button.

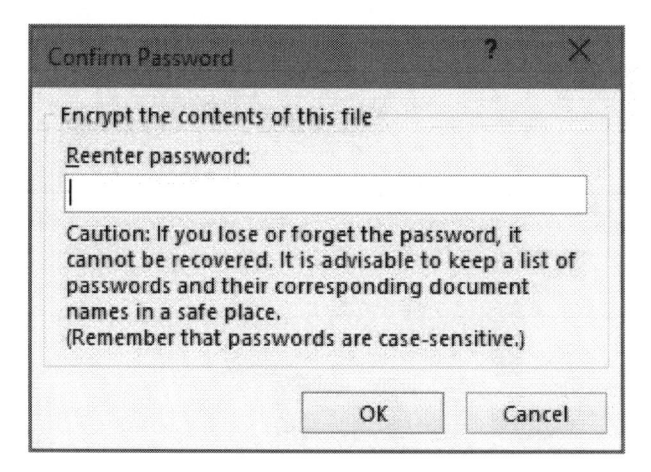

Your document is now protected.

15. Vulnerability: Documents

Encrypt a PDF Document

Microsoft Word allows for creating encrypted PDF documents similar to its own encrypted documents. The encryption standard created by Adobe for PDFs is the same as Microsoft uses for Office documents, AES-128. This standard allows a PDF encrypted by one program to be unencrypted and read by another program, across different platforms and operating systems.

Just as with Microsoft Office documents, Adobe PDF encryption can be broken with an insufficient and weak password.

Assignment: Convert a Document to PDF for Password Protection

1. Open a Microsoft Office document

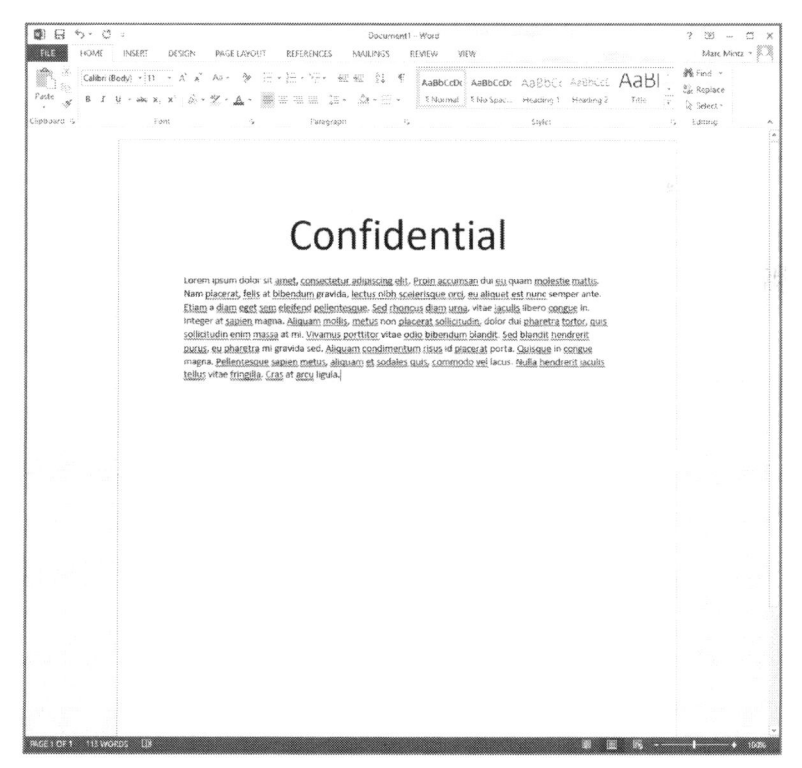

15. Vulnerability: Documents

2. Select the *File* tab > *Export*, and then click the *Create PDF/XPS* button.

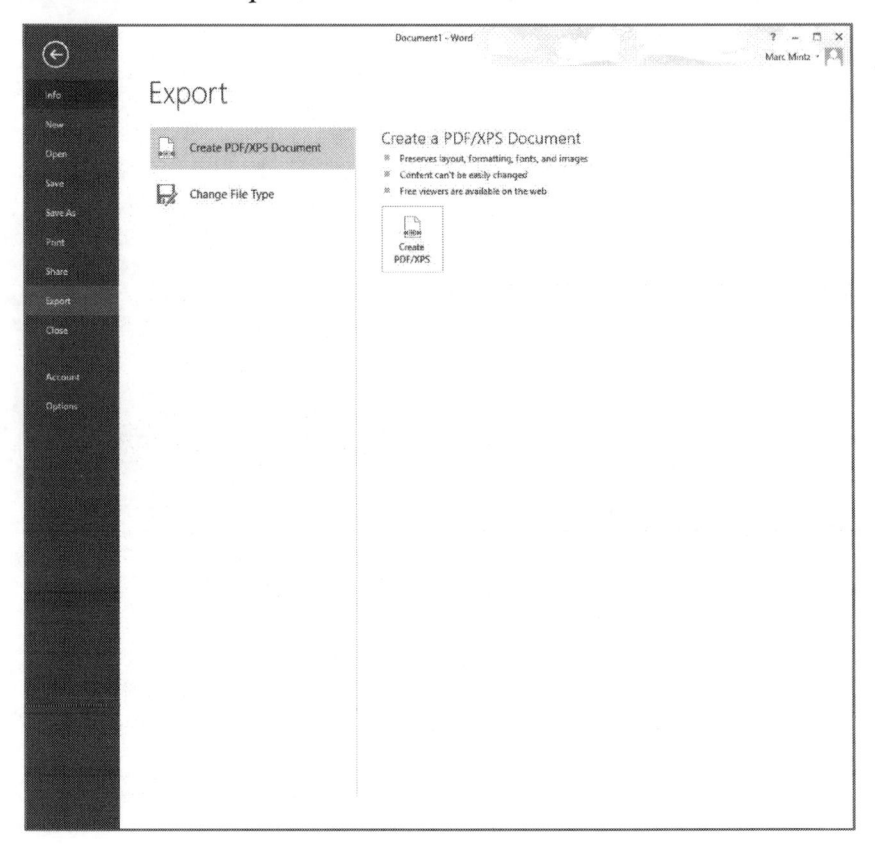

15. Vulnerability: Documents

3. Enter a *File Name* for the PDF, and then select the *Options* button.

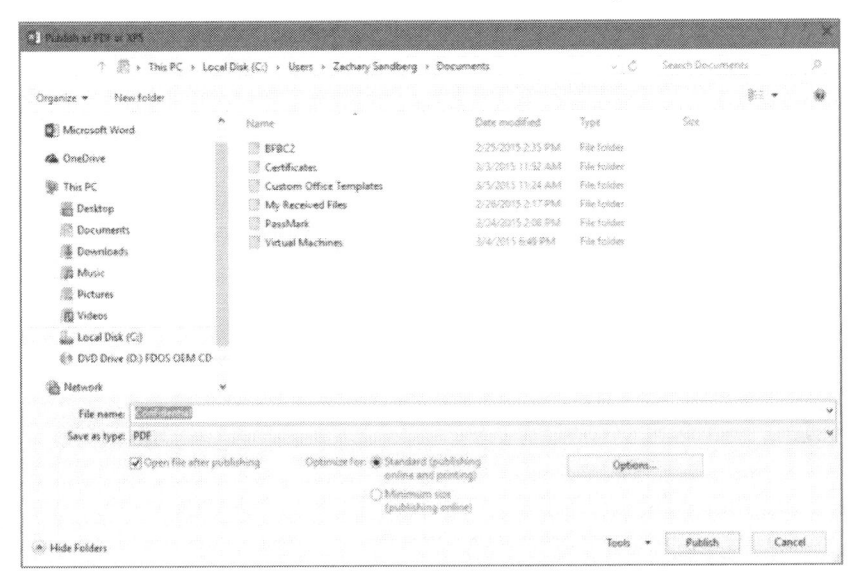

4. In the *Options Menu*, select the *Encrypt the document with a password* checkbox, and then click the *OK* button.

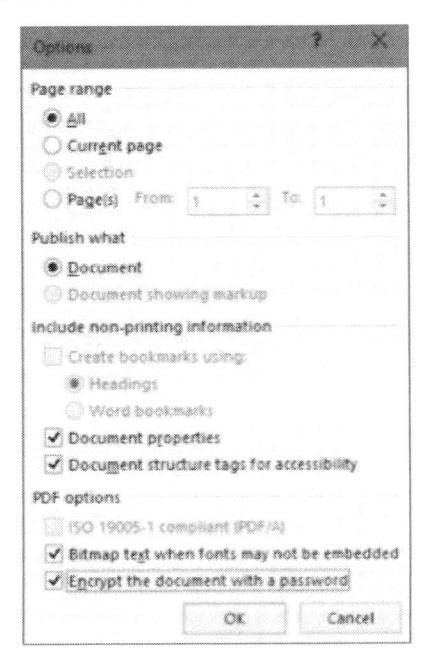

-467-

5. Enter a strong password to encrypt the document, and then click the *OK* button.

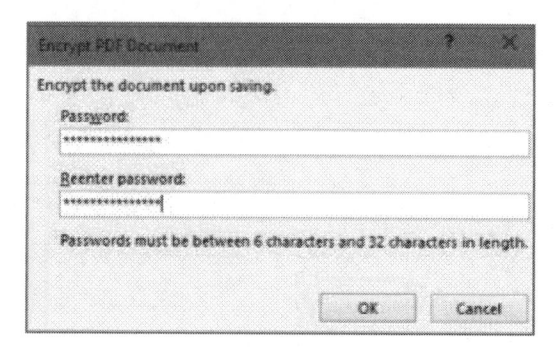

6. Click the *Publish* button on the *File Name* window to finish creating your encrypted PDF file.

The PDF version of the document is now encrypted. If the original document is no longer needed for future editing, it may be trashed.

Encrypt a Folder for Personal use in Windows 10

Perhaps you need to secure an entire folder of files? Well, Windows 10 has a built-in *Folder Encryption* feature to do this for you.

Assignment: Create an Encrypted Windows Folder

1. Right-click the folder that you wish to encrypt and select *Properties*.

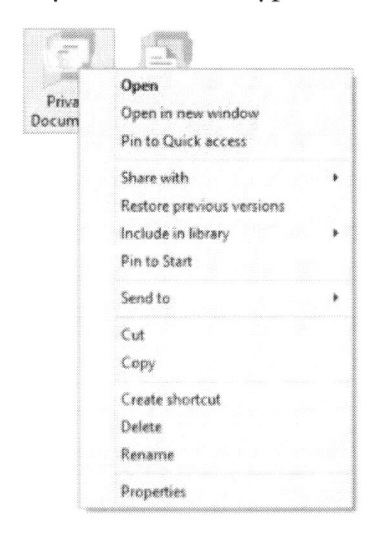

15. Vulnerability: Documents

2. At the bottom of the screen, click the *Advanced* button.

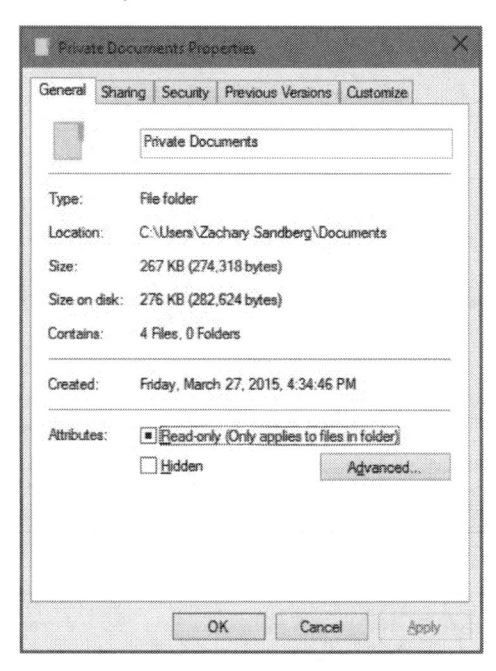

3. The *Advanced Attributes* dialog box appears. Click the checkbox entitled *Encrypt contents to secure data*, and then click the *OK* button.

15. Vulnerability: Documents

4. At the *Properties* window, click *OK*, and then click *OK* again at the *Confirm Attribute Changes* dialog, applying the encryption to the contents of the folder.

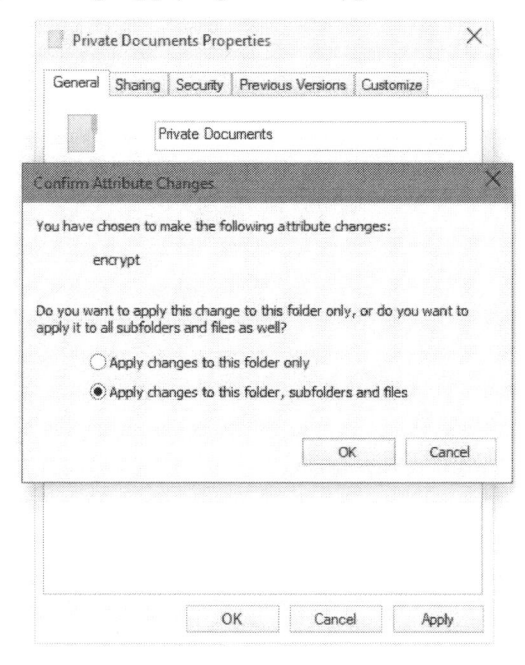

5. When complete, the selected folder text will turn green, signifying that it is fully encrypted.

Assignment: Backup Encryption Keys for the Encrypted Folder

Behind the scenes, Windows has generated a unique folder encryption key to be used during this operation. In the event of a digital catastrophe, it is important to have a backup of this key so you can unencrypt your files.

In this assignment we will back up the encryption keys.

15. Vulnerability: Documents

1. Click the *Start Button,* type *Control Panel* in the search box, and then select the *Control Panel* result in the search return. The *Control Panel* opens.
2. With *Control Panel* open, click the *User Accounts* icon.

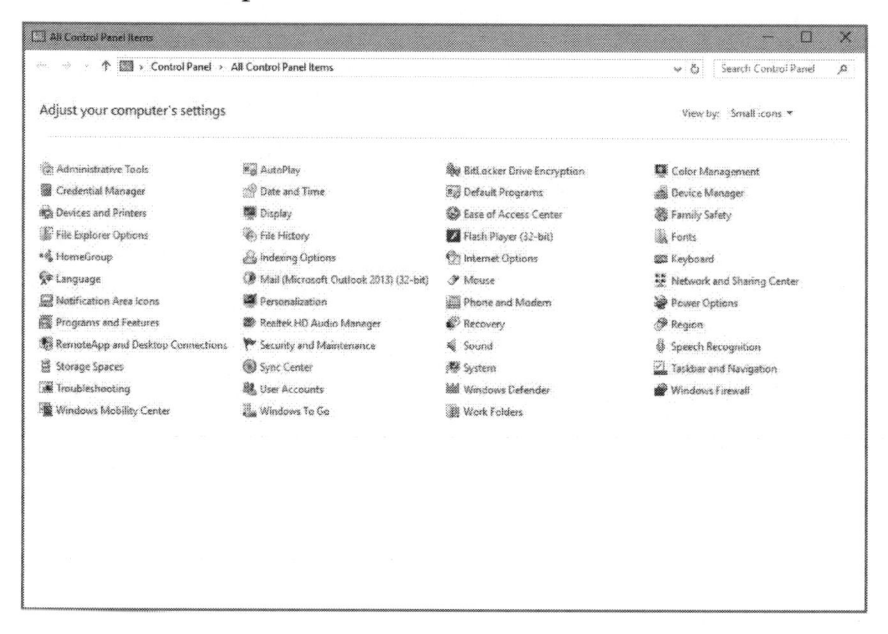

15. Vulnerability: Documents

3. In the *User Accounts* Window, click the sidebar link titled *Manage your file encryption certificates*.

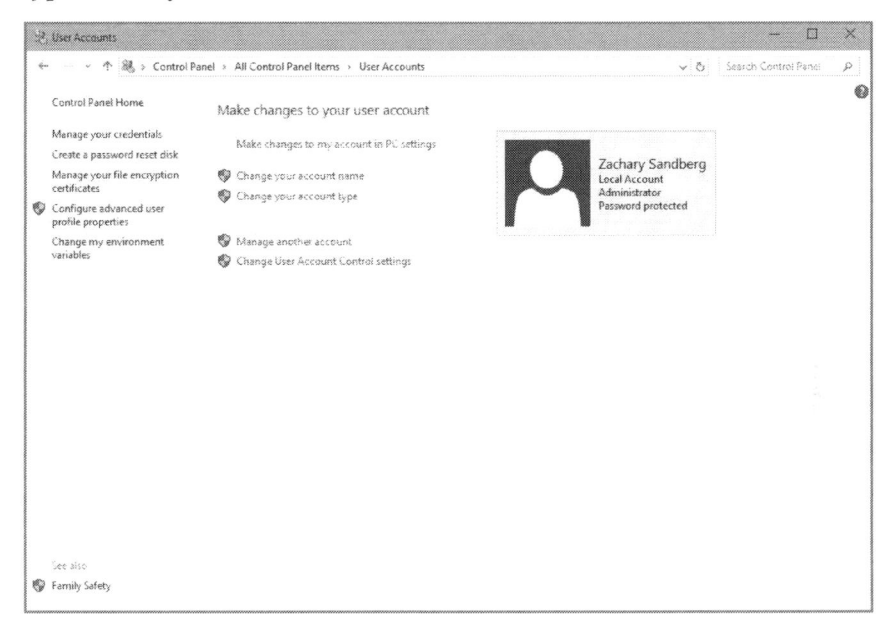

15. Vulnerability: Documents

4. Click *Next* at the *Manage your file encryption certificates* screen.

15. Vulnerability: Documents

5. The certificate listed will likely be the one Windows created during the recent folder encryption process. If for some reason you manage multiple certificates on your computer, click the *Select certificate* to view the available certificates available to you. Make sure the correct one is selected, and then click *Next*.

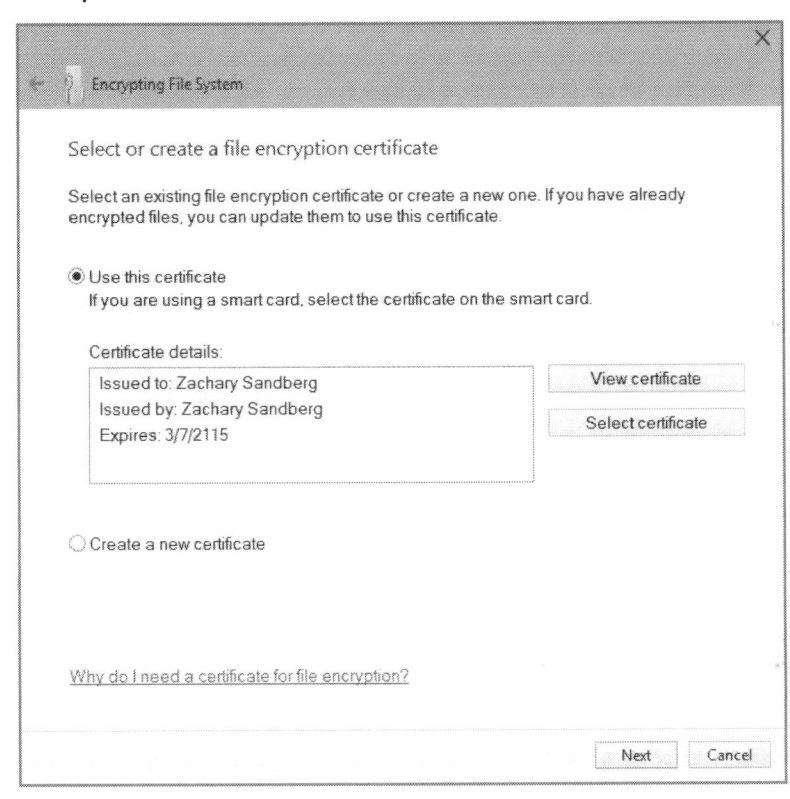

15. Vulnerability: Documents

6. At the *Back up the certificate and key* screen, select the *Back up the certificate and key now* radio button, and then click the *Browse* button.

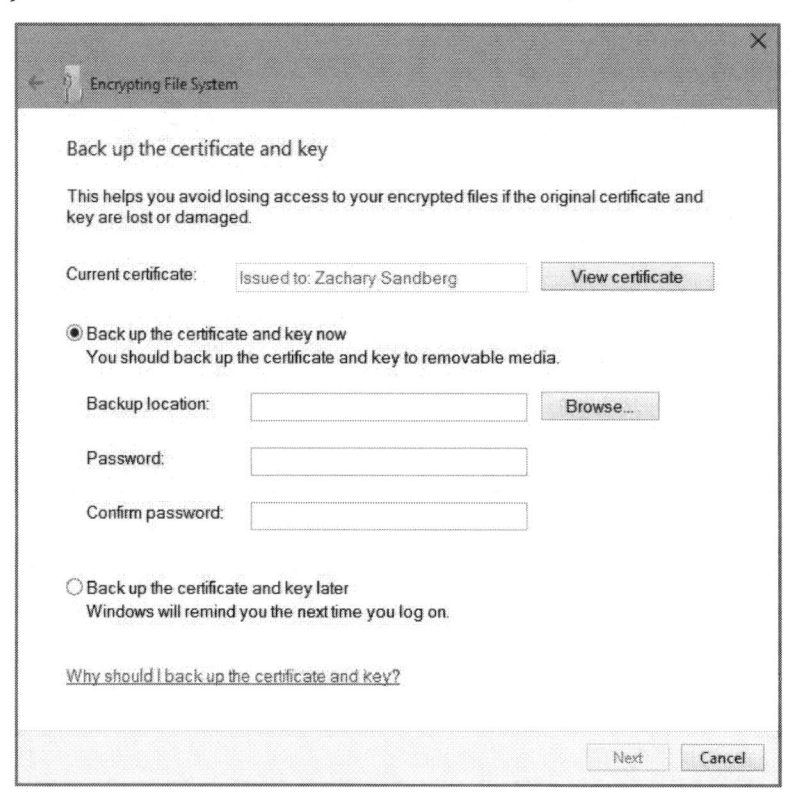

Encrypting File System

Back up the certificate and key

This helps you avoid losing access to your encrypted files if the original certificate and key are lost or damaged.

Current certificate: Issued to: Zachary Sandberg   [View certificate]

⦿ Back up the certificate and key now
  You should back up the certificate and key to removable media.

  Backup location: _____ [Browse...]
  Password: _____
  Confirm password: _____

○ Back up the certificate and key later
  Windows will remind you the next time you log on.

Why should I back up the certificate and key?

[Next] [Cancel]

-476-

15. Vulnerability: Documents

7. Select a safe location to back up your key to. You should also make sure that this key is backed up in a location other than your boot drive in case of a disaster. Click the *Save* button.

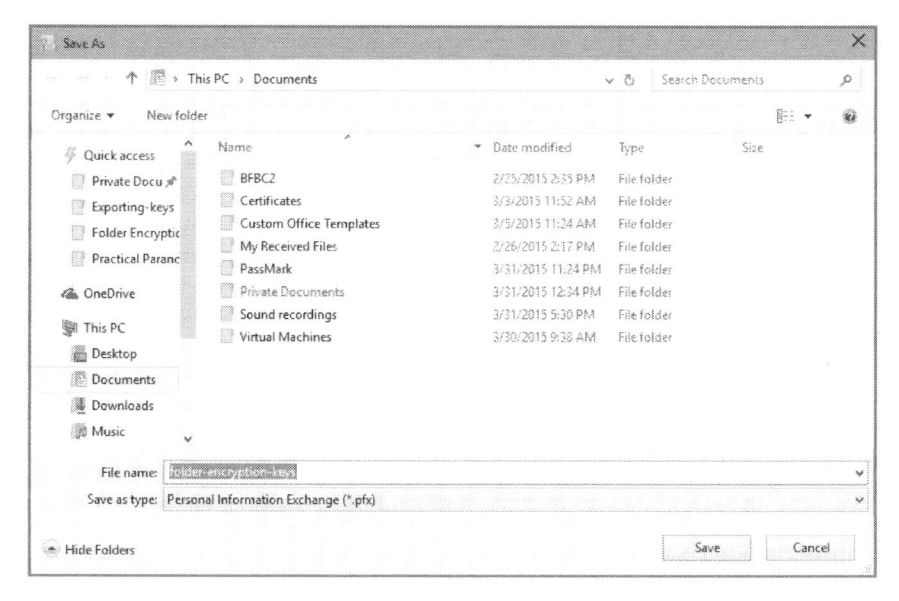

15. Vulnerability: Documents

8. Since we have no files encrypted prior to the preceding exercise, there is no opportunity to update any existing encrypted locations. Click the *Next* button.

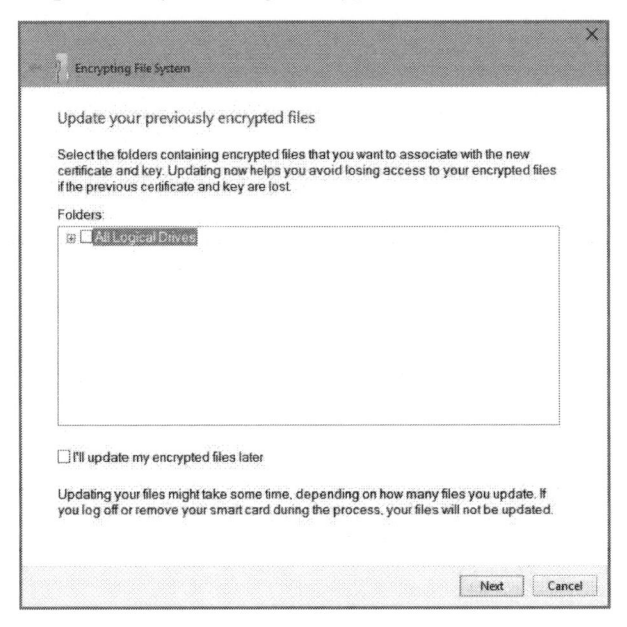

9. At the backup confirmation screen, click the *Close* button.

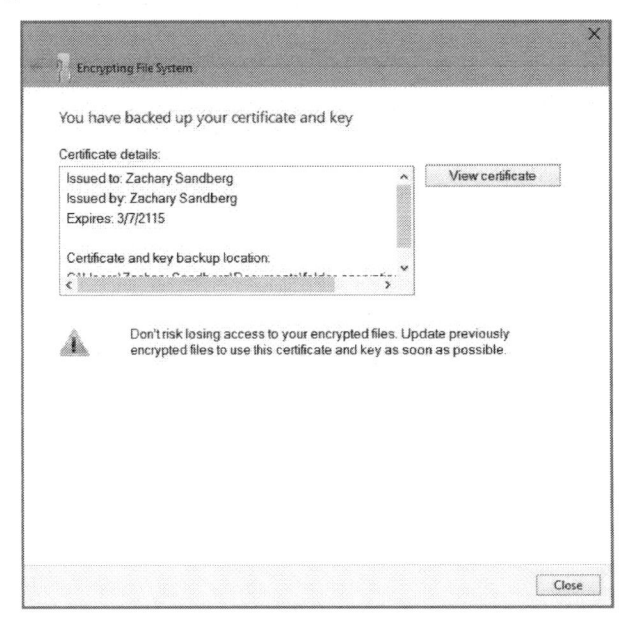

15. Vulnerability: Documents

Congratulations, your File Encryption Certificate has now been exported

Assignment: Import Previously Saved File Encryption Certificates

So, you've just bought a new computer, and after transferring all your files over to the shiny new one, you quickly realize (oh no.) that you cannot view your previously encrypted (green) files & folders.

No worries, as you exported your working encryption certificate to a safe location in the previous assignment. In this assignment, we're going to import that saved certificate to decrypt those green folders.

1. The encrypted files below with green text will need an existing *File Encryption Certificate* to be installed before they can be previewed or opened.

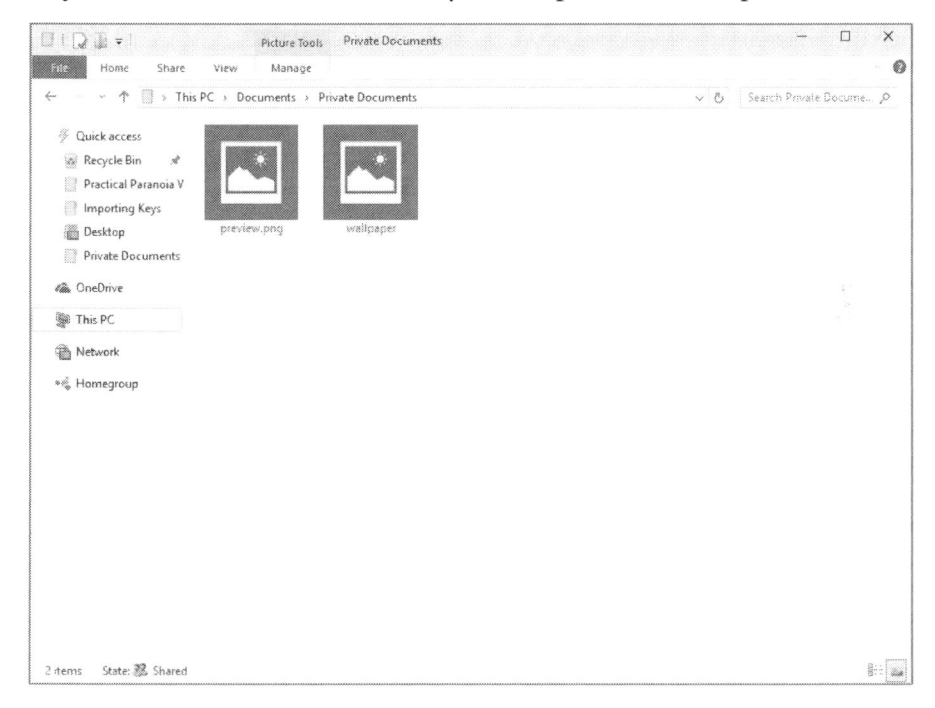

15. Vulnerability: Documents

2. Navigate to the folder where we exported our backup certificate in the previous assignment. In this example, I have my backup file called *Certificate-backup* in my Documents folder ready to be imported. Double click the backup file to open the *Import Wizard*.

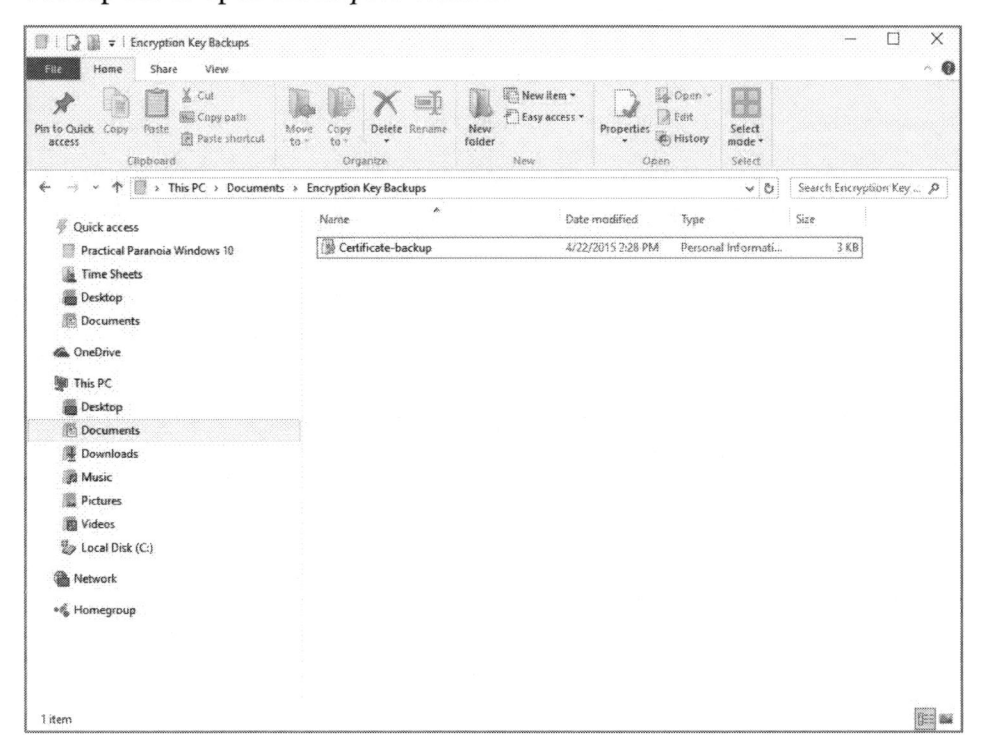

15. Vulnerability: Documents

3. When the *Import Wizard* opens, make sure that the appropriate *Store Location* is selected. If you do not want your key to be accessible to all users on the local machine click *Current User*. This is the default recommendation. Click the *Next* button when complete.

15. Vulnerability: Documents

4. Since the *File to Import* was the certificate that opened the *Import Wizard*, there is no need to select a file to import. Click the *Next* button.

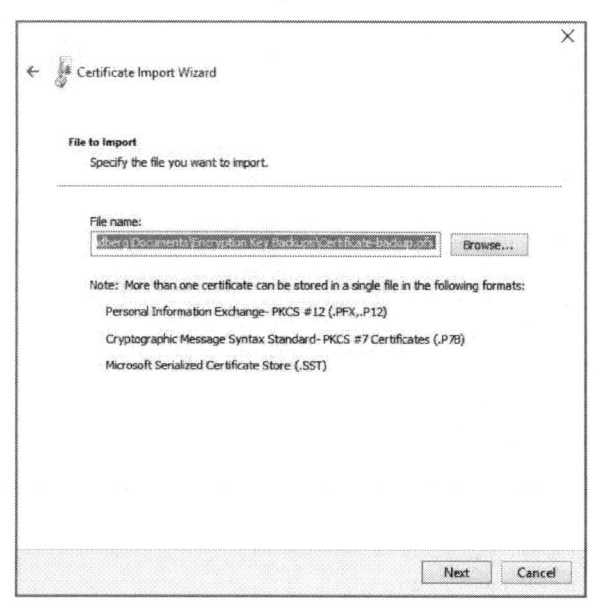

15. Vulnerability: Documents

5. You are prompted to input the password that was previously used when you exported the certificate. Click the checkbox for *Mark this key as exportable...* If you do not enable this, you won't be able to export your private key with certificate in the future. Then click *Next*.

15. Vulnerability: Documents

6. At the next screen, choose the default *Automatically select the certificate based on type of certificate*, and then click the *Next* button.

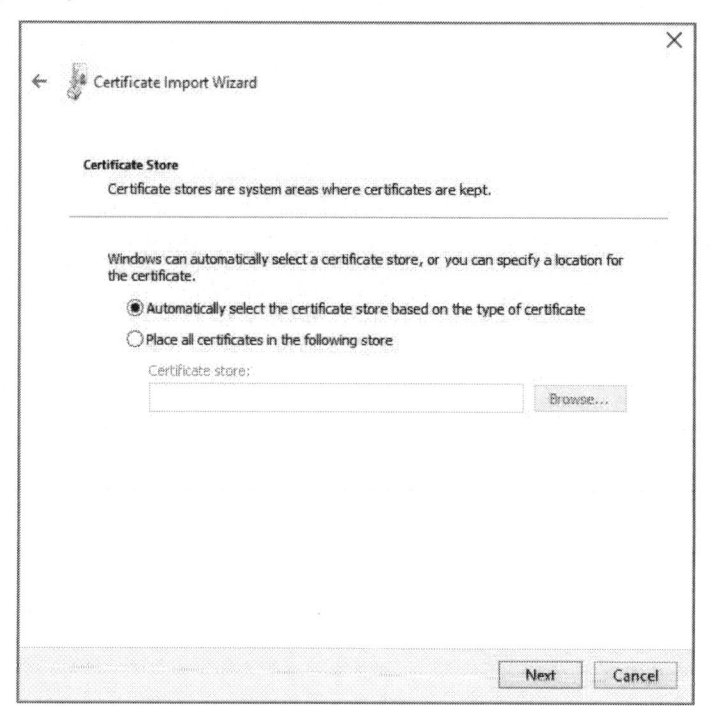

15. Vulnerability: Documents

7. Click the *Finish* button to complete the certificate import.

8. Click *OK* on the confirmation dialog.

Done.

15. Vulnerability: Documents

Encrypt a Folder for Any OS Use with VeraCrypt

If you need to securely exchange a file, files, or folders with others, VeraCrypt http://veracrypt.codeplex.com is a cross-platform solution targeted towards security conscious individuals and organizations.

VeraCrypt is free encryption software developed by *IDRIX* at *https://www.idrix.fr*, a company specializing in security solutions. It is based on *TrueCrypt http://en.wikipedia.org/wiki/TrueCrypt*, which ceased development in 2014.

Although Linux, OS X, and Windows versions are available, no Android or iOS support is offered. Android users may create and decrypt, as well as read and write to VeraCrypt/TrueCrypt files using *EDS* (Encrypted Data Store), available from Google Play. iOS users may use *Disk Decipher,* available from the App Store, to create and decrypt, as well as read and write to VeraCrypt/TrueCrypt files.

VeraCrypt is actually a disk encryption utility, as opposed to file encryption. It creates an encrypted virtual disk, or as it is referred to by VeraCrypt, a container.

VeraCrypt presents a slightly higher level of complexity to the end-user, with a resultant very high level of security. Given the speed of current systems and a strong password, data stored in a container may be considered immune from brute-force attacks.

As VeraCrypt creates a container, you are able to place anything within the container for secure storage. The container may reside on the local drive, placed on a server for network access, or within a cloud storage solution (such as DropBox, Google Drive, etc.) to provide Internet access to files and folders, without the cloud provider (or hacker, malware, or government) being able to view the contents.

15. Vulnerability: Documents

Assignment: Download VeraCrypt

1. Open your browser and go to the VeraCrypt home page at *http://veracrypt.codeplex.com*, and then select the *Download* button.

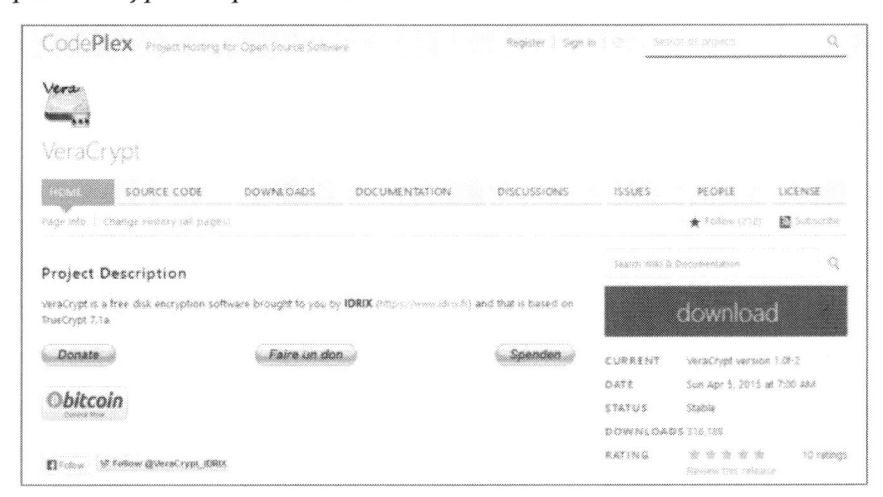

2. Select the version appropriate for your OS. The installer will start to download.

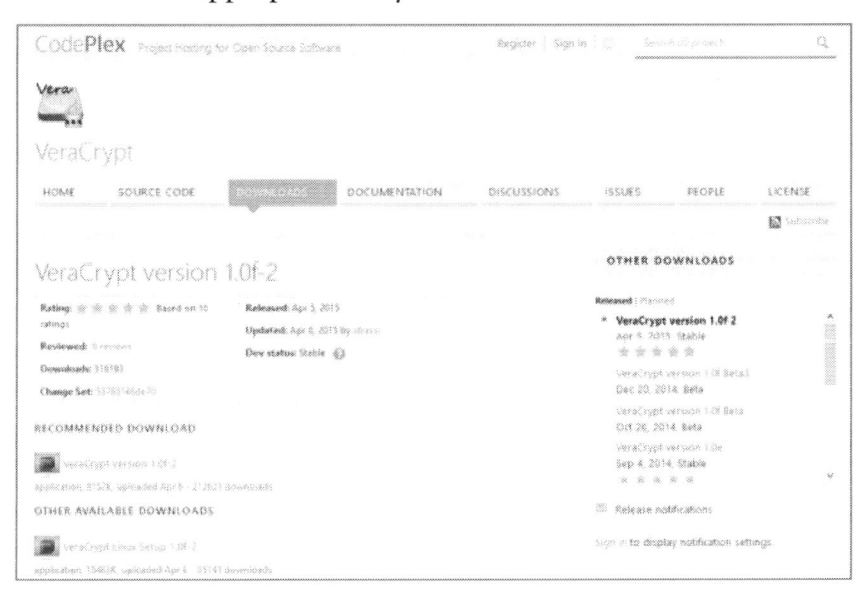

3. Locate VeraCrypt in your Downloads folder, and then double-click to start the installer.

15. Vulnerability: Documents

4. Complete the VeraCrypt installation using the defaults.

Assignment: Configure VeraCrypt

As with most applications, it helps to view and configure VeraCrypt preferences before using it. In this assignment, we will examine VeraCrypt preferences.

1. Open VeraCrypt.
2. Select the *VeraCrypt* menu > *Preferences*. Most of the options may be configured to taste. The exceptions are:
    - *Preserve modification timestamp of file containers*, which should be *disabled* if the containers will be used with cloud-based file storage service (DropBox, Google Drive, Sugar Sync, etc.) as it will conflict with the service's ability to update the timestamp. When complete, select the *OK* button.

15. Vulnerability: Documents

- Under *Default Mount Options* deselect the *TrueCrypt Mode* option should be left deselected unless you will be using software that can only work with the older TrueCrypt mode.

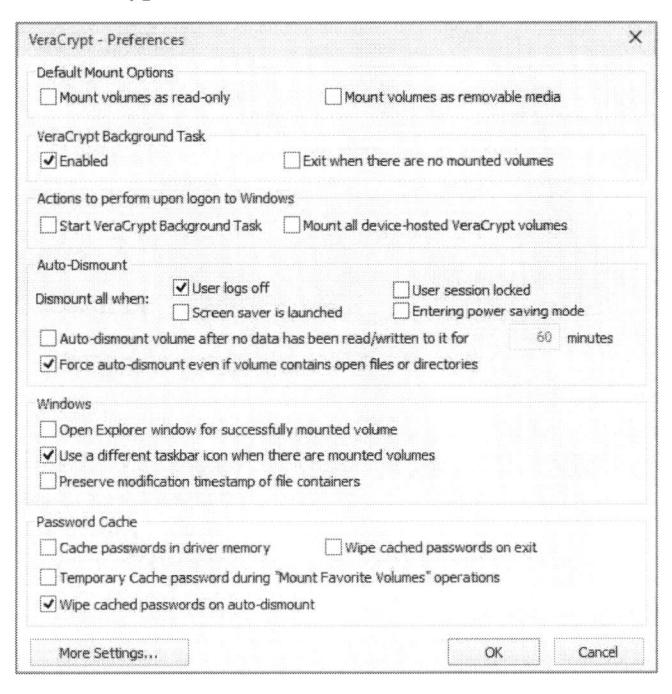

15. Vulnerability: Documents

- In the *Settings > Performance* menu leave *the Hardware acceleration* checkbox selected if your computer supports hardware acceleration of AES encryption protocols. Doing so will improve encryption and decryption speed. When complete, select the *OK* button.

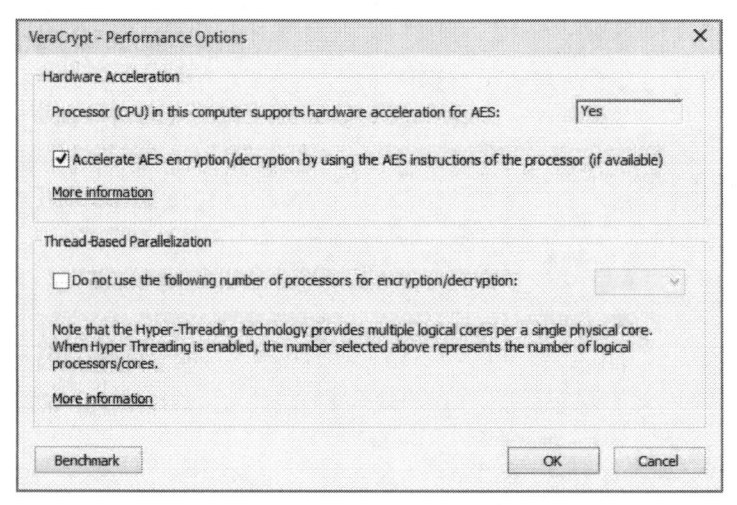

3. The *Keyfiles* tab is an advanced option. Please see the VeraCrypt online documentation *https://veracrypt.codeplex.com/documentation* for additional information.

4. The *Security Tokens* tap is an advanced option. Please see the VeraCrypt online documentation *https://veracrypt.codeplex.com/documentation* for additional information.

5. Close any VeraCrypt *Preferences* windows.

We are now ready to create our first encrypted VeraCrypt container.

Assignment: Create a VeraCrypt Container

Although we will cover the basics of using VeraCrypt, you may find it useful to dive deeper into the topic. Complete VeraCrypt documentation may be found at *https://veracrypt.codeplex.com/documentation*.

15. Vulnerability: Documents

1. Open the *VeraCrypt* application, and then select the *Create Volume* button.

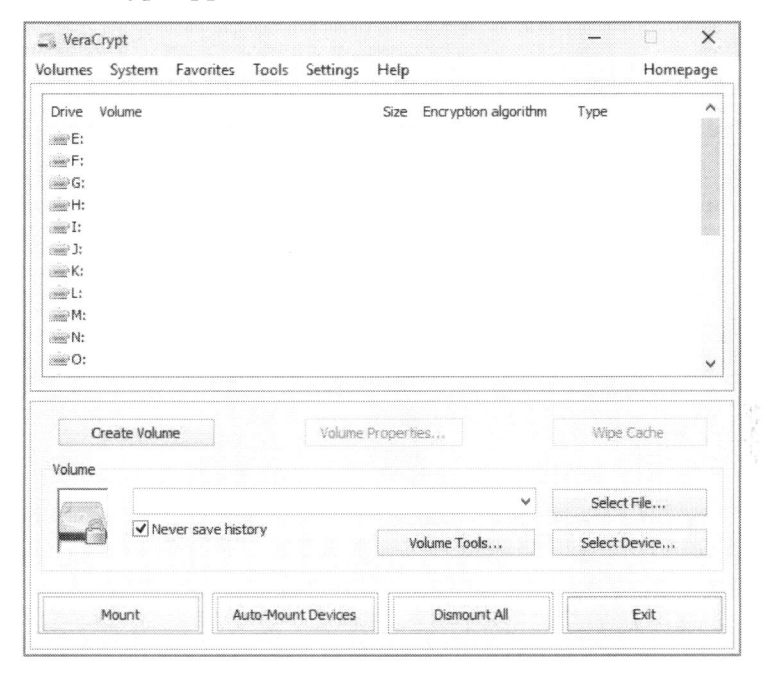

2. To create an encrypted container, at the *VeraCrypt Volume Creation Wizard*, select the *Create an encrypted file container* radio button, and then select the *Next>* button.

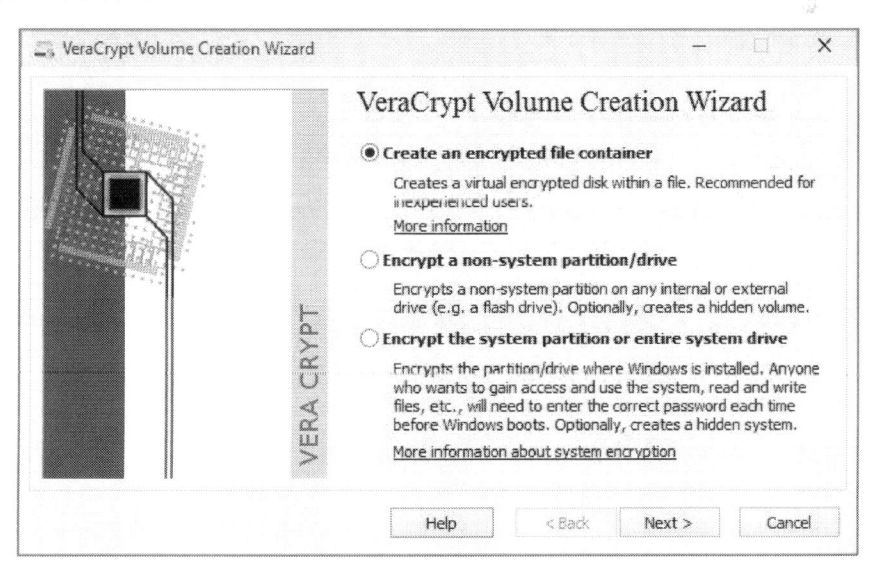

15. Vulnerability: Documents

3. At the *Volume Type* window, select the *Standard VeraCrypt volume* radio button, and then select the *Next>* button.

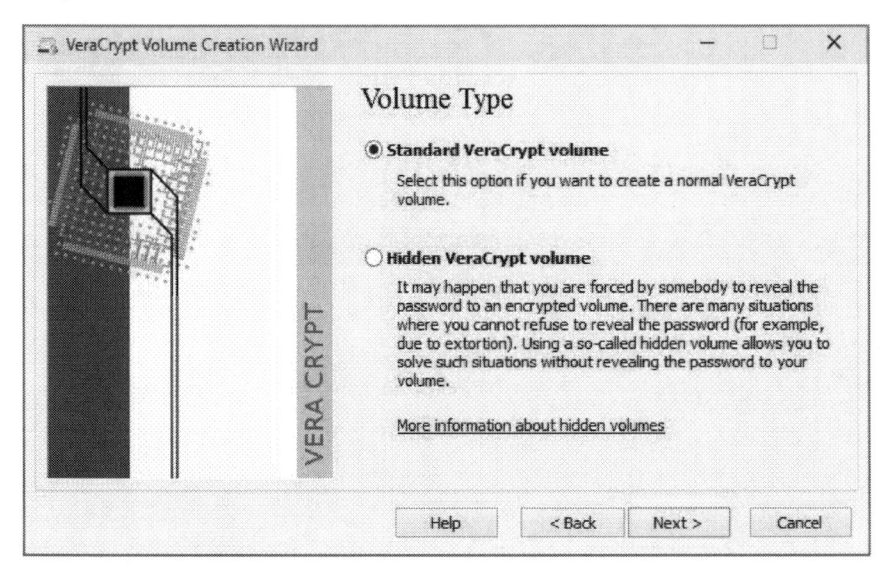

4. At the *Volume Location* window, select the *Select File...* button.

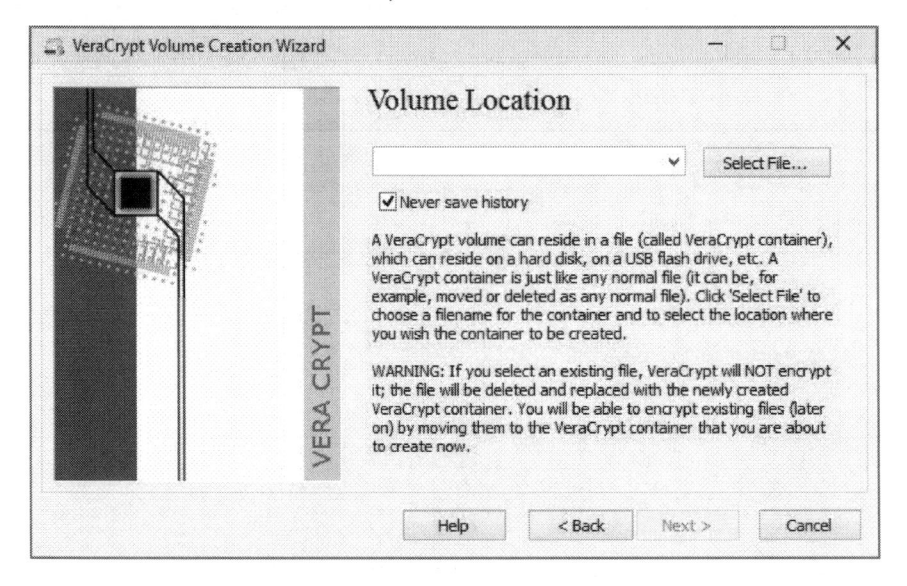

-492-

15. Vulnerability: Documents

5. In the *Save As* field, enter a name for your container, navigate to where you wish to save your container, and then select the *Save* button.

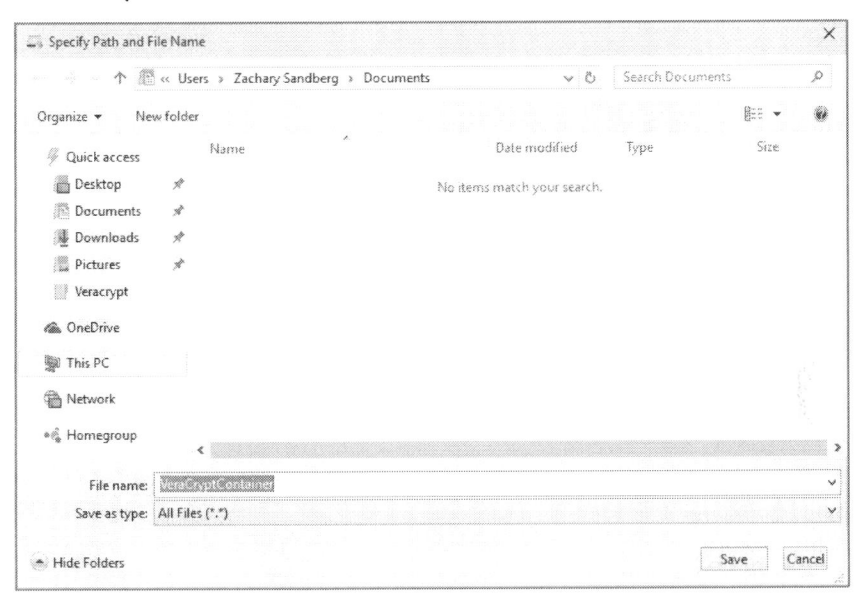

6. When returned to the *Volume Location* window, select the *Next>* button.

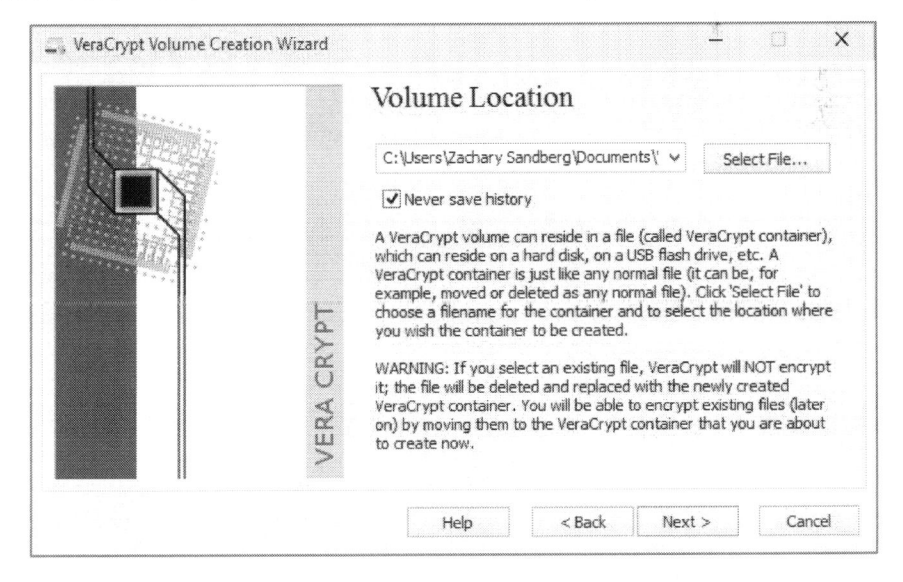

15. Vulnerability: Documents

7. At the *Encryption Options* window, from the *Encryption Algorithm* pop-up menu, select your desired option. *AES* is the industry standard; however, as the NSA and NIST were involved with its acceptance, some experts recommend selecting another option.

8. Then, from the *Hash Algorithm* pop-up menu, select the desired option. *The NSA developed SHA*, so some experts recommend selecting *Whirlpool*. For our example, we will use the industry standards, *AES* and *SHA-512*, and then select the *Next >* button.

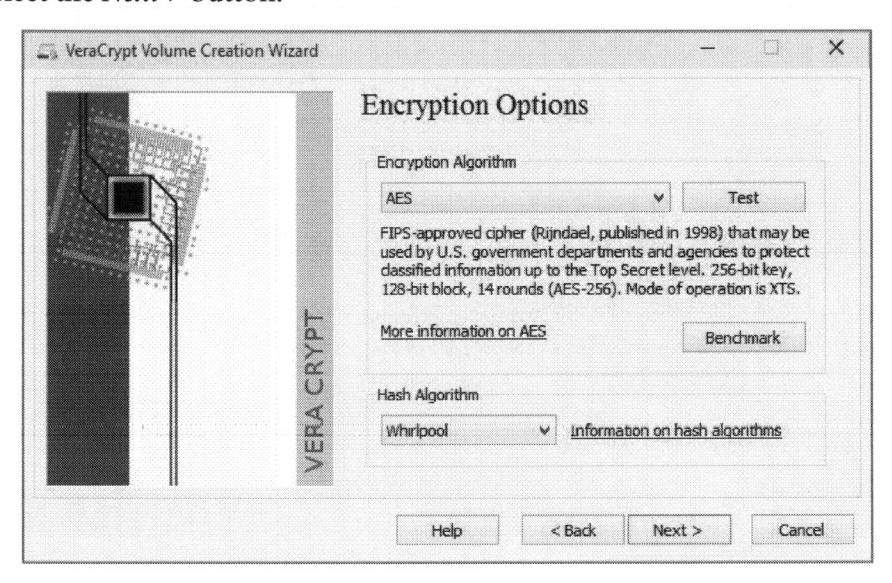

15. Vulnerability: Documents

9. In the *Volume Size* window, set the size of your container. If you intend on emailing, or copying the container to a thumb drive, keep in mind that each email provider has hard limits on the maximum file size that may be sent or received, and a storage device must keep approximately 20% free space for directory and housekeeping needs. Then select the *Next>* button.

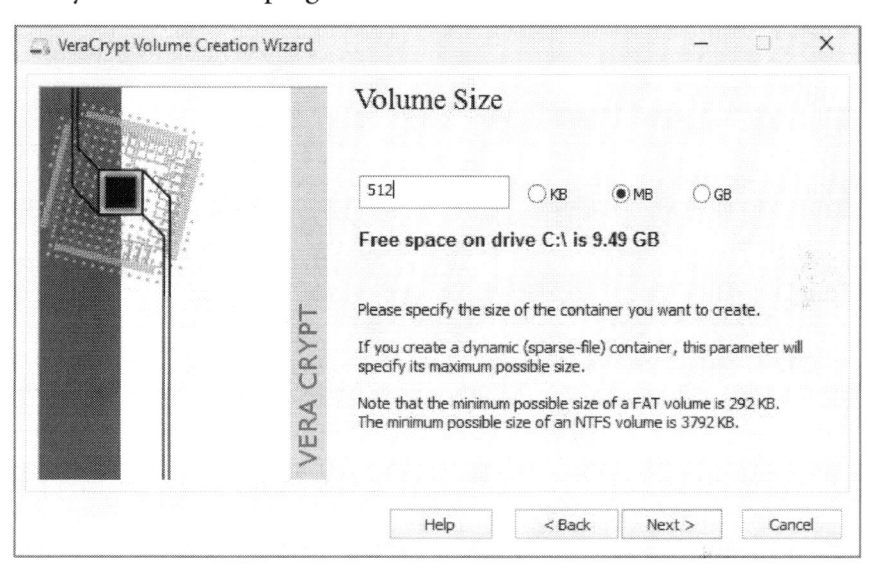

15. Vulnerability: Documents

10. At the *Volume Password* window, in the *Password* and *Confirm Password* fields, enter a strong password for the container, and then select the *Next>* button.

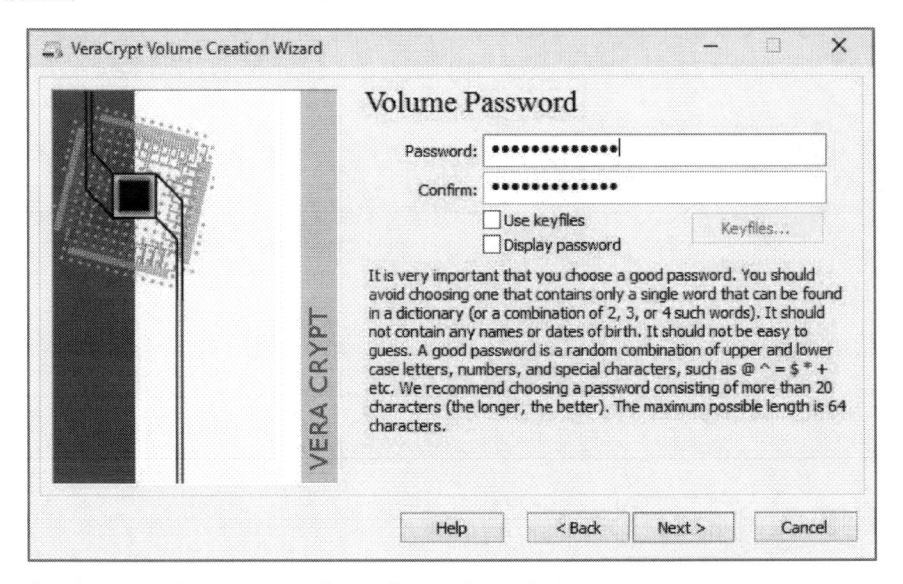

11. At the *Format Options* window, from the *File system type* pop-up menu, select the desired option, and then select the *Next>* button.

    - *FAT* offers full compatibility for Windows, Mac, and Linux use.

    - *NTFS* is the native file system for Windows, however, although OS X and Linux users can read the NTFS file system, OS X and some Linux variants can't write to NTFS without 3rd party software. Choose this option if you want the benefits that NTFS offers and you only plan on using the Windows platform for your VeraCrypt container.

15. Vulnerability: Documents

12. At the *Volume Format* window, move your cursor as randomly as possible within the window for at least 30 seconds, and then select the *Format* button.

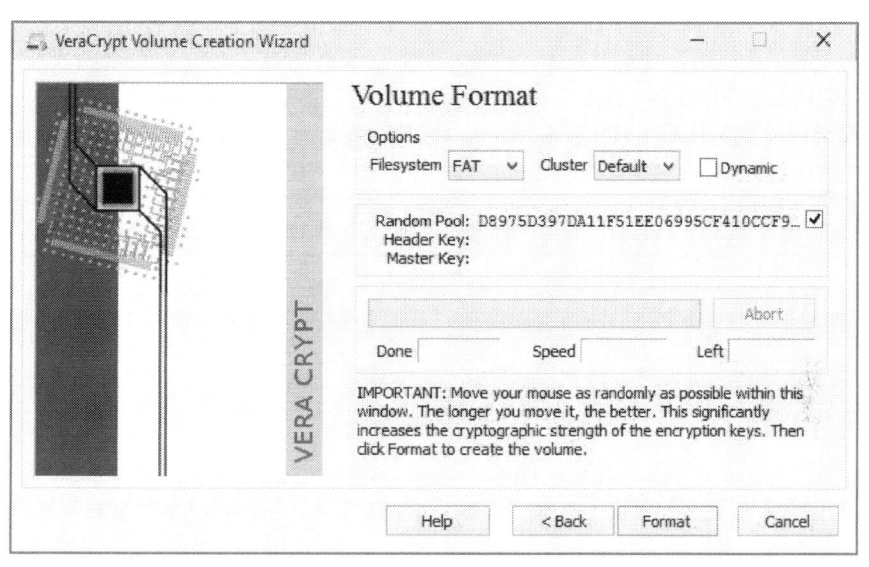

13. Once the container encryption has completed, the *Success* alert appears. Select the *OK* button.

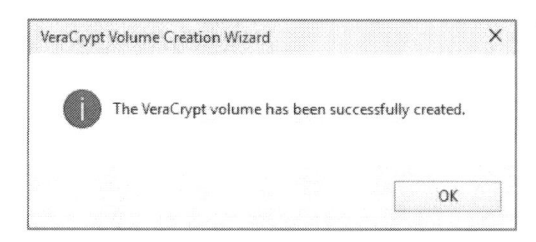

15. Vulnerability: Documents

14. At the *Volume Created* window, select the *Next>* button.

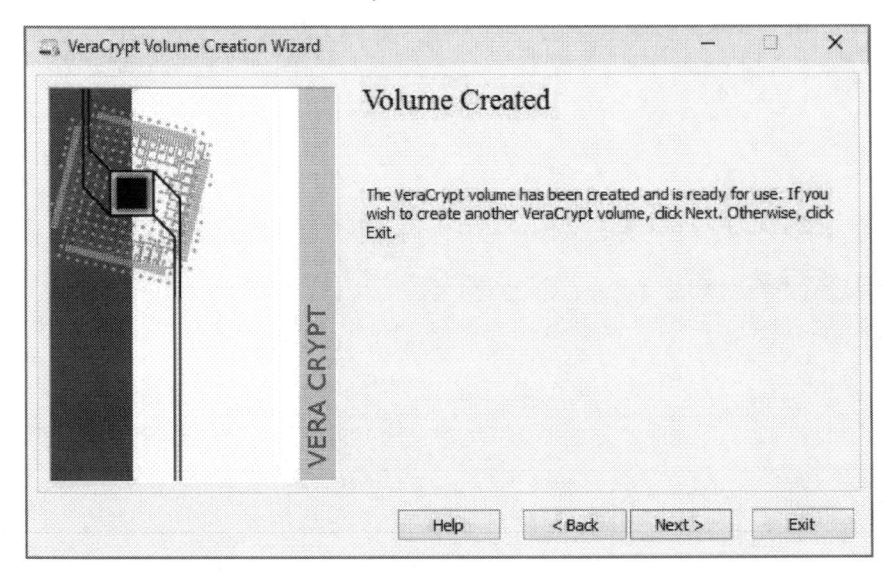

15. You will find yourself at the start of the process again, with VeraCrypt assuming that you wish to create another container. Click *Cancel* to exit the process.

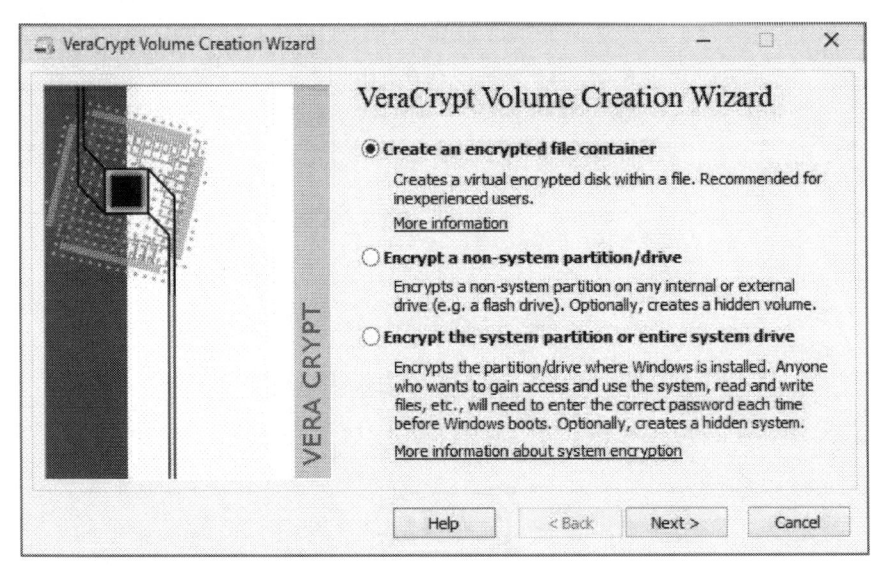

15. Vulnerability: Documents

16. You will now find at the location you specified earlier, the encrypted container.

VeraCryptContainer

Congratulations, you have created your first truly spy-class encryption.

Assignment: Mount an Encrypted VeraCrypt Container

Once you have a VeraCrypt container, you will eventually need to open it to read the contents, add to the container, or make edits to the files. In this assignment, we will mount the VeraCrypt container, which gives you access to all of its data.

1. Open *VeraCrypt,* and then select one of the *Slot* numbers along the left side bar. This will become the temporary number of the VeraCrypt container to be mounted. Select the *Select File…* button.

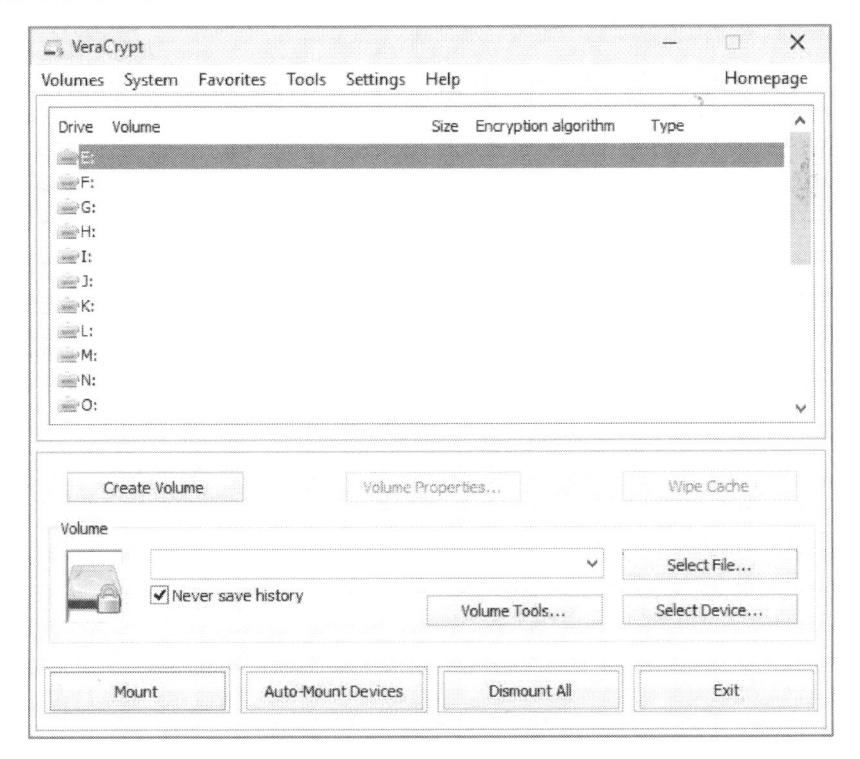

15. Vulnerability: Documents

2. Select the *Select File…* button. The standard *Open* window appears.
3. Navigate to the folder holding the target container. Select the container, and then select the *Open* button.

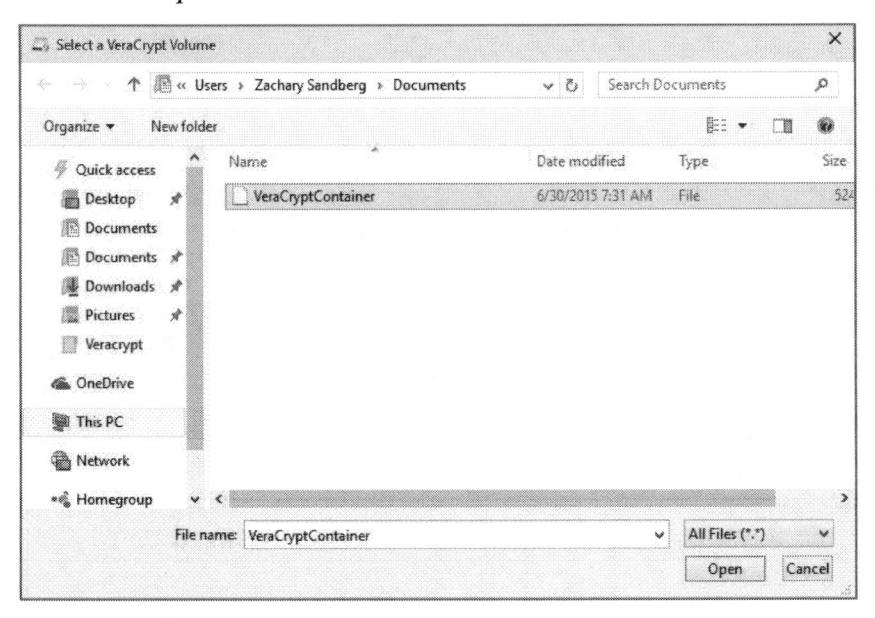

15. Vulnerability: Documents

4. In the VeraCrypt window, select the *Mount* button.

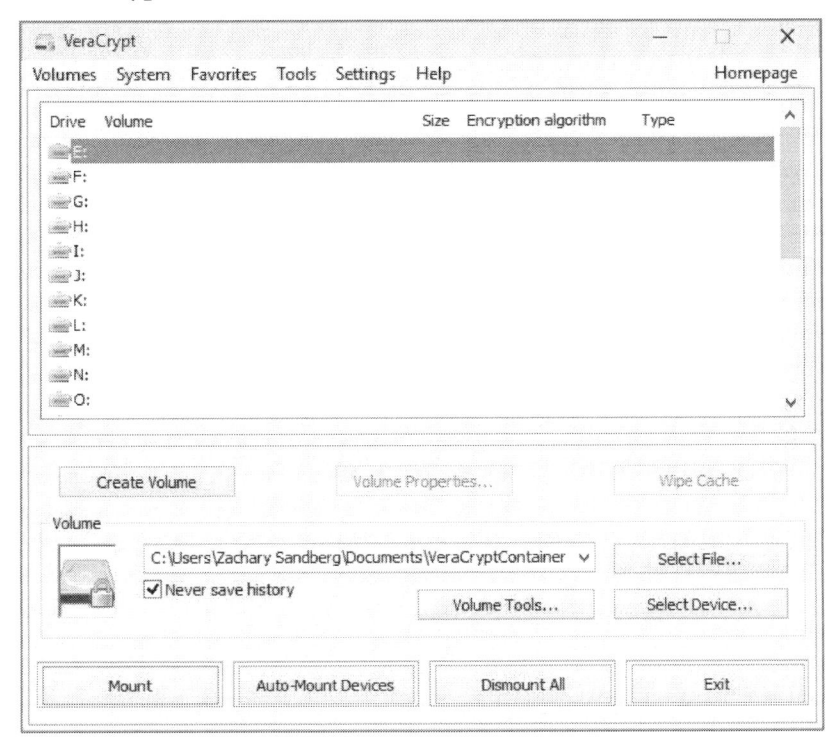

5. The *Enter password* window appears. Enter the password assigned to the container, and then select the *OK* button.

15. Vulnerability: Documents

6. On the main VeraCrypt screen you will see the mounted volume. Double-click to open the volume.

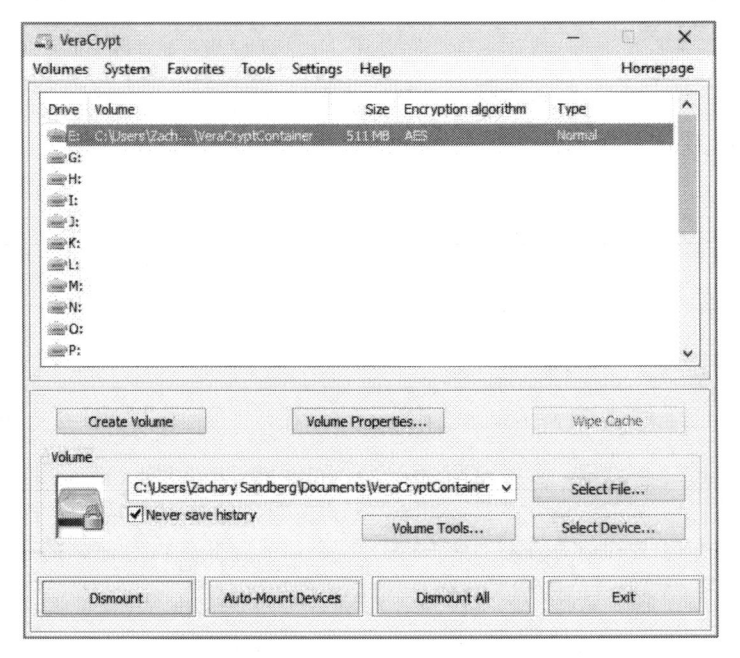

7. You may rename the mounted volume as you would any other item.

8. You may drag and drop or save files and folder into the container.

15. Vulnerability: Documents

9. To unmount, return to the VeraCrypt window, and then select the *Dismount* button. The mounted volume will disappear from VeraCrypt.

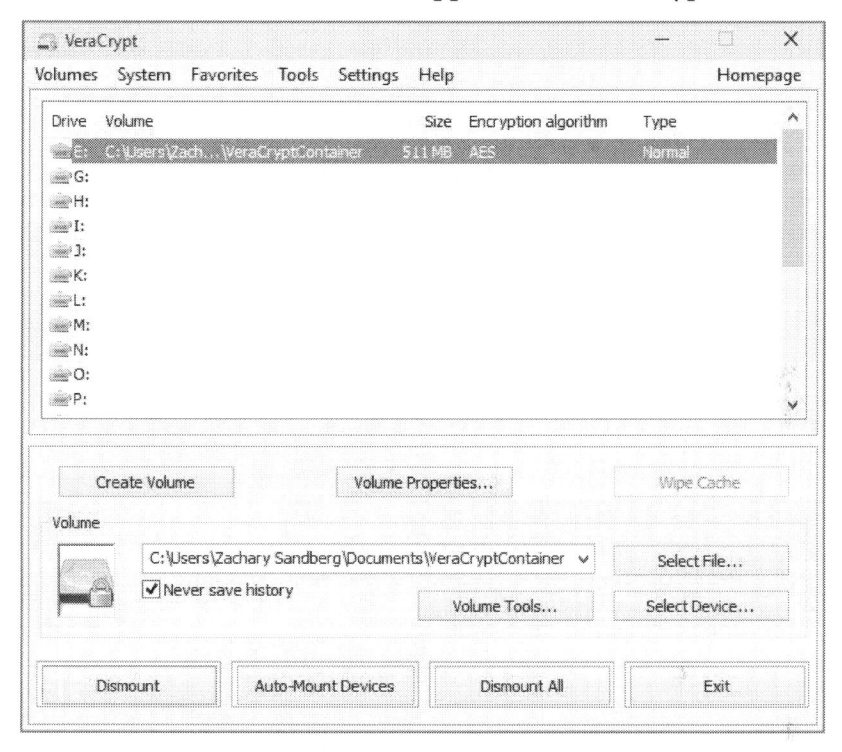

OMG… You *really* are doing high-end security work now. This container may be copied to a thumb drive, optical disc, DropBox, Google Drive, or other Cloud-based storage, and remain secure.

Review Questions

1. The built-in encryption algorithm that is used for modern Microsoft Office and PDF documents is called _____.

2. Password protected Microsoft Office and PDF documents are portable, and can be transferred to a recipient without managing keys or encryption certificates. (True or False)

3. Password protected Windows folders require managing encryption certificates for portability and/or backup purposes.

4. What does a green colored folder or file name indicate?

5. The location to backup and manage your account's encryption certificates is located where?

16. Vulnerability: Storage Device Encryption

There are two types of encryption: one that will prevent your sister from reading your diary and one that will prevent your government.

–Bruce Schneier, American cryptographer, computer security and privacy specialist

BitLocker & UEFI/Legacy BIOS

The UEFI, or Unified Extensible Firmware Interface is a special firmware that has recently replaced the original 30-year old IBM BIOS (Basic Input Output System) used for controlling how computer hardware is seen and managed by the Windows operating system.

When the power button on your computer is pressed, the UEFI firmware takes control of the physical hardware in your computer, acting as a miniature operating system and verifying that the Windows operating system to be booted meets security requirements. Most PCs that shipped with Windows 8 from the factory will be using UEFI, instead of the older, less secure firmware called the BIOS.

Both UEFI and BIOS firmware options are accessed via a special key combination immediately after powering on the computer. These options can be set to allow or disable peripherals (such as webcams, USB ports, Bluetooth, Ethernet ports, etc.)

In the next assignment, we will look at how to set the UEFI menu options for optimal security on your computer. Keep in mind that different manufacturers have different options available. For example, an inexpensive consumer-class laptop from your local retailer might not have the level of UEFI-customization that a business-class laptop has. Business-class laptops are designed with the needs of corporations in mind, meaning that they often contain fine-grained security options.

- Accessing the UEFI Firmware varies from laptop to laptop. If you are unsure how to access your laptop's UEFI, consult the manufacturer's documentation.

- For this assignment, I am using a Lenovo Thinkpad T440s to demonstrate UEFI Firmware security options.

Assignment: Secure UEFI/BIOS Firmware

In this next assignment, we will be learning about UEFI/BIOS Firmware options to maximize the security of your data.

16. Vulnerability: Storage Device Encryption

Listed below are key combinations for accessing the BIOS/UEFI of popular PC manufacturers.

UEFI/Bios Manufacturer Key Command(s)

- **Acer** (Aspire, Power, Veriton, Extensa, Ferrari, TravelMate, Altos): Press [F2] or [Del] immediately after power up

- **Acer** (Altos 600 Server): Press [Ctrl]+[Alt]+[Esc] or [F1] immediately after power up

- **Acer** (Older PC): Press [F1] or [Ctrl]+[Alt]+[Esc] immediately after power up

- **AMI** (American Megatrends AMIBIOS, AMI BIOS): Press [Delete] immediately after power up

- **AMI** (American Megatrends AMIBIOS, AMI BIOS)–Old Version: Press [F1] or [F2] immediately after power up

- **Award BIOS**: Press [Del] immediately after power up

- **Award BIOS**–Old Version: Press [Ctrl]+[Alt]+[Esc] immediately after power up

- **ALR**: Press [Ctrl]+[Alt]+[Esc] or [Ctrl]+[Alt]+[Del] immediately after power up

- **ARI**: Press [Ctrl]+[Alt]+[Esc] or [Ctrl]+[Alt]+[Del] immediately after power up

- **AST** (Advantage): Press [Ctrl]+[Alt]+[Esc] immediately after power up

- **Compaq** (Presario, Prolinea, Deskpro, Systempro, Portable): Press [F10] when blinking cursor jumps to top right corner of screen

- **Compaq** (Presario, Prolinea, Deskpro, Systempro, Portable): Press [F10] When Logo Screen Is Displayed

- **Compaq** (Older Computers): Press [F1], [F2], [F10], or [Del] immediately after power up

- **Cybermax**: Press [Esc] immediately after power up

16. Vulnerability: Storage Device Encryption

- **Dell** (XPS, Dimension, Inspiron, Latitude. OptiPlex, Precision, Vostro): Press F2 When Dell Logo Is Displayed Until "Entering Setup" Appears
- **Dell** (Older 486 Models): Press [Ctrl]+[Alt]+[Enter] immediately after power up
- **Dell** (Some Models): Press Reset Button twice (i.e. Power Reset Button) immediately after power up
- **Dell** (Dimension L566cx System): Press [Del]
- **Dell** (Older Laptop Models) : Press [Fn]+[Esc] or [Fn]+[F1]
- **DTK** (Datatech Enterprises): Press [Esc] immediately after power up
- **EISA Computer**: Press the Reset button on the front of the computer, then press [Ctrl]+[Alt]+[Esc] immediately when the memory count begins or press [Crtl]+[Alt]+[S]
- **eMachines** (eMonster, eTower, eOne, S-Series, T-Series): Press [Tab] or [Del] immediately after power up
- **eMachines** (Some Older Computers): Press [F2]
- **Fujitsu** (LifeBook, Esprimo, Amilo, Tablet, DeskPower): Press [F2] When Fujitsu logo appears
- **Gateway** Using Phoenix BIOS (DX, FX, One, GM, GT, GX, Profile, Astro): Press [F1]
- **Gateway** (Some Older PCs): Press [F2]
- **Hewlett-Parkard** (HP Pavilion, TouchSmart, Vectra, OmniBook, Tablet): Press [F1] immediately after power up
- **Hewlett-Parkard** (HP Alternative): Press [F2] or [Esc] immediately after power up
- **Hewlett-Packard** (HP) Tablet PC: Press [F10] or [F12] immediately after power up
- **IBM** ThinkPad using IBM BIOS (Early Models): Press [Ctrl]+[Alt]+[Ins] When cursor is at upper-right corner

16. Vulnerability: Storage Device Encryption

- **IBM** ThinkPad using IBM BIOS (Later Models): Press and Hold [F1] immediately after power up
- **IBM** ThinkPad using Phoenix BIOS: Press [Ctrl]+[Alt]+[F11] from DOS Prompt
- **IBM** (Older Computers or Notebooks): Press [F2]
- **Lenovo** (ThinkPad, IdeaPad, 3000 Series, ThinkCentre, ThinkStation): Press [F1] or [F2] immediately after power up
- **Lenovo** (Older Products): Press [Ctrl]+[Alt]+[F3], [Ctrl]+[Alt]+[Ins] or [Fn]+[F1] immediately after power up
- **Microid Research** MR BIOS: Press [F1] immediately after power up
- **Micron** (MPC Computers ClientPro, TransPort): Press [F1], [F2] or [Del] immediately after power up
- **NEC** (PowerMate, Versa, W-Series): Press [F2] immediately after power up
- **NEC** Versa Notebook: Press and Hold Down [F1] immediately after power up
- **Olivetti** PC Pro: Press [Ctrl]+[Alt]+[Shift]+[Del](in Num Pad) immediately after power up
- **Packard Bell** (8900 Series, 9000 Series, Pulsar, Platinum, EasyNote, imedia, iextreme): Press [F1], [F2], or [Del] immediately after power up
- **Packard Bell** (Early 386 and 486 Models): Press [Ctrl]+[Alt]+[S] immediately after power up
- **Phoenix BIOS** (Phoenix-Award BIOS): Press [Del] immediately after power up
- **Phoenix BIOS** (Phoenix-Award BIOS)–Old Version: Press [Ctrl]+[Alt]+[S], [Ctrl]+[Alt]+[Esc], [Ctrl]+[Alt]+[Ins] or [Ctrl]+[S] immediately after power up
- **Sharp** (Notebook Laptops, Actius UltraLite): Press [F2] immediately after power up
- **Sharp** (Old PCs): Require Setup Diagnostics disk to access BIOS

16. Vulnerability: Storage Device Encryption

- **Shuttle** (Glamor G-Series, D'vo, Prima P2-Series, Workstation, X Mini XPC, Surveillance): Press [F2] or [Del] immediately after power up
- **Sony** (VAIO, PCG-Series, VGN-Series): Press [F1], [F2] or [F3] immediately after power up
- **Sony** Vaio 320 Series: Press [F2] immediately after power up
- **Tandon** 386: press [Ctrl]+[Shift]+[Esc] Tandon: press [Ctrl]+[Shift]+[Esc] immediately after power up
- **Toshiba** (Portégé, Satellite, Tecra): Press [Esc] immediately after power up
- **Toshiba** (Portégé, Satellite, Tecra with Phoenix BIOS): Press [F1] immediately after power up
- **Zenith**: Press [Ctrl]+[Alt]+[Ins] immediately after power up

16. Vulnerability: Storage Device Encryption

1. Access the UEFI Firmware on your computer. I am using a Lenovo Business-class laptop. To access the UEFI Firmware on it, I press the F1 key immediately after powering on. Your key(s) may be listed in the table above. The main screen below shows my laptop's UEFI version, serial number, model type, CPU model and the amount of memory installed. The keyboard arrow keys must be used to navigate between the top categories and options.

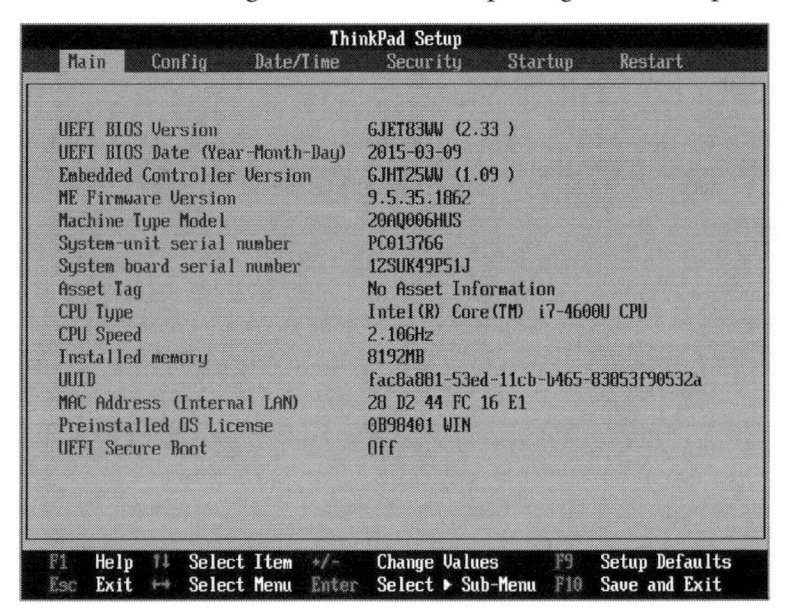

```
                       ThinkPad Setup
    Main    Config    Date/Time    Security    Startup    Restart

    UEFI BIOS Version                GJET83WW (2.33 )
    UEFI BIOS Date (Year-Month-Day)  2015-03-09
    Embedded Controller Version      GJHT25WW (1.09 )
    ME Firmware Version              9.5.35.1862
    Machine Type Model               20AQ006HUS
    System-unit serial number        PC01376G
    System board serial number       12SUK49P51J
    Asset Tag                        No Asset Information
    CPU Type                         Intel(R) Core(TM) i7-4600U CPU
    CPU Speed                        2.10GHz
    Installed memory                 8192MB
    UUID                             facBa801-53ed-11cb-b465-83853f90532a
    MAC Address (Internal LAN)       28 D2 44 FC 16 E1
    Preinstalled OS License          0B90401 WIN
    UEFI Secure Boot                 Off

    F1  Help    ↑↓ Select Item   +/-    Change Values   F9  Setup Defaults
    Esc Exit    ←→ Select Menu   Enter  Select ▶ Sub-Menu  F10 Save and Exit
```

16. Vulnerability: Storage Device Encryption

2. Since we're primarily interested in security, use the right arrow key to select the *Security* tab at the top of the screen. Select *Password*, and then press *Enter*.

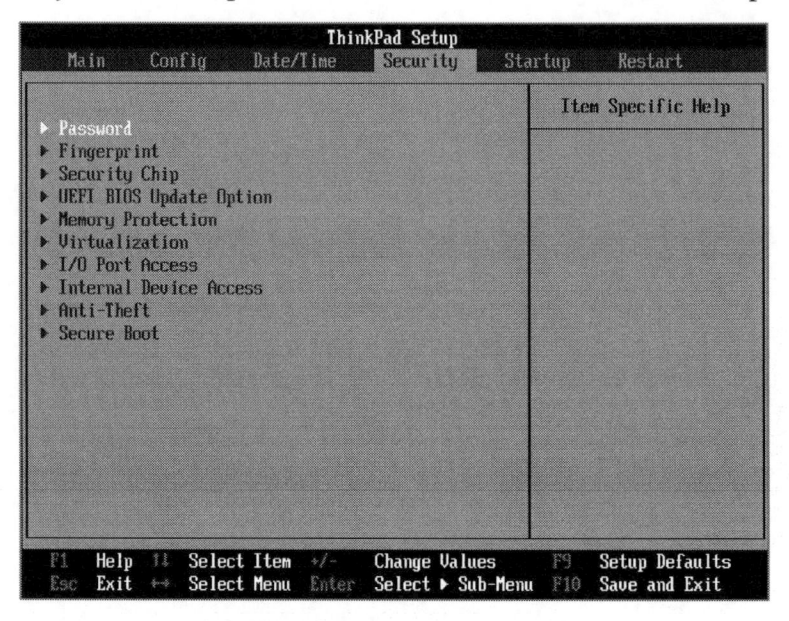

```
                         ThinkPad Setup
     Main      Config      Date/Time    Security    Startup    Restart

                                              Item Specific Help
     ▶ Password
     ▶ Fingerprint
     ▶ Security Chip
     ▶ UEFI BIOS Update Option
     ▶ Memory Protection
     ▶ Virtualization
     ▶ I/O Port Access
     ▶ Internal Device Access
     ▶ Anti-Theft
     ▶ Secure Boot




     F1   Help   ↑↓   Select Item   +/-    Change Values   F9    Setup Defaults
     Esc  Exit   ↔    Select Menu   Enter  Select ▶ Sub-Menu  F10  Save and Exit
```

3. Several different password options are available:

   - **Supervisor Password.** An optional administrator password that can be set to lock out Boot priority lists, and network items.

   - **Power-On Password.** An optional password that must be entered immediately after powering on the computer.

   - **Hard Disk Password.** A recommended password that locks access to the hard drive, so that even if the drive is removed and put into another computer it can't be read. An advanced thief however could pull data from a hard drive's magnetic platters without the password, since the data is (by default) not encrypted.

     If this password is set and used in conjunction with a Self-Encrypting Disk (explained later in this chapter), the contents of the hard drive will be encrypted and completely secured.

16. Vulnerability: Storage Device Encryption

4. To set an optional Supervisor password, use the down arrow key to highlight *Supervisor Password*, and then press the *Enter* key.

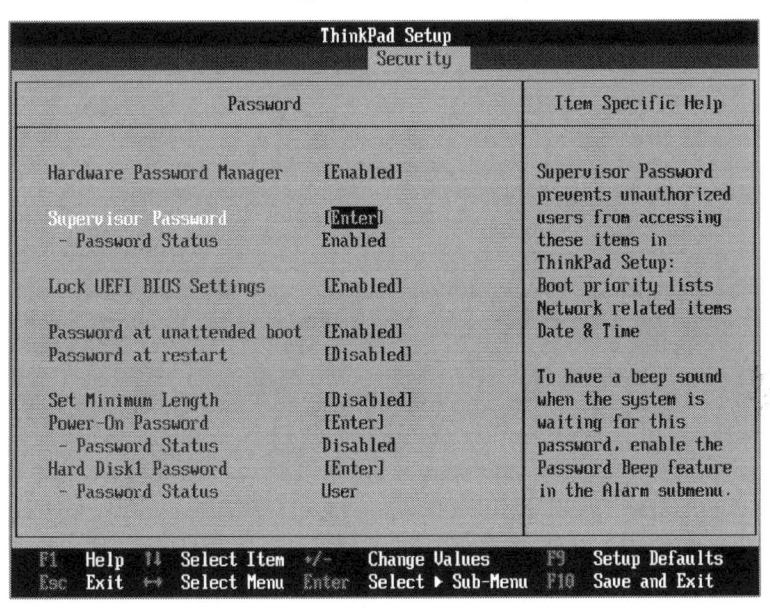

5. Enter a secure password in both of the password fields, and then press the *Enter* key after each field.

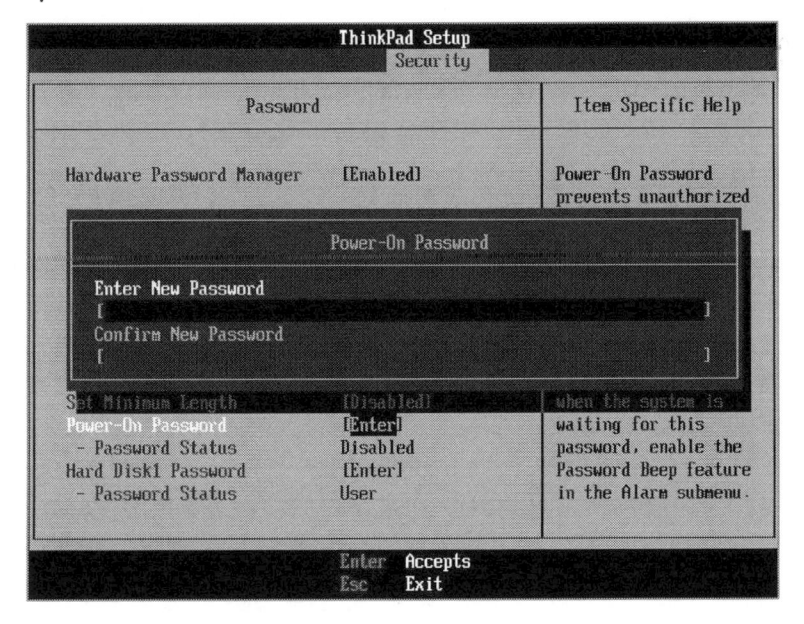

16. Vulnerability: Storage Device Encryption

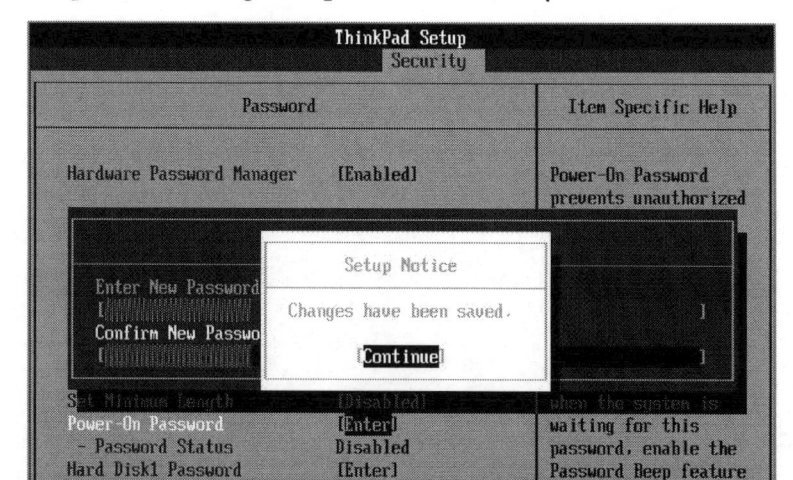

6. At the *Setup Notice* dialog box, press the *Enter* key.

Moving down the page, another important password to set is the *Hard Disk password*. Setting this option will make the computer prompt for credentials on boot to unlock the contents of the hard drive for the UEFI firmware to see the data and load the operating system. If Hard Disk password is set, it will make data recovery impossible if the password is lost. (Computer manufacturers will tell you that the hard disk will need to be replaced if the password is forgotten). Additionally, some newer laptops with *Self-Encrypting Drives* (*SEDs*) use this password to not only lock out the drive at boot, but also encrypt the data with secure 128 or 256-bit AES encryption for an extra level of protection.

Hard drive encryption, even though it's been around for a few years, has yet to be implemented on mainstream consumer hardware. Furthermore, there can be a confusing amount of variables involved, because some Self-Encrypting Drives are designed to also be compatible with traditionally software-based encryption such as Windows BitLocker. This compatibility is known as eDrive. With a non-eDrive Self-Encrypting Drive, enabling Windows BitLocker forces all the data on the hard drive to be read, then manually encrypted using CPU power, then finally written back to the disk in encrypted format. Enabling BitLocker on an eDrive

16. Vulnerability: Storage Device Encryption

disk is instantaneous, and uses no CPU power during the encryption process since it interacts directly with the eDrive firmware.

If your Self-Encrypting Drive is not eDrive compatible, and you do not wish to use slower software-based encryption such as Microsoft BitLocker, then setting the UEFI Hard Disk password is the best option available for instantaneous, transparent encryption. This also holds true if your computer has more than one operating system on it, such as Windows 10 with Windows 7, or Windows 10 with Linux. The UEFI Hard Disk password instantly encrypts the entire disk, including Microsoft and non-Microsoft operating systems alike. By contrast Windows BitLocker only understands newer Windows operating systems and will not work with Linux or older partition formats.

Finally, if your computer lacks a Self-Encrypting Drive, setting the UEFI Hard Disk password will likely prevent a common thief from accessing your drive's data, even if the drive is removed and then transplanted into another computer.

In my own case, the Lenovo Thinkpad we are using for this assignment contains a Self-Encrypting Solid State Disk that is *not* eDrive compatible. My security options are to either use the slower Windows BitLocker encryption, or to set the instantaneous UEFI Hard Disk password (both use the secure AES-256 encryption standard). My decision in this case is to use the simpler, operating-system agnostic UEFI Hard Disk password.

16. Vulnerability: Storage Device Encryption

7. To set a Hard Disk Password, use the arrow keys to highlight the *Hard Disk1 Password* field, and then press the *Enter* Key.

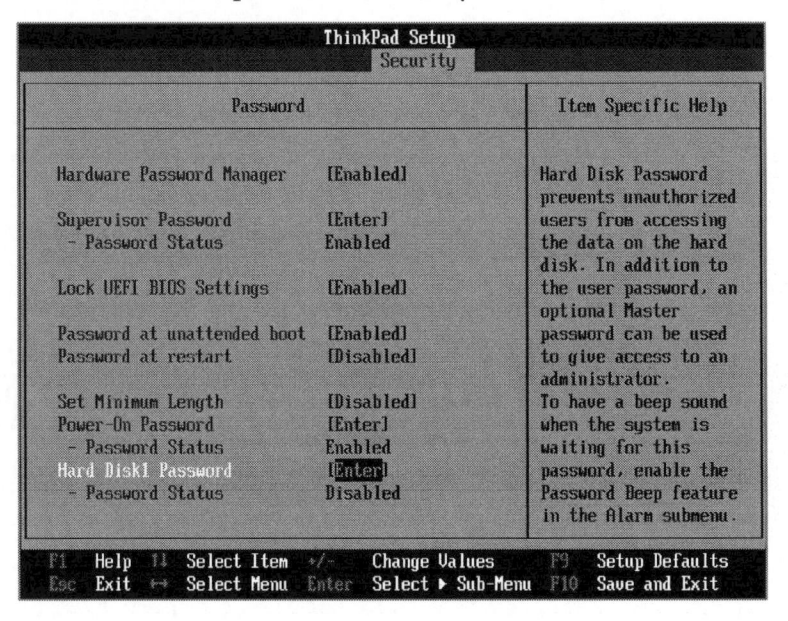

```
                        ThinkPad Setup
                              Security

         Password                            Item Specific Help

   Hardware Password Manager    [Enabled]     Hard Disk Password
                                              prevents unauthorized
   Supervisor Password          [Enter]       users from accessing
    - Password Status           Enabled       the data on the hard
                                              disk. In addition to
   Lock UEFI BIOS Settings      [Enabled]     the user password, an
                                              optional Master
   Password at unattended boot  [Enabled]     password can be used
   Password at restart          [Disabled]    to give access to an
                                              administrator.
   Set Minimum Length           [Disabled]    To have a beep sound
   Power-On Password            [Enter]       when the system is
    - Password Status           Enabled       waiting for this
   Hard Disk1 Password          [Enter]       password, enable the
    - Password Status           Disabled      Password Beep feature
                                              in the Alarm submenu.

   F1   Help    ↑↓  Select Item   +/-    Change Values    F9   Setup Defaults
   Esc  Exit    ←→  Select Menu   Enter  Select ▶ Sub-Menu F10  Save and Exit
```

16. Vulnerability: Storage Device Encryption

8. At the *Setup Confirmation* dialog, select *User,* and then press the *Enter* key.

    - Note: The *User+Master* option is tailored toward corporate environments so that an Administrator (Master) can still access the data on the hard drive even if a User forgets a password. For the home environment, setting the *User* password should be sufficient.

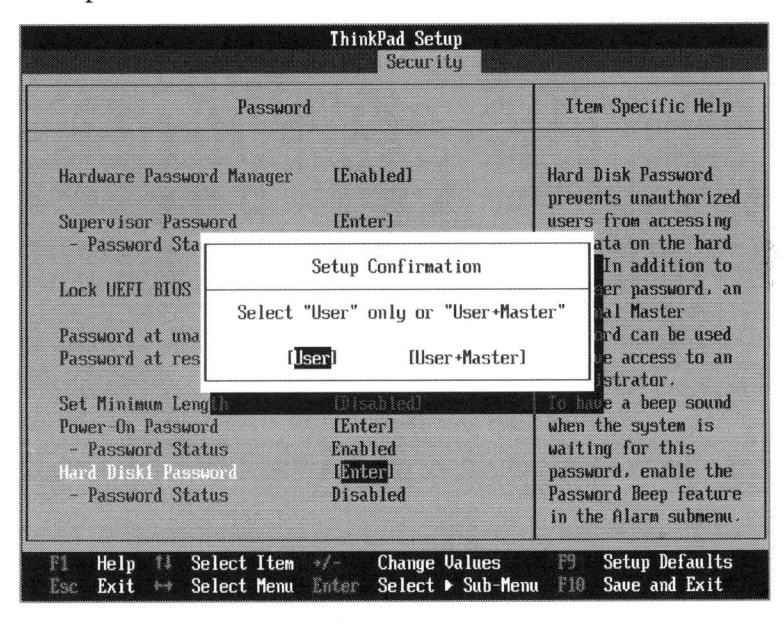

16. Vulnerability: Storage Device Encryption

9. Enter a secure password for the *Hard Disk1 password*. My Lenovo ThinkPad allows for up to 32 characters to be used, however other manufactures may only allow for 8, which is considered to be a very poor design for security. It is recommended that this password be at least 14 characters in length. Press the *Enter Key* after each entry and at the confirmation.

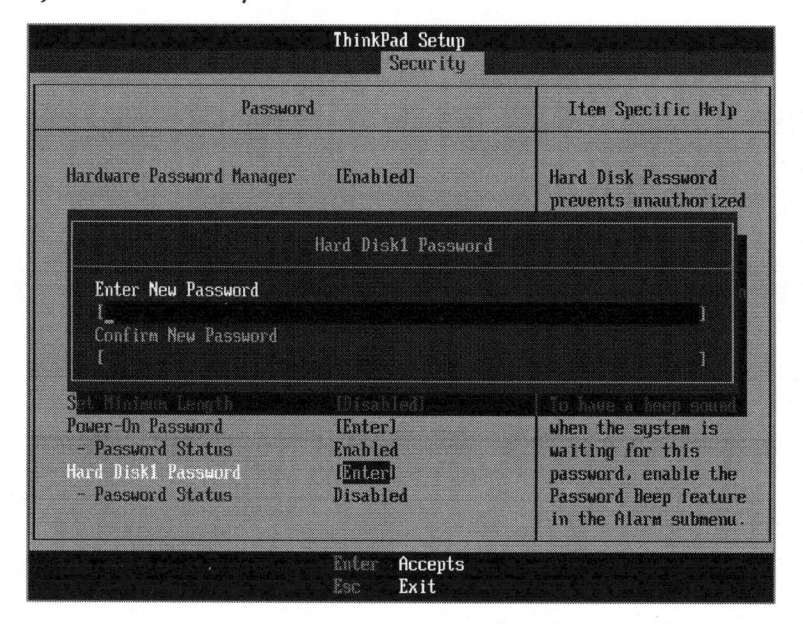

16. Vulnerability: Storage Device Encryption

10. The next option is to enable or disable the integrated *Fingerprint Reader*. Fingerprint readers have been common on many makes and models since IBM introduced the technology to the laptop world in 2004. Using fingerprints as authentication, however, is not as secure as using passwords, since thieves can lift your fingerprints from things you touch and thus fool the sensor into thinking it is you logging on. To maximize security, you can ignore this option (if you have not enrolled fingerprints in Windows), or expressly disable the option by pressing the *Enter* key and selecting *Disable*.

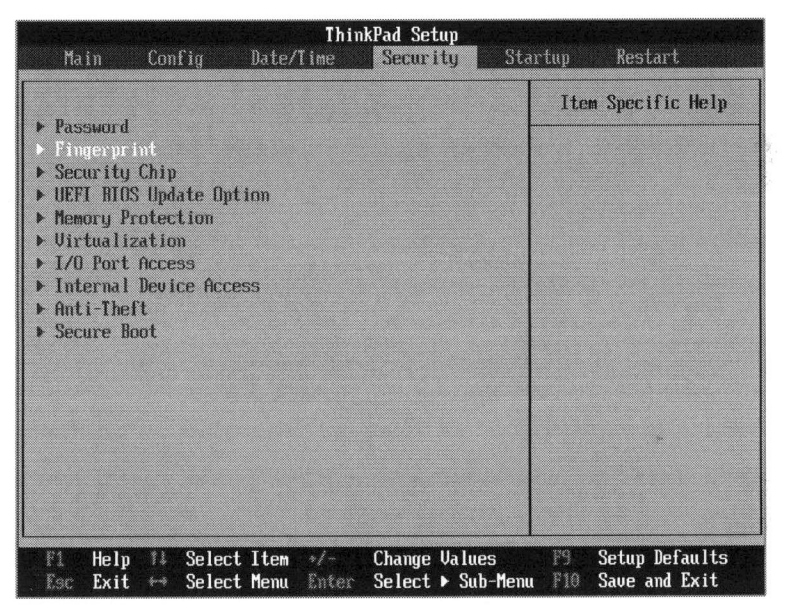

```
                    ThinkPad Setup
   Main    Config    Date/Time   Security    Startup    Restart

                                          Item Specific Help
      ▶ Password
      ▶ Fingerprint
      ▶ Security Chip
      ▶ UEFI BIOS Update Option
      ▶ Memory Protection
      ▶ Virtualization
      ▶ I/O Port Access
      ▶ Internal Device Access
      ▶ Anti-Theft
      ▶ Secure Boot




   F1   Help    ↑↓  Select Item   +/-     Change Values    F9   Setup Defaults
   Esc  Exit    ←→  Select Menu   Enter   Select ▶ Sub-Menu F10  Save and Exit
```

BitLocker UEFI Prep

The next option, entitled *Security Chip,* is to enable or disable the onboard *Trusted Platform Module* or *TPM* for short. The TPM is an encryption chip that acts as a secure storage area between the user and the operating system for management of encryption keys and passwords. Not all existing computers have TPMs, however as of January 1st, 2015, all computers that wish to pass the Windows 8.1 hardware certification must have a TPM.

Historically, TPM chips were introduced in 2001 in the IBM Thinkpad line of laptops, however software support for the technology did not manifest until much

16. Vulnerability: Storage Device Encryption

later. One of the common initial uses of the TPM was to store Fingerprint reader data in the secure "Trusted" location that the Trusted Platform module provided. This prevented malware, or other users from accessing the fingerprints if they were stored on the more vulnerable and volatile hard drive.

Fast-forward to modern times, the TPM is used commonly by Microsoft's BitLocker encryption in Windows 7, Windows 8.x and Windows 10. If BitLocker is enabled on a computer with a present and active TPM chip, the keys that BitLocker generates are stored inside the TPM and away from user access. If BitLocker is enabled on a computer without a present or active TPM, then a user needs to manage his own recovery key by manually printing it out, or by storing it on a USB device. Since this method of storage puts recovery data potentially outside of user control, it is less secure than using a computer with a built-in TPM.

Assignment: Verify TPM is Enabled

1. To make sure that the TPM is enabled for BitLocker encryption, select the *Security Chip* menu item and press the *Enter* key.

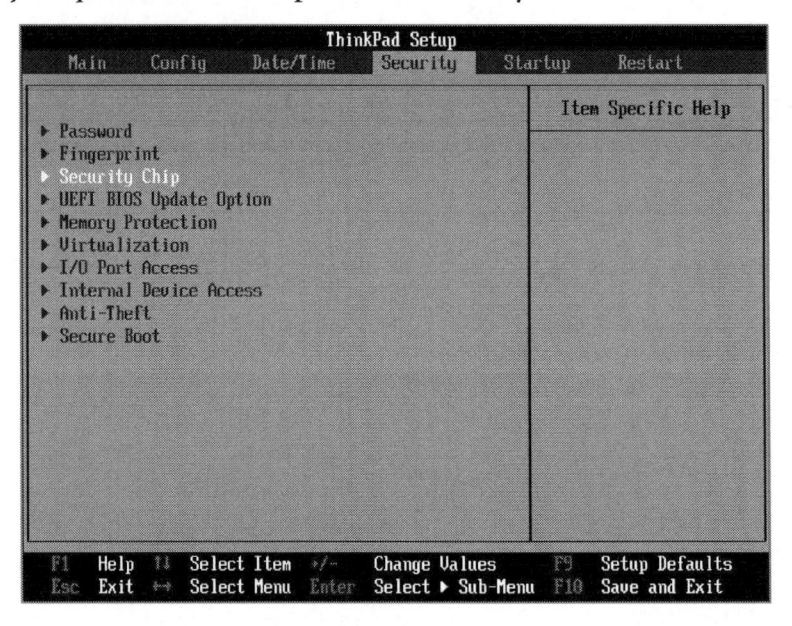

16. Vulnerability: Storage Device Encryption

2. Scroll down to *Security Chip* and change it to *Active*.

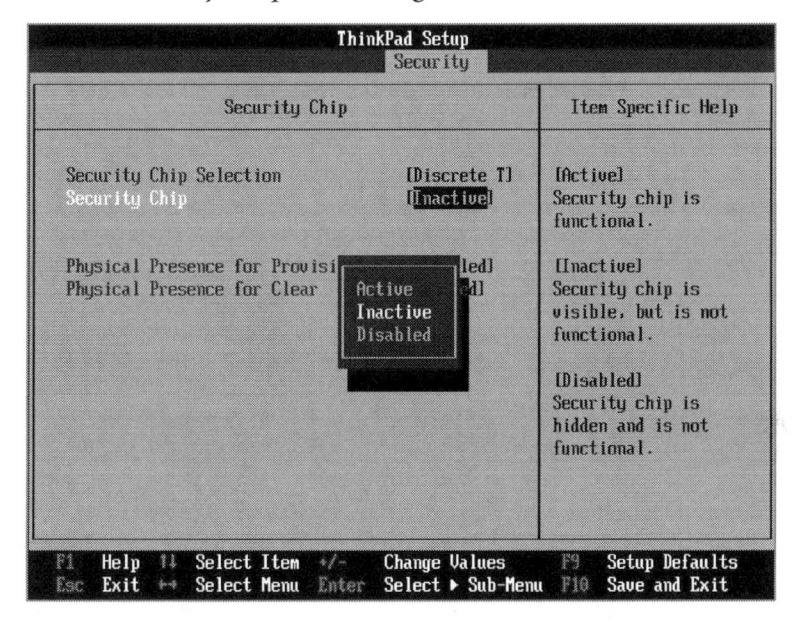

3. Scroll to *Security Chip Selection*, and then press Enter. If you have more than one TPM chip, you can now select which you would like to use. *Discrete TPM* is the more secure if you have multiple TPM chipsets.

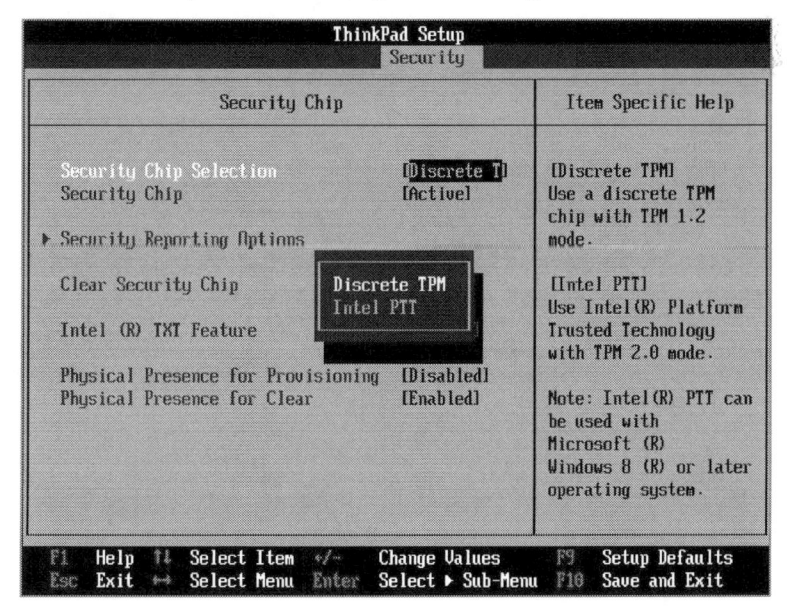

4. Hit escape until you enter the main menu. Scroll to *Restart*, and then select *Exit Saving Changes*.

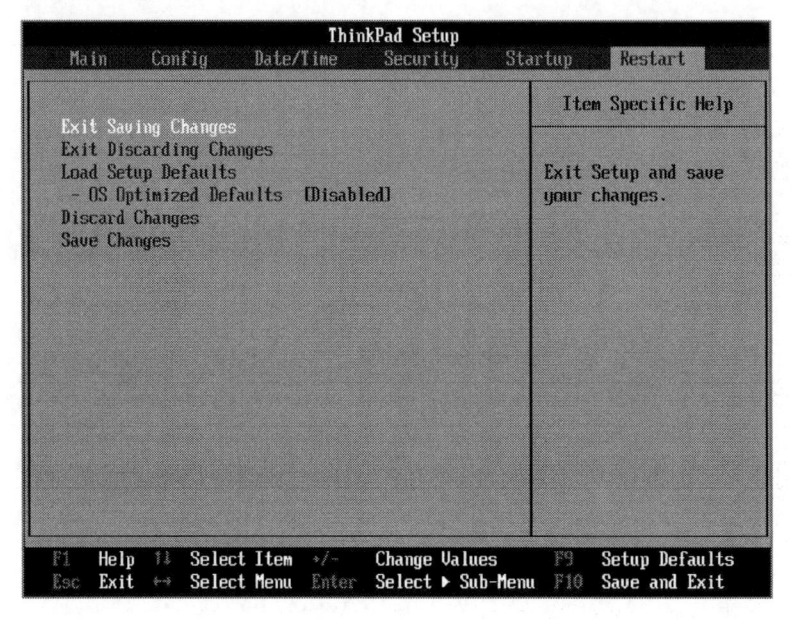

```
                          ThinkPad Setup
     Main    Config    Date/Time    Security    Startup    Restart
                                                    Item Specific Help
     Exit Saving Changes
     Exit Discarding Changes
     Load Setup Defaults                          Exit Setup and save
       - OS Optimized Defaults   [Disabled]       your changes.
     Discard Changes
     Save Changes




     F1   Help   ↑↓  Select Item    +/-     Change Values   F9    Setup Defaults
     Esc  Exit   ↔   Select Menu    Enter   Select ▶ Sub-Menu  F10  Save and Exit
```

Assignment: Test the UEFI/BIOS Password

In this assignment, confirm the UEFI/BIOS password is in place securing your computer:

1. Shut down the PC.

2. Power on the PC.

3. Immediately at the splash screen, hold down the key that allows entry to UEFI/BIOS.

4. At the password prompt, enter the UEFI/BIOS password.

11. The UEFI/BIOS screen will appear.

12. Go to the *Exit* section, and then select *Exit and Do Not Save Changes*. We do not need to save anything since we did not make any changes.

Miscellaneous UEFI/BIOS Security

Depending on the manufacturer of your computer, there may be additional security features within the UEFI/BIOS to configure such as disabling remote management features, disabling ports, or enabling alerts for physical tampering.

As with most technology, different use-cases call for varying methods of security.

Example 1. Perhaps you use your laptop for public presentations, and it occasionally sits on a podium unattended? To prevent a stranger from walking up and sticking in an infected or malicious USB stick, you may find that disabling USB ports along with the SD card reader offers a good physical protection measure against attacks.

Example 2. You have multiple user accounts on your laptop, which you share with colleagues. Since you sometimes work from sensitive areas, you wish to make sure that no software, known or unknown has access to the webcam and microphone. Disabling these two features in the UEFI prevents Windows or any other applications from using them, and offers the highest level of security (aside from removing them completely).

Example 3. As a conspiracy theorist, you are concerned that some three-letter government agency may wish to break into your house while you're away, bugging your computer's hardware in the process. Enabling bottom cover tamper protection to alert you if the computer has been opened may ease your fears (or maybe not).

Assignment: Enabling additional UEFI/BIOS Security Features

1. Shut down the PC.
2. Power on the PC.
3. Immediately at the splash screen, hold down the key that allows entry to UEFI/BIOS.
4. At the password prompt, enter the UEFI/BIOS password.
5. The UEFI/BIOS screen will appear.

Security items to consider optimizing

16. Vulnerability: Storage Device Encryption

- **Intel AMT.** Inside the *Config* menu, an option exists to disable *Intel AMT*, a remote support feature that allows special administration software to completely control your PC (even if it's powered off!). Disabling this option in the UEFI will prevent these management features from working. (Note that the option to *Permanently Disable* the feature also exists, in the event the computer is used in a country or environment that the function is illegal. Unless you have requirements to permanently kill this functionality, it is recommended that this feature just be set to *disabled*.

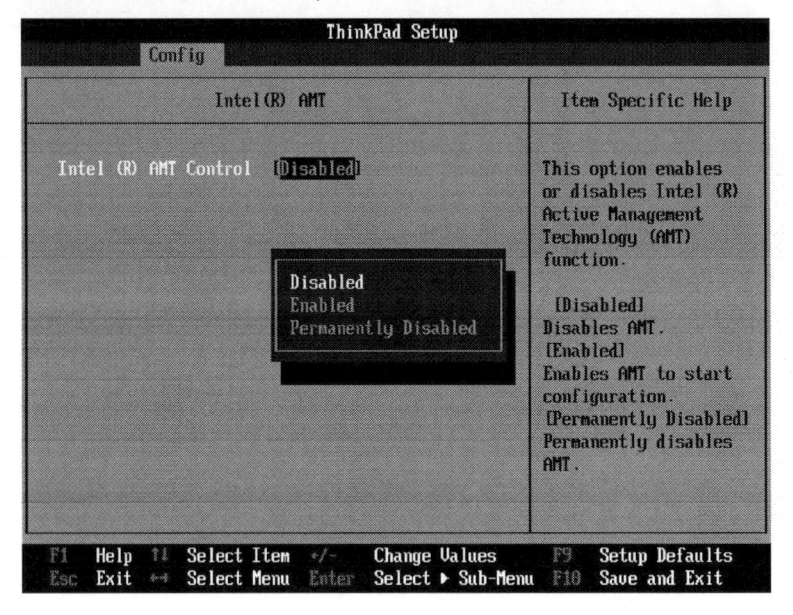

16. Vulnerability: Storage Device Encryption

- **I/O Ports.** Inside the *Security* menu, an option exists to disable Input/Output ports. These ports include the Ethernet Jack, Wireless LAN card, Wireless WAN card (Cellular), Bluetooth, USB Ports, Memory Card slot, Webcam, Microphone, and the Fingerprint reader.

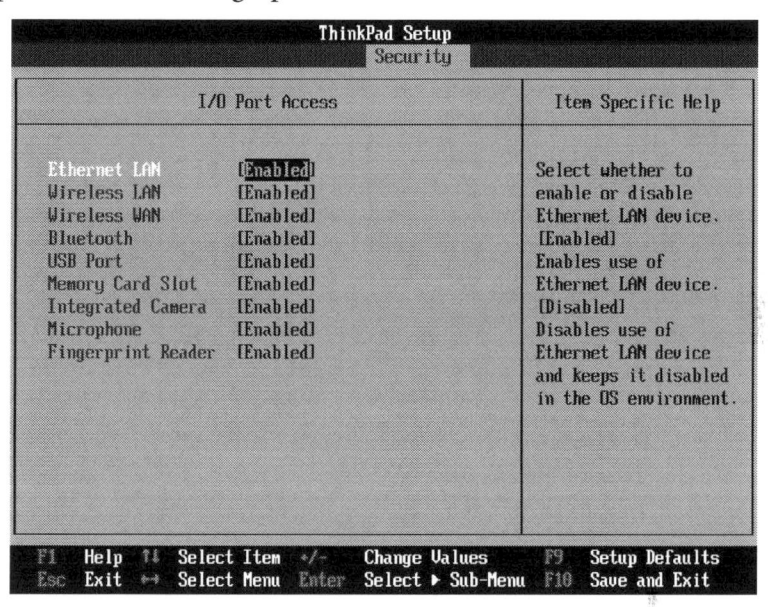

```
                    ThinkPad Setup
                       Security

         I/O Port Access              Item Specific Help

   Ethernet LAN       [Enabled]       Select whether to
   Wireless LAN       [Enabled]       enable or disable
   Wireless WAN       [Enabled]       Ethernet LAN device.
   Bluetooth          [Enabled]       [Enabled]
   USB Port           [Enabled]       Enables use of
   Memory Card Slot   [Enabled]       Ethernet LAN device.
   Integrated Camera  [Enabled]       [Disabled]
   Microphone         [Enabled]       Disables use of
   Fingerprint Reader [Enabled]       Ethernet LAN device
                                      and keeps it disabled
                                      in the OS environment.




   F1   Help    ↑↓  Select Item  +/-    Change Values    F9   Setup Defaults
   Esc  Exit    ↔   Select Menu  Enter  Select ▶ Sub-Menu F10  Save and Exit
```

16. Vulnerability: Storage Device Encryption

- **Bottom Cover Tamper Switch.** Some laptops such as the Lenovo Thinkpad feature an intrusion switch that will display an alert if the switch is tripped. What does this mean? Well if for example, someone removed the screws and opened the bottom cover of the laptop to do something nefarious, the next time the laptop was booted it would display a message that the laptop was tampered with. Assuming that the UEFI password was enabled, the criminals would not be able to reset the tamper switch themselves. You can find the Tamper switch settings in the *Internal Device Access* menu of the *Security* section.

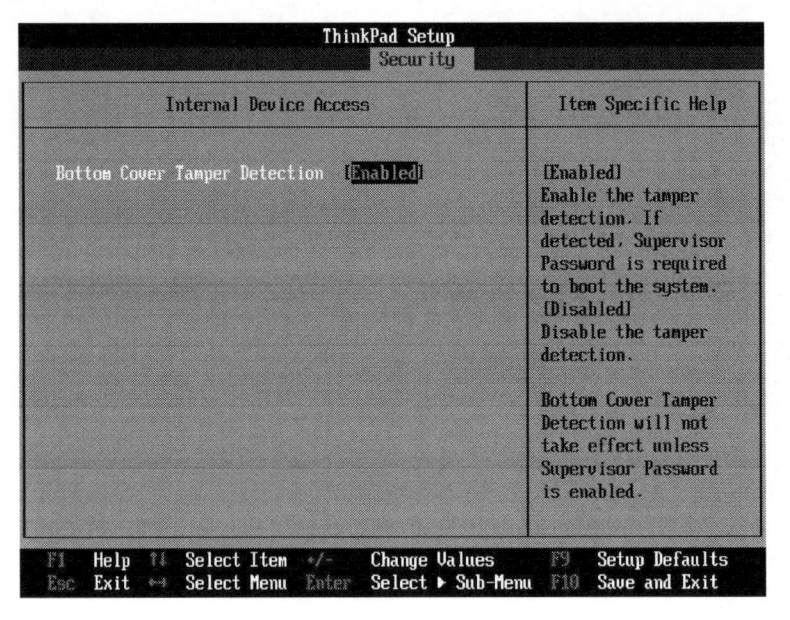

```
                      ThinkPad Setup
                         Security

       Internal Device Access              Item Specific Help

  Bottom Cover Tamper Detection [Enabled]  [Enabled]
                                           Enable the tamper
                                           detection. If
                                           detected, Supervisor
                                           Password is required
                                           to boot the system.
                                           [Disabled]
                                           Disable the tamper
                                           detection.

                                           Bottom Cover Tamper
                                           Detection will not
                                           take effect unless
                                           Supervisor Password
                                           is enabled.

  F1   Help   ↑↓  Select Item   +/-    Change Values    F9   Setup Defaults
  Esc  Exit   ←→  Select Menu   Enter  Select ▶ Sub-Menu F10  Save and Exit
```

16. Vulnerability: Storage Device Encryption

- **UEFI/BIOS Flashing.** Another feature in the *Security* section is the option to disable UEFI/BIOS flashing for anyone who doesn't know the computer's *Supervisor Password*. This can prevent unintended firmware flashing of the device.

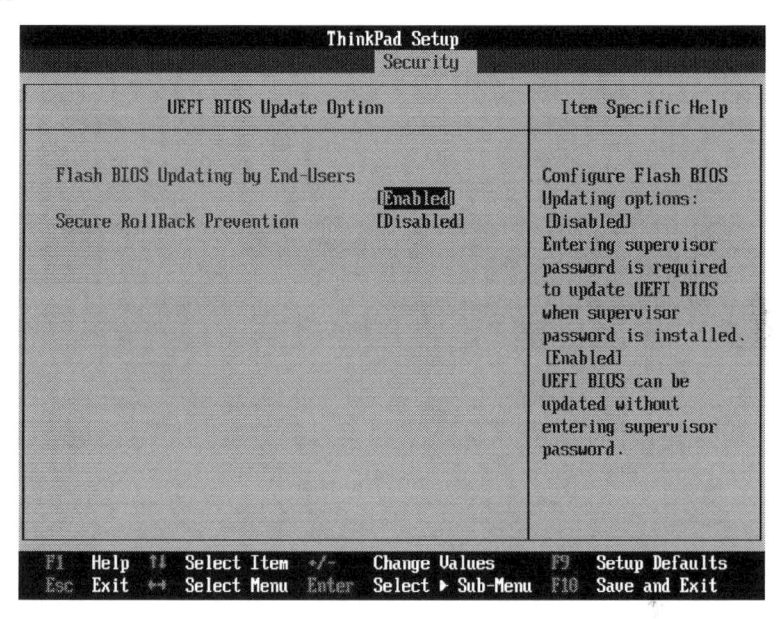

```
                         ThinkPad Setup
                            Security

         UEFI BIOS Update Option              Item Specific Help

   Flash BIOS Updating by End-Users           Configure Flash BIOS
                             [Enabled]        Updating options:
   Secure RollBack Prevention  [Disabled]     [Disabled]
                                              Entering supervisor
                                              password is required
                                              to update UEFI BIOS
                                              when supervisor
                                              password is installed.
                                              [Enabled]
                                              UEFI BIOS can be
                                              updated without
                                              entering supervisor
                                              password.


   F1   Help    ↑↓  Select Item  +/-   Change Values    F9   Setup Defaults
   Esc  Exit    ←→  Select Menu  Enter Select ▶ Sub-Menu F10  Save and Exit
```

16. Vulnerability: Storage Device Encryption

- **Fingerprint Reader.** There are a few options of interest for configuring and managing Fingerprint data. Enabling *Predesktop Authentication* allows the fingerprint reader to authenticate into Windows. The *Security Mode* setting allows the option to force the Supervisor Password to boot a system if no fingerprint is detected. Finally, the option to erase existing stored fingerprints can be found with the *Reset Fingerprint Data* option.

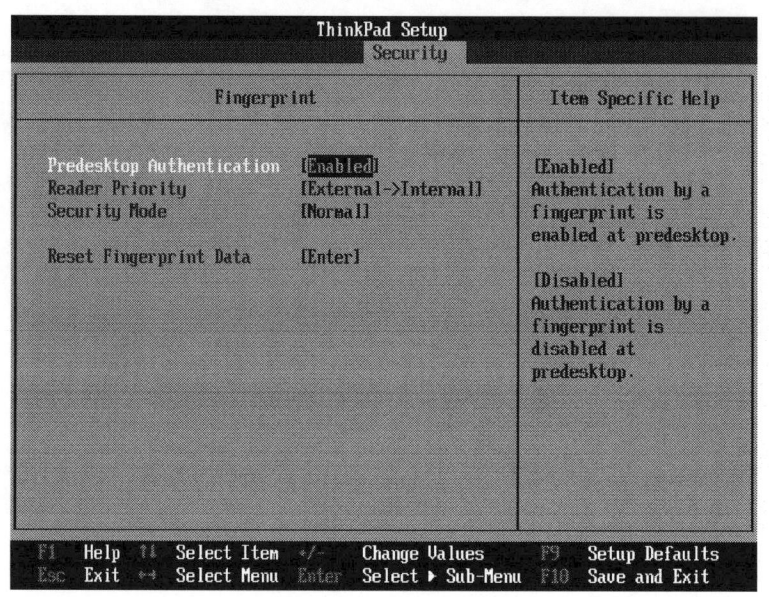

```
                        ThinkPad Setup
                           Security

              Fingerprint                    Item Specific Help

   Predesktop Authentication  [Enabled]      [Enabled]
   Reader Priority            [External->Internal]   Authentication by a
   Security Mode              [Normal]                fingerprint is
                                                      enabled at predesktop.
   Reset Fingerprint Data     [Enter]
                                                     [Disabled]
                                                     Authentication by a
                                                     fingerprint is
                                                     disabled at
                                                     predesktop.




   F1   Help   ↑↓  Select Item   +/-    Change Values    F9   Setup Defaults
   Esc  Exit   ←→  Select Menu   Enter  Select ► Sub-Menu F10  Save and Exit
```

16. Vulnerability: Storage Device Encryption

- **Memory Protection.** Security section option is to enable the *Memory Protection* setting to prevent against buffer overflows in poorly written software.

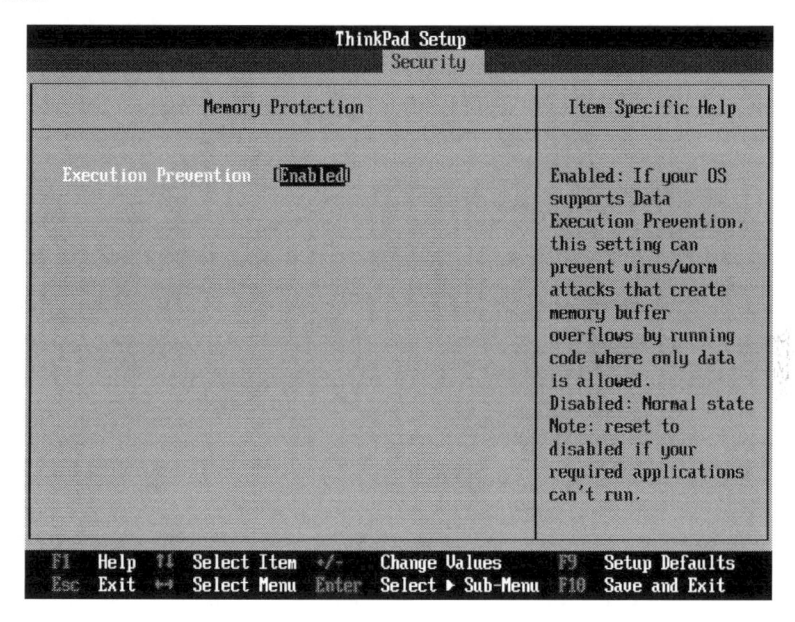

```
                    ThinkPad Setup
                       Security

          Memory Protection          |  Item Specific Help

   Execution Prevention  [Enabled]      Enabled: If your OS
                                        supports Data
                                        Execution Prevention,
                                        this setting can
                                        prevent virus/worm
                                        attacks that create
                                        memory buffer
                                        overflows by running
                                        code where only data
                                        is allowed.
                                        Disabled: Normal state
                                        Note: reset to
                                        disabled if your
                                        required applications
                                        can't run.

   F1   Help    ↑↓  Select Item  +/-   Change Values   F9   Setup Defaults
   Esc  Exit    ↔   Select Menu  Enter Select ▶ Sub-Menu F10  Save and Exit
```

16. Vulnerability: Storage Device Encryption

- **Secure Boot.** Secure Boot is a security feature that should be enabled before installing a fresh copy of Windows (if not currently enabled). Secure Boot creates a trusted environment that prevents malicious software such as rootkits from running. Note that most all computers that have shipped with Windows 8, 8.1, and Windows 10 will have this feature enabled by default. Secure Boot should be disabled if using an older operating system or a version of Linux that does not ship with Microsoft signed keys.

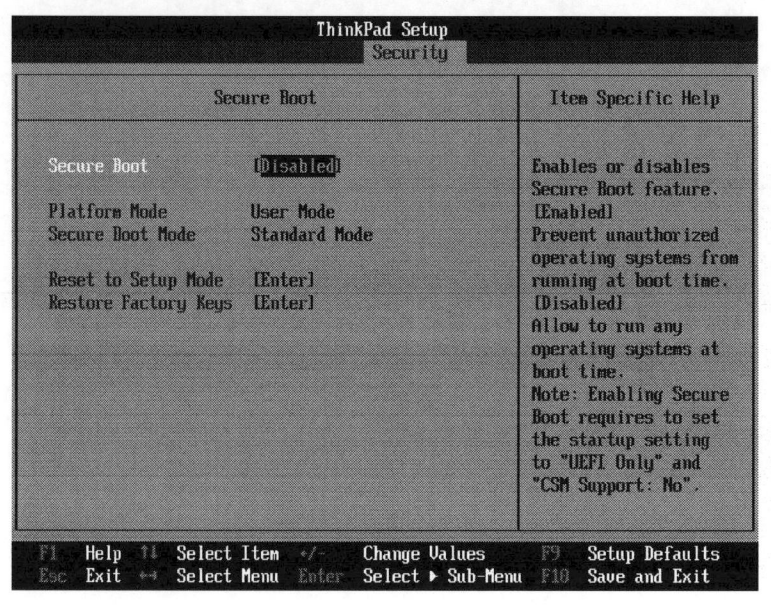

```
                     ThinkPad Setup
                        Security

              Secure Boot                    Item Specific Help

   Secure Boot          [Disabled]      Enables or disables
                                        Secure Boot feature.
   Platform Mode        User Mode       [Enabled]
   Secure Boot Mode     Standard Mode   Prevent unauthorized
                                        operating systems from
   Reset to Setup Mode  [Enter]         running at boot time.
   Restore Factory Keys [Enter]         [Disabled]
                                        Allow to run any
                                        operating systems at
                                        boot time.
                                        Note: Enabling Secure
                                        Boot requires to set
                                        the startup setting
                                        to "UEFI Only" and
                                        "CSM Support: No".

   F1   Help    ↑↓  Select Item  +/-    Change Values    F9   Setup Defaults
   Esc  Exit    ←→  Select Menu  Enter  Select ▶ Sub-Menu F10  Save and Exit
```

16. Vulnerability: Storage Device Encryption

- **Intel AntiTheft**. *Intel AntiTheft* is a now defunct service that Intel once provided with similar functionality to LoJack. It should be in kept in *Disabled* state.

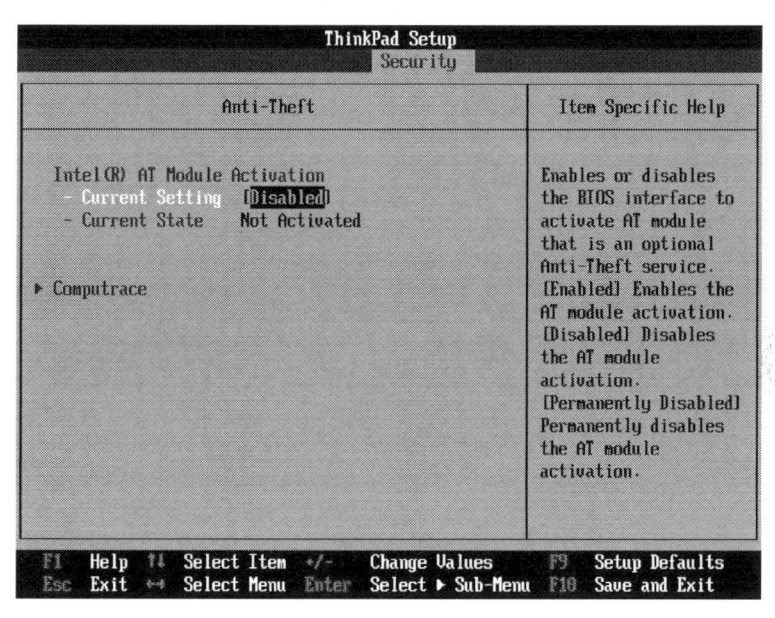

```
                    ThinkPad Setup
                         Security
┌─────────────────────────────────────┬──────────────────────┐
│            Anti-Theft               │   Item Specific Help │
├─────────────────────────────────────┼──────────────────────┤
│                                     │                      │
│ Intel(R) AT Module Activation       │ Enables or disables  │
│  - Current Setting  [Disabled]      │ the BIOS interface to│
│  - Current State    Not Activated   │ activate AT module   │
│                                     │ that is an optional  │
│                                     │ Anti-Theft service.  │
│ ▶ Computrace                        │ [Enabled] Enables the│
│                                     │ AT module activation.│
│                                     │ [Disabled] Disables  │
│                                     │ the AT module        │
│                                     │ activation.          │
│                                     │ [Permanently Disabled]│
│                                     │ Permanently disables │
│                                     │ the AT module        │
│                                     │ activation.          │
│                                     │                      │
├─────────────────────────────────────┴──────────────────────┤
│ F1  Help   ↑↓ Select Item  +/-   Change Values  F9  Setup Defaults │
│ Esc Exit   ←→ Select Menu  Enter Select ▶ Sub-Menu F10 Save and Exit│
└────────────────────────────────────────────────────────────┘
```

16. Vulnerability: Storage Device Encryption

- **Security Chip Management**
    - In a previous section you likely set the security chip status to *Active* for either the discrete (onboard) TPM chip, or the Intel PTT (integrated) chip. Along with enabling their functionality to be used by Window's BitLocker, or other security products, it is possible to enable logging of events as well as set options for physical presence in clearing or provisioning the chips.
    - In the *Security Reporting Options* menu, four different options can be enabled for logging TPM events (normally an advanced user feature).
    - Further down, the option to *Clear Security Chip* should be performed when the laptop is ready to be passed on for sale. This will remove any existing keys from the TPM.
    - The *Intel TXT Feature* is a technology that defends against software attacks that would otherwise compromise a trusted environment. In most cases, it should be *Enabled*.
    - *Physical Presence for Provisioning and Clearing* are both features that require a person to be present to confirm provisioning or clearing of the TPM security chip. This prevents a would-be attacker or malware from remotely running an exploit to either enroll or clear existing TPM keys. This option can safely be set to *Enabled* for both.

16. Vulnerability: Storage Device Encryption

```
                    ThinkPad Setup
                         Security

          Security Chip                    Item Specific Help

 Security Chip Selection        [Discrete T]   [Discrete TPM]
 Security Chip                  [Active]       Use a discrete TPM
                                               chip with TPM 1.2
 ▶ Security Reporting Options                  mode.

 Intel (R) TXT Feature          [Enabled]      [Intel PTT]
                                               Use Intel(R) Platform
 Physical Presence for Provisioning [Disabled] Trusted Technology
 Physical Presence for Clear    [Enabled]      with TPM 2.0 mode.

                                               Note: Intel(R) PTT can
                                               be used with
                                               Microsoft (R)
                                               Windows 8 (R) or later
                                               operating system.

 F1   Help   ↑↓  Select Item  +/-   Change Values   F9   Setup Defaults
 Esc  Exit   ↔   Select Menu  Enter Select ▶ Sub-Menu F10 Save and Exit
```

Review Questions

1. The Unified Extensible Firmware Interface (UEFI) is a replacement for the Basic Input Output System (BIOS) in most 2011+ computers. (True or False)

2. Once way to secure a Self Encrypting Disk (SED) is to set the _____ password in the UEFI to at least 14 characters.

3. Biometrics such as Fingerprint readers are considered secure and should be enabled by default. (True or False)

4. TPM or Trusted Platform Module is used to create secure UEFI passwords. (True or False)

5. It is good security practice to disable unused Input/Output ports in the BIOS or UEFI

6. Boot loader protection known as _____ is used as a security mechanism on Windows 8 and newer operating systems and can be enabled or disabled in the UEFI.

17. Vulnerability: Instant Messaging

The ignorance of one voter in a democracy impairs the security of all.
–John F. Kennedy

Instant Messaging

In 2009 the CTIA reported that on average, U.S. cellphone subscribers send an average of 534 text messages a month. AT&T reported in 2012 that their subscribers under 25 years old averaged 5 times this number.

And if the raw number of texts isn't mind-numbing enough, the topics of discussion most certainly are. With almost nobody giving any thought to the facts that:

- The cellular provider likely archives your text messages for years.
- The government has full access to all of your messages and also archives them.
- The encryption scheme used by cellular providers was broken years ago, and any kid can listen in on your messaging.
- If you are in business, it is possible the competition listens in on your messaging.
- If you are involved with healthcare and text *any* patient information–even to the patient–you are probably in violation of HIPAA compliance and may be subject up to a $50,000 fine.

Unless you are texting innocuous comments, such as: "I love you" (assuming this is a relationship in the open), "remember to bring home milk", or "I'll be home by 6pm", your texting should be secure by way of encryption.

The texting app that is included with Windows 10–*Skype*–does use encryption for voice, video, file transfer, and instant message security. However, the keys to this encryption are held at the same Microsoft servers through which all Skype communication travels. There is strong evidence that Microsoft routinely sniffs through Skype traffic. Microsoft has also demonstrated they sniff through email, and have on at least one occasion, reported their findings to police.

There are only a few cross-platform texting applications that meet military and HIPAA requirements for security and encryption. One of our favorites is *Wickr*. That it works, allows for the sender to set a time of auto-destruct, and is free helps to put it at the top of the list.

18. Vulnerability: Voice and Video Communications

If there is a downside to Wickr, it is that you can only communicate securely with others who are also using Wickr. But this is the nature of the security beast.

Assignment: Install and Configure Wickr

In this assignment we will install and configure Wickr in order to create secure, encrypted text communications.

1. Open a browser, go to *http://wickr.com*, and then click on the *DOWNLOAD* link.

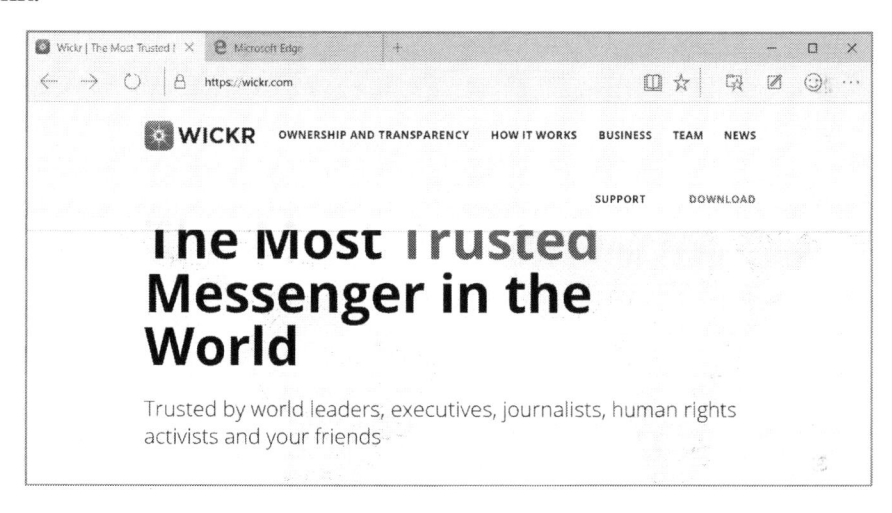

18. Vulnerability: Voice and Video Communications

2. In the *Downloads* page, scroll down to the *Desktop* applications, and then click on the Windows *DOWNLOAD* button.

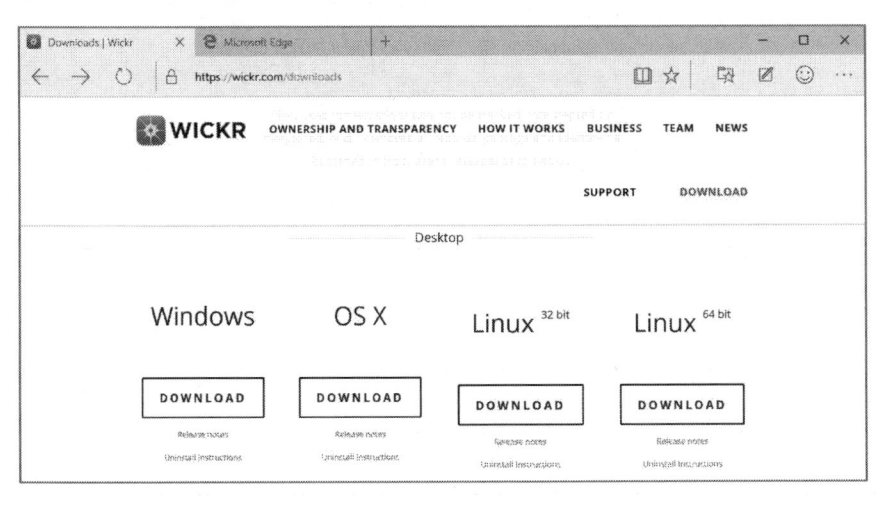

3. The download status window will appear.

4. When the download completes, click the *Run* button to install.

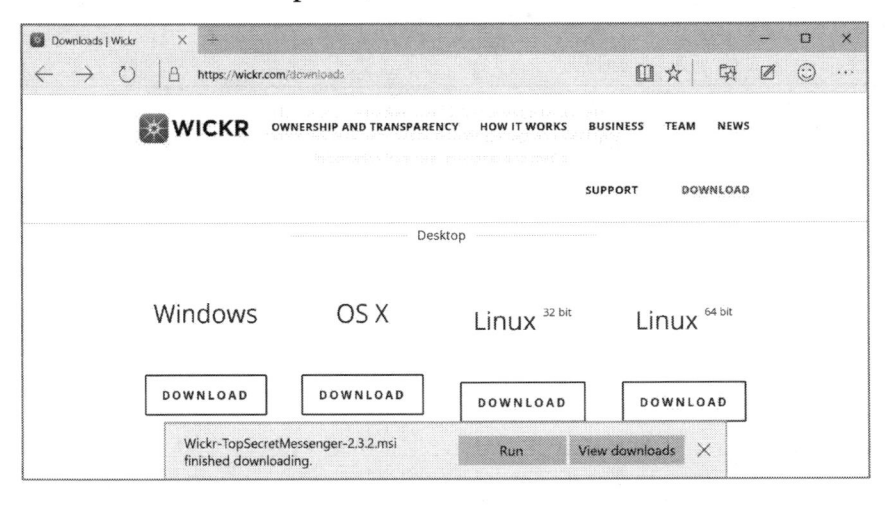

18. Vulnerability: Voice and Video Communications

5. At the *Welcome to the Wickr* window, click *Next*.

6. At the *Select Installation Folder* window, click *Next*.

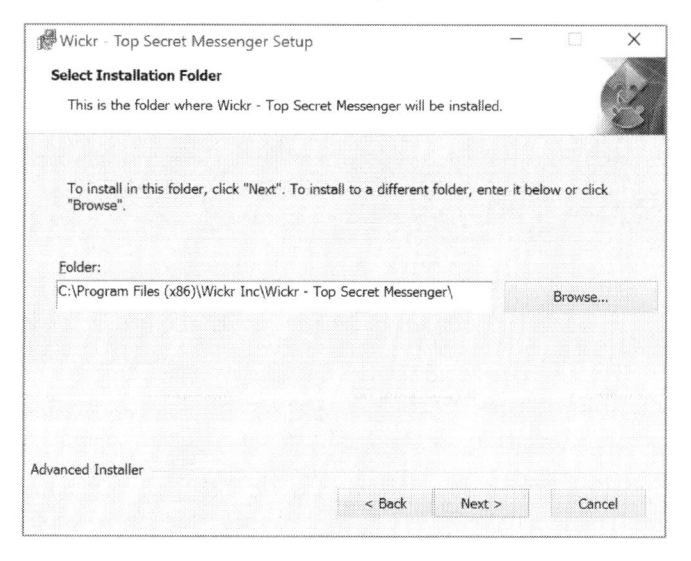

18. Vulnerability: Voice and Video Communications

7. At the *Ready to Install* window, click the *Install* button.

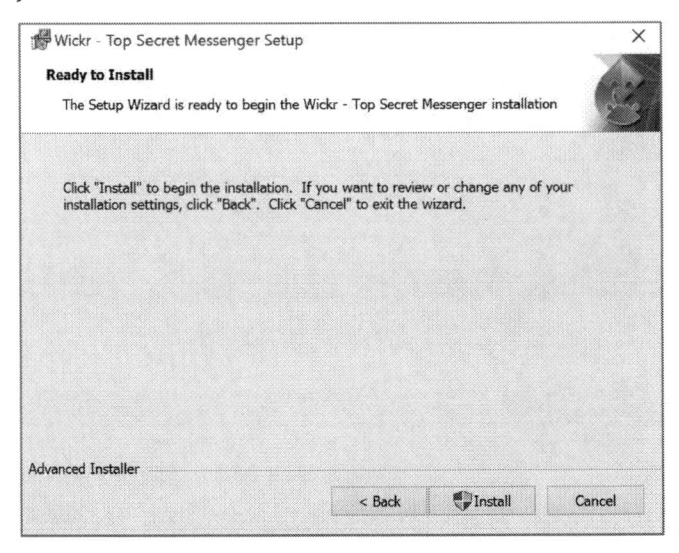

8. At the *Do you want to allow this app to install software on your PC* window, click *Yes* to install.

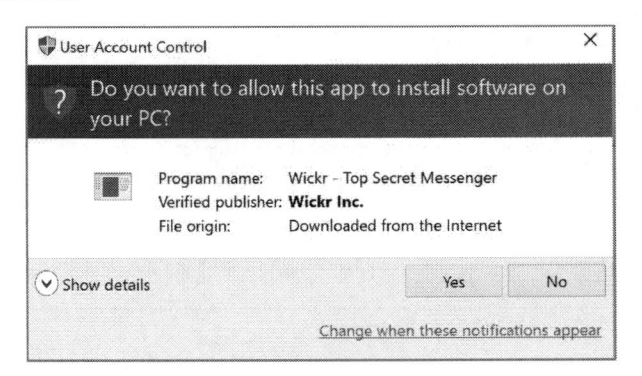

18. Vulnerability: Voice and Video Communications

9. At the *Completing the Wickr* window, enable the *Launch Wickr* checkbox, and then click the *Finish* button.

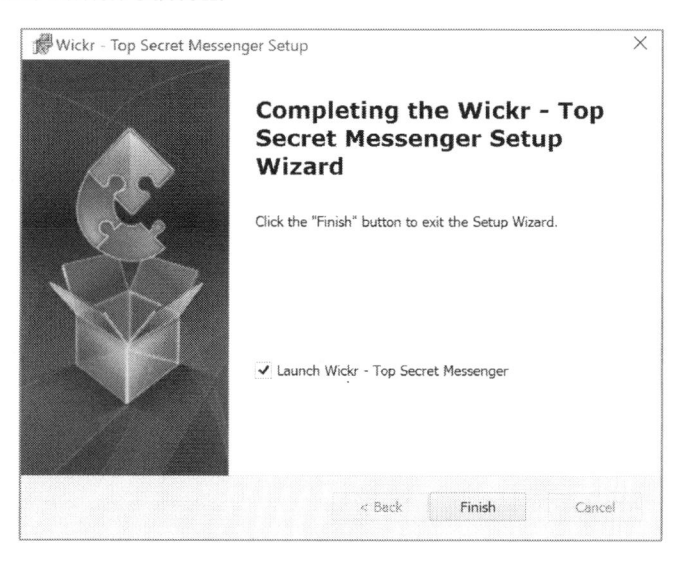

10. The Wickr start window appears. As this is your first time with Wickr, click the *Sign Up* button to create an account.

18. Vulnerability: Voice and Video Communications

11. At the *New Wickr Account* window, complete all fields.

- *Desired Wickr ID*: This would typically be your full name, although you may use any identifier.

- *Password*: Create and enter a strong password

    - **NOTE**: There are no password resets with Wickr. If you forget your password, it is necessary to create a new account.

18. Vulnerability: Voice and Video Communications

12. The Wickr login window opens. Enter your password, and then click the *Login* button.

    - NOTE: Assuming you have followed all the previous guidelines for securing the computer, you may want to enable the *Save* slider, so that you will not need to enter a password every time Wickr is opened.

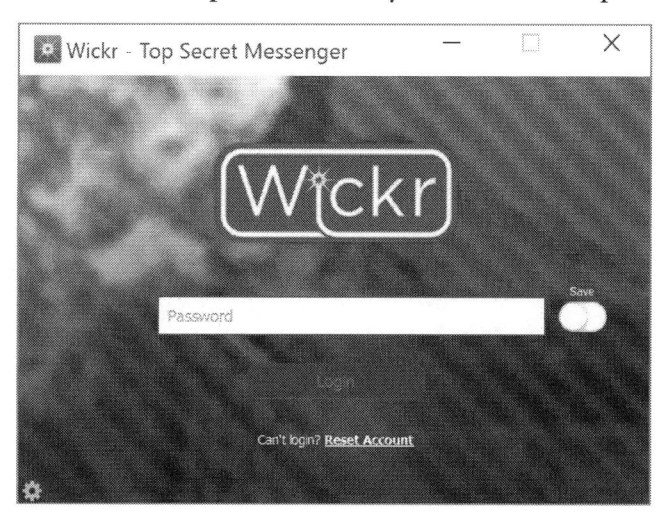

13. In the *Friend Finder* window, you have the option to invite contacts from your Google and Yahoo accounts. If using either Google or Yahoo contacts, turn their switches to *On* to include those contacts in your Wickr friends list.

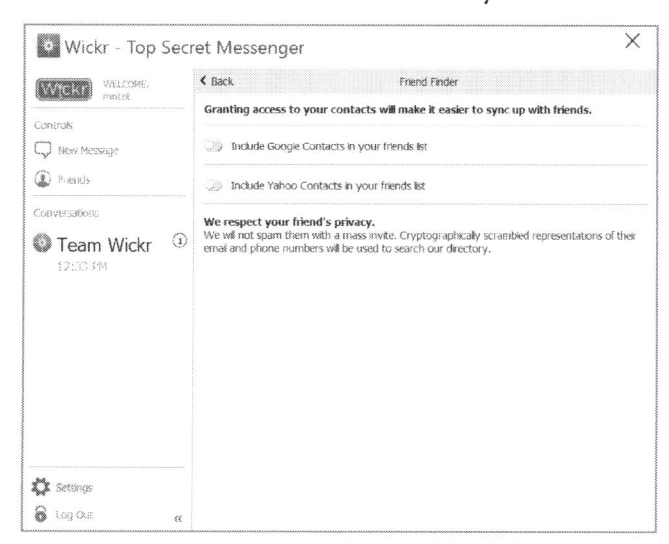

18. Vulnerability: Voice and Video Communications

14. Click the *Settings* button at the bottom left corner. The *Settings* window opens.
15. Click *ID Connections*.

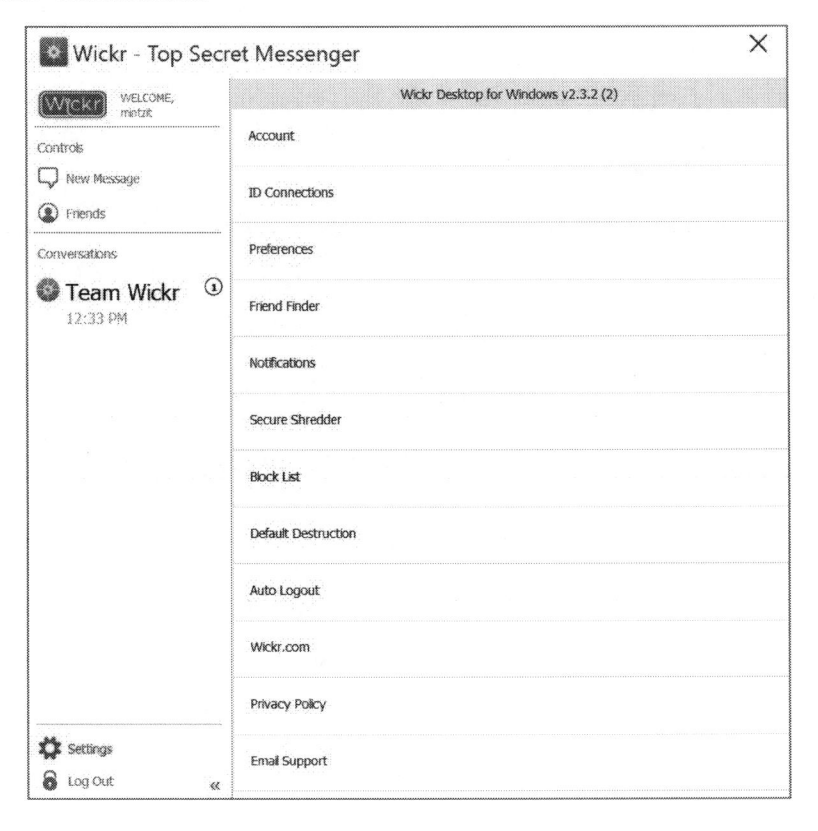

18. Vulnerability: Voice and Video Communications

16. In the *ID Connections* window, enter your *Email* and mobile *Phone* information, which will make it easier for those searching for you on Wicker to find you. When done, click the *Back* button, returning to the *Settings* window.

18. Vulnerability: Voice and Video Communications

17. In the *Settings* window, click *Preferences*. The *Preferences* window opens. Configure to taste. These are my preferences. When done, click *Back* to return to the *Settings* window.

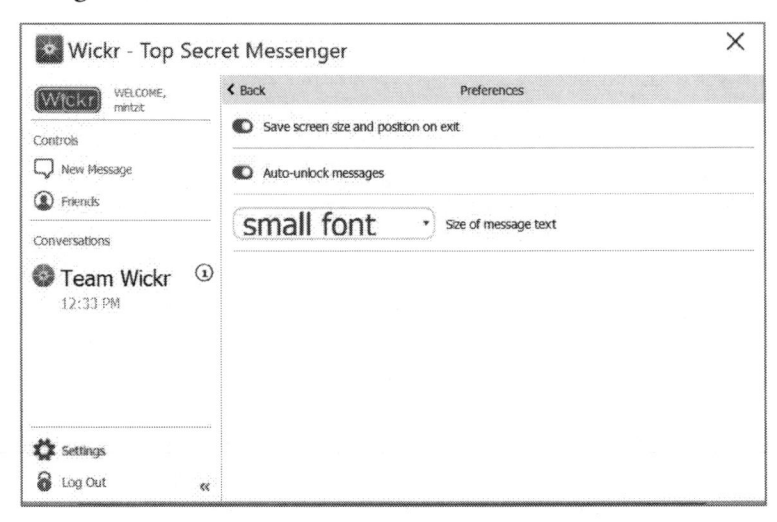

18. In the *Settings* window, click *Notifications*. In the *Notifications* window, configure to taste. These are my settings. When done, click *Back* to return to the *Settings* window.

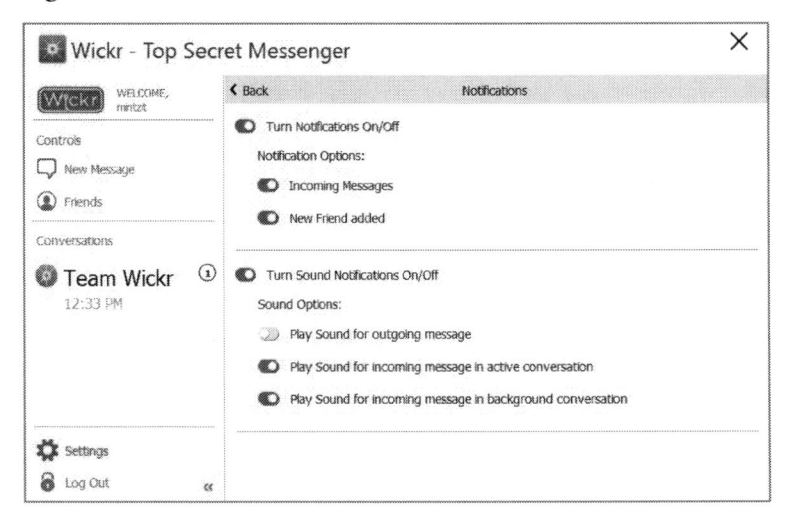

18. Vulnerability: Voice and Video Communications

19. In the *Settings* window, click *Secure Shredder*. This feature performs multiple wipes of any messages you have deleted so they cannot be recovered. Enable the *Turn Background Mode On*. The *Low* to *High* setting determines the CPU priority given to the shredding process. You have the option to perform a shredding anytime you wish by clicking the *Start* button. When done, click *Back* to return to the *Settings* window.

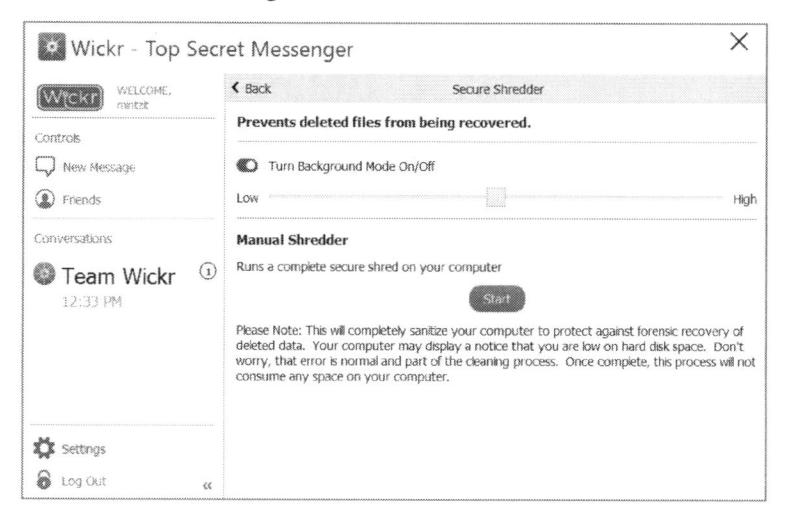

20. In the *Settings* window, select *Default Destruction*. In this window you specify how long a sent message lives until it is auto deleted on the recipient's device. Configure to taste. When done, click *Back* to return to the *Settings* window.

18. Vulnerability: Voice and Video Communications

Wickr is now ready to send and receive text messages.

Assignment: Send a Secure Text Message with Wickr

Once Wickr is configured, it's time to take it out for a test drive. You will need to have at least one friend with a Wickr account to exchange instant messages.

1. Launch Wickr on your device, and then log in.
2. From the sidebar, click *New Message*. The *New Message* window appears.

3. In the *New Message* screen > *To* field, enter the *Wickr ID, email, phone number*, or name of a friend with a Wickr account, and then press the *Return* key.

18. Vulnerability: Voice and Video Communications

4. If the *To* data is found in *Friends* list, the matches will be displayed directly under the *To* field. Select the appropriate match.

   - If the match does not have a Wickr account, an alert will notify you, and the *Create Message* button will remain gray.

   - If the match does have a Wickr account, the *Create Message* button lights up. Click the *Create Message* button.

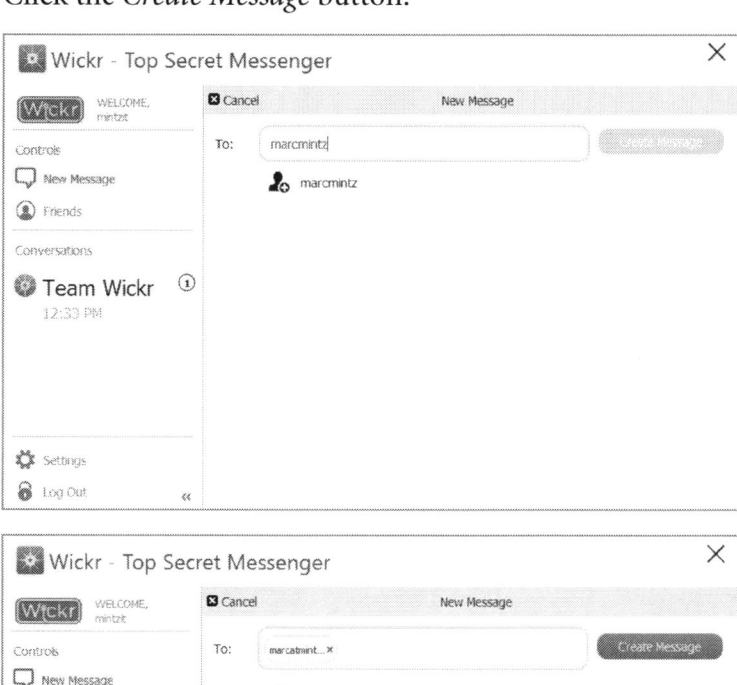

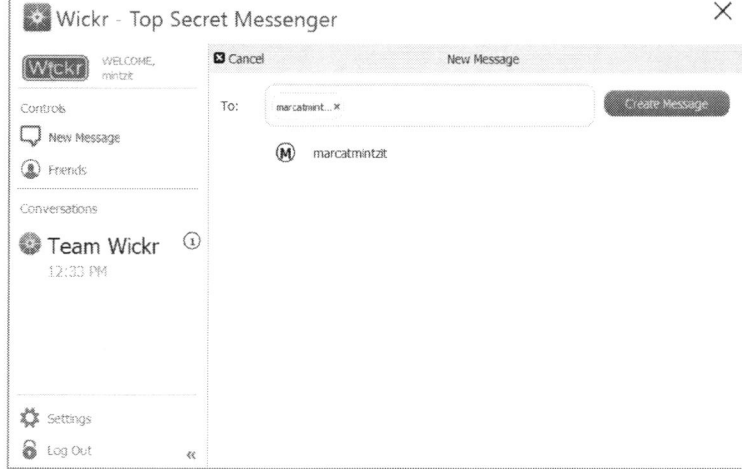

18. Vulnerability: Voice and Video Communications

5. The *Create Message* window opens. Enter your message in the text field at the bottom of the window.

6. The icons immediately above the text field allow you to add a picture, add a voice message, attach a file, and to set the self-destruct time.

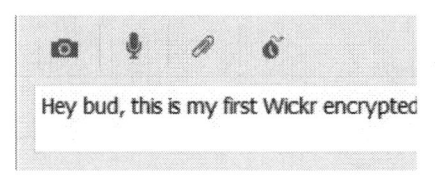

18. Vulnerability: Voice and Video Communications

7. When the message is crafted to taste, press the *Return* key to send. The conversation will display above the text field.

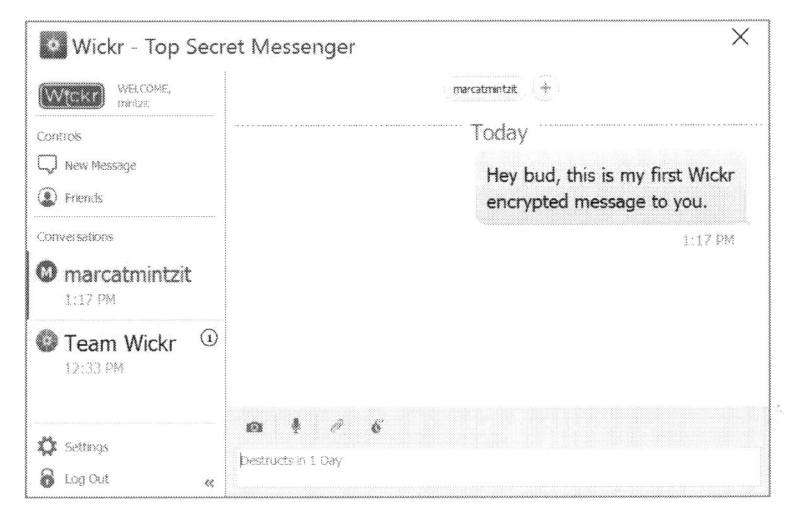

All that is left to do is find a *Man From UNCLE* secret decoder ring.

Review Questions

1. SMS Text Messaging is inherently insecure. (True or False)
2. _____ is an example of a secure messaging application that provides end-to-end encryption and meets government standards such as HIPAA.

18. Vulnerability: Voice and Video Communications

Surveillance technologies now available–including the monitoring of virtually all digital information–have advanced to the point where much of the essential apparatus of a police state is already in place.

- Al Gore

18. Vulnerability: Voice and Video Communications

Voice and Video Communications

Every time you send or receive a text message, phone call, or videoconference on your computer or mobile device, the conversations and metadata are stored by third parties. The carriers (Verizon, AT&T, etc.) for each party have the ability to intercept any traffic that crosses their networks, which may also extend to any third parties that work with your carrier, such as contractors, or subsidiaries.

Aside from the telecom companies themselves, your local and federal government have the ability to monitor in dragnet style snooping.

Online voice & video services such as Facebook messenger and Google Hangouts may be more secure in transit between your computer or device and their servers, but because your conversations are stored on their hardware without end-to-end encryption, there is no guarantee of privacy.

So how can you communicate easily and securely using your computer and mobile device? The common options are:

- *FaceTime*: If you are to videoconference between another iPhone, iPad, or OS X user, you can use the built-in FaceTime app. FaceTime is fully end-to-end encrypted, Apple does not have a back door, so neither does a criminal or government.

    The only downside to FaceTime is that it only works with other Apple devices or computers.

- *Skype*: Skype is Microsoft's premier video conferencing solution that offers voice, video chat and desktop sharing for up to 25 people in a group. Recently setting a record for over 35 million people online simultaneously, Skype is one of Microsoft's core technologies, and is bundled into Windows, XBOX, and Windows mobile.

    It is well known that Skype allows Microsoft and several major governments to listen in on conversations as well as the potential to gain access to files and metadata on the user's computer. As a result, Skype should be treated as a completely insecure service that any number of organizations and governments have access to.

- *Google Hangouts*: In the past several years, other proprietary alternatives to Skype have surfaced, most notably is Google Hangouts. Hangouts tightly integrates Google's social network, Google+, along with Chat, Screen Sharing, and integration with other Google services into a plugin based application. Hangouts is free, and supports up to 10 users simultaneously with any free Google account. Google Business accounts support up to 15 users.

Like Skype, Hangouts has many privacy implications. Google Hangouts doesn't have end-to end encryption, and in a recent online interview with Google's director for law enforcement and information security, it was revealed that Governments, law enforcement and Google itself have access to your chats, and calls.

Secure Alternatives

If you are interested in cross-platform, end-to-end encrypted, voice and video conferencing solutions, there are several alternative services that provide encrypted calls and work with many existing open source clients.

OStel *https://ostel.co* is our choice for end-to-end encrypted voice and video communication. OStel provides encrypted communication to OS X clients using a program called Jitsi. Jitsi is open source communication software that in addition to OStel's SIP protocol, will also handle other popular 3rd party protocols such as Facebook chat, Gchat, XMPP and more.

The only downside to OStel is that it is currently in beta.

Assignment: Sign up for an OStel account

In this assignment we will start the process of creating an OStel account. Getting an OStel account is probably the most painless experience you will ever have. An email address and a password are the only two things you will need to get started.

18. Vulnerability: Voice and Video Communications

1. Open a browser, and then go to *https://ostel.co*. The OStel home page opens. Click the orange *Sign Me Up!* button.

2. In the box provided, type your email address and click *Sign up*.

18. Vulnerability: Voice and Video Communications

3. The confirmation page will display a message at the top telling that your account has been successfully created.

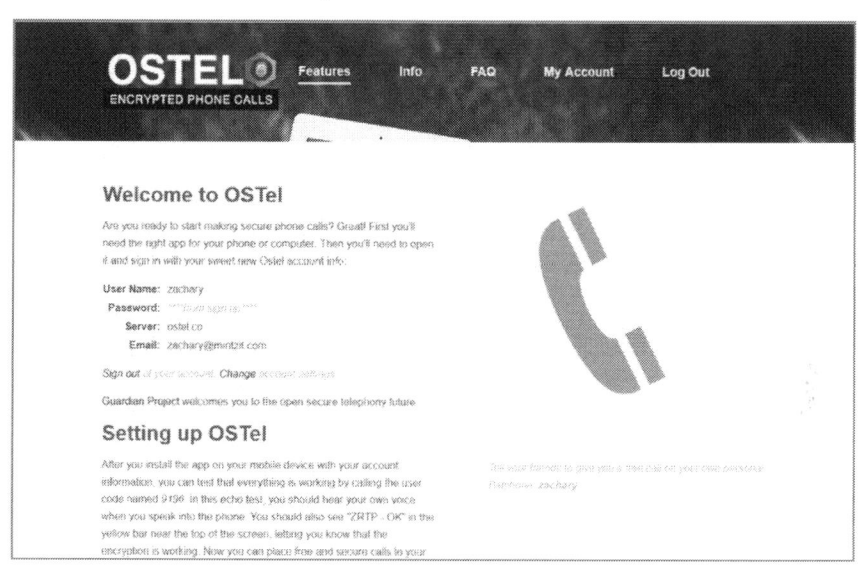

Congratulations. You have successfully created your OStel account, and are now ready to install the software to start making encrypted mobile communications.

Assignment: Install the OStel App–Jitsi

Now that the OStel account set up, we need to download and install the appropriate client app that will allow us to use the OStel network to securely call others.

18. Vulnerability: Voice and Video Communications

1. Scroll down the OStel page you were left on in the previous assignment, to *Download the App* section.

2. Within the section for your target OS and device, click the link to download the appropriate app. In this assignment, this will be the section for *Windows*, with a link for *Jitsi app*.

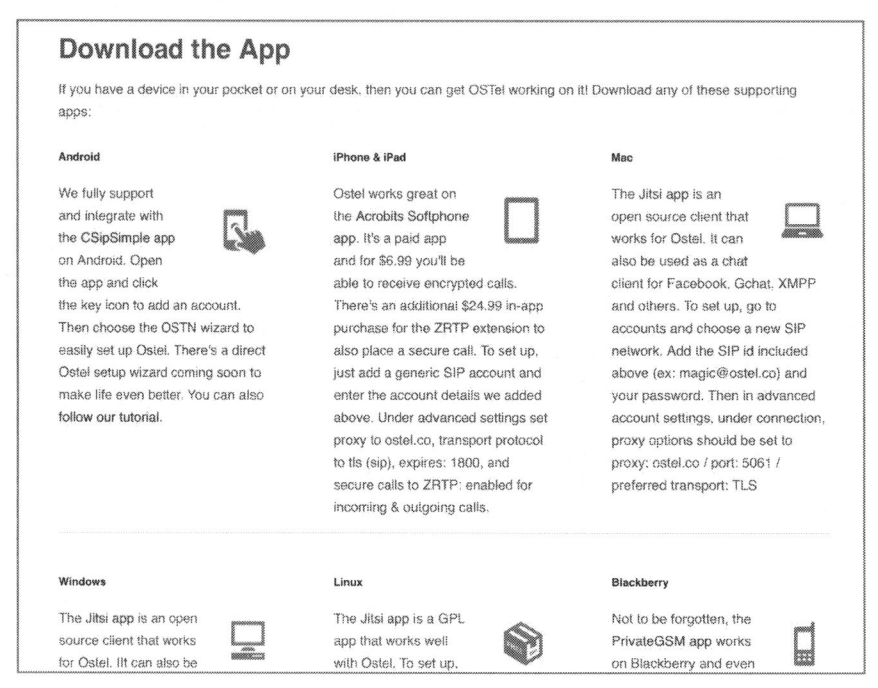

3. At the jitsi.org webpage, click the *Stable Builds* button.

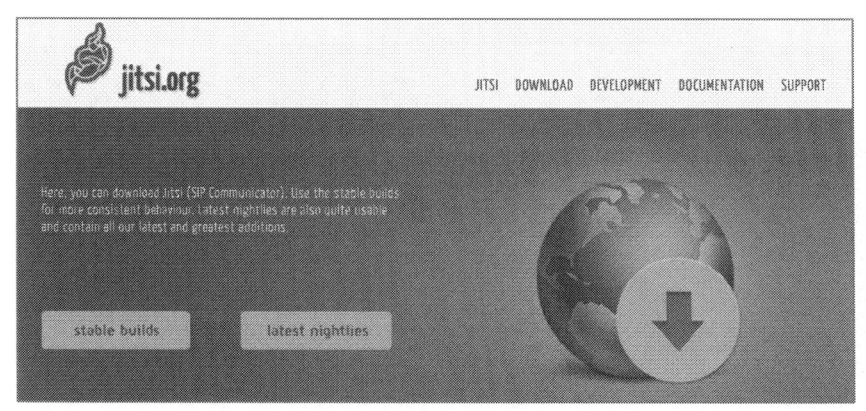

18. Vulnerability: Voice and Video Communications

4. At the *Jitsi Stable Build Line* page, click on the *Microsoft Windows Installers*. The software will begin to download.

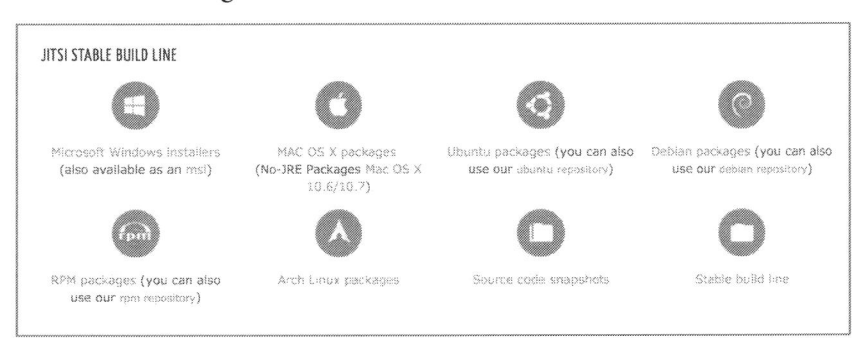

5. After the download completes, run the Jitsi installer, and then click *Next* at the *Setup Wizard Screen*

18. Vulnerability: Voice and Video Communications

6. At the *End-User License Agreement*, accept the license agreement, and then click *Next*.

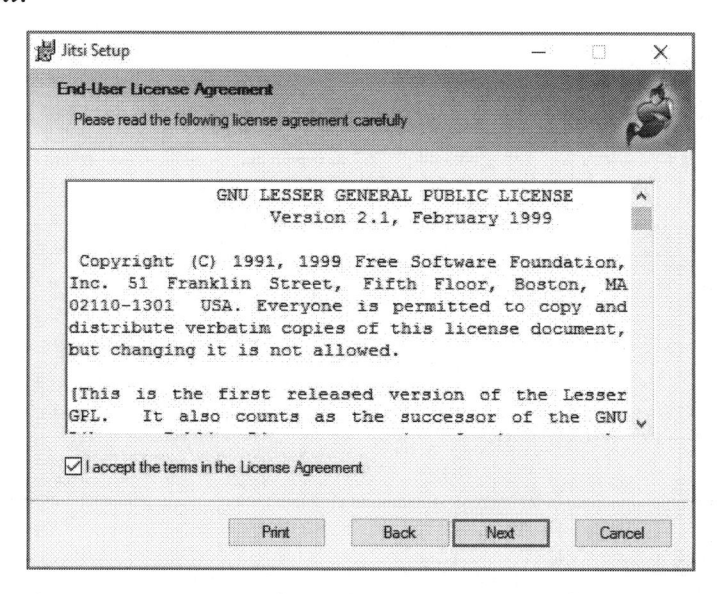

7. In the *Destination Folder* window, leave the default path, and then click Next.

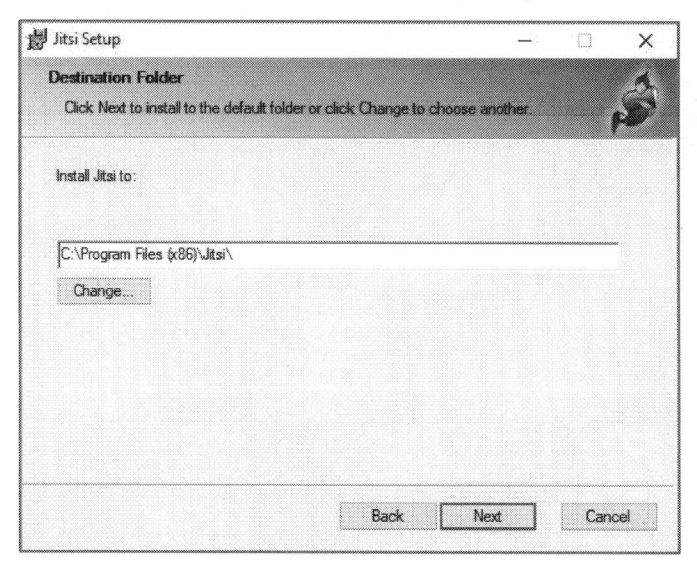

18. Vulnerability: Voice and Video Communications

8. At the *Ready to install Jitsi* window, click *Install*.

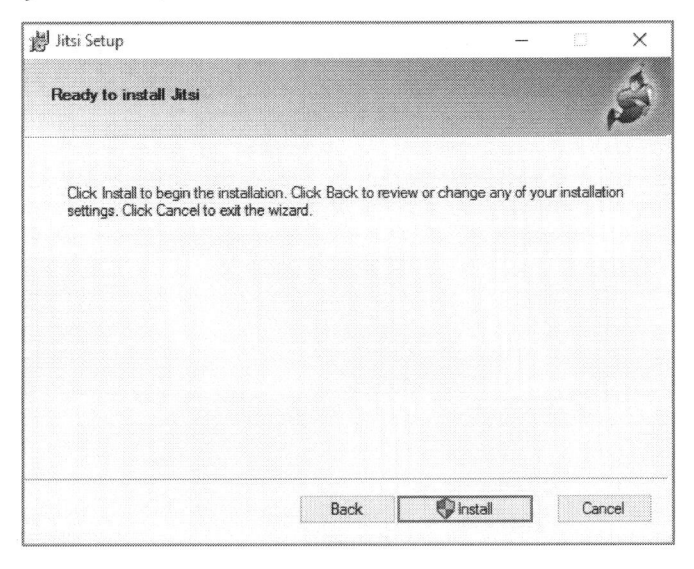

9. When the Jitsi setup completes, click the *Finish* button.

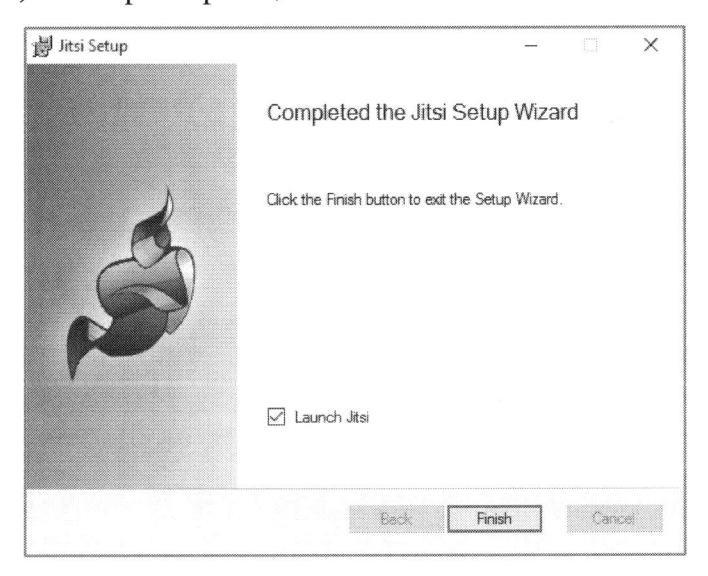

18. Vulnerability: Voice and Video Communications

Assignment: Configure Jetsi

In this assignment, you will configure Jetsi so that you may initiate and receive fully encrypted and secure voice and video communications.

1. Launch the Jitsi client.

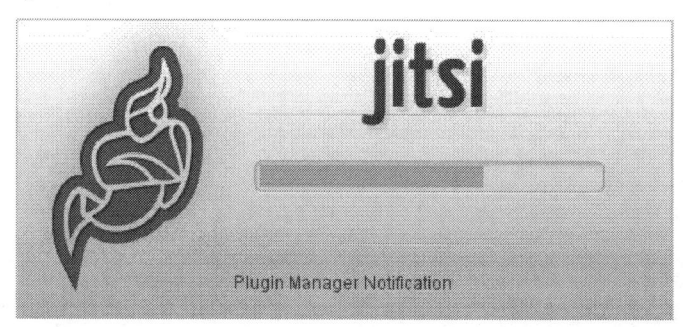

2. The *Accounts* window opens. OStel uses the *SIP* protocol, so add your OStel credentials under the SIP section, and then click *Sign in*.

    - NOTE: Your *SIP Username* and *Password* are the same as you created in the first assignment of this chapter, "*Sign Up For an OStel Account.*"

    - NOTE: The *Username* must have *@ostel.com* as your domain.

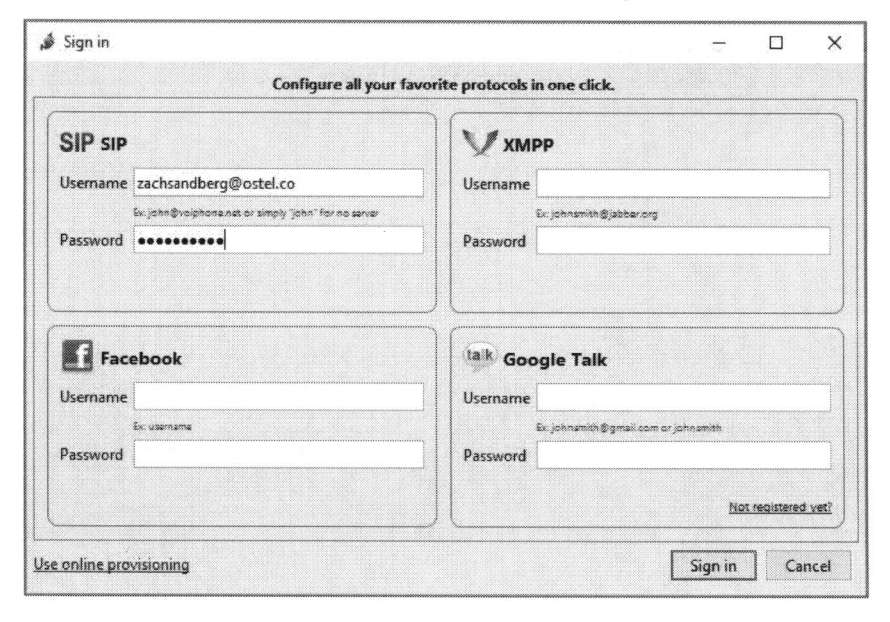

18. Vulnerability: Voice and Video Communications

3. The status in Jitsi will be displayed as *Online*.

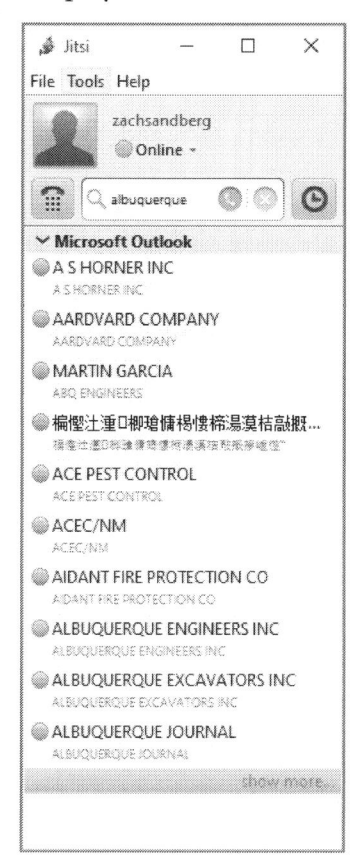

Assignment: Make Your First Encrypted Call

In this assignment, you will make your first secure, encrypted call using OStel and Jitsi.

- Prerequisites: Completion of all previous assignments in this chapter, and a friend who also has an OStel account (or for those of you without friends, another device configured with a different OStel account.)

18. Vulnerability: Voice and Video Communications

1. Look up another member on the OStel network by entering their username in the search box. In the example below, I have located my friend Anthony's username. To initiate a call with Anthony, click the phone icon under his name.

18. Vulnerability: Voice and Video Communications

2. Once the voice call initiates, each participant can share webcam video if desired. Clicking the video icon on the bottom row will start the sharing.

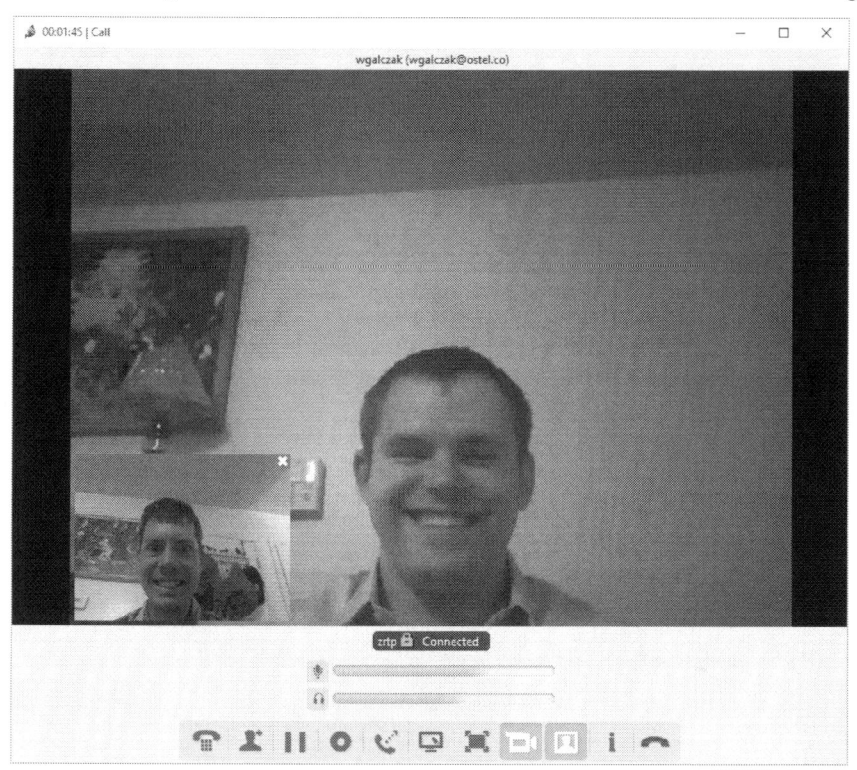

18. Vulnerability: Voice and Video Communications

3. Another feature of Jitsi is desktop sharing. To activate, click the *Desktop* icon in the bottom row. Once initiated, you will be prompted to either allow the other chat member to take control of your computer or to simply view your screen.

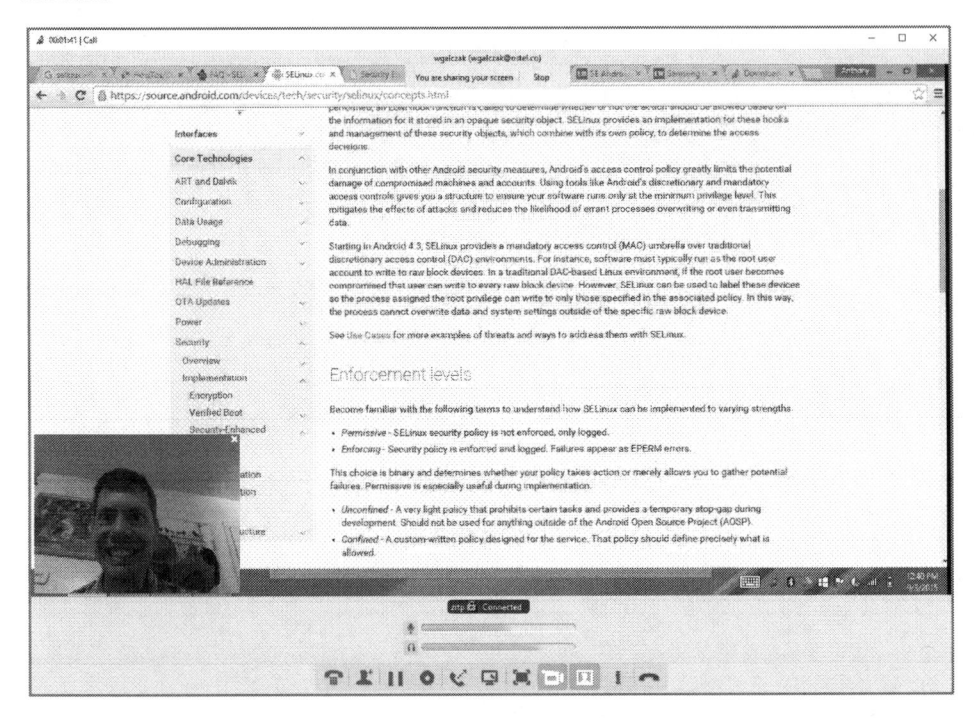

Great work! You are now talking, videoconferencing, and screen sharing in complete privacy and protected from the intrusion of governments, criminals, business competitors, and even Floyd the high school geek.

Review Questions

1. Apple's Facetime is end-to-end encrypted. (True or False)
2. _____ is cross-platform, open source application that works with OStel, an end-to-end encrypted voice, video and chat service.
3. _____ and _____ are examples of popular, non-end-to-end encrypted voice, video and chat services.

19. Vulnerability: Internet Activity

If you go to a coffee shop or at the airport, and you're using open wireless, I would use a VPN service that you could subscribe for 10 bucks a month. Everything is encrypted in an encryption tunnel, so a hacker cannot tamper with your connection.

–Kevin Mitnick, American computer security consultant

19. Vulnerability: Internet Activity

VPN–Virtual Private Network

In case you have been sleep reading through this book, let me repeat my wake-up call: *They are watching you on the Internet. They* may be the automated governmental watchdogs (of your own or another country), government officials (again, of your own or another country), bored staff at an Internet Service Provider or broadband provider, a jealous (and slightly whackadoodle) ex, high school kids driving by your home or office or sitting on a hill several miles away, or criminals.

Regardless, your computer and data are at risk.

Perhaps one of the most important steps that can be taken to protect you is to encrypt the entire Internet experience all the way from your computer, through your broadband provider, to a point where your surfing, chat, webcam, email, etc. cannot be tracked or understood. This is accomplished using a technology called *VPN–Virtual Private Network*.

Gateway VPN

There are two fundamental flavors of VPN *http://en.wikipedia.org/wiki/Virtual_private_network*. The most common is called a *gateway VPN* (mesh VPN is discussed later.) Historically, gateway VPN involved the use of a VPN box resident at an organization. Telecommuting staff is able to use the gateway so the Internet acts like a very long Ethernet cable connecting their computer to the office network. In addition, all data traveling between the user's computer and the gateway is military-grade encrypted. The downside to this strategy is that these boxes are relatively expensive (from $600-several thousand dollars), and they require significant technical experience to configure correctly.

In greater detail, the concept works like this:

1. Your computer has VPN software installed and configured to connect to a VPN server at the office. This server is connected to your office network. OS X comes with VPN software built into the Network System Preferences that works with many of the commercially available VPN servers, including the most popular–Cisco. Other VPN servers require their own proprietary client software to be installed.

2. On your computer you open the VPN software and instruct it to connect to the VPN server. This typically requires entering your authentication credentials of user name and password, along with a long key.

3. The VPN server authenticates you as an allowed account and begins the connection between itself and your computer.

4. As you send data from your computer to the network connected to the VPN server (typically the regular business network), all of it is military-grade encrypted. When the data is received at the VPN server or at your computer, the VPN software decrypts it.

5. Once your data reaches the VPN server, it is then forwarded to the appropriate service on your organizations network (file server, printer, mail server, etc.)

19. Vulnerability: Internet Activity

Although this may sound a bit complex, all a user must do is enter a name, password, and key. Everything else is invisible. The only indicator that anything is different is that speed slower than normal. This is due to the overhead of encryption/decryption process.

We can use this same strategy so that instead of securely exchanging data with our office server, we can securely surf the Internet. The workflow is just slightly different:

1. Your computer has VPN software configured to connect to a VPN server that is not associated with your office, but is just another server "on the Internet."

2. On your computer you open the VPN software and instruct it to connect to the VPN server. If you are using our recommended software, it is pre-configured with all the settings necessary–nothing much more to do but launch.

3. The VPN server authenticates you as an allowed account and begins the connection between itself and your computer.

4. As you surf the web, all data is military-grade encrypted. When the data is received at the VPN server or your computer, the VPN software decrypts it.

5. Once your data reaches the VPN server, it is then forwarded to the appropriate service on the Internet.

Using this strategy (a VPN Internet server), all of your Internet traffic is military-grade encrypted between your computer and the VPN server. It is not possible to decipher any of your traffic (user names, passwords, data) or even the type of data coming and going.

One downside is that once the data exits the VPN server, it is readable. However, your data is intermingled with thousands of other user's data, making the process of tweezing out your data a task that perhaps only the NSA can accomplish.

Another concern is that some VPN providers maintain user activity logs. This is law in most countries, so that government agencies are able to review who is doing what through the VPN. Ideally, you want to work only with VPN providers operating in a country doesn't require logs, and in fact, do not keep logs.

There are thousands of VPN Internet Servers available. Most of them are free. I do not recommend using the free services for two reasons:

19. Vulnerability: Internet Activity

- You get what you pay for (here today/gone tomorrow, unstable, etc.)
- You don't know who is listening at the server side of things. Remember, your data is fully encrypted up to the server. But once the data reaches the server on the way to the Internet, it is readable. There must be a high degree of trust for the administration of the VPN server. I see no reason to place such trust in free services.

When determining the best VPN provider for your use, there are some key variables to look for:

- **Speed**. How fast is your Internet experience? Using VPN introduces a speed penalty due to the encryption/decryption process, as well as the need to process all incoming and outgoing packets through a server instead of point-to-point. VPN providers can reduce this penalty in various ways, including: faster servers, reducing the clients:server ratio, better algorithms, filtering content to remove advertisements and cookies, and faster server internet connections.

- **Logs**. Are logs kept on client activities? In many countries it is required by law that all Internet providers maintain logs of client activities. If so, although the logs may not record what you were doing, they do keep a record of where you traveled. It is ideal to have a VPN provider that keeps no logs whatsoever.

- **Support**. VPN adds a layer of complexity to your Internet activities. Should something not work correctly, you do not want to be the one troubleshooting. Ideally, your VPN provider has 24/7/365 chat support. It is even better if they offer telephone support.

- **Cross-Platform Support**. Most of us have more than one device, perhaps a Windows and OS X computer, an Android phone, and an Apple iPad. It would be madness to have to use a different VPN product for each of these. Look for a provider that supports all your current and potential devices.

- **Multi-Device Support**. Most, but not all, providers now offer concurrent licensing for 3 to 5 devices. This allows your VPN service to be operational on all of your devices at the same time. Providers that offer only single-device licensing may prove quite costly should you have multiple devices.

19. Vulnerability: Internet Activity

- **DNS-Leak Protection**. Although the VPN encrypts all data that comes and goes from your device, before you can reach out to the Internet to connect to your email, a website, or text, your device must connect to a DNS server for guidance on where to find the mail, web, or text server. If you are using your default DNS server (typically one provided by your Internet broadband provider), data between your system and the DNS server is not encrypted and is recorded. It is ideal if your VPN provider offers its own DNS servers. Using this strategy, then the data between your device and the DNS server now is encrypted, or is not logged.

VPNArea

One of our favorite VPN providers is *VPNArea.net*. Although VPNArea.net does not offer a free or trial option, the yearly rate is a reasonable $59. With this you get servers in almost every country you can name, use on 5 devices, unlimited bandwidth, humans on the other end of the tech support call, and highly responsive bandwidth.

The dominant feature of VPNArea is it is registered in Bulgaria, with servers located in Switzerland. Switzerland's national data protection laws are among the strictest in terms of protecting private data, and permitting a VPN provider to not keep logs of client traffic. Other differentiating features include the option to use OpenVPN, L2TP, or PPTP (OpenVPN would be our only choice), 7-day money back guarantee, and their list of over 10,000 DNS servers that do not track or log your activities. This last option is important, because when you are using your ISP, Google, or other common DNS servers, your web travels are logged (called a *DNS Leak*). They also offer the upgrade to your own dedicated VPN server. This provides a significant speed boost, as your server then is not timesharing with dozens or hundreds of other users.

Assignment: Install VPNArea on Windows 10

In this assignment, we will create a paid account (with a 7-day cancellation policy) with *VPNArea.net*, and then configure VPN services.

19. Vulnerability: Internet Activity

1. Open a browser, visit *http://vpnarea.com,* and then select the *Get Started–Prices* button.

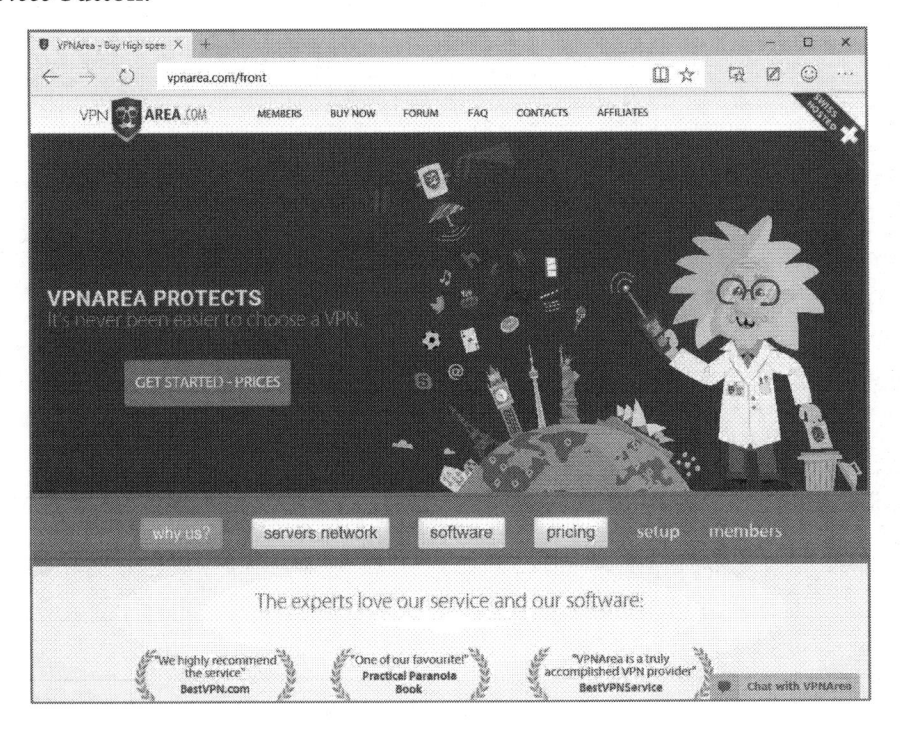

19. Vulnerability: Internet Activity

2. After reviewing the available plans, click the *Buy Now* button for the desired plan.

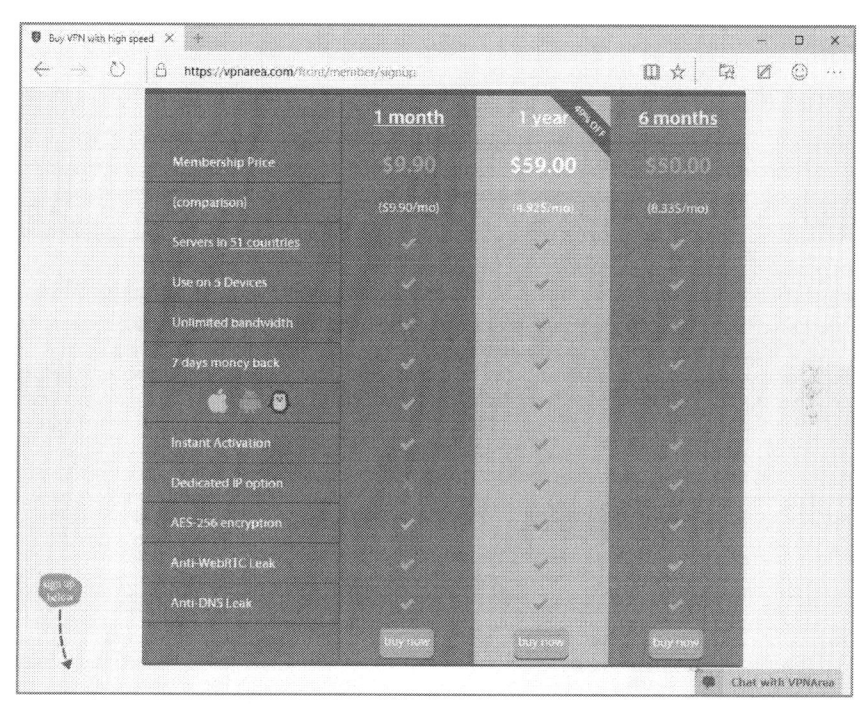

19. Vulnerability: Internet Activity

3. Scroll down the page to the *Sign up in seconds* area. Enter all the requested information, remember to record your *Username* and *password,* and then click the *Buy Now* button.

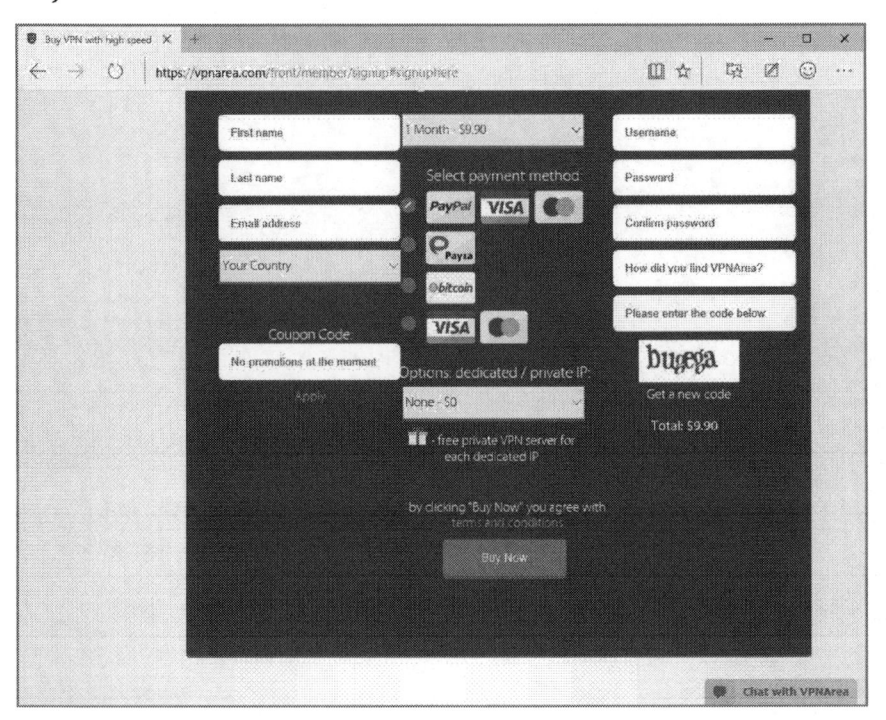

4. After your payment is processed, you are taken to the *Thank You* page. Select the *Go to Members Area* button or *members* button.

19. Vulnerability: Internet Activity

5. In the Members Area page, select the *Windows 8/7/Vista/XP* button.

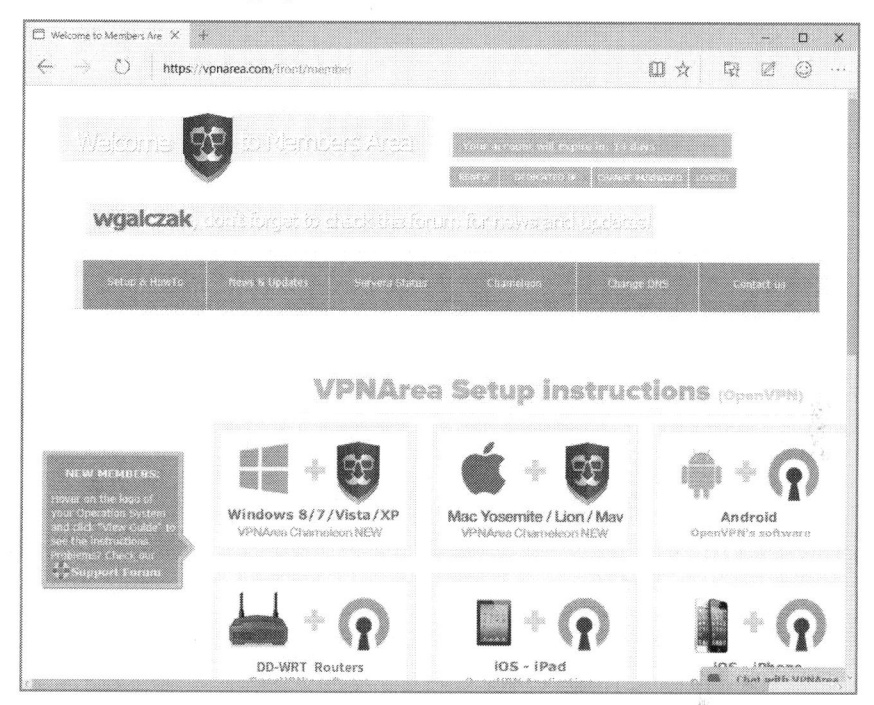

6. In this page will be complete setup instructions. They will be repeated here.

19. Vulnerability: Internet Activity

7. We will download the VPNArea VPN utility *Chameleon*. Select the *Setup File* button to download the file.

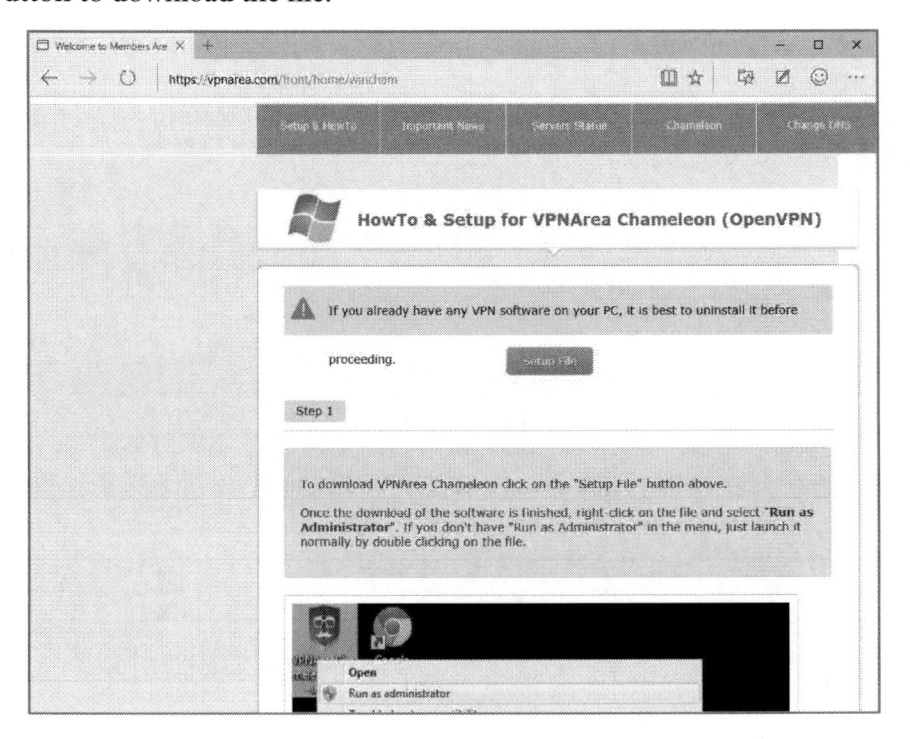

19. Vulnerability: Internet Activity

8. Once the *Chameleon* exe file has downloaded, select *Run* to open and run the installer.

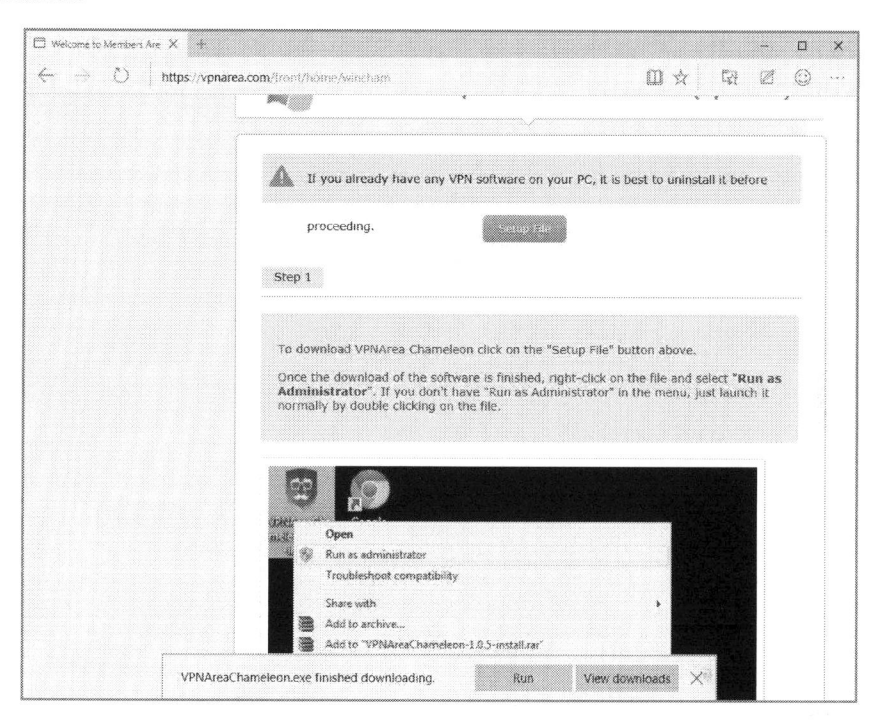

9. Follow the prompts on the installer, and then select *Next* to continue.

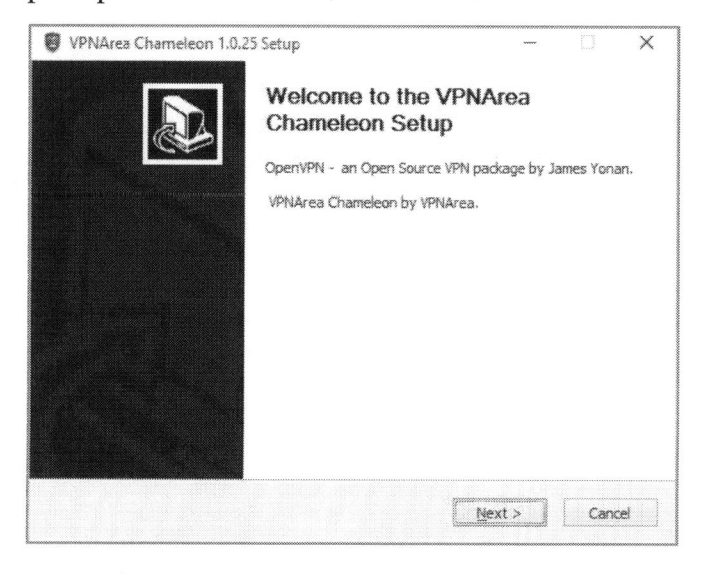

19. Vulnerability: Internet Activity

10. A Windows Security prompt will appear during the installation. Select *Install*. After the installation completes select *Next* and then *Finish*.

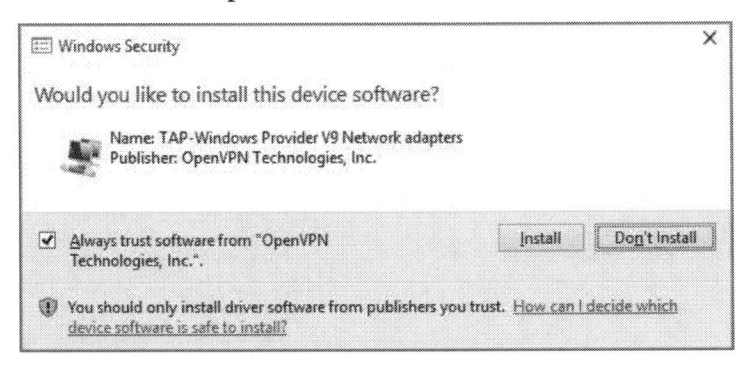

11. *VPNArea Chameleon* will open. Enter your *Username* and *Password* as created when you created your account, from the *Connect with server* pop-up menu, select a server, and then select the *Connect* button.

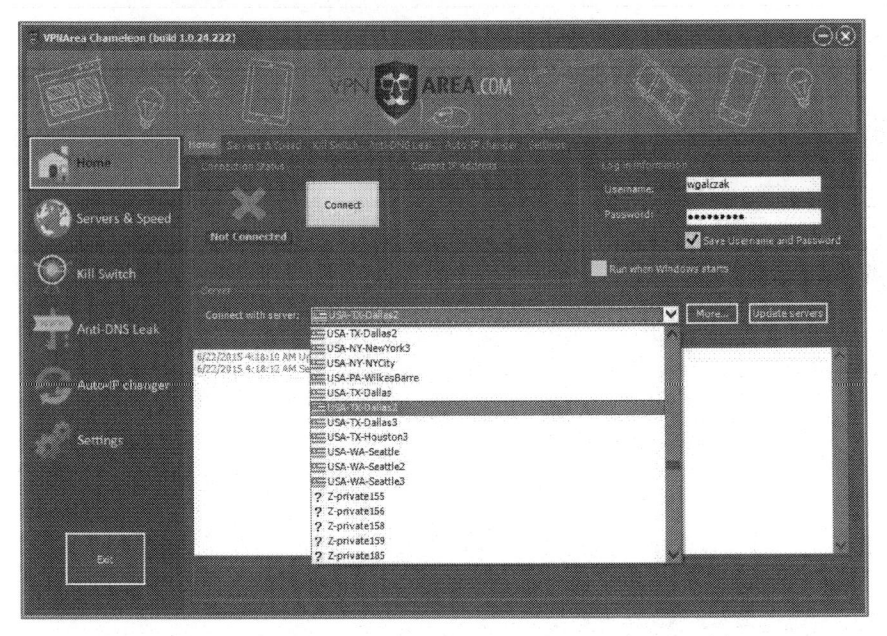

19. Vulnerability: Internet Activity

12. When connected you will see the *Connection Status* change to *Connected*. Also, the *Chameleon* menu item will change to green.

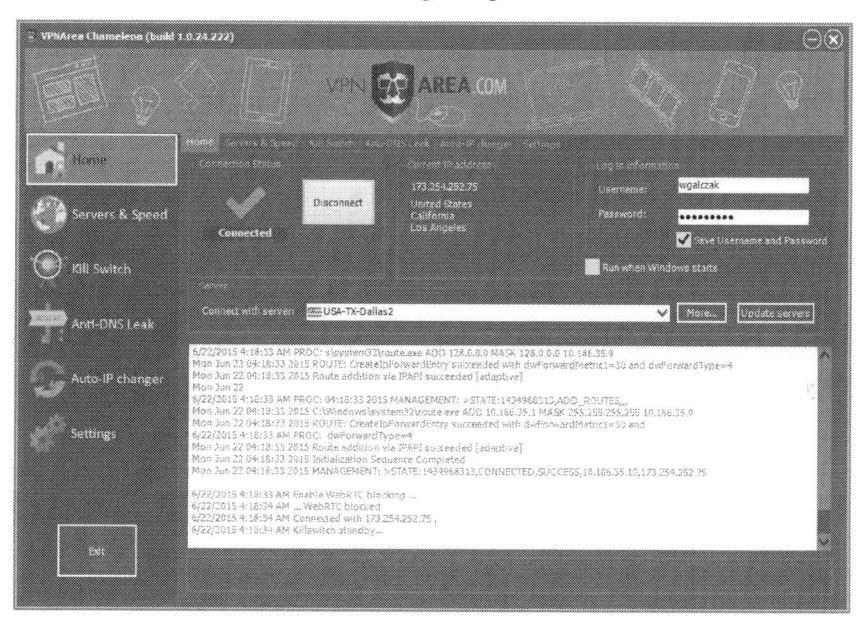

19. Vulnerability: Internet Activity

13. To add extra assurance that you will only ever use VPN when connecting to the Internet, from the *Chameleon* sidebar, select the *Kill Switch* icon, and then enable the *Enabled* checkbox.

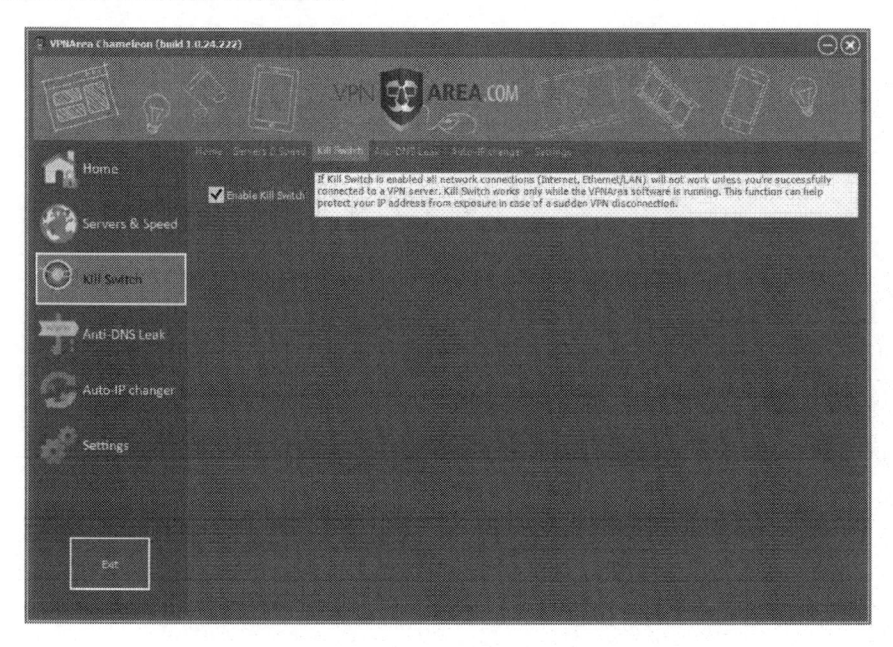

19. Vulnerability: Internet Activity

14. To reduce the possibility that your DNS activity is tracked or recorded (called a *DNS Leak*), you will want to change your DNS Servers when connecting to VPN. With most other VPN providers, this must be done in the *System Preferences > Network > Advanced > DNS* pane. However, VPNArea makes this automatic. To find your desired DNS servers, open a browser and go to *http://vpnarea.com/front/member/dns.* You can get here manually from logging in to *vpnarea.net*, selecting *Members Area,* and then selecting *Change DNS.*

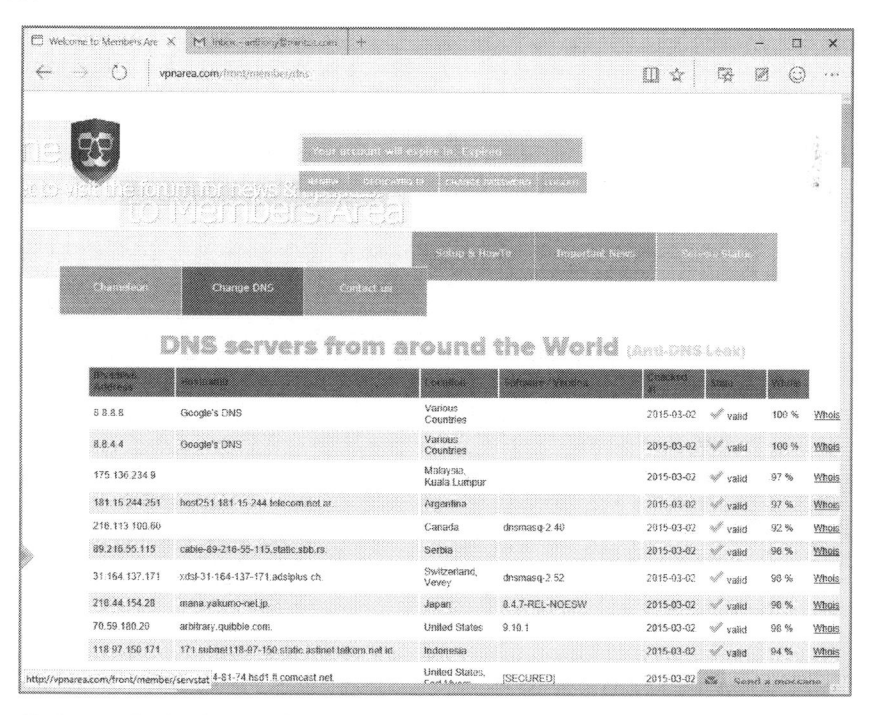

15. Scroll through the list to find a DNS server in the country of choice, and then copy the *IPv4* address from the left column.

19. Vulnerability: Internet Activity

16. Select the *www Anti DNS Leak* icon from the *Chameleon.app* sidebar, click in the *Primary* field, and then *Paste*.

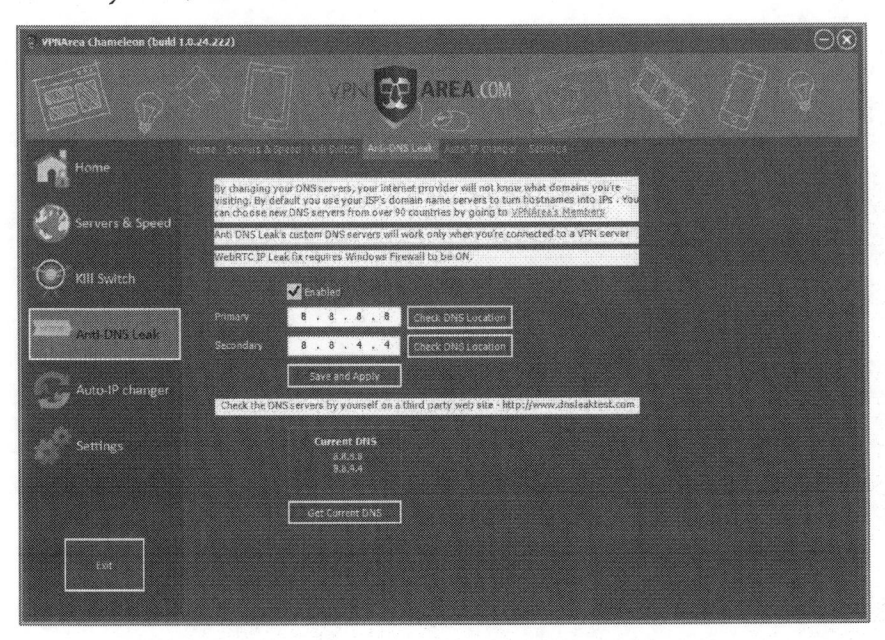

17. Repeat for another DNS server in your desired country, and then *Paste* in the *Secondary* field.

19. Vulnerability: Internet Activity

18. Click the *Check DNS Location* for each DNS server to verify it is working properly. When verified, click the *OK* button.

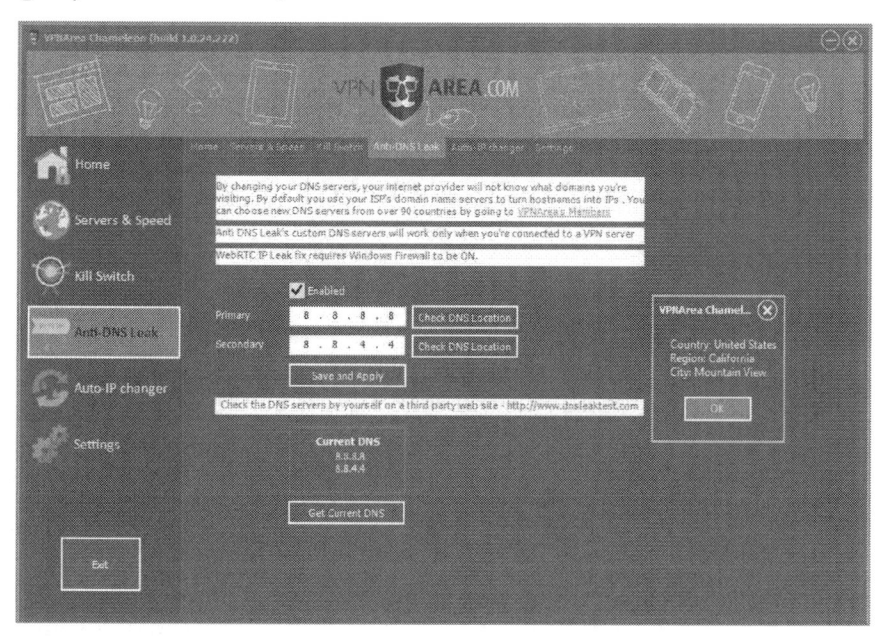

19. Click on *Save and Apply*. Your computer is now using VPN with *Anti-DNS Leak* enabled. Neither your data nor your DNS activity can now be read or tracked.

19. Vulnerability: Internet Activity

20. If at any time you wish to change your VPN server or country, click on the *Servers & Speed* menu item, scroll through the list of servers, and then select the desired server.

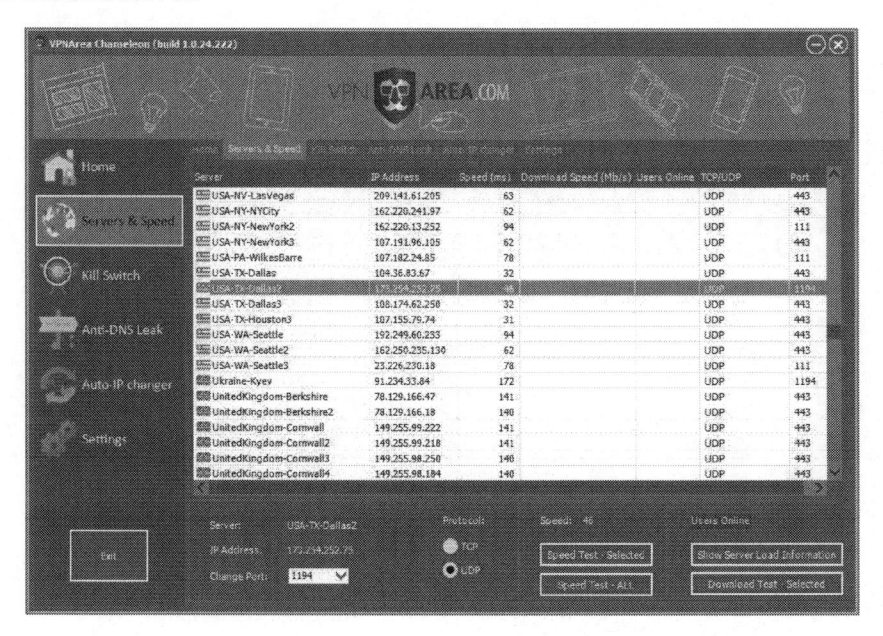

19. Vulnerability: Internet Activity

21. The last piece of configuration is found by selecting the *Settings* icon in the *Chameleon* sidebar. Configure to taste. Shown below are my recommendations:

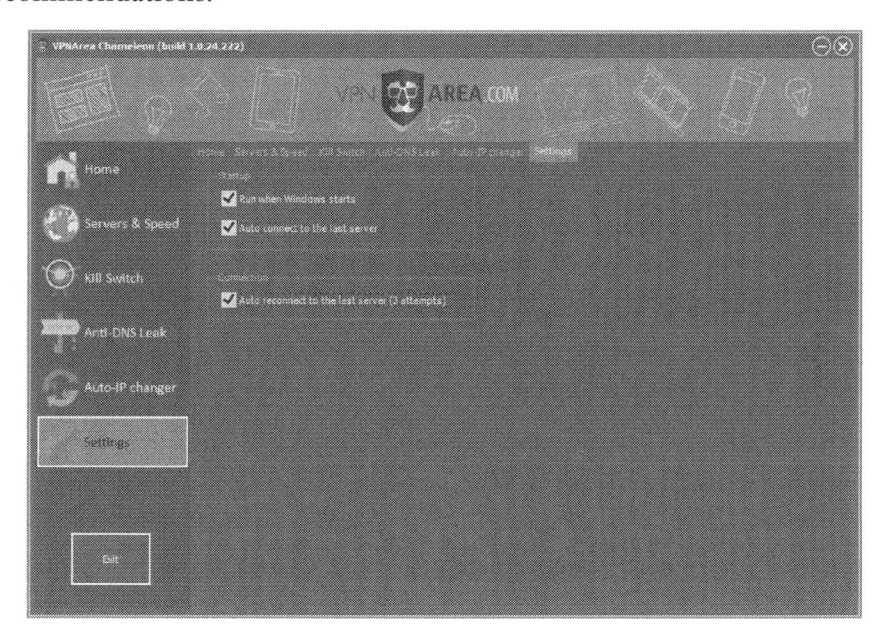

19. Vulnerability: Internet Activity

22. To turn VPN and Anti-DNS Leak off, click on the *Home* menu item, and then select the *Disconnect* button.

23. When you wish to reactivate VPN, open *VPNArea Chameleon.app*. You can see that VPN is active when the *VPNArea* menu icon changes to green.

Congratulations. You have configured VPN so that any time you need complete privacy with your Internet communications, it is ready for you.

19. Vulnerability: Internet Activity

Mesh VPN

Another way in which VPN can be configured is a *mesh VPN*. This strategy places multiple computers within the same virtual network regardless of where they are geographically located on the Internet. All the computers operate as if they are on the same physical network, and all traffic between each of the computers is military-grade encrypted. Mesh VPN is ideal for groups of people to exchange files, screen share, and access databases from each other, while maintaining full privacy from the outside world.

We now have software that enables mesh networks for a trivial cost. Keep in mind that VPN is only as secure as the provider, and the vendor of choice is a U.S. company, subject to U.S. federal laws and National Security Letters which give the NSA full access to logs and data crossing the vendor servers.

LogMeIn Hamachi

LogMeIn at *http://logmein.com* is a US-based company with a line of top-grade cloud services. They are best known for their *LogMeIn* remote support software, allowing technical support staff both attended and unattended access to client and server computers.

One of their lesser-known, but game-changing products is *Hamachi https://secure.logmein.com/products/hamachi/*. Hamachi is a cloud-based VPN that completely eliminates the need for expensive VPN boxes. As if that weren't enough, it also allows for three different types of VPN configurations: Gateway, mesh, and hub & spoke. We will restrict discussion here to the mesh option.

As of this writing, Hamachi is free for use with 5 or fewer nodes (computers). Up to 32 nodes on one network is available for $29/year. Up to 256 nodes on a network is available for $119/year.

Assignment: Create a LogMeIn Hamachi Account

In this assignment, we will create a *LogMeIn Hamachi* account, so that we can deploy a free Hamachi network for up to 5 computers. Should you eventually need more computers on the network, you can upgrade your account at any time.

19. Vulnerability: Internet Activity

4. Open a browser, and go to
   https://secure.logmein.com/products/hamachi/default.aspx. The Hamachi home page opens.

19. Vulnerability: Internet Activity

5. Select the *Try it Free* button. In the *Sign Up* field, enter all requested information, and then select the *Create Account* button.

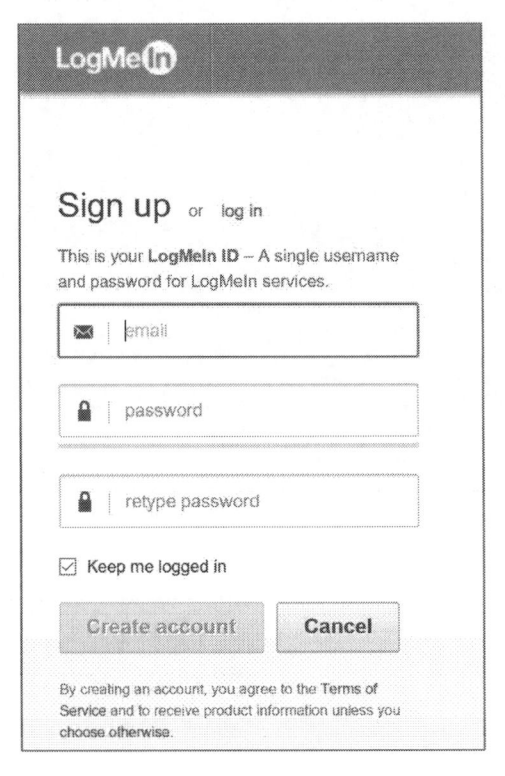

19. Vulnerability: Internet Activity

6. In the *Complete Your Registration* page, enter all requested information, and then select the *Register* button.

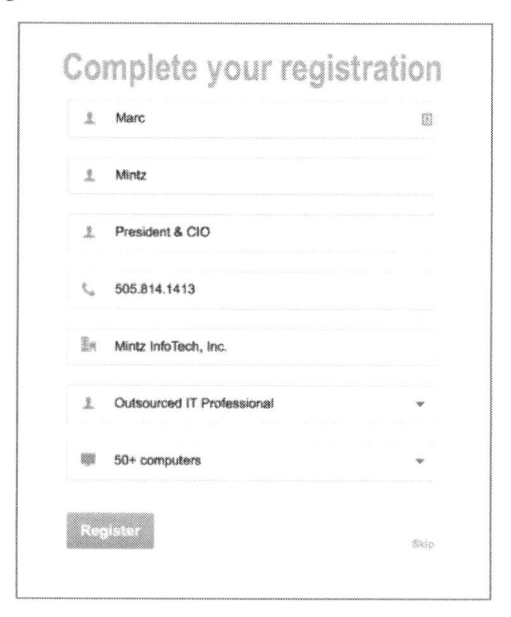

7. At the *Get LogMeIn* page, select the *Download and Install Software* button to install the software on this computer. If you don't need the software on this computer, but want to install on other computers, skip to the next assignment, *Configure the Hamachi Network*.

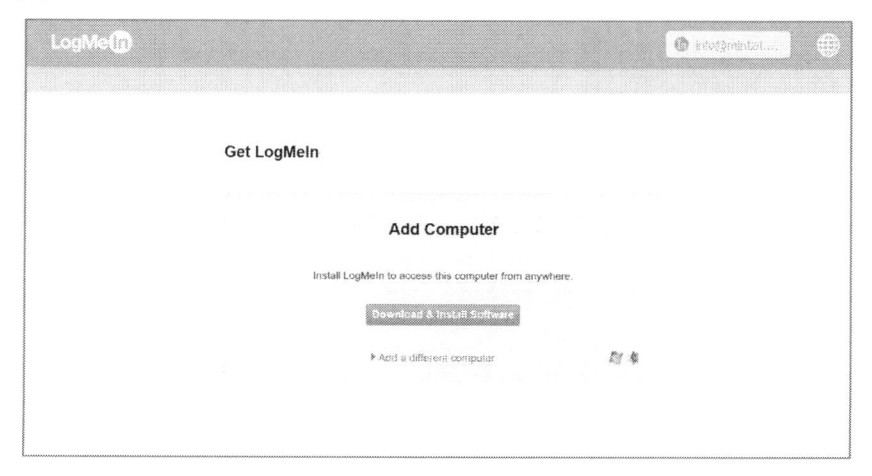

19. Vulnerability: Internet Activity

8. The software will begin to download, and the guide page will appear.

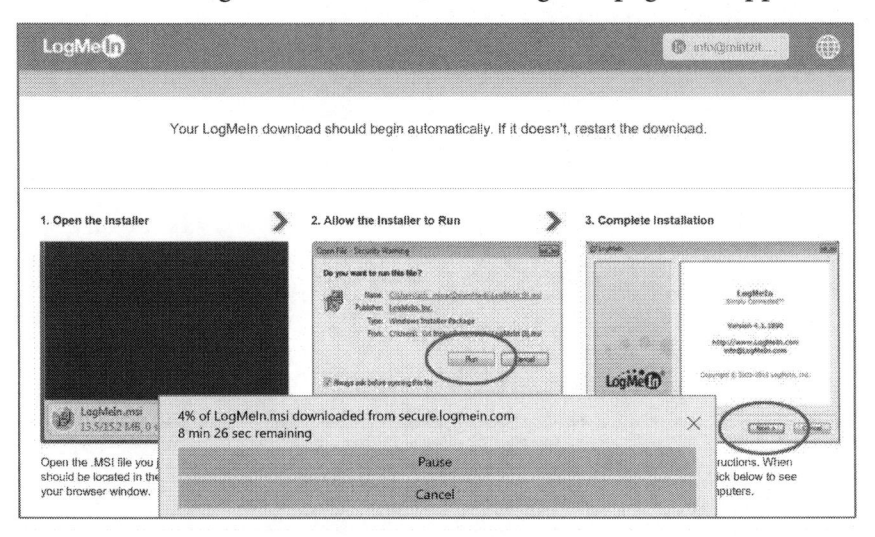

9. When complete, click the *Run* button.

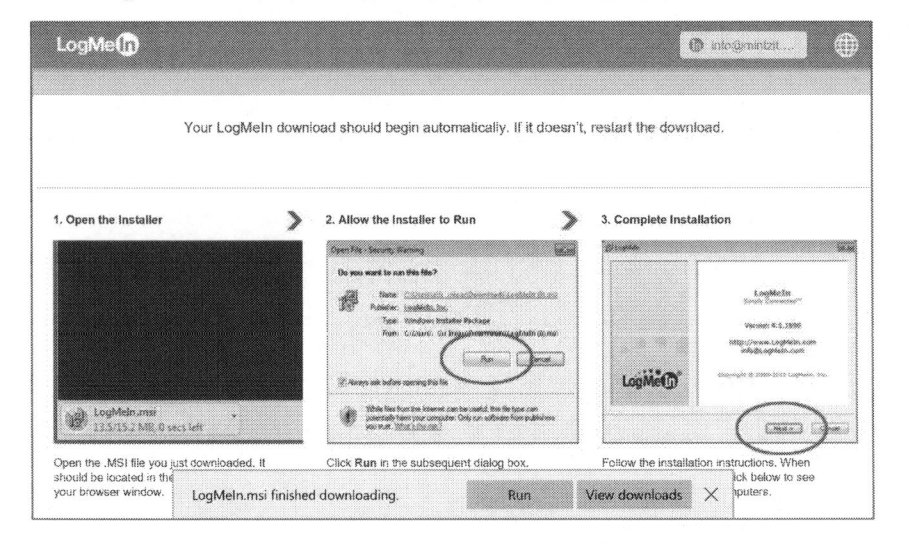

19. Vulnerability: Internet Activity

10. At the LogMeIn installer window, check the *License Agreement* checkbox, and then click *Next*.

11. Select *Next*.

19. Vulnerability: Internet Activity

12. At *Software options*, select the *Typical*, and then click *Next*.

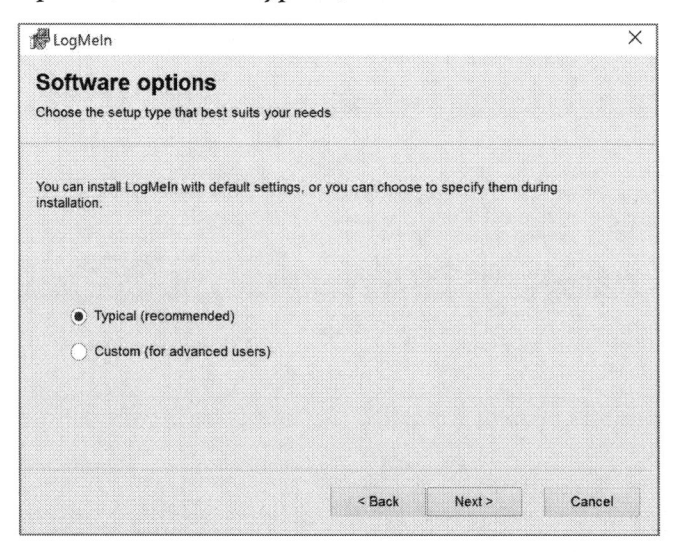

13. In the *Computer Description* window, enter an identifying name for this computer, and then click *Next*.

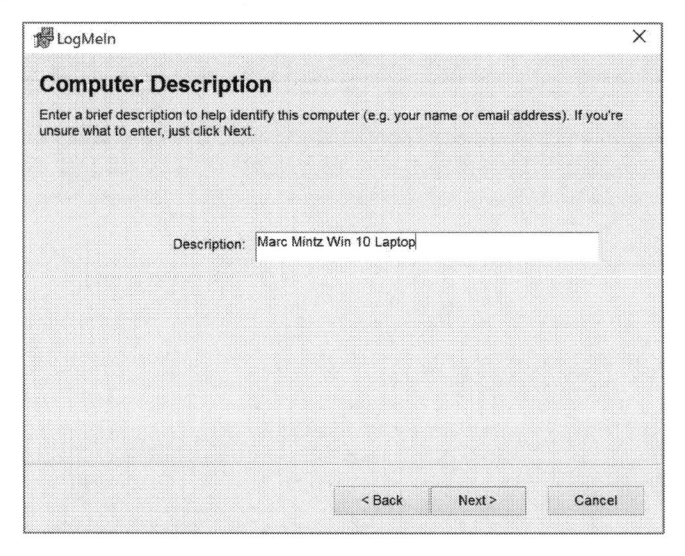

19. Vulnerability: Internet Activity

14. In the *Choose Destination Location*, click *Next*.

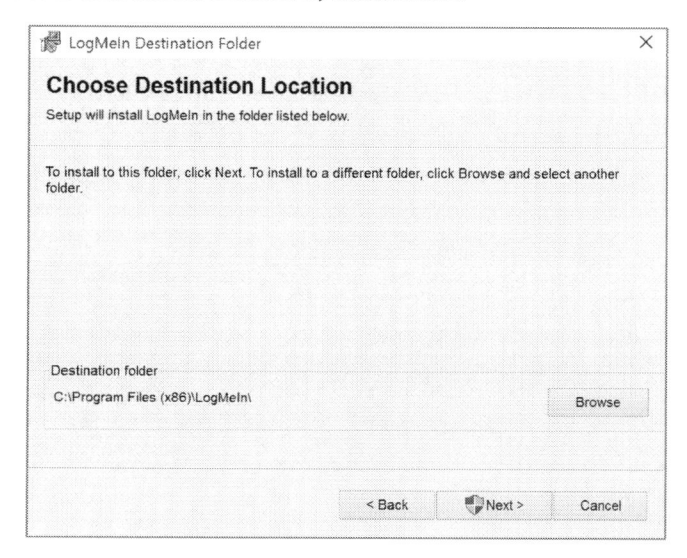

15. When asked *Do you want to allow this app to install software on your PC*, click *Yes*.

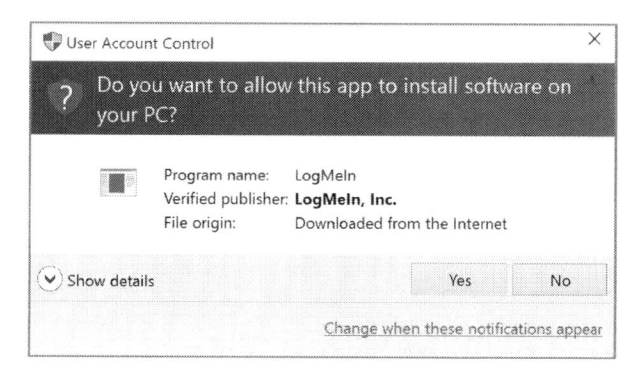

19. Vulnerability: Internet Activity

16. At the *Installation Successful* window, click *Finish*.

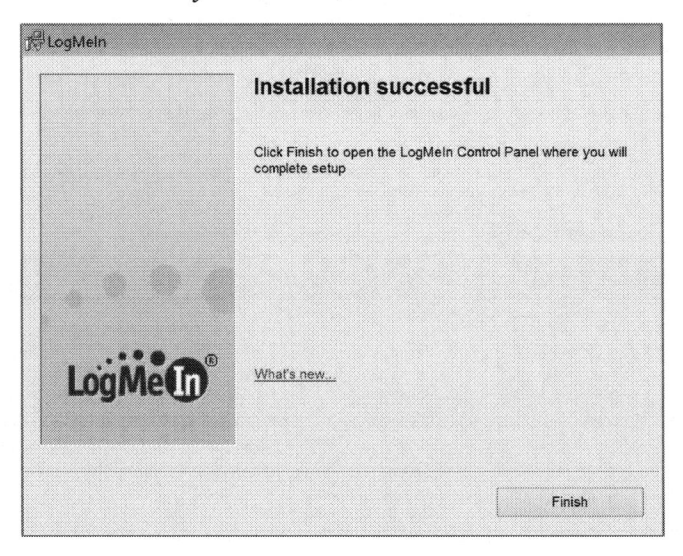

Great. Next, we need to install Hamachi on at least one other device so that a VPN network may be created.

Assignment: Configure the Hamachi Network

In this assignment we will add another device to your Hamachi VPN network.

19. Vulnerability: Internet Activity

1. Open a browser, go to the *LogMeIn* Hamachi home page, *https://secure.logmein.com/products/hamachi/*, and then click the *Log In* button.

2. At the *Log In* window, enter the account credentials, and then click *Log In*.

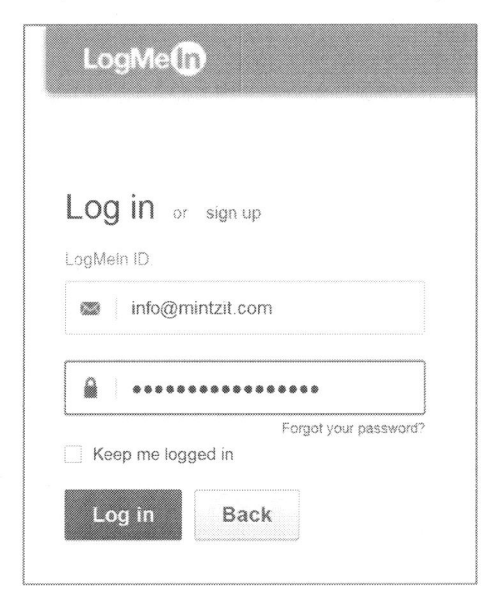

19. Vulnerability: Internet Activity

3. The *LogMeIn Central* window opens. From the sidebar, select *Networks > My Networks*. Then from the main area, select *Create Networks*.

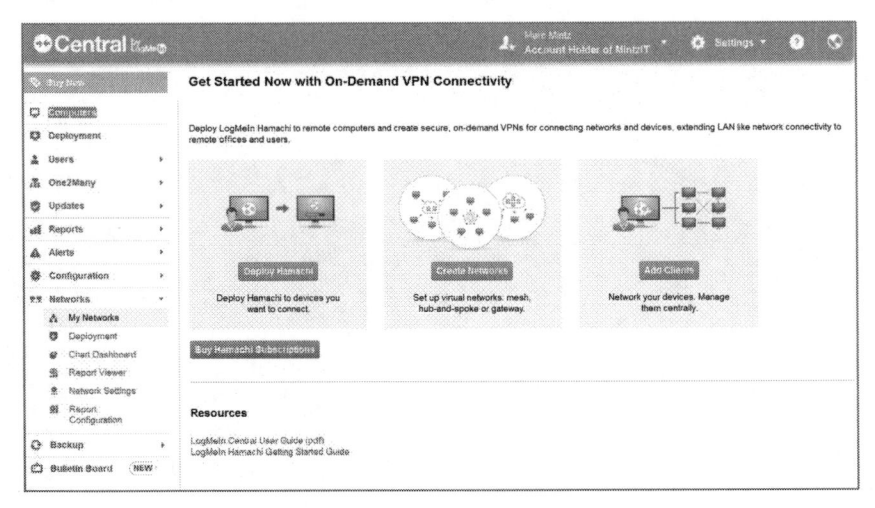

4. In the *Add Network* window, complete to taste, and then click *Continue*.

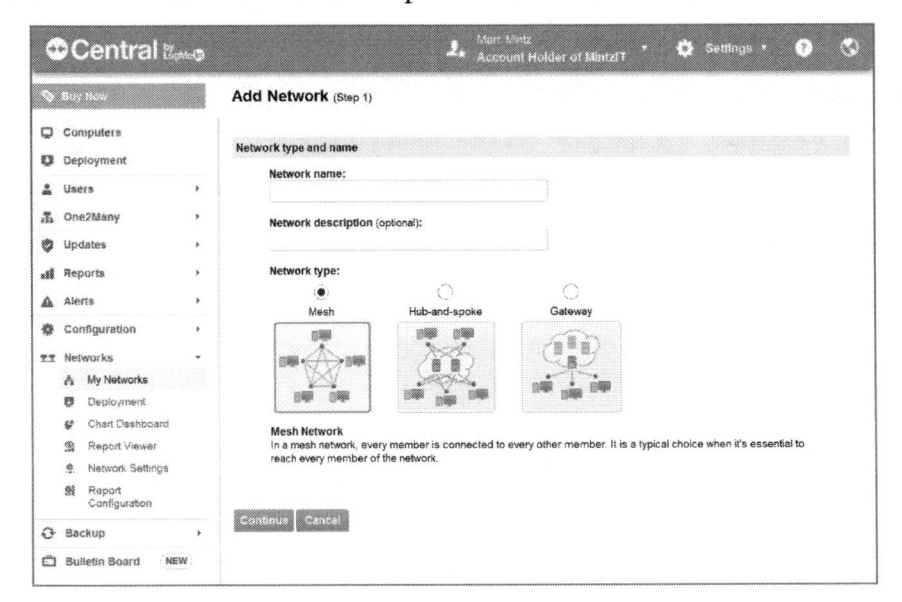

- *Network Name*: Assign a human-readable name to the network.
- *Network Description*: Enter a brief description of the network.

19. Vulnerability: Internet Activity

- *Network Type*: Almost all such networks will be *Mesh* as this allows all members to connect with all other members.

- *NOTE*: Gateway networks are not compatible with OS X.

5. In the *Add Network (step 2)* window, configure to taste, and then click *Continue*.

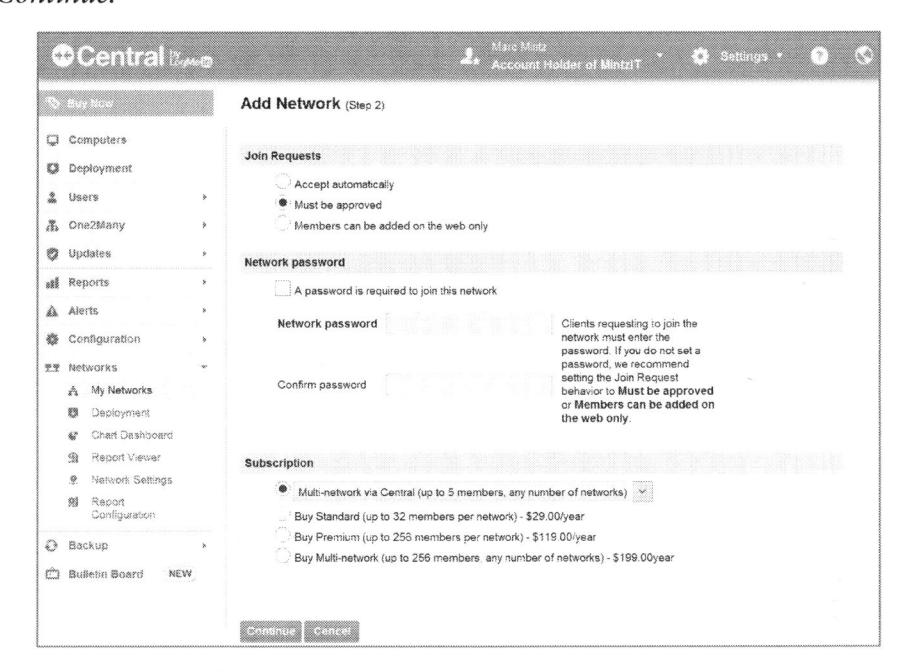

- *Join Requests*: For higher security, set to *Must be approved*. Approval is done from this site.

- *Network Password*: This is an optional method to accept members into the network instead of using *Join Requests*.

- *Subscription*: Select the desired subscription/number of members/networks.

6. At *Add Network (step 3)*, click *Finish*.

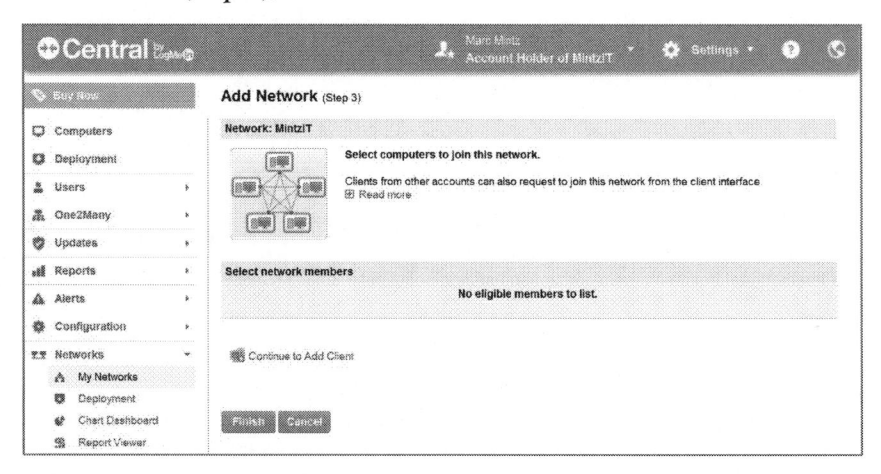

Congratulations, your Hamachi VPN network is now ready to accept members.

Assignment: Add Users to the Hamachi VPN Network

In this assignment we will add users to the Hamachi VPN network created in the previous assignment as an administrator on that computer. To add a user on a computer where you are not physically working, skip to the next assignment, *Deploy Hamachi*. Completion of the previous assignment is a prerequisite.

1. Open a browser and go to *https://secure.logmein.com*, and then login with your username and password. The *LogMeIn Central* page appears.

19. Vulnerability: Internet Activity

2. Select the *Networks > My Networks*. The network created in the previous assignment will appear.

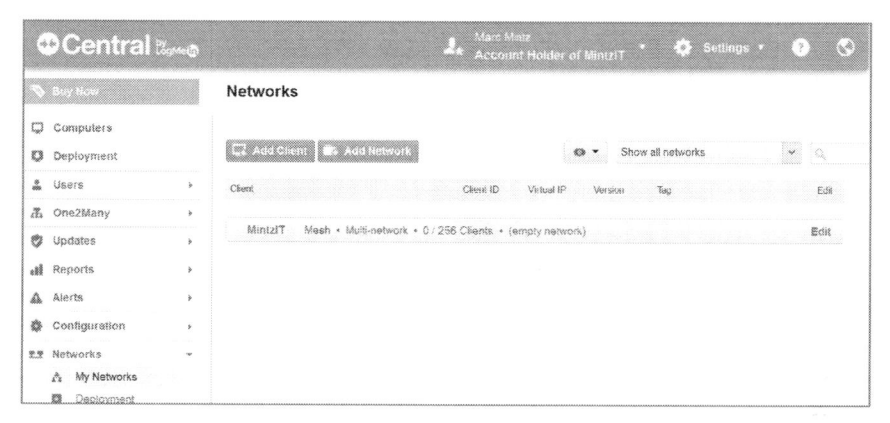

3. Click the *Add Client* button. The *Add Client* window appears. To add this computer to the network, select *Install LogMeIn Hamachi on this computer*, and then click *Continue*. To add a different computer, skip to the next assignment, *Deploy Hamachi*.

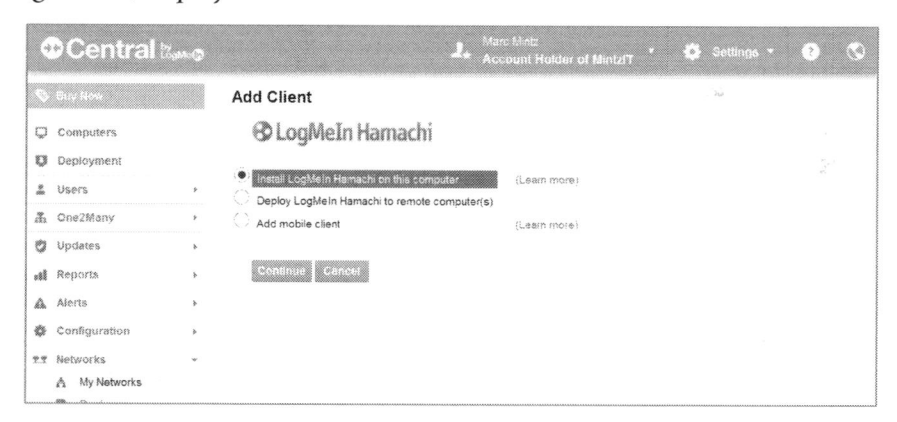

19. Vulnerability: Internet Activity

4. At the *Add Client* window, click the *Download Now* button.

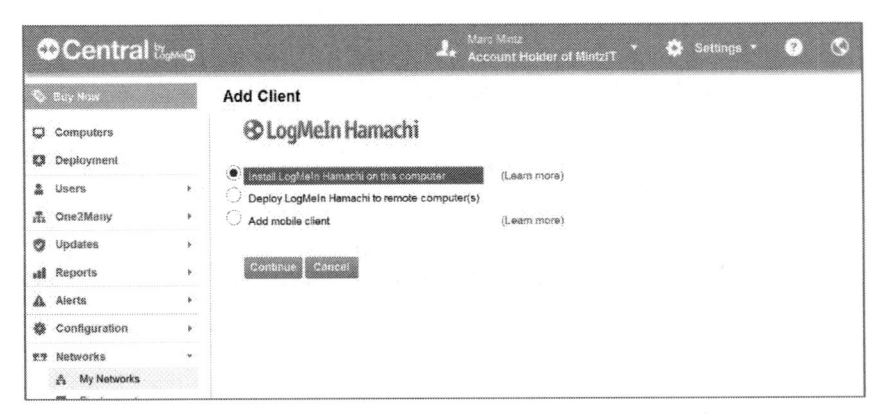

5. At the *Add Client* window, click the *Download Now* button.

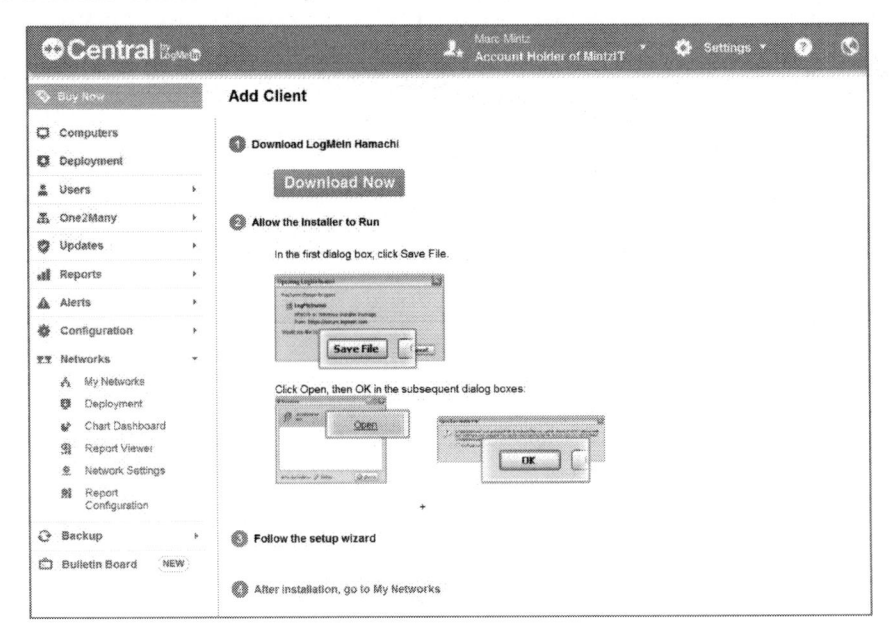

19. Vulnerability: Internet Activity

6. At the *Opening Hamachi.msi* window, select *Save File*.

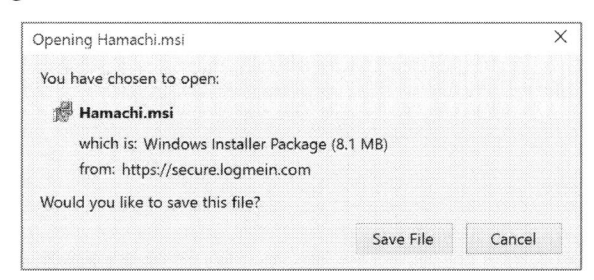

7. Go to your downloads folder, and then double-click the *Hamachi.msi* file.

8. When prompted *Do you want to run this file?* click *Run*.

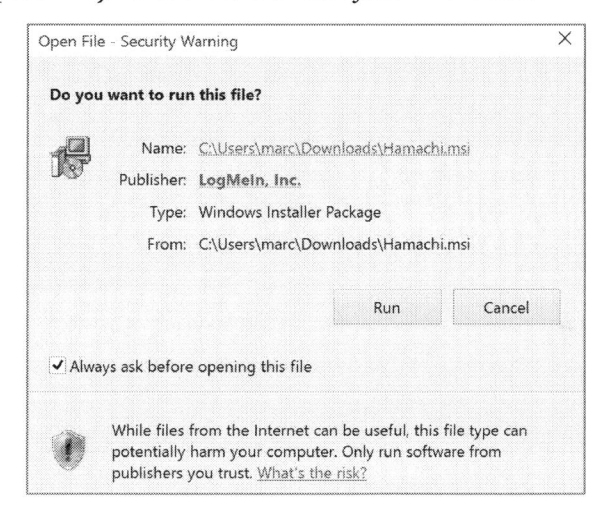

19. Vulnerability: Internet Activity

9. At *Language Selection,* select your desired language, and then click *Next.*

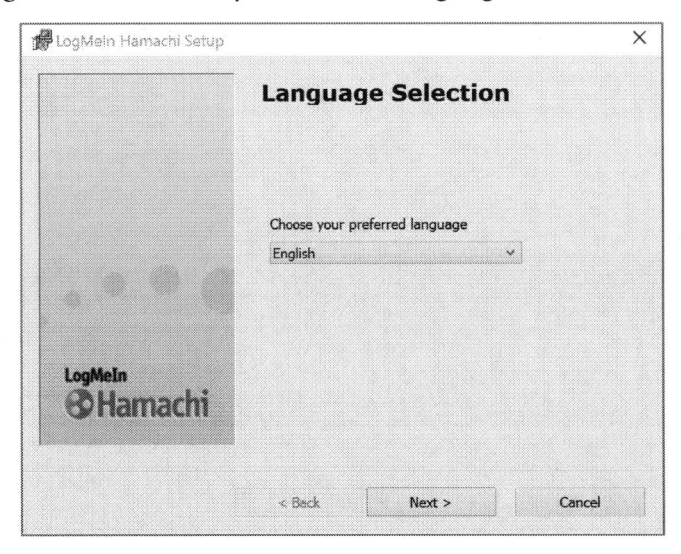

10. At the *Setup* window, click *Next.*

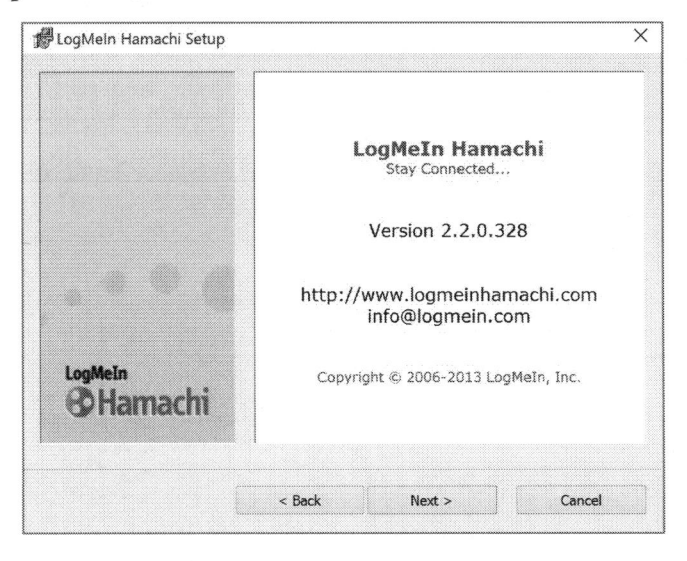

19. Vulnerability: Internet Activity

11. At the *Terms and Conditions of Use*, bring out your team of attorneys, and then click *I Agree*.

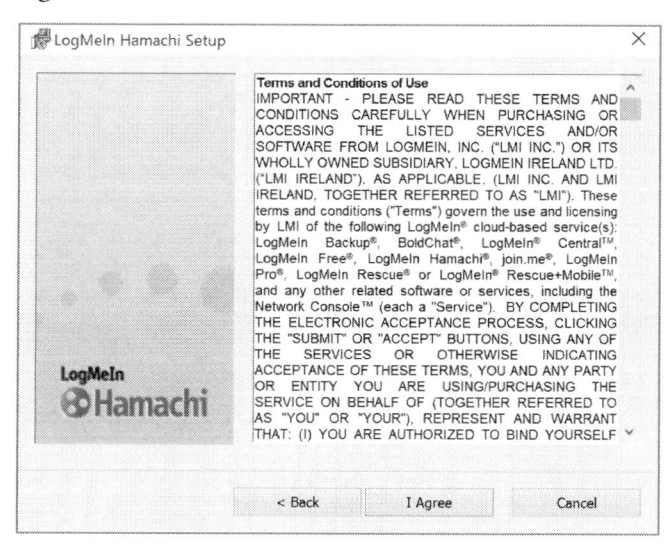

12. At *Attach client to LogMeIn account*, click *Next*.

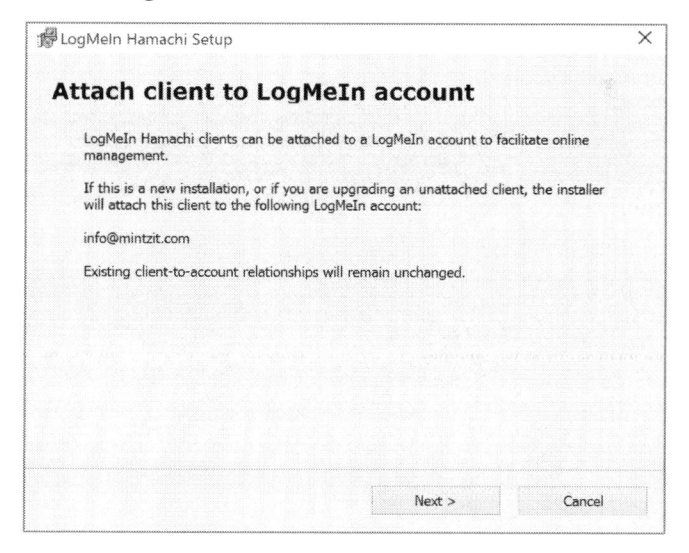

19. Vulnerability: Internet Activity

13. At *Choose Install Options*, check the *Create Shortcut on the Desktop* checkbox, and then click *Install*.

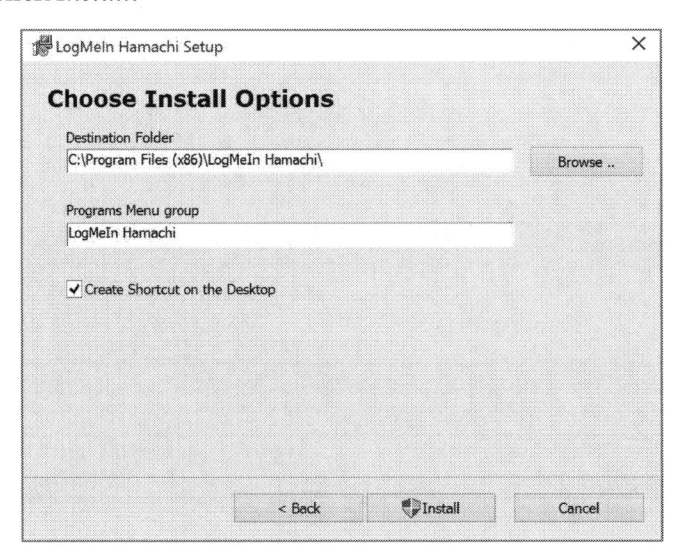

14. When prompted *Do you want to allow this app to install software on your PC*, click *Yes*. The installer will run for a few minutes.

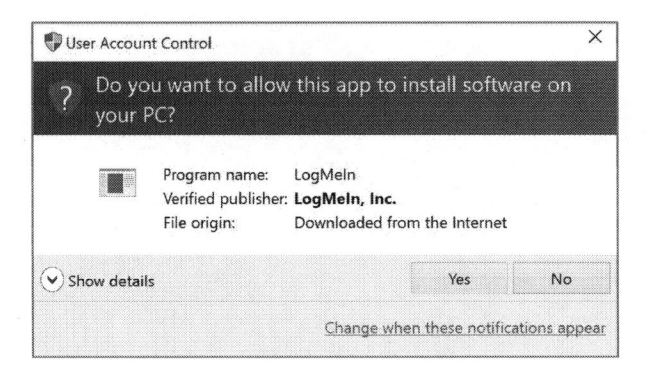

19. Vulnerability: Internet Activity

15. At *LogMeIn Hamachi Setup Complete*, check the *Launch Hamachi* checkbox, and then click *Finish*.

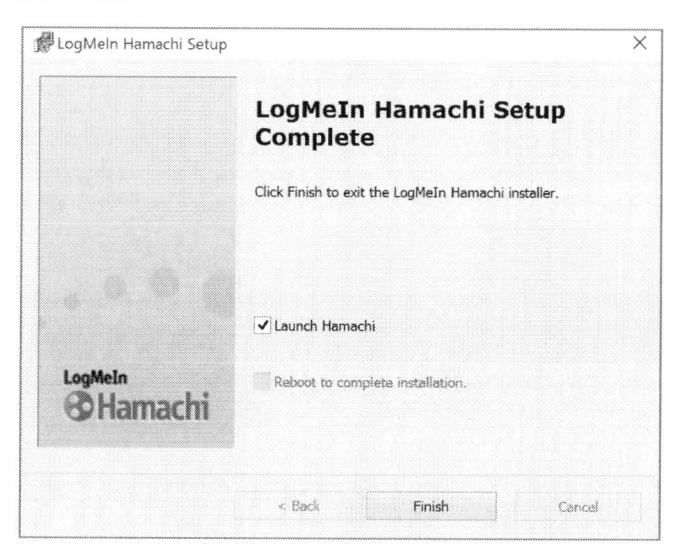

16. The *LogMeIn Hamachi* window will open. As this is the initial launch, select *Join an existing network*.

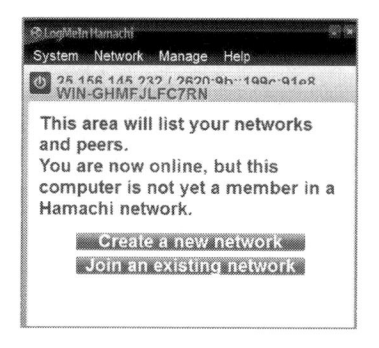

19. Vulnerability: Internet Activity

17. The *Join Network* window opens. Enter the *Network ID* of the target network, and then click *Join*. In my own case, the network I created is named *MintzIT*.

    - **NOTE:** If you receive an error, it is likely because your Hamachi client is not yet approved. If this happens, continue to the next step. If no error, all is rainbows and unicorns, and this computer is now a member of the VPN network.

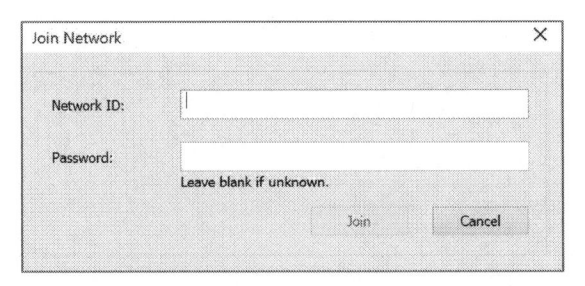

18. Return to your browser and the *LogMeIn Central* website > *Networks* > *My Networks*. Your computer will be listed as a *Non-member*. Click the *Edit* link to the far right of the non-member computer.

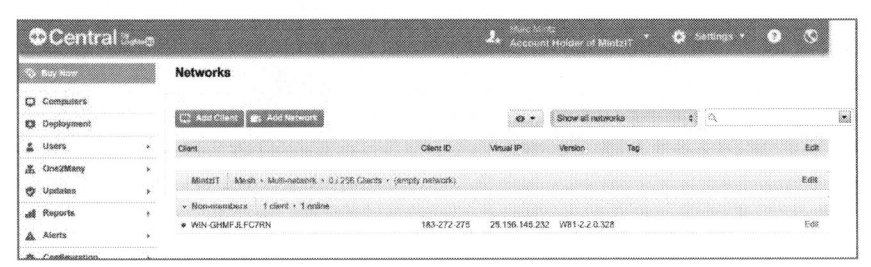

19. Select the *Name* tab. In the *Client Name* field, enter the desired name for this client, click *Save*, and then click the *Networks* tab.

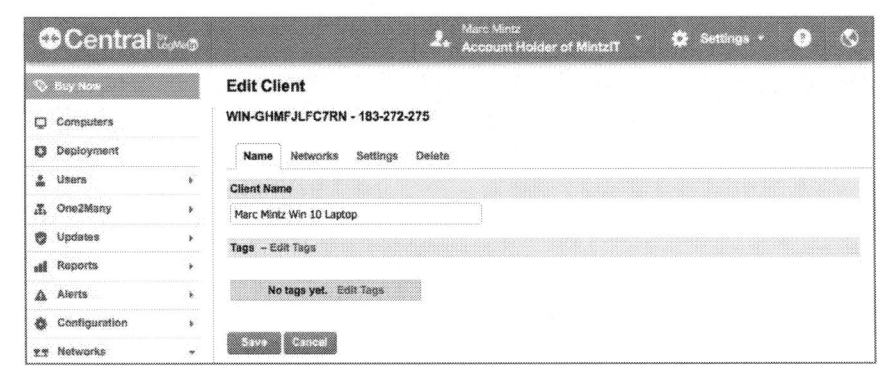

19. Vulnerability: Internet Activity

20. Check the checkbox to the far left of the client, and then click *Save*.

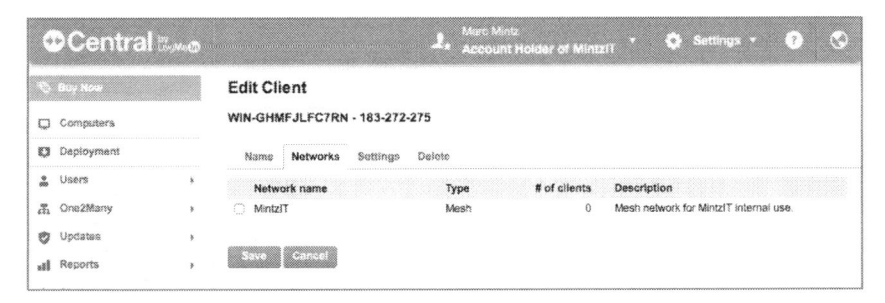

21. Back at your computer, in the LogMeIn Hamachi window, it now reflects that you are a member of this network.

One device down, now let's add another so that we can have a real network.

Assignment: Deploy Hamachi

Once you have created a Hamachi network, and have installed Hamachi on your own computer, deployment to unlimited numbers of computers is only a few clicks away.

In this assignment, we will deploy Hamachi to other computers.

1. Open a browser, visit the LogMeIn log in page at *http://logmein.com*, and then click the *Log In* button.

-613-

19. Vulnerability: Internet Activity

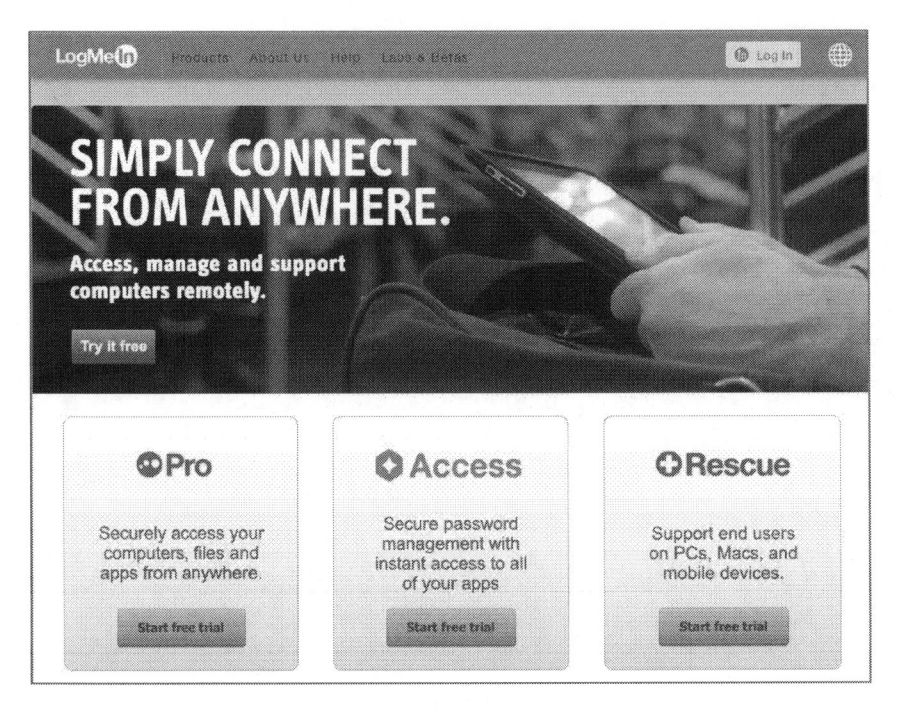

2. At the *Log In* window, enter your credentials, and then click *Log In*.

3. The LogMeIn Central window appears. Select *Networks > My Networks* to display the *Networks* window, and then click the *Add Client* button.

19. Vulnerability: Internet Activity

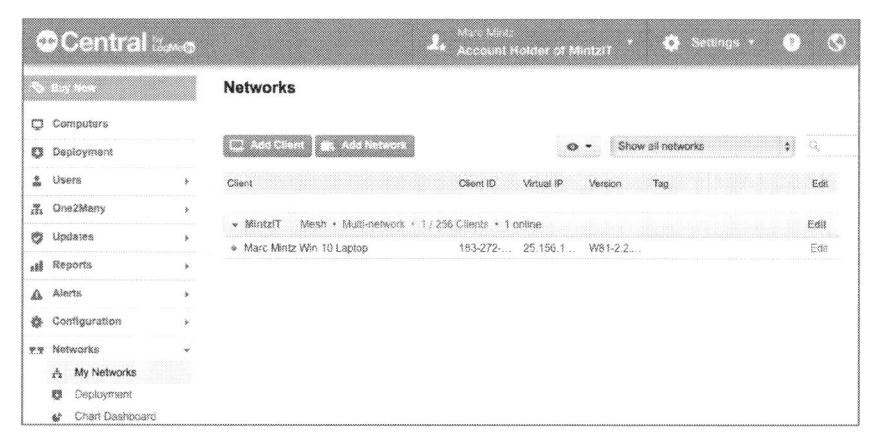

4. In the *Add Client window*, select *Deploy LogMeIn Hamachi to remote computer(s)*, and then click *Continue*.

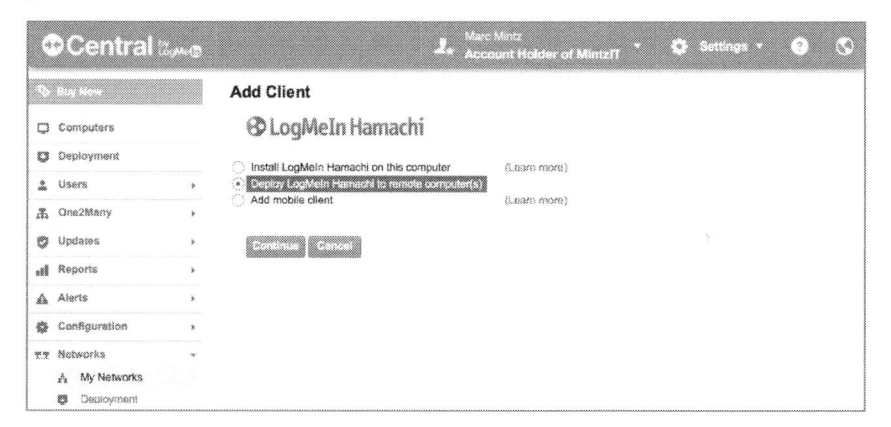

5. In the *Add Client* window, configure to taste, and then click *Continue*.

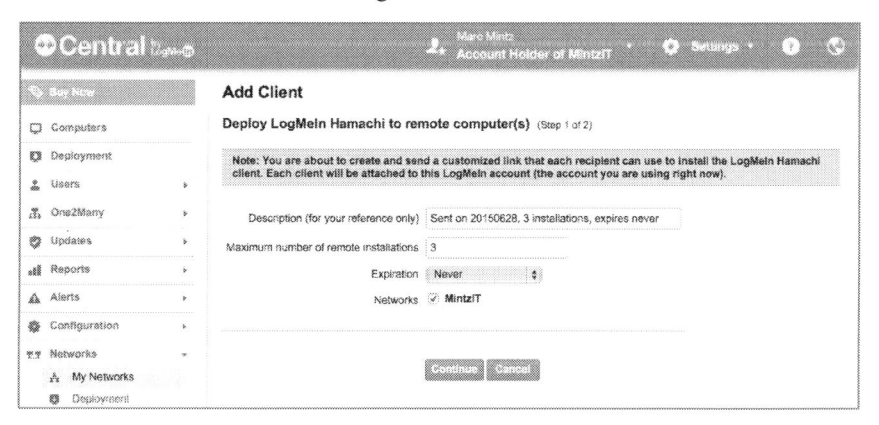

19. Vulnerability: Internet Activity

- *Description*: Enter information to identify this deployment.
- *Maximum number of remote installations*: Places a limit on how many devices can use this installation.
- *Expiration*: Gives you the option of limiting how long the installer will live.
- *Networks*: Specifies for which network(s) the installer will connect to.

6. In *Add Clients (step 2 of 2)*, select how to deploy. For our example, we will select *Send*.

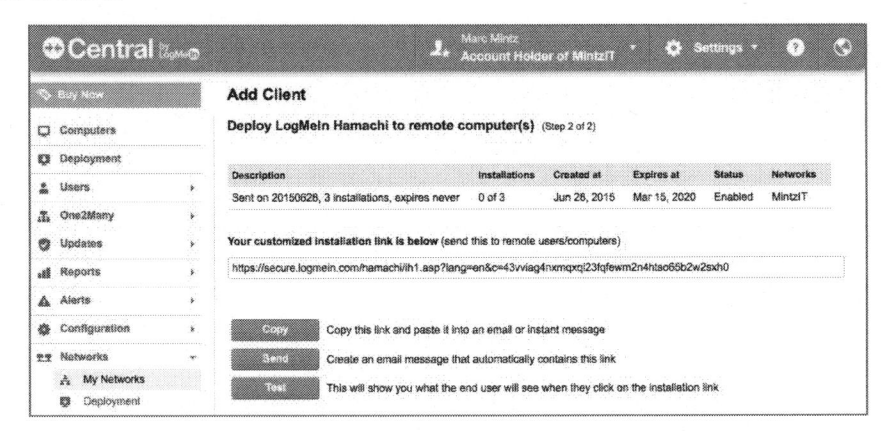

- *Copy*: This will copy the URL link to the installer so that you may paste it into an email or instant message.
- *Send*: Creates an email with the URL link included.
- *Test*: Shows what the end user will see when clicking the URL link to the installer.

7. When clicking *Send*, your email client will open with the URL entered in the body area.

8. Enter recipient addresses, a subject, any additional information within the body, and then click *Send* within your mail application.

19. Vulnerability: Internet Activity

9. The recipient will receive the email.

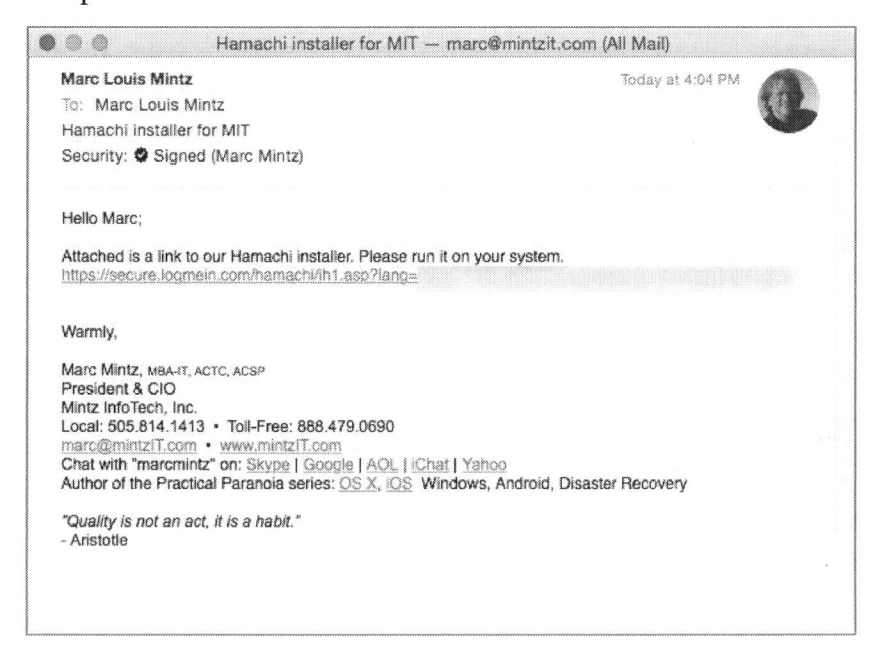

10. The recipient clicks the link in the email. The link opens in a browser. The recipient checks the *I have received this link from a trusted source* checkbox, and then click *Continue*.

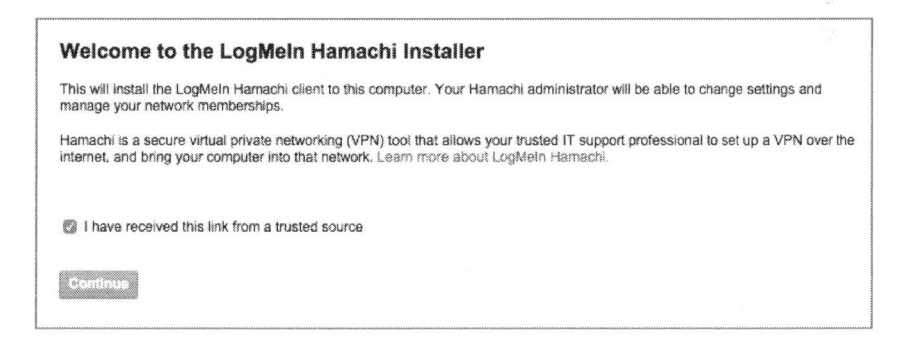

19. Vulnerability: Internet Activity

11. In the *Welcome to the LogMeIn Hamachi Installer* window, the recipient clicks the *Download Now* button.

12. The recipient locates the *Hamachi installer* in their *Downloads* folder, and then launches it (in this example, on an OS X computer).

13. The recipient checks *I have read and agree* checkbox, and then clicks *Install*.

19. Vulnerability: Internet Activity

14. In the *Attach client to LogMeIn account* window, the recipient clicks *Next*.

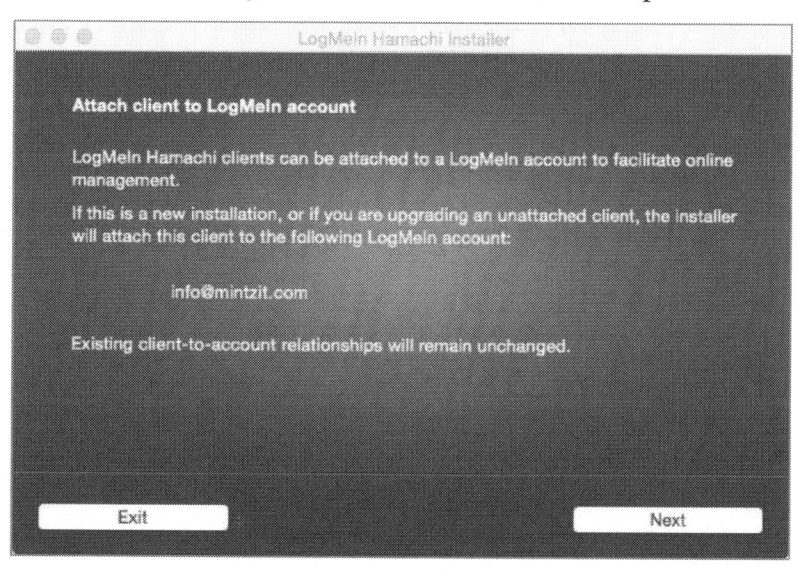

15. At the *Installation was successful* window, the recipient clicks *Finish*.

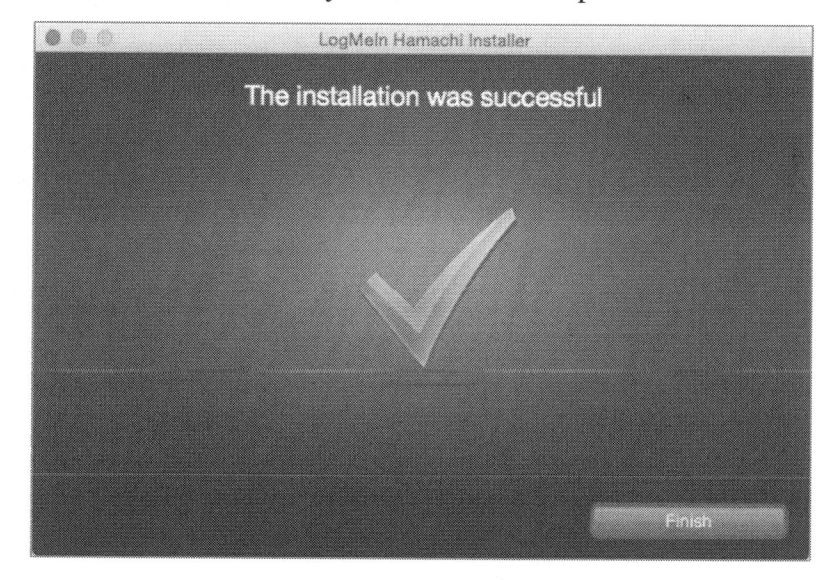

16. The recipient launches the LogMeIn Hamachi application.

The recipient will see the other devices currently active on the LogMeIn Hamachi VPN network within the Hamachi window.

19. Vulnerability: Internet Activity

Assignment: File Sharing Within a Hamachi VPN Network

In this assignment we will file share within a Hamachi VPN network. Completing the previous assignment is a prerequisite.

In the typical Local Area Network (LAN) environment, one computer can see another over the network using an automatic discovery protocol. These protocols aren't in effect over a VPN connection, so we will need a different method of accessing other computers for file sharing and other network activities.

Before we begin, please make sure that any OS X computers within your VPN network have *System Preferences > Sharing > File Sharing* enabled, and that SMB file sharing is enabled.

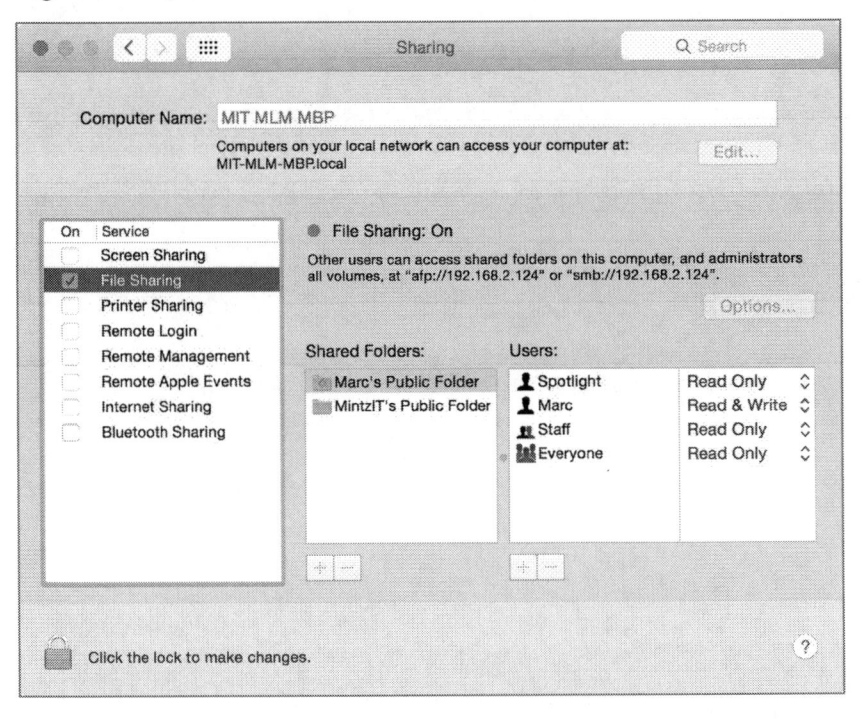

19. Vulnerability: Internet Activity

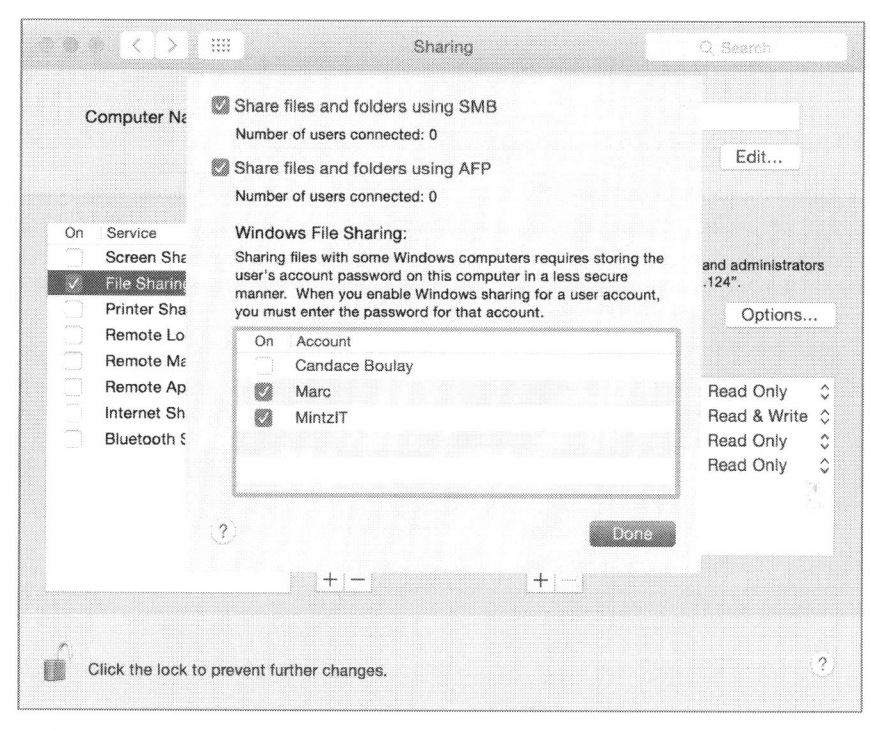

1. Launch *Hamachi*, and verify the target computer is showing as *Online*. In this example, the other computer is named *Stephens-MIT-MacBook-Air.local*.

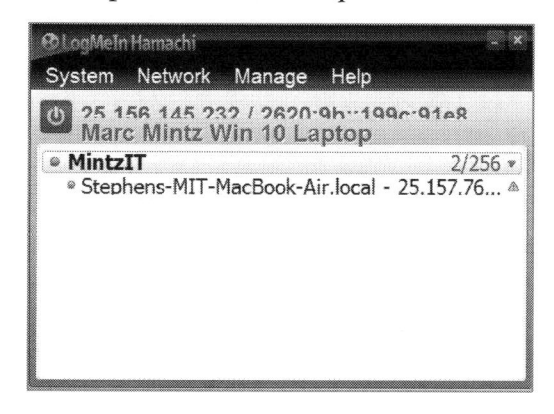

2. Right-click on the name of the target computer (in this example, *Stephens…*). From the pop-up menu, select *Browse*.

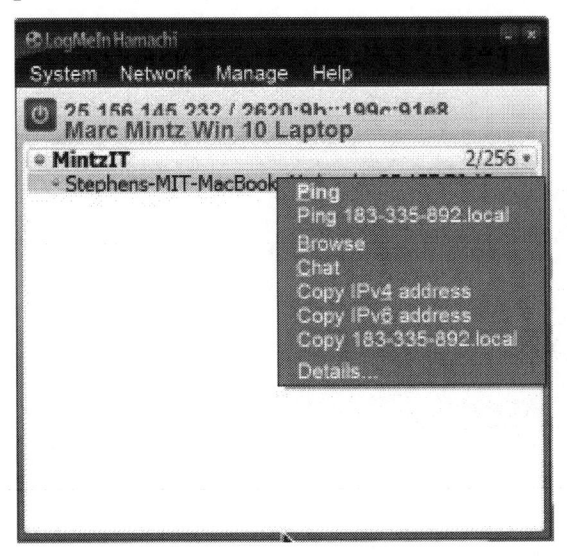

3. At the prompt, enter a username and password that has permissions to file share on the target computer, and then click *Connect*. You will now be able to browse files on the target computer just as you could if on the same physical network.

Assignment: Exit the Hamachi VPN Network

In this assignment we will stop VPN so that we are no longer connected to the VPN network.

19. Vulnerability: Internet Activity

1. On your computer, in the Hamachi window, click on the *Power* icon. The status text will change to *offline*, indicating you are no longer connected.

2. You may now Quit LogMeIn Hamachi.

Great work. You can now create a military-grade, encrypted network, on the fly, so that your friends or business associates can share files, screen share, etc. without fear of data or activities being spied upon.

19. Vulnerability: Internet Activity

Resolving Email Conflicts with VPN

Some email servers will send up a red flag and then block user access to email when the user switches to a VPN connection. This is a good thing as it indicates the email provider is highly sensitive to any possible security breach. In all cases there is a resolution available, although the steps to take will vary with each provider.

The example below outlines what occurs when using VPN with a Gmail account, and how to gain access to your email after the blockage.

1. The user starts a VPN program to encrypt all data between the user's computer and the Internet.

2. The user attempts to receive Gmail using a mail app.

3. Google sees attempted access from an unknown machine (the Proxy Server), and blocks access to the account.

4. Both an email and a text from Google are sent notifying the user of suspicious activity. Select the link in either message.

5. The first support file opens. Select the link.

6. In the authentication window, enter your email and password, and then select the *Sign In* button.

7. Another support window opens, explaining the next steps to take. Select the *Continue* button.

8. The final support window opens. Following the instructions, return to your email application and access your Gmail within 10 minutes. This will provide Google with the authentication to release your account.

Review Questions

1. A _____ VPN connection provides a secure entry point into a network allowing the resources of that network to be shared with remote hosts.

2. For the greatest security, a VPN provider should reside within a country that has strong digital privacy laws. (True or False)

3. A _____ VPN connection allows for two or more computers to access the same de-centralized virtual network.

The Final Word

If you have followed each of the steps outlined in this book, your computer now is secured to a level higher than even the NSA requires for its own staff. Although this won't prevent one of the bad guys from stealing your computer, it will prevent them from accessing your data.

And since you have at least one current backup at the home or office, and one on the Internet, you are still in possession of the item with *real* value: your data.

Mintz InfoTech, Inc.
Windows 10 Security Checklist

Included below is the checklist used by Mintz InfoTech, Inc. consultants when performing security checks for our clients' systems. You should use this same checklist to ensure your own system is fully hardened.

Passwords
Critical
- ☐ Strong account passwords of at least 14 characters
- ☐ All passwords recorded
- ☐ All challenge questions and answers recorded

Optional
- ☐ Install and use LastPass

Updates
Critical
- ☐ All current system updates installed
- ☐ All current application and driver updates installed

Optional
- ☐ Install and use Ninite to keep applications and drivers updated
- ☐ Anti-Virus installed

User Account
- ☐ All users always log in with a non-administrative account
- ☐ Administrative account used to authenticate to perform administrator tasks
- ☐ Configure Application Whitelisting

Storage Device
Optional
- ☐ Block access to external storage devices
- ☐ Enable full disk encryption using BitLocker

Sleep and Screen Saver
- ☐ Require password after sleep or screen saver

Mintz InfoTech, Inc. Windows 10 Security Checklist

Malware
- ☐ Install and configure quality antimalware (Avira for home, Bitdefender for business)
- ☐ After antimalware installation, perform a full scan of all drives

Firewall
- ☐ The built-in Windows 10 firewall is automatically enabled. Do no disable to modify, unless using Bitdefender, which disables the Windows firewall, and installs its own

Data Loss
- ☐ Enable at least one on-site clone backup with Parted Magic or Windows Backup
- ☐ Test the integrity of all on-site backups monthly
- ☐ Enable at least one off-site backup (CrashPlan recommended for home, CrashPlan Pro recommended for business)
- ☐ Test the integrity of all off-site backups monthly
- ☐ Guest User disabled if using BitLocker encryption

Network Security

Critical
- ☐ WPA2 with AES is used for all Wi-Fi networks
- ☐ Strong password in use for Wi-Fi
- ☐ All network passwords recorded
- ☐ Only Ethernet switches in use, no hubs
- ☐ Current router firmware installed
- ☐ Router vulnerability checked for no inappropriate port forwarding
- ☐ Router vulnerability checked for no inappropriate DMZ
- ☐ Router power cycled to remove RAM-resident malware

Optional
- ☐ Use MAC address to limit Wi-Fi access

Web Browsing

- ☐ User educated to never enter sensitive information in an HTTP page, only on an HTTPS page
- ☐ HTTPS Everywhere installed (if using Chrome, Firefox, or Opera browsers)
- ☐ Use browser private browsing to anonymized searches
- ☐ DuckDuckGo configured as the default search engine
- ☐ Configure the browser security settings

Optional

- ☐ *TorBrowser* installed

Email

- ☐ All email accounts use either TLS, SSL or HTTPS

Does client need end-to-end email security?
If No, then skip this section.

If Yes, as appropriate set up with *SendInc, S/MIME* or *GPG*:

- ☐ Create a SendInc.com account and use for all sensitive email

Or:

- ☐ Acquire a Class 1 or 3 S/MIME certificate, install on computer and use for all sensitive email

Or:

- ☐ Install GPG on computer and use for all sensitive email

Documents

Critical

- ☐ Educate the user how to encrypt from within MS Office
- ☐ Educate the user how to encrypt a PDF document
- ☐ Educate the user how to encrypt a Windows folder

Optional

- ☐ Install and educate the user how to create encrypted folders with VeraCrypt

Mintz InfoTech, Inc. Windows 10 Security Checklist

Storage Device Encryption
- ☐ Secure UEFI/BIOS Firmware
- ☐ Enable BitLocker
- ☐ Routinely review your account's activity under the security & privacy section

Instant Messaging
- ☐ Install and configure Wickr

Audio and Video Communications
- ☐ Create an OStel account, and install Jitsi

Internet Activity
- ☐ Install a quality VPN utility to secure all Internet traffic (we recommend only *VPNArea*).
- ☐ Install *LogMeIn Hamachi* to create ad hoc secure networks between a group of computers

Review Answers

1. Vulnerability: Passwords

1. **Q:** Microsoft Recommends at least 12 characters for passwords to meet minimum length requirements. (True or False)
   A: False. Microsoft recommends at least 14 characters for a secure length.

2. **Q:** Two factor authentication ensures that an account is secured using one or more independent verification sources. (True or False)
   A: True.

3. **Q:** It is helpful to pick obscure challenge questions, or provide bogus answers. (True or False)
   A: True.

4. **Q:** What is one website that can be used to test the strength of a password?
   A: https://www.grc.com/haystack.htm

2. Vulnerability: Updates

1. **Q:** What are the three fundamental reasons for security updates and upgrades?
   A: Bug Fixes, Monetization & Security Patches.

2. **Q:** The department of Homeland Security recommends installing updates no later than 72 hours after their release. (True or False)
   A: False. US-CERT recommends patching systems no more than 48 hours after updates are released.

3. **Q:** Name one way in which 3rd party applications can be monitored and patched as needed.
   A: By using a third party application such as Ninite updater.

3. Vulnerability: User Accounts

1. **Q:** What are the four different types of user accounts available in Windows 10?
   A: Administrator, Standard, child, and Microsoft.

2. **Q:** What abilities does the Administrator have that other user accounts don't?
   A: Create new user accounts, Delete user accounts, modify the contents of the root level of the hard drive, and authorize the installation or removal of applications and system updates.

3. **Q:** What are the minimum and maximum number of Administrator accounts?
   A: 1, unlimited.

4. **Q:** What are the minimum and maximum number of Standard accounts?
   A: 0, Unlimited.

5. **Q:** What is the advantage of working in a Standard account?
   A: It is not possible to damage the operating system or applications.

6. **Q:** A Child account is fundamentally a _____ account, with _____ turned on.
   A: Standard, Family Safety controls.

7. **Q:** Family Safety Controls restrict the powers of an account by limiting _____, _____, and _____.
   A: Access to specific applications (Application Whitelisting), access to specific websites or any adult site, and the hours for which the user may stay logged in.

8. **Q:** Microsoft account can only be an Administrator account. (True or False)
   A: False.

9. **Q.** In order to use Family Safety on a Child account, the Administrator of the child account must have a Microsoft or Outlook.com enabled account. (True or False)
   A: True.

4. Vulnerability: Storage Device

1. **Q:** What are the three ways to block access to external storage devices?
   A: Modifying the Registry, disabling USB ports from the device manager, and using commercial software.

2. **Q:** What way(s) can Windows encrypt hard disks?
   A: Hardware encryption and software encryption.

3. **Q:** Hardware encryption is accomplished by using _____.
   A: SED's (Self-Encrypting Drives).

4. **Q:** Software encryption is accomplished by using _____ software that is included with Windows 10.
   A: BitLocker.

5. Vulnerability: Sleep and Screen Saver

1. **Q:** Where do you go to configure requiring a password after X minutes of inactivity?
   A: Control Panel > Appearance and Personalization > Personalization > Change screen saver.

6. Vulnerability: Malware

1. **Q:** According to Wikipedia, there may be as many as _____ malware that impact Windows.
   A: 10,000,000.

2. **Q:** Name a URL of an independent anti-malware testing organization.
   A: http://av-comparatives.org.

3. **Q:** When selecting an anti-malware product, what are some of the selection criteria to consider?
   A: Effectiveness, false-positives, performance are most important. Other considerations may include cost, centralized configuration, and cross-platform compatibility.

7. **Vulnerability: Firewall**

    1. **Q:** Network ports are numbered from _____ to _____.
       A: 1, 65,535.

    2. **Q:** The purpose of a firewall is _____.
       A: To block unwanted attempts to get into or communicate with your computer from the network or Internet.

    3. **Q:** By default, the Windows 10 firewall is off and must be configured to provide protection.
       A: False.

    4. **Q:** Bitdefender installs its own firewall, and deactivates the Windows 10 firewall.
       A: True.

8. **Vulnerability: Data Loss**

    1. **Q:** Best Practices call for at least _____ backups.
       A: 3.

    2. **Q:** The benefits of an on-site backup are _____.
       A: Almost immediate recovery of lost or corrupted documents, and full recovery of the OS, applications, and documents in the event of complete loss of the hard drive.

    3. **Q:** The benefit of an off-site backup is _____.
       A: Data is available even after a catastrophic loss of computer and local backup.

    4. **Q:** Advantages of using Windows Backup for your onsite backup include _____.
       A: Free, reliable and stable, low resource requirements, new files may be added into the backup, can be scheduled, back up to external drive or CD/DVD, and can create a System Image.

    5. **Q:** The advantage of using Parted Magic for your backup is _____.
       A: Creates a bootable clone backup.

6. **Q:** The major advantage of using an Internet-based backup is _____.
   A: As long as you have access to the Internet, you have access to all of your data.

9. **Vulnerability: Recovery Drive**

   1. **Q:** When would you use a Recovery Drive?
      A: When you are unable to boot into your Windows computer due to a virus, bad boot record, or other drive damage.

   2. **Q:** A Recovery Drive should be created on your boot drive. (True or False)
      A: False.

   3. **Q:** Where do you go to create a Recovery Drive?
      A: Control Panel > Recovery > Create a recovery drive.

10. **Vulnerability: Lost or Stolen Device**

    1. **Q:** LoJack can locate a PC using _____.
       A: GPS, Wi-Fi, or IP geolocation.

    2. **Q:** Where is LoJack located on a PC?
       A: UEFI firmware.

    3. **Q:** Prey requires the guest account be enabled. (True or False)
       A: True.

    4. **Q:** What is the URL for Prey?
       A: https://preyproject.com.

    5. **Q:** To use LoJack, a supported UEFI and a subscription are both needed for the service. (True or False)
       A: True.

    6. **Q:** Since LoJack is resident in the UEFI, it can remain on the device even if Windows has been erased, or the hard drive replaced. (True or False)
       A: True.

    7. **Q:** LoJack's primary purpose is theft deterrence. (True or False)
       A: False. LoJack's primary purpose is theft recovery.

8. **Q:** What feature does Prey rely on to allow for a stolen computer to be used and tracked by its owner?
   A: A guest account. Prey will only be useful if a thief can operate the laptop without reformatting the hard drive.

9. **Q:** Prey works in conjunction with full disk encryption software. (True or False)
   A: False.

11. Vulnerability: When It Is Time To Say Goodbye

1. **Q:** When selling, giving away, or trashing your PC, all data on the drive must be made inaccessible, which can be done by _____.
   A: Securely erase the drive, or physically destroy the drive.

2. **Q:** Using a traditional drive wiping utility will securely erase a SSD (True or False)
   A: False.

3. **Q:** To create a bootable USB drive with Parted magic installed, use the _____ utility.
   A: Rufus.

4. **Q:** Secure-Erase and TRIM are controller functions that allow for secure erasure of Solid State Drives (True or False)
   A: True.

12. Vulnerability: Local Network

1. **Q:** The WEP Wi-Fi encryption protocol should be used whenever possible. (True or False)
   A: False.

2. **Q:** The WPA Wi-Fi encryption protocol should be used whenever possible. (True or False)
   A: False.

3. **Q:** The WPA2 Wi-Fi encryption protocol should be used whenever possible. (True or False)
   A: True.

4. **Q:** Of the two encryption algorithms–TKIP and AES–which should be used?
   A: AES.

5. **Q:** The network hardware that decodes and modulates the signal from your Internet provider to your cable or telephone jack is called a _____.
   A: Modem.

6. **Q:** The network hardware that allows hundreds or thousands of devices to interact between the local network and Internet is called a _____.
   A: Router.

7. **Q:** The network hardware or software that inspects data traffic between the Internet and local network devices is called a _____.
   A: Firewall.

8. **Q:** The network hardware that allows multiple devices to connect and interact with each other and the router is called a _____.
   A: Network Switch.

9. **Q:** The network hardware that allows tens or hundreds of wireless devices to connect to a network is called a _____.
   A: Access Point.

10. **Q:** A _____ address includes a unique manufacturer code, and a unique device code.
    A: MAC.

13. **Vulnerability: Web Browsing**

    1. **Q:** HTTPS uses the _____ encryption protocol.
       A: SSL.

    2. **Q:** To ensure your browser goes to https even if entering https, install the _____ plug-in.
       A: HTTPS Everywhere.

    3. **Q:** To ensure your browser doesn't store browsing history, passwords, user names, list of downloads, cookies, or cached files, enable _____ mode.
       A: Private.

4. **Q:** By default, any two people will have the same results for a given Google search. (True or False)
   A: False.

5. **Q:** By default, any two people will have the same results for a given DuckDuckGo search (True or False)
   A: True.

6. **Q:** TOR is based on the _____ browser.
   A: Firefox.

7. **Q:** It is OK to install browser plug-ins to TOR. (True or False)
   A: False.

14. Vulnerability: Email

1. **Q:** The attempt to acquire your personal or sensitive information by appearing as a trustworthy source is called _____.
   A: Phishing.

2. **Q:** Three common protocols to encrypt email between email server and user are _____, _____, and _____.
   A: TLS (Transport Layer Security), SSL (Secure Socket Layer), and HTTPS (Hypertext Transport Layer Secure.)

3. **Q:** The encryption protocol used for web-based email is _____.
   A: HTTPS.

4. **Q:** Email encrypted with either PGP or GPG can be decrypted with either. (True or False)
   A: True.

5. **Q:** S/MIME Class 1 certificate is designed for business use. (True or False)
   A: False.

15. Vulnerability: Documents

1. **Q:** The built-in encryption algorithm that is used for modern Microsoft Office and PDF documents is called _____.
   A: AES-128.

2. **Q:** Password protected Microsoft Office and PDF documents are portable, and can be transferred to a recipient without managing keys or encryption certificates. (True or False)
   A: True.

3. **Q:** Password protected Windows folders require managing encryption certificates for portability and/or backup purposes.
   A: True.

4. **Q:** What does a green colored folder or file name indicate?
   A: That the object is encrypted.

5. **Q:** The location to backup and manage your account's encryption certificates is located where?
   A: Control Panel > User Accounts > Manage your file encryption certificates.

16. **Vulnerability: Storage Device Encryption**

    1. **Q:** The Unified Extensible Firmware Interface (UEFI) is a replacement for the Basic Input Output System (BIOS) in most 2011+ computers. (True or False)
       A: True.

    2. **Q:** Once way to secure a Self Encrypting Disk (SED) is to set the _____ password in the UEFI to at least 14 characters.
       A: Hard Disk.

    3. **Q:** Biometrics such as Fingerprint readers are considered secure and should be enabled by default. (True or False)
       A: False.

    4. **Q:** TPM or Trusted Platform Module is used to create secure UEFI passwords. (True or False)
       A: False. TPM stores and manages encryption keys and biometrics.

    5. **Q:** It is good security practice to disable unused Input/Output ports in the BIOS or UEFI
       A: True.

6. **Q:** Boot loader protection know as _____ is used as a security mechanism on Windows 8 and newer operating systems and can be enabled or disabled in the UEFI.
   A: Secure Boot.

17. Vulnerability: Instant Messaging

1. **Q:** SMS Text Messaging is inherently insecure. (True or False)
   A: True.

2. **Q:** _____ is an example of a secure messaging application that provides end-to-end encryption and meets government standards such as HIPAA.
   A: Wickr.

18. Vulnerability: Voice and Video Communication

1. **Q:** Apple's Facetime is end-to-end encrypted. (True or False)
   A: True.

2. **Q:** _____ is cross-platform, open source application that works with OStel, an end-to-end encrypted voice, video and chat service.
   A: Jitsi.

3. **Q:** _____ and _____ are examples of popular, non-end-to-end encrypted voice, video and chat services.
   A: Skype, Google Hangouts.

19. Vulnerability: Internet Activity

1. **Q:** A _____ VPN connection provides a secure entry point into a network allowing the resources of that network to be shared with remote hosts.
   A: Gateway.

2. **Q:** For the greatest security, a VPN provider should reside within a country that has strong digital privacy laws. (True or False)
   A: True.

3. **Q:** A _____ VPN connection allows for two or more computers to access the same de-centralized virtual network.
   A: Mesh.

Index

802.1x 257, 258
access point 259
administrative 80, 81, 86
administrator 80, 223
Administrator Account 78
AES 258, 494
Al Gore 553
Android 486
Anonymous Internet Browsing .. 313
antenna 256
Anti-malware 88, 151
Antivirus 160
Assignment 33, 36, 41, 49, 57, 61, 63, 69, 73, 81, 86, 89, 98, 109, 114, 115, 116, 119, 121, 126, 127, 142, 151, 159, 160, 179, 184, 192, 196, 202, 205, 214, 222, 236, 238, 245, 246, 249, 260, 263, 267, 272, 279, 287, 288, 290, 292, 295, 298, 301, 302, 305, 307, 313, 324, 341, 345, 348, 350, 352, 353, 357, 367, 372, 374, 382, 387, 392, 395, 397, 400, 415, 422, 434, 444, 449, 453, 462, 465, 469, 471, 479, 487, 488, 490, 499, 506, 520, 522, 523, 537, 548, 555, 557, 562, 575, 592, 600, 604, 613, 620, 622
Aung San Suu Kyi 335
AV Comparatives 148
AVC 148, 150
AV-Comparatives 21

Avira 149, 150, 151, 153, 158, 159, 160
Backblaze 179
backup 176, 177, 178, 196
Backups 176
Ban Ki-moon 113
Benjamin Franklin 277
BIOS 205, 206, 214, 506, 507, 508, 509, 510, 522, 523
Bios Manufacturer Key Command 507
BitDefender 149, 150, 160, 162, 163, 169
BitLocker 127, 128, 132, 133, 134, 186, 187, 188, 214, 222, 236, 245, 246, 506, 514, 515, 519, 520, 630
Blog 26
broadcasting 256
Bruce Schneier 505
Carbonite 179
Certificate Authorities 399
Challenge Questions 47
Chameleon 580, 581, 583, 584, 586, 589
Charles Dickens 67
Child Account 78
Cisco 32
CISPA 21
Clear History 295
clone 178, 179, 196
Comodo 400, 402, 413, 415, 421, 422, 423, 424, 435
Computer theft 176
crack 31

Index

CrashPlan 179
Criminal activities 176
Deep Web 333
Disk Decipher 486
DMZ 272, 274
DoD 234
DoE 234
Douglas MacArthur 255
Dr. Seuss 233
DuckDuckGo 292
Ed Snowden 333
EDS 486
Elayne Boosler 201
Elbert Hubbard 141
Email 624
Encrypt 279, 486
Encrypted Data Store 486
encrypted email .. 344, 347, 356, 357, 399, 449, 452, 453
encryption ... 256, 258, 278, 339, 348, 349, 460, 461, 465
Entropy 176
Ethernet 256, 257
Facebook 26, 32, 61, 62, 63
Facetime 554
Family Safety 78, 88
FBI 21
FileVault 2 460
Find My Mac 214, 222
Fire 176
Firewall 166, 171, 172, 259
Firmware 272, 506, 511, 514
Flash 21
Gateway VPN 571
George Carlin 175
GNU Privacy Guard 349, 356

Google Hangouts 554, 555
GPA 357
GPG 356, 357, 358, 372, 373, 374, 382, 395, 397, 399, 456
GPG Keychain Access 368, 372
GPG Public Key 357
GPG4win 356, 357
GPGMail 374, 382
GpgOL 382, 383
GPGtools 357
Hamachi 592, 593, 604, 620, 621, 622, 623
haystack 32, 33
Henry Ford 77
HIPAA 179, 350, 536
https ... 32, 33, 278, 279, 284, 340, 348
HTTPS Everywhere 279, 315
Incognito Mode 287, 288
infected 32
InPrivate 287, 290, 291
iOS 486
Java 21
Jiddu Krishnamurti 459
Jitsi 555, 557, 558, 559, 561, 562, 563, 566, 632
John F. Kennedy 535
Joseph Heller 17
Keychain 372, 374
Kleopatra 362, 363, 368, 372, 373, 380, 385, 387, 398
LAN 259
LastPass 32, 48, 49, 50, 52, 55, 56, 57, 58, 61, 62, 63, 64
Linux 311, 312, 486
Local Area Network 259
LogMeIn 592, 595, 604, 623

-644-

Index

LoJack 214
MAC Address 267
maintenance 80, 177
malware 80, 148, 176
Media Access Control 267
Mesh VPN 591
Microsoft Account 78, 340, 341
Mintz's extrapolation of Sturgeon's Revelation 20
modem 259
Newsletter 26
Ninite Updater 73, 74
NSA 19, 30, 234, 456, 494
Nwipe 250, 251, 253
Onion Sites 333
oPenGP 356
Ostel 555, 556, 557
Parallels 315
Parental Controls 88
Parted Magic 178, 179, 238, 239, 243, 246, 249
passphrase 32
password 21, 31, 32, 33, 34, 62, 80, 83, 142, 214, 257, 258, 340, 344, 347, 348, 349, 350, 405, 435, 461, 463, 464, 465, 512, 516, 522
Passwords 31
PGP 356, 399, 456
phishing 21, 148
port 119, 172, 272
Port forwarding 272
Power sags 176
Power surges 176
Practical Paranoia Book Upgrades 27
Practical Paranoia Updates 26
Pretty Good Privacy 356

Prey 214, 222, 223
private browsing 287, 290
Public Key 356, 357, 367, 371, 372, 374, 395, 397, 399, 449, 452
RADIUS 257
RAM-Resident Malware 272
Recovery Drive ... 201, 202, 205, 236, 237, 238, 245
recovery key 136, 236, 246, 520
router ... 172, 259, 260, 263, 264, 266, 267, 269, 270, 272
Rufus 240, 241, 245
S/MIME 399, 400, 415, 422, 426, 430, 433, 434, 449, 453, 456
Sabotage 176
SEC 179
SecuMail 356
Secure Erase 236, 238, 245, 249
Secure Socket Layer 278
SendInc 349, 350, 352, 353
Server 256
SHA 496
Skype 554, 555
sleep 570
software 31, 32, 80, 177, 179, 256, 350
solid state drive 238
spyware 148
SSD 139, 238
SSL 278, 340, 341, 344, 345, 349
Standard 492
Standard Account 78
Static electricity 176
Supervisor Password 512, 513
switch 259, 584
Symantec 21
System Image Backup 192, 193

Index

System Updates 68
Tails 311, 312, 313, 315, 332
Terrorist activities 176
theft 21, 177
Theodore Roosevelt 171
Theodore Sturgeon 20
thepracticalparanoid.................... 451
Thomas Jefferson 29
Thomas Sowell............................. 213
TKIP 258
TLS 339, 340, 341, 344, 345
Tor 311, 312, 313, 314, 315, 316, 318, 319, 321, 322, 323, 324, 332, 333
TorBrowser 322, 324
torrent 315
TPM 132, 519, 520
trojan horses............................ 21, 148
TrueCrypt.............................. 486, 489
Trusted Platform Module ... 132, 519
UEFI214, 506, 507, 511, 514, 515, 519, 522, 523
Unified Extensible Firmware Interface.. 506
USB Disabler......................... 121, 126
US-CERT 68

User Accounts................. 78, 472, 473
VeraCrypt.... 486, 487, 488, 490, 491, 492, 496, 498, 499, 501, 502, 503
Virtual Machine 315
Virtual Private Network 279
viruses 21
VPN......279, 569, 570, 571, 572, 573, 574, 575, 580, 584, 585, 587, 588, 590, 591, 592, 600, 604, 612, 619, 620, 622, 624
VPNArea 575, 580, 585, 588, 590
war driving 21
Water damage.............................. 176
WEP 258, 260
Whitelisting..................................... 88
Wickr 536, 537, 548
Wi-Fi.......21, 256, 257, 258, 260, 262
Windows 311, 486, 496
Windows Backup 177, 178, 179, 184, 199
Windows Defender 148
worms 21, 148
WPA..258, 260
WPA2......................................258, 260
zero-day exploits 23

Your Virtual CIO & IT Department

Mintz InfoTech, Inc.
when, where, and how you want IT

Technician fixes problems.
Consultant delivers solutions.

Technician answers questions.
Consultant asks questions, revealing core issues.

Technician understands your equipment.
Consultant understands your business.

Technician costs you money.
Consultant contributes to your success.

Let us contribute to your success.

Mintz InfoTech is uniquely positioned to be your Virtual CIO and provide comprehensive technology support. With the only MBA-IT consultant in New Mexico heading our organization, our mission is to provide small and medium businesses with the same Chief Information and Technology Officer resources otherwise only available to large businesses.

Mintz InfoTech, Inc.
Toll-free: +1 888.479.0690 • Local: +1 505.814.1413
info@mintzIT.com • https://mintzit.com

Index

Practical Paranoia
Security Essentials Workshops & Books
Android, iOS, OS X, Windows

This is an age of government intrusion into every aspect of our digital lives, criminals using your own data against you, and teenagers competing to see who can crack your password the fastest. Every organization, every computer user, every one should be taking steps to protect and secure their digital lives.

The *Practical Paranoia: Security Essentials Workshop* is the perfect environment in which to learn not only *how*, but to actually *do* the work to harden the security of your OS X and Windows computers, and iPhone, iPad, and Android devices.

Workshops are available online and instructor-led at your venue, as well as tailored for on-site company events.

Each Book is designed for classroom, workshop, and self-study. Includes all instructor presentations, hands-on assignments, software links, security checklist, and review questions and answers. Available from Amazon (both print and Kindle format), and all fine booksellers, with inscribed copies available from the author.

Call for more information, to schedule your workshop, or order your books!

Mintz InfoTech, Inc.
Toll-free: +1 888.479.0690 • Local: +1 505.814.1413
info@mintzIT.com • http://thepracticalparanoid.com

Made in the USA
Lexington, KY
09 February 2016